Keep this book. You will need it and use it throughout your career.

About the American Hotel & Motel Association (AH&MA)

Founded in 1910, AH&MA is the trade association representing the lodging industry in the United States. AH&MA is a federation of state lodging associations throughout the United States with 11,000 lodging properties worldwide as members. The association offers its members assistance with governmental affairs representation, communications, marketing, hospitality operations, training and education, technology issues, and more. For information, call 202-289-3100.

LODGING, the management magazine of AH&MA, is a "living textbook" for hospitality students that provides timely features, industry news, and vital lodging information. For information on subscriptions and student rates, call 202-289-3113.

About the Educational Institute of AH&MA (EI)

An affiliate of AH&MA, the Educational Institute is the world's largest source of quality training and educational materials for the lodging industry. EI develops textbooks and courses that are used in more than 1,200 colleges and universities worldwide, and also offers courses to individuals through its Distance Learning program. Hotels worldwide rely on EI for training resources that focus on every aspect of lodging operations. Industry-tested videos, CD-ROMs, seminars, and skills guides prepare employees at every skill level. EI also offers professional certification for the industry's top performers. For information about EI's products and services, call 800-349-0299 or 407-999-8100.

About the American Hotel Foundation (AHF)

An affiliate of AH&MA, the American Hotel Foundation provides financial support that enhances the stability, prosperity, and growth of the lodging industry through educational and research programs. AHF has awarded hundreds of thousands of dollars in scholarship funds for students pursuing higher education in hospitality management. AHF has also funded research projects on topics important to the industry, including occupational safety and health, turnover and diversity, and best practices in the U.S. lodging industry. For information, call 202-289-3100.

HOSPITALITY INDUSTRY MANAGERIAL ACCOUNTING

Educational Institute Books

UNIFORM SYSTEM OF ACCOUNTS FOR THE LODGING
INDUSTRY
Ninth Revised Edition

RESORT DEVELOPMENT AND MANAGEMENT
Second Edition
Chuck Y. Gee

PLANNING AND CONTROL FOR FOOD AND BEVERAGE
OPERATIONS
Fourth Edition
Jack D. Ninemeier

TRAINING FOR THE HOSPITALITY INDUSTRY
Second Edition
Lewis C. Forrest, Jr.

UNDERSTANDING HOSPITALITY LAW
Third Edition
Jack P. Jefferies

SUPERVISION IN THE HOSPITALITY INDUSTRY
Second Edition
Raphael R. Kavanaugh/Jack D. Ninemeier

ENERGY AND WATER RESOURCE MANAGEMENT
Second Edition
Robert E. Aulbach

MANAGEMENT OF FOOD AND BEVERAGE OPERATIONS
Third Edition
Jack D. Ninemeier

MANAGING FRONT OFFICE OPERATIONS
Fifth Edition
Michael L. Kasavana/Richard M. Brooks

STRATEGIC HOTEL/MOTEL MARKETING
Revised Edition
Christopher W. L. Hart/David A. Troy

MANAGING SERVICE IN FOOD AND BEVERAGE
OPERATIONS
Second Edition
Ronald F. Cichy/Paul E. Wise

THE LODGING AND FOOD SERVICE INDUSTRY
Fourth Edition
Gerald W. Lattin

SECURITY AND LOSS PREVENTION MANAGEMENT
Second Edition
Raymond C. Ellis, Jr./David M. Stipanuk

HOSPITALITY INDUSTRY MANAGERIAL ACCOUNTING
Fourth Edition
Raymond S. Schmidgall

PURCHASING FOR HOSPITALITY OPERATIONS
William B. Virts

THE ART AND SCIENCE OF HOSPITALITY MANAGEMENT
Jerome J. Vallen/James R. Abbey

MANAGING COMPUTERS IN THE HOSPITALITY
INDUSTRY
Third Edition
Michael L. Kasavana/John J. Cahill

MANAGING HOSPITALITY ENGINEERING SYSTEMS
Michael H. Redlin/David M. Stipanuk

UNDERSTANDING HOSPITALITY ACCOUNTING I
Fourth Edition
Raymond Cote

UNDERSTANDING HOSPITALITY ACCOUNTING II
Third Edition
Raymond Cote

CONVENTION MANAGEMENT AND SERVICE
Fifth Edition
Milton T. Astroff/James R. Abbey

HOSPITALITY SALES AND ADVERTISING
Third Edition
James R. Abbey

MANAGING HOUSEKEEPING OPERATIONS
Second Edition
Margaret M. Kappa/Aleta Nitschke/Patricia B. Schappert

CONVENTION SALES: A BOOK OF READINGS
Margaret Shaw

DIMENSIONS OF TOURISM
Joseph D. Fridgen

HOSPITALITY TODAY: AN INTRODUCTION
Third Edition
Rocco M. Angelo/Andrew N. Vladimir

MANAGING BAR AND BEVERAGE OPERATIONS
Lendal H. Kotschevar/Mary L. Tanke

ETHICS IN HOSPITALITY MANAGEMENT: A BOOK OF
READINGS
Edited by Stephen S. J. Hall

HOSPITALITY FACILITIES MANAGEMENT AND DESIGN
David M. Stipanuk/Harold Roffmann

MANAGING HOSPITALITY HUMAN RESOURCES
Second Edition
Robert H. Woods

FINANCIAL MANAGEMENT FOR THE HOSPITALITY
INDUSTRY
William P. Andrew/Raymond S. Schmidgall

HOSPITALITY INDUSTRY FINANCIAL ACCOUNTING
Raymond S. Schmidgall/James W. Damitio

INTERNATIONAL HOTELS: DEVELOPMENT AND
MANAGEMENT
Chuck Y. Gee

QUALITY SANITATION MANAGEMENT
Ronald F. Cichy

HOTEL INVESTMENTS: ISSUES & PERSPECTIVES
Second Edition
Edited by Lori E. Raleigh and Rachel J. Roginsky

QUALITY LEADERSHIP AND MANAGEMENT IN THE
HOSPITALITY INDUSTRY
Robert H. Woods/Judy Z. King

MARKETING IN THE HOSPITALITY INDUSTRY
Third Edition
Ronald A. Nykiel

CONTEMPORARY HOSPITALITY MARKETING
William Lazer/Roger Layton

UNIFORM SYSTEM OF ACCOUNTS FOR THE HEALTH,
RACQUET AND SPORTSCLUB INDUSTRY

CONTEMPORARY CLUB MANAGEMENT
Edited by Joe Perdue for the Club Managers Association of America

RESORT CONDOMINIUM AND VACATION OWNERSHIP
MANAGEMENT: A HOSPITALITY PERSPECTIVE
Robert A. Gentry/Pedro Mandoki/Jack Rush

2/00

HOSPITALITY INDUSTRY MANAGERIAL ACCOUNTING

Fourth Edition

Raymond S. Schmidgall, Ph.D., CPA

EDUCATIONAL INSTITUTE
American Hotel & Motel Association

Disclaimer

This publication is designed to provide accurate and authoritative information in regard to the subject matter covered. It is sold with the understanding that the publisher is not engaged in rendering legal, accounting, or other professional service. If legal advice or other expert assistance is required, the services of a competent professional person should be sought.

—*From the Declaration of Principles jointly adopted by the American Bar Association and a Committee of Publishers and Associations*

The author, Raymond S. Schmidgall, is solely responsible for the contents of this publication. All views expressed herein are solely those of the author and do not necessarily reflect the views of the Educational Institute of the American Hotel & Motel Association (the Institute) or the American Hotel & Motel Association (AH&MA).

Nothing contained in this publication shall constitute a standard, an endorsement, or a recommendation of the Institute or AH&MA. The Institute and AH&MA disclaim any liability with respect to the use of any information, procedure, or product, or reliance thereon by any member of the hospitality industry.

Library of Congress Cataloging-in-Publication Data
Schmidgall, Raymond S., 1945–
    Hospitality industry managerial accounting/Raymond S.
Schmidgall.—4th ed.
        p. cm.
    Includes bibliographical references and index.
    ISBN 0-86612-149-8
    1. Hospitality industry—Accounting. 2. Managerial accounting.
I. Title.
HF5686.H75S34   1997
647'.94'0681—dc21   97–23145
                                                             CIP

Editor: Sharon L. Martin

Contents

Preface

Hospitality Industry Managerial Accounting, Fourth Edition, presents managerial accounting concepts and explains how they apply to specific operations within the hospitality industry. This book is written not only for managers in the hospitality industry, but also for hospitality students at both the two-year and four-year college levels. Readers of this textbook should already be familiar with basic accounting concepts and procedures, or have taken an introductory course in basic accounting.

Each chapter begins by posing a number of questions that managers in the hospitality industry may have regarding accounting concepts that will be developed within the chapter. At the close of each chapter, there are a number of review questions and problems designed to test the reader's understanding of the concepts covered within that chapter. Some chapters are followed by appendices that present more detailed approaches to concepts mentioned in the text.

The text consists of 15 chapters. It begins with an overview of accounting in Chapter 1. Chapters 2 through 4 cover the three basic financial statements—the balance sheet, the income statement, and the statement of cash flows, respectively. While the presentations of the balance sheet and the statement of cash flows are similar to the coverage found in most financial accounting texts, the presentation of the income statement is based on various schedules from the *Uniform System of Accounts for the Lodging Industry.*

Chapter 5 focuses on ratio analysis as a means of interpreting information reported on financial statements. For each ratio presented, the chapter outlines its purpose, the sources of data needed for the ratio's calculation, the formula by which it is calculated, and the interpretation of the ratio results from the varying viewpoints of owners, creditors, and managers.

Chapters 6, 7, and 8 cover basic cost concepts, cost-volume-profit analysis, and cost approaches to pricing. Chapter 6 presents the various types of costs and how managers can identify the relevant costs in particular decision-making situations. The discussion of cost-volume-profit analysis in Chapter 7 is presented in both equation and graphic form. In addition, this chapter discusses and illustrates the determination of each break-even point. Chapter 8 takes a cost approach to pricing and includes pricing examples for food, beverages, and rooms.

Forecasting methods and operations budgeting are the subjects of Chapters 9 and 10, respectively. Chapter 9 focuses on basic mathematical models for forecasting sales. This chapter also presents hospitality industry examples of sales forecasting procedures at Hilton Hotels, ARAMARK Corporation, and Pizza Hut. Chapter 10 discusses how budgets are prepared, how budgets are used for control operations, and how the operations budgeting process may take different forms at multi-unit and single-unit hospitality enterprises. Several exhibits for this chapter have been provided by ITT Sheraton Corporation.

Chapter 11 covers cash management and includes sections on cash budgeting and managing working capital. Chapter 12 presents basic requirements of internal accounting control for various accounting functions, including cash receipts, cash disbursements, accounts receivable, accounts payable, inventories, payroll, fixed assets, and marketable securities. Capital budgeting is the subject of Chapter 13. The capital budgeting models presented include payback, accounting rate of return, net present value, and internal rate of return.

The final two chapters deal with lease accounting and income taxes. Although both of these topics are generally found in financial accounting texts, they are addressed here because managers of hospitality operations should have some knowledge in each of these areas. The chapter on lease accounting includes illustrations of accounting for various types of leases. The chapter on income taxes does not dwell on tax details. Instead, it provides an overview of the elements of taxes, discusses tax avoidance, and presents the advantages and disadvantages of various forms of business organization from a tax point of view.

I am grateful for the industry support that makes this book possible. Exhibits throughout the book are courtesy of several hospitality companies and companies serving the hospitality industry, including Hilton Hotels, Pizza Hut, ARAMARK Corporation, PKF Consulting, Marriott International, and ITT Sheraton.

In addition, many users of this textbook, especially professors in hospitality management programs, have provided helpful suggestions for revision. Rather than try to list them all and err in leaving someone out, I simply say thank you to the entire group of hospitality educators teaching hospitality accounting.

Finally, I thank my wife, Barbara; my daughters, Erica, Monica, Kristina, and Joanna; and my sons-in-law, Jeremy and Bryan, who have been patient during the long time periods it has taken me to write and revise this book.

Dedication

In memory of Raymond Klein Schmidgall, loving father, entrepreneur, and leader of people by example.

About the Author

Raymond S. Schmidgall

RAYMOND S. SCHMIDGALL is a professor in the School of Hotel, Restaurant and Institutional Management at Michigan State University. He holds a B.B.A. in accounting from Evangel College and an M.B.A. and a Ph.D. in accounting from Michigan State University. He is also a Certified Public Accountant. He has published articles in *Lodging, Club Management, Michigan Hospitality, The Bottomline, The Consultant, Restaurant Business*, the *Cornell Hotel and Restaurant Administration Quarterly*, the *Journal of Hospitality and Tourism Research*, the *International Journal of Hospitality Management*, and the *Journal of Hospitality Financial Management*. Dr. Schmidgall has also written accounting textbooks oriented to the hospitality industry, including basic texts on financial management, financial accounting, and managerial accounting. He is active in the Association of Hospitality Financial Management Educators, the International Association of Hospitality Accountants, and the American Hotel & Motel Association's financial management committee. He is the treasurer of the International Council on Hotel, Restaurant and Institutional Education (International CHRIE) and serves on the editorial board of International CHRIE's *Journal of Hospitality and Tourism Research*. He has worked as a financial controller and public accountant and is also a member of several accounting associations.

Chapter 1 Outline

Overview of the Hospitality Industry
    Seasonality of Business
    Short Distribution Chain and Time Span
    A Labor-Intensive Industry
    Major Investment in Fixed Assets
The Accounting Function in the Hospitality Industry
    Uniform Systems of Accounts
Principles of Accounting
    The Cost Principle
    Business Entity
    Continuity of the Business Unit (Going Concern)
    Unit of Measurement
    Objective Evidence
    Full Disclosure
    Consistency
    Matching
    Conservatism
    Materiality
    Cash Versus Accrual Accounting
Branches of Accounting
Review of Accounting Mechanics
    Debit and Credit
The Accounting Cycle
Forms of Business Organization
Ethics and Hospitality Accounting
Computer Applications

1

Introduction to Managerial Accounting

$\mathbf{H}$OSPITALITY IS A HUGE and growing industry. A property manager needs more knowledge today than ever before and will need even more tomorrow. Managerial accounting focuses upon those aspects of accounting that concern hospitality managers most. These aspects include internal financial statements, budgeting, internal control, and costs. This introductory chapter will provide answers to many questions, including the following:

1. How does the hospitality industry differ from many other industries?
2. Why are food and beverage inventories relatively low in hospitality operations?
3. What are three aspects of seasonality in lodging properties?
4. What is the scope of the accounting function in hotels?
5. What are the major principles of accounting?
6. What are the various branches of accounting?
7. Why are rooms, in essence, perishable inventory?
8. What are the four forms of business organization?

This chapter will present an overview of the hospitality industry and then focus on the accounting function within the industry. We will briefly review the principles, branches, and mechanics of accounting, discuss the accounting cycle, and describe the four forms of business organization.

Overview of the Hospitality Industry

The hospitality industry consists of several different types of operations providing both products and services to its clients or guests. It includes hotels, motels, motor hotels, inns, quick-service restaurants, fine dining restaurants, cafeterias, resorts, country clubs, and city clubs, to mention a few. These hospitality operations serve both the traveling public and local residents. While this is particularly true of food and beverage operations, many lodging properties also market their accommodations to local residents by promoting "weekend escape" packages.

Properties in the lodging segment of the hospitality industry range from single-unit operations of fewer than 10 rooms to Hospitality Franchise Systems, the largest chain operation in the world, with over eight brand names, 5,400 hotels, and 490,000 rooms. In 1996, there were over 80 mega-hotels—hotels with 1,000 or more rooms—in the United States.[1] The American Hotel & Motel Association estimates that there are 3.5 million rooms in 46,000 lodging establishments in 1996. The differences among lodging operations are vast. At one extreme, there are budget hotels and motels providing only rooms, and at the other, luxury properties providing nearly every imaginable service a guest might desire.

There are also many different types of food service operations. Properties in the food and beverage segment of the hospitality industry range from the single-unit operation with only window service to the McDonald's Corporation with over 13,000 restaurants throughout the world. In the club segment of the hospitality industry, there are some operations with fewer than 200 members and others with over 15,000 members.

Lodging facilities in the United States took in more than $66 billion in a recent year, while food service establishments took in over $300 billion in revenues. The total revenue of these two segments of the hospitality industry approximates 5% of the U.S. gross national product.

Exhibits 1 and 2 provide further insights into financial aspects of the hospitality industry. Exhibit 1 illustrates what happens to the average revenue dollar in the lodging industry—where it comes from and where it goes. Exhibit 2 illustrates this for the average revenue dollar in four segments of the food service industry. Notice that in the lodging industry, food sales are the second largest source of total revenues. Also notice that the largest category of expense for lodging operations is payroll and related expenses, while for the restaurant industry, payroll costs are generally second only to the cost of food. Finally, note that for food service operations, net income before taxes represents a relatively small percentage of total revenues.

Seasonality of Business

Although both manufacturing firms and hospitality operations frequently experience seasonal fluctuations in sales volume, hospitality operations also deal with activity variations throughout the day. Check-in times vary, but many hotels are busiest with check-ins between 3 and 5 P.M. Check-out at many hotels is extremely busy between 7 and 9 A.M. and between 11 A.M. and 1 P.M. Similarly, some food service operations may be full from 7:30 to 8:30 A.M., 11:30 A.M. to 1:30 P.M., and 6 to 8 P.M., and nearly empty during other hours of the day. Hospitality business may also vary during the week.

A common measure of activity for lodging operations is paid occupancy percentage. Paid occupancy percentage indicates what percentage of the rooms available for sale are actually sold. It is calculated by dividing the number of rooms sold by the number of rooms available. Transient hotels—that is, hotels catering primarily to business people—may experience 100% occupancy Monday through Thursday and 30% occupancy Friday through Sunday, averaging 70% for the week. Weekly seasonality for many resort hotels results in the opposite distribution; their busiest periods are usually weekends rather than weekdays. In addition, their multiple occupancy, determined by dividing the number of rooms with more than one guest by the total number of rooms occupied, is higher than that of transient hotels. Generally, multiple occupancy is highest at resort hotels and lowest at transient hotels.[2]

Exhibit 1   U.S. Lodging Industry Dollar

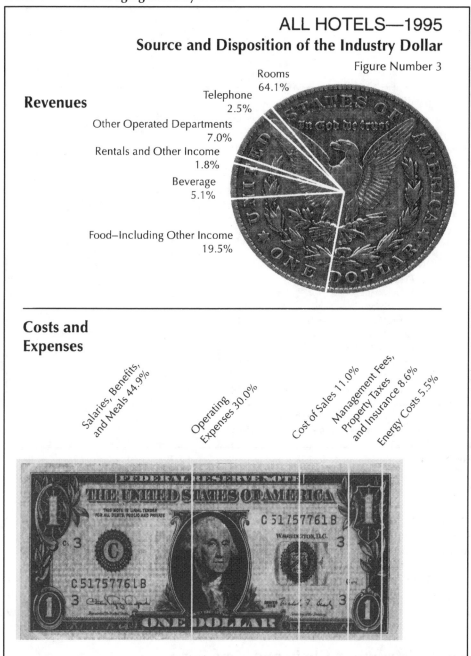

ALL HOTELS—1995
Source and Disposition of the Industry Dollar

Figure Number 3

Revenues

Rooms
64.1%

Telephone
2.5%

Other Operated Departments
7.0%

Rentals and Other Income
1.8%

Beverage
5.1%

Food–Including Other Income
19.5%

Costs and Expenses

Salaries, Benefits, and Meals 44.9%

Operating Expenses 30.0%

Cost of Sales 11.0%

Management Fees, Property Taxes, and Insurance 8.6%

Energy Costs 5.5%

Source: *Trends in the Hotel Industry—USA Edition 1996* (San Francisco: PKF Consulting, 1996), p. 51.

Exhibit 2   U.S. Restaurant Industry Dollar

	Full Service Restaurants (Average Check Per Person Under $10)	Full Service Restaurants (Average Check Per Person Over $10)	Limited Service Fast Food Restaurants
Where It Came From*			
Food Sales	87.2%	76.5%	96.4%
Beverage Sales (alcoholic)	12.8	23.5	3.6
Where It Went**			
Cost of Food Sold	28.2	26.8	31.2
Cost of Beverages Sold	3.5	6.6	0.9
Salaries and Wages	29.9	28.5	24.4
Employee Benefits	3.8	4.4	2.7
Direct Operating Expenses	6.7	7.3	7.4
Music and Entertainment	0.3	0.7	0.1
Marketing	3.5	2.6	5.3
Utility Services	3.0	2.5	2.7
Restaurant Occupancy Costs	5.8	5.3	6.4
Repairs and Maintenance	1.7	2.0	1.6
Depreciation	2.1	2.1	1.7
Other Operating Expense/(Income)	0.4	(0.2)	(2.1)
General and Administrative	3.3	4.5	5.7
Corporate Overhead	1.8	1.5	1.9
Interest	0.6	0.6	1.0
Other	0.2	0.5	0.1
Income Before Income Tax	5.2%	4.3%	9.0%

*All figures are weighted averages based on 1995 data.
**All amounts are reflected as a percentage of total sales.

Source: National Restaurant Association and Deloitte & Touche, *Restaurant Industry Operations Report 1996,* p. 11.

Seasonality throughout the year is a serious factor for many hotels. Many resorts are open for only one season of the year. Other lodging establishments, although open all year, have much more sales activity during certain times of the year. For example, the occupancy of many Florida hotels is higher during the winter months as vacationers from the north descend on Florida to enjoy its warmth and sunshine.

Exhibit 3 shows the monthly occupancy rates in selected U.S. cities for 1996. Boston hotels registered 91% occupancy in October and 52% in December, while hotels in Honolulu registered a high of 93% in February and a low of 74% in May. Thus, Exhibit 3 reveals both seasonal fluctuations and large differences among cities.

Short Distribution Chain and Time Span

In a food service operation, there is a relatively fast conversion of raw materials into a finished product and of the product into cash. Like manufacturing operations,

Exhibit 3   Selected Monthly Occupancy Rates

	Average For Year 1996	1996											
		Jan.	Feb.	Mar.	Apr.	May	June	July	Aug.	Sept.	Oct.	Nov.	Dec.
Atlanta	68	67	80	76	74	72	68	75	70	65	68	64	47
Boston	74	52	59	67	72	77	85	81	85	85	91	73	52
Chicago	72	53	58	71	72	77	83	77	82	82	83	72	55
Dallas	70	71	70	76	70	73	76	72	69	67	77	68	53
Los Angeles	68	61	66	71	67	67	71	72	76	70	71	64	58
Minneapolis	70	54	63	70	69	69	81	80	84	75	78	66	51
New Orleans	71	57	70	84	76	76	70	70	75	67	78	76	52
New York City	80	64	70	78	81	82	84	78	84	87	92	86	78
Honolulu	81	84	93	82	74	74	83	83	86	81	75	77	76
Orlando	80	76	81	90	88	79	81	87	84	73	81	71	69
San Francisco	79	64	69	75	73	80	87	84	91	89	90	78	63
Washington, D.C.	68	45	58	72	80	81	80	74	70	72	78	64	47

Source: *Smith Travel Research.*

food service operations must offer products that meet the consumer's expectations. However, the distribution chain and time span is considerably shorter for hospitality "products" than for most consumer goods.

For example, a new automobile purchased from a dealer may have been assembled several months before the sale, thousands of miles away, by a different company using finished parts supplied by more than 50 companies. In hospitality operations, inventory is often purchased one day and sold the next. The product is produced, sold, and consumed at the same location, often in less than two hours, sometimes within minutes. The food service "manufacturer" purchases the raw ingredients, prepares them to suit the consumer's tastes, and serves the finished product on the premises. The food service operator will in many cases receive immediate feedback on the quality of the food and service product, especially if it failed to meet the consumers' expectations.

As a result of this short distribution chain and time span, hospitality operations do little advance production. Thus, they maintain a minimal inventory of the goods they provide. This is reflected in the fact that major operations in the hospitality industry generally have less than 5% of their total assets invested in inventory of goods for resale. In contrast, the inventory of many major manufacturing firms equals at least 30% of their total assets.

A Labor-Intensive Industry

There is another important difference between the hospitality and manufacturing industries. In the manufacturing sector, automatic equipment has reduced the need for labor. This is not the case in the hospitality industry. As we have already seen, payroll expense is a major element in the cost of sales for both the lodging and food service segments of the hospitality industry. The seasonality of hospitality sales also contributes to the labor intensity of the industry. The busy check-in and check-out times during daily hotel operations require much labor to provide quality service. Similarly, food service operations have increased labor needs for spurts of activity throughout the day. Scheduling personnel for busy times is important if a hospitality operation is to generate profits while meeting guests' needs and wants.

Another important dimension of food and beverage operations in lodging facilities is the need to provide service even when it may not be profitable. For example, food service must be provided to guests even on low-occupancy days, and room service must always be available in first-class properties.

The short distribution chain and time span characteristic of the delivery and consumption of hospitality products and services also contributes to the industry's labor intensity. Personnel must prepare, produce, sell, and serve the operation's offerings. Labor must be available to prepare food when a guest wants it. Some food service operations promise the finished product within minutes after the guest's order is taken. Such prompt guest-oriented service can only be provided by a large and efficient staff. The total labor cost may be as low as 20% of the total revenue dollar at a quick-service restaurant or over 50% at a private club. Controlling labor costs while satisfying the needs and wants of guests is crucial to the success of any hospitality operation.

Major Investment in Fixed Assets

In addition to being labor-intensive, hospitality properties are, for the most part, fixed-asset–intensive. Lodging facilities provide rooms for guests to relax, rest, entertain, and conduct business in. The room as a product is carried as a fixed asset, and its cost is written off (depreciated) over time. The basic cost of the room is the same whether or not it is occupied. In this sense, a room is the most perishable product a lodging operation has, because the revenue lost from an unsold room can never be regained. The construction cost of lodging facilities, including the furniture and fixtures, may vary between $10,000 and $400,000 per room. The cost of rooms represents a major investment by lodging operations, and the fixed assets of major hotels range between 55% and 85% of their total assets. In contrast, the fixed assets of many manufacturing companies approximate only 30% of their total assets.

This overview of the hospitality industry has described many of the different types of hospitality operations and indicated the impressive dimensions of the industry. As we have seen, the hospitality industry is greatly affected by seasonal (daily, weekly, monthly, and yearly) sales fluctuations, by the short distribution chain and quick consumption of its offerings, by the need for a large, efficient work force, and by large investment in fixed assets. These characteristics of hospitality operations give shape to the challenges which the accounting function must face within the industry.

The Accounting Function in the Hospitality Industry

The accounting function in hospitality industry properties is performed by a group of specialists ranging from bookkeepers to executives with such titles as Executive Vice-President and Controller (or Comptroller). Chief accounting executives are responsible for typical accounting functions such as receivables, payables, payroll, and, in some cases, storage and security. Exhibit 4 summarizes the results of a

Exhibit 4   Responsibilities of Hotel Controllers

Area	Percentage Reporting Responsibility
General Accounting	92%
Accounts Payable	92%
Accounts Receivable	91%
Computer System Accounting	88%
Payroll	87%
Night Audits	80%
Cash Managment	77%
Beverage Controls	67%
Food Controls	65%
Cashiers	64%
Tax Returns	61%
Purchasing	60%
Computer System Front Office Reservations	58%
Receiving	52%
Storage	52%
Investments	42%
Security	22%

survey of 278 hotel *property* (as opposed to *corporate*) controllers and shows a wide range of reported responsibilities.

The size of an accounting staff may vary widely—from a part-time bookkeeper in a 10-room motel to several hundred people in a large hotel or restaurant chain. The size of the accounting staff at an individual property varies with the size and diversity of the hotel's operations. The accounting staff at hotels with more than 1,000 rooms ranges from 30 to 50 people. The accounting staff at one major world-wide hotel company totals approximately 250, while the corporate accounting staff (accounts payable, payroll, internal audit, tax, and so forth) at a major food service headquarters totals 150. Exhibit 5 is a sample organization chart for the accounting function at a large hotel.

The accounting function within a lodging property is information-oriented—that is, its major role is providing information to users. For external users such as financial institutions, accounting usually communicates through financial statements. Internally, accounting provides a wide variety of financial reports, including operating statements. The operating statements are formatted to reflect revenues and related expenses by areas of responsibility. In addition to the income statement of the property as a whole, departmental statements are prepared for each department generating revenues and incurring expenses, such as rooms, food and beverage, and telephone. Service centers such as marketing and property operation and maintenance also provide separate statements.

Regardless of the size of an operation's accounting department, the diversity of its responsibilities, or the number and types of reports produced, the accounting staff

Exhibit 5   Controller's Department Organization Chart

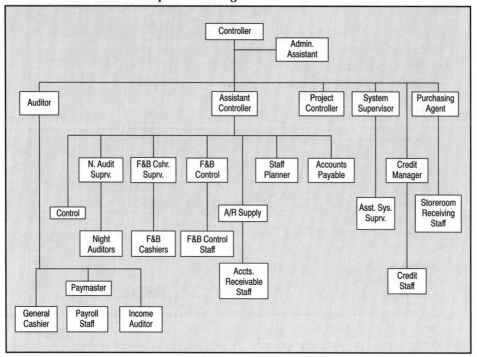

is responsible for providing *service.* The accounting staff must work closely with operating management and other service departments in order for the hospitality property to meet its objectives. Exhibit 6, an organization chart of a major hotel, reflects the relative position of the controller and his/her staff within the hotel's organization.

Uniform Systems of Accounts

For internal purposes (that is, for management use), uniform accounting systems, commonly called *uniform systems of accounts,* have been developed. These systems are popular among hospitality organizations because they provide a turnkey accounting system. Uniform systems have been tested over time and refined to meet the ever-changing needs of management.

Principles of Accounting

In order to understand accounting methods, you must understand basic accounting principles. These **generally accepted accounting principles** (often referred to by the acronym *GAAP*) provide a uniform basis for preparing financial statements. Although not "etched in stone," accounting principles have become accepted over time through common usage and also through the work of such major accounting bodies as the American Institute of Certified Public Accountants, the American Accounting Association, and the Financial Accounting Standards Board (FASB).

Exhibit 6   Organization Chart for a Large Lodging Establishment

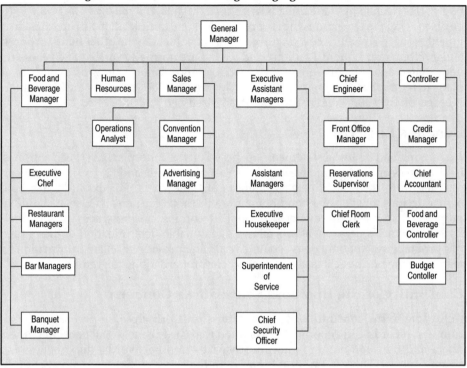

Students of hospitality accounting may often wonder why an accounting transaction is recorded in a particular way at a particular time or why some asset value is not changed at some point. Generally, the reasons relate to accounting principles. The following sections briefly discuss several generally accepted accounting principles.

The Cost Principle

The **cost principle** states that when a transaction is recorded, it is the transaction price or cost that establishes the accounting value for the product or service purchased. For example, if a restaurateur buys a dishwasher, the agreed-upon price between the restaurant and the supplier determines the amount to be recorded. If the agreed-upon price is $5,000, then the dishwasher is initially valued at $5,000 in the restaurant's accounting records. The supplier may have acquired the dishwasher from the manufacturer for $4,000 and the restaurant may receive an offer of $5,500 for it the day it is purchased; however, it is the actual cost that establishes the amount to be recorded. If amounts other than cost (such as estimates or appraisals) were used to record transactions, then accounting records would lose their usefulness. When cost is the basis for recording a transaction, the buyer and seller determine the amount to be recorded. This amount is generally an objective and fair measure of the value of the goods or services purchased.

When the value of *current* assets is clearly less than the cost recorded on the books, this decline in value must be recognized. Thus, the *conservatism principle* (to be discussed later) overrides the cost principle. For example, many properties carry inventory at the lower of cost or current market value. On the other hand, property and equipment (frequently called fixed assets) are normally carried at cost less the depreciated amounts and are not reduced to market value as long as management plans to retain them for their useful life. This treatment of property and equipment is based on the *going-concern principle* (also discussed later).

Business Entity

Accounting and financial statements are based on the concepts that (1) each business is a **business entity** that maintains its own set of accounts and (2) these accounts are separate from the other financial interests of the owners. For example, if a hotel owner decides to take some food home from the hotel for personal use, it should be properly charged to the owner's account. Recording business activity separately from the owner's personal affairs allows a reasonable determination of the property's profitability. Not only does separate recording provide excellent information for managing the business, it is also necessary for properly filing tax returns.

Continuity of the Business Unit (Going Concern)

According to the **continuity of the business unit principle**, in preparing the accounting records and reports, it is assumed that the business will continue indefinitely and that liquidation is not in prospect—in other words, the business is a **going concern**. This assumption is based on the concept that the real value of the hotel or motel is its ability to earn a profit, rather than the value its assets would bring in liquidation. According to this concept, the market value of the property and equipment need not appear on the financial statements, and prepaid expenses are considered assets. If there is a reasonable chance the hospitality property may be unable to continue operations in the near future, allowance for this future event should be reflected in the financial statements. This may be best accomplished by reducing asset values to their market values.

Unit of Measurement

The financial statements are based on transactions expressed in monetary terms. The monetary unit is assumed to represent a stable unit of value so that transactions from past periods and the current period can be included on the same statement.

In the late 1970s and early 1980s, annual inflation (as measured by the Consumer Price Index) exceeded 10%. The FASB responded by requiring large hospitality firms to show current replacement cost of their property and equipment in footnotes to their financial statements. For some lodging properties, the current values of property and equipment exceeded twice the amount of the fixed assets carried on the books. Since inflation has been relatively low for the past several years, the FASB has rescinded this reporting requirement.

Throughout the 1980s, some hospitality businesses, such as Hilton Hotels Corporation, provided financial information in addition to that required by the FASB.

Hilton provided the traditional financial statements based on historical cost, as well as certain figures to reflect current replacement cost. It also provided certain figures based on the present value of income streams from their fixed assets.

Objective Evidence

Accounting transactions and the resulting accounting records should be based as much as possible on **objective evidence**. Generally, this evidence is an invoice and/or a canceled check. However, estimates must be assumed in the absence of such objective evidence. For example, suppose that the owner of a restaurant contributes equipment, purchased several years ago for personal use, to a restaurant corporation in exchange for 100 shares of stock. Further assume that there is no known market value for the restaurant corporation's stock. The owner may believe the equipment is worth $1,200, while the original catalog shows the cost several years ago of $1,400, and an appraiser appraises the equipment at $850. In this example, the most objective estimate of its value today would be the appraiser's estimate of $850.

Full Disclosure

The financial statements must provide information on all the facts pertinent to the interpretation of the financial statements. This **full disclosure** is accomplished either by reporting the information in the body of the financial statements or in footnotes to the financial statements. Footnote disclosures might include the accounting methods used, changes in accounting methods, contingent liabilities, events occurring after the financial statement date, and unusual and non-recurring items. An example of each type of disclosure is presented in Exhibit 7.

Consistency

Several accounting methods are often available for reporting a specific kind of activity. Management chooses the method most appropriate under the circumstances. For example, there are several ways to determine inventory values, and there are several methods of depreciating fixed assets. The **consistency principle** requires that, once an accounting method has been adopted, it should be followed from period to period unless a change is warranted and disclosed. The consistency principle allows a user of financial information to make reasonable comparisons between periods. Without consistent accounting, trends indicated by supposedly comparable financial statements might be misleading. When it becomes necessary to change to another method, the change must be disclosed and the dollar effect on earnings and/or the balance sheet must be reported.

The consistency principle does *not* dictate that an operation must or even should use the same accounting methods for preparing tax returns that it uses to prepare financial statements for external users. The principle does not even require that a method selected for one element of a company be used for all similar elements. For example, the straight-line method of depreciation may be used to depreciate one hotel and an accelerated method of depreciation may be used to depreciate another hotel owned by the same company.

Exhibit 7   Types of Disclosure

Type of Disclosure	Example
Accounting methods used	Straight-line method of depreciation
Change in the accounting methods	A change from depreciating a fixed asset using the straight-line method to using the double declining balance method
Contingent liability	A lawsuit against the company for alleged failure to provide adequate security for a guest who suffered personal injury
Events occurring after the financial statement date	A fire destroys significant assets of the hotel company one week after the end of the year
Unusual and non-recurring items	A hotel firm in Michigan suffers significant losses due to an earthquake

Matching

The **matching principle** refers to relating expenses to revenues. For example, suppose that a hotel purchases a computerized reservations system which will benefit the hotel for several years. The cost is therefore recorded as a fixed asset and the cost of the system is written off over the system's life. The result is a partial write-off of the fixed asset each year against the revenues generated in part by using the system. This process is referred to as matching and is the basis for adjusting entries at the end of each accounting period. The matching principle is used when transactions are recorded on an accrual rather than cash basis. The accrual basis and cash basis of accounting are discussed later in this chapter.

Conservatism

The **conservatism principle** calls for recognizing expenses as soon as possible, but delaying the recognition of revenues until they are ensured. The practical result is to be conservative (low) in recognizing net income for the current year. It is not proper to deliberately understate net income; however, many accountants wish to be cautious in recognizing revenues and "generous" in recognizing expenses.

A good example of this is the accounting treatment of lawsuits. If a hotel is a plaintiff in a lawsuit and its legal counsel indicates the case will be won and estimates the amount of settlement, the amount is not recorded as revenue until a judgment is rendered. On the other hand, if the same hotel is a defendant in a lawsuit and its legal counsel indicates the hotel will lose the lawsuit and most likely will pay a stated amount, this "expense" is recognized immediately.

Conservatism is apparent in the valuation of inventory at the lower of cost or current market value and the recognition of non-refundable deposits for future banquets as a liability until the banquet is catered.

Materiality

According to the **materiality principle**, events or information must be accounted for if they "make a difference" to the user of the financial information. An item is material in comparison to a standard. Some accountants have attempted to establish materiality by rules of thumb; for example, an item may be recognized if it exceeds a certain percentage of total assets or total income. However, this approach fails to address an item's relative importance over time. In addition, several immaterial items may be material when viewed collectively.

The materiality principle is often applied to fixed assets. Tangible items with useful lives beyond one year are commonly recorded as fixed assets. However, when such items cost less than a certain amount (specified by the board of directors of the purchasing organization), they are expensed because the cost is considered immaterial. An example would be a wastebasket. A $39 wastebasket might have a useful life of ten years, but if the company has set a $100 limit for recording expenditures as fixed assets, the cost of the wastebasket would be immaterial and the wastebasket would be expensed.

When a hospitality property provides footnotes to supplement its financial statement, only material or potentially material items are presented.

Cash Versus Accrual Accounting

The cash and accrual bases of accounting are two methods of determining when to record a transaction.

Cash basis accounting recognizes an accounting transaction at the point of cash inflow or outflow. For example, cash received in 19X2 for rooms sold in 19X1 would be treated as 19X2 revenues. Likewise, expenses incurred in 19X1 for which cash was disbursed in 19X2 would be treated as 19X2 expenses. Because of these improper assignments of revenues and expenses, cash basis accounting is generally not a fair reflection of business operations. Cash basis accounting usually violates the generally accepted accounting principles discussed earlier. However, using this method is acceptable if the results do not differ *materially* from those that accrual basis accounting would produce. This method is used only by very small hospitality operations.

The more commonly used **accrual basis accounting** recognizes revenues when earned (regardless of when cash is received) and expenses when incurred (regardless of when cash is disbursed). For example, suppose that a hotel room is sold for the period of December 30, 19X1, through January 2, 19X2, and the hotel guest pays the bill of $240 ($60 per night for four nights) on the morning of January 3, 19X2. Under accrual basis accounting, two days of rooms revenue are recorded in December and two days of rooms revenue are recorded in January.

Expenses must be recognized periodically (because of the matching principle) even when no transaction has occurred. Examples of non-transaction expense recognition include depreciation of property and equipment, reduction of prepaid insurance, accrual of payroll, and provisions of an allowance for uncollectible receivables.

For example, insurance coverage may be purchased twelve months in advance. Accrual basis accounting would recognize insurance expense over the 12-month period rather than when the cash is disbursed. The vehicle for this recognition is *adjusting entries,* which are briefly discussed later in this chapter.

Branches of Accounting

Accountants classify accounting activities in a variety of ways. However, most agree that there are distinct (though overlapping) branches. These branches are financial accounting, cost accounting, managerial accounting, tax accounting, auditing, and accounting systems.

Financial accounting refers to accounting for revenues, expenses, assets, and liabilities. It involves the basic accounting processes of recording, classifying, and summarizing transactions. This area is often limited to the accounting necessary to prepare and distribute financial reports. Financial accounting is historical in nature; that is, it deals with past events. Managerial accounting, on the other hand, deals with proposed events.

Cost accounting is the branch of accounting dealing with the recording, classification, allocation, and reporting of current and prospective costs. Cost accountants determine costs by departments, functions, responsibilities, and products and services. The chief purpose of cost accounting is to help operations personnel control operations.

Managerial accounting is the branch of accounting designed to provide information to various management levels for the purpose of enhancing controls. Management accountants prepare performance reports, including comparisons to the budget. One major purpose of these reports is to provide in-depth information as a basis for management decisions. Although managerial accounting may vary among segments of the hospitality industry and certainly among different establishments, many management accountants use various statistical techniques.

Tax accounting is the branch of accounting relating to the preparation and filing of tax forms with governmental agencies. Tax planning to minimize tax payments is a significant part of the tax accountant's work. Tax accounting usually focuses on income tax at the federal, state, and local levels, but may also include sales, excise, payroll, and property taxes. Many hospitality operations employ tax accountants. Some operations contract the services of tax accountants employed by certified public accounting firms.

Auditing is the branch of accounting involved with reviewing and evaluating documents, records, and control systems. Auditing may be either external or internal. It is most often associated with the independent, external audit called a **financial audit**. The external auditor reviews the financial statements of the hospitality operation, its underlying internal control system, and its accounting records (journals, vouchers, invoices, checks, bank statements, and so forth) in order to render an opinion of the financial statements. The auditor usually then provides recommendations for strengthening the operation's internal controls. Financial audits may only be conducted by certified public accounting firms.

Over the past several years, hospitality operations have increasingly employed internal auditors, whose primary purpose is to review and evaluate internal control systems. Many large hospitality firms have a full staff of internal auditors who conduct audits at individual properties to help management maintain the internal control system.

The final branch of accounting is accounting systems. Accounting systems personnel review the information systems of hospitality organizations. Information systems include not only the accounting system but other elements such as reservations. Because many hospitality operations are now computerized, many accounting systems experts are electronic data processing specialists, such as programmers and systems analysts. The trend toward larger accounting systems staffs in hospitality organizations will continue as the information revolution extends into the twenty-first century.

Review of Accounting Mechanics

Introductory accounting textbooks use several chapters to cover the mechanics of accounting, from the fundamental accounting equation to the preparation of the financial statements. Let us briefly review these topics.[3]

The **fundamental accounting equation** is simply *assets equal liabilities plus owners' equity*. The equation is a balance to be tested and proven, not a formula to be calculated. This equality is reflected in the balance sheet prepared at the end of each accounting period. **Assets**, simply defined, are things owned by the hospitality operation, including cash, inventory, accounts receivable, land, buildings, and equipment. **Liabilities**, simply stated, are obligations to outside parties and include accounts payable, notes payable, income tax payable, long-term debt payable, and accrued payroll. **Owners' equity** is the residual claims owners have on assets. In other words, assets less liabilities equals owners' equity. After each business transaction is recorded, the total assets must equal the total of liabilities and owners' equity.

There are two major sub-classifications of owners' equity—**permanent accounts** and **temporary accounts**. An **account** is simply a device for showing increases and/or decreases in an individual asset, liability, or owners' equity item. For example, a hospitality operation would have an account for cash in its bank account called "cash in bank." Permanent owners' equity accounts are not closed at the end of an accounting period. They include accounts for recording capital stock and retained earnings. Temporary owners' equity accounts are closed out at the end of each fiscal year and include all revenue and expense accounts. Revenues increase owners' equity, while expenses decrease owners' equity.

The fundamental accounting equation can now be expanded as follows:

Assets (A) = Liabilities (L)
+ Permanent Owners' Equity Accounts (POEA)
+ Temporary Owners' Equity Accounts (TOEA)

Revenues (R) and expenses (E) can be substituted for the TOEA, producing the following equation:

$$A = L + POEA + R - E$$

Debit and Credit

The left side of any account is called the **debit** side and the right side is the **credit** side. To debit an account means to record an amount on the left side, while to credit an account means to record an amount on the right side. The difference between the total debits and total credits of an account is called the **balance**. The normal balance of an account is the kind of balance, either debit or credit, which the account generally shows. The major classes of accounts have normal balances as follows:

Type of Account	Normal Balance
Asset	Debit
Liability	Credit
Owners' Equity:	
Permanent	Credit
Revenue	Credit
Expense	Debit

Each transaction is recorded with equal dollar amounts of debits and credits in **ledger accounts**. This equality of debits and credits in ledger accounts is tested by preparing a **trial balance**, which will be discussed later.

Debits (dr) and credits (cr) increase (+) and decrease (−) the various classes of accounts as follows:

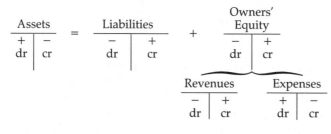

The Accounting Cycle ————————————————

In every accounting period (generally one year), an **accounting cycle** begins, starting with recording transactions and ending with a post-closing trial balance. Each step in the cycle will be defined and discussed briefly.

There are five common transactions in a hospitality operation:

1. Sales of products and services

2. Cash receipts

3. Purchases of products and services

4. Payroll

5. Cash disbursements

With each transaction, documents are prepared and/or received from which bookkeepers record the transaction. Exhibit 8 lists a few key documents for each type of transaction.

Exhibit 8   Documents and Transactions

	Documents	
Type of Transaction	Prepared by Firm	Prepared Outside of Firm
Sales of products and services	Food guest check Telephone voucher Laundry voucher	—
Cash receipts	Cash register tape	Checks
Purchases of products and services	Purchase order	Suppliers' invoices
Payroll	Time cards Payroll checks	—
Cash disbursements	Check	—

Step 1 in the accounting cycle is recording the transactions in journals. **Journals** are simply books used for initially recording individual transactions. There is generally a separate journal (generically called a **specialized journal**) for each type of transaction. In addition, each establishment maintains a **general journal** for recording entries not recorded in specialized journals. The process of recording requires that each transaction be analyzed and that a minimum of two accounts be affected. For example, a cash sales transaction results in increases to the cash account and the sales account.

Step 2 in the accounting cycle is transferring the amounts from the journals to the ledger accounts. This process, called **posting**, tracks individual accounts. For example, assume that cash at the beginning of the period is $1,000, cash receipts for the month total $50,000 (per the cash receipts journal), and cash disbursements equal $45,000 (per the cash disbursements journal). The cash account after these postings would show the following:

CASH

Date	P/R	Debit	Credit	Balance
Bal.		1,000		1,000
EOM	CR	50,000		51,000
EOM	CD		45,000	6,000

Normally, the columns of each specialized journal are totaled and these totals are posted to the proper accounts at the end of the month (EOM). Amounts recorded in the general journal, however, are posted individually. The example shows posting references (P/R) of CR for the cash receipts journal and CD for the cash disbursements journal. The beginning cash balance of $1,000 increased to $6,000 by the end of the month because $50,000 was received and $45,000 disbursed.

Step 3 in the accounting cycle is preparing a trial balance. The trial balance is simply a listing of all account balances, with debit balance accounts and credit balance accounts in separate columns. The totals of each column should be equal and prove the equality of debits and credits. Exhibit 9 presents the Mason Motel's trial balance for the month ended December 31, 19X1. Notice that the debit and credit columns both total $488,000.

Exhibit 9   Mason Motel Trial Balance

Mason Motel
Trial Balance
December 31, 19X1

	Debits	Credits
Cash	$ 5,000	
Marketable Securities	10,000	
Accounts Receivable	8,000	
Cleaning Supplies	2,500	
Prepaid Insurance	4,500	
Furniture	40,000	
Accumulated Depreciation, Furniture		$ 20,000
Equipment	10,000	
Accumulated Depreciation, Equipment		5,000
Building	300,000	
Accumulated Depreciation, Building		100,000
Land	20,000	
Accounts Payable		5,000
Notes Payable		5,000
Mortgage Payable		100,000
Melvin Mason, Capital		103,000
Room Revenue		150,000
Manager's Salary	15,000	
Assistant Manager's Salary	7,500	
Maids' Wages	15,000	
Payroll Taxes	3,000	
Cleaning Supplies Expense	2,000	
Office Supplies	1,000	
Utilities	5,000	
Advertising	500	
Repairs and Maintenance	9,000	
Property Taxes	22,000	
Interest Expense	8,000	
Total	$488,000	$488,000

Step 4 in the accounting cycle is preparing **adjusting entries**. Adjusting entries are required to adjust accounts to reflect the proper account balances. The adjusting entries are recorded in the general journal at the end of the accounting period. The major categories of adjusting entries, along with examples, are shown in Exhibit 10.

Step 5 is posting the adjusting entries. All adjusting entries are posted individually from the general journal. All adjustments are different, so there are no common accounts affected by the adjustments (in contrast to the entries recorded in specialized journals).

Step 6 in the accounting cycle is preparing an adjusted trial balance. After the adjusting entries are posted to the accounts, an adjusted trial balance is prepared to once

Exhibit 10   Major Categories of Adjusting Entries

		Accounts	
Category	Examples	Debited	Credited
1. Prepaid expense	a. Reduction of prepaid insurance	Insurance Expense	Prepaid Insurance
	b. Reduction of prepaid rent	Rent Expense	Prepaid Rent
2. Accrued expense	a. Accrual of payroll	Payroll Expense	Accrued Payroll
	b. Accrual of interest expense on a note payable	Interest Expense	Interest Payable
3. Unearned revenue	Reduction of unearned rent	Unearned Rent	Rental Revenue
4. Accrued revenue	Accrual of interest earned on note receivable	Interest Receivable	Interest Income
5. Estimated items	Depreciation expense	Depreciation Expense	Accumulated Depreciation, Fixed Assets
6. Inventory adjustment	Recording of ending inventory from physical inventory. (Note: other account balances such as Purchases are also transferred to the Cost of Goods Sold account.)	Inventory end of month	Cost of Goods Sold

again test the equality of debit and credit accounts. This process may be facilitated by using a worksheet (see Exhibit 11).

Step 7 is the preparation of the financial statements. Using a worksheet approach, the accountant simply extends all figures from the adjusted trial balance to the proper income statement and balance sheet columns. Exhibit 11 reveals that the difference between the debit and credit columns under the "income statement" results in net income. For the Mason Motel, revenues of $150,000 exceeded expenses of $105,350, resulting in net income of $44,650. Net income of $44,650 added to the total credits of $353,150 (balance sheet columns) equals total debits of $397,800 (balance sheet columns).

The accountant then prepares a formal income statement and balance sheet in accordance with generally accepted accounting principles (especially the full disclosure principle). This process may include footnotes to the statements and additional financial statements, such as the statement of cash flows.

In Step 8, after preparation of the financial statements, the revenue and expense accounts are closed. These temporary owners' equity accounts are closed into retained earnings. The closing entries either increase retained earnings (if the hospitality operation earned a profit) or decrease retained earnings (if a loss was suffered). The closing entries result in zero balances in all revenue and expense accounts. The closing entries are recorded in the general journal and posted to the proper accounts.

Exhibit 11 Mason Motel Worksheet

Mason Motel
Work Sheet
For the year ended December 31, 19X1

Account Title	Trial Balance Debit	Trial Balance Credit	Adjustments Debit	Adjustments Credit	Adjusted Trial Balance Debit	Adjusted Trial Balance Credit	Income Statement Debit	Income Statement Credit	Balance Sheet Debit	Balance Sheet Credit
Cash	5000				5000				5000	
Marketable Securities	10000				10000				10000	
Accounts Receivable	8000				8000				8000	
Cleaning Supplies	2500			(b) 700	1800				1800	
Prepaid Insurance	4500			(a) 1500	3000				3000	
Furniture	40000				40000				40000	
Accumulated Depreciation, Furniture		20000		(c) 4000		24000				24000
Equipment	10000				10000				10000	
Accumulated Depreciation, Equipment		5000		(d) 1000		6000				6000
Building	3000000				300000				300000	
Accumulated Depreciation, Building		100000		(e) 10000		110000				110000
Land	20000				20000				20000	
Accounts Payable		5000				5000				5000
Notes Payable		5000				5000				5000
Mortgage Payable		100000				100000				100000
Melvin Manson, Capital		103000				103000				103000
Room Revenue		150000				150000		150000		
Managers Salary	15000				15000		15000			
Assistant Managers Salary	7500				7500		7500			
Maids' Wages	15000		(f) 150		15150		15150			
Payroll Taxes	3000				3000		3000			
Cleaning Supplies Expense	2000		(b) 700		2700		2700			
Office Supplies	1000				1000		1000			
Utilities	5000				5000		5000			
Advertising	500				500		500			
Repairs & Maintenance	9000				9000		9000			
Property Taxes	22000				22000		22000			
Interest Expense	8000				8000		8000			
	488000	488000								
Insurance Expense			(a) 1500		1500		1500			
Depreciation Expense, Furniture			(c) 4000		4000		4000			
Depreciation Expense, Equipment			(d) 1000		1000		1000			
Depreciation Expense, Building			(e) 10000		10000		10000			
Accrued Wages				(f) 150		150				150
			17350	17350	5031150	5031150	105350	150000	353150	353150
Net Income							44650			44650
							150000	150000	397800	397800

Step 9, the final step in the accounting cycle, is the preparation of a post-closing trial balance. This balance is prepared to prove once again the equality of debits and credits.

Forms of Business Organization

There are four basic forms of business organization: the sole proprietorship, the partnership, the corporation, and the limited liability company. The business entity principle applies to all businesses. That is, all four forms of business organization are separate from other business entities and separate from their owners for accounting purposes.

A **sole proprietorship** is a business owned by a single person who generally (but not necessarily) manages the business. Many small lodging and food service businesses are organized as sole proprietorships. There are no legal formalities in organizing these businesses; thus, formation is quick and easy. The owner is held legally responsible for all debts of the business. However, the operation is, for accounting purposes, a separate business entity.

A **partnership** is a business owned by two or more people who often manage the business. Partnerships are created by either an oral or written agreement. The written agreement is preferable, as it provides a permanent record of the terms of the partnership. The written agreement includes the duties and initial investment of each partner and the sharing of profits and losses. Each partner is responsible for the debts of the business. As with the sole proprietorship, for accounting purposes, the partnership is a separate business entity.

A **limited partnership** is a form of partnership that offers the protection of limited liability to its **limited partners**. In order to have limited liability, limited partners may not actively participate in managing the business. A limited partnership must have at least one **general partner** who is responsible for the debts of the partnership—that is, the general partner has unlimited liability.

A **corporation** is a business organization incorporated under the laws of one of the United States. The corporation differs from the other forms of business organization because it is a *legal* business entity separate from its owners. Its continued existence depends on its charter from the state, not the lives of its owners. With the exception of the S corporations described on the next page, corporations (known as C corporations) may have any number of owners.

The owners of the C corporation are stockholders who buy shares of stock in the corporation. The stockholders are not responsible for the debts of the corporation, and, should the corporation fail, the stockholders lose only the amount they have paid for their shares. In contrast to the personal assets of sole proprietors and partners (or general partners in limited partnerships), the stockholders' personal assets are protected from the corporation's creditors.

The stockholders do not directly manage the lodging corporation, but rather elect a board of directors to represent their interests. The board selects officers (such as president and vice-president) who manage the corporation. Payments to the stockholders from the corporation's profits are called **dividends**. Once the board of directors declares dividends, the dividends are legal liabilities of the corporation and must be paid.

Exhibit 12   Comparative Features of Business Formats

	Limited Number of Owners	Limited Liability	Double Taxation	Management Participation
Sole Proprietorship	yes	no	no	yes
Partnership				
Limited partners	no	yes	no	no
General partners	no	no	no	yes
Limited Liability Co.	no	yes	no	yes
Corporation				
S Corporation	yes	yes	no	yes
C Corporation	no	yes	yes	yes

A special type of corporation is the S corporation. It enjoys favorable tax treatment under the Internal Revenue Code. The S corporation offers limited liability and its owners may participate in management; however, unlike the C corporation, it is not subject to double taxation. The major limitations of a business organized as an S corporation are that it may not have more than 75 stockholders, its stockholders must be U.S. citizens, and its stockholders may not in general include other corporations.

A **limited liability company (LLC)** is a relatively new form of business organization now available in a majority of U.S. states. The LLC has been gaining in popularity because it combines the corporate feature of limited liability with the favorable tax treatment of partnerships and sole proprietorships. The LLC, unlike the S corporation, may have an unlimited number of owners (who are referred to as members) and is not restricted to one class of stock.

Exhibit 12 reflects major aspects of the types of organizational formats.

Ethics and Hospitality Accounting

In recent years, considerable attention has been devoted to ethics, both in classrooms and boardrooms. Many major corporations have a code of ethics, and their managers are required to sign a statement saying that they will abide by the firm's code of ethics. Failure to follow the code often results in termination. Studies of the codes of ethics in America's largest corporations reveal the following common elements: (1) privacy of communication, (2) conflict of interests, (3) political contributions in the United States, (4) company records, (5) gifts, favors, entertainment, trips, and outings, (6) use of company assets, (7) anti-trust laws, (8) relations with competitors, (9) relations with suppliers, and (10) relations with customers.[4]

In the book *Ethics in Hospitality Management* by Stephen S. J. Hall, the role of ethics in accounting is discussed. The topic is divided into two sections: (1) the impact of ethics on accounting and (2) the marriage of theory and practice. The first section includes several ethical conflicts commonly encountered by hospitality accountants. For example:

A management company president, whose incentive compensation is based on a percentage of income before fixed charges, directs that all repair and maintenance items costing more than $500 be capitalized as capital improvements.

Clearly, this practice will result in greater management fees for the management company when revenue expenditures (expenditures that should be expensed) are accounted for as capital expenditures.

The second section under ethics in accounting states that it is unwise to separate ethical theories and practices. Theories of ethical behavior that are applied to situations at home and church should also be practiced in business. In accounting, "creativity" is allowed in certain situations if it is clearly explained. For example, different accounting methods can be used for various purposes, such as using an accelerated depreciation method for tax purposes and the straight-line method of depreciation for book purposes. However, this same "creativity" in accounting can lead to unethical practices if it does not reflect reality or is intended to deceive.

When faced with an ethical dilemma, the following questions can be used to make an appropriate decision:

1. Is the decision legal?

2. Is the decision fair?

3. Does the decision hurt anyone?

4. Have I been honest with those affected?

5. Can I live with my decision?

6. Am I willing to publicize my decision?

7. What if everyone did what I did?

If a decision can pass this seven-step test, it will most likely be considered ethical. [5]

Computer Applications

Less than 30 years ago, computers were almost unknown in the hospitality industry; they were usually found only at corporate headquarters. Now, they are increasingly common even in the smallest hospitality operations. Originally used to process accounts payable, accounts receivable, and general ledger transactions, computers are now used to process payroll, make reservations, post charges to guest accounts, and even report rooms ready for occupancy. Restaurants are using computers to record reservations, control food costs, and even notify the maître d' when a table is ready.

Two types of computers are often used in hospitality operations—the minicomputer and the personal computer (PC). Larger computers, or mainframe computers, can also be used for most business applications. However, they are expensive to own and operate and are still not common in most hotel properties. Minicomputers and personal computers generally do not require a data processing staff to operate them. In fact, the personal computer is so sophisticated it often allows the user, without any knowledge of computer programming, to make the machine do what is needed. For example, the user simply instructs the computer in easily understood commands to add, subtract, or calculate the present value and the machine does the rest.

A word of caution is appropriate, however. If the user does not understand the principles of accounting, a computer can provide incorrect results. It is critical that management understand the principles of accounting and what the machine should be doing. Without this knowledge, inaccurate financial results can be reported. In addition, employees who understand what the machine should be doing may be able to commit fraud. The computer must be considered a management tool. If management does not know how to use the tool properly, it may be useless or even harmful.

Summary

The major objectives of this chapter have been to provide a brief overview of the hospitality industry and a review of basic accounting procedures and concepts. Businesses in the hospitality industry, although different in several respects from firms in many other industries, maintain their accounts according to the same basic principles. A hospitality manager should therefore be well versed in general accounting and the special accounting considerations of a hospitality operation.

Hotels and restaurants may experience large fluctuations in demand and often maintain very perishable products. Although a manufacturing firm's inventory may have a shelf life of several years, a restaurant's inventory will perish after a few days and an unsold hotel room night can never be recovered. Hospitality operations do not maintain extensive inventories, so labor must be readily available to prepare and serve food and other products. This labor force must be able to satisfy many ranges of seasonality; different times of the day, days of the week, and seasons of the year will generate different levels of sales.

In order to reflect accurately the operations of these businesses and to ensure consistent recording between periods and properties, hospitality accountants follow generally accepted accounting principles. The cost principle stipulates that items be recorded at the amount for which they are purchased. The continuity of the business unit principle assumes that the organization is a going concern which is not threatened by having to liquidate immediately. The property must be treated as an entity separate from its owners according to the business entity principle. Other requirements are that accountants use objective evidence whenever possible and fully disclose financial items of significance to the users of the financial statements. If these principles are adhered to, the resultant statements will more accurately report the property's operations and financial position.

This chapter also provided a brief overview of basic accounting mechanics. Assets are items owned by the property and have debit balances; liabilities are amounts the property owes and have credit balances. The difference between assets and liabilities is owners' equity—the amount of residual claims owners have on assets. The final section of this chapter included a brief description of the four types of business organization: sole proprietorships, partnerships, corporations and limited liability companies.

Endnotes

1. *1996 Directory of Hotel & Motel Systems,* 65th ed. (Washington, D.C.: American Hotel & Motel Association, 1996).

2. *Trends in the Hotel Industry—USA Edition 1996* (San Francisco: PKF Consulting, 1996).

3. This text assumes that the reader has read an introductory accounting text or has access to one. *Hospitality Industry Financial Accounting* by Raymond S. Schmidgall and James W. Damitio (East Lansing, Mich.: Educational Institute of the American Hotel & Motel Association, 1994) contains several chapters which provide detailed coverage of the concepts in this section. Another appropriate text is Raymond Cote's *Understanding Hospitality Accounting I,* 3d ed. (East Lansing, Mich.: Educational Institute of the American Hotel & Motel Association, 1995).

4. W. F. Edmonson, *A Code of Ethics: Do Corporate Executives and Employees Need It?* (Fulton, Miss.: Itawamba Community College Press, 1990).

5. Stephen S. J. Hall, *Ethics in Hospitality Management* (East Lansing, Mich.: Educational Institute of the American Hotel & Motel Association, 1992).

Key Terms

account—A record containing information regarding a particular type of business transaction.

accounting cycle—Sequence of principal accounting procedures of a fiscal period; analyzing transactions, journal entry, posting to ledger, trial balance, adjustments, preparation of periodic financial statements, account closing, post-closing trial balance.

accrual basis accounting—System of reporting revenues and expenses in the period in which they are considered to have been earned or incurred, regardless of the actual time of collection or payment.

adjusting entries—Entries required at the end of an accounting period to record internal transactions.

assets—Resources available for use by the business; that is, anything owned by the business that has monetary value.

balance—The difference between the total debits and total credits of an account.

business entity principle—The generally accepted accounting principle that requires that a business maintain its own set of accounts that are separate from other financial interests of its owners.

cash basis accounting—Reporting of revenues and expenses at the time they are collected or paid.

conservatism principle—The generally accepted accounting principle that requires accounting procedures that recognize expenses as soon as possible, but delay the recognition of revenues until they are ensured. For example, non-refundable deposits for future services should be recognized as a liability until the service is actually performed.

consistency principle—The generally accepted accounting principle that requires that once an accounting method has been adopted, it should be followed from period to period in the future unless a change in accounting methods is warranted and disclosed.

continuity of the business unit principle—The generally accepted accounting principle that requires the assumption in preparing the accounting records and reports that the business will continue indefinitely and that liquidation is not in prospect—in other words, that the business is a going concern. Also called the going concern principle.

corporation—A form of business organization that provides a separate legal entity apart from its owners.

cost principle—The generally accepted accounting principle that requires recording the value of transactions for accounting purposes at the actual transaction price (cost).

credit—Decrease in an asset or increase in a liability or capital—entered on the right side of an account; such amounts are said to be credited to the account.

debit—Increase in an asset or decrease in a liability or capital—entered on the left side of an account; such amounts are said to be debited or charged to the account.

dividends—Distributions of earnings to owners of a corporation's stock.

financial audit—An independent, external audit.

full disclosure principle—The generally accepted accounting principle that requires that financial statements must provide information on all the significant facts that have a bearing on their interpretation. Types of disclosures include the accounting methods used, changes in the accounting methods, contingent liabilities, events occurring subsequent to the financial statement date, and unusual and nonrecurring items.

fundamental accounting equation—Assets equal liabilities plus owners' equity. This equation is a balance to be tested and proven, not a formula to be calculated.

general journal—Record of all accounting transactions.

general partner—A member of a partnership with unlimited liability for the debts of the partnership.

generally accepted accounting principles—Accounting principles that have become accepted over time through common usage and also through the work of major accounting bodies. They provide a uniform basis for preparing financial statements.

going concern principle—The generally accepted accounting principle that requires the preparation of accounting records and reports under the assumption that the business will continue indefinitely and that liquidation is not in prospect; also referred to as continuity of the business unit.

journals—Accounting records of business transactions.

ledger—A group of related accounts that constitute a complete unit.

liabilities—Obligations of a business; largely indebtedness related to the expenses incurred in the process of generating income.

limited liability company—A form of business organization that combines the corporate feature of limited liability with the favorable tax treatment of partnerships and sole proprietorships. May have an unlimited number of owners (who are referred to as members) and is not restricted to one class of stock.

limited partner—A member of a limited partnership having limited liability. Limited partners may not actively participate in managing the business.

limited partnership—A form of business organization consisting of a partnership between two or more individuals having at least one general partner and one limited partner in which the latter's liabilities are limited to investments.

matching principle—The generally accepted accounting principle that requires recording expenses in the same period as the revenues to which they relate.

materiality principle—The generally accepted accounting principle that requires that events be recognized and recorded by accounting procedures if they make a difference as determined by some relative standard of comparison. For example, materiality may be established by a rule of thumb which states that an item is recognized if it exceeds $x\%$ or more of total assets or income.

objective evidence—The preferred basis of accounting transactions and the resulting accounting records.

owners' equity—Financial interest of the owners of a business; assets minus liabilities.

partnership—A form of business organization involving two or more owners that is not incorporated.

permanent accounts—A classification of owners' equity accounts that are not closed at the end of an accounting period; for example, accounts for recording capital stock and retained earnings.

posting—Transferring data entered in a journal to the appropriate account.

sole proprietorship—An unincorporated business organized by one person.

specialized journal—A journal used to accelerate the recording of specific kinds of accounting transactions.

temporary accounts—A classification of owners' equity accounts that are closed out at the end of each fiscal year; for example, all revenue and expense accounts.

trial balance—Listing and totaling of all the general ledger accounts on a worksheet.

unit of measurement principle—The accounting principle that the monetary values stated in financial statements should represent a stable unit of value so that meaningful comparisons of current and past periods are possible.

? Review Questions

1. What are some differences between hospitality operations and manufacturing firms?

2. What types of seasonality would a transient hotel most likely experience?

3. Approximately what percentage of total revenues is labor cost in the hospitality industry?

4. What is the matching principle?

5. How does inflation affect the unit of measurement principle?

6. What accounts are included in the Temporary Owners' Equity Accounts?

7. What is posting?

8. What are the five types of accounts which are included in the general ledger of all hospitality firms?

9. What is the concept of materiality?

10. What are the six branches of accounting and the major responsibilities of each?

Problems

Problem 1

What is the normal balance of each account listed below?

1.	Cash	6.	Mortgage payable
2.	G. Williams, Capital	7.	Equipment
3.	Accounts payable	8.	Room sales
4.	Inventory	9.	Payroll taxes expense
5.	Cost of food sold	10.	Accounts receivable

Problem 2

The Williamston Cafe experienced several cash transactions on July 1, 19X4, as follows:

1. Received cash on account for $300.
2. Received cash from sales of July 1, 19X4, for $700.
3. Paid payroll taxes of $450.
4. Purchased a new range costing $6,000 by paying $1,000 and signing a note payable for $5,000 with the supplier.
5. Received cash of $5,000 from an investor in the business.
6. Paid a food supplier $2,000 on account.

Required:

Determine the balance of the cash account at the end of the day. The cash balance at the beginning of the day was $650.

Problem 3

Which business organization format is most desirable for each independent situation below?

1. The quickest and easiest business format is desired.
2. The five owners will use a corporate approach but want to avoid double taxation.
3. The general partner has investors who have no interest in operations. Only a significant return is desired.
4. The owner of this operation wants total control. He is not concerned about limiting his liability.
5. The owners want to tap the capital markets for millions of dollars from thousands of investors.
6. The two owners in this firm will both be very active in operating the business. They have no concerns about limiting their liability but do want to minimize their taxes.

Problem 4

Multiple choice: Select the best response in each item below.

1. An entry to increase the accumulated depreciation account is recorded with a _____ entry.

   a. debit
   b. credit
   c. either debit or credit

2. Food inventory is reduced on the books to its market value when it is lower than cost due to the _____ principle.

   a. cost
   b. going concern
   c. business entity
   d. none of the above

3. Which of the following items is *not* recorded at the end of the accounting period because of the matching principle?

   a. accrual of unpaid wages
   b. recognition of expired insurance coverage
   c. increase in the allowance for doubtful accounts
   d. recording of the dividend declared by the board of directors
   e. all of the above

4. The branch of accounting involved with reviewing and evaluating documents, records, and control systems is _____.

   a. cost
   b. managerial
   c. auditing
   d. accounting systems

5. Which of the following forms of business formats has a limited number of owners?

   a. C corporation

b. S corporation
c. limited partnership
d. limited liability company
e. both c and d

6. The Triple-Z Ranch purchased a three-year insurance policy on June 1, 19X1 for $36,000. The coverage was for the period of July 1, 19X1 through June 30, 19X4. The amount of prepaid insurance that should be shown on the ranch's balance sheet as a current asset as of December 31, 19X1 is _____.

a. $0
b. $6,000
c. $12,000
d. $24,000
e. $30,000

7. The Zebra Inn sold 10,000 shares of its common stock for $20 per share. Its common stock has a par value of $1 per share. Which of the following statements is false?

a. Cash of $200,000 was received.
b. The common stock account increased by $200,000.
c. The additional paid-in capital account increased by $190,000.
d. Retained earnings is not affected by this transaction.

Problem 5

Fill in the blanks below with the accounting principle that best applies.

A. Cost principle
B. Business entity
C. Conservatism
D. Full disclosure
E. Materiality
F. Continuity of the business unit
G. Consistency
H. Matching
I. Unit of measurement
J. Objective evidence

1. A restaurant records accrued wages at the end of the fiscal year because of the _____ principle.

2. A hotel reduces its inventory values to reflect the market value of its food stocks, which are lower than the original cost, because of the _____ principle.

3. A motel does *not* reduce the value of its glassware to liquidation value because of the _____ principle.

4. The cost of ten replacement wastebaskets is expensed rather than recorded as equipment due to the _____ principle.

5. The method of depreciation used is reflected in the financial report because of the _____ principle.

6. When one method of inventory valuation is used at the end of 19X5 and another method is used at the end of 19X6, this violates the _____ principle.

7. The cost of steaks taken home by the owner for personal use is recorded as a "withdrawal" because of the _____ principle.

8. A boat dock is recorded at $22,500 (the amount paid) rather than the original contract price of $25,000 because of the _____ principle.

Problem 6

Which branch of accounting is described by each statement below?

1. This branch of accounting prepares the independent review of a firm's financial statements.

2. The chief purpose of this branch of accounting is to assist operations personnel in controlling operations.

3. The nature of this branch of accounting is historical.

4. This branch of accounting deals with proposed events.

5. Reports prepared by this branch of accounting should greatly assist management in making future decisions.

6. The focus of this branch of accounting is to minimize taxes paid.

7. This branch of accounting focuses on the review and evaluation of internal control systems.

8. In this branch of accounting, some members are likely to be systems analysts.

Problem 7

Mr. Gregory Vain is a successful business person who does not fully understand the fundamental accounting equation and how various transactions affect it. You have been hired to share your knowledge with him.

Required:

1. State the basic equation and briefly explain each element of it.

2. Explain how each type of account could be increased and illustrate with examples. Be sure to describe all the effects of your examples.

   Example: Asset accounts would increase when a new hotel is purchased. However, in order to remain in equilibrium, another asset account, "cash," would decrease if the hotel is purchased with cash.

3. State how temporary accounts relate to the fundamental accounting equation.

Problem 8

Browny Brad's Beach Motel (BBBM), a 40-room lodging facility, has operated for the past three years. BBBM's night auditor has kept accurate records over the past year but has not analyzed any of these data. The following is a summary of the rooms sold by month:

Rooms sold:

January	400	March	700	May	960
February	600	April	840	June	980

July	992	September	800	November	650
August	973	October	705	December	500

Assume there are 365 days in the year and that the summer months include May, June, July, and August. The off-season comprises all other months.

Required:

Determine the paid occupancy percentage for the summer months, the off-season, and the entire year.

Problem 9

Julie Bickley desires to organize her lodging business to minimize her taxes, minimize her legal liability, and maintain control. She is willing to include additional investors.

Required:

1. Discuss the organizational format you recommend and state the reasoning behind your recommendations.
2. If she is highly successful and decides to expand into several adjoining states or provinces, would you recommend a change? Explain why or why not.

Problem 10

Below is a list of the 19X3 activities/transactions for Emily's Eatery.

1. A fire insurance policy for July 1, 19X3, through June 30, 19X4, was purchased on May 15, 19X3. The premium paid totaled $24,000 and was recorded as prepaid insurance.
2. The operation purchased a new cash register costing $12,000 on September 1, 19X3, and recorded it in the equipment account. The cash register is expected to have a useful life of seven years and a salvage value of $1,000. No depreciation has been recorded. Emily's uses the straight-line method of depreciation.
3. The employees were paid for their work through December 26. They worked 300 hours for the period of December 27–31, 19X3, and will be paid on January 10, 19X4. The average hourly wage is $6.00.
4. Sales for the year totaled $800,000. The allowance for doubtful accounts has a December 31 balance of $1,000. The allowance should be adjusted at year-end to $1/2\%$ of sales for the year.
5. The electric bill for the period of December 5, 19X3, through January 4, 19X4, totaled $620. It has not been recorded and will be paid on January 10, 19X4.

Required:

For each situation, prepare the adjusting entry to record the proper expense for 19X3.

Problem 11

The following balance sheet for the Sundowner Motel has several accounts that require adjusting before preparation of the December 31, 19X5, financial statements.

Balance Sheet
The Sundowner Motel
November 30, 19X5

Assets

Current Assets:

Cash	$ 15,000
Accounts Receivable	108,000
Allowance for Doubtful Accounts	(6,000)
Food Inventory	4,000
Prepaid Insurance	3,000
Total Current Assets	124,000

Property and Equipment:

Land	50,000
Building	1,440,000
Equipment	400,000
Accumulated Depreciation	(490,000)
Total Property and Equipment	1,400,000
Total Assets	$1,524,000

Liabilities and Owners' Equity

Current Liabilities:

Notes Payable	$ 5,000
Accounts Payable	10,000
Wages Payable	12,000
Taxes Payable	17,000
Total Current Liabilities	44,000

Long-term Liabilities:

Mortgage Payable	600,000

Owners' Equity:

James Sun, Capital	880,000
Total Liabilities and Owners' Equity	$1,524,000

Additional information:

1. The allowance for doubtful accounts is calculated as 5.5% of the total accounts receivable and then rounded to the next $100. The accounts receivable at December 31, 19X5, totaled $123,200.

2. The annual insurance premium of $6,000 was paid on May 15 for the period of June 1, 19X5, through May 31, 19X6.

3. The physical food inventory at December 31, 19X5, totaled $3,800.

4. The building is depreciated over 30 years using the straight-line (SL) method (assume a salvage value of $100,000). The equipment is depreciated over five years using the SL method (assume a salvage value of zero). For purposes of depreciation calculation, assume that the equipment was purchased on January 1, 19X3. Calculate depreciation expense for the month of December only.

Required:

Prepare the adjusting entries for The Sundowner Motel.

Problem 12

Robbie Hanson owns a resort on an excellent fishing lake. Her busy season begins May 15 and extends through mid-fall. During the winter, she engaged a contractor to build a boat house and dock for a total price of $25,000. The contract called for completion by May 15 because the resort was completely booked for the week of May 15 to 22, the opening week of the fishing season. Because the completion date was so important to Hanson, she specified in the contract that if the construction was not completed by May 15, the price would be reduced by $100 per day until completion.

The construction was not completed until June 9, at which time Hanson paid the contract price of $22,500, deducting $100 for each day's delay. Hanson is convinced that she lost goodwill because the resort's facilities were inadequate and that several of her guests shortened their stays because the facilities were still under construction.

Hanson included the boat house and dock as assets valued at $25,000 on the balance sheet prepared on September 30, the end of her fiscal year. Included in her revenues was an item "Penalty payments received in lieu of lost revenue—$2,500."

The auditor who examined Hanson's report objected to this treatment and insisted that the facilities be recorded at their actual cost, $22,500. Hanson stated that she could not understand the logic of this position. "Accounting principles are out of tune with reality," she complained. "What if the contract had been 250 days late and the boat house and dock had cost me nothing; would you record on my balance sheet that I had no asset? I lost at least $100 per day in revenues because of the construction delay."

Required:

At what amount should these facilities be reported on the balance sheet of September 30? (You may ignore depreciation from June 9 to September 30.) Explain your position in terms of accounting principles.

Chapter 2 Outline

Purposes of the Balance Sheet
Limitations of the Balance Sheet
Balance Sheet Formats
Content of the Balance Sheet
    Current Accounts
        Current Assets
        Current Liabilities
    Noncurrent Receivables
    Investments
    Property and Equipment
    Other Assets
    Long-Term Liabilities
    Owners' Equity
    Footnotes
    Consolidated Financial Statements
Balance Sheet Analysis
    Horizontal Analysis
    Vertical Analysis
    Base-Year Comparisons
Computer Applications

2

The Balance Sheet

THE BALANCE SHEET IS A MAJOR financial statement prepared at the end of each accounting period. It reflects a balance between an organization's assets and claims to its assets called liabilities and owners' equity. This statement is also referred to as a statement of financial position. It contains answers to many questions that managers, owners (investors), and creditors may have, such as:

1. How much cash was on hand at the end of the period?

2. What was the total debt of the hospitality operation?

3. What was the mix of internal and external financing at the end of the period?

4. How much was owed to the hotel by guests?

5. What amount of taxes was owed to the various governmental tax agencies?

6. What was the operation's ability to pay its current debt?

7. What was the financial strength of the operation?

8. How much interest do stockholders have in the operation's assets?

This chapter addresses the purposes and limitations of the balance sheet. We will also consider the formats and contents of balance sheets with special attention to the suggested balance sheet from the *Uniform System of Accounts for the Lodging Industry (USALI)*.[1] In addition, we will discuss the kinds and purposes of footnotes attached to balance sheets. Finally, we will consider techniques for analyzing the financial information contained in a balance sheet. The Appendix at the end of this chapter includes the financial statements for the Hilton Hotels Corporation from its 1996 annual report.

Purposes of the Balance Sheet

Other major financial statements—the income statement, the statement of retained earnings, and the statement of cash flows—pertain to a period of time. The balance sheet reflects the financial position of the hospitality operation—its assets, liabilities, and owners' equity—at a given date. It is the financial statement that reflects, or tests and proves, the fundamental accounting equation (assets equal liabilities plus owners' equity).

Management, although generally more interested in the income statement and related department operations statements, will find balance sheets useful for conveying financial information to creditors and investors. In addition, management must determine if the balance sheet reflects to the best extent possible the financial position of the hospitality operation. For example, many long-term loans specify a required **current ratio** (which is current assets divided by current liabilities). Failure to meet the requirement may result in all long-term debt being reclassified as current and thus due immediately. Since few operations could raise large sums of cash quickly, bankruptcy could result. Therefore, management must carefully review the balance sheet to determine that the operation is in compliance. For example, assume that at December 31, 19X1 (year-end), a hotel has $500,000 of current assets and $260,000 of current liabilities. Further assume that the current ratio requirement in a bank's loan agreement with the hotel is 2 to 1. The required current ratio can be attained simply by taking the appropriate action. In this case, the payment of $20,000 of current liabilities with cash of $20,000 results in current assets of $480,000 and current liabilities of $240,000, resulting in a current ratio of 2 to 1.

Creditors are interested in the hospitality operation's ability to pay its current and future obligations. The ability to pay its current obligations is shown, in part, by a comparison of current assets and current liabilities. The ability to pay its future obligations depends, in part, on the relative amounts of long-term financing by owners and creditors. Everything else being the same, the greater the financing from investors, the higher the probability that long-term creditors will be paid and the lower the risk that these creditors take in "investing" in the enterprise.

Investors are most often interested in earnings that lead to dividends. To maximize earnings, an organization should have financial flexibility, which is the operation's ability to change its cash flows to meet unexpected needs and take advantage of opportunities. Everything else being the same, the greater the financial flexibility of the hospitality operation, the greater its opportunities to take advantage of new profitable investments, thus increasing net income and, ultimately, cash dividends for investors.

In addition, the balance sheet reveals the liquidity of the hospitality operation. **Liquidity** measures the operation's ability to convert assets to cash. Even when a property's past earnings have been substantial, this does not in itself guarantee that the operation will be able to meet its obligations as they become due. The hospitality operation should have sufficient liquidity not only to pay its bills, but also to provide its owners with adequate dividends.

Analysis of several balance sheets for several periods will yield trend information that is more valuable than single period figures. In addition, comparison of balance sheet information with projected balance sheet numbers (when available) will reveal management's ability to meet various financial goals.

Limitations of the Balance Sheet

As useful as the balance sheet is, it is generally considered less useful than the income statement to investors, long-term creditors, and especially to management. Since the balance sheet is based on the cost principle, it often does not reflect current values of some assets, such as property and equipment. For hospitality operations whose assets are appreciating rather than depreciating, this difference may be significant. Hilton Hotels Corporation may be a fair reflection of this difference. In the most recent annual report that disclosed market values, Hilton revealed the current value of its assets (footnote disclosure only) to be $4.03 billion, while its balance sheet showed the book value of its assets to be $1.89 billion. The difference between current value and book value was $2.14 billion. The assets reflected in the balance sheet for Hilton were only 47% of their current value.[2] This "understatement," if unknown or ignored by management, investors, and creditors, could lead to less than optimal use of Hilton's assets.

Another limitation of balance sheets is that they fail to reflect many elements of value to hospitality operations. Most important to hotels, motels, restaurants, clubs, and other sectors of the hospitality industry are people. Nowhere in the balance sheet is there a reflection of the human resource investment. Millions of dollars are spent in recruiting and training to achieve an efficient and highly motivated work force, yet this essential ingredient for successful hospitality operations is not shown as an asset. Other valuable elements not directly shown on the balance sheet include such things as goodwill, superior location, loyal customers, and so on. Understandably, it may be difficult to assign an objective value to these elements. Nevertheless, they are not only critical to an operation's success—they are also of significant value. An exception to this is purchased goodwill, which is shown on the balance sheet. This goodwill results when a purchaser of a hospitality operation is unable to assign the entire purchase price to the operation's individual assets. The excess of the purchase price over the dollars assigned to the individual assets is labeled goodwill. For example, if a hotel costs $10 million, $8 million of that price may be assigned to the building, $1 million may be assigned to the land, and $600,000 may be assigned to furniture, fixtures, and equipment. The remaining $400,000 may be assigned to goodwill. Self-generated goodwill, which for many hospitality operations is significant, is not shown on the balance sheet.

Balance sheets are limited by their static nature; that is, they reflect the financial position for only a moment. Thereafter, they are less useful because they become outdated. Thus, the user of the balance sheet must be aware that the financial position reflected at year-end may be quite different one month later. For example, a hospitality operation with $1,000,000 of cash may seem financially strong at year-end, but if it invests most of this cash in fixed assets two weeks later, its financial flexibility and liquidity are greatly reduced. This situation would generally only be known to the user of financial documents if a balance sheet and/or other financial statements were available for a date after this investment had occurred.

Finally, the balance sheet, like much of accounting, is based on judgments; that is, it is *not* exact. Certainly, assets equal liabilities plus owners' equity. However, several balance sheet items are based on estimates. The amounts shown as accounts receivable (net) reflect the estimated amounts to be collected. The amounts shown as inventory reflect the lower of the cost or market (that is, the lower of original cost and current replacement cost) of the items expected to be sold, and the amount shown as property and equipment reflects the cost less estimated depreciation. In each case, accountants use estimates to arrive at values. To the degree that these estimates are in error, the balance sheet items will be wrong.

Balance Sheet Formats

The balance sheet can be arranged in either the account or report format. The **account format** lists the asset accounts on the left side of the page and the liability and owners' equity accounts on the right side. Exhibit 1 illustrates this arrangement.

Exhibit 1   Balance Sheet Account Format

Mason Motel				
Balance Sheet				
December 31, 19X1				
ASSETS			**LIABILITIES AND OWNERS' EQUITY**	
Current Assets:			Current Liabilities:	
Cash	$ 2,500		Notes Payable	$ 23,700
Accounts Receivable	5,000		Accounts Payable	8,000
Cleaning Supplies	2,500		Wages Payable	300
Total	10,000		Total	32,000
Property & Equipment:			Long-Term Liabilities:	
Land	20,000		Mortgage Payable	120,000
Building	300,000		Total Liabilities	152,000
Furnishings and Equipment	50,000			
	370,000		Melvin Mason, Capital at	
			January 1, 19X1	64,500
Less: Accumulated			Net Income for 19X1	38,500
Depreciation	125,000		Melvin Mason, Capital at	
			December 31, 19X1	103,000
Net Property &				
Equipment	245,000		**Total Liabilities**	
Total Assets	**$ 255,000**		**and Owners' Equity**	**$ 255,000**

The **report format** shows assets first, followed by liabilities and owners' equity. The group totals on the report form can show either that assets equal liabilities and owners' equity or that assets minus liabilities equal owners' equity. Exhibit 2 illustrates the report format.

Content of the Balance Sheet

The balance sheet consists of assets, liabilities, and owners' equity. Simply stated, assets are things owned by the firm, liabilities are claims of outsiders to assets, and owners' equity is claims of owners to assets. Thus, assets must equal (balance) liabilities and owners' equity. Assets include various accounts such as cash, inventory for resale, buildings, and accounts receivable. Liabilities include accounts such as accounts payable, wages payable, and mortgage payable. Owners' equity includes capital stock and retained earnings. These major elements are generally divided into various classes as shown in Exhibit 3. While balance sheets may be organized differently, most hospitality operations follow the order shown in Exhibit 3.

Current Accounts

Under both "assets" and "liabilities and owners' equity" is a current classification. **Current assets** normally refer to items to be converted to cash or used in operations

Exhibit 2   Balance Sheet Report Format

Mason Motel
Balance Sheet
December 31, 19X1

ASSETS

Current Assets:		
Cash		$ 2,500
Accounts Receivable		5,000
Cleaning Supplies		2,500
Total Current Assets		10,000
Property and Equipment:		
Land	$ 20,000	
Building	300,000	
Furnishings and Equipment	50,000	
Less: Accumulated Depreciation	125,000	
Net Property and Equipment		245,000
Total Assets		**$255,000**

LIABILITIES AND OWNERS' EQUITY

Current Liabilities:		
Notes Payable	$ 23,700	
Accounts Payable	8,000	
Wages Payable	300	$ 32,000
Long-Term Liabilities:		
Mortgage Payable		120,000
Total Liabilities		152,000
Owners' Equity:		
Melvin Mason, Capital at January 1, 19X1	64,500	
Net Income for 19X1	38,500	
Melvin Mason, Capital at December 31, 19X1		103,000
Total Liabilities and Owners' Equity		**$255,000**

within one year or in a normal operating cycle. **Current liabilities** are obligations that are expected to be satisfied either by using current assets or by creating other current liabilities within one year or a normal operating cycle.

Exhibit 4 reflects a normal operating cycle which includes (1) the purchase of inventory for resale and labor to produce goods and services, (2) the sale of goods and services, and (3) the collection of accounts receivable from the sale of goods and services.

A normal operating cycle may be as short as a few days, as is common for many quick-service restaurants, or it may extend over several months for some hospitality

Exhibit 3   Major Elements of the Balance Sheet

Assets	Liabilities and Owners' Equity
Current Assets	Current Liabilities
Noncurrent Assets:	Long-Term Liabilities
Noncurrent Receivables	Owners' Equity
Investments	
Property and Equipment	
Other Assets	

Exhibit 4   Normal Operating Cycle

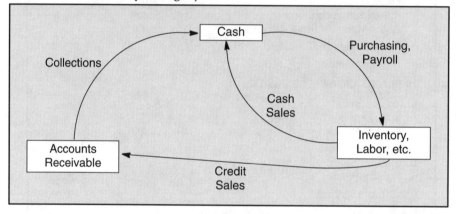

operations. It is common in the hospitality industry to classify assets as current/noncurrent on the basis of one year rather than on the basis of the normal operating cycle.

Current Assets. Current assets, listed in the order of liquidity, generally consist of cash, marketable securities, receivables, inventories, and prepaid expenses. Cash consists of cash in house banks, cash in checking and savings accounts, and certificates of deposit. The exception is cash restricted for retiring long-term debt, which should be shown under other assets. Cash is shown in the balance sheet at its face value.

Marketable securities are shown as current assets when they are available for conversion to cash. Marketable securities that are not available for conversion to cash are considered investments. Generally, the critical factor in making this current/noncurrent decision is management's intent. Marketable securities should be shown on the balance sheet at market value.

The current asset category of receivables consists of accounts receivable—trade and notes receivable. Accounts receivable—trade are open accounts carried by a hotel or motel on the guest, city, or rent ledgers. Notes receivable due within one year are also listed, except for notes from affiliated companies, which should be shown under "Investments." Receivables should be stated at the amount estimated to be collectible. An allowance for doubtful accounts, the amount of receivables estimated to be uncollectible, should be subtracted from receivables to provide a net receivables amount.

Inventories of a hospitality operation primarily consist of merchandise held for resale. Inventories are generally an insignificant percentage of the total assets of a hospitality operation and may be valued at cost. If the amount of inventory is material and the difference between cost and market is significant, then the inventory should be stated at the lower of cost or market.

The final current asset category is prepaid expenses. Prepaid expenses represent purchased goods and services to be used by the hospitality operation within one year. For example, assume that a fire insurance premium of $6,000 affords insurance protection for one year after the transaction. At the date of the expenditure, the $6,000 is classified as prepaid insurance and, thereafter, is amortized by a monthly reduction of $500 ($1/12$ of $6,000) which is shown on the income statement as insurance expense. Other prepaid expenses include prepaid rent, prepaid property taxes, prepaid interest, and prepaid maintenance and service contracts.

Prepaid expenses that will benefit the operation beyond one year from the balance sheet date should be classified as other assets. For example, assume that a three-year fire insurance policy costs $18,000. The entry to record the cash disbursement would be to debit prepaid insurance for $6,000 (the cost of coverage for the next 12 months) and to debit deferred charges—insurance for $12,000 (the cost of insurance coverage paid that benefits the operation for periods beyond 12 months from the balance sheet date).

Current Liabilities. Current liabilities are obligations at the balance sheet date that are expected to be paid by converting current assets or by creating other current liabilities within one year. They generally consist of one of the four following types:

1. Payables resulting from the purchase of goods, services, and labor and from the applicable payroll taxes

2. Amounts received in advance of the delivery of goods and services, such as advance deposits on rooms and banquet deposits

3. Obligations to be paid in the current period relating to fixed asset purchases or to reclassification of long-term debt as current

4. Dividends payable and income taxes payable

The major classifications of current liabilities according to the *USALI* are notes payable, current maturities of long-term debt, income taxes payable, deferred income taxes, accrued expenses, advance deposits, and accounts payable. Notes payable include short-term notes which are due within 12 months. Current maturities of long-term debt include the principal payments of long-term debt such as notes and similar liabilities, sinking fund obligations, and the principal portion of capitalized leases due within 12 months. Accounts payable include amounts due to creditors for merchandise, services, equipment, or other purchases. Deferred income taxes—current include amounts that represent the tax effects of timing differences attributable to current assets and current liabilities that are accounted for differently for financial and income tax reporting purposes. Accrued expenses are expenses incurred before the balance sheet date that are not due until after the balance sheet date. Advance deposits include amounts received for services that have not been provided as of the balance sheet date.

Obligations to be paid with **restricted cash** (that is, cash that has been deposited in separate accounts, often for the purpose of retiring long-term debt) should not be classified as current, but rather as long-term.

Current liabilities are often compared with current assets. The difference between the two is commonly called **working capital.** The current ratio results from dividing current assets by current liabilities. Many hospitality properties operate successfully with a current ratio approximating 1 to 1, compared with a reasonable current ratio for many other industries of 2 to 1. The major reason for this difference lies with the relatively low amount of inventories required and relatively high turnover of receivables by hospitality operations as compared with many other industries.

Noncurrent Receivables

Noncurrent receivables include both accounts and notes receivable that are not expected to be collected within one year from the balance sheet date. If any collectibility is uncertain regarding noncurrent receivables, an allowance for doubtful noncurrent receivables should be used (similar to the allowance account for current receivables) and subtracted from total noncurrent receivables to provide net noncurrent receivables.

Investments

Investments generally includes debt or equity securities and ownership interests that are expected to be held on a long-term basis. Investments in marketable equity securities and debt securities, where there is not the intent and ability to hold such securities to maturity, should be considered "available for sale" and reflected at market value with unrealized gains and losses being shown, net of tax effects, as a separate component of equity. Investment in debt securities where there is the intent and ability to hold such securities to maturity should be considered "held to maturity" and reflected at amortized cost. Investments in affiliated entities should be shown separately, unless insignificant. Investments in property for future development generally should also be accounted for as investments. The method of accounting for and the basis for valuing investments should be disclosed in Notes to the Financial Statements.

Property and Equipment

Property and equipment consists of fixed assets including land, buildings, furnishings and equipment, construction in progress, leasehold improvements, and china, glassware, silver, linens, and uniforms.[3] Property and equipment under capital leases should also be shown in this section of the balance sheet. With the exception of land, the cost of all property and equipment is written off to expense (depreciation expense) over time due to the matching principle. Depreciation methods used should be disclosed in a footnote to the balance sheet. The depreciation method used for financial reporting to outsiders and that used for tax purposes may differ, resulting in deferred income taxes. Deferred income taxes are generally a liability and will be discussed later in the chapter. On the balance sheet, fixed assets are shown at cost and are reduced by the related accumulated depreciation and amortization.

Other Assets

Other assets consist of all noncurrent assets not included in the aforementioned categories. Other assets include:

Goodwill. Goodwill represents the excess of the purchase price over the fair value of the net assets acquired in the purchase of a business. Goodwill should be amortized over the period during which it is expected to benefit the business. Accumulated Amortization should be shown and the amortization method and period disclosed in the Notes to Financial Statements.

Cash Surrender Value of Life Insurance. Some organizations purchase life insurance on the lives of key individuals. Many of these policies have a cash surrender value that should be recorded as an asset. Changes in the amount of the Cash Surrender Value should be reflected as adjustments to Insurance Expense.

Deferred Charges. Deferred Charges typically relates to financing activities and represents direct costs of obtaining financing such as loan fees and bond issuance costs. Such costs are usually amortized over the life of the related financing. The method and period of amortization should be disclosed in Notes to the Financial Statements.

Deferred Income Taxes—Noncurrent. Deferred Income Taxes—Noncurrent represents the tax effects of temporary differences between the bases of Noncurrent Assets and Noncurrent Liabilities for financial and income tax reporting purposes. For example, if a liability is accrued that will not be paid for an extended period and the expense is deductible only when paid for tax purposes, the accrual will result in a Noncurrent Deferred Income Tax asset. Noncurrent Deferred Income Taxes are presented as net noncurrent assets or net noncurrent liabilities as circumstances dictate.

Other assets also include the costs to organize the hospitality operation (organization costs), security deposits, and unamortized franchise costs. The initial franchise fee paid by the franchisee should be recorded as an other asset and amortized against revenue over the life of the franchise agreement.

Long-Term Liabilities

Long-term liabilities are obligations at the balance sheet date that are expected to be paid beyond the next 12 months or, if paid in the current year, will be paid from restricted funds. Common long-term liabilities consist of notes payable, mortgages payable, bonds payable, capitalized lease obligations, and deferred income taxes. Any long-term debt to be paid with current assets within the next year is reclassified as current liabilities. Still, long-term debt per the *USALI* is reported on the balance sheet in total with the amount due within 12 months subtracted as "Less Current Maturities."

Lease obligations reported as long-term liabilities generally cover several years, while short-term leases are usually expensed when paid. Deferred income taxes result from timing differences in reporting for financial and income tax purposes—that is, the accounting treatment of an item for financial reporting purposes results in a different amount of expense (or revenue) than that used for tax purposes. Generally, the most significant timing difference for hotels and motels relates to depreciation, since many operations use the straight-line method for financial reporting purposes and an accelerated method for income tax purposes.

For example, suppose a hotel decides to depreciate a fixed asset on a straight-line basis at $15,000 a year for reporting purposes, and depreciate the same asset $25,000 for the year using an accelerated method for tax purposes. If the firm's marginal tax rate is 25%, then the difference in depreciation expense of $10,000 ($25,000 − $15,000) times 25% results in $2,500 cash saved and reported as a noncurrent liability. The book entry to record this savings is as follows:

Income Tax Expense	$2,500	
Deferred Income Taxes		$2,500

Owners' Equity

The **owners' equity** section of the balance sheet reflects the owner's interest in the operation's assets. The detail of the owners' equity section is a function of the organization of the business. The four major types of business organization are sole proprietorships, partnerships, limited liability companies, and corporations. The owners' equity section of a corporation includes capital stock, additional paid-in capital, retained earnings, and treasury stock. **Capital stock** for most hospitality operations is **common stock**; however, a few operations have also issued **preferred stock.** When more than one type of stock has been issued, each should be reported separately. Capital stock is the product of the number of shares outstanding and the par value of the shares.

The **additional paid-in capital** category consists of payments for capital stock in excess of the stated and/or par value of the capital stock. For example, cash of $50 received from the sale of common stock with a par value of $10 would be recorded as $10 to the common stock account and the remainder ($40) as "additional paid-in capital" or "paid-in capital in excess of par."

Retained earnings reflect earnings generated but not distributed as dividends. Changes in this account during the year are commonly shown on a statement of retained earnings.

Treasury stock represents the property's own capital stock that has been repurchased but not retired. The cost of the treasury shares is shown as a reduction of owners' equity.

Exhibit 5 shows the prescribed formats of the assets section and the liabilities and owners' equity section of the balance sheet from the *USALI*. Note that the owners' equity section of the balance sheet pertains to a lodging operation organized as a corporation.

When a lodging operation is organized as a sole proprietorship, all the owner's equity is reflected in one account as illustrated in Exhibit 1, Melvin Mason, Capital. The $103,000 of capital of Melvin Mason would have been spread across at least two accounts, capital stock and retained earnings, if the Mason Motel had been incorporated.

Exhibit 5   Balance Sheet

BALANCE SHEET

Assets

	Current Year	Prior Year
CURRENT ASSETS		
Cash		
House Banks	$	$
Demand Deposits		
Temporary Cash Investments		
Total Cash		
Short-Term Investments		
Receivables		
Accounts Receivable		
Notes Receivable		
Current Maturities of Noncurrent Receivables		
Other		
Total Receivables		
Less Allowance for Doubtful Accounts		
Net Receivables		
Inventories		
Prepaid Expenses		
Deferred Income Taxes, Current		
Other		
Total Current Assets		
NONCURRENT RECEIVABLES, Net of Current Maturities		
INVESTMENTS		
PROPERTY AND EQUIPMENT		
Land		
Leaseholds and Leasehold Improvements		
Furnishings and Equipment		
Buildings		
Construction in Progress		
China, Glassware, Silver, Linen and Uniforms		
Total Property and Equipment		
Less: Accumulated Depreciation and Amortization		
Net Property and Equipment		
OTHER ASSETS		
Goodwill		
Cash Surrender Value of Life Insurance		
Deferred Charges		
Deferred Income Taxes—Noncurrent		
Other		
Total Other Assets		
TOTAL ASSETS	$	$

Exhibit 5   *(continued)*

BALANCE SHEET

Liabilities and Owners' Equity

	Current Year	Prior Year
CURRENT LIABILITIES		
Notes Payable		
Banks	$	$
Others		
Total Notes Payable		
Accounts Payable		
Accrued Expenses		
Advance Deposits		
Income Taxes Payable		
Deferred Income Taxes—Current		
Current Maturities of Long-Term Debt		
Other		
Total Current Liabilities		
LONG-TERM DEBT, Net of Current Maturities		
Mortgage Notes, other notes, and similar liabilities		
Obligations Under Capital Leases		
Total Long-Term Debt		
OTHER LONG-TERM LIABILITIES		
DEFERRED INCOME TAXES—Noncurrent		
COMMITMENTS AND CONTINGENCIES		
*OWNERS' EQUITY		
_____% Cumulative Preferred Stock, $_____ par value, authorized _____ shares; issued and outstanding _____ shares		
Common Stock, $_____ par value, authorized _____ shares; issued and outstanding _____ shares		
Additional Paid-In Capital		
Retained Earnings		
Less: Treasury Stock, _____ shares of Common Stock, at cost		
Total Owners' Equity		
TOTAL LIABILITIES AND OWNERS' EQUITY	$	$

*The line items of this section reflect a corporate form of business organization. For line items appropriate to proprietorships and partnerships, see the explanatory notes for this section.

Finally, many lodging businesses are organized as partnerships. The owners' equity section of a partnership should reflect each partner's equity. The balance sheet for a partnership with many partners simply will refer to a supplementary schedule showing each partner's share. The owners' equity section of a business organized as a partnership by its three owners is illustrated as follows:

M. Kass, Capital	$ 50,000
J. Ninety, Capital	25,000
R. Chicklets, Capital	25,000
Total Owners' Equity	$ 100,000

Footnotes

The balance sheets of hospitality operations, although packed with financial information, are not complete without the other financial statements (income statement and statement of cash flows) and footnotes. Footnotes are discussed below.

The full disclosure principle requires that financial information be sufficient to inform the users—creditors, owners, and others. This can only be accomplished by providing footnote disclosure in addition to the financial statements. Thus, footnotes are an integral part of the financial statements of a hospitality operation. They should contain additional information not presented in the body of the financial statements. They should not contradict or soften the disclosure of the financial statements, but rather provide needed explanations. The financial statements of publicly-held companies generally include the following footnotes:

1. Summary of Significant Accounting Policies

2. Accounts and Notes Receivable

3. Inventories

4. Investments

5. Property and Equipment

6. Current Liabilities

7. Long-Term Debt

8. Income Taxes

9. Capital Stock

10. Employee Benefit Plans

11. Leases

12. Segments of Business

13. Supplementary Financial Information

14. Commitments and Contingent Liabilities

Consolidated Financial Statements

Many major hospitality companies consist of several corporations. For example, the hypothetical XYZ Hotel Company consists of a parent corporation, XYZ Hotel Company, and three separately incorporated hotels—Hotel X, Hotel Y, and Hotel Z. The XYZ Hotel Company owns 100% of the capital stock of each of the three hotels. Each hotel has its own set of financial statements, but for purposes of financial reporting, they are combined with the parent's financial statements. The combined statements are referred to as **consolidated financial statements.** Generally, the first footnote includes a brief description of the principles of consolidation used to combine the statements of a parent corporation and its subsidiary corporations.

In effect, consolidated financial statements reflect a single economic unit rather than the legal separate entities resulting from separate corporations. Generally, more than 50% of the voting stock of a subsidiary should be owned by the holding company or by the same interests if the associated companies' financial statements are to be combined. Accounting procedures related to financial statement consolidations are covered in advanced accounting textbooks.

Balance Sheet Analysis

The information shown on the balance sheet is most useful when it is properly analyzed. The analysis of a balance sheet may include the following:

1. Horizontal analysis (**comparative statements**)

2. Vertical analysis (**common-size statements**)

3. Base-year comparisons

4. Ratio analysis

In the remainder of this chapter, the first three techniques will be discussed.

Horizontal Analysis

Horizontal analysis compares two balance sheets—the current balance sheet and the balance sheet of the previous period. In this analysis, the two balance sheets are often referred to as comparative balance sheets. This represents the simplest approach to analysis and is essential to the fair reporting of the financial information. Often included for management's analysis are the two sets of figures with the changes from one period to the next expressed both in absolute and relative terms.

Absolute changes show the change in dollars between two periods. For example, assume that cash was $10,000 at the end of year 19X1 and $15,000 at the end of year 19X2. The absolute change is the difference of $5,000.

The relative change (also called the percentage change) is found by dividing the absolute change by the amount for the previous period. The relative change, using the cash example above, is 50% ($5,000 ÷ $10,000). The $5,000 absolute change may not seem significant by itself, but viewed as a relative change, it is a 50% increase over the previous year.

Examine the comparative balance sheets for the Stratford Hotel found in Exhibit 6. Comparative analysis shows that marketable securities increased by $629,222 in absolute terms and 404.7% in relative terms. The increase is substantial. In light of these figures, a manager would desire answers to several questions, including the following:

1. Are the marketable securities readily convertible to cash?

Exhibit 6   Comparative Balance Sheets

Comparative Balance Sheets
Stratford Hotel

	December 31		Change from 19X1 to 19X2	
ASSETS	19X2	19X1	Amount	Percentage
Current Assets:				
Cash	$ 104,625	$ 85,600	$ 19,025	22.2%
Marketable Securities	784,687	155,465	629,222	404.7
Accounts Receivable (net)	1,615,488	1,336,750	278,738	20.9
Inventories	98,350	92,540	5,810	6.3
Other	12,475	11,300	1,175	10.4
Total	2,615,625	1,681,655	933,970	55.5
Property and Equipment:				
Land	905,700	905,700	0	0
Buildings	5,434,200	5,434,200	0	0
Furnishings and Equipment	2,617,125	2,650,500	(33,375)	(1.3)
Less: Accumulated Depreciation	1,221,490	749,915	471,575	62.9
Total	7,735,535	8,240,485	(504,950)	(6.1)
Other Assets	58,350	65,360	(7,010)	(10.7)
Total Assets	$ 10,409,510	$ 9,987,500	$ 422,010	4.2%
LIABILITIES				
Current Liabilities:				
Accounts Payable	$ 1,145,000	$ 838,000	$ 307,000	36.6%
Current Maturities of Long-Term Debt	275,000	275,000	0	0
Income Taxes Payable	273,750	356,000	(82,250)	(23.1)
Total	1,693,750	1,469,000	224,750	15.3
Long-Term Debt				
Notes Payable	50,000	0	50,000	N.M.
Mortgage Payable	1,500,000	1,775,000	(275,000)	(15.5)
Less: Current Maturities	275,000	275,000	0	0
Total	1,275,000	1,500,000	(225,000)	(15.0)
Total Liabilities	2,968,750	2,969,000	(250)	0
OWNERS' EQUITY				
Common Stock	1,750,000	1,750,000	0	0
Additional Paid-In Capital	250,000	250,000	0	0
Retained Earnings	5,440,760	5,018,500	422,260	8.4
Total	7,440,760	7,018,500	422,260	6.0
Total Liabilities and Owners' Equity	$ 10,409,510	$ 9,987,500	$ 422,010	4.2%

N.M. = not meaningful

2. Is the amount invested in marketable securities adequate for cash needs in the next few months?

3. Should some of the dollars invested in marketable securities be moved to less liquid, but higher rate-of-return investments?

Significant changes in other accounts should be similarly investigated.

To explain the drastic change in some balance sheet items, a **fluctuation explanation** may be prepared. This explanation provides detail not available on the balance sheet. Exhibit 7 illustrates a fluctuation explanation of marketable securities for the Stratford Hotel.

Exhibit 7   Fluctuation Explanation

Fluctuation Explanation—Marketable Securities Stratford Hotel			
	Balance at Dec. 31		Increase
	19X2	19X1	(Decrease)
Marketable Securities			
Commercial Paper	$240,000	$ 90,000	$150,000
Bank Repurchase Agreements	44,687	15,465	29,222
Treasury Bills	150,000	25,000	125,000
Treasury Bonds	150,000	25,000	125,000
Corporate Stocks & Bonds	200,000	0	200,000
	$784,687	$155,465	$629,222

Vertical Analysis

Another approach to analyzing balance sheets is to reduce them to percentages. This **vertical analysis,** often referred to as common-size statement analysis, is accomplished by having total assets equal 100% and individual asset categories equal percentages of the total 100%. Likewise, total liabilities and owners' equity equal 100% and individual categories equal percentages of 100%.

Common-size balance sheets permit a comparison of amounts relative to a base within each period. For example, assume that cash at the end of year 19X1 is $10,000 and total assets are $100,000. At the end of year 19X2, assume that cash is $15,000 and total assets are $150,000. Horizontal analysis shows a $5,000/50% increase. But cash at the end of each year is 10% of the total assets ($10,000 divided by $100,000 equals 10%; $15,000 divided by $150,000 equals 10%). What first appears to be excessive cash at the end of year 19X2 ($5,000) may not be excessive since cash is 10% of total assets in both cases. However, only a detailed investigation would resolve whether cash equal to 10% of total assets is required in each case.

Examine the Stratford Hotel's common-size balance sheets (Exhibit 8). Notable changes include marketable securities (1.6% to 7.5%), total current assets (16.9% to 25.1%), accumulated depreciation (−7.5% to −11.7%), and accounts payable (8.4% to 11.0%). Management should investigate significant changes such as these to determine if they are reasonable. If the changes are found to be unreasonable, management should attempt to remedy the situation.

Common-size statement comparisons are not limited strictly to internal use. Comparisons may also be made against other operations' financial statements and against industry averages. Common-size figures are helpful in comparing hospitality operations that differ materially in size. For example, assume that a large hospitality operation has current assets of $500,000, while a much smaller operation's current assets are $50,000 and that both figures are for the same period. If total assets equal $1,500,000 for the large operation and $150,000 for the small enterprise, then both operations have current assets equaling 33.3% of total assets. These percentages provide

Exhibit 8   Common-Size Balance Sheets

	Common-Size Balance Sheets Stratford Hotel				
		December 31		Common Size	
ASSETS		19X2	19X1	19X2	19X1
Current Assets:					
Cash	$	104,625	$ 85,600	1.0%	0.9%
Marketable Securities		784,687	155,465	7.5	1.6
Accounts Receivable (net)		1,615,488	1,336,750	15.5	13.4
Inventories		98,350	92,540	1.0	0.9
Other		12,475	11,300	0.1	0.1
Total		2,615,625	1,681,655	25.1	16.9
Property and Equipment:					
Land		905,700	905,700	8.7	9.1
Buildings		5,434,200	5,434,200	52.2	54.4
Furnishings and Equipment		2,617,125	2,650,500	25.1	26.5
Less: Accumulated Depreciation		1,221,490	749,915	(11.7)	(7.5)
Total		7,735,535	8,240,485	74.3	82.5
Other Assets		58,350	65,360	0.6	0.6
Total Assets		$10,409,510	$ 9,987,500	100.0%	100.0%
LIABILITIES					
Current Liabilities:					
Accounts Payable	$	1,145,000	$ 838,000	11.0%	8.4%
Current Maturities of Long-Term Debt		275,000	275,000	2.6	2.8
Income Taxes Payable		273,750	356,000	2.6	3.6
Total		1,693,750	1,469,000	16.2	14.8
Long-Term Debt					
Notes Payable		50,000	0	0.5	0
Mortgage Payable		1,500,000	1,775,000	14.4	17.8
Less: Current Maturities		275,000	275,000	(2.6)	(2.8)
Total		1,275,000	1,500,000	12.3	15.0
Total Liabilities		2,968,750	2,969,000	28.5	29.8
OWNERS' EQUITY					
Common Stock		1,750,000	1,750,000	16.8	17.5
Additional Paid-In Capital		250,000	250,000	2.4	2.5
Retained Earnings		5,440,760	5,018,500	52.3	50.2
Total		7,440,760	7,018,500	71.5	70.2
Total Liabilities and Owners' Equity		$10,409,510	$ 9,987,500	100.0%	100.0%

a more meaningful comparison than the dollar amount of the current assets when comparing financial statements of the two companies.

Base-Year Comparisons

A third approach to analyzing balance sheets is **base-year comparisons**. This approach allows a meaningful comparison of the balance sheets for several periods. A base period is selected as a starting point, and all subsequent periods are compared with the base. Exhibit 9 illustrates the base-year comparisons of the Stratford Hotel's current assets for the years 19X0–19X2.

Exhibit 9   Base-Year Comparisons

	19X2	19X1	19X0
	Base-Year Comparisons		
	Current Assets		
	Stratford Hotel		
Cash	126.30%	103.33%	100.00%
Marketable Securities	339.32%	67.23%	100.00%
Accounts Receivable (net)	124.39%	102.92%	100.00%
Inventories	110.55%	104.02%	100.00%
Other	114.11%	103.37%	100.00%
Total Current Assets	152.71%	98.18%	100.00%

The base-year comparisons of the Stratford Hotel use 19X0 as the base. Total current assets for 19X2 are 152.71% of the total current assets for 19X0. The user of this analysis is quickly able to determine the changes of current assets over a period of time. For example, cash increased only 26.30% from the end of 19X0 to the end of 19X2, while marketable securities increased 239.32%.

Computer Applications

The balance sheet preparation was one of the first activities to be computerized. There are software programs (general ledger packages) available which require that the bookkeeper enter all of the journal entries as they occur, and which use this information to generate the financial statements at the end of the period. Many of these packages require sophisticated hardware to operate. However, in recent years, more packages for minicomputers and personal computers have been developed.

Even if a general ledger package is not used by a hospitality operation, the computer can be used as a tool in the balance sheet preparation. For example, a property's fixed assets can be maintained on the computer and the depreciation expense calculated with a spreadsheet program. Exhibit 10 is a partial listing of the Lincoln Motel's fixed assets. Using this spreadsheet, an accountant could merely enter the fixed asset's name, cost, purchase date, and expected life, and the computer could then generate the depreciation amounts (straight-line with no salvage value) in the following years. The sum of each individual asset's depreciation is automatically calculated for the income statement's depreciation expense. With a more sophisticated spreadsheet, the user could record accumulated depreciation, make use of salvage values, and even calculate depreciation using different methods such as double declining balance or sum-of-the-years' digits.

Summary

Although the balance sheet may not play the vital role in management decision-making that other financial statements play, it is still an important tool. By examining

Exhibit 10   Lincoln Motel's Computerized Depreciation Schedule

	Cost	Year Purchased	Year Life		19X1	19X2	19X3	19X4
				XX		Year's Depreciation		
				XX				
				XX				
Building	$1,000,000	19X1	40	XX	$25,000	$25,000	$25,000	$25,000
Furniture	200,000	19X1	10	XX	20,000	20,000	20,000	20,000
Truck	15,000	19X2	3	XX		5,000	5,000	5,000
				XX				
				XX				
				XX				
				XX				
				XX				
				XX				
				XX				
Total F/A	$1,215,000			XX				
				XX				
				XX				
				XX				
TOTAL DEPRECIATION EXPENSE:					$45,000	$50,000	$50,000	$50,000

it, managers, investors, and creditors may determine the financial position of the hospitality operation at a given point in time. It is used to help determine an operation's ability to pay its debts, offer dividends, and purchase fixed assets.

The balance sheet is divided into three major categories: assets, liabilities, and owners' equity. Assets are the items owned by the operation, while liabilities and owners' equity represent claims to the operation's assets. Liabilities are amounts owed to creditors. Owners' equity represents the residual interest in assets for investors. Both assets and liabilities are divided into current and noncurrent sections. Current assets are cash and other assets that will be converted to cash or used in the property's operations within the next year. Current liabilities represent present obligations that will be paid within one year. The major categories of noncurrent assets include noncurrent receivables, investments, property and equipment, and other assets. Long-term liabilities are present obligations expected to be paid beyond the next 12 months from the date of the balance sheet.

Owners' equity generally includes common stock, paid-in capital in excess of par, and retained earnings. Common stock is the product of the number of shares outstanding and the par value of the shares. Paid-in capital in excess of par is the amount over the par value paid by investors when they purchased the stock from the hospitality property. Retained earnings are the past earnings generated by the operation but not distributed to the stockholders in the form of dividends.

As assets are the items owned by the property, and liabilities and owners' equity are claims to the assets, the relationship involving the three is stated as follows: Assets = Liabilities + Owners' Equity. The balance sheet is prepared either with assets on one side of the page and liabilities and owners' equity on the other (account format) or with the three sections in one column (report format).

In order to gain more information from the balance sheet, it is frequently compared to the balance sheet prepared at the end of the previous period. One tool used is horizontal analysis, which calculates absolute and relative differences between the the current year's data and the data from the prior period. Significant differences are generally analyzed. Another type of analysis is vertical analysis, which states all accounts as percentages of either total assets or total liabilities and owners' equity. Differences between the end results of two periods can then be examined. Alternatively, the balance sheet figures for the particular hospitality operation may be compared with data from other properties or with averages for the hospitality industry as a whole. These comparisons can highlight differences and help management identify areas of concern. A third type of analysis is called base-year comparisons. This approach expresses changes over two or more years as percentages of a base year.

Endnotes

1. *Uniform System of Accounts for the Lodging Industry, 9th rev. ed.* (East Lansing, Mich.: Educational Institute of the American Hotel & Motel Association, 1996).

2. *Hilton Hotels Corporation 1988 Annual Report* (Beverly Hills, Calif.: Hilton Hotels Corp., 1989), pp. 32, 44.

3. The detailed accounting for these items (capitalization, depreciation, amortization) is covered in Raymond S. Schmidgall and James W. Damitio, *Hospitality Industry Financial Accounting* (East Lansing, Mich.: Educational Institute of the American Hotel & Motel Association, 1994).

Key Terms

account format—A possible arrangement of a balance sheet that lists the asset accounts on the left side of the page and the liability and owners' equity accounts on the right side.

additional paid-in capital—Payments for capital stock in excess of the stated and/or par value of the capital stock. Also called paid-in capital in excess of par.

balance sheet—Statement of the financial position of the hospitality establishment at a given date, giving the account balances for assets, liabilities, and ownership equity.

base-year comparison—An analytical tool that allows a meaningful comparison of financial statements for several periods by using a base period as a starting point (set at 100%) and comparing all subsequent periods with the base.

capital stock—Shares of ownership of a corporation.

common stock—Capital stock of a corporation that generally allows its holders to have voting rights.

common-size balance sheets—Balance sheets used in vertical analysis whose information has been reduced to percentages to facilitate comparisons.

common-size statements—Financial statements used in vertical analysis whose information has been reduced to percentages to facilitate comparisons.

comparative balance sheets—Balance sheets from two or more successive periods used in horizontal analysis.

comparative statements—The horizontal analysis of financial statements from the current and previous periods in terms of both absolute and relative variances for each line item.

consolidated financial statements—The combined financial statements of a parent corporation and its subsidiary corporations.

current assets—Resources of cash and items that will be converted to cash or used in generating income within a year through normal business operations.

current liabilities—Obligations that are due within a year.

current ratio—Ratio of total current assets to total current liabilities expressed as a coverage of so many times; calculated by dividing current assets by current liabilities.

fluctuation explanation—A document providing detail not available on the balance sheet that explains drastic changes in balance sheet items.

goodwill—The excess of a hospitality operation's purchase price over the dollars assigned to its individual assets.

horizontal analysis—Comparing financial statements for two or more accounting periods in terms of both absolute and relative variances for each line item.

liquidity—The ability of an operation to meet its short-term (current) obligations by maintaining sufficient cash and/or investments easily convertible to cash.

long-term liabilities—Obligations at the balance sheet date which are expected to be paid beyond the next 12 months, or if paid in the next year, they will be paid from restricted funds; also called noncurrent liabilities.

noncurrent receivables—Accounts and notes receivable that are not expected to be collected within one year from the balance sheet date.

owners' equity—Financial interest of the owners of a business; assets minus liabilities.

preferred stock—Stock issued by a corporation that provides preferential treatment on dividends, but may not give the stockholder voting rights.

report format—A possible arrangement of a balance sheet that lists assets first, followed by liabilities and owners' equity.

restricted cash—Cash that has been deposited in separate accounts, often for the purpose of retiring long-term debt.

retained earnings—An account for recording undistributed earnings of a corporation.

treasury stock—Capital stock of a corporation that the corporation has repurchased for future issuance.

vertical analysis—Analyzing individual financial statements by reducing financial information to percentages of a whole; that is, income statement line items are expressed as percentages of total revenue; balance sheet assets are expressed as percentages of total assets; and so forth.

working capital—Current assets minus current liabilities.

Review Questions

1. How do creditors and investors use the balance sheet?

2. What are some of the limitations of the balance sheet?

3. What are the differences and similarities between the account and report formats of the balance sheet?

4. What are assets, liabilities, and owners' equity? What is the relationship among the three?

5. What is meant by the phrase "the lower of cost or market"? When is it used?

6. What are deferred income taxes? Where are they recorded on the balance sheet?

7. What are the differences between a comparative balance sheet and a common-size balance sheet?

8. What is the order of liquidity for the following accounts (most liquid first): marketable securities, prepaid expenses, cash, inventories, and receivables?

9. How do the terms "current" and "long-term" relate to the balance sheet?

10. How is the current ratio determined? What does it reflect?

Problems

Problem 1

The Cooper Cafe's balance sheet contains several assets as listed below. Identify the major classification of each based on the *USALI* balance sheet (see Exhibit 5).

> Construction in progress
> Cash advance to affiliated company
> Petty cash
> Trade receivables
> Building
> Cash surrender value of life insurance
> Notes receivable—long-term
> Office supplies
> Land
> Unamortized franchise costs
> Organizational costs
> Food inventory
> Prepaid insurance
> Leasehold improvements

Problem 2

Using major classifications from the *USALI* balance sheet (see Exhibit 5), classify each account below:

>Food inventory
>Front office computer
>Utility deposits
>State income taxes payable
>Bonds payable (long-term)

>Treasury stock
>Prepaid insurance
>Leased equipment under capital leases
>Petty cash
>Kitchen utensils

>Paid-in capital in excess of par
>Banquet deposits
>James Smith, Capital
>Goodwill
>Deferred insurance

>Investment in GM stock (100 shares)
>Loan to James Smith (owner)
>Land (10 acres—undeveloped)
>Accrued payroll

>Cash—First National Bank
>Retained earnings

Problem 3

Anna Williams incorporated her lodging business at the beginning of 19X1. Transactions and information regarding the owners' equity accounts are as follows:

- Preferred stock: 100,000 shares of $1 par value stock have been authorized for sale by the State of Delaware. Ten thousand shares have been sold and issued for $10 per share.

- Common stock: 500,000 shares of $5 par value stock have been authorized for sale. One hundred thousand shares have been sold and issued for $20 per share.

- Treasury stock: At the end of 19X1, 1,000 shares of common stock were repurchased for $25 per share and are being held for future reissue.

- Retained earnings: Williams' lodging business generated net income of $7,500 for 19X1 and no dividends have been declared.

Required:

Prepare the owners' equity section of the balance sheet at the end of 19X1 in accordance with the *USALI* (see Exhibit 5).

Problem 4

Listed below are asset, liability, and owners' equity accounts for Sue & Jerry's Sleepy Hollow as of December 31, 19X1.

Common Stock	$ 44,600
Inventories	23,241
Treasury Stock	7,278
Land	111,158
House Banks	11,738
Deferred Income Taxes (noncurrent/credit balance)	190,038
Paid-in Capital in Excess of Par	115,501
Notes Payable	42,611
Retained Earnings	327,137
Demand Deposits	8,803
Dividends Payable	21,246
Accounts Receivable	128,179
Accrued Salaries	78,293
Certificates of Deposit	2,934
Prepaid Expenses	13,499
Notes Receivable	22,420
Building	682,093
Marketable Securities	134,634
Long-Term Debt	262,930
Investments	30,049
Accounts Payable	58,690
Allowance for Doubtful Accounts	16,316
Deferred Expenses	12,794
Advance Deposits—Banquets	14,203
Current Maturities on Long-Term Debt	25,824
Security Deposits	8,569

Required:

Prepare the current assets section of the balance sheet for Sue & Jerry's Sleepy Hollow in accordance with the *USALI* (see Exhibit 5).

Problem 5

Using the data from Problem 4:

1. Prepare the liabilities section of the balance sheet in accordance with the *USALI* (see Exhibit 5).

2. Determine the current ratio.

Problem 6

Using the data from Problem 4, prepare the owners' equity section of the balance sheet in accordance with *USALI* (see Exhibit 5).

Problem 7

The Spartan Inn, a sole proprietorship, has several accounts as follows:

Room sales	$1,000,000
Land	80,000
Cash	5,000
Accounts payable	20,000
Inventories	15,000
Accounts receivable	80,000
Bonds payable (long-term)	300,000
Jerry Spartan, Capital (1/1/19X4)	300,000
Accrued expenses	10,000
Prepaid expenses	8,000
Temporary investments	25,000
Building	500,000
Equipment and furnishings	200,000
Franchise fees (deferred)	15,000
Accumulated depreciation	150,000
Income tax payable	10,000
Deferred income taxes (noncurrent/ credit balance)	20,000
Interest expense	25,000

Other information is as follows:

The Spartan Inn's net income for 19X4 was $145,000, and Jerry Spartan withdrew $27,000 for personal use during 19X4.

Required:

Prepare a balance sheet for the Spartan Inn as of December 31, 19X4 in accordance with the *USALI* (see Exhibit 5).

Problem 8

The following information is KRS, Inc.'s balance sheet account balances as of December 31, 19X1 and 19X2. You have been hired by Kermit Smith, the owner, to prepare a financial package for a bank loan including comparative balance sheets.

Assets	19X1	19X2
Cash	$ 16,634	$ 20,768
Accounts Receivable	16,105	11,618
Marketable Securities	10,396	10,496
Inventories	14,554	18,554
Prepaid Expenses	4,158	3,874
Land	116,435	116,435
Building	1,007,090	1,007,090
China, Glass, etc.	269,255	284,934
Accumulated Depreciation	453,263	537,849

Liabilities & Owners' Equity

Accounts Payable	13,265	12,945
Accrued Expenses	2,047	1,039
Deferred Income Taxes (noncurrent)	8,163	7,927
Current Portion of Long-Term Debt	20,407	20,060
Long-Term Debt	553,429	533,369
Retained Earnings	192,853	149,380
Common Stock	211,200	211,200

Required:

Prepare comparative balance sheets for December 31, 19X1 and 19X2, in accordance with the *USALI*. Note: the comparative approach is shown in Exhibit 6.

Problem 9

Mrs. Wolf, the owner of the Foxtail, a small lodging operation, has asked for your help in understanding the balance sheets for 19X1 and 19X2. She is able to present you with the condensed balance sheets as follows:

The Foxtail
Condensed Balance Sheets
December 31, 19X1 and 19X2

	19X1	19X2
Cash	$ 10,000	$ 12,000
Accounts Receivable	26,500	18,500
Investments	10,000	20,000
Equipment	200,000	325,000
Accumulated Depreciation	(20,000)	(64,000)
Total Assets	$ 226,500	$ 311,500
Current Liabilities:		
Accounts Payable	$ 18,000	$ 21,000
Mortgage Payable (current)	5,000	22,000
Dividends Payable	5,000	8,000
Noncurrent Liabilities:		
Mortgage Payable	75,000	110,000
Notes Payable	20,000	0
Common Stock	70,000	100,000
Treasury Stock	(20,000)	(30,000)
Retained Earnings	53,500	80,500
Total Liabilities and Owners' Equity	$ 226,500	$ 311,500

Required:

Answer the following questions.

1. What amount of existing debt must be paid during 19X3?

2. What is the total of current assets at the end of 19X2?

3. What is the amount of net working capital at the end of 19X2?

4. How has the change in accounts receivable during 19X2 affected cash at the end of 19X2?

5. How much does the Foxtail owe its stockholders at the end of 19X2?

6. What is the net book value of the Foxtail's fixed assets at the end of 19X2?
7. What amount of past earnings are available for distribution to the Foxtail's owners at the end of 19X2?

Problem 10

Noreen Bayley, the owner/manager of Winkie's Motel, has come to you with some accounting questions. As a result of a fire at the motel, many of the records as of December 31, 19X2, were either burned or soaked by the sprinkler system. You are to help her determine the following balances:

1. In one report, the current ratio for the motel is 1.2 to 1. In addition, you have determined the amount of current liabilities (including $14,736 of current portion of long-term debt) to be $105,380 and long-term debt to be $60,000. What is the amount of current assets for Winkie's Motel?
2. Ms. Bayley has her December 31, 19X2 bank statement which says she has $49,765 in her savings account and $36,072 in her checking account. She has a copy of the inventory sheet which states total inventory on December 31, 19X2, of $15,491. Assuming that the only current assets are cash, inventory, and accounts receivable, what is the total accounts receivable owed to Ms. Bayley?
3. Ms. Bayley has a copy of the balance sheet from November 30, 19X2, which states that current assets were 30% of the total assets. Assuming this relationship is the same at December 31, 19X2, what are the total assets as of December 31, 19X2?
4. Based on the information in parts 1 through 3, what is the Owners' Equity as of December 31, 19X2?

Problem 11

James Strat, the owner of the Molehill, a small lodging operation, has asked for your help in answering a few selected questions. He is able to present you with the condensed balance sheets and some additional information, as follows:

The Molehill
Condensed Balance Sheets
December 31, 19X1 and 19X2

	19X1	19X2
Cash	$ 10,000	$ 8,000
Accounts Receivable	26,500	22,500
Investments	10,000	20,000
Equipment	200,000	320,000
Accumulated Depreciation	(20,000)	(59,000)
Total Assets	$ 226,500	$ 311,500
Current Liabilities:		
Accounts Payable	$ 18,000	$ 21,000
Mortgage Payable (current)	5,000	22,000
Dividends Payable	5,000	8,000
Noncurrent Liabilities:		
Mortgage Payable	75,000	110,000
Common Stock	50,000	70,000
Retained Earnings	73,500	80,500
Total Liabilities and Owners' Equity	$ 226,500	$ 311,500

Additional information regarding activities for 19X2:

a. Equipment costing $20,000 and fully depreciated (to $0) was sold for $5,000.

b. Long-term investments costing $10,000 were sold for $12,000.

c. Common stock was sold and long-term debt was borrowed during 19X2. There were no noncash financing or investing activities during 19X2.

d. Income before gain on the sale of equipment and investments for 19X2 totaled $15,000. The firm's average and marginal tax rates are 15% and 20%, respectively.

e. Assume all current liabilities are paid on a timely basis.

f. Assume retained earnings is affected only by net earnings and dividends declared.

Required:

Answer the following questions.

1. What was the change in cash during 19X2?

2. What amount of investments were purchased during 19X2?

3. What was the total cost of equipment purchases during 19X2?

4. What was the net book value of fixed assets at the beginning of 19X2?

5. What was the amount of the mortgage payment, excluding interest expense, during 19X2?

6. What were the net earnings for 19X2?

7. What were the amount of dividends declared during 19X2?

8. What were the amount of dividends paid during 19X2?

Problem 12

The trial balance of balance sheet accounts of Lancer's, a popular casual dining spot, as of December 31, 19X3, is as follows:

	Debits	Credits
Cash	$ 5,000	
Marketable securities	10,000	
Accounts receivable	100,000	
Allowance for doubtful accounts		$ 5,000
Food inventory	15,000	
Prepaid rent	5,000	
Prepaid insurance	8,000	
Investments	50,000	
Land	80,000	
Building	420,000	
Equipment	100,000	
Accumulated depreciation		100,000
Accounts payable		15,000
Income taxes payable		-0-
Accrued expenses		25,000
Dividends payable		-0-

Long-term debt	300,000
Capital stock	89,000
Paid-in capital in excess of par	68,000
Retained earnings (1/1/X3)	61,000

Additional information:

1. Dividends declared during 19X3 totaled $30,000. Only $20,000 of the dividends declared in 19X3 have been paid as of December 31, 19X3. The unpaid dividends have not been recorded.

2. Operations generated $800,000 of revenue for 19X3. Expenses recorded totaled $650,000. Additional adjustments required are as follows:

   A. The allowance for doubtful accounts should be adjusted to 10% of accounts receivable.

   B. Prepaid insurance of $8,000 is the premium paid for insurance coverage for July 1, 19X3, through June 30, 19X4.

   C. Unrecorded depreciation expense for 19X3 totals $41,000.

   D. Income taxes have not been recorded. Lancer's average rate is 20%.

3. The long-term debt account includes $50,000 which must be paid on June 30, 19X4.

Required:

Prepare a balance sheet according to the *USALI* (see Exhibit 5).

Problem 13

Below is selected information from the comparative and common-size asset portion of balance sheets for Martin's Motel.

Martin's Motel

	December 31		Dollar	Common-Size
	19X1	19X2	Difference	(Dec. 31, 19X2)
Current Assets:				
Cash				
House Bank	$ _____	$ _____	$ (10)	_____ %
Demand Deposit	_____	60		.6
Total Cash	_____	_____	(10)	1.0
Accounts Receivable	1,241	_____	_____	14.0
Inventories	_____	_____		
Total Current Assets	_____	1,620	201	_____
Investments	_____	_____	25	2.0
Property & Equipment (net):				
Land	957	1,030	_____	_____
Building	4,350	_____	_____	_____
Furniture	_____	_____	(75)	25.0
Other Assets	49	_____	_____	.5
Total Assets	$_____	$_____	$_____	_____ %

Required:

Fill in the blanks above. Round all amounts to the nearest dollar.

Problem 14

Below is selected information from the comparative and common-size asset section of the balance sheets December 31, 19X1 and 19X2 of the Gordon Lodge.

	December 31 19X1	December 31 19X2	Dollar Difference	Common-Size (Dec. 31, 19X1)
Current Liabilities:				
Notes Payable	$ 5,000	$ _____	$ _____	1.0 %
Accounts Payable	_____	8,000	1,000	_____
Taxes Payable	——	——	500	0.6
Wages Payable	_____	_____	1,000	_____
Total	20,000	18,000	_____	_____
LTD:				
Mortgage Payable	$_____	$ _____	$ (20,000)	40.0 %
Deferred Taxes	_____	80,000	_____	_____
Total	280,000	_____	(20,000)	_____
Owners' Equity:				
Common Stock	$_____	$ _____	$ 10,000	30.0 %
Retained Earnings	_____	80,000	20,000	_____
Treasury Stock	_____	_____	–0–	_____
Total	_____	_____	_____	_____
Total Liabilities and Owners' Equity	$ 500,000	$ _____	$ _____	_____ %

Required:

Fill in the blanks above. Round all amounts to the nearest dollar.

Problem 15

Below is selected information from the comparative and common-size asset section of the balance sheets of Dec. 31, 19X1 and 19X2 of the Longstreth Lodge.

	December 31		%	Common-Size
	19X1	19X2	Difference	(Dec. 31, 19X2)
Current Assets:				
Cash	$ _____	$ 1,000	25.0%	_____ %
Accounts Receivable	30,000	_____	_____ %	5.0 %
Inventories	500	_____	10.0%	0.1 %
Prepaid Expenses	_____	_____	10.0%	1.0 %
Total Current Assets	_____	_____	_____ %	_____ %
Property & Equipment:				
Land	100,000	_____	–0– %	_____ %
Building	_____	400,000	–0– %	_____ %
Equipment	_____	_____	–0– %	10.0 %
Accumulated Depreciation	(35,000)	_____	_____ %	(8.0)%
Net Property & Equipment	_____	_____	_____ %	_____ %
Other Assets	_____	_____	_____ %	_____ %
Total Assets	$562,000	$ _____	_____ %	_____ %

Required:

Fill in the blanks above. Round all percentages to the nearest .1%

Appendix

Hilton Hotels Corporation and Subsidiaries

Consolidated Statements of Income

(in millions, except per share amounts)	Year Ended December 31, 1996	1995	1994
Revenue			
Rooms	$1,734	1,562	1,445
Food and beverage	857	782	738
Casino	857	791	729
Franchise fees	43	39	37
Other	449	381	352
	3,940	3,555	3,301
Expenses			
Rooms	508	484	462
Food and beverage	674	625	601
Casino	466	400	344
Other expenses, including remittances to owners	1,911	1,659	1,580
Corporate expense	52	32	28
	3,611	3,200	3,015
Operating Income	329	355	286
Interest and dividend income	38	35	22
Interest expense	(88)	(93)	(87)
Interest expense, net, from equity investments	(12)	(17)	(12)
Income Before Income Taxes and Minority Interest	267	280	209
Provision for income taxes	106	102	85
Minority interest, net	5	5	2
Income Before Extraordinary Item	156	173	122
Extraordinary loss on extinguishment of debt, net of tax benefit of $52	(74)	—	—
Net Income	$ 82	173	122
Earnings Per Share			
Income before extraordinary item	$ .79	.89	.63
Extraordinary loss	(.38)	—	—
Net Income Per Share	$ .41	.89	.63

See notes to consolidated financial statements

Hilton Hotels Corporation and Subsidiaries ⅃

Consolidated Balance Sheets

(in millions)	December 31, 1996	1995
Assets		
Current Assets		
Cash and equivalents	$ 388	433
Temporary investments	50	101
Accounts receivable, net	430	348
Other current assets	283	218
Total current assets	1,151	1,100
Investments, Property and Other Assets		
Equity investments	277	576
Other investments	96	19
Property and equipment, net	4,698	1,696
Goodwill	1,295	—
Other assets	60	52
Total investments, property and other assets	6,426	2,343
Total Assets	$7,577	3,443
Liabilities and Stockholders' Equity		
Liabilities		
Current liabilities	$ 998	917
Long-term debt	2,606	1,070
Deferred income taxes	598	124
Insurance reserves and other	164	78
Total liabilities	4,366	2,189
Commitments and Contingencies		
Stockholders' Equity		
8% PRIDES convertible preferred stock	15	—
Common stock, 249 million and 193 million		
shares outstanding, respectively	627	494
Additional paid-in capital	1,745	—
Retained earnings	931	909
Other	4	(7)
	3,322	1,396
Less treasury shares, at cost	111	142
Total stockholders' equity	3,211	1,254
Total Liabilities and Stockholders' Equity	$7,577	3,443

See notes to consolidated financial statements

Hilton Hotels Corporation and Subsidiaries   **X**

Consolidated Statements of Cash Flow

(in millions)	Year Ended December 31, 1996	1995	1994
Operating Activities			
Net income	$ 82	173	122
Adjustments to reconcile net income to net			
cash provided by operating activities:			
Extraordinary loss on extinguishment of debt	74	—	—
Depreciation and amortization	178	142	133
Non-cash charges	23	—	—
Amortization of debt issue costs	1	1	1
Change in working capital components:			
Inventories	23	(11)	(37)
Accounts receivable	(43)	(41)	(73)
Other current assets	(19)	25	(23)
Accounts payable and accrued expenses	9	71	131
Income taxes payable	43	4	(1)
Change in deferred income taxes	(22)	1	(21)
Change in other liabilities	20	(14)	8
Distributions from equity investments in excess of earnings	33	30	6
Gain from property transactions	(5)	(1)	(1)
Other	41	—	8
Net cash provided by operating activities	438	380	253
Investing Activities			
Capital expenditures	(242)	(186)	(265)
Additional investments	(104)	(98)	(157)
Decrease in long-term marketable securities	—	1	63
Change in temporary investments	83	139	(119)
Payments on notes and other	21	17	61
Acquisitions, net of cash acquired	(288)	—	—
Net cash used in investing activities	(530)	(127)	(417)
Financing Activities			
Change in commercial paper borrowings			
and revolving loans	1,041	189	(113)
Long-term borrowings	492	1	170
Reduction of long-term debt	(1,457)	(192)	(32)
Issuance of common stock	31	11	12
Cash dividends	(60)	(58)	(58)
Net cash provided by (used in) financing activities	47	(49)	(21)
(Decrease) Increase in Cash and Equivalents	(45)	204	(185)
Cash and Equivalents at Beginning of Year	433	229	414
Cash and Equivalents at End of Year	$ 388	433	229

See notes to consolidated financial statements

Hilton Hotels Corporation and Subsidiaries

Consolidated Statements of Stockholders' Equity

(in millions, except per share amounts)	PRIDES Convertible Preferred Stock	Common Stock	Additional Paid-in Capital	Retained Earnings	Other	Treasury Shares
Balance, December 31, 1993	$—	494	2	732	(2)	(169)
Exercise of stock options	—	—	(2)	(1)	—	15
Cumulative translation adjustment, net of deferred tax	—	—	—	—	1	—
Unrealized loss on marketable securities, net of deferred tax benefit	—	—	—	—	(5)	—
Net income	—	—	—	122	—	—
Dividends ($.30 per share)	—	—	—	(58)	—	—
Balance, December 31, 1994	—	494	—	795	(6)	(154)
Exercise of stock options	—	—	—	(1)	—	12
Cumulative translation adjustment, net of deferred tax benefit	—	—	—	—	(1)	—
Net income	—	—	—	173	—	—
Dividends ($.30 per share)	—	—	—	(58)	—	—
Balance, December 31, 1995	—	494	—	909	(7)	(142)
Exercise of stock options	—	—	—	—	—	31
Bally acquisition	15	133	1,735	—	—	—
Cumulative translation adjustment, net of deferred tax	—	—	—	—	6	—
Realized loss on marketable securities, net of deferred tax	—	—	—	—	5	—
Deferred compensation	—	—	10	—	—	—
Net income	—	—	—	82	—	—
Dividends ($.305 per share)	—	—	—	(60)	—	—
Balance, December 31, 1996	$15	627	1,745	931	4	(111)

See notes to consolidated financial statements

Chapter 3 Outline

Major Elements of the Income Statement
Relationship with the Balance Sheet
Income Statements for Internal and External Users
Uniform Systems of Accounts
Approach to Hospitality Industry Income Statements
Contents of the Income Statement
Departmental Statements
Lodging Industry Operating Statistics
Analysis of Income Statements
Uniform System of Accounts for Restaurants
Computer Applications

The Income Statement

THE INCOME STATEMENT, ALSO CALLED the statement of earnings, the profit and loss (or P & L) statement, the statement of operations, and various other titles, reports the success of the hospitality property's operations for a period of time. This statement may be prepared on a weekly or monthly basis for management's use and quarterly or annually for outsiders such as owners, creditors, and governmental agencies.

Users of financial statements examine an operation's income statements for answers to many questions, such as:

1. How profitable was the hospitality operation during the period?

2. What were the total sales for the period?

3. How much was paid for labor?

4. What is the relationship between sales and cost of sales?

5. How much have sales increased over last year?

6. What is the utilities expense for the year and how does it compare with the expense of a year ago?

7. How much was spent to market the hospitality operation's services?

8. How does net income compare with total sales for the period?

These and many more questions can be answered by reviewing the income statements that cover several periods of time. Income statements, including statements by individual departments called **departmental income statements,** are generally considered to be the most useful financial statements for management's review of operations. Owners and creditors, especially long-term creditors, find that the income statement yields significant information for determining investment value and creditworthiness. However, when analyzing the operating results of any entity, an income statement should be considered in conjunction with other financial statements as well as with the footnotes to those financial statements.

In this chapter, we will address the major elements of the income statement and consider its relationship with the balance sheet. We will also note the differences between income statements prepared for internal users and those for external users. The uniform system of accounts and the general approach to income statements in the hospitality industry will also be discussed. We will provide an in-depth discussion of the contents of the income statement, consider the uses of departmental statements and industry operating statistics, and discuss guidelines and techniques for analyzing income statements. Finally, a brief overview of the income statement based on the *Uniform System of Accounts for Restaurants (USAR)* will be presented.

Major Elements of the Income Statement

The income statement reflects the revenues, expenses, gains, and losses for a period of time. **Revenues** represent the inflow of assets, reduction of liabilities, or a combination of both resulting from the sale of goods or services. For a hospitality operation, revenues generally include food sales, beverage sales, room sales, interest and dividends from investments, and rents received from lessees of retail space.

Expenses are defined as the outflow of assets, increase in liabilities, or a combination of both in the production and rendering of goods and services. Expenses of a hospitality operation generally include cost of goods sold (for example, food and beverages), labor, utilities, advertising, depreciation, and taxes, to list a few.

Gains are defined as increases in assets, reductions in liabilities, or a combination of both resulting from a hospitality operation's incidental transactions and from all other transactions and events affecting the operation during the period, except those that count as revenues or investments by owners. For example, there may be a gain on the sale of equipment. Equipment is used by the business to provide goods and services and, when sold, only the excess proceeds over its net book value (purchase price less accumulated depreciation) is recognized as gain.

Finally, **losses** are defined as decreases in assets, increases in liabilities, or a combination of both resulting from a hospitality operation's incidental transactions and from other transactions and events affecting the operation during a period, except those that count as expenses or distributions to owners. In the equipment example above, if the proceeds were less than the net book value, a loss would occur and would be recorded as "loss on sale of equipment." Another example would be a loss from an act of nature, such as a tornado or hurricane. The loss reported is the reduction of assets less insurance proceeds received.

In the income statement for hospitality operations, revenues are reported separately from gains, and expenses are distinguished from losses. These distinctions are important in determining management's success in operating the hospitality property. Management is held accountable primarily for operations (revenues and expenses) and only secondarily (if at all) for gains and losses. Generally, gains and losses are shown near the bottom of the income statement before income taxes.

Relationship with the Balance Sheet

The income statement covers a period of time, while the balance sheet is prepared as of the last day of the accounting period. Thus, the income statement reflects operations of the hospitality property for the period between balance sheet dates. The result of operations—net income or loss for the period—is added to the proper equity account and shown on the balance sheet at the end of the accounting period.

Income Statements for Internal and External Users

Hospitality properties prepare income statements for both internal users (management) and external users (creditors, owners, and so forth). These statements differ substantially. The income statements provided to external users are relatively brief, providing only summary detail about the results of operations. Income statements for external users are often called **summary income statements,** even though the word "summary" does not usually appear on the form. Exhibit 1 is the income statement presentation of Marriott International, Inc. and Subsidiaries from a recent annual report. Marriott's income statement shows the following:

- Sales by segment

- Operating expenses by segment

- Operating income by segment (sales less operating expenses)

- Interest expense

- Interest income

- Income taxes

- Net income

- Earnings per share

We have already stated that footnotes, which generally appear after the financial statements in the financial report, are critical to interpreting the numbers reported on the income statement. Note that Marriott International notifies readers of the importance of footnotes on the same page as the income statement.

Although the amount of operating information shown in the income statement and accompanying footnotes may be adequate for external users to evaluate the hospitality property's operations, management requires considerably more information. Management also needs this information more frequently than outsiders. In general, the more frequent the need to make decisions, the more frequent the need for financial information. Management's information needs are met, in part, by detailed monthly income statements that reflect budget numbers and report performance for the most recent period, the same period a year ago, and year-to-date numbers for both the current and past year.

If any difference between the year-to-date numbers and the originally budgeted numbers is expected, the income statements of many firms in the hospitality industry also show the latest forecast of results (reforecasting). Management is then able to compare actual results against the most recent forecasts.

Management's need for financial information on a monthly basis may be met, to a large degree, by using an income statement and accompanying departmental statements that are contained in the various uniform systems of accounts. In addition to the monthly income statement, a more frequent major report prepared for management is the **daily report of operations.**

Ultimately, however, hospitality managers require even more information than is provided by daily reports and monthly statements. Exhibit 2 lists various management reports and the frequency, content, comparisons, intended readers, and purpose of each report. Even this list does not include all reports required by the various levels of management in a hospitality operation. For example, two major financial statements, the balance sheet and the statement of cash flows, are absent from the list.

Exhibit 1   Sample Income Statement

CONSOLIDATED STATEMENT OF INCOME

MARRIOTT INTERNATIONAL, INC. AND SUBSIDIARIES

Fiscal years ended January 3, 1997, December 29, 1995 and December 30, 1994	1996	1995	1994
(dollars in millions, except per share amounts)	*(53 weeks)*	*(52 weeks)*	*(52 weeks)*
Sales			
Lodging			
Rooms	**$ 3,619**	$3,273	$3,036
Food and beverage	**1,361**	1,289	1,210
Other	**874**	765	703
	5,854	5,327	4,949
Contract Services	**4,318**	3,634	3,466
	10,172	8,961	8,415
Operating Costs and Expenses			
Lodging			
Departmental direct costs			
Rooms	**843**	772	727
Food and beverage	**1,038**	973	922
Other operating expenses, including remittances to hotel owners	**3,521**	3,222	2,998
	5,402	4,967	4,647
Contract Services	**4,141**	3,504	3,355
	9,543	8,471	8,002
Operating Profit			
Lodging	**452**	360	302
Contract Services	**177**	130	111
Operating profit before corporate expenses and interest	**629**	490	413
Corporate expenses	**(79)**	(64)	(68)
Interest expense	**(85)**	(53)	(32)
Interest income	**37**	39	29
Income Before Income Taxes	**502**	412	342
Provision for income taxes	**196**	165	142
Net Income	**$ 306**	$ 247	$ 200
Earnings Per Share	**$ 2.24**	$ 1.87	$ 1.51

See notes to consolidated financial statements.

Courtesy of Marriott International, Inc., Washington, D.C.

Exhibit 2 Management Reports

Report	Frequency	Content	Comparisons	Who Gets It	Purpose
Daily Reports of Operations	Daily, on a cumulative basis for the month, the year to date.	Occupancy, average rate, revenue by outlet, and pertinent statistics.	To operating plan for current period and to prior year results.	Top management and supervisors responsible for day to day operation.	Basis for evaluating the current health of the enterprise.
Weekly Forecasts	Weekly.	Volume in covers, occupancy.	Previous periods.	Top management and supervisory personnel.	Staffing and scheduling; promotion.
Summary Report— Flash	Monthly at end of month (prior to monthly financial statement).	Known elements of revenue and direct costs; estimated departmental indirect costs.	To operating plan; to prior year results.	Top management and supervisory personnel responsible for function reported.	Provides immediate information on financial results for rooms, food and beverages, and other.
Cash Flow Analysis	Monthly (and on a revolving 12-month basis).	Receipts and disbursements by time periods.	With cash flow plan for month and for year to date.	Top management.	Predicts availability of cash for operating needs. Provides information on interim financing requirements.
Labor Productivity Analysis	Daily, weekly, monthly.	Dollar cost; manpower hours expended; hours as related to sales and services (covers, rooms occupied, etc.).	To committed hours in the operating plan (standards for amount of work to prior year statistics).	Top management and supervisory personnel.	Labor cost control through informed staffing and scheduling. Helps refine forecasting.
Departmental Analysis	Monthly (early in following month).	Details on main categories of income; same on expense.	To operating plan (month and year to date) and to prior year.	Top management and supervisors by function (e.g., rooms, each food and beverage outlet, laundry, telephone, other profit centers).	Knowing where business stands, and immediate corrective actions.
Room Rate Analysis	Daily, monthly, year to date.	Actual rates compared to rack rates by rate category or type of room.	To operating plan and to prior year results.	Top management and supervisors of sales and front office operations.	If goal is not being achieved, analysis of strengths and weaknesses is prompted.
Return on Investment	Actual computation, at least twice a year. Computation based on forecast, immediately prior to plan for year ahead.	Earnings as a percentage rate of return on average investment or equity committed.	To plan for operation and to prior periods.	Top management.	If goal is not being achieved, prompt assessment of strengths and weaknesses.
Long-Range Planning	Annually.	5-year projections of revenue and expenses. Operating plan expressed in financial terms.	Prior years.	Top management.	Involves staff in success or failure of enterprise. Injects more realism into plans for property and service modifications.
Exception Reporting	Concurrent with monthly reports and financial statements.	Summary listing of line item variances from predetermined norm.	With operating budgets.	Top management and supervisors responsible for function reported.	Immediate focusing on problem before more detailed statement analysis can be made.
Guest History Analysis	At least semi-annually; quarterly or monthly is recommended.	Historical records of corporate business, travel agencies, group bookings.	With previous reports.	Top management and sales.	Gives direction to marketing efforts.
Future Bookings Report	Monthly.	Analysis of reservations and bookings.	With several prior years.	Top management, sales and marketing, department management.	Provides information on changing guest profile. Exposes strong and weak points of facility. Guides (1) sales planning and (2) expansion plans.

Uniform Systems of Accounts ———————————————————

Uniform systems of accounts are standardized accounting systems prepared by various segments of the hospitality industry.[1] A uniform system of accounts provides a turnkey system for new entrants into the hospitality industry by offering detailed information about accounts, classifications, formats, and the different kinds, contents, and uses of financial statements and reports. For example, the *Uniform System of Accounts for the Lodging Industry (USALI)* contains not only the basic financial statements, but also over 25 supplementary departmental operating statements and appendices covering budgeting and forecasting, a discussion of compiling revenues by market source, forms of statements, breakeven analysis, and a uniform account numbering system.

A uniform system of accounts also allows for a more reasonable comparison of the operational results of similar hospitality properties. When various establishments follow a uniform system of accounts, the differences in accounting among these hospitality properties are minimized, thus ensuring comparability.

A uniform system of accounts is a time-tested system. The *Uniform System of Accounts for Hotels (USAH)* was first produced in 1925-26 by a designated group of accountants for the Hotel Association of New York City. Since then, the *USAH* has been revised many times by committees, beginning with New York City accountants and, later, by accountants from across the United States. In 1961, to meet the needs of its members, the American Hotel & Motel Association appointed the National Association of Accountants to develop the *Uniform System of Accounts and Expense Dictionary for Small Hotels, Motels, and Motor Hotels (USASH)*, which also was revised a number of times. Then, in 1996, the Hotel Association of New York City and the American Hotel & Motel Association combined their efforts to produce a single, updated, and authoritative uniform system of accounts—the *Uniform System of Accounts for the Lodging Industry (USALI)*.

This uniform system of accounts can be adapted for use by large and small hospitality operations. The *USALI* contains many more accounts and classifications than will generally be used by a single hotel or motel. Therefore, each facility simply selects the schedules and accounts that are required for its use and ignores the others.

The *USALI* is designed to be used at the property level rather than the corporate level of a hotel. The format of the income statement is based on **responsibility accounting.** That is, the presentation is organized to focus attention on departmental results such as the rooms and food departments. The income statements prepared at the corporate level, where more than one lodging property is owned by the lodging corporation, would probably be considerably different and would include sale of properties, corporate overhead expenses, and so on, not necessarily shown on an individual lodging property's income statement. Our discussion of income statements for management will focus primarily on the *USALI*, although, as stated earlier, the *USAR* will also be presented near the end of this chapter.

Approach to Hospitality Industry Income Statements

In many industries, the basic income statement format consists of the following:

	Revenues
Less:	Cost of goods sold
Equals:	Gross profit
Less:	Overhead expenses
Equals:	Net income

For wholesale and retail firms, the cost of goods sold is the cost of goods purchased for resale, while for manufacturers, it is a combination of labor, raw materials, and overhead expenses incurred in the manufacturing process. The expenses subtracted from gross profit to equal net income consist of all other expenses such as administration and selling expenses, depreciation, and income taxes.

By contrast, the income statement format in the *USALI* approach consists of the following:

	Revenues
Less:	Direct operating expenses
Equals:	Departmental operating income
Less:	Overhead expenses
Equals:	Net income

Direct operating expenses include not only the cost of goods sold, but also the direct labor expense and other direct expenses. Direct labor expense is the expense of personnel working in the profit centers, such as the rooms department and the food department. Other direct expenses include supplies used by these revenue-producing departments. Therefore, everything else being the same, gross profit would exceed departmental operating income, since direct operating expenses include direct labor and other direct expenses in addition to cost of goods sold.

The income statements based on the *USALI* provide separate line reporting by profit center, that is, sales and direct expenses are shown separately for the rooms department, the food department, the beverage department, and so forth. In addition, the overhead expenses are divided among undistributed operating expenses, management fees, and fixed charges. The undistributed operating expenses are further detailed on the income statement by major service centers such as marketing and data processing. The detail provided by both profit centers and service centers reflects reporting by areas of responsibility and is commonly referred to as responsibility accounting.

Thus, the *USALI* income statement is useful to managers in the hospitality industry because it is designed to provide the information necessary to evaluate the performance of managers of the lodging facility by area of responsibility.

Contents of the Income Statement

The income statement per the *USALI* (see Exhibit 3) is divided into three major sections—operated departments, undistributed operating expenses, and the final section which includes management fees, fixed charges, gain or loss on sale of property, and income tax. (See also the Appendix to this chapter, which presents the *USALI*'s versions of the various departmental statements used to support the income statement; these statements are discussed next.)

Exhibit 3   Income Statement

SUMMARY STATEMENT OF INCOME

	SCHEDULE	NET REVENUES	COST OF SALES	PAYROLL AND RELATED EXPENSES	OTHER EXPENSES	INCOME (LOSS)
OPERATED DEPARTMENTS		$	$	$	$	$
Rooms	1					
Food	2					
Beverage	3					
Telecommunications	4					
Garage and Parking	5					
Golf Course	6					
Golf Pro Shop	7					
Guest Laundry	8					
Health Center	9					
Swimming Pool	10					
Tennis	11					
Tennis Pro Shop	12					
Other Operated Departments	13					
Rentals and Other Income	14					
Total Operated Departments						
UNDISTRIBUTED OPERATING EXPENSES[1]						
Administrative and General	15					
Human Resources	16					
Information Systems	17					
Security	18					
Marketing	19					
Franchise Fees	19a					
Transportation	20					
Property Operation and Maintenance	21					
Utility Costs	22					
Total Undistributed Operating Expenses						
TOTALS		$	$	$	$	
INCOME AFTER UNDISTRIBUTED OPERATING EXPENSES						
Management Fees	23					
Rent, Property Taxes, and Insurance	24					
INCOME BEFORE INTEREST, DEPRECIATION AND AMORTIZATION, AND INCOME TAXES[2]						
Interest Expense	25					
INCOME BEFORE DEPRECIATION, AMORTIZATION AND INCOME TAXES						
Depreciation and Amortization	26					
Gain or Loss on Sale or Property						
INCOME BEFORE INCOME TAXES						
Income Taxes	27					
NET INCOME						$

(1)A separate line for preopening expenses can be included if such costs are captured separately.
(2)Also referred to as EBITDA—Earnings before Interest, Taxes, Depreciation and Amortization

The first section, operated departments, reports net revenue by department for every major revenue-producing department. Net revenue is the result of subtracting allowances from related revenues. Allowances include refunds and overcharges at the time of sale that are subsequently adjusted. For example, hotel guests may have been charged $100 for their rooms when they should have been charged a group rate of $80. The subsequent adjustment of $20 the following day is treated as an allowance. Revenues earned from non-operating activities such as investments are shown with rentals. If these amounts are significant, they should be reported separately.

For each department generating revenues, direct expenses are reported. These expenses relate directly to the department incurring them and consist of three major categories: cost of sales, payroll and related expenses, and other expenses. Cost of sales is normally determined as follows:

	Beginning inventory
Plus:	Inventory purchases
Equals:	Goods available for sale
Less:	Ending inventory
Equals:	Cost of goods consumed
Less:	Goods used internally
Equals:	Cost of goods sold

Cost of sales is determined by starting first with beginning inventory. The beginning inventory is the value of the inventory at the start of the accounting period. Inventory purchases include the purchase cost of goods for sale plus the related shipping cost. An important, but relatively small, category of direct expense is "goods used internally." For example, food may be provided free of charge to employees (employee meals), to entertainers (entertainers—complimentary food), to guests for promotional purposes (promotion—food), or to other departments (transfers to the beverage department). In each case, the cost of food transferred must be charged to the proper account of the benefiting department and subtracted in the calculation of cost of food sold. For example, cost of employee meals for the rooms department is subtracted to determine cost of food sold. The cost of employee meals for rooms department employees is shown as an expense in the rooms department.

The second major direct expense category of operated departments is "payroll and related expenses." This category includes the salaries and wages of employees working in the designated operated departments (for example, servers in the food department). Salaries, wages, and related expenses of departments not generating revenues but providing service, such as marketing, are recorded by service departments. The category of "related expenses" includes all payroll taxes and benefits relating to employees of each operated department. For example, in the rooms department, the front office manager's salary and related payroll taxes and benefits would be included in the "payroll and related expenses" of the rooms department.

The final major expense category for the operated departments is "other expenses." This category includes only other direct expenses. For example, the 14 major other expense categories for the rooms department (per the *USALI*) are cable/satellite television, commissions, complimentary guest services, contract services, guest relocation, guest transportation, laundry and dry cleaning, linen, operating supplies, reservations, telecommunications, training, uniforms, and other. Expenses such as marketing, administration, and transportation are recorded as expenses of service departments. They benefit the rooms department and other profit centers but only on an indirect basis.

Net revenue less the sum of cost of sales, payroll and related expenses, and other expenses results in departmental income or loss. The departmental income or loss is shown on the income statement (see schedules 1–14 in Exhibit 3) for each operated department.

The second major section of the income statement is undistributed operating expenses. This section includes nine general categories: administrative and general expenses, human resources, information systems, security, marketing, franchise fees, transportation, property operation and maintenance, and utility costs. These expense categories are related to the various service departments. In the income statement, two of the expense elements—payroll and related expenses, and other expenses—are shown for each category. The administrative and general expense category includes service departments such as the general manager's office and the accounting office. In addition to salaries, wages, and related expenses of service department personnel covered by administrative and general, other expenses include, but are not limited to, insurance—general, professional fees, and provision for doubtful accounts. The administrative and general statement in the Appendix to this chapter details the several categories for such expenses.

The *USALI* recommends a separate departmental accounting of information systems expenses for those lodging operations with significant investments in information systems. As with most other service centers, the two major sections of expense are payroll and related expenses, and other expenses. If information systems expenses are not considered significant, then the *USALI* recommends information systems expenses be included as part of administrative and general expenses.

Another service center for which the *USALI* recommends separate departmental accounting is the human resources department. This schedule includes labor costs of departmental personnel and other expenses such as employee housing, recruiting expenses, costs of relocating employees, and training costs.

The fourth service department is security. The purpose of this service department is to provide security services for the lodging facility and the guests. The expenses to be included on the security department schedule include payroll and related expenses, and other expenses such as armored car service, operating supplies, safety and lock boxes, and training. If security expenses are not considered significant, then the *USALI* recommends security expenses be included as part of the administrative and general expenses.

Marketing expenses include costs relating to personnel working in marketing areas of sales, advertising, and merchandising. In addition, other marketing expenses include advertising and merchandising expenses such as direct mail, in-house graphics, point-of-sale materials, and print, radio, and television advertising. Agency fees and other fees and commissions are also included as marketing expenses. Franchise fees, when applicable and significant, should be listed as a separate line item on the summary statement of income. If the franchise fees are insignificant, they would be included as part of the marketing expenses.

The transportation service department provides transportation services for lodging guests, such as transportation to and from the airport. The expenses to be included on the transportation department schedule include payroll and related expenses, and other expenses such as fuel, operating supplies, and repairs and maintenance. If guest transportation expenses are not considered significant, then the *USALI* recommends transportation expenses be included as part of the rooms department expenses.

The eighth major category of undistributed operating expenses is property operation and maintenance. Included in property operation and maintenance are salaries and related payroll costs of the property operation and maintenance personnel and the various supplies used to maintain the buildings, grounds, furniture, fixtures, and equipment.

The final category of undistributed operating expenses is utility costs. The recommended schedule includes separate listings of the various utilities, such as electricity and water. Sales by the hotel to tenants and charges to other departments are subtracted in determining net utility costs.

Subtracting the total undistributed operating expenses from the total operated departments income results in income after undistributed operating expenses. Many industry personnel continue to refer to this difference between operating revenue and expense as gross operating profit, or simply GOP, but this is terminology from an earlier edition of *USALI*'s format for the income statement.

Operating management is considered fully responsible for all revenues and expenses reported to this point on the income statement, as they generally have the authority to exercise their judgment to affect all these items. However, the management fees and the fixed charges that follow in the next major section of the income statement are the responsibility primarily of the hospitality property's board of directors. The expenses listed on this part of the statement generally relate directly to decisions by the board, rather than to management decisions.

Management fees are the cost of using an independent management company to operate the hotel or motel. Management fees often consist of a basic fee calculated as a percentage of sales and an incentive fee calculated as a percentage of income after undistributed operating expenses.

Fixed charges are also referred to as **capacity costs,** as they relate to the physical plant or the capacity to provide goods and services to guests. Fixed charges include rent, property taxes, insurance, interest, and depreciation and amortization. Rent includes the cost of renting real estate, computer equipment, and other major items that, if they had been purchased, would have been recorded as fixed assets. Rental of miscellaneous equipment for specific functions such as banquets is to be shown as a direct expense of the food and beverage department.

Property taxes include real estate taxes, personal property taxes, taxes assessed by utilities, and other taxes (but not income and payroll taxes) that cannot be charged to guests. Insurance expense is the cost of insuring the facilities, including contents for damage caused by fire or other catastrophes, and the cost of liability insurance.

Interest expense is the cost of borrowing money and is based on the amounts borrowed, the interest rate, and the length of time for which the funds are borrowed.

Generally, loans are approved by the operation's board of directors, as most relate to the physical plant. Thus, interest expense is considered to be a fixed charge.

Depreciation of fixed assets and amortization of other assets are shown on the income statement as fixed charges. The depreciation methods and useful lives of fixed assets are normally disclosed in footnotes.

The income statement per the *USALI* then shows gains or losses on the sale of property and equipment. A gain or loss on sale of property results from a difference between the proceeds from the sale and the carrying value (net book value) of the fixed asset. For example, suppose that a 15-unit motel that cost $300,000 and was depreciated by $150,000 was sold for $200,000. The gain in this case is determined as follows:

$$\begin{aligned}
\text{Net Book Value} \quad &= \quad \text{Cost } - \text{ Accumulated Depreciation} \\
&= \quad \$300,000 - \$150,000 \\
&= \quad \underline{\underline{\$150,000}} \\
\text{Gain} \quad &= \quad \text{Proceeds } - \text{ Net Book Value} \\
&= \quad \$200,000 - \$150,000 \\
&= \quad \underline{\underline{\$50,000}}
\end{aligned}$$

In the *USALI*'s income statement, gains are added while losses are subtracted in determining income before income taxes.

Finally, income taxes are subtracted from income before income taxes to determine net income.

Departmental Statements

Departmental statements, supplementary to the income statement and referred to as **schedules,** provide management with detailed information by operated departments and service centers. The classifications listed in the income statement suggest up to 27 schedules and the *USALI* provides additional schedules for greater detail. Each of these schedules is included in the Appendix to this chapter.

Exhibit 4 illustrates an operated department schedule using the rooms department of the Vacation Inn. The operated department schedule reflects both revenues and direct expenses.

The expenses are subdivided on the rooms department schedule between "payroll and related expenses" and "other expenses." Under payroll and related, salaries and wages and employee benefits are shown. Employee benefits include both payroll taxes and benefits, such as cost of health insurance paid by the lodging operation and similar benefits.

Other expenses include direct expenses of the rooms department. According to the *USALI*, 14 expense categories are shown under other expenses of the rooms department. All other room department expenses should be classified in these 14 categories if the *USALI* is to be followed. When a classification is not used, it should not be shown on the rooms department schedule. Exhibit 4 does not include a few categories (as shown in the rooms department schedule in the Appendix). For example,

Exhibit 4   Rooms Department Schedule

Vacation Inn Rooms For the year ended December 31, 19X1	Schedule 1
Revenue	
Transient—Regular	$ 543,900
Transient—Group	450,000
Permanent	48,000
Other	2,000
Allowances	(2,700)
Net Revenue	1,041,200
Expenses	
Salaries and Wages	159,304
Employee Benefits	26,030
Total Payroll and Related Expenses	185,334
Other Expenses	
Cable/Satellite Television	4,900
Commissions	5,124
Contract Cleaning	3,200
Contract Services	3,100
Laundry and Dry Cleaning	12,706
Linen	9,494
Operating Supplies	12,742
Reservations	9,288
Telecommunications	4,685
Training	4,315
Uniforms	1,400
Other	8,126
Total Other Expenses	79,080
Total Expenses	264,414
Departmental Income	$ 776,786

guest transportation is not included in this schedule because transportation is treated as a separate department as reflected on the income statement in Exhibit 5.

Totals from the rooms department schedule and other operated department schedules are reflected on the income statement. In the rooms department illustration in Exhibit 4, the following totals are carried from the department schedule to the property's income statement:

- Net Revenue $1,041,200
- Payroll and Related Expenses $ 185,334
- Other Expenses $ 79,080
- Departmental Income $ 776,786

Exhibit 5 Summary Income Statement—Vacation Inn

Vacation Inn
Summary Income Statement
For the year ended December 31, 19X1

	Schedule	Net Revenue	Cost of Sales	Payroll and Related Expenses	Other Expense	Income (Loss)
Operated Departments						
Rooms	1	$1,041,200	$ 0	$ 185,334	$ 79,080	$ 776,786
Food	2	420,100	160,048	160,500	44,013	55,539
Beverage	3	206,065	48,400	58,032	22,500	77,133
Telephone	4	52,028	46,505	14,317	6,816	(15,610)
Total Operated Departments		1,719,393	254,953	418,183	152,409	893,848
Undistributed Operating Expenses						
Administrative and General	5			47,787	24,934	72,721
Information Systems	6			20,421	11,622	32,043
Human Resources	7			22,625	4,193	26,818
Transportation	8			13,411	7,460	20,871
Marketing	9			33,231	33,585	66,816
Property Operation and Maintenance	10			31,652	49,312	80,964
Utility Costs	11			0	88,752	88,752
Total Undistributed Operating Expenses				169,127	219,858	388,985
Income After Undistributed Operating Expenses		$1,719,393	$254,953	$ 587,310	$372,267	504,863
Rent, Property Taxes, and Insurance	12					200,861
Interest	12					52,148
Depreciation and Amortization	13					115,860
Income Before Income Taxes						135,994
Income Tax	14					48,707
Net Income						$ 87,287

Exhibit 5 is the Vacation Inn's summary income statement. The above figures from the rooms department schedule are reflected in the top row of figures on the income statement.

In contrast to the profit center schedules prepared by the revenue-producing operated departments of a hospitality operation, a service center schedule reports only expenses by area of responsibility. Although these activity areas do not generate revenues, they do provide service to the operated departments and, in some cases, to other service centers. Exhibit 6 illustrates a service center departmental schedule by using the property operation and maintenance schedule of the Vacation Inn. The three numbers that are carried over to the Vacation Inn's income statement (Exhibit 5) for this department are total payroll and related expenses of $31,652, other expenses of $49,312, and total expenses of $80,964. Notice that the total expenses of service departments are shown on the income statement under the Income (Loss) column.

The number and nature of the supporting schedules reported in a lodging facility depends on the size and organization of the establishment. A small lodging property that provides very limited guest transportation services would not have a separate transportation department (as does the Vacation Inn in Exhibit 5). In this case, the relatively minor transportation expenses would be shown in the rooms department schedule.

Exhibit 6 Property Operation and Maintenance Schedule

Vacation Inn	Schedule 10
Property Operation and Maintenance	
For the year ended December 31, 19X1	
Salaries and Wages	$ 27,790
Employee Benefits	3,862
Total Payroll and Related Expenses	31,652
Other Expenses	
Building Supplies	8,900
Electrical and Mechanical Equipment	8,761
Engineering Supplies	1,981
Furniture, Fixtures, Equipment, and Decor	14,322
Grounds and Landscaping	6,241
Operating Supplies	2,651
Removal of Waste Matter	2,499
Swimming Pool	2,624
Uniforms	652
Other	681
Total	49,312
Total Property Operation and Maintenance	**$ 80,964**

Lodging Industry Operating Statistics

A sale of $x by any operated department increases total revenues by that amount, but the increase in the total operated department *income* from additional sales of $x depends on the operated department making the sale. The different effects on the bottom line are caused by the direct expenses of the department generating the sale.

The difference between an operated department's revenues and its direct expenses is referred to as departmental income. The operated department contributing most to the lodging property's ability to pay overhead costs and generate profit is the one that has the greatest departmental income.

PKF Consulting, an international firm providing specialized services to establishments in the hospitality industry, recently released figures showing that the average hotel reports rooms departmental income of 73.2% of total room revenues, while the food and beverage departmental income is only approximately 20.8% of total food and beverage revenues.[2] Historically, the telephone departments of most hotels have experienced losses from operations, although recently they have shown relatively minor profits from operations. Therefore, all things being the same, a manager would rather have an additional sale of $x made in the rooms department than in any other operated department, because the contribution toward overhead costs and profit would be greater than from any other operated department. That is, based on PKF's figures, a sale of $100 in the rooms department would result in a departmental income of approximately $73.20. A similar sale in the food and beverage department would result in a departmental income of only approximately $20.80.

Within the food and beverage department, the gross profit (sales less cost of sales) generally differs substantially between food sales and beverages sales. According to PKF's statistics, the gross profit of food sales is 69.8% compared with 77.9% for beverage sales.[3] PKF does not separate payroll and related expenses or other direct expenses of the food and beverage department between food operations and beverage operations as it does cost of sales. However, if we assume that these expenses relate proportionately to sales, then from a profit perspective, increased beverage sales are more desirable than increased food sales. For example, $100 of food sales and $100 of beverage sales result in a food contribution margin of $69.80 and a beverage contribution margin of $77.90—a difference of $8.10 per $100 of sales.

Exhibit 7 provides statistics revealing the percentage distribution of revenues and expenses for the average hotel/motel. These statistics support the preceding discussion of the greater desirability of beverage sales compared with food sales, and the increased desirability of rooms sales compared with sales in any other department. However, do not consider these averages to be the norm. They are only averages and are based on lodging establishments that PKF selected on a judgmental, not random, basis. The operated departments of a particular hotel will most likely produce different percentages. However, of more than 2,800 hotels and motels in the PKF study, significant numbers noted in Exhibit 7 include:

- Rooms revenues approximate 64.1% of total revenues

- Food revenues approximate 19.5% of total revenues

- Beverage revenues approximate 5.1% of total revenues

- Total operated department income approximates 57.4% of total revenues

- Undistributed operating expenses approximate 24.9% of total revenues

Finally, industry averages vary widely by type of lodging establishment. Exhibit 8 is a comparison of statistics covering full-service, limited-service, resort, suite, and convention hotels. Again, the reader is cautioned that the percentages shown are not norms or standards but statistics based on a judgmental sample.

Hospitality industry statistics for the various segments of the industry are published annually by PKF Consulting and Smith Travel Research and are listed in Exhibit 9. These publications are generally available upon request to hospitality industry executives.

Analysis of Income Statements

The analysis of income statements enhances the user's knowledge of the hospitality property's operations. This can be accomplished by horizontal analysis, vertical analysis, base-year comparisons, and ratio analysis. Since much less financial information is available to owners (stockholders and partners who are not active in the operation) and creditors than is available to management, their analytical approaches will generally differ.

Horizontal analysis compares income statements for two accounting periods in terms of both absolute and relative variances for each line item in a way similar to the analysis of comparative balance sheets. The user should investigate any significant

Exhibit 7 Comparative Results of Operations

	1995	1994
Revenues:		
Rooms	64.1%	63.5%
Food—Including Other Income	19.5	19.7
Beverage	5.1	5.5
Telephone	2.5	2.5
Other Operated Departments	7.0	7.0
Rentals and Other Income	1.8	1.9
Total Revenues	100.0%	100.0%
Departmental Costs and Expenses:		
Rooms	17.2%	17.4%
Food and Beverage	19.9	20.6
Telephone	1.3	1.4
Other Operated Departments	4.2	4.3
Total Costs and Expenses	42.6%	43.6%
Total Operated Departmental Income	57.4%	56.4%
Undistributed Operating Expenses:**		
Administrative and General	8.5%	8.7%
Franchise Fees	0.9	0.9
Marketing and Guest Entertainment	6.1	6.4
Property Operation and Maintenance	5.2	5.3
Energy Costs	4.0	4.3
Other Unallocated Operated Departments	0.1	0.2
Total Undistributed Expenses	24.9%	25.8%
Income Before Fixed Charges	32.5%	30.6%
Management Fees, Property Taxes, and Insurance:**		
Management Fees	2.6%	2.6%
Property Taxes and Other Municipal Charges	3.2	5.3
Insurance on Buildings and Contents	0.7	0.7
Total Management Fees, Property Taxes, and Insurance	6.4%	6.7%
Income Before Other Fixed Charges***	26.1%	23.9%
Percentage of Occupancy	71.6%	70.7%
Average Daily Rate per Occupied Room	$85.32	$80.31
Average Size (Rooms)	211	210

	1995	1994
Rooms Department:		
Rooms Net Revenue	100.0%	100.0%
Departmental Expenses:		
Salaries and Wages including Vacation	13.0%	13.4%
Payroll Taxes and Employee Benefits	4.6	4.8
Subtotal	17.6%	18.2%
Laundry, Linen, and Guest Supplies	2.9	3.1
Commissions and Reservation Expenses	2.7	2.6
Complimentary Food and/or Beverage Expenses	0.5	0.7
All Other Expenses	3.1	2.8
Total Rooms Expense	26.8%	27.4%
Rooms Departmental Income	73.2%	72.6%
Food Department:		
Food Net Revenue	100.0%	100.0%
Cost of Food Consumed	32.1%	32.5%
Less: Cost of Employees' Meals	2.0	2.0
Net Cost of Food Sales	30.2%	30.4%
Food Gross Profit	69.8%	69.6%
Beverage Department:		
Beverage Net Revenue	100.0%	100.0%
Cost of Beverage Sales	22.1	21.8
Beverage Gross Profit	77.9%	78.2%
Food and Beverage Department:		
Food and Beverage Revenue	100.0%	100.0%
Net Cost of Food and Beverage Sales	28.4	28.4
Gross Profit on Combined Sales	71.6%	71.6%
Public Room Rentals	2.6	2.5
Other Income	4.0	4.2
Gross Profit and Other Income	78.3%	78.3%
Departmental Expenses:		
Salaries and Wages including Vacation	34.4%	34.8%
Payroll Taxes and Employee Benefits	12.9	13.3
Subtotal	47.3%	48.0%
Laundry and Dry Cleaning	1.1	1.1
China, Glassware, Silver, and Linen	1.5	1.4
Contract Cleaning	0.5	0.5
All Other Expenses	7.2	7.7
Total Food and Beverage Expenses	57.5%	58.8%
Food and Beverage Departmental Income	20.8%	19.5%

** Averages based on total groups, although not all establishments reported data.
***Income before deducting Depreciation, Rent, Interest, Amortization, and Income Taxes.
Note: Payroll Taxes and Employee Benefits distributed to each department.

Source: *Trends in the Hotel Industry—USA Edition 1996* (San Francisco: PKF Consulting, 1996), p. 53.

Exhibit 8 Sales and Expenses as a Percentage of Total Sales

SUMMARY STATEMENT OF INCOME

	Full-Service Hotels	Limited-Service Hotels	Resort Hotels	Suite Hotels	Convention Hotels
			Ratio to Sales		
Revenue					
Rooms	61.5%	95.5%	58.8%	84.9%	52.7%
Food—including Other Income	24.3	—	22.4	7.7	20.1
Beverage	6.4	—	6.4	1.7	5.1
Telephone	2.8	2.4	1.8	2.9	2.3
Other Operated Departments	3.4	0.8	8.3	1.9	17.4
Rentals and Other Income	1.6	1.2	2.3	0.8	2.3
Total Revenue	100.0%	100.0%	100.0%	100.0%	100.0%
Departmental Costs and Expenses					
Rooms	16.5%	23.2%	16.2%	21.4%	15.3%
Food and Beverage	24.7	—	23.6	7.8	20.2
Telephone	1.5	1.5	1.0	1.3	1.1
Other Operated Departments	2.3	0.6	5.5	1.3	9.6
Total Costs and Expenses	45.0%	25.3%	46.3%	31.7%	46.2%
Total Operated Departmental Income	55.0%	74.7%	53.7%	68.3%	53.8%
Undistributed Operating Expenses**					
Administrative and General	9.3%	9.0%	7.9%	8.3%	7.3%
Franchise Fees	1.2	1.9	0.3	1.5	0.1
Marketing and Guest Entertainment	6.2	3.7	6.8	7.3	6.1
Property Operation and Maintenance	5.2	5.6	5.8	5.0	4.9
Energy Costs	4.3	5.0	3.9	4.1	3.2
Other Unallocated Operated Departments	0.1	—	0.1	0.1	—
Total Undistributed Expenses	26.3%	25.1%	24.8%	26.3%	21.7%
Income Before Fixed Charges	28.7%	49.6%	28.9%	42.0%	32.1%
Management Fees, Property Taxes, and Insurance**					
Management Fees	2.6%	2.8%	3.2%	3.9%	1.6%
Property Taxes and Other Municipal Charges	2.9	4.0	2.6	4.0	3.3
Insurance on Buildings and Contents	0.8	1.1	0.6	0.9	0.3
Total Management Fees, Property Taxes, and Insurance	6.3%	7.8%	6.5%	8.8%	5.3%
Income Before Other Fixed Charges***	22.4%	41.8%	22.4%	33.3%	26.8%

*Average for top 25% based on Income per Available Room before Other Fixed Charges.
**Averages based on total groups, although not all establishments reported data.
***Income before deducting Depreciation, Rent, Interest, Amortization, and Income Taxes.
NOTE: Payroll Taxes and Employee Benefits distributed to each department.

Exhibit 9   Major Hospitality Statistical Publications

Publication	Industry Segment	Firm
Trends in the Hotel Industry—Worldwide	Lodging	PKF
Trends in the Hotel Industry—USA	Lodging	PKF
Clubs in Town and Country	Clubs	PKF
Hotel Operating Statistics	Lodging	Smith Travel Research
Restaurant Industry Operations Report	Restaurant	NRA

differences. Another common comparative analysis approach is to compare the most recent period's operating results with the budget by determining absolute and relative variances.

Exhibit 10 illustrates the horizontal analysis of operating results of the Vacation Inn for years 19X1 and 19X2. In this comparative analysis, 19X1 is considered the base. Because the revenues for 19X2 exceed revenues for 19X1, the dollar difference is shown as positive. If 19X2 revenues had been less than 19X1 revenues, the difference would have been shown as negative. Actual 19X2 expenses increased compared to 19X1, resulting in a positive difference. This should be expected, since as revenues increase, expenses should also increase. If actual 19X2 expenses had decreased compared to 19X1, the differences would have been shown as negative. The percentage differences in this statement are determined by dividing the dollar difference by the base (that is, the 19X1 numbers).

Another approach in analyzing income statements is vertical analysis. The product of this analysis is also referred to as common-size statements. These statements result from reducing all amounts to percentages using total sales as a common denominator. Exhibit 11 illustrates two **common-size income statements** for the Vacation Inn.

Vertical analysis allows for more reasonable comparisons of two or more periods when the activity for the two periods was at different levels. For example, assume the following:

	19X1	19X2
Food sales	$500,000	$750,000
Cost of food sales	150,000	225,000

A $75,000 increase in cost of sales may at first appear to be excessive. However, vertical analysis reveals the following:

	19X1	19X2
Food sales	100%	100%
Cost of food sales	30%	30%

In this example, vertical analysis suggests that despite the absolute increase in cost of sales from 19X1 to 19X2, the cost of food sales has remained constant at 30% of

Exhibit 10   Comparative Income Statements

	19X1	19X2	Difference $	Difference %
	Vacation Inn **Comparative Income Statements**			
Total Revenue	$ 1,719,393	$ 1,883,482	$ 164,089	9.54%
Rooms—Revenue	1,041,200	1,124,300	83,100	7.98
Payroll & Related Expenses	185,334	192,428	7,094	3.83
Other Expenses	79,080	84,624	5,544	7.01
Department Income	776,786	847,248	70,462	9.07
Food—Revenue	420,100	460,115	40,015	9.53
Cost of Sales	160,048	173,359	13,311	8.32
Payroll & Related Expenses	160,500	181,719	21,219	13.22
Other Expenses	44,013	50,178	6,165	14.01
Department Income	55,539	54,859	(680)	(1.22)
Beverage—Revenue	206,065	237,126	31,061	15.07
Cost of Sales	48,400	62,072	13,672	28.25
Payroll & Related Expenses	58,032	67,901	9,869	17.01
Other Expenses	22,500	26,497	3,997	17.76
Department Income	77,133	80,656	3,523	4.57
Telephone—Revenue	52,028	61,941	9,913	19.05
Cost of Sales	46,505	50,321	3,816	8.21
Payroll & Related Expenses	14,317	16,289	1,972	13.77
Other Expenses	6,816	7,561	745	10.93
Department Income	(15,610)	(12,230)	3,380	21.65
Total Operated Department Income	893,848	970,533	76,685	8.58
Undistributed Operating Expenses				
Administrative and General	72,721	79,421	6,700	9.21
Information Systems	32,043	35,213	3,170	9.89
Human Resources	26,818	28,942	2,124	7.92
Transportation	20,871	21,555	684	3.28
Marketing	66,816	79,760	12,944	19.37
Property Operation and Maintenance	80,964	84,465	3,501	4.32
Utility Costs	88,752	96,911	8,159	9.19
Total Undistributed Operating Expenses	388,985	426,267	37,282	9.58
Income After Undistributed Operating Expenses	504,863	544,266	39,403	7.80
Rent, Property Taxes, and Insurance	200,861	210,932	10,071	5.01
Interest	52,148	61,841	9,693	18.59
Depreciation and Amortization	115,860	118,942	3,082	2.66
Income Before Income Taxes	135,994	152,551	16,557	12.17
Income Taxes	48,707	57,969	9,262	19.02
Net Income	$ 87,287	$ 94,582	$ 7,295	8.36%

sales for both years. The relatively large dollar increase from 19X1 to 19X2 can be attributed to the higher level of activity during the 19X2 period rather than to unreasonable increases in the cost of sales.

Vertical analysis allows more meaningful comparisons among hospitality operations in the same industry segment but differing substantially in size. This

Exhibit 11   Common-Size Income Statements

			Percentages	
Vacation Inn **Common-Size Income Statements**				
	19X1	**19X2**	**19X1**	**19X2**
Total Revenue	$ 1,719,393	$ 1,883,482	100.0%	100.0%
Rooms—Revenue	1,041,200	1,124,300	60.6	59.7
Payroll & Related Expenses	185,334	192,428	10.8	10.2
Other Expenses	79,080	84,624	4.6	4.5
Department Income	776,786	847,248	45.2	45.0
Food—Revenue	420,100	460,115	24.4	24.4
Cost of Sales	160,048	173,359	9.3	9.2
Payroll & Related Expenses	160,500	181,719	9.3	9.6
Other Expenses	44,013	50,178	2.6	2.7
Department Income	55,539	54,859	3.2	2.9
Beverage—Revenue	206,065	237,126	12.0	12.6
Cost of Sales	48,400	62,072	2.8	3.3
Payroll & Related Expenses	58,032	67,901	3.4	3.6
Other Expenses	22,500	26,497	1.3	1.4
Department Income	77,133	80,656	4.5	4.3
Telephone—Revenue	52,028	61,941	3.0	3.3
Cost of Sales	46,505	50,321	2.7	2.7
Payroll & Related Expenses	14,317	16,289	0.8	0.9
Other Expenses	6,816	7,561	0.4	0.4
Department Income	(15,610)	(12,230)	(0.9)	(0.7)
Total Operated Department Income	893,848	970,533	52.0	51.5
Undistributed Operating Expenses				
Administrative and General	72,721	79,421	4.2	4.2
Information Systems	32,043	35,213	1.9	1.9
Human Resources	26,818	28,942	1.6	1.5
Transportation	20,871	21,555	1.2	1.1
Marketing	66,816	79,760	3.9	4.2
Property Operation and Maintenance	80,964	84,465	4.7	4.5
Utility Costs	88,752	96,911	5.1	5.1
Total Undistributed Operating Expenses	388,985	426,267	22.6	22.6
Income After Undistributed Operating Expenses	504,863	544,266	29.4	28.9
Rent, Property Taxes, and Insurance	200,861	210,932	11.7	11.2
Interest	52,148	61,841	3.0	3.3
Depreciation and Amortization	115,860	118,942	6.7	6.3
Income Before Income Taxes	135,994	152,551	8.0	8.1
Income Taxes	48,707	57,969	2.8	3.1
Net Income	$ 87,287	$ 94,582	5.1%	5.0%

common-size analysis also allows comparisons to industry standards, as discussed previously. However, a note of caution is offered at this point. Industry averages are simply that—averages. They include firms of all sizes from vastly different locations operating in entirely different markets. The industry averages reflect neither any particular operation nor an average operation, and they certainly do not depict an ideal operation.

A third approach to analyzing income statements is base-year comparisons. This approach allows a meaningful comparison of income statements for several periods. A base period is selected as a starting point and its figures are assigned a value of 100%. All subsequent periods are compared with the base on a percentage basis. Exhibit 12 illustrates the base-year comparison of the Vacation Inn for 19X0–19X2 (with 19X0 as the base). Note that some percentages increase quite dramatically.

A fourth approach to analyzing income statements is ratio analysis. Ratio analysis gives mathematical expression to a relationship between two figures and is computed by dividing one figure by the other figure. Financial ratios are compared with standards in order to evaluate the financial condition of a hospitality operation. Since vertical analysis is a subset of ratio analysis, there is considerable overlap between these two approaches.

Uniform System of Accounts for Restaurants

Operations of a commercial food service operation differ from operations of a lodging business or a club, and therefore, the financial information as presented in financial statements also differs. The income statement recommended for commercial food service operations is prescribed in the *Uniform System of Accounts for Restaurants (USAR)* published by the National Restaurant Association.

The benefits of the *USAR* are similar to those of the *USALI*. That is, the *USAR:*

- Provides for uniform classification and presentation of operating results.

- Allows for easier comparisons to food service industry statistics.

- Provides a turnkey accounting system.

- Is a time-tested system prepared by some of the food service industry's best accounting minds.

Exhibit 13 is the summary statement of income for the hypothetical Steak-Plus Restaurant. As with the *USALI*'s income statement, there are several recommended subsidiary schedules to this summary statement of income. Although they are not shown here, they provide supplementary information, as do the subsidiary schedules for the *USALI*'s income statement.

The basic similarities and differences between the *USAR*'s and *USALI*'s income statement formats are as follows:

	USALI	USAR
Sales segmented	yes	yes
Cost of sales segmented	yes	yes
Payroll and related costs segmented	yes	no
Other direct costs segmented	yes	no
Controllable expenses separated from fixed charges	yes	yes
Fixed charges segmented	yes	yes

Exhibit 12   Base-Year Comparison Income Statements

Vacation Inn
Base-Year Comparison Income Statements

	19X0	19X1	19X2
Total Revenue	100.0%	107.5%	117.7%
Rooms—Revenue	100.0%	104.1%	112.4%
Payroll & Related Expenses	100.0%	103.1%	106.9%
Other Expenses	100.0%	105.4%	112.8%
Department Income	100.0%	104.3%	113.7%
Food—Revenue	100.0%	105.0%	115.0%
Cost of Sales	100.0%	101.3%	109.7%
Payroll & Related Expenses	100.0%	103.5%	117.2%
Other Expenses	100.0%	110.0%	125.4%
Department Income	100.0%	118.2%	116.7%
Beverage—Revenue	100.0%	103.0%	118.6%
Cost of Sales	100.0%	105.2%	134.9%
Payroll & Related Expenses	100.0%	101.8%	119.1%
Other Expenses	100.0%	107.1%	126.2%
Department Income	100.0%	101.5%	106.1%
Telephone—Revenue	100.0%	104.1%	123.9%
Cost of Sales	100.0%	103.3%	111.8%
Payroll & Related Expenses	100.0%	110.1%	125.3%
Other Expenses	100.0%	113.6%	126.0%
Department Income	100.0%	111.5%	87.4%
Total Operated Department Income	100.0%	110.9%	120.4%
Undistributed Operating Expenses			
Administrative and General	100.0%	103.9%	113.5%
Information Systems	100.0%	106.8%	117.4%
Human Resources	100.0%	103.1%	111.3%
Transportation	100.0%	104.4%	107.8%
Marketing	100.0%	102.8%	122.7%
Property Operation and Maintenance	100.0%	101.2%	105.6%
Utility Costs	100.0%	103.2%	112.7%
Total Undistributed Operating Expenses	100.0%	103.2%	113.1%
Income Before Fixed Charges	100.0%	117.7%	126.9%
Rent, Property Taxes, and Insurance	100.0%	100.4%	105.5%
Interest	100.0%	94.1%	111.6%
Depreciation and Amortization	100.0%	99.9%	102.5%
Income Before Income Taxes	100.0%	236.1%	264.8%
Income Taxes	100.0%	281.9%	335.5%
Net Income	100.0%	216.5%	234.6%

Computer Applications

As they do with the balance sheet, larger hospitality operations often produce the income statement using a general ledger package. As personal computers become more sophisticated, smaller operations will also be able to use these packages.

Exhibit 13   *USAR* **Summary Statement of Income**

Summary Statement of Income
Steak-Plus Restaurant
For the year ended December 31, 19X1

	Exhibit	Amounts	Percentages
Sales:			
Food	D	$ 1,045,800	75.8%
Beverage	E	333,000	24.2
Total Sales		1,378,800	100.0
Cost of Sales:			
Food		448,000	32.5
Beverage		85,200	6.2
Total Cost of Sales		533,200	38.7
Gross Profit		845,600	61.3
Operating Expenses:			
Salaries and Wages	F	332,200	24.1
Employee Benefits	G	57,440	4.2
Direct Operating Expenses	H	88,400	6.4
Music and Entertainment	I	14,200	1.0
Marketing	J	30,000	2.2
Utility Services	K	37,560	2.7
General and Administrative Expenses	L	56,400	4.1
Repairs and Maintenance	M	28,600	2.1
Occupancy Costs	N	82,200	6.0
Depreciation	N	31,200	2.3
Other Income	O	(5,400)	(0.4)
Total Operating Expenses		752,800	54.6
Operating Income		92,800	6.7
Interest	P	21,600	1.6
Income Before Income Taxes		71,200	5.2
Income Taxes		22,000	1.6
Net Income		$ 49,200	3.6%

In the meantime, there are many computer applications for the income statement. For example, Exhibit 14 was produced by a spreadsheet program that helps prepare the amounts for common-size statements. The user only had to enter the separate revenue and expense amounts; the computer calculated all totals (such as Department Income) and all percentages.

In addition, many software packages have extensive graphics capabilities. The phrase "a picture is worth a thousand words" applies here. Although graphs do not usually provide detail, managers can more easily track recent performance trends by showing results in line graphs. Departmental expenses can be shown using pie charts. Departmental revenues for several years can be shown using bar charts. These charts are easy to understand, and they can be used as management tools to show employees the operation's results more effectively than the traditional financial statements, which sometimes seem like a confusing list of numbers.

Exhibit 14   Sample Spreadsheet Printout

	DOLLARS		PERCENTAGES	
VACATION INN COMMON-SIZE INCOME STATEMENTS	19X1	19X2	19X1	19X2
TOTAL REVENUE	$1,719,393	$1,883,482	100.0%	100.0%
Rooms—Revenue	1,041,200	1,124,300	60.6	59.7
Payroll & Related Expenses	185,334	192,428	10.8	10.2
Other Expenses	79,080	84,624	4.6	4.5
Department Income	776,786	847,248	45.2	45.0
Food—Revenue	420,100	460,115	24.4	24.4
Cost of Sales	160,048	173,359	9.3	9.2
Payroll & Related Expenses	160,500	181,719	9.3	9.6
Other Expenses	44,013	50,178	2.6	2.7
Department Income	55,539	54,859	3.2	2.9
Beverage—Revenue	206,065	237,126	12.0	12.6
Cost of Sales	48,400	62,072	2.8	3.3
Payroll & Related Expenses	58,032	67,901	3.4	3.6
Other Expenses	22,500	26,497	1.3	1.4
Department Income	77,133	80,656	4.5	4.3
Telephone—Revenue	52,028	61,941	3.0	3.3
Cost of Sales	46,505	50,321	2.7	2.7
Payroll & Related Expenses	14,317	16,289	0.8	0.9
Other Expenses	6,816	7,561	0.4	0.4
Department Income	(15,610)	(12,230)	(0.9)	(0.7)
Total Operated Department Income	893,848	970,533	52.0	51.5
Undistributed Operating Expenses				
Administrative and General	72,721	79,421	4.2	4.2
Information Systems	32,043	35,213	1.9	1.9
Human Resources	26,818	28,942	1.6	1.5
Transportation	20,871	21,555	1.2	1.1
Marketing	66,816	79,760	3.9	4.2
Property Operation and Maintenance	80,964	84,465	4.7	4.5
Utility Costs	88,752	96,911	5.1	5.1
Total Undistributed Operating Expenses	388,985	426,267	22.6	22.6
Income After Undistributed Operating Expenses	504,863	544,266	29.4	28.9
Rent, Property Taxes, and Insurance	200,861	210,932	11.7	11.2
Interest	52,148	61,841	3.0	3.3
Depreciation and Amortization	115,860	118,942	6.7	6.3
Income Before Income Taxes	135,994	152,551	8.0	8.1
Income Taxes	48,707	57,969	2.8	3.1
Net Income	$ 87,287	$ 94,582	5.1%	5.0%

Summary

The income statement, complete with all departmental statements, is generally considered the most useful financial statement for management. It highlights the important financial aspects of the property's operations over a period of time.

The income statement shows four major elements: revenues, expenses, gains, and losses. Revenues (increases in assets or decreases in liability accounts) and expenses (decreases in assets or increases in liability accounts) are directly related to operations, while gains and losses result from transactions incidental to the property's major operations.

In order to standardize income statements within the hospitality industry, the original *Uniform System of Accounts for Hotels* was written in 1925-26. Since then, there have been changes and revisions, the most recent being the ninth edition, the *Uniform System of Accounts for the Lodging Industry*, published in 1996. By using an accounting system based on a uniform system of accounts, the management of a new hotel has a turnkey accounting system for a complete and systematic accounting for the hotel's operations. The various uniform systems also facilitate comparison among operations of varying sizes in the hospitality industry.

In order to enhance the usefulness of the income statement, the format set up by the *USALI* includes statements of departmental income showing the revenues produced by each profit center (operated department) and subtracting from each the corresponding direct operating expenses. Included in the direct operating expenses are not only the cost of goods sold, but also the direct payroll and other direct expenses. Next, undistributed operating expenses, which consist of nine major service center categories—administrative and general expenses, human resources, information systems, security, marketing, franchise fees, transportation, property operation and maintenance, and utility costs—must be subtracted to determine "income after undistributed operating expenses." This is followed by management fees and fixed charges, which include rent, property taxes, fire insurance, interest, depreciation, and amortization. Next, gain (loss) on sale of property and equipment is added (subtracted) to determine income before income taxes. Finally, income taxes are subtracted to determine net income.

As a supplement to the income statement, several departmental income statements should be presented. These offer management additional insight into the operation of each department. The number of schedules necessary depends on the complexity of the lodging facility; the more cost and profit centers operated, the more supplemental statements should be presented. These departmental statements can be very useful for management. First, they can be used to compare the hotel's operations with industry averages, prior performance, and, most important, budgeted standards or goals. Also, the relative profitability of various departments can be compared.

There are four major methods management can use to analyze the income statement. The first method is horizontal analysis, which considers both the relative and absolute changes in the income statement between two periods and/or between the budgeted and actual figures. Any major variances exceeding levels predefined by management can be further investigated to determine their causes. The next type of analysis is the vertical analysis, which reduces all items to a percentage of sales. These percentages, often referred to as common-size statements, can then be used to compare the results of the property's operations with either those of other lodging facilities or with industry standards. Again, any significant differences should be studied. The third method is base-year comparisons, in which two or more years are compared on a percentage basis with a base year set at 100%. The final method, ratio analysis, gives mathematical expression to a relationship between two figures and is computed by dividing one figure by the other figure. Financial ratios are compared with standards in order to evaluate the financial condition of a hospitality operation.

Endnotes

1. Uniform systems of accounts are available as follows:

   Uniform System of Accounts for the Lodging Industry, 9th rev. ed. (East Lansing, Mich.: Educational Institute of the American Hotel & Motel Association, 1996).

   Uniform System of Accounts for Clubs (Washington, D.C.: Club Managers Association of America, 1982).

   Uniform System of Accounts for Restaurants, 6th rev. ed. (Washington, D.C.: National Restaurant Association, 1990).

2. *Trends in the Hotel Industry—USA Edition 1996* (San Francisco: PKF Consulting, 1996).

3. *Trends.*

Key Terms

capacity costs—Fixed charges relating to the physical plant or the capacity to provide goods and services to guests.

common-size income statements—Income statements used in vertical analysis whose information has been reduced to percentages to facilitate comparisons.

comparative income statements—Horizontal analysis of income statements for two accounting periods in terms of both absolute and relative variances for each line item.

daily report of operations—A frequent major report prepared for management.

departmental income statements—Supplements to the income statement that provide management with detailed financial information for each operating department and service center; also referred to as schedules.

expenses—Costs incurred in providing the goods and services offered.

gain—An increase in assets, a reduction in liabilities, or a combination of both resulting from incidental transactions and from all other transactions and events affecting the operation during the period, except those that count as revenues or investments by owners.

income statement—A report on the profitability of operations, including revenues earned and expenses incurred in generating the revenues for the period of time covered by the statement.

loss—A decrease in assets, an increase in liabilities, or a combination of both resulting from incidental transactions and from other transactions and events affecting the operation during a period, except those that count as expenses or distributions to owners.

responsibility accounting—The organization of accounting information (as on an income statement) that focuses attention on departmental results such as the rooms and food departments.

revenue—The amount charged to customers in exchange for goods and services.

schedules—See departmental income statements.

summary income statement—An income statement intended for external users that lacks the detail of supporting schedules.

uniform systems of accounts—Standardized accounting systems prepared by various segments of the hospitality industry offering detailed information about accounts, classifications, formats, the different kinds, contents, and uses of financial statements and reports, and other useful information.

Review Questions

1. What are the major differences between the balance sheet and the income statement?

2. Why are creditors interested in the income statement?

3. What are the major differences between a revenue and a gain?

4. What are three examples of direct operating expenses for the rooms department?

5. What is the difference between the income statement used in many non-hospitality industries and one prepared by a lodging facility?

6. How is the cost of food sold determined?

7. What are the advantages of the uniform system of accounts?

8. What detailed expenses are included in the property operation, maintenance, and energy costs of the income statement?

9. Why are supplemental statements valuable to management?

10. What are the different techniques of income statement analysis?

11. How is the Summary Statement of Income per the *USAR* similar to and different from the *USALI*'s income statement?

Problems

Problem 1

Bibicoff's Cafe sold two pieces of equipment during 19X2. Relevant information is as follows:

1. Sale of range

   Selling price = $500

   Original cost = $3,000

   Accumulated depreciation = $2,700

2. Sale of van

   Selling price = $3,500

Original cost = $20,000

Accumulated depreciation = $15,000

Required:

Determine the gain or loss on the sale of each piece of equipment.

Problem 2

The Tong Lee Inn had total revenues of $600,000 for the month of June. Assume that the Tong Lee Inn's percentages for June were the same as the comparative results of operations information shown in Exhibit 7 for 1995.

Required:

Determine the amount of each of the following for June:

1. Rooms revenue
2. Total rooms expenses
3. Energy costs
4. Administrative and general expenses
5. Beverage gross profit
6. Total food and beverage expenses

Problem 3

Marita Lo, the owner of the MaLo Diner, has requested your assistance in determining some monthly expenses. She provides you with the following information:

	Food	Beverages
Beginning inventory 1/1	$ 8,000	$ 3,000
Ending inventory 1/31	$10,000	$ 3,500
Purchases	$40,000	$20,000
Employee meals	$ 500	—
Food transfers to beverage department	$ 300	—

Required:

Determine the following:

1. Cost of food used
2. Cost of food sold
3. Cost of beverages sold

Problem 4

As the controller for Kelly's, a hotel with a large restaurant operation, you are responsible for monitoring costs. You have collected the following information concerning the food inventory and need to calculate the cost of food sold for the month of December.

Inventory, December 1, 19X1	$12,376
Inventory, December 31, 19X1	15,845

Purchases	76,840
Employee Meals:	
A. General Manager	85
B. Food Department	648
Transfers from the Bar to Kitchen	46
Promotional Meals	256

Required:

1. Calculate the cost of food sold for December 19X1.
2. To which departments would each expense be charged?

Expense	Department
1. Cost of food sold	_____
2. Employee meals—general manager	_____
3. Employee meals—food department	_____
4. Promotional meals	_____

Problem 5

Several accounts from the Hilltop Motel's general ledger that pertain to the rooms department are listed below. The accounts are in random order as follows:

Sales—transient—regular	$ 100,000
Salaries	10,000
Commissions	1,000
Uniforms	500
Linen expense	1,000
Sales—transient—groups	50,000
Wages	15,000
Payroll taxes	2,000
Operating supplies	1,500
Contract cleaning	1,800
Dry cleaning	1,200
Fringe benefits	3,000
Other revenues	2,000
Allowances—rooms	500
Laundry	3,000
Other expenses	1,800

Required:

Prepare a rooms department schedule following the *USALI*. Use only classifications as shown on the prescribed schedule. See Exhibit 4 as a guide.

Problem 6

The Warwick Motel's income statement for 19X6 is provided below:

Warwick Motel
Income Statement
For the year ended December 31, 19X6

	Net Revenue	Cost of Sales	Payroll & Related Expenses	Other Expenses	Income (Loss)
OPERATED DEPARTMENTS					
Rooms	$ 380,000	$ —	$ 92,000	$ 30,000	$ 258,000
Food	180,000	54,000	69,000	20,000	37,000
Other Income	1,000	—	—	—	1,000
Total Operated Departments	561,000	54,000	161,000	50,000	296,000
UNDISTRIBUTED OPERATING EXPENSES					
Administrative and General			63,250	10,000	73,250
Marketing					10,000
Property Operation and Maintenance					30,000
Energy Costs					27,000
Total Undistributed Operating Expenses			63,250	10,000	140,250
Income After Undistributed Operating Expenses	$ 561,000	$ 54,000	$ 224,250	$ 60,000	155,750
Rent, Property Taxes, and Insurance					17,000
Interest Expense					21,000
Depreciation					30,000
INCOME BEFORE INCOME TAXES					87,750
Income Tax					21,938
NET INCOME					$ 65,812

Required:

Answer the following questions.

1. What was the total gross profit for 19X6?
2. What were the total fixed charges for 19X6?
3. What is the average tax rate for 19X6?
4. What is the amount of income the general manager is most likely responsible for during 19X6?
5. What is the total of overhead expenses for 19X6?
6. What is the payroll cost percentage for 19X6?
7. What is the food cost percentage for 19X6?

Problem 7

The Salazar Sunset Inn (SSI) has three major operated departments—rooms, food, and beverages. The following information is supplied to you as of December 31, 19X6:

Account	Account Balance
Insurance (fire)	$ 20,000
Rooms department—salaries and wages	150,000
Food department—salaries and wages	160,000
Beverage department—salaries and wages	40,000
Management fees	50,000
Supplies—food department	40,000
Cost of food sold	180,000
Cost of beverages sold	60,000
Room sales	1,000,000
Dividend income	15,000
Interest expense	85,000
Food sales	540,000
Beverage sales	200,000
A & G—wages	80,000
Supplies—beverage department	15,000
Advertising	30,000
Maintenance—contract	60,000
Depreciation	50,000
Heat	40,000
Franchise fees	25,000
Power and lights	30,000
Amortization of franchise initial fee	5,000
Supplies & other—rooms department	80,000
Property taxes	50,000
A & G—other expense	40,000
Room—allowances	2,000

Required:

Prepare a summary income statement in accordance with the *USALI*. Assume an average tax rate of 25%.

Problem 8

The general ledger of Ramsey's, a 100-seat restaurant, as of December 31, 19X3, includes revenue and expense accounts as follows:

Salaries	$ 150,000
Wages	280,000
Payroll taxes	30,000
Fringe benefits (excludes employee meals)	50,000
Employee meals	5,000
Food sales	1,200,000
Beverage sales	500,000
Food purchases	460,000

Beverage purchases	130,000
Other sales	20,000
Direct operating expenses	100,000
Music	20,000
Marketing	30,000
Heat, light and power	35,000
Rent	152,000
Interest expense	20,000
Depreciation	50,000
Repairs	30,000
Administrative & general	92,000

Other information:

Income tax rate—30% on pretax income

Inventories	1/1/X3	12/31/X3
Food	$20,000	$22,000
Beverage	15,000	17,000

Required:

Prepare Ramsey's statement of income for 19X3 in accordance with the *USAR*. See Exhibit 13 as a guide.

Problem 9

The Wilson Motel has two major operated departments—rooms and food. The following information is supplied to you as of December 31, 19X6:

Account	Account Balance
Insurance (fire)	$ 5,000
Rooms department—salaries and wages	80,000
Food department—salaries and wages	60,000
Supplies—food department	20,000
Food purchases	55,000
Room sales	380,000
Interest income	1,000
Interest expense	??
Cost of food sold	??
Food sales	180,000
A & G—wages	50,000
Advertising	10,000
Maintenance—contract	30,000
Depreciation	50,000
Heat	15,000
Power and lights	12,000
Franchise fee	30,000
Supplies and other—rooms department	30,000

Property taxes	12,000
A & G—other expense	10,000

Other information:

1. The Wilson Motel borrowed $50,000 two years ago from the Wilmore Savings and Loan. On June 30, 19X6, the first non-interest payment is made to Wilmore of $10,000. The funds were borrowed at an interest rate of 10%.

2. The beginning and ending inventories of food were $2,000 and $3,000 respectively. Food consumed by the food and rooms department employees during the year (free of charge) totaled $500 and $300, respectively.

3. Benefits and payroll taxes for all employees, excluding free food, are 20% of gross salaries and wages.

4. The Wilson Motel pays an average of 25% of its pretax income to the various governmental units in the form of income taxes.

5. The management fee to be paid to the management company is 3% of room sales and 10% of total income after undistributed operating expenses.

Required:

Prepare an income statement for the Wilson Motel based on the *USALI*.

Problem 10

Tim's Tasty Tidbits' August and September 19X1 condensed income statements are as follows:

	August	September
Food Sales	$80,000	$82,000
Cost of Food Sales	24,000	25,000
Labor	25,500	28,800
Laundry	4,000	4,200
China, glass, silver	1,000	1,100
Other	16,000	15,500
Total Expenses	70,500	74,600
Net Income	$ 9,500	$ 7,400
Customers were served as follows:		
Food	14,000	15,000

Required:

1. Convert the two income statements to common-size income statements.

2. Based on the information provided (including customer information), comment regarding the operating performance of Tim's Tasty Tidbits for the two months.

Problem 11

Pat Mulhurn, the founder of Pat's Place, wants to analyze the year's operations for 19X2 by comparing them with the 19X1 results. To aid him, prepare a comparative income statement using the 19X1 and 19X2 information available.

Pat's Place
Income Statement
For the years ending December 31, 19X1 and 19X2

	19X1	19X2
Revenues		
Rooms	$ 976,000	$1,041,000
Food	604,000	626,000
Telephone	50,000	52,000
Total	1,630,000	1,719,000
Direct Expenses		
Rooms	250,000	264,000
Food	476,000	507,000
Telephone	68,000	68,000
Total Operated Department Income	836,000	880,000
Undistributed Operating Expenses		
Administrative and General	195,000	206,000
Marketing	65,000	68,000
Property Operation & Maintenance	69,000	68,000
Utility Costs	101,000	102,000
Income After Undistributed Operating Expenses	406,000	436,000
Rent, Property Taxes, & Insurance	200,000	201,000
Interest	55,000	52,000
Depreciation and Amortization	116,000	116,000
Income Before Income Taxes	35,000	67,000
Income Taxes	7,000	17,000
Net Income	$ 28,000	$ 50,000

Required:

Prepare the comparative income statement for Pat's Place. Note: Rearrange the income statement to conform to the *USALI* format as reflected in Exhibit 10.

Problem 12

The Black Beach Motel (BBM) has three operated departments—rooms, food, and telephone. The following information is supplied to you as of December 31, 19X1.

Account	Account Balance
Insurance (fire)	$ 20,000
Rooms department—salaries and wages	100,000
Food department—salaries and wages	80,000
Telephone department—salaries and wages	5,000
Supplies—food department	30,000
Food purchases	80,000
Room sales	600,000
Interest income	??
Interest expense	50,000

Cost of food sold	??
Food sales	300,000
A & G—wages	40,000
Advertising	8,000
Maintenance—contract	40,000
Depreciation	60,000
Heat	15,000
Power and lights	12,000
Supplies and other—rooms department	40,000
Property taxes	12,000
A & G—other expenses	20,000
Telephone sales	16,000
Cost of calls	10,000
Telephone—other expenses	3,000
Management fee	??
Marketing—wages	20,000
Rent	5,000

Other information:

1. The BBM invested $100,000 on April 1, 19X1, in a certificate of deposit earning an annual rate of 8%.

2. The beginning and ending inventories of food were $4,000 and $6,000 respectively. Food consumed by the department employees during the year (free of charge) was as follows:

Rooms	$ 600
Food	1,000
A & G	300

3. Benefits and payroll taxes for all employees, excluding free food, are 25% of gross salaries and wages.

4. The BBM pays an average of 30% of its pretax income to the various governmental units in the form of income taxes.

5. The management fee to be paid to the management company is 5% of total sales and 8% of total income before management fees and fixed charges.

Required:

Prepare an income statement for 19X1 for the Black Beach Motel based on the *USALI.*

Problem 13

The Bush Beach Motel (BBM) has two major operated departments—rooms and food. The following information is supplied to you as of December 31, 19X2:

Account	Account Balance
Insurance (fire)	$?
Rooms department—salaries and wages	90,000
Food department—salaries and wages	60,000
Supplies & other—food department	20,000

Food purchases	65,000
Room sales	550,000
Interest income	?
Cost of food sold	?
Food sales	250,000
A & G—salaries	60,000
Advertising	12,000
Maintenance—contract	40,000
Depreciation	40,000
Electricity	15,000
Heating oil	12,000
Amortization of intangible asset	5,000
Supplies & other—rooms department	30,000
Property taxes	15,000
A & G—other expense	15,000
Franchise fees	?
Room—allowances	1,000

Other information is as follows:

1. The BBM invested $30,000 on July 1, 19X2 in Daytona Aircraft Bonds. The funds were invested at an annual interest rate of 12%.

2. The beginning and ending inventories of food were $5,000 and $4,000, respectively. Food consumed by the food and rooms department employees during the year (free of charge) totaled $500 and $300, respectively.

3. Fringe benefits and payroll taxes for all employees, inclusive of employee meals, are 20% of gross salaries and wages.

4. The BBM pays an average of 30% of its pre-tax income to the various governmental units in the form of income taxes.

5. The management fee to be paid to the management company is 2% of net room sales and 6% of total income before management fees and fixed charges.

6. Fire insurance protection was secured on June 1, 19X1 for a two-year period of coverage from July 1, 19X1 through June 30, 19X3. The two-year premium was $36,000.

7. Franchise fees (a marketing expense) is paid to Best Eastern Corporation at a rate of 3% of net room sales and 2% of net food sales.

8. A range that cost $5,000 was sold for $2,000. The range had been depreciated by 80% of its cost.

Required:

Prepare an income statement for 19X2 for the BBM based on the *USALI* format.

Problem 14

The Wilkin Inn's partially completed condensed comparative income statements are as follows:

	19X1	19X2	Difference $	%
Total Revenues	$ 1,000,000	$1,200,000		
Rooms—Revenues	600,000			25.0
Payroll & Related Expenses		100,000	10,000	
Other Expense	50,000			10.0
Department Income				
Food—Revenues	350,000			
Cost of Sales		130,000	15,000	
Payroll & Related Expenses	75,000			10.0
Other Expense			3,500	10.0
Department Income				
Telephone—Revenues		60,000		
Cost of Sales	40,000			12.0
Payroll & Related Expenses			2,000	14.0
Other Expense		8,000	1,000	
Department Income				
Total Operated Department Income				
Undistributed Operating Expenses:				
Administrative & General	100,000			11.0
Marketing		60,000	5,000	
Property Operation and Maintenance			10,000	
Utility Costs				12.0
Total Undistributed Operating Expenses	250,000		32,000	
Income After Undistributed Operating Expenses				
Management Fees		30,000	3,000	
Income Before Fixed Charges				
Rent, Property Taxes, and Insurance	100,000			6.0
Interest		80,000	20,000	
Depreciation			5,000	20.0
Income Before Income Taxes				
Income Taxes			6,000	10.0
Net Income				

Required:

Complete the above comparative income statements.

Problem 15

Listed below is financial information for the Harby Hotel for the year ended December 31, 19X2.

Account	Account Balance
Commissions—Rooms Department	$ 23,500
Marketing Expense	111,800
Ending Food Inventory	53,000
Depreciation and Amortization Expense	91,000
Net Room Revenue	1,560,000
Cost of Sales—Rental and Other Income	9,360
Rent Expense	148,200
Reservation Expense	13,500
Fire Insurance Expense	10,400
Income Taxes—40% pretax rate	??
Employee Benefits—Rooms Department	51,000
Food Revenues	858,000
Proceeds from Sale of Equipment*	10,000
Other Expense—Telephone Department	6,240
Contract Cleaning—Rooms Department	5,800
Administrative and General Expenses (total)	270,400
Property Taxes	70,200
Food Purchases	328,400
Payroll—Telephone Department	15,600
Linen Expense—Rooms Department	8,600
Other Expense—Rental and Other Income	9,360
Beginning Food Inventory	38,900
Revenues—Rental and Other Income	119,600
Revenues—Telephone Department	62,400
Data Processing Expenses (total)	34,320
Human Resources Expenses (total)	32,614
Salaries and Wages—Rooms Department	209,000
Interest Expenses	98,800
Payroll—Rental and Other Income	20,800
Free Food—Employees**	12,300
Laundry and Dry Cleaning—Rooms Department	24,800
Other Expenses—Food Department	93,600
Other Expenses—Rooms Department	130,000
Property Operation and Maintenance (total)	112,200
Cost of Sales—Telephone Department	46,800
Payroll—Food Department	93,600
Utility Costs (total)	159,500

*   Equipment sold cost $15,000 and had been depreciated by $8,000.

**   This has already been recorded as expense in the appropriate departments, except in the determination of the cost of food sold.

Required:

1. Prepare a rooms departmental statement in accordance with the *USALI*.
2. Determine the cost of food sold.
3. Prepare a summary income statement following the *USALI*.

Appendix
Uniform Systems Schedules

Directly below is the income statement for the Eatonwood Hotel for the year ended 12/31/19X8. The following pages present the nine supporting schedules referenced on the income statement below.

Eatonwood Hotel
Summary Statement of Income
For the year ended 12/31/19X8

	SCHEDULE	NET REVENUE	COST OF SALES	PAYROLL & RELATED EXPENSES	OTHER EXPENSES	INCOME (LOSS)
OPERATED DEPARTMENTS						
ROOMS	1	$ 6,070,356		$ 1,068,383	$ 473,487	$ 4,528,486
FOOD	2	2,017,928	$ 733,057	617,705	168,794	498,372
BEVERAGE	3	778,971	162,258	205,897	78,783	332,033
TELECOMMUNICATIONS	4	213,744	167,298	31,421	17,309	-2,284
RENTALS AND OTHER INCOME	5	188,092				188,092
TOTAL OPERATED DEPARTMENTS		9,269,091	1,062,613	1,923,406	738,373	5,544,699
UNDISTRIBUTED OPERATING EXPENSES						
ADMINISTRATIVE AND GENERAL	6			227,635	331,546	559,181
MARKETING	7			116,001	422,295	538,296
PROPERTY OPERATION AND MAINTENANCE	8			204,569	163,880	368,449
UTILITY COSTS	9				546,331	546,331
TOTAL UNDISTRIBUTED OPERATING EXPENSES				548,205	1,464,052	2,012,257
TOTALS		$ 9,269,091	$ 1,062,613	$ 2,471,611	$ 2,202,425	
INCOME AFTER UNDISTRIBUTED OPERATING EXPENSES						3,532,442
RENT, PROPERTY TAXES, AND INSURANCE						641,029
INCOME BEFORE INTEREST, DEPRECIATION AND AMORTIZATION, AND INCOME TAXES						2,891,413
INTEREST EXPENSE						461,347
INCOME BEFORE DEPRECIATION AMORTIZATION, AND INCOME TAXES						2,430,066
DEPRECIATION AND AMORTIZATION						552,401
GAIN ON SALE OF PROPERTY						1,574
INCOME BEFORE INCOME TAXES						1,879,239
INCOME TAXES						469,810
NET INCOME						$ 1,409,429

Note: The Statement of Income format as shown in the 9th revised edition of the *USALI* also includes additional operated departments, undistributed operating expenses, and management fees. However, these other departments are not used by the hypothetical Eatonwood Hotel.

Rooms—Schedule #1
Eatonwood Hotel
For the year ended 12/31/19X8

	Current Period
REVENUE	$6,124,991
ALLOWANCES	54,635
NET REVENUE	6,070,356
EXPENSES	
Salaries and Wages	855,919
Employee Benefits	212,464
Total Payroll and Related Expenses	1,068,383
Other Expenses	
Cable/Satellite Television	20,100
Commissions	66,775
Complimentary Guest Services	2,420
Contract Services	30,874
Guest Relocation	1,241
Guest Transportation	48,565
Laundry and Dry Cleaning	42,495
Linen	12,140
Operating Supplies	122,600
Reservations	40,908
Telecommunications	12,442
Training	7,122
Uniforms	60,705
Other	5,100
Total Other Expenses	473,487
TOTAL EXPENSES	1,541,870
DEPARTMENTAL INCOME (LOSS)	$4,528,486

Food—Schedule #2
Eatonwood Hotel
For the year ended 12/31/19X8

	Current Period
TOTAL REVENUE	$2,017,928
REVENUE	$1,974,318
ALLOWANCES	7,864
NET REVENUE	1,966,454
COST OF SALES	
Cost of Food	743,260
Less Cost of Employee Meals	9,830
Less Food Transfers to Beverage	2,118
Plus Beverage Transfers to Food	1,035
Net Cost of Food	732,347
Other Cost of Sales	710
Total Cost of Sales	733,057
GROSS PROFIT (LOSS) ON FOOD SALES	1,233,397
OTHER INCOME	
Meeting Room Rentals	3,400
Miscellaneous Banquet Income	15,129
Service Charges	32,945
Total Other Income	51,474
GROSS PROFIT (LOSS) AND OTHER INCOME	1,284,871
EXPENSES	
Salaries and Wages	488,266
Employee Benefits	129,439
Total Payroll and Related Expenses	617,705
Other Expenses	
China, Glassware, Silver, and Linen	20,152
Contract Services	20,464
Laundry and Dry Cleaning	8,427
Licenses	1,300
Miscellaneous Banquet Expense	14,559
Music and Entertainment	4,618
Operating Supplies	57,512
Telecommunications	7,971
Training	8,400
Uniforms	15,200
Other	10,191
Total Other Expenses	168,794
TOTAL EXPENSES	786,499
DEPARTMENTAL INCOME (LOSS)	$ 498,372

Beverage—Schedule #3
Eatonwood Hotel
For the year ended 12/31/19X8

	Current Period
TOTAL REVENUE	$778,971
REVENUE	774,101
ALLOWANCES	4,618
NET REVENUE	769,483
COST OF SALES	
Cost of Beverage	160,905
Less Beverage Transfers to Food	1,035
Plus Food Transfers to Beverage	2,118
Net Cost of Beverage	161,988
Other Cost of Sales	270
Total Cost of Sales	162,258
GROSS PROFIT (LOSS) ON BEVERAGE SALES	607,225
OTHER INCOME	
Cover Charges	1,966
Service Charges	7,522
Total Other Income	9,488
GROSS PROFIT (LOSS) AND OTHER INCOME	616,713
EXPENSES	
Salaries and Wages	162,753
Employee Benefits	43,144
Total Payroll and Related Expenses	205,897
Other Expenses	
China, Glassware, Silver, and Linen	6,718
Contract Services	7,624
Gratis Food	1,914
Laundry and Dry Cleaning	3,088
Licenses	6,375
Music and Entertainment	18,975
Operating Supplies	14,200
Telecommunications	1,378
Training	3,600
Uniforms	7,830
Other	7,081
Total Other Expenses	78,783
TOTAL EXPENSES	284,680
DEPARTMENTAL INCOME (LOSS)	$332,033

Telecommunications—Schedule #4
Eatonwood Hotel
For the year ended 12/31/19X8

	Current Period
REVENUE	$214,810
ALLOWANCES	1,066
NET REVENUE	213,744
COST OF CALLS	
Long-Distance	124,966
Local	36,415
Utility Tax	4,602
Other	1,315
Total Cost of Calls	167,298
GROSS PROFIT (LOSS)	46,446
EXPENSES	
Salaries and Wages	25,566
Employee Benefits	5,855
Total Payroll and Related Expenses	31,421
Other Expenses	
Contract Services	6,250
Printing and Stationery	3,566
Telecommunications	1,714
Training	815
Other	4,964
Total Other Expenses	17,309
TOTAL EXPENSES	48,730
DEPARTMENTAL INCOME (LOSS)	$ (2,284)

Rentals and Other Income—Schedule #5
Eatonwood Hotel
For the year ended 12/31/19X8

	Current Period
Space Rentals and Concessions	$68,750
Commissions	32,471
Interest Income	83,500
Other	3,371
TOTAL RENTALS AND OTHER INCOME	$188,092

Administrative and General—Schedule #6
Eatonwood Hotel
For the year ended 12/31/19X8

	Current Period
PAYROLL AND RELATED EXPENSES	
Salaries and Wages	$ 182,108
Employee Benefits	45,507
Total Payroll and Related Expenses	227,635
OTHER EXPENSES	
Bank Charges	2,115
Cash Overages and Shortages	816
Communication Systems	8,454
Contract Services	1,609
Credit and Collection	15,746
Credit Card Commissions	62,906
Donations	10,000
Dues and Subscriptions	7,283
Head Office	8,919
Human Resources	30,349
Information Systems	12,140
Internal Audit	3,600
Internal Communications	7,400
Loss and Damage	1,615
Meals and Entertainment	3,200
Operating Supplies and Equipment	15,914
Postage	7,421
Printing and Stationery	8,972
Professional Fees	4,619
Provision for Doubtful Accounts	22,406
Security	42,911
Telecommunications	15,841
Training	7,500
Transportation	3,918
Travel	14,200
Other	11,692
Total Other Expenses	331,546
TOTAL ADMINISTRATIVE AND GENERAL EXPENSES	$ 559,181

Marketing—Schedule #7
Eatonwood Hotel
For the year ended 12/31/19X8

	Current Period
SELLING	
PAYROLL AND RELATED EXPENSES	
Salaries and Wages	$ 57,658
Employee Benefits	14,415
Total Payroll and Related Expenses	72,073
OTHER EXPENSES	
Complimentary Guest Services	1,562
Contract Services	1,815
Dues and Subscriptions	6,679
Meals and Entertainment	7,482
Printing and Stationery	8,419
Postage	5,900
Trade Shows	12,500
Telecommunications	12,213
Training	3,347
Travel	16,424
Other	7,172
Total Other Expenses	84,513
TOTAL SELLING EXPENSES	156,586
ADVERTISING AND MERCHANDISING	
PAYROLL AND RELATED EXPENSES	
Salaries and Wages	35,128
Employee Benefits	8,800
Total Payroll and Related Expenses	43,928
OTHER EXPENSES	
Collateral Material	28,793
Contract Services	4,916
Direct Mail	77,398
Frequent Stay Programs	25,941
In-House Graphics	36,223
Media	102,059
Outdoor	15,914
Point-of-Sale Material	9,286
Telecommunications	6,014
Other	4,615
Total Other Expenses	311,159
TOTAL ADVERTISING AND MERCHANDISING EXPENSES	355,087
FEES AND COMMISSIONS	
Agency Fees	5,574
Other	649
Total Fees and Commissions	6,223
OTHER MARKETING EXPENSES	20,400
TOTAL MARKETING EXPENSES	$538,296

Property Operation and Maintenance—Schedule #8
Eatonwood Hotel
For the year ended 12/31/19X8

	Current Period
PAYROLL AND RELATED EXPENSES	
Salaries and Wages	$163,899
Employee Benefits	40,670
Total Payroll and Related Expenses	204,569
OTHER EXPENSES	
Building Supplies	12,460
Contract Services	10,100
Curtains and Draperies	3,415
Electrical and Mechanical Equipment	4,892
Elevators	10,619
Engineering Supplies	10,117
Floor Covering	12,924
Furniture	15,141
Grounds and Landscaping	6,152
Heating, Ventilating, and Air Conditioning Equipment	6,967
Kitchen Equipment	2,015
Laundry Equipment	1,914
Life/Safety	4,570
Light Bulbs	3,418
Locks and Keys	2,618
Operating Supplies	6,529
Painting and Decorating	8,915
Removal of Waste Matter	10,996
Swimming Pool	5,602
Telecommunications	6,118
Training	3,441
Uniforms	2,615
Vehicle Maintenance	8,911
Other	3,431
Total Other Expenses	163,880
TOTAL PROPERTY OPERATION AND MAINTENANCE EXPENSES	$368,449

Utility Costs—Schedule #9
Eatonwood Hotel
For the year ended 12/31/19X8

	Current Period
UTILITY COSTS	
Electricity	$ 226,514
Gas	236,100
Oil	8,500
Water	62,524
Other Fuels	13,053
Total Utility Costs	$ 546,331

In addition to the schedules used in the preceding example, the *Uniform System of Accounts for the Lodging Industry,* 9th rev. ed., contains several other schedules that can be used when circumstances warrant their use. Blank versions of these schedules are presented in the remainder of this Appendix.

GARAGE AND PARKING

	Current Period
REVENUE	$
ALLOWANCES	
NET REVENUE	
COST OF MERCHANDISE SOLD	
GROSS PROFIT (LOSS)	
EXPENSES	
Salaries and Wages	
Employee Benefits	
Total Payroll and Related Expenses	
Other Expenses	
Contract Services	
Licenses	
Management Fee	
Operating Supplies	
Telecommunications	
Training	
Uniforms	
Other	
Total Other Expenses	
TOTAL EXPENSES	
DEPARTMENTAL INCOME (LOSS)	$

GOLF COURSE

	Current Period
REVENUE	$
ALLOWANCES	_____
NET REVENUE	
EXPENSES, EXCLUDING COURSE MAINTENANCE	
Salaries and Wages	
Employee Benefits	
Total Payroll and Related Expenses	_____
Other Expenses	
Contract Services	
Gasoline and Lubricants	
Golf Car Batteries/Electricity	
Golf Car Repairs and Maintenance	
Laundry and Dry Cleaning	
Operating Supplies	
Professional Services	
Telecommunications	
Tournament Expenses	
Training	
Other	
Total Other Expenses	_____
TOTAL EXPENSES EXCLUDING COURSE MAINTENANCE	_____
COURSE MAINTENANCE EXPENSES	
Salaries and Wages	
Employee Benefits	
Total Payroll and Related Expenses	_____
Other Expenses	
Contract Services	
Fertilizers, Insecticides, and Topsoil	
Gasoline and Lubricants	
Repairs and Maintenance	
General	
Irrigation	
Machinery and Equipment	
Refuse Removal	
Sand and Top Dressing	
Seeds, Flowers, and Shrubs	
Telecommunications	
Training	
Uniforms	
Water	
Other	
Total Other Expenses	_____
TOTAL COURSE MAINTENANCE EXPENSES	_____
TOTAL GOLF COURSE EXPENSES	_____
DEPARTMENTAL INCOME (LOSS)	$ _____

GOLF PRO SHOP

	Current Period
TOTAL REVENUE	$ _____
REVENUE	$ _____
ALLOWANCES	
NET REVENUE	
COST OF MERCHANDISE SOLD	_____
GROSS PROFIT (LOSS)	
OTHER INCOME	
GROSS PROFIT (LOSS) AND OTHER INCOME	
EXPENSES	
Salaries and Wages	
Employee Benefits	
Total Payroll and Related Expenses	_____
Other Expenses	
Contract Services	
Operating Supplies	
Telecommunications	
Training	
Other	_____
Total Other Expenses	_____
TOTAL EXPENSES	_____
DEPARTMENTAL INCOME (LOSS)	$ _____

GUEST LAUNDRY (A)

	Current Period
REVENUE	$
ALLOWANCES	_____
NET REVENUE	
EXPENSES	
Salaries and Wages	
Employee Benefits	
Total Payroll and Related Expenses	_____
Other Expenses	
Contract Services	
Laundry Supplies	
Operating Supplies	
Telecommunications	
Training	
Uniforms	
Other	_____
Total Other Expenses	_____
TOTAL EXPENSES	_____
DEPARTMENTAL INCOME (LOSS)	$ _____

GUEST LAUNDRY (B)
(where only one laundry is operated)

REVENUE	$
ALLOWANCES	_____
NET REVENUE	
COST OF LAUNDERING	_____
DEPARTMENTAL INCOME (LOSS)	$ _____

HEALTH CENTER

	Current Period
REVENUE	$
ALLOWANCES	_____
NET REVENUE	
COST OF MERCHANDISE SOLD	_____
GROSS PROFIT (LOSS)	
EXPENSES	
Salaries and Wages	
Employee Benefits	_____
Total Payroll and Related Expenses	_____
Other Expenses	
Contract Services	
Laundry and Dry Cleaning	
Licenses	
Linen	
Maintenance	
Operating Supplies	
Professional Services	
Telecommunications	
Training	
Uniforms	
Other	_____
Total Other Expenses	_____
TOTAL EXPENSES	_____
DEPARTMENTAL INCOME (LOSS)	$ =========

SWIMMING POOL

	Current Period
REVENUE	$
ALLOWANCES	————
NET REVENUE	
EXPENSES	
Salaries and Wages	
Employee Benefits	————
Total Payroll and Related Expenses	————
Other Expenses	
Chemicals	
Contract Services	
Laundry and Dry Cleaning	
Linen	
Operating Supplies	
Professional Services	
Telecommunications	
Training	
Uniforms	
Other	————
Total Other Expenses	————
TOTAL EXPENSES	————
DEPARTMENTAL INCOME (LOSS)	$ ————

TENNIS

	Current Period
REVENUE	$
ALLOWANCES	
NET REVENUE	
EXPENSES	
Salaries and Wages	
Employee Benefits	
Total Payroll and Related Expenses	
Other Expenses	
Contract Services	
Court Maintenance	
Nets and Tapes	
Operating Supplies	
Professional Services	
Telecommunications	
Tournament Expense	
Training	
Other	
Total Other Expenses	
TOTAL EXPENSES	
DEPARTMENTAL INCOME (LOSS)	$

TENNIS PRO SHOP

	Current Period
REVENUE	$
ALLOWANCES	_____
NET REVENUE	
COST OF MERCHANDISE SOLD	_____
GROSS PROFIT (LOSS)	
OTHER INCOME	
GROSS PROFIT (LOSS) AND OTHER INCOME	
EXPENSES	
Salaries and Wages	
Employee Benefits	
Total Payroll and Related Expenses	_____
Other Expenses	
Contract Services	
Operating Supplies	
Telecommunications	
Training	
Other	
Total Other Expenses	_____
TOTAL EXPENSES	_____
DEPARTMENTAL INCOME (LOSS)	$ _____

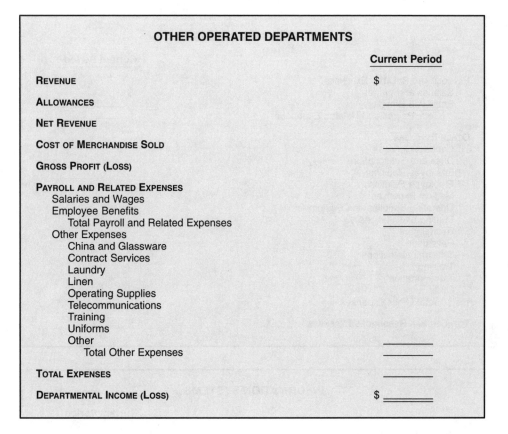

OTHER OPERATED DEPARTMENTS

	Current Period
REVENUE	$
ALLOWANCES	
NET REVENUE	
COST OF MERCHANDISE SOLD	
GROSS PROFIT (LOSS)	
PAYROLL AND RELATED EXPENSES	
Salaries and Wages	
Employee Benefits	
Total Payroll and Related Expenses	
Other Expenses	
China and Glassware	
Contract Services	
Laundry	
Linen	
Operating Supplies	
Telecommunications	
Training	
Uniforms	
Other	
Total Other Expenses	
TOTAL EXPENSES	
DEPARTMENTAL INCOME (LOSS)	$

HUMAN RESOURCES

	Current Period
PAYROLL AND RELATED EXPENSES	
Salaries and Wages	$ _____
Employee Benefits	_____
Total Payroll and Related Expenses	_____
OTHER EXPENSES	
Contract Services	
Dues and Subscriptions	
Employee Housing	
Employee Relations	
Medical Expenses	
Operating Supplies and Equipment	
Printing and Stationery	
Recruitment	
Relocation	
Telecommunications	
Training	
Transportation	
Other	_____
Total Other Expenses	_____
TOTAL HUMAN RESOURCES EXPENSES	$ _____

INFORMATION SYSTEMS

	Current Period
PAYROLL AND RELATED EXPENSES	
Salaries and Wages	$ _____
Employee Benefits	_____
Total Payroll and Related Expenses	_____
OTHER EXPENSES	
Contract Services	
Equipment Maintenance	
Operating Supplies	
Printing and Stationery	
Software—Commercial Applications	
Telecommunications	
Training	
Other	_____
Total Other Expenses	_____
TOTAL INFORMATION SYSTEMS EXPENSES	$ _____

SECURITY

	Current Period
PAYROLL AND RELATED EXPENSES	
Salaries and Wages	$
Employee Benefits	
Total Payroll and Related Expenses	
OTHER EXPENSES	
Armored Car Service	
Contract Services	
Operating Supplies	
Safety and Lock Boxes	
Telecommunications	
Training	
Uniforms	
Other	
Total Other Expenses	
TOTAL SECURITY EXPENSES	$

FRANCHISE FEES

	Current Period
FRANCHISE FEES	$

TRANSPORTATION

	Current Period
PAYROLL AND RELATED EXPENSES	
Salaries and Wages	$
Employee Benefits	
Total Payroll and Related Expenses	
OTHER EXPENSES	
Contract Services	
Fuel and Oil	
Insurance	
Operating Supplies	
Repairs and Maintenance	
Telecommunications	
Training	
Uniforms	
Other	
Total Other Expenses	
TOTAL TRANSPORTATION EXPENSES	$

MANAGEMENT FEES

	Current Period
BASE FEES	$ _____
INCENTIVE FEES	_____
TOTAL MANAGEMENT FEES	$ _____

RENT, PROPERTY TAXES, AND INSURANCE

	Current Period
RENT	
Land and Buildings	$
Information Systems Equipment	
Telecommunications Equipment	
Other Property and Equipment	_____
Total Rent Expense	
PROPERTY TAXES	
Real Estate Taxes	
Personal Property Taxes	
Business and Transient Occupation Taxes	
Utility Taxes	
Other	_____
Total Property Tax Expense	
INSURANCE	
Building and Contents	
Liability	_____
Total Insurance	_____
TOTAL RENT, PROPERTY TAXES, AND INSURANCE	$ _____

INTEREST EXPENSE

	Current Period
Amortization of Deferred Financing Costs	$
Mortgages	
Notes Payable	
Obligation Under Capital Leases	
Other Long-term Debt	
Other	_____
TOTAL INTEREST EXPENSE	$ _____

DEPRECIATION AND AMORTIZATION

	Current Period
Assets Held Under Capital Leases	$
Buildings	
Furnishings and Equipment	
Leaseholds and Leasehold Improvements	
Intangibles	
Other	_____
TOTAL DEPRECIATION AND AMORTIZATION	$ _____

FEDERAL AND STATE INCOME TAXES

	Current Period
FEDERAL	
Current	
Deferred	$ _____
Total Federal	_____
STATE	
Current	_____
Deferred	_____
Total State	
TOTAL FEDERAL AND STATE INCOME TAXES	$ _____

HOUSE LAUNDRY

	Current Period
PAYROLL AND RELATED EXPENSES	
Salaries and Wages	$
Employee Benefits	_____
Total Payroll and Related Expenses	_____
OTHER EXPENSES	
Cleaning Supplies	
Contract Services	
Laundry Supplies	
Printing and Stationery	
Telecommunications	
Training	
Uniforms	
Other	_____
Total Other Expenses	_____
TOTAL EXPENSES	
CREDITS	
Cost of Guest and Outside Laundry	
Concessionaires' Laundry	
Total Credits	_____
COST OF HOUSE LAUNDRY	_____
CHARGED TO:	
Rooms	
Food	
Beverage	
Golf Course	
Health Center	
Swimming Pool	
Other Operated Departments	_____
Total	$ =========

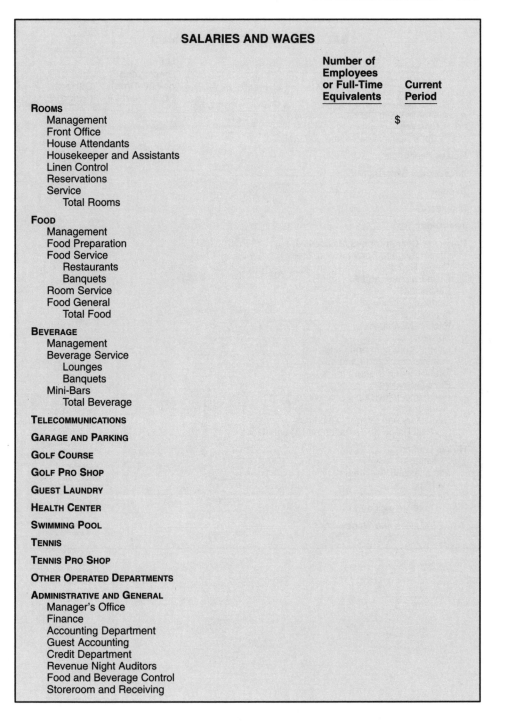

SALARIES AND WAGES

	Number of Employees or Full-Time Equivalents	Current Period
ROOMS		
Management		$
Front Office		
House Attendants		
Housekeeper and Assistants		
Linen Control		
Reservations		
Service		
Total Rooms		
FOOD		
Management		
Food Preparation		
Food Service		
Restaurants		
Banquets		
Room Service		
Food General		
Total Food		
BEVERAGE		
Management		
Beverage Service		
Lounges		
Banquets		
Mini-Bars		
Total Beverage		
TELECOMMUNICATIONS		
GARAGE AND PARKING		
GOLF COURSE		
GOLF PRO SHOP		
GUEST LAUNDRY		
HEALTH CENTER		
SWIMMING POOL		
TENNIS		
TENNIS PRO SHOP		
OTHER OPERATED DEPARTMENTS		
ADMINISTRATIVE AND GENERAL		
Manager's Office		
Finance		
Accounting Department		
Guest Accounting		
Credit Department		
Revenue Night Auditors		
Food and Beverage Control		
Storeroom and Receiving		

SALARIES AND WAGES *(continued)*

	Number of Employees or Full-Time Equivalents	Current Period

ADMINISTRATIVE AND GENERAL *(continued)*
  Purchasing $
    Total Administrative and General

HUMAN RESOURCES

INFORMATION SYSTEMS

SECURITY

MARKETING

TRANSPORTATION

PROPERTY OPERATION AND MAINTENANCE
  Carpenters and Furniture Repairers
  Carpet Repairers
  Chief Engineer and Assistants
  Electricians
  General Mechanical
  Grounds and Landscaping
  Kitchen Mechanics
  Masons
  Office, Storeroom and Other
  Painters and Paperhangers
  Plumbers and Steam Fitters
  Plant Operators
  Radio and Television
  Refrigeration
  Upholstery and Drapery Repairers
    Total Property Operation and Maintenance

HOUSE LAUNDRY
  Finishing
  Manager and Assistants
  Washing
  Other
    Total House Laundry

TOTAL SALARIES AND WAGES $

PAYROLL TAXES AND EMPLOYEE BENEFITS

	Current Period
PAYROLL TAXES	
Federal Retirement (FICA)	$
Federal Unemployment (FUTA)	
Medicare (FICA)	
State Disability	
State Unemployment (SUTA)	————
Total Payroll Taxes	
EMPLOYEE BENEFITS	
Auto Allowance	
Child Care	
Contributory Savings Plan (401K)	
Dental Insurance	
Disability Pay	
Group Life Insurance	
Health Insurance	
Meals	
Nonunion Insurance	
Nonunion Pension	
Profit Sharing	
Stock Benefits	
Union Insurance	
Union Pension	
Workers' Compensation Insurance	
Other	————
Total Employee Benefits	————
TOTAL PAYROLL TAXES AND EMPLOYEE BENEFITS	$ ————
Charged to	
Rooms	
Food	
Beverage	
Telecommunications	
Garage and Parking	
Golf Course	
Golf Pro Shop	
Guest Laundry	
Health Center	
Swimming Pool	
Tennis	
Tennis Pro Shop	
Other Operated Departments	
Administrative and General	
Human Resources	
Information Systems	
Security	
Marketing	
Transportation	
Property Operation and Maintenance	
House Laundry	
Total	$

Chapter 4 Outline

The Purpose of the Statement of Cash Flows
    The SCF in Relation to Other Financial Statements
Classification of Cash Flows
Conversion of Accrual Income to Net Cash Flows from Operations
    Direct and Indirect Methods
Preparing the SCF
    Step 1: Net Cash Flows from Operating Activities
    Step 2: Net Cash Flows from Investing Activities
    Step 3: Net Cash Flows from Financing Activities
    Step 4: Presenting Cash Flows by Activity
A Comprehensive Illustration
    Interpreting the Results
Analysis of Statements of Cash Flow

The Statement of Cash Flows

TRADITIONALLY, THE PRINCIPAL financial statements used by hospitality operations have been the income statement and the balance sheet. The balance sheet shows the financial position of the business at the end of the accounting period. The income statement reflects the results of operations for the accounting period. Although these statements provide extensive financial information, they do not provide answers to such questions as:

1. How much cash was provided by operations?
2. What amount of property and equipment was purchased during the year?
3. How much long-term debt was borrowed during the year?
4. What amount of funds was raised through the sale of capital stock?
5. What amount of dividends was paid during the year?
6. How much was invested in long-term investments during the year?

The **statement of cash flows (SCF)** is designed to answer these questions and many more. The Financial Accounting Standards Board (FASB), which is the current accounting rule-making body, has mandated that the SCF be included with the other financial statements issued to external users only since 1988. It replaces the infamous statement of changes in financial position, which generally focused on working capital rather than cash.

Our discussion of this most recent addition to the collection of major financial statements will address the definition of cash, the relationship of the SCF to other financial statements, the purposes and uses of the SCF, a classification of cash flows, alternative formats which may be used for the SCF, a four-step approach for preparing the SCF, and a comprehensive illustration of the preparation of the statement.

The Purpose of the Statement of Cash Flows

The statement of cash flows shows the effects on cash of a business's operating, investing, and financing activities for the accounting period. It explains the change in cash for the accounting period; that is, if cash increases by $5,000 from January 1, 19X1 (the beginning of the accounting period) to December 31, 19X1 (the end of the accounting period), the SCF will reflect the increase in the sum of cash from the firm's various activities.

For purposes of this statement, cash is defined to include both cash and cash equivalents. **Cash equivalents** are short-term, highly liquid investments such as U.S. Treasury bills and money market accounts. Firms use cash equivalents for investing funds temporarily not needed for operating purposes. Generally, these short-term investments are made for 90 days or less. Since cash and cash equivalents are considered to be the same, transfers between cash and cash equivalents are not considered to be cash receipts or cash disbursements for SCF purposes.

The major purpose of the SCF is to provide relevant information regarding the cash receipts and disbursements of a hospitality business to help users (investors, creditors, managers, and others) to:

1. Assess the organization's ability to generate positive future net cash flows. Although users of financial statements are less interested in the past than in the future, many users, especially external users, must rely on historical financial information to assess an operation's future abilities. Thus, the investor interested in future cash dividends will review the SCF to determine past sources and uses of cash to evaluate the firm's ability to pay future dividends.

2. Assess the firm's ability to meet its obligations. Users of financial statements want to determine the firm's ability to pay its bills as they come due. If a firm has little likelihood of being able to pay its bills, then suppliers will most likely not be interested in selling the firm their goods and services.

3. Assess the difference between the enterprise's net income and cash receipts and disbursements. The SCF allows a user to quickly determine the major net sources of cash and how much relates to the enterprise's operations. Investors, creditors, and other users generally prefer enterprises which are able to generate cash from operations (that is, from their primary purpose for being in business), as opposed to those generating cash solely from financing and investing activities (that is, activities which are incidental to the primary purpose).

4. Assess the effect of both cash and noncash investing and financing during the accounting period. Investing activities relate to the acquisition and disposition of noncurrent assets, such as property and equipment. Financing activities relate to the borrowing and payment of long-term debt and sale and purchase of capital stock. Noncash activities (that is, transactions involving no cash) include such transactions as the acquisition of a hotel in exchange for stock or long-term debt.

The three major user groups of the SCF are management (internal) and investors and creditors (external). Management may use the SCF to (1) assess the firm's liquidity, (2) assess its financial flexibility, (3) determine its dividend policy, and (4) plan investing and financing needs. Investors and creditors will most likely use the SCF to assess the firm's (1) ability to pay its bills as they come due, (2) ability to pay dividends, and (3) need for additional financing, including borrowing debt and selling capital stock.

The SCF in Relation to Other Financial Statements

The relationship of the SCF to other financial statements is shown in Exhibit 1. The statement of retained earnings, mentioned in Exhibit 1, reflects results of operations and dividends declared, and reconciles the retained earnings accounts of two successive balance sheets. Net income from the income statement is transferred to

Exhibit 1 Relationship of SCF to Other Financial Statements

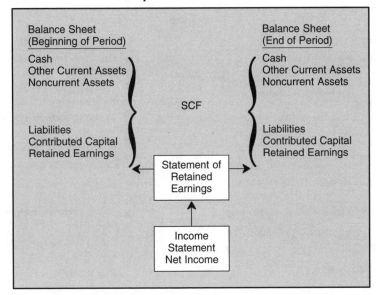

the retained earnings account when the temporary accounts (revenues and expenses) are closed at the end of the accounting period. In addition, net income is shown on the SCF when the SCF is prepared using the indirect approach (which is discussed later in this chapter). Finally, the SCF indirectly reconciles most accounts other than cash on the balance sheet by showing the sources and uses of cash.

Classification of Cash Flows

The SCF classifies cash receipts and disbursements as operating, investing, and financing activities. Both **cash inflows** and **cash outflows** are included within each category. Exhibit 2 presents classifications of cash flows under the various activities, which are further described below:

- **Operating Activities:** This category includes cash transactions related to revenues and expenses. Revenues (cash inflows) include sales of food, beverages, other goods and services to lodging guests, as well as interest and dividend income. Expenses (cash outflows) are for operational cash expenditures, including payments for salaries, wages, taxes, supplies, and so forth. Interest expense is also included as an operations cash outflow.

- **Investing Activities:** These activities relate primarily to cash flows from the acquisition and disposal of all noncurrent assets, especially property, equipment, and investments. Also included are cash flows from the purchase and disposal of marketable securities (short-term investments).

- **Financing Activities:** These activities relate to cash flows from the issuance and retirement of debt and the issuance and re-purchase of capital stock. Cash

Exhibit 2   Classification of Cash Flows

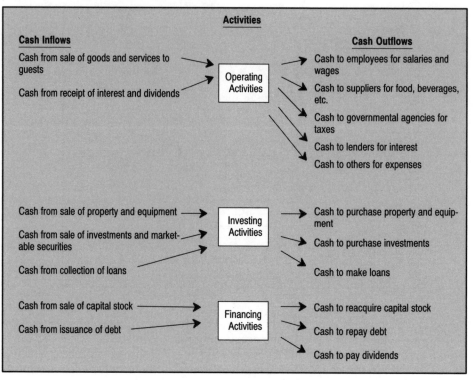

inflows include cash received from issues of stock and both short-term and long-term borrowing. Cash outflows include repayments of loans (although the interest expense portion of the debt payment is an operating activity) and payments to owners for both dividends and any re-purchase of stocks. Payments of accounts payable, taxes payable, and the various accrued expenses, such as wages payable, are not payments of loans under financing activities, but they are classified as cash outflows under operating activities.

Finally, hospitality enterprises engage in noncash investing and financing activities, such as the exchange of capital stock for a hotel building. Since this represents only an exchange, no cash transaction has occurred. Therefore, these noncash activities are not shown on the SCF. However, since a major purpose of the SCF is to include financing and investing activities, and since these activities will affect future cash flows, they must be disclosed on a separate schedule to the SCF. Thus, the user of financial information is provided with a complete presentation of investing and financing activities. Exhibit 3 is an example of a supplementary schedule of noncash investing and financing activities of the Gateway Inn.

The basic format of the SCF is shown in Exhibit 4. Generally, cash flows from operating activities are shown first. The indirect or direct approaches (to be discussed later) may be used to show cash flows from operating activities. Cash flows

Exhibit 3   Schedule of Noncash Investing and Financing Activities—Gateway Inn

Common stock exchanged for long-term debt	$100,000
Capital lease obligations incurred for use of equipment	50,000
Total	$150,000

Exhibit 4   Basic Format of the SCF

Cash Flows from Operating Activities	$XX
(direct or indirect approaches may be used)	
Cash Flows from Investing Activities	XX
(list cash inflows and outflows)	
Cash Flows from Financing Activities	
(list cash inflows and outflows)	XX
Net Increase (Decrease) in Cash	XX
Cash at the beginning of the period	XX
Cash at the end of the period	$XX
Schedule of Noncash Investing and Financing Transactions	
List individual transactions $XX	

from investing and financing activities follow. Individual cash outflows and inflows are shown in each section. For example, long-term debt may increase by $100,000 due to the payment of $50,000 and subsequent borrowing of $150,000. Each cash flow should be shown rather than netting the two flows. Finally, as stated above, a supplementary schedule of noncash investing and financing activities to the SCF must be included.

Conversion of Accrual Income to Net Cash Flows from Operations

A major purpose of the SCF is to show net cash flows from operations. The income statement is prepared on an **accrual basis**; that is, revenues are recorded when earned, not when cash is received from guests, and expenses are recorded when incurred, not necessarily when cash is disbursed. Consequently, there may be little correlation between net income and cash flow. Consider the hypothetical Wales Inn which had $2,000,000 sales for 19X1. Its accounts receivable (AR) from guests totaled $100,000 at the beginning of the year and $110,000 at the end of the year. The cash received from sales during 19X1 is determined as follows:

$$\text{Cash receipts from sales} = \begin{array}{l} \text{Sales} - \text{increase in AR} \\ \qquad or \; + \; \text{decrease in AR} \end{array}$$

$$= \$2,000,000 - \$10,000$$

$$= \underline{\underline{\$1,990,000}}$$

Thus, even though the Wales Inn had sales of $2,000,000 as reported on its income statement, it would show cash receipts from sales on its SCF as $1,990,000.

Direct and Indirect Methods

There are two methods for converting net income to net cash flow from operations—the direct and the indirect methods. The **direct method** shows cash receipts from sales and cash disbursements for expenses. This method requires that each item on the income statement be converted from an accrual basis to a cash basis, as were the sales of the Wales Inn above. Another example of this conversion process for the Wales Inn is payroll expense. Assume that the Wales Inn reported $700,000 as payroll expense for 19X1, and its balance sheet's accrued payroll account at the beginning of the year showed $15,000 and at the end of the year showed $20,000. Its cash disbursements for payroll for 19X1 is determined as follows:

$$\begin{array}{l} \text{Cash Disbursement} \\ \text{for Payroll} \\ \text{Expense} \end{array} = \begin{array}{l} \text{Payroll Expense} - \text{increase in Accrued Payroll} \\ \qquad or \; + \; \text{decrease in Accrued Payroll} \end{array}$$

$$= \$700,000 - \$5,000$$

$$= \underline{\underline{\$695,000}}$$

So, even though payroll expense for the year totaled $700,000 as shown on the income statement, only $695,000 was disbursed during the year.

Some expenses shown on the income statement do not involve any direct cash disbursement and are simply ignored when using the direct method. For example, depreciation expense is only an adjustment to help match expenses to revenues. Depreciation does not entail any cash, so it is ignored when using the direct method. The same approach is taken for amortization expense and gains and losses on the sale of property and equipment. The basic formats of cash flows from the operating activities section of the SCF for both the direct and indirect methods are shown in Exhibit 5.

The FASB prefers the direct approach. However, most hospitality businesses use the indirect method because the information needed to prepare it is more readily available than that needed for using the direct method. For that reason, the major focus in this chapter will be the indirect method.

The **indirect method** for determining net cash flows from operations starts with net income. Net income is then adjusted for noncash items included on the income statement. The commonest noncash expense deducted to determine net income is depreciation. Therefore, since depreciation is subtracted to compute net income on the income statement, it is added back to net income to compute net cash flows from operating activities. Other items on the income statement that must be

Exhibit 5   Basic Formats of the Net Cash Flow from Operating Activities Sections

Operating Activities

Direct Method

Cash Flows from Operating Activities:

Cash receipts from sales		$ XXX
Interest and dividends received		XXX
Total		XXX

Cash Disbursements for:

Payroll	$ XXX	
Purchases of inventory	XXX	
Other expenses	XXX	
Interest expense	XXX	
Income taxes	XXX	XXX
Net Cash Flows from Operating Activities		$ XXX

Indirect Method

Cash Flows from Operating Activities:

Net Income		$ XXX
Adjustments to reconcile net income to net cash flows from operating activities:		
Depreciation expense	$ XXX	
Gain on sale of property	(XXX)	
Loss on sale of investments	XXX	
Increase in accounts receivable	(XXX)	
Decrease in inventories	XXX	
.		
.		
.		
Increase in accrued payroll	XXX	XXX
Net Cash Flows from Operating Activities		$ XXX

added or subtracted include amortization expense and gains and losses on the sale of noncurrent assets and marketable securities.

To illustrate the addback of a loss on the sale of investments, assume that the Wales Inn sold a parcel of undeveloped land (an investment) in 19X1 for $200,000 which originally cost $250,000. The journal entry to record the sale was as follows:

Cash	$200,000	
Loss on sale of investments	50,000	
Investment in land		$250,000

The $200,000 of cash inflow will be shown as an investing activity on the SCF; however, the loss on sale of investments of $50,000 was included on the income statement in determining net income. Since it was subtracted in determining the Wales Inn's net income and it did not use cash, it must be added back to net income to determine the net cash flows from operating activities for the SCF.

In addition, in order to determine the net cash flows from operating activities using the indirect method, the Wales Inn's net income must be adjusted for sales that were recorded but which guests did not pay for during 19X1. This adjustment is accomplished by subtracting the increase in accounts receivable of $10,000 from net income on the SCF (as discussed previously). There are several similar adjustments that must be made using the indirect method. These will be discussed in detail and illustrated in the next section of this chapter.

Regardless of the method used, the result will show the same amount of net cash provided by operating activities. The FASB requires that firms using the indirect method report the amount of interest expense and taxes paid in separate disclosures.

Preparing the SCF

The principal sources of information needed for preparing the SCF are the income statement, the statement of retained earnings, and two successive balance sheets from the beginning and end of the accounting period. In addition, details of transactions affecting any change in noncurrent balance sheet accounts must be reviewed. For example, if a comparison of two successive balance sheets shows the building account has increased by $5,000,000, the account must be analyzed to determine the reason(s) for the changes. Simply reflecting the net change of $5,000,000 on the SCF is generally not acceptable.

A four-step approach for preparing the SCF is as follows:

1. Determine the net cash flows from operating activities.

2. Determine the net cash flows from investing activities.

3. Determine the net cash flows from financing activities.

4. Present the cash flows by activity on the SCF.

Exhibits 6 and 7 contain balance sheets and a condensed income statement and statement of retained earnings for the Simple Hotel. These will be used to illustrate this four-step approach. (A more comprehensive illustration will be shown later in the chapter.) The preparation of the SCF is illustrated using the indirect method for showing net cash flows from operating activities.

Step 1: Net Cash Flows from Operating Activities

To determine the net cash flow from operating activities using the indirect method, we focus first on the income statement by starting with net income of $500,000. Next, we need to adjust net income for items on the income statement that did not provide or use cash. In particular, depreciation expense and the gain on the sale of the investment are considered. Since depreciation was subtracted on the income

Exhibit 6   Balance Sheets for the Simple Hotel

Simple Hotel
Balance Sheets
December 31, 19X1 and 19X2

Assets		19X1	19X2
Current Assets:			
Cash		$ 5,000	$ 10,000
Accounts Receivable		30,000	26,000
Inventory		10,000	12,000
	Total	45,000	48,000
Investments		50,000	300,000
Property and Equipment:			
Land		200,000	200,000
Building		10,000,000	10,000,000
Equipment		1,000,000	1,100,000
Less: Accum. Depreciation		(5,000,000)	(5,500,000)
	Total	6,200,000	5,800,000
Total Assets		$ 6,295,000	$ 6,148,000
Liabilities and Owners' Equity			
Current Liabilities:			
Accounts Payable		$ 6,000	$ 6,500
Accrued Payroll		4,000	4,500
Income Taxes Payable		7,000	6,000
Dividends Payable		10,000	15,000
	Total	27,000	32,000
Long-Term Debt		4,500,000	3,750,000
Owners' Equity:			
Capital Stock		1,000,000	1,250,000
Retained Earnings		768,000	1,116,000
	Total	1,768,000	2,366,000
Total Liabilities and Owners' Equity		$ 6,295,000	$ 6,148,000

statement to determine net income, it must be added to net income on the SCF to determine net cash flow from operating activities. Since the gain on the sale of investments is not a cash flow (the proceeds from the sale of investments of $150,000 are an investing activity on the SCF and will be discussed later), the gain of $100,000 must be subtracted from net income on the SCF. Thus, the net cash flows from operating activities are determined at this point as follows:

Exhibit 7   Income Statement and Statement of Retained Earnings for the Simple Hotel

Simple Hotel
Condensed Income Statement and Statement of Retained Earnings
For the Year Ended December 31, 19X2

Sales	$7,000,000
Cost of Goods Sold	1,000,000
Payroll Expenses	2,450,000
Other Expenses	2,400,000
Depreciation Expense	500,000
Income Taxes	250,000
Gain on the Sale of Investments	100,000
Net Income	500,000
Retained Earnings—12/31/X1	768,000
Dividends Declared	152,000
Retained Earnings—12/31/X2	$1,116,000

Other Information:

1. No property and equipment were disposed of during 19X2.

2. Investment and equipment purchases during 19X2 were made with cash. No funds were borrowed.

3. Investments costing $50,000 were sold for $150,000, resulting in a $100,000 gain on the sale of investments during 19X2.

4. Long-term debt of $250,000 was converted to capital stock in a noncash transaction during 19X2. No other capital stock was issued, and there were no repurchases of capital stock.

5. Interest expense paid during the year totaled $400,000.

Net Cash Flows from Operating Activities:		
Net income		$500,000
Adjustments to Reconcile Net Income to Net Cash Flows from Operating Activities:		
Depreciation expense	$500,000	
Gain on sale of investments	(100,000)	400,000
Partial net cash flows from operating activities		$900,000

The second type of adjustment includes changes in current accounts from the balance sheet. The cash account is not considered, since we are essentially looking at all other balance sheet accounts to determine what caused the change in cash for purposes of the SCF. In addition, the current liability account dividends payable is not considered in determining cash flows from operating activities, as dividends payable relate to financing activities and will be considered later. The change in the remaining five current accounts is fully considered as follows:

Account	Balances—December 31		Change in Account Balance
	19X1	19X2	
Current Assets:			
Accounts Receivable	$30,000	$26,000	$4,000 (dec.)
Inventory	$10,000	$12,000	$2,000 (inc.)
Current Liabilities:			
Accounts Payable	$ 6,000	$ 6,500	$ 500 (inc.)
Accrued Payroll	$ 4,000	$ 4,500	$ 500 (inc.)
Income Taxes Payable	$ 7,000	$ 6,000	$1,000 (dec.)

A brief explanation follows for each of the above current accounts, including how the change affects net cash flow from operating activities.

Accounts receivable relate directly to sales, which were $7,000,000 for the Simple Hotel for 19X2. Sales on account result in cash inflows when the hotel guests pay their bills. However, under accrual accounting, the sale is recorded when services are provided. Most of the sales during 19X2 resulted in cash as the guests paid their accounts, but at year end, the accounts receivable account balance was $26,000. Analysis of the account will reveal how much cash resulted from sales as follows:

Accounts Receivable

12/31/X1 Balance	30,000	Cash received	7,004,000
Sales to hotel guests	7,000,000		
12/31/X2 Balance	26,000		

Alternatively, the cash receipts from hotel guests could be determined as follows:

$$\text{Cash Receipts from Hotel Guests} = \text{AR Beginning Balance} + \text{Sales} - \text{AR Ending Balance}$$

$$= \$30,000 + \$7,000,000 - \$26,000$$

$$= \$7,004,000$$

In preparing the SCF, we need to show a decrease in accounts receivable of $4,000, which is added to net income as an increase in cash to determine net cash flows from operating activities.

The change in the balances of the inventory account is an increase of $2,000. Inventory relates to the purchases and cost of goods sold (food and beverages) accounts. Remember, cost of goods sold is the cost of food and beverage inventory sold, not the cash disbursed for purchases. Therefore, we need to determine the purchases for the year as follows:

Ending inventory	$ 12,000
+ Cost of goods sold	1,000,000
Goods available for sale	1,012,000
− Beginning inventory	10,000
Purchases	$1,002,000

The $2,000 increase in inventory causes the accrual-basis cost of goods sold to be $2,000 less than purchases. By assuming that purchases is the cash amount paid for purchases, we must show a decrease in cash flows from operating activities of $2,000.

However, not all purchases were made for cash. The $500 increase in accounts payable represents the difference between purchases on account and cash paid to suppliers during 19X2. An increase in accounts payable means the amount of cash paid was less than the amount of purchases. Thus, the $500 increase in accounts payable must be added back to the accrual-basis net income to determine net cash flows from operating activities. An analysis of the accounts payable account shows this as follows:

Accounts Payable

		1/1/X2 Balance	6,000
		Purchases	1,002,000
Payments to suppliers	1,001,500		
		12/31/X2 Balance	6,500

The increase in the accrued payroll account of $500 represents the difference between the accrual basis payroll costs of $2,450,000 and the cash payments to personnel of $2,449,500. This determination is apparent in the analysis of the accrued payroll account as follows:

Accrued Payroll

		12/31/X1 Balance	4,000
		Payroll expense	2,450,000
Payments for payroll	2,449,500		
		12/31/X2 Balance	4,500

Since the payroll payments were $500 less than the payroll expense, the $500 increase in accrued payroll is added back to the accrual-basis net income to determine net cash flows from operations.

Finally, the decrease of $1,000 in income taxes payable represents the difference between the accrual basis income taxes of $250,000, shown on the condensed income statement of the Simple Hotel, and the $251,000 paid, as determined by the analysis of the income taxes payable account as follows:

Income Taxes Payable

		12/31/X1 Balance	7,000
		Income tax expense	250,000
Income taxes paid	251,000		
		12/31/X2 Balance	6,000

In reality, the $7,000 of income taxes due at the beginning of 19X1 were paid along with $244,000 of income taxes for 19X2. The remaining $6,000 of taxes for 19X2 will be paid in early 19X3. However, since income taxes paid during 19X2 exceed income tax expenses for 19X2 by $1,000, the $1,000 must be subtracted from the accrual-basis net income to determine the net cash flows from operations.

In addition to differences from year to year in the payment of income taxes, a hospitality enterprise may have deferred income taxes over several years. The details of the account for deferred income taxes are beyond the scope of this chapter.

The Simple Hotel's SCF's net cash flows from operating activities based on the above would reflect the following:

Net Cash Flows from Operating Activities:		
Net income		$500,000
Adjustments to Reconcile Net		
Income to Net Cash Flows from		
Operating Activities:		
Depreciation expense	$500,000	
Gain on sale of investments	(100,000)	
Decrease in accounts receivable	4,000	
Increase in inventory	(2,000)	
Increase in accounts payable	500	
Increase in accrued payroll	500	
Decrease in income taxes payable	(1,000)	402,000
Net Cash Flows from Operating		
Activities		$902,000

In general, the rules for accounting for changes in current accounts in determining net cash flows provided by operating activities are as follows:

• A decrease in a current asset is added to net income.

• An increase in a current asset is deducted from net income.

• A decrease in a current liability is deducted from net income.

• An increase in a current liability is added to net income.

Step 2: Net Cash Flows from Investing Activities

Step 2 of the four-step approach to preparing an SCF focuses on investing activities. In general, attention must be directed to noncurrent assets of the Simple Hotel.

The investment account increased by $250,000. Further analysis of this account is as follows:

Investments

12/31/X1 Balance	50,000	Sale of investments	50,000
Purchase of investments	300,000		
12/31/X2 Balance	300,000		

The analysis reveals both a sale of $50,000 of investments and a purchase of investments of $300,000. Thus, cash of $300,000 was used to purchase investments, which is a use of cash in the investing activities section of the SCF. However, further analysis of the sale of investments shows the journal entry to record this transaction as follows:

Cash	$150,000
Investments	$ 50,000
Gains on sale of investments	$100,000

The entry clearly shows a cash inflow of $150,000. Thus, this source of cash should be shown as an investing activity. Notice that the cost of investments sold ($50,000) and the gain on the sale of investments ($100,000) has no impact on net cash flow from investing activities.

There were no changes in the land and building accounts, as no purchases or sales were made during 19X2. Therefore, cash was not affected.

We will look next at the equipment account. According to note #1 under other information, no equipment was disposed of during 19X2. Thus, the $100,000 difference must be due to purchases of equipment. The $100,000 of equipment is shown as a use of cash in determining net cash flows from investing activities.

The Simple Hotel's final noncurrent account is accumulated depreciation, which increased by $500,000, the exact amount of depreciation expense for the year. Because depreciation does not affect cash, under the indirect method the $500,000 is added back to the accrual-basis net income as discussed under Step 1. The change in no way affects investing activities of the Simple Hotel.

Now that the noncurrent asset accounts of the Simple Hotel have been analyzed, the investing activities section of the SCF would reflect the following:

Net Cash Flows from Investing Activities:	
Proceeds from sale of investments	$ 150,000
Purchase of investments	(300,000)
Purchase of equipment	(100,000)
Net cash flows from investing activities	$(250,000)

Step 3: Net Cash Flows from Financing Activities

To determine the net cash flows from financing activities, we must turn our attention to the noncurrent liabilities and owners' equity accounts. First, the change in the long-term debt account is a decrease of $750,000. The analysis of the long-term debt is as follows:

Long-Term Debt (LTD)

		12/31/X1 Balance	4,500,000
Conversion to Common Stock	250,000		
Payment of LTD	500,000		
		12/31/X2 Balance	3,750,000

The above analysis is based on notes #2 and #4 under other information. Note #4 reveals that $250,000 of LTD was converted to capital stock. This is a noncash transaction and will be shown only in a supplementary schedule to the SCF. Note #2 indicates no funds were borrowed; therefore, the remaining $500,000 reduction in LTD had to be due to payment of LTD. The $500,000 payment is a cash outflow from financing activities.

The next account to be analyzed is capital stock. The increase for 19X2 is $250,000, which is due to the exchange of capital stock for LTD, as discussed above. According to the note #4 under other information, there were no other capital stock transactions. Since this change in capital stock did not involve cash, it is not shown on the SCF. However, since it is a financing activity, it is shown on a supplementary schedule as mentioned above.

The final account to be analyzed is retained earnings. The statement of retained earnings at the bottom of the income statement reflects the detailed changes in this account as follows:

Retained Earnings

		12/31/X1 Balance	768,000
		Net income	500,000
Dividends declared	152,000		
		12/31/X2 Balance	1,116,000

The net income has already been accounted for in the SCF as an operating activity. The declaration of $152,000 of dividends is not a cash activity by itself. For the SCF, the focus is on dividend payments, not dividend declaration. When dividends are declared, they are recorded as a reduction in retained earnings and as an increase in dividends payable, a current liability account. Therefore, to determine the amount of dividends paid during 19X2, we analyze the dividends payable account as follows:

Dividends Payable

		12/31/X1 Balance	10,000
		Dividends declared	152,000
Dividends paid	147,000		
		12/31/X2 Balance	15,000

Effectively, the $5,000 increase in the dividends payable account results in dividends declared during 19X2 exceeding dividends paid by $5,000. The $147,000 of dividends paid is shown in the SCF as a financing activity.

The Simple Hotel's SCF financing activity section would show the following:

Net Cash Flows from Financing Activities:	
Payment of long-term debt	$(500,000)
Payment of cash dividends	(147,000)
Net cash flows from financing activities	$(647,000)

Exhibit 8   SCF for the Simple Hotel

**Simple Hotel
Statement of Cash Flows
For the Year Ended December 31, 19X2**

Net Cash Flow From Operating Activities:		
Net income		$ 500,000
Adjustments to reconcile net income to		
net cash flows from operating activities:		
Depreciation	$ 500,000	
Gain on sale of investments	(100,000)	
Decrease in accounts receivable	4,000	
Increase in inventory	(2,000)	
Increase in accounts payable	500	
Increase in accrued payroll	500	
Decrease in income taxes payable	(1,000)	402,000
Net cash flow from operating activities		902,000
Net Cash Flow From Investing Activities:		
Sale of investments	$ 150,000	
Purchase of investments	(300,000)	
Purchase of equipment	(100,000)	
Net cash flow from investing activities		(250,000)
Net Cash Flow From Financing Activities:		
Payment of long-term debt	$ (500,000)	
Dividends paid	(147,000)	
Net cash flow from financing activities		(647,000)
Net Increase in Cash During 19X2		5,000
Cash at the beginning of 19X2		5,000
Cash at the end of 19X2	$	10,000

Supplementary Schedule of Noncash Financing and Investing Activities

Exchange of capital stock for long-term debt	$ 250,000	

Supplementary Disclosure of Cash Flow Information:

Cash paid during the year for:		
Interest	$ 400,000	
Income Taxes	$ 251,000	

Step 4: Presenting Cash Flows by Activity

We now are ready to prepare the SCF based on the analysis in Steps 1–3. The SCF for the Simple Hotel is shown in Exhibit 8. The three activities show cash flows as follows:

Operating activities provided cash	$902,000
Investing activities used cash	(250,000)
Financing activities used cash	(647,000)
Total	$ 5,000

The result is a bottom line of $5,000 cash inflow. The Simple Hotel's operating activities provided large enough cash inflows to cover the outflows for investing and financing.

In the preparation of the SCF, the net increase in cash of the Simple Hotel per the SCF is added to the Simple Hotel's cash at the beginning of 19X2 to equal the cash at the end of 19X2. The $5,000 net increase in cash per the SCF equals the $5,000 increase in cash per the Simple Hotel's successive balance sheets (Exhibit 6). This does not *prove* that the SCF is prepared correctly; however, if the $5,000 increase per the SCF had *not* been equal to the change per the successive balance sheets, we would know that we had improperly prepared the SCF. We would then need to locate our mistake and make the correction. Thus, this is at least a partial check on the SCF's accuracy.

Further, notice the supplementary schedule to the SCF, which shows the noncash exchange of capital stock of $250,000 for long-term debt and the supplementary disclosure of the amounts of interest and income taxes paid during 19X2.

A Comprehensive Illustration

To provide a comprehensive illustration of the preparation of an SCF with accompanying explanations, the Evangel Inn's financial statements, as shown in Exhibits 9 and 10, will be used. The Evangel Inn's SCF for 19X7 is shown in Exhibit 11.

The net cash flows provided by operating activities for the Evangel Inn for 19X7 are $700,000. The explanation and/or source is as follows:

Item	Explanation and/or Source
1. Net income $330,000	From 19X7 income statement.
2. Depreciation expense $340,000	Depreciation is a noncash flow shown on the income statement. It must be added back to net income, as it was subtracted from revenues to determine net income. To confirm this amount, the accumulated depreciation account is analyzed as follows:

Accumulated Depreciation

		12/31/X6 Balance	1,000,000
Accumulated Depreciation written off with sale of equipment	40,000	Depreciation expense	340,000
		12/31/X7 Balance	1,300,000

Exhibit 9   **Evangel Inn Balance Sheets**

Evangel Inn Balance Sheets December 31, 19X6 and 19X7		
Assets	19X6	19X7
Current Assets:		
Cash	$ 20,000	$ 60,000
Marketable Securities	20,000	25,000
Accounts Receivable	90,000	115,000
Inventory	15,000	20,000
Prepaid Expenses	15,000	5,000
Total Current Assets	160,000	225,000
Investments	150,000	450,000
Property and Equipment:		
Land	450,000	450,000
Buildings	2,000,000	2,000,000
Equipment	500,000	610,000
Less: Accum. Depr.	(1,000,000)	(1,300,000)
Net Property and Equipment	1,950,000	1,760,000
Other Assets—Franchise Fees	100,000	90,000
Total Assets	$2,360,000	$2,525,000
Liabilities and Owners' Equity		
Current Liabilities:		
Accounts Payable	$ 25,000	$ 35,000
Current Maturities of Long-Term Debt	50,000	50,000
Wages Payable	15,000	15,000
Dividends Payable	20,000	15,000
Total Current Liabilities	110,000	115,000
Long-Term Debt	1,000,000	1,050,000
Owners' Equity:		
Common Stock	1,160,000	1,285,000
Retained Earnings	100,000	225,000
Less: Treasury Stock	(10,000)	(150,000)
Total Owners' Equity	1,250,000	1,360,000
Total Liabilities and Owners' Equity	$2,360,000	$2,525,000

3. Amortization expense $10,000

The amortization expense relates to write-off of franchise fees recorded originally as an other asset. Like depreciation, it is a non-cash expense subtracted to determine net income; therefore, it must be added back to net income to determine net cash flows provided by operating activities.

Exhibit 10   Evangel Inn Income Statement

Evangel Inn
Condensed Income Statement
For the Year Ended 19X7

Revenues:

Sales	$2,700,000
Interest Income	80,000
Total Revenues	2,780,000

Expenses:

Salaries and Wages	750,000
Depreciation	340,000
Amortization (franchise fees)	10,000
Interest Expense	100,000
Other Expenses	1,140,000
Income Before Gain and Losses and Income Taxes	440,000
Gain on Sale of Equipment	20,000
Loss on Sale of Investments	(50,000)
Income Taxes	80,000
Net Income	$ 330,000

Other Information:

1. Equipment costing $100,000 was sold for $80,000 during 19X7.
2. Investments costing $100,000 were sold during 19X7 for a loss of $50,000.
3. Dividends of $205,000 were declared during 19X7.
4. Treasury stock of $140,000 was purchased during 19X7.
5. Long-term debt of $100,000 was converted to common stock during 19X7.
6. Common stock of $35,000 was sold during 19X7.
7. Long-term debt of $200,000 was borrowed during 19X7.
8. Marketable securities of $5,000 were purchased during 19X7.

4. Gain on sale of
   equipment $20,000

The sale of equipment resulted in a gain of $20,000, as shown on the income statement. The $80,000 received per note #1 is shown as an investing activity. The gain shown on the income statement is not a cash figure, so the $20,000 must be subtracted from net income in the SCF.

5. Loss on sale of
   investments $50,000

The loss on the sale of investments is shown as an investing activity. The loss shown is not a cash figure, so the $50,000 must be added to net income in the SCF.

Exhibit 11   Evangel Inn SCF

**Evangel Inn
Statement of Cash Flows
For the Year of 19X7**

Cash Flow Provided by Operating Activities:

Net Income		$ 330,000
Adjustments to Reconcile Net Income to Net Cash Flows Provided by Operating Activities:		
Depreciation expense	$ 340,000	
Amortization expense	10,000	
Gain on sale of equipment	(20,000)	
Loss on sale of investments	50,000	
Increase in accounts receivable	(25,000)	
Increase in inventory	(5,000)	
Decrease in prepaid expenses	10,000	
Increase in accounts payable	10,000	370,000
Net Cash Flows from Operating Activities		700,000
Cash Flow Provided by Investing Activities:		
Proceeds from sale of equipment	$ 80,000	
Proceeds from sale of investment	50,000	
Purchase of marketable securities	(5,000)	
Purchase of equipment	(210,000)	
Purchase of investments	(400,000)	
Net Cash Flows from Investing Activities		(485,000)
Cash Flow Provided by Financing Activities:		
Payment of long-term debt	$ (50,000)	
Borrowing—long-term debt	200,000	
Purchase of treasury stock	(140,000)	
Proceeds from sale of common stock	25,000	
Payment of dividends	(210,000)	
Net Cash Flows from Financing Activities		(175,000)
Increase in Cash		40,000
Cash at the beginning of 19X7		20,000
Cash at the end of 19X7		$ 60,000

Supplementary Schedule of Noncash Investing and Financing Activities

Exchange of Common Stock for Long-Term Debt		$ 100,000

Supplementary Disclosure of Cash Flow Information:

Cash paid during the year for:		
Interest	$ 100,000	
Income Taxes	$ 80,000	

6. Changes in current assets and liabilities:

The changes in the current accounts are added or subtracted from net income as follows:

Increase in accounts receivable $25,000; increase in inventory $5,000; decrease in prepaid expenses $10,000; increase in accounts payable $10,000.

1) *increases* in current assets and *decreases* in current liabilities are *subtracted;*

2) *decreases* in current assets and *increases* in current liabilities are *added.* The marketable securities current asset account, current maturities of long-term debt, and dividends payable are considered in preparing the investing and financing activity sections of the SCF, as these accounts do not relate to operating activities.

The investing activities section of the SCF relates to investment and property and equipment for the Evangel Inn. The activity to be shown in the SCF relates to investment and equipment transactions as follows:

Item	Discussion
1. Proceeds from sale of equipment	According to note #1, equipment was sold for $80,000.
2. Purchase of equipment	The equipment account, as shown on the successive balance sheets for 19X6 and 19X7, shows a $110,000 increase in 19X7. However, since equipment costing $100,000 was sold during 19X7, then $210,000 was purchased in 19X7. Analysis of the equipment account below supports this conclusion.

Equipment

Balance 12/31/X6	500,000	Cost of equipment sold	100,000
Purchases during 19X7	210,000		
Balance 12/31/X7	610,000		

Item	Discussion
3. Proceeds from sale of investments $50,000	According to note #2, $100,000 of investments were sold at a loss of $50,000. Therefore, the proceeds are determined by subtracting the loss from the cost as follows:

Cost of investments sold	$100,000
Loss on sale of investments	(50,000)
Proceeds from sale	$ 50,000

Item	Discussion
4. Purchase of investments $400,000	Investments, according to the 19X6 and 19X7 balance sheets, increased by $300,000; however, during 19X7, $100,000 of investments were sold. Thus, purchases were $400,000, based on the analysis of the investment account as follows:

Investments

Balance 12/31/X6	150,000		
Purchase of investments	400,000	Sale of investments	100,000
Balance 12/31/X7	450,000		

5. Purchase of marketable securities

According to note #8, marketable securities of $5,000 were purchased in 19X7.

The financing activities of the Evangel Inn during 19X7 resulted in a net cash outflow of $175,000, as well as the noncash exchange of $100,000 of Evangel's common stock for long-term debt as shown on the Supplementary Schedule of Noncash Investing and Financing Activities at the bottom of Exhibit 11. The individual sources and uses of cash flows in the financing activities section of the Evangel Inn's SCF are explained as follows:

Item

Discussion

1. Payment of long-term debt $50,000

The payment of debt is determined by analyzing both the LTD and current maturities of LTD accounts as follows:

Current Maturities of LTD

Payment of LTD	50,000	12/31/X6 Balance	50,000
		Reclassification of LTD	50,000
		12/31/X7 Balance	50,000

Long-Term Debt

Reclassification of LTD	50,000	12/31/X6 Balance	1,000,000
		Borrowing during 19X7	200,000
Converted to common stock	100,000		
		12/31/X7 Balance	1,050,000

The current maturities of LTD account showed $50,000 payable on December 31, 19X6. By definition, current liabilities must be paid within one year; therefore, we can safely assume that the $50,000 balance at December 31, 19X6, was paid in 19X7. The balance at the end of 19X7 is a $50,000 reclassification of LTD which occurred during 19X7. In other words, the $50,000 of LTD due in 19X8 is shown as current maturities of LTD on December 31, 19X7.

2. Borrowed long-term debt $200,000

Note #7 reports $200,000 was borrowed during 19X7. The analysis of the long-term debt above confirms the $200,000 of new debt.

3. Purchase of treasury stock $140,000

The analysis of the treasury stock account confirms the purchase, according to note #4, of $140,000 as follows:

Treasury Stock

	12/31/X6 Balance	10,000
	Purchase	140,000
	12/31/X7 Balance	150,000

4. Proceeds from sale of common stock $25,000

Note #6 reveals $25,000 of common stock was sold during 19X7. This is confirmed by analyzing the common stock account as follows:

Common Stock

	12/31/X6 Balance	1,160,000
	Issued to retire LTD	100,000
	Issued for cash	25,000
	12/31/X7 Balance	1,285,000

The $100,000 of common stock issued for debt is a noncash transaction and is reported on the Schedule of Noncash Investing and Financing Activities shown at the bottom of Exhibit 11.

5. Payment of dividends $210,000

During 19X7, $205,000 of dividends were declared; however, for the SCF purposes, the $210,000 amount paid must be determined and shown. Analysis of the dividends payable account reveals that $210,000 was paid as follows:

Dividends Payable

		12/31/X6 Balance	20,000
		Dividends declared	205,000
Dividends paid	210,000		
		12/31/X7 Balance	15,000

In essence, the dividends declared in 19X6 and payable at the end of 19X6 of $20,000 were paid in 19X7. In addition, $190,000 of the $205,000 of dividends declared in 19X7 were paid in 19X7, leaving $15,000 dividends to be paid in 19X8 and shown as a current liability on Evangel Inn's balance sheet at the end of 19X7.

Thus, the net total of cash flows for operating, investing, and financing activities for the Evangel Inn for 19X7 is $40,000, which equals the increase in cash of $40,000 as reflected on the Evangel Inn's 19X6 and 19X7 balance sheets.

Interpreting the Results

The Evangel Inn's SCF lends insight to the user as follows:

- While net income increased by $330,000, cash flows from operations increased by $700,000. The major difference as shown on the SCF is depreciation expense of $340,000.

- Cash flows from operations were sufficient to allow the Evangel Inn to (1) use $485,000 in net investing activities, (2) use $175,000 in net financing activities, and (3) provide an increase in cash of $40,000 during 19X7.

- In addition, noncash activities occurred in the noncash exchange of $100,000 of common stock for $100,000 of long-term debt.

Analysis of Statements of Cash Flow

Unlike the balance sheet and income statement, the SCF is generally not analyzed by itself. Rather, figures from the SCF are compared with specific balance sheet and income statement numbers. For example, the operating cash flow to total liabilities ratio is determined by dividing operating cash flows from the SCF by average total liabilities from the balance sheet.

A few reasons appear to exist for the comparatively little analysis of the SCF. First, management tends to focus on operations (which are reflected on the income statement) and on resources used in operations (which are shown on the balance sheet). Though cash is critical to business, corporate officials often handle the cash activities. Second, the SCF is relatively new. The FASB has required that this statement be issued only since 1988. As we continue to issue this statement, more analysis will no doubt be conducted on the cash flow numbers.

Though a common-size SCF could possibly be prepared, it may be useless. What figure would be the base figure of 100%? Net sales and total assets from the income statement and balance sheet, respectively, serve that purpose. However, since the SCF is divided into three distinct, independent sections, no similar base figure appears reasonable. A comparative SCF could also be prepared. However, the results reflecting details of some sections would be relatively useless. For example, how would the change in accounts receivable be shown? Assume that in 19X1 accounts receivable increased by $10,000 and that during 19X2 accounts receivable decreased by $15,000. On the SCF, the increase is shown as a negative figure, while the decrease is shown as a positive figure. The change over the two periods is $25,000, yet the change in accounts receivable balance over the two periods is a decrease of $5,000.

Useful analysis over time on a comparative basis would examine the changes in the net cash flows from each activity. An example is as follows:

	19X1	19X2	Difference $	Difference %
Net cash flows from:				
Operations	$300,000	$350,000	$ 50,000	16.67%
Investing	(400,000)	(300,000)	100,000	25.00%
Financing	150,000	100,000	(50,000)	33.33%
Change in cash	$ 50,000	$150,000	$100,000	200.00%

This analysis clearly reflects the changes in cash from the major activities. The user does not get lost in meaningless detail.

Summary

The SCF is an FASB-mandated financial statement that must be issued with other financial statements released to external users. It reflects the inflow and outflow of cash for a period of time.

The SCF must show operating, investing, and financing activities. Operating activities reflect cash flows as they relate to revenues and expenses. Investing activities relate to changes in marketable securities and noncurrent asset accounts. Commonly included in these activities are the purchase and sale of property and equipment. Financing activities relate to changes in dividends payable, current maturities of long-term debt, long-term debt, and equity accounts. The sale of common stock and payment of long-term debt are two examples of financing activities. The net sum of the three activities shown on the SCF must equal the change in the cash amount shown on the two successive balance sheets.

There are two basic approaches to preparing the SCF—the direct and indirect methods. The difference between the two approaches is reflected only in the operating activities section of the SCF. The indirect approach starts with net income and includes various adjustments made to determine net income which did not affect cash. Other adjustments for the indirect approach are the changes in current accounts related to operations. The direct approach shows the direct sources of cash, such as cash receipts from sales, and direct uses of cash, such as disbursements for payroll. Most hospitality firms use the indirect approach because it is easier to prepare.

Key Terms

accrual basis accounting—System of reporting revenues and expenses in the period in which they are considered to have been earned or incurred, regardless of the actual time of collection or payment.

cash equivalents—Short-term, highly liquid investments such as U.S. Treasury bills and money market accounts.

cash inflows—Cash received by a hospitality organization during an accounting period.

cash outflows—Cash disbursed by a hospitality organization during an accounting period.

direct method—One of two methods for converting net income to net cash flow from operations. This method shows cash receipts from sales and cash disbursements for expenses and requires that each item on the income statement be converted from an accrual basis to a cash basis.

indirect method—One of two methods for converting net income to net cash flow from operations. This method starts with net income and then adjusts for noncash items included on the income statement.

statement of cash flows—Explains the change in cash for the accounting period by showing the effects on cash of a business's operating, investing, and financing activities for the accounting period.

Review Questions

1. What is the major purpose of the SCF?

2. How do different users of the SCF use this statement?

3. What are the three major classifications of cash flows in the SCF?

4. What are the two alternative approaches to preparing the SCF?

5. How do the two methods of preparing the SCF differ?

6. What supplementary information must be provided when the indirect approach is used in preparing the SCF?

7. How are changes in the various current balance sheet accounts shown on an SCF prepared using the indirect approach?

8. Where is the $10,000 loss on the sale of an investment shown on the SCF prepared using the indirect approach?

9. How does the sum of the cash flows from the three major classifications on the SCF relate to the change in balance sheet accounts from two successive balance sheets?

10. How is the exchange of common stock for long-term debt shown on the SCF?

Problems

Problem 1

The Spartan Corporation has engaged in several transactions listed below:

1. Sold food and beverages for cash

2. Purchased investments

3. Exchanged its common stock for long-term bonds

4. Sold common stock

5. Issued a stock dividend

6. Paid salaries and wages

7. Sold investments at a loss

8. Paid a cash dividend
9. Purchased a 60-day treasury bill
10. Sold land for a gain
11. Paid interest
12. Received dividends from an investment
13. Paid for food and beverage supplies
14. Paid long-term debt
15. Purchased equipment

Required:

Identify each transaction as (1) an operating activity, (2) an investing activity, (3) a financing activity, (4) a noncash transaction, or (5) none of the above.

Problem 2

The Nittany Lion Motel Corporation has engaged in various activities listed below:

1. Sold food on account
2. Received interest income
3. Purchased underdeveloped land
4. Opened a payroll checking account
5. Declared a cash dividend
6. Purchased food on account
7. Paid income taxes
8. Exchanged 1,000 shares of common stock for a long-term note
9. Reclassified long-term debt as current debt
10. Collected cash on a noncurrent note receivable
11. Recorded depreciation
12. Sold equipment at a loss
13. Sold preferred stock
14. Paid a food supplier
15. Paid interest on long-term debt

Required:

Identify each activity for SCF purposes as (1) an operating activity, (2) an investing activity, (3) a financing activity, (4) a noncash transaction, or (5) none of the above.

Problem 3

The Pennsy Inn has incurred various activities described in each situation below:

1. During 19X2, the Pennsy Inn's total payroll expense was $805,000. The payroll payable account at the beginning and end of 19X2 equaled $6,000 and $8,000, respectively. What were the total cash disbursements for payroll during 19X2?

2. The insurance expense for 19X2 was $15,000. Prepaid insurance was $3,000 at the beginning of 19X2 and $5,000 at the end of 19X2. The prepaid insurance account is debited when insurance premiums are paid, and insurance expense is recorded as time passes. What was the amount of total insurance premiums paid during 19X2?

3. The utility expense was $30,000 during 19X2. The accrued utility expense was $3,000 and $4,000 at the beginning and end of the year, respectively. What was the total amount paid to the utility company during 19X2?

4. During 19X2, all equipment purchased was obtained by using excess cash of the Pennsy Inn. The equipment account had a beginning balance of $200,000 and an ending balance of $250,000. During 19X2, equipment which cost $20,000 was sold for $5,000. A loss of $2,000 was recorded on this sale. How much was expended during the year for equipment?

5. The balance of marketable securities was $20,000 and $25,000 at the beginning and end of 19X2, respectively. Marketable securities were sold during 19X2 for $8,000 and a gain on the sale of $3,000 was recorded. How much was expended during 19X2 for marketable securities?

Problem 4

The Eppley Hotel has incurred various activities as described in each situation below:

1. During 19X3, the Eppley Hotel had cash sales of $800,000 and sales on account of $2,540,000. During the same year, accounts receivable—hotel guests increased by $10,000. Determine the cash received from hotel guests during 19X3.

2. During 19X3, the Eppley Hotel's Board of Directors declared cash dividends of $120,000. The dividends payable account was $10,000 at the beginning of the year and $15,000 at the end of the year. Determine the dividends paid by the Eppley Hotel during 19X3.

3. During 19X3, the Eppley Hotel had cost of food used of $400,000. During the year, food inventory increased by $8,000 and the related suppliers payable accounts decreased by $5,000. Determine the cash payments for food purchases during 19X3.

4. During the year, the Eppley Hotel's long-term debt of $1,000,000 on January 1, 19X3, increased by $500,000 to $1,500,000 on December 31, 19X3. Also during 19X3, $200,000 of long-term debt was converted to common stock, and $50,000 of long-term debt was reclassified as current debt. Determine the amount of cash that was borrowed and recorded as long-term debt during 19X3.

5. The Eppley Hotel's income tax expense for 19X3 was $25,000. Its income taxes payable account on the balance sheet was $4,000 at the beginning of the year and $5,000 at the end of the year. Determine the amount of income taxes paid during 19X3.

Problem 5

During 19X4, the Kellogg Inn had net income of $50,000. Included on its income statement for 19X4 was depreciation expense of $100,000 and amortization expense of $5,000. Current accounts changed during 19X4 as follows:

Cash	$ 5,000 increase
Marketable securities	30,000 decrease
Accounts receivable	10,000 increase
Inventory	5,000 decrease
Prepaid expenses	4,000 increase

Accounts payable	10,000 increase
Accrued payroll	2,000 increase
Income taxes payable	3,000 decrease
Dividends payable	5,000 decrease

In addition, sales of equipment, marketable securities, and investments during 19X4 were as follows:

1. Equipment costing $100,000 with accumulated depreciation of $80,000 was sold for $25,000.

2. Investments that cost $150,000 were sold for $200,000.

3. Marketable securities of $30,000 were sold for $25,000.

Required:

Prepare the schedule of cash flows from operating activities using the indirect method.

Problem 6

The Owen Resort had several transactions as shown below. In the columns to the right, describe the type of activity for each transaction and what amount (if any) would be shown on the SCF prepared according to the indirect method. (For example, the payment of utilities is not shown on the SCF because it is subtracted from sales to determine net income which is shown on the SCF.)

Transaction			Type of Activity	Amount Shown on SCF
1. Cash	$ 125,000			
Common stock		$ 100,000		
Paid-in capital				
in excess of par		25,000	_____	_____
2. Cash	$ 25,000			
Accum. Depr.	60,000			
Equipment		$ 80,000		
Gain on sale of				
equipment		5,000	_____	_____
3. Cash	$ 125,000			
Treasury stock		$ 100,000		
Retained				
earnings		25,000	_____	_____
4. Notes payable	$ 75,000			
Common stock		$ 60,000		
Paid-in capital				
in excess of par		150,000	_____	_____
5. Notes payable	$ 100,000			
Interest expense	20,000			
Cash		$ 120,000	_____	_____

6. Cash	$ 10,000			
Accounts Receivable	30,000			
Sales		$ 40,000	_____	_____
7. Salaries and wages	$ 20,000			
Cash		$ 20,000	_____	_____
8. Cash	$ 5,000			
Dividend income		$ 5,000	_____	_____
9. Cash	$ 40,000			
Loss on sale of				
investments	10,000			
Investments		$ 50,000	_____	_____
10. Equipment	$ 15,000			
Notes payable		$ 15,000	_____	_____

Problem 7

You have been hired by D. Smith, a successful entrepreneur, to prepare a statement of cash flows for his two-year-old hotel, the Illini Inn. The following are copies of the condensed balance sheets and the income statement of the Illini Inn.

Illini Inn
Condensed Balance Sheets
December 31, 19X1 and 19X2

	19X1	19X2
Cash	$ 30,000	$ 40,000
Accounts Receivable	190,000	225,000
Inventory	30,000	35,000
Property and Equipment (net)	1,400,000	1,500,000
Other Assets	200,000	100,000
Total Assets	$1,850,000	$1,900,000
Accounts Payable	$ 140,000	$ 185,000
Wages Payable	10,000	15,000
Current Maturities-LTD	50,000	50,000
Long-Term Debt	1,000,000	950,000
Total Liabilities	1,200,000	1,200,000
Owners' Equity	650,000	700,000
Total Liabilities and Owners' Equity	$1,850,000	$1,900,000

Illini Inn
Condensed Income Statement
For the year ended December 31, 19X2

Sales	$1,600,000
Cost of Goods Sold	200,000
Contribution Margin	1,400,000
Undistributed Operating Expenses	950,000
Income After Undistributed Operating Expenses	450,000
Depreciation Expense	200,000
Amortization Expense	100,000
Income Before Tax	150,000
Income Tax	50,000
Net Income	$ 100,000

Additional information:

1. Equipment was purchased for $300,000.

2. Dividends of $50,000 were declared and paid during 19X2.

3. Long-term debt of $50,000 was reclassified as current at the end of 19X2.

Required:

Prepare the SCF, with supplementary disclosures, for the Illini Inn using the indirect method.

Problem 8

The operations of the Molehill, a small lodging operation, are becoming more complex. Susan Strat, the owner, has asked for your help in preparing her statement of cash flows. She is able to present you with condensed balance sheets and some additional information.

The Molehill
Condensed Balance Sheets
December 31, 19X1 and 19X2

	19X1	19X2
Cash	$ 10,000	$ 8,000
Accounts Receivable	26,500	22,500
Investments	10,000	20,000
Equipment	200,000	320,000
Accumulated Depreciation	(20,000)	(59,000)
Total Assets	$ 226,500	$ 311,500
Current Liabilities:		
Accounts Payable	$ 18,000	$ 21,000
Mortgage Payable (current)	5,000	22,000
Dividends Payable	5,000	8,000
Noncurrent Liabilities:		
Mortgage Payable	75,000	110,000
Common Stock	50,000	70,000
Retained Earnings	73,500	80,500
Total Liabilities and Owners' Equity	$ 226,500	$ 311,500

Additional information:

1. Equipment costing $20,000 and fully depreciated (to $–0–) was sold for $5,000.

2. Long-term investments costing $10,000 were sold for $12,000.

3. Common stock was sold and long-term debt was borrowed during 19X2. There were no non-cash financing or investing activities during 19X2.

4. Income before gain on the sale of equipment for 19X2 totaled $15,000. The firm's average tax rate is 15%.

5. Assume all current liabilities are paid on a timely basis.

6. Assume all long-term debt is reclassified as a current liability on December 31 of the year prior to its payment.

7. Assume the change in retained earnings is due only to dividends declared and net income from operations. Dividends declared during 19X2 totaled $10,000.

Required:

Prepare the SCF using the indirect method.

Problem 9

The operations of The Freida, a small lodging operation, are becoming more complex. Ms. Martin, the owner, has asked for your help in preparing her statement of cash flows. She is able to present you with condensed balance sheets and some additional information.

The Freida
Condensed Balance Sheets
December 31, 19X1 and 19X2

	19X1	19X2
Cash	$ 10,000	$ 6,000
Accounts Receivable	26,500	25,500
Investments	10,000	5,000
Equipment	200,000	325,000
Accumulated Depreciation	(20,000)	(40,000)
Total Assets	$ 226,500	$ 321,500
Current Liabilities:		
Accounts Payable	$ 18,000	$ 21,000
Mortgage Payable (current)	5,000	5,000
Dividends Payable	5,000	5,000
Noncurrent Liabilities:		
Mortgage Payable	75,000	70,000
Notes Payable	–0–	40,000
Common Stock	50,000	100,000
Retained Earnings	73,500	80,500
Total Liabilities and Owners' Equity	$ 226,500	$ 321,500

Additional information:

1. Equipment costing $20,000, depreciated to one half its cost, was sold for $8,000.

2. Common stock, purchased as a long-term investment for $5,000, was sold for $8,000.

3. Dividends declared during 19X2 totaled $7,000.
4. Equipment costing $145,000 was purchased during 19X2.
5. Depreciation expense for 19X2 totaled $30,000.
6. Long-term debt of $5,000 was reclassified as current at the end of 19X2.
7. Common stock of $50,000 was sold and long-term debt of $40,000 (note payable) was borrowed during 19X2.
8. The Freida generated net income of $14,000 during 19X2.

Required:

Prepare the SCF as requested by Ms. Martin using the indirect method.

Problem 10

The condensed balance sheets of the Spartan Inn are as follows:

Spartan Inn
Condensed Balance Sheets
December 31, 19X1 and 19X2

Assets	19X1	19X2
Current Assets:		
Cash	$ 30,000	$ 40,000
Marketable Securities	50,000	50,000
Accounts Receivable	100,000	95,000
Inventory	20,000	25,000
Total Current Assets	200,000	210,000
Investments	100,000	60,000
Property and Equipment:		
Land	500,000	500,000
Building	5,000,000	6,000,000
Equipment	1,000,000	1,100,000
Accumulated Depreciation	(1,600,000)	(2,000,000)
Net Property and Equipment	4,900,000	5,600,000
Total Assets	$5,200,000	$5,870,000
Liabilities and Owners' Equity		
Current Liabilities:		
Accounts Payable	$ 60,000	$ 70,000
Dividends Payable	30,000	50,000
Current Portion of LTD	100,000	130,000
Total	190,000	250,000
Long-Term Debt	4,000,000	4,370,000
Capital Stock	700,000	700,000
Retained Earnings	310,000	550,000
Total Liabilities and Owners' Equity	$5,200,000	$5,870,000

Spartan Inn
Condensed Income Statement
For the year ended December 31, 19X2

Sales	$6,000,000
Cost of Sales	1,000,000
Gross Profit	5,000,000
Depreciation	400,000
Other Expenses (except depreciation)	4,500,000
Net Operating Income	100,000
Gain on Sales of Investments	300,000
Income Taxes	110,000
Net Income	$ 290,000

Additional information:

1. Dividends declared during 19X2 totaled $50,000.
2. No investments were purchased during 19X2.
3. The current portion of long-term debt at the end of 19X2 was reclassified from noncurrent during 19X2.
4. No equipment or buildings were sold during 19X2.
5. Long-term debt was borrowed to partially finance the building purchase.

Required:

Prepare the Spartan Inn's SCF for 19X2 using the indirect method.

Problem 11

Use the information in Problem 10 for the Spartan Inn. Additional information is as follows:

Total labor expense for 19X2 was $2,000,000.

Interest expense for 19X2 was $450,000.

Required:

Prepare the Spartan Inn's SCF for 19X2 using the direct method.

Problem 12

The operations of the Fishtail, a small food service operation, are becoming more complex. Treva Trout, the owner, has asked for your help in understanding the condensed balance sheets and additional information provided.

The Fishtail
Condensed Balance Sheets
December 31, 19X1 and 19X2

	19X1	19X2
Cash	$ 10,000	$ 12,000
Accounts Receivable	15,000	18,500
Prepaid Expenses	21,500	20,000
Equipment	200,000	325,000
Accumulated Depreciation	(20,000)	(64,000)
Total Assets	226,500	311,500
Current Liabilities:		
Accounts Payable	18,000	21,000
Mortgage Payable (current)	5,000	15,000
Dividends Payable	5,000	18,000
Noncurrent Liabilities:		
Mortgage Payable	95,000	110,000
Common Stock	90,000	100,000
Treasury Stock	(40,000)	(30,000)
Retained Earnings	53,500	77,500
Total Liabilities and Owners' Equity	$ 226,500	$ 311,500

Additional information:

a. A range costing $8,000 with a net book value of $3,000 was sold for $4,000.

b. Dividends paid during 19X2 totaled $20,000.

c. There were no noncash transactions during 19X2.

d. Retained earnings is only affected by the results of operations (net income) and dividends declared.

Required:

1. What amount of dividends were declared in 19X2?
2. What was the net income for 19X2?
3. What was the depreciation expense for 19X2?
4. What were the equipment purchases for 19X2?
5. What was the amount of funds borrowed during 19X2?

Problem 13

The operations of Rosa's Cafe, a small food service operation, are becoming more complex. Rosa Soliz, the owner, has asked for your help in preparing her statement of cash flows. She is able to present you with condensed balance sheets and some additional information.

Rosa's Cafe
Condensed Balance Sheets
December 31, 19X1 and 19X2

	19X1	19X2
Cash	$ 15,000	$ 15,000
Marketable Securities	5,000	5,000
Accounts Receivable	14,000	15,000
Inventory	20,000	19,000
Investments (noncurrent)	10,000	10,000
Equipment	320,000	320,000
Accumulated Depreciation	(50,000)	(50,000)
Total Assets	334,000	334,000
Current Liabilities:		
Accounts Payable	$ 18,000	$ 19,000
Dividends Payable	20,000	20,000
Mortgage Payable (current)	20,000	20,000
Noncurrent Liabilities:		
Mortgage Payable	160,000	160,000
Common Stock	100,000	100,000
Retained Earnings	16,000	15,000
Total Liabilities & Owners' Equity	$ 334,000	$ 334,000

Additional information about activities in 19X2:

1. Investments costing $15,000 were sold for $10,000.
2. Dividends declared during 19X2 totaled $30,000.
3. The cafe's van, which cost $25,000, was sold at a gain of $5,000. Its net book value on the date of sale was $10,000.
4. Marketable securities that cost $5,000 were sold for $10,000.
5. Common stock of $20,000 was exchanged for equipment in a noncash transaction.
6. Assume current liabilities are paid on a timely basis.

Required:

Prepare the statement of cash flows for 19X2.

Problem 14

The operations of the Bloated Goat Cafe, a small food service operation, are becoming more complex. Sharon Nanny, the owner, has asked for your help in understanding the condensed balance sheets and the additional information provided.

The Bloated Goat Cafe
Condensed Balance Sheets
December 31, 19X1 and 19X2

	19X1	19X2
Cash	$ 15,000	$ 12,000
Accounts Receivable	15,000	14,000
Inventory	25,000	20,000
Investments (noncurrent)	10,000	5,000
Equipment	240,000	320,000
Accumulated Depreciation	(20,000)	(50,000)
Total Assets	$285,000	$321,000

	19X1	19X2
Current Liabilities:		
Accounts Payable	$ 18,000	$ 10,000
Mortgage Payable (current)	10,000	10,000
Dividends Payable	5,000	10,000
Noncurrent Liabilities:		
Mortgage Payable	152,000	171,000
Common Stock	100,000	100,000
Treasury Stock	(40,000)	(50,000)
Retained Earnings	40,000	70,000
Total Liabilities and Owners' Equity	$285,000	$321,000

Additional information:

a. Investments costing $10,000 were sold for $15,000.

b. Dividends paid during 19X2 totaled $10,000.

c. The cafe's van, which cost $20,000, was sold for $5,000. Its net book value on the date of sale was $3,000.

d. Assume that the retained earnings account is affected only by dividends declared and the results of operations (net income).

e. Assume current liabilities are paid on a timely basis.

Required:

1. What amount of dividends was declared during 19X2?

2. What amount of the mortgage payable was paid during 19X2?

3. What impact did the change in inventory during 19X2 have on cash?

4. What impact did the change in accounts payable during 19X2 have on cash?

5. What were the results of operations for 19X2?

6. What amount of investments were purchased during 19X2?

7. What was the depreciation expense for 19X2?

Problem 15

The Hawkeye Hotel's balance sheet for December 31, 19X5, is provided below.

Hawkeye Hotel
Balance Sheet
December 31, 19X2

Current Assets		
Cash	$	12,540
Marketable Securities		100,000
Accounts Receivable		73,811
Food Inventory		10,833
Prepaid Insurance		4,318
Total Current Assets		201,502
Property and Equipment, at Cost		
Land		262,000
Building		1,572,805
Equipment		213,843
		2,048,648
Less Accumulated Depreciation		303,227
		1,745,421
Total Assets		$1,946,923
Current Liabilities		
Notes Payable	$	–0–
Mortgage Payable—Current		50,000
Accounts Payable		18,776
Accrued Wages		6,843
Total Current Liabilities		75,619
Long-Term Liabilities		
Mortgage Payable		950,695
Owners' Equity		
Common Stock, No Par, Authorized 100,000		
Shares, Issued 75,000 Shares		750,000
Retained Earnings		170,609
Total Liabilities and Owners' Equity		$1,946,923

The Hawkeye Hotel's general ledger as of December 31, 19X6, contained the following accounts:

	DR	CR
Cash	$ 19,278	
Accounts receivable	75,000	
Allowance for doubtful accounts		$ 1,211
Food inventory	11,936	
Prepaid insurance	4,667	
Land	262,000	
Building	1,927,817	
Equipment	241,470	
Accumulated depreciation		411,137
Accounts payable		6,821
Accrued wages		7,953
Notes payable		25,000
Mortgage payable (current)		50,000
Mortgage payable (long-term)		1,105,399
Common stock		750,000
Retained earnings		107,109
Room revenues		1,349,866
Food revenues		753,722
Telephone revenues		73,936
Other sales		1,006
Interest income		785
Room expenses:		
Labor	450,000	
Other	115,037	
Food expenses:		
Cost of sales	225,000	
Labor	250,000	
Other	149,161	
Telephone expenses:		
Cost of calls	52,470	
Labor	22,000	
Other	2,000	
Administrative & general:		
Labor	150,677	
Other	100,000	
Marketing expense	45,000	
Property operation & maintenance:		
Labor	42,000	
Other	10,000	

	DR	CR
Utilities	57,478	
Property taxes	80,000	
Fire insurance expense	31,462	
Interest expense	161,087	
Depreciation expense	110,225	
Gain on sale of equipment		3,000
Income taxes	51,180	
Total	$4,646,945	$4,646,945

Additional information:

1. Equipment costing $6,750 with accumulated depreciation of $2,315 was sold for $7,435.
2. The mortgage payable—current balance of $50,000 at the end of 19X6 was reclassified from noncurrent liabilities during 19X6.
3. An addition to the building during 19X6 cost $355,012.
4. Equipment purchases during 19X6 totaled $34,377.
5. Dividends paid during 19X6 totaled $63,500.

Required:

1. Prepare a comparative balance sheet for the Hawkeye Hotel.
2. Prepare the Hawkeye Hotel's income statement for 19X6 in accordance with the *USALI*.
3. Prepare the SCF for the Hawkeye Hotel for 19X6 using the indirect approach.

Chapter 5 Outline

Ratio Standards
Purposes of Ratio Analysis
What Ratios Express
Classes of Ratios
Liquidity Ratios
    Current Ratio
    Acid-Test Ratio
    Operating Cash Flows to Current Liabilities Ratio
    Accounts Receivable Turnover
    Average Collection Period
    Working Capital Turnover Ratio
Solvency Ratios
    Solvency Ratio
    Debt-Equity Ratio
    Long-Term Debt to Total Capitalization Ratio
    Number of Times Interest Earned Ratio
    Fixed Charge Coverage Ratio
    Operating Cash Flows to Total Liabilities Ratio
Activity Ratios
    Inventory Turnover
    Property and Equipment Turnover
    Asset Turnover
    Paid Occupancy Percentage
    Complimentary Occupancy
    Average Occupancy per Room
    Multiple Occupancy
Profitability Ratios
    Profit Margin
    Operating Efficiency Ratio
    Return on Assets
    Gross Return on Assets
    Return on Owners' Equity
    Return on Common Stockholders' Equity
    Earnings per Share
    Price Earnings Ratio
    Viewpoints Regarding Profitability Ratios
    Profitability Evaluation of Segments
Operating Ratios
    Mix of Sales
    Average Room Rate
    Revenue per Available Room
    Average Food Service Check
    Food Cost Percentage
    Beverage Cost Percentage
    Labor Cost Percentage
Limitations of Ratio Analysis
Usefulness of Financial Ratios
Computer Applications

Ratio Analysis

FINANCIAL STATEMENTS ISSUED BY hospitality establishments contain a lot of financial information. A thorough analysis of this information requires more than simply reading the reported facts. Users of financial statements need to be able to interpret the reported facts to discover aspects of the hospitality property's financial situation that could otherwise go unnoticed. This is accomplished through **ratio analysis,** which is the comparison of related facts and figures, most of which appear on the financial statements. A ratio gives mathematical expression to a relationship between two figures and is computed by dividing one figure by the other figure. By bringing the two figures into relation with each other, ratios generate new information. In this way, ratio analysis goes beyond the figures reported in a financial statement and makes them more meaningful, more informative, and more useful. In particular, ratio analysis generates indicators for evaluating different aspects of a financial situation.

Ratio analysis can provide users of financial statements with answers to such questions as:

1. Is there sufficient cash to meet the establishment's obligations for a given time period?

2. Are the profits of the hospitality operation reasonable?

3. Is the level of debt acceptable in comparison with the stockholders' investment?

4. Is the inventory usage adequate?

5. How do the operation's earnings compare with the market price of the hospitality property's stock?

6. Are accounts receivable reasonable in light of credit sales?

7. Is the hospitality establishment able to service its debt?

In this chapter, we will first explain the different kinds of standards against which ratios are compared in order to evaluate the financial condition of a hospitality operation. We will also discuss the variety of functions or purposes that ratio analysis serves in interpreting financial statements and the ways in which different ratios are expressed in order to make sense of the information they provide. Most of this chapter then is devoted to a detailed discussion of the ratios most commonly used in the hospitality industry.

Ratio Standards

Ratio analysis is used to evaluate the favorableness or unfavorableness of various financial conditions. However, the computed ratios alone do not say anything about what is good or bad, acceptable or unacceptable, reasonable or unreasonable. By themselves, ratios are neutral and simply express numerical relationships between related figures. In order to be useful as indicators or measurements of the success or well-being of a hospitality operation, the computed ratios must be compared against some standard. Only then will the ratios become meaningful and provide users of financial statements with a basis for evaluating the financial conditions.

There are basically three different standards that are used to evaluate the ratios computed for a given operation for a given period: ratios from a past period, industry averages, and budgeted ratios. Many ratios can be compared with corresponding ratios calculated for the prior period in order to discover any significant changes. For example, paid occupancy percentage (discussed later in this chapter) for the current year may be compared with paid occupancy percentage of the prior year in order to determine whether the lodging operation is succeeding in selling more of its available rooms this year than it had previously. This comparison may be useful in evaluating the effectiveness of the property's current marketing plans.

Industry averages provide another useful standard against which to compare ratios. After calculating the return on investment (discussed later in this chapter) for a given property, investors may want to compare this with the average return for similar properties in their particular industry segment. This may give investors an indication of the ability of the property's management to use resources effectively to generate profits for the owners in comparison with other operations in the industry. In addition, managers may want to compare the paid occupancy percentage or food cost percentage for their own operation with industry averages in order to evaluate their abilities to compete with other operations in their industry segment. Published sources of average industry ratios are readily available.

While ratios can be compared against results of a prior period and against industry averages, ratios are best compared against planned ratio goals. For example, in order to more effectively control the cost of labor, management may project a goal for the current year's labor cost percentage (also discussed in this chapter) that is slightly lower than the previous year's levels. The expectation of a lower labor cost percentage may reflect management's efforts to improve scheduling procedures and other factors related to the cost of labor. By comparing the actual labor cost percentage with the planned goal, management is able to assess the success of its efforts to control labor cost.

Different evaluations may result from comparing ratios against these different standards. For example, a food cost of 33% for the current period may compare favorably with the prior year's ratio of 34% and with an industry average of 36%, but may be judged unfavorably when compared with the operation's planned goal of 32%. Therefore, care must be taken when evaluating the results of operations using ratio analysis. It is necessary to keep in mind not only which standards are being used to evaluate the ratios, but the purposes of the ratio analysis as well.

Purposes of Ratio Analysis

Managers, creditors, and investors often have different purposes in using ratio analysis to evaluate the information reported in financial statements.

Ratios help managers monitor the operating performances of their operations and evaluate their success in meeting a variety of goals. By tracking a limited number of ratios, hospitality managers are able to maintain a fairly accurate perception of the effectiveness and efficiency of their operations. In a food service operation, most managers compute food cost percentage and labor cost percentage in order to monitor the two largest expenses of their operations. In lodging operations, occupancy percentage is one of the key ratios that managers use on a daily basis. Management often uses ratios to express operational goals. For example, management may establish ratio goals as follows:

- Maintain a 1.25 to 1 current ratio.

- Do not exceed a debt-equity ratio of 1 to 1.

- Maintain return on owners' equity of 15%.

- Maintain property and equipment turnover of 1.2 times.

These ratios, and many more, will be fully explained later in this chapter. The point here is to notice that ratios are particularly useful to managers as indicators of how well goals are being achieved. When actual results fall short of goals, ratios help indicate where a problem may be. In the food cost percentage example presented earlier in which an actual ratio of 33% compared unfavorably against the planned 32%, additional research is required to determine the cause(s) of the 1% variation. This 1% difference may be due to cost differences, sales mix differences, or a combination of the two. Only additional analysis will determine the actual cause(s). Ratio analysis can contribute significant information to such an investigation.

Creditors use ratio analysis to evaluate the solvency of hospitality operations and to assess the riskiness of future loans. For example, the relationship of current assets to current liabilities, referred to as the current ratio, may indicate an establishment's ability to pay its upcoming bills. In addition, creditors sometimes use ratios to express requirements for hospitality operations as part of the conditions set forth for certain financial arrangements. For example, as a condition of a loan, a creditor may require an operation to maintain a current ratio of 2 to 1.

Investors and potential investors use ratios to evaluate the performance of a hospitality operation. For example, the dividend payout ratio (dividends paid divided by earnings) indicates the percentage of earnings paid out by the hospitality establishment. Potential investors primarily interested in stock growth may shy away from investing in properties that pay out large dividends.

Ratios are used to communicate financial performance. Different ratios communicate different results. Individually, ratios reveal only part of the overall financial condition of an operation. Collectively, however, ratios are able to communicate a great deal of information that may not be immediately apparent from simply reading the figures reported in financial statements.

What Ratios Express

In order to understand the information communicated by the different kinds of ratios used in ratio analysis, it is necessary to understand the various ways in which ratios express financial information. Different ratios are read in different ways. For example, many ratios are expressed as *percentages*. An illustration is the food cost percentage, which expresses the cost of food sold in terms of a percentage of total food sales. If total food sales for a given year are $430,000, while the cost of food sold is $135,000, then the result of dividing the cost of food sold by the total food sales is .314. Because the food cost percentage is a ratio expressed as a percentage, this figure is multiplied by 100 to yield a 31.4% food cost. Another example is paid occupancy percentage, resulting from rooms sold divided by rooms available for sale. If a lodging property has 100 rooms available for sale and sells only 50 of them, then 50 divided by 100 yields .5, which is then multiplied by 100 to be expressed as a percentage (50%).

Some other ratios are expressed on a *per unit basis*. For example, the average breakfast check is a ratio expressed as a certain sum per breakfast served. It is calculated by dividing the total breakfast sales by the number of guests served during the breakfast period. Thus, on a given day, if 100 guests were served breakfast and the total revenue during the breakfast period amounted to $490, then the average breakfast check would be $4.90 per meal ($490 ÷ 100).

The proper way to express still other ratios is as a *turnover* of so many times. **Seat turnover** is one such ratio, determined by dividing the number of guests served during a given period by the number of restaurant seats. If the restaurant in the previous example had a seating capacity of 40 seats, then seat turnover for the breakfast period in which it served 100 guests would be 2.5 (100 ÷ 40). This means that, during that breakfast period, the restaurant used its entire seating capacity 2.5 times.

Finally, some ratios are expressed as a *coverage* of so many times. The denominator of such a ratio is always set at 1. The current ratio, determined by dividing current assets by current liabilities, is one of the ratios expressed as a coverage of so many times. For example, if a hospitality operation reported current assets of $120,000 and current liabilities of $100,000 for a given period, then the operation's current ratio at the balance sheet date would be 1.2 to 1 (120,000 ÷ 100,000). This means that the hospitality operation possessed sufficient current assets to cover its current liabilities 1.2 times. Put another way, for every $1 of current liabilities, the operation had $1.20 of current assets.

The proper way to express the various ratios used in ratio analysis depends entirely on the particular ratio and the nature of the significant relationship it expresses between the two facts it relates. The ways in which different ratios are expressed are a function of how we use the information that they provide. As we discuss the ratios commonly used in the hospitality industry, pay attention to how each is expressed.

Classes of Ratios

Ratios are generally classified by the type of information that they provide. Five common ratio groupings are as follows:

1. Liquidity

2. Solvency

3. Activity

4. Profitability

5. Operating

Liquidity ratios reveal the ability of a hospitality establishment to meet its short-term obligations. **Solvency ratios**, on the other hand, measure the extent to which the enterprise has been financed by debt and is able to meet its long-term obligations. **Activity ratios** reflect management's ability to use the property's assets, while several **profitability ratios** show management's overall effectiveness as measured by returns on sales and investments. Finally, **operating ratios** assist in the analysis of hospitality establishment operations.

The classification of certain ratios may vary. For example, some texts classify the inventory turnover ratio as a liquidity ratio, but this text and some others consider it to be an activity ratio. Also, profit margin could be classified as an operating ratio, but it is generally included with the profitability ratios.

Knowing the meaning of a ratio and how it is used is always more important than knowing its classification. We will now turn to an in-depth discussion of individual ratios. For each ratio discussed, we will consider its purpose, the formula by which it is calculated, the sources of data needed for the ratio's calculation, and the interpretation of ratio results from the varying viewpoints of owners, creditors, and management.

Exhibits 1 through 4, financial statements of the hypothetical Grand Hotel, will be used throughout our discussion of individual ratios.

Liquidity Ratios

The ability of a hospitality establishment to meet its current obligations is important in evaluating its financial position. For example, can the Grand Hotel meet its current debt of $214,000 as it becomes due? Several ratios can be computed that suggest answers to this question.

Current Ratio

The commonest liquidity ratio is the **current ratio**, which is the ratio of total current assets to total current liabilities and is expressed as a coverage of so many times. Using figures from Exhibit 1, the 19X2 current ratio for the Grand Hotel can be calculated as follows:

$$\text{Current Ratio} = \frac{\text{Current Assets}}{\text{Current Liabilities}}$$

$$= \frac{\$338,000}{\$214,000}$$

$$= \underline{1.58} \text{ times or 1.58 to 1}$$

Exhibit 1   Balance Sheets

Balance Sheets
Grand Hotel
December 31, 19X0, 19X1, 19X2

ASSETS	19X0	19X1	19X2
Current Assets:			
Cash	$ 20,000	$ 21,000	$ 24,000
Marketable Securities	60,000	81,000	145,000
Accounts Receivable (net)	100,000	90,000	140,000
Inventories	14,000	17,000	15,000
Prepaid Expenses	13,000	12,000	14,000
Total Current Assets	$ 207,000	$ 221,000	$ 338,000
Investments	43,000	35,000	40,000
Property and Equipment:			
Land	68,500	68,500	68,500
Buildings	810,000	850,000	880,000
Furniture and Equipment	170,000	190,000	208,000
	1,048,500	1,108,500	1,156,600
Less: Accumulated Depreciation	260,000	320,000	381,000
China, glassware, silver, linen, and uniforms	11,500	20,500	22,800
Total Property and Equipment	800,000	809,000	798,300
Total Assets	$ 1,050,000	$ 1,065,000	$ 1,176,300
LIABILITIES AND OWNERS' EQUITY			
Current Liabilities:			
Accounts Payable	$ 60,000	$ 53,500	$ 71,000
Accrued Income Taxes	30,000	32,000	34,000
Accrued Expenses	70,000	85,200	85,000
Current Portion of Long-Term Debt	25,000	21,500	24,000
Total Current Liabilities	185,000	192,200	214,000
Long-Term Debt:			
Mortgage Payable	425,000	410,000	400,000
Deferred Income Taxes	40,000	42,800	45,000
Total Long-Term Debt	465,000	452,800	445,000
Total Liabilities	650,000	645,000	659,000
Owners' Equity:			
Common Stock	55,000	55,000	55,000
Paid-in Capital in Excess of Par	110,000	110,000	110,000
Retained Earnings	235,000	255,000	352,300
Total Owners' Equity	400,000	420,000	517,300
Total Liabilities and Owners' Equity	$ 1,050,000	$ 1,065,000	$ 1,176,300

This result shows that for every $1 of current liabilities, the Grand Hotel has $1.58 of current assets. Thus, there is a cushion of $.58 for every dollar of current debt. A considerable shrinkage of inventory and receivables could occur before the Grand Hotel would be unable to pay its current obligations. By comparison, the 19X1 current ratio for the Grand Hotel was 1.15. An increase in the current ratio from 1.15 to

Exhibit 2   Income Statements

Income Statements
Grand Hotel
For the years ended December 31, 19X1 and 19X2

	19X1	19X2
Total Revenue	$ 1,300,000	$ 1,352,000
Rooms:		
Revenue	$ 780,000	$ 810,000
Payroll and Related Costs	135,000	145,000
Other Direct Expenses	62,500	60,000
Departmental Income	582,500	605,000
Food and Beverages:		
Revenue	430,000	445,000
Cost of Sales	142,000	148,000
Payroll and Related Costs	175,000	180,000
Other Direct Expenses	43,400	45,000
Departmental Income	69,600	72,000
Telephone:		
Revenue	40,000	42,000
Cost of Sales	30,000	31,000
Payroll and Related Costs	10,000	10,500
Other Direct Expenses	5,000	4,500
Departmental Income	(5,000)	(4,000)
Rentals and Other Income Revenue	50,000	55,000
Total Operated Departments Income	697,100	728,000
Undistributed Operating Expenses:		
Administrative & General	105,000	108,500
Marketing	51,500	55,000
Property Operation & Maintenance	65,250	67,500
Utility Costs	80,250	81,500
Total Undistributed Operating Expenses	302,000	312,500
Income After Undistributed Operating Expenses	395,100	415,500
Rent	20,000	20,000
Property Taxes	20,000	24,000
Insurance	5,500	6,000
Interest	54,000	60,000
Depreciation	60,000	61,000
Total Fixed Charges	159,500	171,000
Income Before Income Taxes	235,600	244,500
Income Taxes	94,300	97,800
Net Income	$ 141,300	$ 146,700

Note: Information systems, human resources, security, and transportation expenses are insignificant and are not shown as separate cost centers.

Exhibit 3   Statement of Cash Flows

Statement of Cash Flows
Grand Hotel
For the years ended December 31, 19X1 and 19X2

	19X1	19X2
Cash Flows from Operating Activities	$ 141,300	$ 146,700
Net Income		
Adjustments to reconcile net income to net cash provided by operations:		
Depreciation expense	60,000	61,000
Inc./Dec. in accounts receivable (net)	10,000	(50,000)
Inc./Dec. in inventories	(3,000)	2,000
Inc./Dec. in prepaid expenses	1,000	(2,000)
Inc./Dec. in accounts payable	(6,500)	17,500
Increase in income taxes	2,000	2,000
Inc./Dec. in accrued expenses	15,200	(200)
Inc./Dec. in deferred taxes	2,800	2,200
Net cash from operating activities	222,800	179,200
Cash Flows from Investing Activities:		
Purchase of marketable securities	(21,000)	(64,000)
Sale of investments	8,000	–0–
Purchase of buildings	(40,000)	(30,000)
Purchase of furniture and equipment	(20,000)	(18,000)
Purchase of china, etc.	(9,000)	(2,300)
Purchase of investments	–0–	(5,000)
Net cash from investing activities	(82,000)	(119,300)
Cash Flows from Financing Activities:		
Payment of dividends	(121,300)	(49,400)
Payment of long-term debt	(25,000)	(21,500)
Borrowed long-term debt	6,500	14,000
Net cash from financing activities	(139,800)	(56,900)
Net Increase in Cash	$ 1,000	$ 3,000

Additional information
Investments of $8,000 were sold at cost in 19X1.

1.58 within one year is considerable and would no doubt please creditors. However, would a current ratio of 1.58 please all interested parties?

Owners/stockholders normally prefer a low current ratio to a high one, because stockholders view investments in most current assets as less productive than investments in noncurrent assets. Since stockholders are primarily concerned with profits, they prefer a relatively low current ratio.

Creditors normally prefer a relatively high current ratio, as this provides assurance that they will receive timely payments. A subset of creditors, lenders of funds,

Exhibit 4   Statement of Retained Earnings and Other Information

Grand Hotel Statement of Retained Earnings and Other Information
December 31, 19X1 and 19X2

	19X1	19X2
Retained earnings—beginning of the year	$ 235,000	$ 255,000
Net income	141,300	146,700
Dividends declared	121,300	49,400
Retained earnings—end of the year	$ 255,000	$ 352,300

Other Information

	19X1	19X2
Rooms Sold	20,500	21,000
Paid Guests	23,500	24,000
Rooms Occupied by Two or More People	2,400	2,500
Complimentary Rooms	150*	160*
Shares of Common Stock Outstanding	55,000	55,000
Food Covers	55,500	56,000
Food Sales	$ 280,000	$ 300,000
Beverage Sales	$ 150,000	$ 145,000

*Assume one guest per complimentary room.

believe adequate liquidity is so important that they often incorporate a minimum working capital requirement or a minimum current ratio in loan agreements. Violation of this loan provision could result in the lender demanding full payment of the loan.

Management is caught in the middle, trying to satisfy both owners and lenders while, at the same time, maintaining adequate working capital and sufficient liquidity to ensure the smooth operation of the hospitality establishment. Management is able to take action affecting the current ratio. In the case of the Grand Hotel, a current ratio of 2 could be achieved by selling $90,000 worth of marketable securities on the last day of 19X2 and paying current creditors.[1] Other possible actions to increase a current ratio include:

- Obtain long-term loans.

- Obtain new owner equity contributions.

- Convert noncurrent assets to cash.

- Defer declaring dividends and leave the cash in the business.

An extremely high current ratio may mean that accounts receivable are too high because of liberal credit policies and/or slow collections, or it may indicate that inventory is excessive. Since ratios are indicators, management must follow through by analyzing possible contributing factors.

Acid-Test Ratio

A more stringent test of liquidity is the **acid-test ratio.** The acid-test ratio measures liquidity by considering only "quick assets"—cash and near-cash assets. Excluded from current assets are inventories and prepaid expenses in determining the total quick assets. In many industries, inventories are significant and their conversion to cash may take several months. The extremes appear evident in the hospitality industry. In some hospitality operations, especially quick-service restaurants, food inventory may be entirely replenished twice a week. On the other hand, the stock of certain alcoholic beverages at some food service operations may be replaced only once in three months.

The difference between the current ratio and the acid-test ratio is a function of the amount of inventory relative to current assets. In some operations, the difference between the current ratio and the acid-test ratio will be minor, while in others, it will be significant. Using relevant figures from Exhibit 1, the 19X2 acid-test ratio for the Grand Hotel is computed as follows:

$$\text{Acid-Test Ratio} = \frac{\text{Cash, Marketable Securities, Notes Receivable \& Accounts Receivable}}{\text{Current Liabilities}}$$

$$= \frac{\$309,000}{\$214,000}$$

$$= \underline{\underline{1.44}} \text{ times}$$

The 19X2 acid-test ratio reveals quick assets of $1.44 for every $1.00 of current liabilities. This is an increase of .44 times over the 19X1 acid-test ratio. Although the acid-test ratio was 1.0 for 19X1, the Grand Hotel was not in difficult financial straits. Many hospitality establishments are able to operate efficiently and effectively with an acid-test ratio of 1 or less, for they have minimal amounts of both inventory and accounts receivable.

The viewpoints of owners, creditors, and managers toward the acid-test ratio parallel those held toward the current ratio. That is, owners of hospitality operations prefer a low ratio (generally less than 1), creditors prefer a high ratio, and management is again caught in the middle.

Operating Cash Flows to Current Liabilities Ratio

A fairly new ratio made possible by the statement of cash flows is **operating cash flows to current liabilities.** The operating cash flows are taken from the statement of cash flows, while current liabilities come from the balance sheet. This measure of liquidity compares the cash flow from the firm's operating activities to its obligations at the balance sheet date that must be paid within twelve months. Using the relevant figures from Exhibits 1 and 3, the 19X2 operating cash flows to current liabilities ratio is computed as follows:

$$\text{Operating Cash Flows to} \atop \text{Current Liabilities Ratio} \quad = \quad \frac{\text{Operating Cash Flows}}{\text{Average Current Liabilities}}$$

$$= \quad \frac{\$179,200}{.5(\$192,200 + \$214,000)}$$

$$= \quad .882 \text{ or } \underline{\underline{88.2\%}}$$

The 19X2 ratio of 88.2% shows that only $.882 of cash flow from operations was provided by the Grand Hotel during 19X2 for each $1.00 of current debt at the end of 19X2. The prior year's ratio was 118%. This dramatic change should cause management to consider reasons for the change and be prepared to take appropriate action.

All users of ratios would prefer to see a high operating cash flow to current liabilities, as this suggests operations are providing sufficient cash to pay the firm's current liabilities.

Accounts Receivable Turnover

In hospitality operations that extend credit to guests, accounts receivable is generally the largest current asset. Therefore, in an examination of a property's liquidity, the "quality" of its accounts receivable must be considered.

In the normal operating cycle, accounts receivable are converted to cash. The **accounts receivable turnover** measures the speed of the conversion. The faster the accounts receivable are turned over, the more credibility the current and acid-test ratios have in financial analysis.

This ratio is determined by dividing revenue by average accounts receivable. A refinement of this ratio uses only charge sales in the numerator; however, quite often charge sales figures are unavailable to outsiders (stockholders, potential stockholders, and creditors). Regardless of whether revenues or charge sales are used as the numerator, the calculation should be consistent from period to period. Average accounts receivable is the result of dividing the sum of the beginning-of-the-period and end-of-the-period accounts receivable by two. When a hospitality operation has seasonal sales fluctuations, a preferred approach (when computing the *annual* accounts receivable turnover) is to sum the accounts receivable at the end of each month and divide by 12 to determine the average accounts receivable.

Exhibit 5 uses relevant figures from Exhibits 1 and 2 to calculate the accounts receivable turnover for 19X2 of the Grand Hotel. The accounts receivable turnover of 11.76 indicates that the total revenue for 19X2 is 11.76 times the average receivables. This is lower than the 19X1 accounts receivable turnover of the Grand Hotel of 13.68. Management would generally investigate this difference. The investigation may reveal problems or that changes in the credit policy and/or collection procedures significantly contributed to the difference.

Although the accounts receivable turnover measures the overall rapidity of collections, it fails to address individual accounts. This matter is resolved by preparing an aging of accounts receivable schedule which reflects the status of each account. In an aging schedule, each account is broken down to the period when the

Exhibit 5   Accounts Receivable Turnover

$$\text{Accounts Receivable Turnover} = \frac{\text{Total Revenue}}{\text{Average Accounts Receivable*}}$$

$$= \frac{\$1,352,000}{\$115,000}$$

$$= \underline{\underline{11.76 \text{ times}}}$$

$$\text{*Average Accounts Receivable} = \frac{\text{Accounts Receivable at Beginning and End of Year}}{2}$$

$$= \frac{\$90,000 + \$140,000}{2}$$

$$= \underline{\underline{\$115,000}}$$

charges originated. Like credit sales, this information is generally available only to management. Exhibit 6 illustrates an aging of accounts receivable schedule.

Since few hospitality establishments charge interest on their accounts receivable, the opportunity cost of credit sales is the investment dollars that could be generated by investing cash. However, credit terms are extended with the purpose of increasing sales. Therefore, theoretically, credit should be extended to the point where the bad debt and additional collection costs of extending credit to one more guest equal the additional profit earned by extending credit to one more guest.

Owners prefer a high accounts receivable turnover as this reflects a lower investment in nonproductive accounts receivable. However, they understand how a tight credit policy and an overly aggressive collections effort may result in lower sales. Nonetheless, everything else being the same, a high accounts receivable turnover indicates that accounts receivable are being managed well. Suppliers, like owners, prefer a high accounts receivable turnover, because this means that hospitality establishments will have more cash readily available to pay them. Long-term creditors also see a high accounts receivable turnover as a positive reflection of management.

Management desires to maximize the sales of the hospitality operation. Offering credit helps maximize sales. However, management also realizes that offering credit to maximize sales may result in more accounts receivable and in selling to some less creditworthy customers. One result of management's decision to offer credit is a lower accounts receivable turnover. On the other hand, while management may see a lower accounts receivable turnover as a consequence of higher sales, it does not lose sight of the fact that it also must maintain the operation's cash flow—that is, it must effectively collect on the credit sales.

Exhibit 6   Aging of Accounts Receivable Schedule

Aging of Accounts Receivable Schedule
Grand Hotel
December 31, 19X2

Firm Name	Total	0–30	31–60	61–90	91–120	Over 120 days
Ace Co.	$600	$400	$200	$–0–	$–0–	$–0–
Acem Corp.	400	100	–0–	300	–0–	–0–
Ahern, Jim	100	100	–0–	–0–	–0–	–0–
America, Inc.	1,000	950	–0–	–0–	–0–	50
Armadillo Co.	50	–0–	–0–	–0–	50	–0–
.						
.						
.						
Zebra Zoo Equip.	80	80	–0–	–0–	–0–	–0–
Total	**$145,000**	**$115,000**	**$18,000**	**$7,000**	**$4,000**	**$1,000**

Average Collection Period

A variation of the accounts receivable turnover is the **average collection period,** which is calculated by dividing the accounts receivable turnover into 365 (the number of days in a year). This conversion simply translates the turnover into a more understandable result. For the Grand Hotel, the average collection period for 19X2 is as follows:

$$\text{Average Collection Period} = \frac{365}{\text{Accounts Receivable Turnover}}$$

$$= \frac{365}{11.76}$$

$$= \underline{\underline{31}} \text{ days}$$

The average collection period of 31 days means that on an average of every 31 days throughout 19X2, the Grand Hotel was collecting all its accounts receivable. The 31 days is a four-day increase over the 19X1 average collection period of 27 days.

What should be the average collection period? Generally, the time allowed for average payments should not exceed the terms of sale by more than 7 to 10 days. Therefore, if the terms of sale are $n/30$ (entire amount is due in 30 days), the maximum allowable average collection period is 37 to 40 days.

The above discussion assumes that all sales are credit sales. However, many hospitality operations have both cash and credit sales. Therefore, the mix of cash and credit sales must be considered when the accounts receivable turnover ratio uses

Exhibit 7   Working Capital Turnover

$$\text{Working Capital Turnover} = \frac{\text{Revenue}}{\text{Average Working Capital}}$$

$$= \frac{\$1,352,000}{\$76,400^*}$$

$$= \underline{17.70} \text{ times}$$

	Working Capital (WC)	=	Current Assets − Current Liabilities
WC (19X2)	$124,000	=	$338,000 − $214,000
WC (19X1)	28,800	=	221,000 − 192,200

*Average Working Capital = $124,000 + $28,800 divided by 2 = $76,400

revenue, rather than credit sales, in the numerator. This is accomplished by allowing for cash sales. For example, if sales are 50% cash and 50% credit, then the maximum allowable average collection period should be adjusted. An adjusted maximum allowable average collection period is calculated by multiplying the maximum allowable average collection period by credit sales as a percentage of total sales.

In the previous example of a maximum allowable collection period of 37 to 40 days and 50% credit sales, the adjusted maximum allowable average collection period is 18.5 to 20 days (37 to 40 days × .5). Generally, only management can make this adjustment, because the mix of sales is unknown by other interested parties.

The average collection period preferred by owners, creditors, and management is similar to their preferences for the accounts receivable turnover, because the average collection period is only a variation of the accounts receivable turnover. Therefore, owners and creditors prefer a lower number of days, while management prefers a higher number of days (as long as cash flow is sufficient).

Working Capital Turnover Ratio

The final liquidity ratio presented here is the **working capital turnover ratio,** which compares working capital (current assets less current liabilities) to revenue. For most businesses, the higher the revenue, the greater the amount of working capital required. Thus, as the revenue rises, working capital is expected to rise also. Exhibit 7 uses relevant figures from Exhibits 1 and 2 to calculate the working capital turnover ratio in 19X2 for the Grand Hotel.

For the Grand Hotel, a working capital turnover of 17.70 means that working capital of $76,400 was "used" 17.70 times during the year. Everything else being the same, the lower the current ratio, the greater the working capital turnover ratio. Therefore, those establishments in segments of the hospitality industry with virtually no credit sales and a low level of inventory will generally have an extremely high working capital ratio.

Owners prefer this ratio to be high, as they prefer a low current ratio, thus low working capital. Creditors prefer a lower working capital turnover ratio than owners, because they prefer a relatively high current ratio. Management's preferences fall between owners and creditors. Management desires to maintain an adequate amount of working capital to cover unexpected problems, yet management also desires to maximize profits by using available funds to make long-term investments.

Solvency Ratios

Solvency ratios measure the degree of debt financing by a hospitality enterprise and are partial indicators of the establishment's ability to meet its long-term debt obligations. These ratios reveal the equity cushion that is available to absorb any operating losses. Primary users of these ratios are outsiders, especially lenders, who generally prefer less risk rather than more risk. High solvency ratios generally suggest that an operation has the ability to weather financial storms.

Owners like to use debt instead of additional equity to increase their return on equity already invested. This process is commonly referred to as **financial leverage.** Financial leverage is used when the return on the investment exceeds the cost of the debt used to finance an investment. When using debt to increase their leverage, owners are, in essence, transferring part of their risk to creditors.

As a further explanation of the concept of leverage, let us consider the following example. Assume that total assets of a lodging facility are $100 and earnings before interest and taxes (EBIT) are $50, and interest is 15% of debt. Further assume that two possible combinations of debt and equity are $80 of debt and $20 of equity, and the reverse ($80 of equity and $20 of debt). Further assume a tax rate of 40%. The return on equity for each of the two combinations is calculated in Exhibit 8.

The calculations in Exhibit 8 reveal that each $1 invested by stockholders in the high debt/low equity combination earns $1.14, while every $1 invested by stockholders in the low debt/high equity combination earns only $.35.

This class of ratios includes two groups—those based on balance sheet information and those based on income statement information. The first three ratios to be examined (the solvency ratio, the debt-equity ratio, and long-term debt to total capitalization) are based on balance sheet information. The following two ratios, the number of times interest earned ratio and the fixed charge coverage ratio, are based on information from the income statement. The final ratio relates operating cash flows to total liabilities.

Solvency Ratio

A hospitality enterprise is solvent when its assets exceed its liabilities. Therefore, the **solvency ratio** is simply total assets divided by total liabilities. The solvency ratio in 19X2 for the Grand Hotel is determined as follows:

$$\text{Solvency Ratio} = \frac{\text{Total Assets}}{\text{Total Liabilities}}$$

$$= \frac{\$1,176,300}{\$659,000}$$

$$= \underline{1.78} \text{ times}$$

Exhibit 8   Return on Equity

	High Debt/ Low Equity	High Equity/ Low Debt
Debt	$ 80	$ 20
Equity	$ 20	$ 80
EBIT	$ 50	$ 50
Interest (15%)	12*	3**
Income before taxes	38	47
Income taxes	− 15.20	− 18.80
	$ 22.80	$ 28.20

Return per $1 of equity:

$$\frac{\text{Net income}}{\text{equity}} = \frac{\$22.80}{\$20} = \$1.14 \qquad \frac{\$28.20}{\$80} = \$.35$$

*Debt times interest rate = interest expense   **$20 × .15 = $ 3
        $80 × .15 = $12

Thus, at the end of 19X2, the Grand Hotel has $1.78 of assets for each $1.00 of liabilities or a cushion of $.78. The Grand Hotel's assets could be discounted substantially ($.78 ÷ $1.78 = 43.8%) and creditors could still be fully paid. The Grand Hotel's solvency ratio at the end of 19X1 was 1.65 times. The 19X2 ratio would be considered more favorable from the perspective of creditors.

The greater the leverage (use of debt to finance the assets) used by the hospitality establishment, the lower its solvency ratio. Owners prefer to use leverage in order to maximize their return on their investments. This occurs as long as the earnings from the creditor-financed investment exceed the cost of the establishment's borrowing. Creditors, on the other hand, prefer a high solvency ratio, as it provides a greater cushion should the establishment experience losses in operations. Managers must satisfy both owners and creditors. Thus, they desire to finance assets so as to maximize the return on owners' investments, while not unduly jeopardizing the establishment's ability to pay creditors.

Debt-Equity Ratio

The **debt-equity ratio,** one of the commonest solvency ratios, compares the hospitality establishment's debt to its net worth (owners' equity). This ratio indicates the establishment's ability to withstand adversity and meet its long-term debt obligations. Figures from Exhibit 1 can be used to calculate the Grand Hotel's debt-equity ratio for 19X2:

$$\text{Debt-Equity Ratio} \quad = \quad \frac{\text{Total Liabilities}}{\text{Total Owners' Equity}}$$

$$= \quad \frac{\$659,000}{\$517,300}$$

$$= \quad \underline{\underline{1.27 \text{ to } 1}}$$

The Grand Hotel's debt-equity ratio of 1.27 to 1 at the end of 19X2 indicates for each $1 of owners' net worth, the Grand Hotel owed creditors $1.27. The debt-equity ratio for 19X1 for the Grand Hotel was 1.54 to 1. Thus, relative to its net worth, the Grand Hotel reduced its 19X1 debt.

Owners view this ratio similarly to the way they view the solvency ratio. That is, they desire to maximize their return on investment by using leverage. The greater the leverage, the higher the debt-equity ratio. Creditors generally would favor a lower debt-equity ratio because their risk is reduced as net worth increases relative to debt. Management, as with the solvency ratio, prefers a middle position between creditors and owners.

Long-Term Debt to Total Capitalization Ratio

Still another solvency ratio is the calculation of long-term debt as a percentage of the sum of long-term debt and owners' equity, commonly called total capitalization. This ratio is similar to the debt-equity ratio except that current liabilities are excluded in the numerator, and long-term debt is added to the denominator of the debt-equity ratio. Current liabilities are excluded because current assets are normally adequate to cover them, therefore, they are not a long-term concern. Figures from Exhibit 1 can be used to calculate the 19X2 **long-term debt to total capitalization ratio** for the Grand Hotel:

$$\text{Long-Term Debt to Total Capitalization Ratio} \quad = \quad \frac{\text{Long-Term Debt}}{\text{Long-Term Debt and Owners' Equity}}$$

$$= \quad \frac{\$445,000}{\$962,300}$$

$$= \quad \underline{\underline{46.24\%}}$$

Long-term debt of the Grand Hotel at the end of 19X2 is 46.24% of its total capitalization. This can be compared to 51.88% at the end of 19X1. Creditors would prefer the lower percentage because it would indicate a reduced risk on their part. Owners, on the other hand, would prefer the higher percentage because of their desire for high returns through the use of leverage.

Number of Times Interest Earned Ratio

The **number of times interest earned ratio** is based on financial figures from the income statement and expresses the number of times interest expense can be covered.

The greater the number of times interest is earned, the greater the safety afforded the creditors. Since interest is subtracted to determine taxable income, income taxes are added to net income and interest expense (earnings before interest and taxes, abbreviated as EBIT) to form the numerator of the ratio, while interest expense is the denominator. Figures from Exhibit 2 can be used to calculate the 19X2 number of times interest earned ratio for the Grand Hotel:

$$\text{Number of Times Interest Earned Ratio} = \frac{\text{EBIT}}{\text{Interest Expense}}$$

$$= \frac{\$304,500}{\$60,000}$$

$$= \underline{\underline{5.08 \text{ times}}}$$

The result of 5.08 times shows that the Grand Hotel could cover its interest expense by over five times. The number of times interest earned ratio in 19X1 for the Grand Hotel was 5.36 times. This two-year trend suggests a slightly riskier position from a creditor's viewpoint. However, in general, a number of times interest earned ratio of greater than 4 reflects a sufficient amount of earnings for a hospitality enterprise to cover the interest expense of its existing debt.

All parties (owners, creditors, and management) prefer a relatively high ratio. Owners are generally less concerned about this ratio than creditors, as long as interest obligations are paid on a timely basis and leverage is working to their advantage. Creditors and especially lenders also prefer a relatively high ratio, because this indicates that the establishment is able to meet its interest payments. To the lender, the higher this ratio, the better. Management also prefers a high ratio. However, since an extremely high ratio suggests leverage is probably not being optimized for the owners, management may prefer a lower ratio than do lenders.

The number of times interest earned ratio fails to consider fixed obligations other than interest expense. Many hospitality firms have long-term leases which require periodic payments similar to interest. This limitation of the number of times interest earned ratio is overcome by the fixed charge coverage ratio.

Fixed Charge Coverage Ratio

The **fixed charge coverage ratio** is a variation of the number of times interest earned ratio that considers leases as well as interest expense. Hospitality establishments that have obtained the use of property and equipment through leases may find the fixed charge coverage ratio to be more useful than the number of times interest earned ratio. This ratio is calculated the same as the number of times interest earned ratio, except that lease expense (rent expense) is added to both the numerator and denominator of the equation.

Exhibit 9 uses figures from Exhibit 2 to calculate the 19X2 fixed charge coverage ratio for the Grand Hotel. The result indicates that earnings prior to lease expense, interest expense, and income taxes cover lease and interest expense 4.06 times. The Grand Hotel's fixed charge coverage ratio for 19X1 was 4.18 times. The change of 0.12 times reflects a minor decrease in the Grand Hotel's ability to cover its fixed costs of

Exhibit 9   Fixed Charge Coverage Ratio

$$\text{Fixed Charge Coverage Ratio} = \frac{\text{EBIT} + \text{Lease Expense}}{\text{Interest Expense and Lease Expense}}$$

$$= \frac{\$304,500 + \$20,000}{\$60,000 + \$20,000}$$

$$= \frac{\$324,500}{\$80,000}$$

$$= \underline{4.06} \text{ times}$$

interest and lease expense. The viewpoints of owners, creditors, and management are similar to the views they hold regarding changes in the number of times interest earned ratio.

Operating Cash Flows to Total Liabilities Ratio

The final solvency ratio presented in this chapter uses figures from both the statement of cash flows and the balance sheet by comparing operating cash flows to average total liabilities. Both the debt-equity and long-term debt to total capitalization ratios are based on static numbers from the balance sheet. This ratio overcomes the deficiency of using debt at a point in time by considering cash flow for a period of time.

Figures from Exhibits 1 and 3 are used to calculate the 19X2 **operating cash flows to total liabilities ratio** for the Grand Hotel as follows:

$$\text{Operating Cash Flow to Total Liabilities Ratio} = \frac{\text{Operating Cash Flows}}{\text{Average Total Liabilities}}$$

$$= \frac{\$179,200}{.5(\$645,000 + \$659,000)}$$

$$= .275 \text{ or } \underline{27.5\%}$$

The 19X1 operating cash flows to total liabilities ratio is 34.4%; thus, the Grand Hotel's ability to meet its long-term obligations with operating cash flows has deteriorated from 19X1 to 19X2.

All users of financial information prefer this ratio to be relatively high; that is, the cash flow from operations should be high relative to total liabilities, given that the amount of debt used is optimal.

Exhibit 10   Condensed Food and Beverage Department Statement

Condensed Food and Beverage Department Statement
Grand Hotel
For the year 19X2

	Food	Beverage
Sales	$ 300,000	$ 145,000
Cost of sales:		
Beginning inventory	11,000	6,000
Purchases	120,000	28,000
Less: Ending inventory	9,000	6,000
Cost of goods used	122,000	28,000
Less: Employee meals	2,000	0
Cost of goods sold	120,000	28,000
Gross Profit	180,000	117,000
Expenses:		
Payroll and related expenses	135,000	45,000
Other expenses	30,000	15,000
Total expenses	165,000	60,000
Departmental income	$ 15,000	$ 57,000

Activity Ratios

Activity ratios measure management's effectiveness in using its resources. Management is entrusted with inventory and fixed assets (and other resources) to generate earnings for owners while providing products and services to guests. Since the fixed assets of most lodging facilities constitute a large percentage of the operation's total assets, it is essential to use these resources effectively. Although inventory is generally not a significant portion of total assets, management must adequately control it in order to minimize the cost of sales.

Inventory Turnover

The **inventory turnover** shows how quickly the inventory is being used. All things being the same, generally, the quicker the inventory turnover the better, because inventory can be expensive to maintain. Maintenance costs include storage space, freezers, insurance, personnel expense, recordkeeping, and, of course, the opportunity cost of the funds tied up in inventory. Inventories held by hospitality operations are highly susceptible to theft and must be carefully controlled.

Inventory turnovers should generally be calculated separately for food supplies and for beverages. Some food service operations will calculate several beverage turnovers based on the types of beverages available.

Exhibit 10 is a condensed food and beverage department statement of the Grand Hotel with food and beverage operations for 19X2 shown separately. Figures from this statement will be used to illustrate the food and beverage turnover ratios.

Exhibit 11   Food Inventory Turnover

$$\text{Food Inventory Turnover} = \frac{\text{Cost of Food Used}}{\text{Average Food Inventory*}}$$

$$= \frac{\$122,000}{\$10,000}$$

$$= \underline{\underline{12.2 \text{ times}}}$$

$$\text{*Average Food Inventory} = \frac{\text{Beginning and Ending Inventories}}{2}$$

$$= \frac{\$11,000 + \$9,000}{2}$$

$$= \underline{\underline{\$10,000}}$$

Exhibit 11 calculates the 19X2 food inventory turnover for the Grand Hotel. The food inventory turned over 12.2 times during 19X2, or approximately once per month. The speed of food inventory turnover generally depends on the type of food service operation. A quick-service restaurant generally experiences a much faster food turnover than does a fine dining establishment. In fact, a quick-service restaurant may have a food inventory turnover in excess of 200 times for a year. A norm used in the hotel industry for hotels that have several different types of restaurants and banquets calls for food inventory to turn over four times per month.

Although a high food inventory turnover is desired because it means that the food service establishment is able to operate with a relatively small investment in inventory, too high a turnover may indicate possible stockout problems. Failure to provide desired food items to guests may not only immediately result in disappointed guests, but may also result in negative goodwill if this problem persists. Too low an inventory turnover suggests that food is overstocked, and, in addition to the costs to maintain inventory previously mentioned, the cost of spoilage may become a problem.

Exhibit 12 uses figures from Exhibit 10 to calculate the 19X2 beverage turnover for the Grand Hotel. The beverage turnover of 4.67 means that the beverage inventory of $6,000 required restocking approximately every 78 days. This is calculated by dividing 365 days in the year by the beverage turnover of 4.67. Not all beverage items are sold evenly; thus, some items would have to be restocked more frequently. A norm used in the hotel industry for hotels having several different types of lounges and banquets calls for beverage inventory to turn over 1.25 times per month or 15 times per year.

Exhibit 12   Beverage Turnover

$$\text{Beverage Turnover} = \frac{\text{Cost of Beverage Used}}{\text{Average Beverage Inventory*}}$$

$$= \frac{\$28,000}{\$6,000}$$

$$= \underline{4.67 \text{ times}}$$

$$\text{*Average Beverage Inventory} = \frac{\text{Beginning and Ending Inventories}}{2}$$

$$= \frac{\$6,000 + \$6,000}{2}$$

$$= \underline{\$6,000}$$

All parties (owners, creditors, and management) prefer high inventory turnovers to low ones, as long as stockouts are avoided. Ideally, as the last inventory item is sold, the shelves are being restocked.

Property and Equipment Turnover

The **property and equipment turnover** (sometimes called the fixed asset turnover) is determined by dividing average total property and equipment into total revenue for the period. A more precise measurement would be to use only revenues related to property and equipment usage in the numerator. However, revenue by source is not available to many financial analysts, so total revenue is generally used.

This ratio measures management's effectiveness in using property and equipment. A high turnover suggests the hospitality enterprise is using its property and equipment effectively to generate revenues, while a low turnover suggests the establishment is not making effective use of its property and equipment and should consider disposing of part of them.

A limitation of this ratio is that it places a premium on using older (depreciated) property and equipment, since their book value is low. Further, this ratio is affected by the depreciation method employed by the hospitality operation. For example, an operation using an accelerated method of depreciation will show a higher turnover than an operation using the straight-line depreciation method, all other factors being the same.

Exhibit 13 uses figures from Exhibits 1 and 2 to calculate the 19X2 property and equipment turnover ratio for the Grand Hotel. The turnover of 1.68 reveals that revenue was 1.68 times the average total property and equipment. For 19X1, the Grand

Exhibit 13   Property and Equipment Turnover

$$\text{Property and Equipment Turnover} = \frac{\text{Total Revenue}}{\text{Average Property and Equipment*}}$$

$$= \frac{\$1,352,000}{\$803,650}$$

$$= \underline{1.68 \text{ times}}$$

$$\text{*Average Property and Equipment} = \frac{\text{Total Property and Equipment at Beginning and End of Year}}{2}$$

$$= \frac{\$809,000 + \$798,300}{2}$$

$$= \underline{\$803,650}$$

Hotel's property and equipment turnover was 1.62 times. The change of .06 times, although minor, is viewed as a positive trend.

All parties (owners, creditors, and management) prefer a high property and equipment turnover. Management, however, should resist retaining old and possibly inefficient property and equipment, even though they result in a high property and equipment turnover. The return on assets ratio (discussed under profitability ratios) is a partial check against this practice.

Asset Turnover

Another ratio to measure the efficiency of management's use of assets is the **asset turnover**. It is calculated by dividing total revenue by average total assets. The two previous ratios presented, inventory turnover and property and equipment turnover, concern a large percentage of the total assets. The asset turnover examines the use of total assets in relation to total revenue. Limitations of the property and equipment ratio are also inherent in this ratio to the extent that property and equipment make up total assets. For most hospitality establishments, especially lodging businesses, property and equipment constitute the majority of the operation's total assets.

Exhibit 14 uses figures from Exhibits 1 and 2 to calculate the 19X2 asset turnover ratio for the Grand Hotel. The asset turnover of 1.21 indicates that each $1 of assets generated $1.21 of revenue in 19X2. The asset turnover ratio for 19X1 was 1.23. Thus, there was virtually no change for the two years.

As with the property and equipment turnover, all concerned parties (owners, creditors, and management) prefer this ratio to be high, because a high ratio means effective use of assets by management, subject to the limitations of using old (depreciated) assets as discussed previously.

Exhibit 14   Asset Turnover

$$\text{Asset Turnover Ratio} = \frac{\text{Total Revenues}}{\text{Average Total Assets*}}$$

$$= \frac{\$1,352,000}{\$1,120,650}$$

$$= \underline{\underline{1.21 \text{ times}}}$$

$$\text{*Average Total Assets} = \frac{\text{Total Assets at Beginning and End of Year}}{2}$$

$$= \frac{\$1,065,000 + \$1,176,300}{2}$$

$$= \underline{\underline{\$1,120,650}}$$

Both the property and equipment turnover and the asset turnover ratios are relatively low for most hospitality segments, especially for hotels and motels. The relatively low ratios are due to the hospitality industry's high dependence on fixed assets and its inability to quickly increase output to meet maximum demand. It is common for many hotels and motels to turn away guests four nights a week due to excessive demand, and operate at an extremely low level of output (less than 50%) the three remaining nights.

Four additional measures of management's ability to efficiently use available assets are paid occupancy percentage, complimentary occupancy, average occupancy per room, and multiple occupancy percentage. Although these ratios are not based on financial information, they are viewed as excellent measures of management's effectiveness in selling space, whether it be rooms in a lodging facility or seats in a food service establishment.

Paid Occupancy Percentage

Paid occupancy is a major indicator of management's success in selling its "product." It refers to the percentage of rooms sold in relation to rooms available for sale in hotels and motels. In food service operations, it is commonly referred to as seat turnover, and is calculated by dividing the number of people served by the number of seats available. Seat turnover is commonly calculated by meal period. In most food service facilities, different seat turnovers are experienced for different dining periods. The occupancy percentage for lodging facilities and the seat turnovers for food service facilities are key measures of facility utilization.

Using the "Other Information" listed in Exhibit 4, the annual paid occupancy of the Grand Hotel can be determined by dividing total paid rooms occupied by

Exhibit 15   Paid Occupancy Percentage

$$\text{Paid Occupancy} = \frac{\text{Paid Rooms Occupied}}{\text{Available Rooms*}}$$

$$= \frac{21,000}{29,200}$$

$$= \underline{71.92\%}$$

$$\text{*Available Rooms} = \text{Rooms Available per Day} \times \text{365 Days}$$

$$= 80 \times 365$$

$$= \underline{\underline{29,200}}$$

available rooms for sale. If the Grand Hotel had 80 rooms available for sale each day, its paid occupancy percentage for 19X2 is calculated as indicated in Exhibit 15.

The Grand Hotel's 19X2 annual paid occupancy percentage of 71.92% was an improvement over the 19X1 annual occupancy percentage of 70.21%, when 20,500 rooms were sold. This percentage does not mean that every day 70.21% of the available rooms were sold, but rather that on the average 70.21% were sold. For example, a hotel experiencing 100% paid occupancy Monday through Thursday and 33% paid occupancy Friday through Sunday would end up with a combined result of 71.29%.

There are many factors affecting paid occupancy rates in the lodging industry, such as location within an area, geographic location, seasonal factors (both weekly and yearly), rate structure, and type of lodging facility, to mention a few.

Complimentary Occupancy

Complimentary occupancy, as stated in the *Uniform System of Accounts for the Lodging Industry,* is determined by dividing the number of complimentary rooms for a period by the number of rooms available. Using figures from the "Other Information" section of Exhibit 4, the 19X2 complimentary occupancy for the Grand Hotel is calculated as follows:

$$\text{Complimentary Occupancy} = \frac{\text{Complimentary Rooms}}{\text{Rooms Available}}$$

$$= \frac{160}{29,200}$$

$$= \underline{.55\%}$$

Average Occupancy per Room

Another ratio to measure management's ability to use the lodging facilities is the **average occupancy per room**. This ratio is the result of dividing the number of guests by the number of rooms occupied. Generally, as the average occupancy per room increases, the room rate also increases.

Using figures from the "Other Information" section of Exhibit 4, the 19X2 average occupancy per room for the Grand Hotel can be calculated as follows:

$$\text{Average Occupancy per Room} = \frac{\text{Number of Guests}}{\text{Number of Rooms Occupied by Guests}}$$

$$= \frac{24,160}{21,160}$$

$$= \underline{\underline{1.14}} \text{ Guests}$$

The Grand Hotel's 19X2 average occupancy per room was 1.14 guests. The 19X1 average occupancy per room was slightly higher at 1.15 guests.

The average occupancy per room is generally the highest for resort properties, where it can reach levels in excess of two guests per room, and is lowest for transient lodging facilities.

Multiple Occupancy

Another ratio used to measure multiple occupancy of rooms is **multiple occupancy,** sometimes less accurately called **double occupancy.** This ratio is similar to the average occupancy per room. It is determined by dividing the number of rooms occupied by more than one guest by the number of rooms occupied by guests.

Using figures from the "Other Information" section of Exhibit 4, the multiple occupancy of the Grand Hotel for 19X2 can be calculated as follows:

$$\text{Multiple Occupancy} = \frac{\text{Rooms Occupied by Two or More People}}{\text{Rooms Occupied by Guests}}$$

$$= \frac{2,500}{21,160}$$

$$= \underline{\underline{11.81\%}}$$

The multiple occupancy for the Grand Hotel during 19X2 indicates 11.81% of the rooms sold were occupied by more than one guest. The 19X1 multiple occupancy for the Grand Hotel was 11.62%; therefore, a minor increase in multiple occupancy has occurred.

Owners, creditors, and management all prefer high occupancy ratios—paid occupancy percentage, average occupancy per room, and multiple occupancy. The higher the occupancy ratios, the greater the use of the facilities. These ratios are considered to be prime indicators of a lodging facility's level of operations. Occupancy ratios are generally computed on a daily basis and are recorded on the daily report of operations.

Profitability Ratios

Profitability ratios reflect the results of all areas of management's responsibilities. All the information conveyed by liquidity, solvency, and activity ratios affect the profitability of the hospitality enterprise. The primary purpose of most hospitality operations is the generation of profit. Owners invest for the purpose of increasing their wealth through dividends and through increases in the price of capital stock. Both dividends and stock price are highly dependent upon the profits generated by the operation. Creditors, especially lenders, provide resources for hospitality enterprises to use in the provision of services. Generally, future profits are required to repay these lenders. Managers are also extremely interested in profits because their performance is, to a large degree, measured by the operation's bottom line. Excellent services breed goodwill, repeat customers, and other benefits which ultimately increase the operation's profitability.

The profitability ratios we are about to consider measure management's overall effectiveness as shown by returns on sales (profit margin and operating efficiency ratio), returns on assets (return on assets and net return on assets), return on owners' equity (return on owners' equity and return on common stockholders' equity), and the relationship between net income and the market price of the hospitality establishment's stock (price earnings ratio).

Profit Margin

Hospitality enterprises are often evaluated in terms of their ability to generate profits on sales. **Profit margin**, a key ratio, is determined by dividing net income by total revenue. It is an overall measurement of management's ability to generate sales and control expenses, thus yielding the bottom line. In this ratio, net income is the income remaining after all expenses have been deducted, both those controllable by management and those directly related to decisions made by the board of directors.

Using figures from Exhibit 2, the 19X2 profit margin of the Grand Hotel can be determined as follows:

$$\text{Profit Margin} \quad = \quad \frac{\text{Net Income}}{\text{Total Revenue}}$$

$$= \quad \frac{\$146,700}{\$1,352,000}$$

$$= \quad \underline{10.85}$$

The Grand Hotel's 19X2 profit margin of 10.85% has remained nearly constant from the 19X1 figure of 10.87%. The 10.85% is very good compared with a pretax income industry average of approximately 9.6% for full service properties.[2]

If the profit margin is lower than expected, then expenses and other areas should be reviewed. Poor pricing and low sales volume could be contributing to the low ratio. To identify the problem area, management should analyze both the overall profit margin and the operated departmental margins. If the operated departmental margins are satisfactory, the problem would appear to be with overhead expense.

Operating Efficiency Ratio

The **operating efficiency ratio** (also known as **gross operating profit ratio**) is a better measure of management's performance than the profit margin. This ratio is the result of dividing income after undistributed operating expenses by total revenue. Income after undistributed operating expenses is the result of subtracting expenses generally controllable by management from revenues. Nonoperating expenses include management fees and fixed charges. These expenses are directly related to decisions made by the board of directors, not management. Fixed charges are expenses relating to the capacity of the hospitality firm, including rent, property taxes, insurance, depreciation, and interest expense. Although these expenses are the result of board of directors' decisions and thus beyond the direct control of active management, management can and should review tax assessments and insurance policies and quotations, and make recommendations to the board of directors that can affect the facility's total profitability. In calculating the operating efficiency ratio, income taxes are also excluded, since fixed charges directly affect income taxes.

Using figures from Exhibit 2, the 19X2 operating efficiency ratio of the Grand Hotel can be calculated as follows:

$$\text{Operating Efficiency Ratio} = \frac{\text{Income After Undistributed Operating Expenses}}{\text{Total Revenue}}$$

$$= \frac{\$415,500}{\$1,352,000}$$

$$= \underline{\underline{30.73\%}}$$

The operating efficiency ratio shows that nearly $.31 of each $1 of revenue is available for fixed charges, income taxes, and profits. The Grand Hotel's operating efficiency ratio was 30.39% for 19X1.

The next group of profitability ratios compares profits to either assets or owners' equity. The result in each case is a percentage and is commonly called a return.

Return on Assets

The **return on assets (ROA)** ratio is a general indicator of the profitability of the hospitality enterprise's assets. Unlike the two preceding profitability ratios drawn only from income statement data, this ratio compares bottom line profits to the total investment, that is, to the total assets. It is calculated by dividing net income by average total assets. This ratio, or a variation of it, is used by several large conglomerates to measure the performances of their subsidiary corporations operating in the hospitality industry.

Exhibit 16   Return on Assets

$$\text{Return on Assets (ROA)} = \frac{\text{Net Income}}{\text{Average Total Assets*}}$$

$$= \frac{\$146,700}{\$1,120,650}$$

$$= \underline{13.09\%}$$

$$\text{*Average Total Assets} = \frac{\text{Total Assets at Beginning and End of Year}}{2}$$

$$= \frac{\$1,065,000 + \$1,176,300}{2}$$

$$= \underline{\$1,120,650}$$

Using figures from Exhibits 1 and 2, the Grand Hotel's 19X2 return on assets is calculated in Exhibit 16. The Grand Hotel's 19X2 ROA is 13.09%, which means there was 13.09 cents of profit for every dollar of average total assets. The 19X1 ROA was 13.36%. Therefore, there was a slight decline in ROA from 19X1 to 19X2.

A very low ROA may result from inadequate profits or excessive assets. A very high ROA may suggest that older assets require replacement in the near future or that additional assets need to be added to support growth in revenues. The determination of low and high is usually based on industry averages and the hospitality establishment's own ROA profile that is developed over time.

ROA may also be calculated by multiplying the profit margin ratio by the asset turnover ratio:

Profit Margin	×	Asset Turnover	=	ROA
$\dfrac{\text{Net Income}}{\text{Total Revenue}}$	×	$\dfrac{\text{Total Revenue}}{\text{Average Total Assets}}$	=	$\dfrac{\text{Net Income}}{\text{Average Total Assets}}$

Gross Return on Assets

Calculating the **gross return on assets (GROA)** is a variation of the ROA. This ratio measures the rate of return on assets regardless of financing methods. The calculation of ROA uses net income as its numerator and, therefore, includes the cost of debt financing of the assets. The computation of the GROA, on the other hand, ignores any debt financing by using income before interest and income taxes (EBIT) as its numerator. Interest is excluded because it is a financing cost. Income taxes are not considered because interest expense is deductible in calculating the operation's tax liability.

Exhibit 17   Return on Owners' Equity

$$
\begin{array}{rcl}
\text{Return on Owners' Equity} & = & \dfrac{\text{Net Income}}{\text{Average Owners' Equity*}} \\[2mm]
\text{(ROE)} & & \\[4mm]
& = & \dfrac{\$146,700}{\$468,650} \\[4mm]
& = & \underline{31.30\%}
\end{array}
$$

$$
\begin{array}{rcl}
\text{*Average Owners' Equity} & = & \dfrac{\text{Owners' Equity at Beginning and End of Year}}{2} \\[4mm]
& = & \dfrac{\$420,000 + \$517,300}{2} \\[4mm]
& = & \underline{\$468,650}
\end{array}
$$

Using figures from Exhibits 1 and 2, the Grand Hotel's GROA for 19X2 can be calculated as follows:

$$
\begin{array}{rcl}
\text{Gross Return on Assets} & = & \dfrac{\text{EBIT}}{\text{Average Total Assets}} \\[4mm]
& = & \dfrac{\$304,500}{\$1,120,650} \\[4mm]
& = & \underline{27.17\%}
\end{array}
$$

The Grand Hotel's GROA of 27.17% indicates a gross return of 27.17 cents for each dollar of average total assets for 19X2. This is a slight decline from 19X1 when GROA was 27.39%.

Return on Owners' Equity

A key profitability ratio is the **return on owners' equity (ROE)**. The ROE ratio compares the profits of the hospitality enterprise to the owners' investment. It is calculated by dividing net income by average owners' equity. Included in the denominator are all capital stock and retained earnings.

Exhibit 17 uses relevant figures from Exhibits 1 and 2 to calculate the 19X2 ROE for the Grand Hotel. In 19X2, for every one dollar of owners' equity, 31.30 cents was earned. The 19X1 ROE for the Grand Hotel was even higher at 34.46%. To the owner, this ratio represents the end result of all management's efforts. The ROE reflects management's ability to produce for the owners.

An alternative calculation of ROE considers both ROA and average total assets to average owners' equity. For 19X2, the calculation for the Grand Hotel is as follows:

$$\text{ROE} = \text{ROA} \times \frac{\text{Average Total Assets}}{\text{Average Total Owners' Equity}}$$

$$= 13.09\% \times \frac{\$1,120,650}{\$468,650}$$

$$= \underline{\underline{31.30\%}}$$

Thus, the lower the owners' equity relative to total assets (that is, the greater the financial leverage), the greater the ROE.

Return on Common Stockholders' Equity

A few hospitality enterprises have issued preferred stock in addition to common stock. When preferred stock has been issued, a variation of the ROE is the **return on common stockholders' equity**. It is necessary to compute this ratio only when more than one class of stock has been issued. Common stockholders are concerned with what is available to them—net income less preferred dividends paid to preferred stockholders. The ROE ratio is adjusted as follows:

$$\frac{\text{Return on Common}}{\text{Stockholders Equity}} = \frac{\text{Net Income} - \text{Preferred Dividends}}{\text{Average Common Stockholders' Equity}}$$

Since the Grand Hotel has not issued preferred stock, the calculation of this ratio is not further illustrated, because it would be the same as the previously calculated ROE.

The return to common stockholders is enhanced with the issuance of preferred stock when the return on investment from the use of the preferred stockholders' funds exceeds the dividends paid to preferred stockholders. From a common stockholder's viewpoint, any time debt or preferred stock can be issued at a "cost" less than the return from investing these "outside funds," the return to common stockholders is increased.

Earnings per Share

A common profitability ratio shown on hospitality establishments' income statements issued to external users is **earnings per share (EPS)**. The EPS calculation is a function of the capital structure of the hospitality enterprise. If only common stock has been issued (that is, there are no preferred stock or convertible debt or similar dilutive securities), then EPS is determined by dividing net income by the average common shares outstanding. When preferred stock has been issued, preferred dividends are subtracted from net income and the result is divided by the average number of common shares outstanding. If any dilutive securities have been issued, the EPS calculation is much more difficult and is beyond the scope of this chapter.[3]

Using figures from Exhibits 2 and 4, the 19X2 EPS for the Grand Hotel can be calculated as follows:

$$\text{Earnings per Share} \quad = \quad \frac{\text{Net Income}}{\text{Average Common Shares Outstanding}}$$

$$= \quad \frac{\$146,700}{\$55,000}$$

$$= \quad \underline{\$2.67} \text{ per share}$$

In 19X1, the Grand Hotel's EPS was $2.57. Thus, the Grand Hotel's EPS has increased by $.10 from 19X1 to 19X2.

An increase in EPS must be viewed cautiously. The reduction of common stock outstanding by the issuing establishment's purchase of its own stock (treasury stock) will also result in an increased EPS, all other things being equal. Further, EPS is expected to increase as a hospitality enterprise reinvests earnings in its operations because a larger profit can then be generated without a corresponding increase in shares outstanding.

Price Earnings Ratio

Financial analysts often use the **price earnings (PE) ratio** in presenting investment possibilities in hospitality enterprises. The PE ratio is shown daily in the *Wall Street Journal* for all stocks listed on the New York and American Stock Exchanges. It is computed by dividing the market price per share by the EPS.

Assume that the market price per share of the Grand Hotel is $25.00 at the end of 19X2. The PE ratio for the Grand Hotel at the end of 19X2 is calculated as follows:

$$\text{Price Earnings Ratio} \quad = \quad \frac{\text{Market Price per Share}}{\text{Earnings per Share}}$$

$$= \quad \frac{\$25}{\$2.67}$$

$$= \quad \underline{9.36}$$

The Grand Hotel's PE ratio of 9.36 indicates that if the 19X2 EPS ratio is maintained, it would take 9.36 years for earnings to equal the market price per share at the end of 19X2.

The PE ratio for different hospitality enterprises may vary significantly. Factors affecting these differences include relative risk, stability of earnings, perceived earnings trend, and perceived growth potential of the stock.

Viewpoints Regarding Profitability Ratios

Owners, creditors, and management obviously prefer high profitability ratios. Owners prefer high profitability ratios because they indicate the return they are receiving from their investments. They will be most concerned about ROE (return on common stockholders' equity if preferred stock has been issued), because ROE measures the precise return on their investments. Although other profitability measures are important to the owner, the ROE is the "bottom line." Other profitability ratios may be relatively low and the ROE may still be excellent. For example, the profit margin could be only 2%, but the ROE could be 20%, based on the following:

Sales	$100
Net Income	$ 2
Owners' Equity	$ 10
Profit Margin	2%
ROE	20%

If the profitability ratios are not as high as other available investments (with similar risks), stockholders may become dissatisfied and eventually move their funds to other investments. This move, if not checked, will result in lower stock prices, and may pose difficulties for the hospitality enterprise when it desires to raise funds externally.

Creditors also prefer high, stable, or even growing profitability ratios. Although they desire stockholders to receive an excellent return (as measured by ROE), they will look more to the ROA ratio because this ratio considers all assets, not simply claims to a portion of the assets as does ROE. A high and growing ROA represents financial safety and, further, indicates competent management. A high ROA also generally means high profits and cash flow, which suggests safety to the creditor and low risk to the lender.

Managers must keep both creditors and owners happy. Therefore, all profitability ratios are especially important to them. Everything else being the same, the higher the profitability ratios, the better. High ratios also indicate that management is performing effectively and efficiently.

Profitability Evaluation of Segments

In chain operations, hotel managers may be evaluated based on the ROA of their individual hotels. A hotel manager may hesitate to replace inefficient equipment with new, more efficient equipment because the replacement may lower income and ROA through an increased asset base and increased depreciation. Rather than using ROA to evaluate the performance of individual hotels, corporate headquarters should consider using **residual income** as an alternative measure. Simply stated, residual income is the excess of a hotel's net income over a minimum return set by the holding company. The minimum return is calculated as a percentage of the hotel's asset base. When residual income is the basis of hotel management performance evaluation, hotel managers are encouraged to maximize residual income rather than ROA.

To illustrate this concept, assume that A&B Corporation owns two hotels—Hotel A and Hotel B—and requires a 10% return on Hotel A's average total assets. Further assume that Hotel A has $5,000,000 of average assets and generates net income of $600,000. The residual income of $100,000 is determined as follows:

Exhibit 18   Investment Evaluations: ROA versus Residual Income

Hotel A	Current	Proposed	Total
Net Income	$600,000	$110,000	$710,000
Average Total Assets	$5,000,000	$1,000,000	$6,000,000
ROA	12%	11%	11.83%
Hotel B			
Average Total Assets	$4,000,000	$1,000,000	$5,000,000
Net income	$ 480,000	$ 110,000	$ 590,000
Minimum required return (.10 × aver. total assets)	(400,000)	(100,000)	(500,000)
Residual income	$ 80,000	$ 10,000	$ 90,000

Hotel A's net income	$600,000
Less: Minimum required return:	
$5,000,000 × .10	(500,000)
Residual Income	$100,000

Now let us assume for purposes of illustration that Hotel B is evaluated on its residual income base, while Hotel A is evaluated on an ROA of 10%. Further assume that each hotel is earning an ROA of 12% prior to proposed rooms expansions at the beginning of the year, costing $1,000,000 each, which are expected to yield $110,000 at each property.

If Hotel A makes the $1,000,000 investment and $110,000 of profits are earned (which is an 11% return), Hotel A's ROA will slip from 12% to 11.83% as shown in Exhibit 18. It appears that Hotel A's manager performance is lower. Therefore, since Hotel A's manager is evaluated based on ROA, he or she probably will reject the expansion opportunity, even though overall profits would be increased.

On the other hand, Hotel B's general manager, being evaluated on residual income, would welcome the expansion opportunity since the residual income for Hotel B increases by $10,000 as shown in Exhibit 18.

Although residual income appears to resolve the problem of evaluating managers using ROA, its major disadvantage is that it cannot be used to compare the performance of hospitality operations of different sizes.

Operating Ratios

Operating ratios assist management in analyzing the operations of a hospitality establishment. Detailed information necessary for computing these ratios is normally not available to creditors or even owners not actively involved in management. These ratios reflect the actual mix of sales (revenues) and make possible comparisons to sales mix objectives. Further, operating ratios relate expenses to revenues and are useful for control purposes. For example, food cost percentage is calculated and compared to the budgeted food cost percentage to evaluate the overall control of food costs. Any significant deviation is investigated to determine the cause(s) for the variation between actual results and planned goals.

There are literally hundreds of operating ratios that could be calculated. Consider the following:

- Departmental revenues as a percentage of total revenue (sales mix)

- Expenses as a percentage of total revenue

- Departmental expenses as a percentage of departmental revenues

- Revenues per room occupied, meal sold, and so forth

- Annual expenses per room, and so forth

Exhibit 19 suggests over 200 useful operating ratios.

This section will consider only some of the most critical ratios, several relating to revenues and several relating to expenses. The revenue ratios include the mix of sales, average room rate, revenue per available room, and average food service check. The expense ratios include food cost percentage, beverage cost percentage, and labor cost percentage.

Mix of Sales

Hospitality establishments, like enterprises in other industries, attempt to generate sales as a means of producing profits. In the lodging segment of the hospitality industry, sales by the rooms department provide a greater contribution toward overhead costs and profits than the same amount of sales in other departments. In a food service operation, the sales mix of entrées yields a given contribution. The same sales total in a different sales mix will yield a different (possibly lower) contribution toward overhead and profits. Therefore, it is essential for management to obtain the desired sales mix. To determine the sales mix, departmental revenues are totaled and percentages of the total revenue are calculated for each operated department.

Using figures from Exhibits 2 and 4, Exhibit 20 shows the 19X2 sales mix for the Grand Hotel. The sales mix of a hospitality operation is best compared with the establishment's objectives as revealed in its budget. A second standard of comparison is the previous period's results. A third involves a comparison with industry averages.

An evaluation of revenue by department is accomplished by determining each department's average sale. For the rooms department, the ratio is the average room rate. For the food service department, it is the average food service check.

Average Room Rate

A key rooms department ratio is the **average room rate**, often called the **average daily rate** or simply **ADR**. Most hotel and motel managers calculate the ADR even though rates within a property may vary significantly from single rooms to suites,

Exhibit 19   Selected Operating Ratios Useful in Analysis

CERTAIN OPERATING RATIOS USEFUL IN ANALYSIS	% of Total Revenues	% of Depart. Revenues	% of Depart. Total Cost	% Change from Prior Period	% Change from Budget	Per Available Room	Per Occupied Room	Per Available Seats	Per Cover/Guest	Per Square Foot	Per Full-time Equiv. Employee	% of Total Salaries & Wages	Per Unit Produced or Used
Total Revenues				•	•	•	•				•	•	
Rooms													
Revenue	•			•	•	•	•				•		
Salary, Wages & Burden		•	•	•	•	•	•					•	
Other Expenses		•	•	•	•	•	•						
Departmental Profit		•		•	•	•	•						
Food													
Revenue	•			•	•	•	•	•	•	•	•		
Cost of Sales		•	•	•					•				
Salary, Wages & Burden		•	•	•	•			•	•			•	
Other Expenses		•	•	•	•				•				
Departmental Profit		•		•	•			•	•	•	•		
Beverage													
Revenue	•			•	•	•	•	•	•	•	•		
Cost of Sales		•	•	•									
Salary, Wages & Burden		•	•	•	•			•				•	
Other Expenses		•	•	•	•								
Departmental Profit		•		•	•			•		•	•		
Minor Departments													
Revenue	•			•	•								
Cost of Sales		•		•	•								
Salary, Wages & Burden		•		•	•							•	
Other Expenses		•		•	•								
Departmental Profit		•		•	•								
Administrative & General													
Salary, Wages & Burden	•			•	•	•	•					•	
Other Expenses	•			•	•	•	•						
Departmental Total Cost	•			•	•	•	•						
Marketing													
Salary, Wages & Burden	•			•	•	•	•					•	
Other Expenses	•			•	•	•	•						
Departmental Total Cost	•			•	•	•	•						

Exhibit 19   *(continued)*

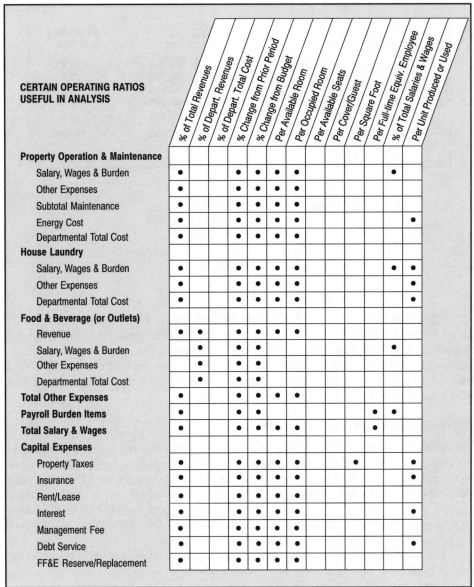

CERTAIN OPERATING RATIOS USEFUL IN ANALYSIS	% of Total Revenues	% of Depart. Revenues	% of Depart. Total Cost	% Change from Prior Period	% Change from Budget	Per Available Room	Per Occupied Room	Per Available Seats	Per Cover/Guest	Per Square Foot	Per Full-time Equiv. Employee	% of Total Salaries & Wages	Per Unit Produced or Used
Property Operation & Maintenance													
Salary, Wages & Burden	•			•	•	•	•				•		
Other Expenses	•			•	•	•	•						
Subtotal Maintenance	•			•	•	•	•						
Energy Cost	•			•	•	•	•						•
Departmental Total Cost	•			•	•	•	•						
House Laundry													
Salary, Wages & Burden	•			•	•	•	•					•	•
Other Expenses	•			•	•	•	•						•
Departmental Total Cost	•			•	•	•	•						•
Food & Beverage (or Outlets)													
Revenue	•	•		•	•	•	•						
Salary, Wages & Burden		•		•	•						•		
Other Expenses		•		•	•								
Departmental Total Cost		•		•	•								
Total Other Expenses	•			•	•	•	•						
Payroll Burden Items	•			•	•						•	•	
Total Salary & Wages	•			•	•	•	•				•		
Capital Expenses													
Property Taxes	•			•	•	•	•			•			•
Insurance	•			•	•	•	•						•
Rent/Lease	•			•	•	•	•						
Interest	•			•	•	•	•						•
Management Fee	•			•	•	•	•						
Debt Service	•			•	•	•	•						•
FF&E Reserve/Replacement	•			•	•	•							

from individual guests to groups and conventions, from weekdays to weekends, and from busy seasons to slack seasons.

Using figures from Exhibits 2 and 4, the 19X2 ADR for the Grand Hotel can be calculated as follows:

Exhibit 20   Sales Mix

Departments	Sales	Percentage of Total
Rooms:	$ 810,000	59.9%
Food	300,000	22.2
Beverage	145,000	10.7
Telephone	42,000	3.1
Rentals and Other Income	55,000	4.1
Total	$1,352,000	100.0%

$$\text{ADR} = \frac{\text{Rooms Revenue}}{\text{Number of Rooms Sold}}$$

$$= \frac{\$810,000}{21,000}$$

$$= \underline{\$38.57}$$

The ADR for 19X2 is a $.52 improvement over the 19X1 ADR of $38.05 ($780,000 ÷ 20,500 rooms sold). The best standard of comparison to use in evaluating an actual average room rate is the rate budgeted as the goal for the rooms department's operation during the period. This average rate should also be calculated individually for each market segment: business groups, tourists, airline crews, and other categories of guests served.

Revenue per Available Room

Traditionally, many hoteliers have placed heavy reliance on paid occupancy percentage as a quick indicator of activity and possibly performance. Others have looked at the ADR as an indication of the quality of its operation. However, paid occupancy percentage and average room rate by themselves are somewhat meaningless. A hotel may have a paid occupancy of 80% and an ADR of $40, while a close competitor has a paid occupancy of 70% and an ADR of $60. Which hotel is in the preferable condition?

The combining of paid occupancy percentage and ADR is called **revpar** (revenue per available room) and is calculated as follows:

$$\text{Revpar} = \frac{\text{Rooms Revenue}}{\text{Available Rooms}}$$

or

$$\text{Revpar} = \text{Paid Occupancy Percentage} \times \text{ADR}$$

Using the above example, the hotel with an 80% paid occupancy and the $40 ADR has a revpar of $32 ($40 × 80%), while its competitor has a revpar of $42

(70% × $60). Everything else being the same, one prefers the hotel with the higher revpar. In this example, the revpar leads us to choose the hotel with the higher ADR, but this will not always be the case. Suppose, for example, that the second hotel in the above example had a paid occupancy of 50% instead of 70%; its revpar would then be $30 ($60 × 50%) and the revpar ratio would then favor the hotel with the higher occupancy percentage.

Based on information in Exhibits 2, 4, and 15, the Grand Hotel's revpar for 19X2 is $27.74, while its revpar for 19X1 is $26.71. Thus, revpar increased by $1.03 in 19X2 over 19X1.

Revpar is an improvement over simply looking at occupancy percentage or ADR separately. Many industry executives prefer this combined statistic.

Average Food Service Check

A key food service ratio is the average food service check. This ratio is determined by dividing total food revenue by the number of food covers sold during the period.

Using figures from Exhibit 4, the average food service check for 19X2 for the Grand Hotel can be calculated as follows:

$$\text{Average Food Service Check} = \frac{\text{Total Food Revenue}}{\text{Number of Food Covers}}$$

$$= \frac{\$300,000}{\$56,000}$$

$$= \underline{\$5.36}$$

The $5.36 average food service check in 19X2 is a $.31 increase over the Grand Hotel's average food service check of $5.05 for 19X1 ($280,000 ÷ 55,500 food covers). The average food service check is best compared with the budgeted amount for 19X2. An additional comparison relates this ratio to industry averages.

Additional average checks should be calculated for beverages. Management may even desire to calculate the average check by different dining areas and/or by various meal periods.

Food Cost Percentage

The **food cost percentage** is a key food service ratio that compares the cost of food sold to food sales. Most food service managers rely heavily on this ratio for determining whether food costs are reasonable.

Using figures from Exhibit 10, the 19X2 food cost percentage for the Grand Hotel is determined as follows:

$$\text{Food Cost Percentage} = \frac{\text{Cost of Food Sold}}{\text{Food Sales}}$$

$$= \frac{\$120,000}{\$300,000}$$

$$= \underline{40\%}$$

The Grand Hotel's 19X2 food cost percentage of 40 indicates that of every $1 of food sales, $.40 goes toward the cost of food sold. This is best compared with the budgeted percentage for the period. A significant difference in either direction should be investigated by management. Management should be just as concerned about a food cost percentage that is significantly lower than the budgeted goal as it is about a food cost percentage that exceeds budgeted standards. A lower food cost percentage may indicate that the quality of food served is lower than desired, or that smaller portions are being served than are specified by the standard recipes. A food cost percentage in excess of the objective may be due to poor portion control, excessive food costs, theft, waste, spoilage, and so on.

Beverage Cost Percentage

A key ratio for beverage operations is the **beverage cost percentage**. This ratio results from dividing the cost of beverages sold by beverage sales.

Using figures from Exhibit 10, the 19X2 beverage cost percentage for the Grand Hotel can be calculated as follows:

$$\text{Beverage Cost Percentage} = \frac{\text{Cost of Beverages Sold}}{\text{Beverage Sales}}$$

$$= \frac{\$28,000}{\$145,000}$$

$$= \underline{19.31\%}$$

The 19X2 beverage cost percentage of 19.31% for the Grand Hotel means that for each $1 of beverage sales, $.19 is spent on the cost of beverages served. As with the food cost percentage ratio, this ratio is best compared with the goal set for that period. Likewise, any significant variances must be investigated to determine the cause(s). Refinements of this ratio would be beverage cost percentage by type of beverage sold and by beverage outlet.

Labor Cost Percentage

The largest expense in hotels, motels, clubs, and many restaurants is labor. Labor expense includes salaries, wages, bonuses, payroll taxes, and fringe benefits. A general **labor cost percentage** is determined by dividing total labor costs by total revenue. This general labor cost percentage is simply a benchmark for making broad comparisons. For control purposes, labor costs must be analyzed on a departmental basis. The rooms department labor cost percentage is determined by dividing rooms department labor cost by room revenue. The food and beverage department labor cost percentage is determined by dividing food and beverage department labor cost by food and beverage revenue. Other operated department labor cost percentages are similarly determined.

Exhibit 21 uses figures from Exhibit 2 to calculate the 19X2 operated department labor cost percentages for the Grand Hotel. The 19X2 labor cost percentages for the Grand Hotel show the food and beverage department with the highest labor cost

Exhibit 21   Operated Department Labor Cost Percentages

$$\text{Labor Cost Percentage} = \frac{\text{Labor Cost by Departments}}{\text{Department Revenues}}$$

Department	Total Labor Cost	÷	Total Revenue	=	Labor Cost Percentage
Rooms	$145,000		$ 810,000		17.90%
Food & Beverage	180,000		445,000		40.45%
Telephone	10,500		42,000		25.00%

percentage at 40.45%. In most lodging firms, this is the case. The standard of comparison for these ratios is the budgeted percentages. Since labor costs are generally the largest expense, they must be tightly controlled. Management must carefully investigate any significant differences between actual and budgeted labor cost percentages.

Ratios for other expenses are usually computed as a percentage of revenues. If the expenses are operated department expenses, then the ratio is computed with the operated department revenues in the denominator and the expense in the numerator. An overhead expense ratio will consist of the overhead expense divided by total revenue. For example, marketing expense percentage is determined by dividing the marketing expense by total revenue. Using figures for the Grand Hotel in 19X2 found in Exhibit 2, the marketing expense percentage is 4.07% (marketing expenses of $55,000 ÷ total revenue of $1,352,000).

Limitations of Ratio Analysis

Ratios are extremely useful to owners, creditors, and management in evaluating the financial condition and operations of hospitality establishments. However, ratios are only indicators. Ratios do not resolve problems or even reveal exactly what the problem is. At best, when they vary significantly from past periods, budgeted standards, or industry averages, ratios only indicate that there *may be* a problem. Much more investigation and analysis are required.

Ratios are meaningful when they result from comparing two *related* numbers. Food cost percentage is meaningful because of the direct relationship between food costs and food sales. A goodwill to cash ratio may be somewhat meaningless due to the lack of any direct relationship between goodwill and cash.

Ratios are most useful when compared with a standard. A food cost percentage of 32% has little usefulness until it is compared with a standard such as past performance, industry averages, or the budgeted percentages.

Ratios are often used to compare different hospitality establishments. However, many ratios, especially operating ratios, will not result in meaningful comparisons if the two firms are in completely different segments of the industry. For example, comparing ratios for a luxury hotel to ratios for a quick-service restaurant would serve no meaningful purpose.

In addition, if the accounting procedures used by two separate hospitality establishments differ in several areas, then a comparison of their ratios will likely show differences related to accounting procedures as well as to financial positions or operations.

No single ratio tells the entire story. Several ratios are often useful in understanding the financial picture of a hospitality business. Generally, the same ratios should be viewed over a series of time periods.

The analyst also must be aware of events that do not directly affect the financial statements. For example, unrecorded contracts, lawsuits, lines of credit, and hotel group reservations will affect a company's financial condition, often with no immediate direct impact on the financial statements. The analyst must carefully weigh these matters and their potential impact on the firm's financial statements.

Finally, financial ratios are generally computed from figures in the financial statements. These figures are based on historical costs. Over time, the effects of inflation render these figures less useful. For example, an ADR of $55 in 19X9 for a given lodging property is not necessarily a better performance than $40 in 19X1; if the inflation rate was greater than 37.5% for the 19X1–19X9 time period, $55 in 19X9 is worth less than $40 in 19X1. Ratios that are most affected by inflation include those that contain property, equipment, or owners' equity in either the numerator or denominator. In addition, depreciation, since it relates to the historical cost of property and equipment, is often "understated," so income figures involving depreciation expense are often "overstated."

Accountants have used some fairly sophisticated techniques, such as restating the financial statements in constant dollars of equal purchasing power, to overcome this limitation in ratio analysis. However, as desirable as this correction is, it is often not used because of the major effort and time required to use it. An alternative approach is to apply an inflation correction factor to ratios that are affected by inflation. For example, using the above ADR example, assume that inflation for the 19X1–19X9 period was 50%. The comparison of ADRs for 19X1 and 19X9 would be as follows:

19X1 (historical)	$40
19X1 (adjusted)	$60*
19X9	$55
*$40 × 150% = $60	

Thus, it is clear that the 19X1 ADR is preferred to the 19X9 ADR when inflation is considered.

Even though these limitations are present, a careful use of ratios that acknowledges their shortcomings will result in an enhanced understanding of the financial position and operations of hospitality establishments.

Usefulness of Financial Ratios

Research has been conducted to determine the usefulness of ratios to various users.[4] The following results are based on surveys of hotel general managers (GMs) and financial controllers who were requested to rate individually the usefulness of

45 different ratios to potential users of these ratios. Specifically, they were asked to rate the usefulness of each of these ratios to GMs, corporate executives, owners, and bankers on a scale of most important to least important. The results were then compiled by class of ratios and by users and are summarized as follows:[5]

| | | Users | | |
Class of Ratios	GMs	Corporate Executives	Owners	Bankers
Operating	1 (1)	2 (2)	3 (5)	4 (4)
Solvency	4 (5)	3 (3)	1 (2)	1 (1)
Activity	1 (2)	2 (5)	3 (4)	4 (5)
Profitability	4 (3)	2 (1)	1 (1)	3 (2)
Liquidity	3 (4)	1 (4)	2 (3)	4 (3)

The interpretation of the above table is as follows:

- The parenthetic numbers show the relative ranking of usefulness of the classes of ratios to each user group. For example, GMs considered operating ratios most useful (1), followed by activity ratios (2) and so forth.

- The non-parenthetic numbers reveal the relative usefulness of a class of ratios across the various user groups. For example, the survey results suggest operating ratios are considered most useful by general managers, followed by corporate executives, then owners and bankers.

- Owners and bankers are tied in their rating of solvency ratios.

In addition, the survey of GMs revealed that across all user groups the ten most useful ratios were:

1. Profit margin

2. Occupancy percentage—month-to-date

3. Cost of labor percentage

4. Daily occupancy percentage

5. ADR

6. Total revenue percentage change from budget

7. Cost of food sold percentage

8. Cost of beverage sold percentage

9. Room sales to total sales

10. Operating efficiency ratio

Computer Applications

Liquidity, solvency, activity, profitability, and operating ratios are by-products of the financial statements. Therefore, computers can automatically calculate and report these important statistics. The speed of the computers will allow these statistics to be created almost at will, assuming the financial data is stored in the computer.

However, many ratios need not be calculated on a daily basis. In fact, if they cover too short a period, they may not provide important information at all. Although it is difficult for many managers to do, it is important that they determine the key ratios to be calculated and the frequency with which they should be provided. If all the ratios were calculated daily, there would be the risk of "information overload." So much information (and so many reams of paper) would be provided that the manager would not have the time—or the desire—to look through it to find the valuable items.

Unlike many other ratios, operating ratios may be very useful when they are prepared frequently. For example, knowing food cost on a daily or weekly basis might be of great assistance to management. If food cost changes significantly for any day, management will want to know it in order to determine the cause(s) so that corrective action can be taken. Computers can play a major role in information gathering and the preparation of operating ratios. For example, when a hotel's night audit is computerized, many of the lodging statistics are a by-product of the process: average daily rate, occupancy percentage, double occupancy percentage, and so forth. These statistics can then be compared with the budget to give management a timely and convenient measure of the operation's success.

In addition, many other operating ratios can be generated quickly and with almost no manual intervention. The following example shows how this might work. Assume that the Grand Hotel has a computerized time clock system. The clocks record the time in and time out for employees as they enter and leave the building. Once a day, a computer in the accounting department receives the previous day's employee data from the clocks and calculates the total time for each employee. Departmental labor costs can then be determined based upon each employee's hourly rate, which is in the payroll system. The computer can even determine overtime, vacation, holiday, and sick pay. It can then report the payroll cost by department and job classification to management. If daily sales are entered into the computer, it would also be possible to track labor cost as a percentage of sales. Similar applications exist for food cost, preventive maintenance, and energy costs.

Summary

Ratio analysis permits investors, creditors, and operators to receive more valuable information from the financial statements than they could receive from reviewing the absolute numbers reported in the documents. Vital relationships can be monitored to determine solvency and risk, performance in comparison with other periods, and dividend payout ratios. A combination of ratios can be used to efficiently and effectively communicate more information than that provided by the statements from which they are calculated.

There are five major classifications of ratios: liquidity, solvency, activity, profitability, and operating. Although there is some overlap among these categories, each has a special area of concern. Exhibit 22 lists the 34 ratios presented in this chapter and the formulas by which they are calculated. It is important to be familiar with

Exhibit 22   List of Ratios

Ratio	Formula
1. Current ratio	Current assets/current liabilities
2. Acid-test ratio	Cash, marketable securities, notes and accounts receivable/current liabilities
3. Operating cash flows to current liabilities ratio	Operating cash flows/average current liabilities
4. Accounts receivable turnover	Revenue/average accounts receivable
5. Average collection period	365/accounts receivable turnover
6. Working capital turnover	Revenue/average working capital
7. Solvency ratio	Total assets/total liabilities
8. Debt-equity ratio	Total liabilities/total owners' equity
9. Long-term debt to total capitalization ratio	Long-term debt/long-term debt and owners' equity
10. Number of times interest earned ratio	EBIT/interest expense
11. Fixed charge coverage ratio	EBIT + lease expense/interest expense and lease expense
12. Operating cash flows to total liabilities ratio	Operating cash flows/average total liabilities
13. Inventory turnover:	
Food inventory turnover	Cost of food used/average food inventory
Beverage turnover	Cost of beverages used/average beverage inventory
14. Property and equipment turnover	Total revenue/average property and equipment
15. Asset turnover	Total revenues/average total assets
16. Paid occupancy percentage	Paid rooms occupied/rooms available
17. Complimentary occupancy	Complimentary rooms/rooms available
18. Average occupancy per room	Number of room guests/number of rooms occupied
19. Multiple occupancy percentage	Rooms occupied by two or more people/rooms occupied by guests
20. Profit margin	Net income/total revenue
21. Operating efficiency ratio	Income after undistributed operating expenses/total revenue
22. Return on assets	Net income/average total assets
23. Gross return on assets	EBIT/average total assets
24. Return on owners' equity	Net income/average owners' equity
25. Return on common stockholders' equity	Net income − preferred dividend/average common stockholders' equity
26. Earnings per share	Net income/average common shares outstanding
27. Price earnings ratio	Market price per share/earnings per share
28. Mix of sales	Departmental revenues are totaled; percentages of total revenue are calculated for each
29. ADR	Room revenue/number of rooms sold
30. Revpar	Paid occupancy percentage × ADR
31. Average food service check	Total food revenue/number of food covers
32. Food cost percentage	Cost of food sold/food sales
33. Beverage cost percentage	Cost of beverages sold/beverage sales
34. Labor cost percentage	Labor cost by department/department revenues

the types of ratios in each category, to know what each ratio measures, and to be aware of the targets or standards against which they are compared.

For example, a number of liquidity ratios focus on the hospitality establishment's ability to cover its short-term debts. However, each person examining the establishment's financial position will have a desired performance in mind. Creditors desire high liquidity ratios indicating that loans will probably be repaid. Investors, on the other hand, like lower liquidity ratios since current assets are not as profitable as long-term assets. Management reacts to these pressures by trying to please both groups.

The five ratio classifications vary in importance among the three major users of ratios. Creditors focus on solvency, profitability, and liquidity; investors and owners consider these ratios, but highlight the profitability ratios. Management uses all types of ratios, but is especially concerned with operating and activity ratios which can be used in evaluating the results of operations.

It is important to realize that a percentage by itself is not meaningful. It is only useful when it is compared with a standard: an industry average, a ratio from a past period, or a budgeted ratio. It is the comparison against budget ratios that is the most useful for management. Any significant difference should be analyzed to determine its probable cause(s). Once management has fully investigated areas of concern revealed by the ratios, then corrective action can be taken to rectify any problems.

Endnotes

1. This may be determined mathematically using the following formula:

    $$\frac{CA - x}{CL - x} =$$ desired current ratio where x indicates the amount of current assets which would be used to retire current liabilities. The calculation for the Grand Hotel is as follows:

    $$\frac{338,000 - x}{214,000 - x} = 2; \qquad x = 90,000; \qquad \frac{248,000}{124,000} = 2 \text{ times}$$

2. *Hotel Operating Statistics—1996*, Smith Travel Research.

3. The interested student is referred to intermediate accounting texts, most of which contain a full discussion of EPS calculations in various situations.

4. Raymond S. Schmidgall, "Financial Ratios: Perceptions of Lodging Industry General Managers and Financial Executives," *FIU Hospitality Review*, Fall 1989, pp. 1–9.

5. As a note of caution, the research is based on perceptions of lodging general managers and financial controllers and does not necessarily reflect the actual views of corporate executives, owners, and bankers. Nonetheless, the great consistency of answers among all respondents suggests that this information is reliable.

Key Terms

accounts receivable turnover—A measure of the rapidity of conversion of accounts receivable into cash; calculated by dividing revenue by average accounts receivable.

acid-test ratio—Ratio of total cash and near-cash current assets to total current liabilities.

activity ratios—A group of ratios that reflect management's ability to use the property's assets and resources.

asset turnover—An activity ratio. Total revenues divided by average total assets.

average collection period—The average number of days it takes a hospitality operation to collect all its accounts receivable; calculated by dividing the accounts receivable turnover into 365 (the number of days in a year).

average daily rate (ADR)—A key rooms department operating ratio. Rooms revenue divided by number of rooms sold. Also called average room rate.

average occupancy per room ratio—An activity ratio measuring management's ability to use the lodging facilities. The number of guests divided by the number of rooms sold.

average room rate (ADR)—See average daily rate.

beverage cost percentage—A ratio comparing the cost of beverages sold to beverage sales; calculated by dividing the cost of beverages sold by beverage sales.

complimentary occupancy—The number of complimentary rooms for a period divided by the number of rooms available.

current ratio—Ratio of total current assets to total current liabilities expressed as a coverage of so many times; calculated by dividing current assets by current liabilities.

debt-equity ratio—Compares the debt of a hospitality operation to its net worth (owners' equity) and indicates the operation's ability to withstand adversity and meet its long-term obligations; calculated by dividing total liabilities by total owners' equity.

double occupancy—The number of rooms occupied by more than one guest divided by the number of rooms occupied by guests. More accurately called multiple occupancy.

earnings per share (EPS)—A ratio providing a general indicator of the profitability of an operation by comparing net income to the average common shares outstanding. If preferred stock has been issued for the operation, then preferred dividends are subtracted from net income before calculating EPS.

financial leverage—The use of debt in place of equity dollars to finance operations and increase the return on the equity dollars already invested.

fixed charge coverage ratio—A variation of the number of times interest earned ratio that considers leases as well as interest expense. Lease expenses and earnings before interest and income taxes divided by interest expense and lease expense.

food cost percentage—A ratio comparing the cost of food sold to food sales; calculated by dividing the cost of food sold by total food sales.

gross operating profit ratio—See operating efficiency ratio.

gross return on assets (GROA)—Measures the rate of return on assets regardless of financing methods. Earnings before interest and income taxes divided by average total assets.

inventory turnover—A ratio showing how quickly a hospitality operation's inventory is moving from storage to productive use; calculated by dividing the cost of food or beverages used by the average food or beverages inventory.

labor cost percentage—A ratio comparing the labor expense for each department by the total revenue generated by the department; total labor cost by department divided by department revenues.

liquidity ratios—A group of ratios that reveal the ability of an establishment to meet its short-term obligations.

long-term debt to total capitalization ratio—A solvency ratio showing long-term debt as a percentage of the sum of long-term debt and owners' equity. Long-term debt divided by long-term debt and owners' equity.

multiple occupancy—The number of rooms occupied by more than one guest divided by the number of rooms occupied by guests. Sometimes called double occupancy.

number of times interest earned ratio—A solvency ratio expressing the number of times interest expense can be covered. Earnings before interest and taxes divided by interest expense.

operating cash flows to current liabilities ratio—A liquidity ratio that compares the cash flow from the firm's operating activities to its obligations at the balance sheet date that must be paid within twelve months. Operating cash flows divided by average current liabilities.

operating cash flows to total liabilities ratio—A solvency ratio that uses figures from both the statement of cash flows and the balance sheet. Operating cash flows divided by average total liabilities.

operating efficiency ratio—A measure of management's ability to generate sales and control expenses; calculated by dividing income after undistributed operating expenses by total revenue. Also called gross operating profit ratio.

operating ratios—A group of ratios that assist in the analysis of hospitality establishment operations.

paid occupancy—A measure of management's ability to efficiently use available assets. The number of rooms sold divided by the number of rooms available for sale.

price earnings (PE) ratio—A profitability ratio used by financial analysts when presenting investment possibilities. The market price per share divided by the earnings per share.

profit margin—An overall measure of management's ability to generate sales and control expenses; calculated by dividing net income by total revenue.

profitability ratios—A group of ratios which reflect the results of all areas of management's responsibilities.

property and equipment turnover—A ratio measuring management's effectiveness in using property and equipment to generate revenue; calculated by dividing average total property and equipment into total revenue generated for the period. Sometimes called fixed asset turnover.

ratio analysis—The comparison of related facts and figures.

residual income—The excess of a hotel's net income over an established minimum return.

return on assets (ROA)—A ratio providing a general indicator of the profitability of a hospitality operation by comparing net income to total investment; calculated by dividing net income by average total assets.

return on common stockholders' equity—A variation of return on owners' equity that is used when preferred stock has been issued. Net income less preferred dividends paid to preferred stockholders divided by average common stockholders' equity.

return on owners' equity (ROE)—A ratio providing a general indicator of the profitability of an operation by comparing net income to the owners' investment; calculated by dividing net income by average owners' equity.

revpar—Revenue per available room. A combination of paid occupancy percentage and average daily rate. Room revenues divided by available revenues or, alternatively, paid occupancy percentage times average daily rate.

seat turnover—An activity ratio measuring the rate at which people are served. The number of people served divided by the number of seats available.

solvency ratio—A measure of the extent to which an operation is financed by debt and is able to meet its long-term obligations; calculated by dividing total assets by total liabilities.

solvency ratios—A group of ratios that measure the extent to which the enterprise has been financed by debt and is able to meet its long-term obligations.

working capital turnover ratio—A liquidity ratio that compares working capital (current assets less current liabilities) to revenue.

Review Questions

1. How does ratio analysis benefit creditors?

2. If you are investing in a hotel, which ratios would be most useful? Why?

3. What are the limitations of ratio analysis?

4. How do the three user groups of ratio analysis react to the solvency ratios?

5. What is leverage, and why may owners want to increase it?

6. What do activity ratios highlight?

7. How is the profit margin calculated? How is it used?

8. Which standard is the most effective for comparison with ratios?

9. What does the ratio expression "turnover" mean?

10. Of what value is the food sales/total sales ratio to the manager of a hotel? To a creditor?

Problems

Problem 1

Indicate the effects of the transactions listed below on each of the following: total current assets, working capital (CA − CL), and current ratio. Indicate increase with " +," indicate decrease with " −" and indicate no effect or effect cannot be determined with "0." Assume an initial current ratio of greater than 1.0.

	Total Current Assets	Working Capital	Current Ratio
1. Food is sold for cash.	_____	_____	_____
2. Equipment is sold at less than its net book value.	_____	_____	_____
3. Beverages are sold on account.	_____	_____	_____
4. A cash dividend is declared.	_____	_____	_____
5. Accrued payroll is paid.	_____	_____	_____
6. Treasury stock is purchased.	_____	_____	_____
7. A fully depreciated fixed asset is retired.	_____	_____	_____
8. Equipment is purchased with long-term notes.	_____	_____	_____
9. Utility expenses are paid (they were not previously accrued).	_____	_____	_____
10. A cash dividend is paid.	_____	_____	_____

Problem 2

Selected financial ratios of the Razorback Hotel for 19X1 through 19X3 are as follows:

	19X1	19X2	19X3
Current ratio	1.6	1.7	1.8
Acid-test ratio	1.3	1.35	1.4
Accounts receivable turnover	24	20	16
Inventory turnover	20	22	24

Required:

Comment on the changing liquidity of the Razorback Hotel from 19X1 to 19X3. Be specific using the above ratios.

Problem 3

A. The Mountaintop Inn consists of 200 guestrooms. During June, on the average, two rooms per day are out-of-order for legitimate reasons. On the average, 1% of the guestrooms are comped for valid business reasons, and 1% are comped to friends of management. During June, 5,000 rooms were sold. Of the rooms sold, 3,200 were doubles.

Required:

1. Determine the paid occupancy percentage.
2. Determine the double occupancy percentage.

B. The Blue Devil Cafe had a beginning food inventory of $4,500 and ending food inventory of $4,000. During the month, its food sales equaled $60,000 and food purchases were $20,500. Food transfers to the beverage department totaled $100, and employee meals equaled $400 for the month.

Required:

Determine the food cost percentage.

Problem 4

The Reese Ranch provides several outdoor activities for its guests. It has 50 guestrooms, including singles and doubles, and, of course, a food service operation.

Required:

Answer each question below using your knowledge of ratio analysis.

1. During June, the multiple occupancy percentage was 40%, and 1,400 guests stayed in the ranch. Assume two guests stayed in each double and one guest in each single. How many rooms were sold?
2. The ranch has a current ratio of 1.5, an acid-test ratio of 1.2, and total current assets of $120,000 at the end of 19X4. What are its total quick assets?
3. The ranch had a food inventory turnover of 24 times for 19X4 when its average food inventory was $4,000 and the cost of employee meals was $1,000. If cost of food sales percentage was 30%, what were total food sales?

Problem 5

The Kluzinski Cafe is a 100-seat restaurant oriented to family dining. Selected information is provided from operations in four short scenarios.

Required:

Answer the question for each scenario.

1. The cafe had a beginning food inventory of $8,000 and ending food inventory of $10,000 for 19X2. The inventory turnover was 24, and employee food expense was $3,000 for the year. What was the total cost of food sold?
2. The cafe had food sales during June, 19X2, of $60,000, of which 40% were during lunch. If the cafe was open 26 days of the month and the average seat turnover was 1.5 per lunch period, what was the average lunch food service check?

3. The cafe's cost of food sold percentage was 34% during April, 19X2. Total food sales in April were $80,000. The cost of employee meals for April totaled $200. What was the cost of food used?

4. The cost of food sold during July totaled $30,000. The beginning food inventory equaled $9,000 and the food inventory turnover was 3.1 times. If the cost of employee meals was $300 for the month, what was the ending food inventory?

Problem 6

The Hershiser Hotel is considering expansion. The proposed expansion is estimated to cost $20,000,000. Alternative financing arrangements are (1) all equity, (2) all debt, and (3) one-half debt and one-half equity. The expected annual income from the expansion before any interest and income taxes is $2,000,000. Assume an annual interest rate of 8% and a marginal tax rate of 30%. Further assume that 500,000 shares of common stock are outstanding, that additional shares can be sold for $100 per share with any equity financing, and that forecasted net income for the year related to current operations (before any expansion) is $2.00 per share based on the 500,000 shares outstanding.

Required:

Determine the expected annual increase in earnings per share for the Hershiser Hotel for each of the financing alternatives.

Problem 7

The Duke Snyder Motel has operated for several years as you become the new manager. In order to better understand the financial situation, you are to examine the financial statements for the year just ended (19X4) and perform ratio analysis. The motel's balance sheet and condensed income statement are below:

Duke Snyder Motel
Balance Sheet
December 31, 19X4

Assets

Current Assets:	
Cash	$ 95,000
Accounts Receivable	100,000
Inventories	5,000
Total Current Assets	200,000

Property and Equipment:

Land	60,000
Building (net)	300,000
Furniture & Equipment (net)	80,000
Total Property and Equipment	440,000
Total Assets	$ 640,000

Liabilities and Owners' Equity

Current Liabilities	$ 210,000
Long-Term Liabilities:	
Note from Owner	40,000
Mortgage Payable	80,000
Total Liabilities	330,000
Owners' Equity	
Common Stock	100,000
Retained Earnings	210,000
Total Owners' Equity	310,000
Total Liabilities and Owners' Equity	$ 640,000

Duke Snyder Motel
Condensed Income Statement
For the year ended December 31, 19X4

Sales	$1,500,000
Cost of Goods Sold	200,000
Operating Expenses	800,000
Contribution Margin	500,000
Undistributed Operating Expenses	125,000
Income After Undistributed Operating Expenses	375,000
Interest	120,000
Other Fixed Charges	162,000
Income Before Taxes	93,000
Income Tax	27,900
Net Income	$ 65,100

Required:

Calculate the following ratios:

1. Current ratio
2. Acid-test ratio
3. Debt-equity ratio
4. Number of times interest earned ratio
5. Operating efficiency ratio
6. Profit margin
7. Return on owners' equity (assume that the only change in owners' equity during 19X4 is the net income of $65,100)
8. Return on total assets (assume that total assets were $640,000 on January 1, 19X4)

Problem 8

The following information applies to the Maris Restaurant:

Cash and marketable securities	$10,000
Property and equipment	$1,500,000
Total sales	$2,000,000
Profit margin	5%
Acid-test	1.2 to 1
Current ratio	1.5 to 1
ROE	10%
Accounts receivable turnover	20 times

Assume the following:

1. The accounts receivable turnover is based on total sales.
2. Total assets are equal to current assets plus property and equipment.
3. The balances of balance sheet accounts at the beginning of the year are the same as the end of the year.

Required:

Determine the following:

1. Total current assets
2. Total current liabilities
3. Net income
4. Asset turnover
5. Total owners' equity
6. Long-term debt
7. Return on assets
8. Debt-equity ratio

Problem 9

The Hodges, a 300-room hotel, has provided you with the following data for the months of June and July:

	June	July
Single rooms sold	2,400	2,418
Double rooms sold	4,200	4,278
Room revenue	$396,000	$339,000
Number of paid guests	9,900	9,910

Required:

1. Compute the following for June and July:
   a. Paid occupancy percentage
   b. Multiple occupancy percentage
   c. Average number of guests per double room sold (assume that only one guest stayed in each single room sold)
   d. Monthly ADR
   e. Monthly revpar

2. Was the Hodges' financial performance better in June or July? (Assume that fixed costs were constant and that the variable costs per room sold remained constant. Support your answer with detailed discussion.)

Problem 10

The Gibson Hotel is a 250-room facility with several profit centers. The hotel is open throughout the year, and generally about 2% of the rooms are being repaired or renovated at all times; therefore, assume that they are unavailable for sale. During 19X1, the hotel sold 77,800 rooms and experienced an average occupancy per room of 1.32 people. The accounting department has supplied the following information concerning the food department:

Ending Inventory	$35,000
Consumption by Employees (free of charge)	5,000
Cost of Sales	312,000
Food Cost Percentage	40%
Food Inventory Turnover	10 times

Required:

Determine the following:

1. Occupancy rate for 19X1
2. Number of paid guests for 19X1
3. Beginning inventory of food
4. Food sales
5. Multiple occupancy percentage (assume that no more than two persons occupied a double room)

Problem 11

Donna Drysdale, co-owner of Drysdale Pizza, provides you with information as follows for 19X3 and 19X4:

	19X3	19X4
Food sales	$800,000	$850,000
Other sales	50,000	60,000
Total sales	850,000	910,000
Cost of food sold	160,000	170,000
Cost of other sales	20,000	24,000
Total cost of sales	180,000	194,000
Gross profit	670,000	716,000
Controllable expenses:		
Salaries and wages	160,000	170,000
Employee benefits	50,000	55,000
Other expenses	150,000	170,000
Income before occupation costs, interest, and depreciation	310,000	321,000
Depreciation expense	80,000	80,000
Interest expense	80,000	75,000
Occupation costs	40,000	45,000
Income before income taxes	110,000	121,000
Income taxes	30,000	35,000
Net income	$ 80,000	$ 86,000

Other data:	19X2	19X3	19X4
Rent expense	--	$10,000	$11,000
Food customers served	--	66,667	65,385
Food inventory at year-end	$ 4,800	$ 5,000	$ 5,300
Employee meals*	--	$ 1,500	$ 1,550

*Included as part of employee benefits.

Required:

1. Determine the following for 19X3 and 19X4:

   a. Average food service check

   b. Food cost percentage

   c. Labor cost percentage

   d. Labor cost per customer served

   e. Number of times interest earned

   f. Operating efficiency ratio

   g. Fixed charge coverage ratio

   h. Profit margin

2. Was Drysdale Pizza more efficient in 19X3 or 19X4? Support your answer with figures and discussion.

Problem 12

Some of the Evangel Inn's financial statements from 19X6 and 19X7 are listed below.

Evangel Inn
Balance Sheets
December 31, 19X6 and 19X7

Assets	19X6	19X7
Current Assets:		
Cash	$ 20,000	$ 60,000
Marketable Securities	20,000	25,000
Accounts Receivable	90,000	115,000
Inventory	15,000	20,000
Prepaid Expenses	15,000	5,000
Total Current Assets	160,000	225,000
Investments	150,000	450,000
Property and Equipment:		
Land	450,000	450,000
Buildings	2,000,000	2,000,000
Equipment	500,000	610,000
Less: Accumulated Depreciation	(1,000,000)	(1,300,000)
Net Property and Equipment	1,950,000	1,760,000
Other Assets—Franchise Fees	100,000	90,000
Total Assets	$2,360,000	$2,525,000
Liabilities and Owners' Equity		
Current Liabilities:		
Accounts Payable	$ 25,000	$ 35,000
Current Maturities of Long-Term Debt	50,000	50,000
Wages Payable	15,000	15,000
Dividends Payable	20,000	15,000
Total Current Liabilities	110,000	115,000
Long-Term Debt	1,000,000	1,050,000
Owners' Equity:		
Common Stock	1,160,000	1,285,000
Retained Earnings	100,000	225,000
Less: Treasury Stock	(10,000)	(150,000)
Total Owners' Equity	1,250,000	1,360,000
Total Liabilities and Owners' Equity	$2,360,000	$2,525,000

Evangel Inn
Condensed Income Statement
For the year ended 19X7

Revenues	
Sales	$2,700,000
Interest Income	80,000
Total Revenues	2,780,000
Expenses	
Salaries and Wages	750,000
Depreciation	340,000
Amortization (franchise fees)	10,000
Interest Expense	100,000
Other Expenses	1,140,000
Income Before Gain and Losses and Income Taxes	440,000
Gain on Sale of Equipment	20,000
Loss on Sale of Investments	(50,000)
Income Taxes	80,000
Net Income	$ 330,000

Additional information:

1.   Equipment costing $100,000 was sold for $80,000 during 19X7.
2.   Investments costing $100,000 were sold during 19X7 for a loss of $50,000.
3.   Dividends of $205,000 were declared during 19X7.
4.   Treasury stock of $140,000 was purchased during 19X7.
5.   Long-term debt of $100,000 was converted to common stock during 19X7.
6.   Common stock of $35,000 was sold during 19X7.
7.   Long-term debt of $200,000 was borrowed during 19X7.
8.   Marketable securities of $5,000 were purchased during 19X7.

Evangel Inn
Statement of Cash Flows
For the year 19X7

Cash Flow Provided by Operating Activities:

Net Income		$ 330,000

Adjustments to Reconcile Net Income
to Net Cash Flows Provided by
Operating Activities:

Depreciation expense	$ 340,000	
Amortization expense	10,000	
Gain on sale of equipment	(20,000)	
Loss on sale of investments	50,000	
Increase in accounts receivable	(25,000)	
Increase in inventory	(5,000)	
Decrease in prepaid expenses	10,000	
Increase in accounts payable	10,000	370,000

Net Cash Flows from Operating
Activities: 700,000

Cash Flow Provided by Investing Activities:

Proceeds from sale of equipment	80,000	
Proceeds from sale of investments	50,000	
Purchase of marketable securities	(5,000)	
Purchase of equipment	(210,000)	
Purchase of investments	(400,000)	

Net Cash Flows from Investing
Activities: (485,000)

Cash Flow Provided by Financing Activities:

Payment of long-term debt	(50,000)	
Borrowing—long-term debt	200,000	
Purchase of treasury stock	(140,000)	
Proceeds from sale of common stock	25,000	
Payment of dividends	(210,000)	

Net Cash Flows from Financing
Activities: (175,000)

Increase in Cash	40,000
Cash at the beginning of 19X7	20,000
Cash at the end of 19X7	$ 60,000

Supplementary Schedule of Noncash Investing and Financing Activities
   Exchange of Common Stock for Long-Term Debt

Supplementary Disclosure of Cash Flow Information
   Cash paid during the year for:

Interest	100,000
Income Taxes	80,000

Required:

Compute the following ratios for the Evangel Inn:

1.   Current ratio for 19X6 and 19X7
2.   Acid-test ratio for 19X6 and 19X7
3.   Accounts receivable turnover for 19X7
4.   Return on assets for 19X7
5.   Return on owners' equity for 19X7
6.   Labor cost percentage for 19X7
7.   Average tax rate for 19X7
8.   Solvency ratio for 19X6 and 19X7
9.   Operating cash flows to total liabilities ratio for 19X7
10.   Operating cash flows to current liabilities for 19X7
11.   Profit margin for 19X7

Problem 13

The Mantle Inn commenced operations on January 1, 19X1, and has been operating for two years. Assume that you are the new assistant manager and desire to gain some insight into financial relationships of your new employer. Balance sheets and condensed income statements for the first two years are provided below.

Balance Sheets
Mantle Inn
December 31, 19X1 and 19X2

Assets	19X1	19X2
Current Assets:		
Cash	$ 10,000	$ 15,000
Marketable Securities	-0-	50,000
Accounts Receivable	55,000	60,000
Inventories	10,000	12,000
Total Current Assets	75,000	137,000
Property and Equipment:		
Land	100,000	100,000
Building (net)	1,950,000	1,900,000
Furniture & Equipment (net)	240,000	200,000
Total Property & Equipment	2,290,000	2,200,000
Total Assets	$2,365,000	$2,337,000
Liabilities and Owners' Equity		
Current Liabilities	$ 55,000	$ 60,000
Long-Term Debt	1,300,000	1,250,000
Total Liabilities	1,355,000	1,310,000
Owner's Equity		
Common Stock	1,000,000	1,000,000
Retained Earnings	10,000	27,000
Total Owners' Equity	1,010,000	1,027,000
Total Liabilities and Owners' Equity	$2,365,000	$2,337,000

Condensed Income Statements
Mantle Inn
For the years ended December 31, 19X1 and 19X2

	19X1	19X2
Sales	$1,200,000	$1,400,000
Operated Department Expense	620,000	700,000
Operated Department Income	580,000	700,000
Undistributed Operating Expenses	380,000	400,000
Total Income After Undistributed Operating Expenses	200,000	300,000
Fixed Charges	185,000	200,000
Income Taxes	5,000	45,000
Net Income	$ 10,000	$ 55,000

Required:

1. Calculate the following ratios for both years:

   a. Current ratio

   b. Solvency ratio

   c. Profit margin

   d. Operating efficiency

2. Calculate for 19X2 the following ratios:

   a. Property and equipment turnover ratio

   b. Total assets turnover ratio

   c. Accounts receivable turnover ratio

   d. Number of days accounts receivable outstanding

   e. Return on total assets

   f. Return on owners' equity

Problem 14

Musial Enterprises consists of four hotels. The corporation's required annual return for each hotel is 12% of each hotel's average total assets. The net income and average total assets for each hotel are as follows:

	Gibson Hotel	Brock Hotel	Smith Hotel	Carey Hotel
Net income	$ 2,700,000	$ 4,500,000	$ 3,000,000	$ 3,000,000
Average total assets	$20,000,000	$15,000,000	$25,000,000	$18,000,000

Each hotel has the opportunity to expand. The cost of expansion per hotel is $5,000,000, and the expected annual after-tax profit per hotel is $650,000.

Required:

1. Determine the ROA for each hotel before the expansion consideration.
2. If the expansion is based on maintaining or improving a hotel's ROA, which hotels would be expanded? Why?
3. Calculate the residual income for each hotel before and after the proposed expansion.

Problem 15

The owner of the Martin Motel and Restaurant has asked you to prepare an income statement and balance sheet based on the following:

1. Accounts receivable = $10,000
2. Accounts payable = $15,000
3. Current assets consist of cash, accounts receivable, and inventory.
4. Current liabilities consist of only accounts payable.
5. Current ratio = 1.2 to 1
6. Acid-test ratio = .8 to 1
7. Accounts receivable turnover = 30 times (all sales are credit sales)
8. Food inventory turnover = 9.625 times
9. Beverage inventory turnover = 6.3525 times
10. Property and equipment turnover = $1\,^3/47$ times
11. Depreciation expense = 10% of book value at year-end
12. Long-term debt = 9 times accounts payable
13. Interest rate = 10%
14. Tax rate = 20%
15. Average room rate = $20.00
16. Average food and beverage check = $5.00
17. Size of motel = 25 rooms
18. Occupancy percentage = 80%
19. Number of food and beverage checks = 30,800
20. Undistributed Operating Expenses = $33\,^1/3$% of total revenue
21. Food cost percentage = 40%
22. Beverage cost percentage = 22%
23. Food and beverage labor and other cost percentage = 30%
24. Rooms labor and other cost percentage = 40%
25. Food sales = $62\,^1/2$% of total food and beverage sales
26. Debt-equity ratio = 1 to 1
27. Return on owners' equity = 1.330667%

Assume that the balance sheet at the beginning of the year is the same as at the end of the year.

Note: For this problem, food and beverage is a single combined department.

Chapter 6 Outline

General Nature of Cost
Costs in Relation to Sales Volume
    Fixed Costs
    Variable Costs
    Step Costs
    Mixed Costs
    Total Costs
Determination of Mixed Cost Elements
    High/Low Two-Point Method
    Scatter Diagram
    Regression Analysis
    Evaluation of the Results
Fixed Versus Variable Costs
Direct and Indirect Costs
Overhead Costs
    Allocation of Overhead Costs
    After Cost Allocation
Controllable Costs
Differential Costs
Relevant Costs
Sunk Costs
Opportunity Costs
Average and Incremental Costs
Standard Costs
Decision-Making Situations
    Illustration of Relevant Costs in Management Decisions
Computer Applications

6

Basic Cost Concepts

THE WORD *COST* IS USED in many different contexts and may convey very different meanings. For example, each of the following expressions uses the term to refer to something different: the cost of a dishwasher was $5,000; the labor cost for the period was $10,000; the cost of damages to the hotel from the hurricane approximated $10,000. In the first expression, cost refers to the purchase price of an asset; one asset (cash) was given in exchange for another asset (the dishwasher). The second expression uses cost to refer to an expense for the period; cash (an asset) was paid to employees for services they provided. In this case, assets were not directly exchanged; rather, cash was paid for labor services rendered by employees to generate revenues and accounts receivable. The accounts receivable, when collected, result in cash. In the third expression, the cost due to the hurricane refers to a loss—a dissipation of assets without the receipt of other assets either directly or indirectly. Obviously, the term cost may have a variety of meanings. In this chapter, we will generally use cost to mean expenses.

Managers must understand many cost concepts, including those in the following questions:

1. What are the hotel's fixed costs?
2. Which costs are relevant to purchasing a new microcomputer?
3. What are the variable costs of serving a steak dinner?
4. What is the opportunity cost of adding 25 rooms to the motel?
5. What is the standard cost of catering a banquet for 500 people?
6. What are the hotel's controllable costs?
7. How are fixed cost portions of mixed costs determined?
8. How are costs allocated to operated departments?
9. Which costs are sunk costs in considering a future purchase?
10. Which costs are relevant to pricing a lobster dinner?

In this chapter, we will discuss a variety of cost concepts. We will consider costs in relation to sales volume and operated departments. We will also discuss the separation of mixed costs into fixed and variable elements, provide a simplified approach to the problem of cost allocation, and consider the concept of relevant costs in decision-making. The Appendix to this chapter contains a detailed discussion of more advanced approaches to cost allocation, including illustrations of the direct and step methods of cost allocation.

Exhibit 1   Fixed Costs: Total and Per Unit

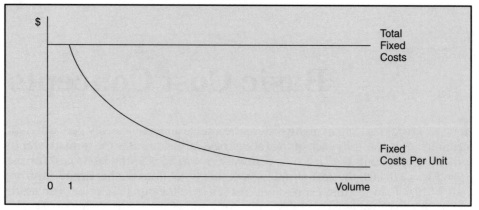

General Nature of Cost

Cost, considered as an expense, is the reduction of an asset, generally for the ultimate purpose of increasing revenues. Costs include cost of food sold, labor expense, supplies expense, utilities expense, marketing expense, rent expense, depreciation expense, insurance expense, and many others. Because the profit margin for most hospitality operations is less than 10%, more than 90% of their revenues (ultimately cash) is used to pay these expenses or costs. From management's viewpoint, there are several different types of costs. It is essential that managers understand both the types of costs and their applications.

Costs in Relation to Sales Volume

One way of viewing costs is to understand how they change with changes in the activity (sales) of the hospitality operation. In this context, costs can be seen as fixed, variable, step, or mixed (partly fixed and partly variable).

Fixed Costs

Fixed costs are those that remain constant in the short run, even when sales volume varies. For example, room sales may increase by 5% or food sales may decline by 10% while, in both cases, the fixed costs remain constant. The graph in Exhibit 1 plots costs along the vertical axis and sales volume along the horizontal axis. The graph shows that total fixed costs remain constant even when sales volume increases.

Common examples of fixed costs include salaries, rent expense, insurance expense, property taxes, depreciation expense, and interest expense. Certain fixed costs may be reduced if a lodging facility closes for part of the year. For example, insurance and labor expenses may be avoided during the shut-down. Fixed costs that may be avoided when a company shuts down are called **avoidable costs**.

Fixed costs are often classified as either capacity or discretionary costs. **Capacity fixed costs** relate to the ability to provide goods and services. For a hotel, the capacity fixed costs relate to the ability to provide a number of rooms for sale. The fixed costs include, but are not limited to, depreciation, property taxes, interest, and certain salaries. There is a quality dimension related to capacity fixed costs. For example, if the hotel were to eliminate its swimming pool or air conditioning system, it could still provide the same number of rooms, but at a lower level of service.

Discretionary fixed costs do not affect a lodging establishment's current capacity. They are costs that managers may choose to avoid during the short run, often to meet a budget. However, continued avoidance will generally cause problems for the hospitality operation. Discretionary fixed costs include educational seminars for executives, charitable contributions, employee training programs, and advertising. Generally, reducing such costs has no immediate effect on operations. However, if these programs continue to be curtailed, sales and various expenses may be seriously affected. During a financial crisis, discretionary fixed costs are likelier to be cut than capacity fixed costs because they are easier to restore and have less immediate impact.

Fixed costs can also be related to sales volume by determining the average fixed cost per unit sold. For example, if fixed costs total $10,000 for a period in which 2,000 rooms are sold, the average fixed cost per room sold is $5.00 ($10,000 ÷ 2,000 rooms). However, if 3,000 rooms are sold during the period, then the average fixed cost per room sold is $3.33 ($10,000 ÷ 3,000 rooms). As the sales volume increases, the fixed cost per unit decreases. The graph in Exhibit 1 also illustrates this relationship.

Although they are constant in the short run, all fixed costs change over longer periods. For example, the monthly lease payment on a machine may increase about once a year. Therefore, from a long-term perspective, all fixed costs may be viewed as variable costs.

Variable Costs

Variable costs change proportionally with the volume of business. For example, if food sales increase by 10%, the cost of food sold may also be expected to increase by 10%. Exhibit 2 depicts total variable costs and variable costs per unit as each relates to sales volume. Total variable costs (TVC) are determined by multiplying the variable cost per unit by the number of unit sales. For example, the TVC for a food service operation with a variable cost per meal of $3 and 1,000 projected meal sales would be $3,000.

Theoretically, total variable costs vary with total sales, whereas unit variable costs remain constant. For example, if the cost of food sold is 35%, then the unit cost per $1 of sales is $.35, regardless of sales volume. The graph in Exhibit 2 shows that unit variable costs are really fixed—that is, the cost per sales dollar remains constant. In actuality, of course, a business should be able to take advantage of volume discounts as its sales increase beyond some level. When this occurs, the cost of sales should increase at a slower rate than sales.

In truth, few costs, if any, vary in *exact* proportion to total sales. However, several costs come close to meeting this criterion and may be considered variable costs. Examples include the cost of food sold, cost of beverages sold, some labor costs, and supplies used in production and service operations.

Exhibit 2 Variable Costs: Total and Per Unit

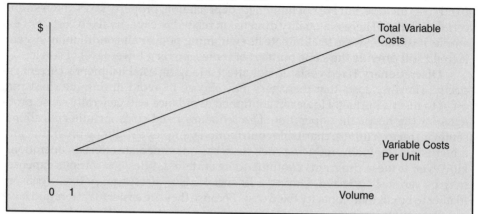

Exhibit 3 Step Costs

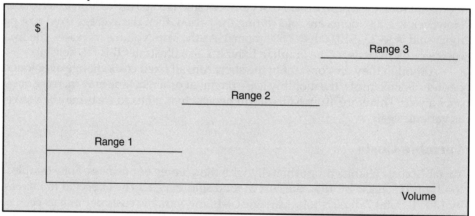

Step Costs

Step costs are constant within a range of activity but different among ranges of activity. Exhibit 3 illustrates this relationship. Supervisor salaries are typical step costs. For example, if a housekeeping supervisor is able to oversee no more than 15 room attendants, then the operation must add another supervisor upon adding the sixteenth room attendant. This new supervisor would be able to supervise an additional 14 room attendants.

Step costs resemble fixed costs when one step includes the operation's probable range of activity. In Exhibit 3, for example, range 2 might be a hotel's expected range of activity. In such cases, step costs are considered fixed costs for analytical purposes. When there are many steps and the cost differences between steps are small, then step costs, for analytical purposes, are considered mixed costs (to be discussed next).

Exhibit 4   Total Mixed Costs

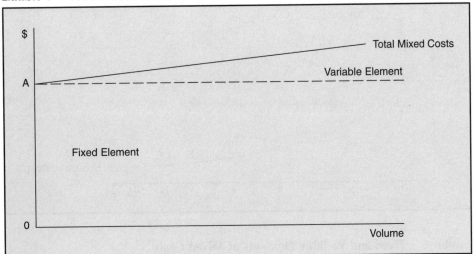

Mixed Costs

Many costs are partly fixed and partly variable—that is, they are a mix of both fixed and variable cost elements. These costs are sometimes referred to as semi-variable or semi-fixed. In this chapter, we will refer to costs that are partly fixed and partly variable as **mixed costs**.

The mixed cost's fixed element is determined independently of sales activity, while the variable element is assumed to vary proportionally with sales volume. As with variable costs, the variable element of mixed costs may not vary in exact proportion to sales activity. However, the assumption of a linear relationship between variable cost elements and sales volume is generally accepted because any difference is usually considered insignificant. However, this assumption is reasonable only across a relevant range of activity. For example, the relevant range for a hotel *may* be paid occupancy levels between 40% and 95%. Outside of this range, the variable cost–sales relationship *may* be different.

The graph in Exhibit 4 depicts the two elements (fixed and variable) of mixed costs. The portion of the vertical axis below point A represents fixed costs, while the difference between the slopes of the total mixed costs and fixed cost lines reflects the variable element of total mixed costs. The graph in Exhibit 5 shows a decrease in unit mixed costs as sales volume increases. This decrease is not as dramatic as the decrease in fixed costs per sales unit (Exhibit 1) because the variable element in mixed costs increases with each unit sold, therefore increasing total mixed costs.

Several examples of mixed costs, including a brief discussion of their fixed and variable elements, are listed in Exhibit 6.

Total mixed costs (TMC) for any cost can be estimated with the following equation:

Exhibit 5   Mixed Costs per Sales Unit

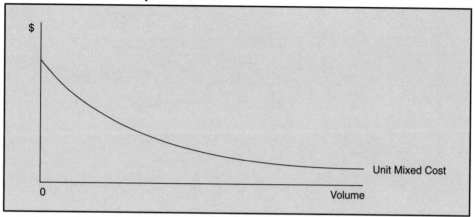

Exhibit 6   Fixed and Variable Elements of Mixed Costs

	Elements	
Mixed Cost	**Fixed**	**Variable**
1. Telephone expense	Cost of system/rental of system	Cost of calls
2. Building lease	Fixed cost per square foot of space rented	Percentage of revenue in addition to fixed amount
3. Automobile lease	Fixed cost/day	Additional charge per mile automobile is driven
4. Executive remuneration	Base pay	Bonuses based on sales
5. Repair and maintenance	Minimum amount required to maintain lodging firm at low occupancy	Additional maintenance required with higher occupancy levels

$$\text{TMC} = \text{fixed costs} + (\text{variable cost per unit} \times \text{unit sales})$$

Thus, a hotel with a franchise fee of $1,000 per month and $3 per room sold would estimate its franchise fees (a mixed cost) for a month with 3,500 projected room sales as follows:

$$
\begin{aligned}
\text{Franchise fees} \quad &= \quad \$1,000 + (3,500 \times \$3) \\
&= \quad \underline{\underline{\$11,500}}
\end{aligned}
$$

Total Costs

Total costs (TC) for a hospitality establishment consist of the sum of its fixed, variable, step, and mixed costs. If step costs are included in either fixed or mixed costs, the TC may be determined by the following equation:

Exhibit 7   Total Costs

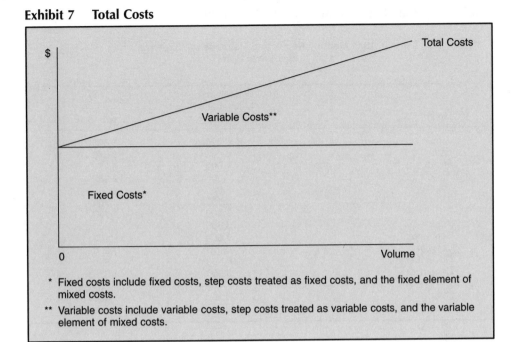

* Fixed costs include fixed costs, step costs treated as fixed costs, and the fixed element of mixed costs.

** Variable costs include variable costs, step costs treated as variable costs, and the variable element of mixed costs.

$$TC = \text{fixed costs} + (\text{variable cost per unit} \times \text{unit sales})$$

An estimation of TC for a rooms-only lodging operation that sells 1,000 rooms and has total fixed costs of $20,000 and variable costs per unit of $20, is $40,000.

$$
\begin{aligned}
TC &= \$20{,}000 + (1{,}000 \times \$20) \\
&= \underline{\$40{,}000}
\end{aligned}
$$

Total costs are depicted graphically in Exhibit 7.

The equation for TC corresponds to the general equation for a straight line, which is as follows:[1]

$$y = a + bx$$

where y = value of the dependent variable (total costs)
a = the constant term (total fixed costs)
b = slope of the line (variable cost per unit)
x = the value of the independent variable (units sold)

Determination of Mixed Cost Elements

When making pricing, marketing, and expansion decisions, management needs to estimate the fixed and variable elements of each mixed cost. We will consider three

Exhibit 8 Monthly Repair and Maintenance Expense

19X1 Monthly Repair and Maintenance Expense
Mayflower Hotel

Month	Repair and Maintenance Expense	Rooms Sold
January	$ 6,200	1,860
February	6,100	1,820
March	7,000	2,170
April	7,500	2,250
May	8,000	2,480
June	8,500	2,700
July	7,900	2,790
August	8,600	2,800
September	7,000	2,100
October	6,000	1,900
November	6,500	1,800
December	5,900	1,330
Total	$85,200	26,000

methods of estimating mixed cost elements: the high/low two-point method, the scatter diagram, and regression analysis. The maintenance and repair expense of the hypothetical Mayflower Hotel for 19X1 will be used to illustrate all three methods. Exhibit 8 presents the monthly repair and maintenance expense together with rooms sold by month for the Mayflower Hotel.

High/Low Two-Point Method

The simplest approach to estimating the fixed and variable elements of a mixed cost is the **high/low two-point method**. This approach is simple because it bases the estimation on data from only two periods in the entire time span of an establishment's operations. The method consists of the following eight steps:

1. Select the two extreme periods (such as months) of sales activity (for example, rooms sold) in the time span under consideration (such as one year). If an extreme value is due to an event beyond management's control and does not represent normal operations, consider the next value. For example, if a country club is closed for the month of January, the value for the next lowest month should be used. Extreme values may only be apparent when charted on a scatter diagram, which we will discuss shortly.

2. Calculate the differences in total mixed cost and activity for the two periods.

3. Divide the mixed cost difference by the activity difference to determine the variable cost per activity unit (for example, each room sold).

4. Multiply the variable cost per activity unit by the total activity for the period of lowest (or highest) sales to arrive at the total variable cost for the period of lowest (or highest) activity.

5. Subtract the result in Step 4 from the total mixed cost for the period of lowest activity to determine the fixed cost for that period.

6. Check the answer in Step 5 by repeating Steps 4 and 5 for the period with the greatest activity.

7. Multiply the fixed cost per period by the number of periods in the time span to calculate the fixed costs for the entire time period.

8. Subtract the total fixed costs from the total mixed costs to determine the total variable costs.

The high/low two-point method is illustrated below using data from Exhibit 8.

1. High month—August
   Low month—December

2.

	Repair and Maintenance Expense	Rooms Sold
August	$8,600	2,800
December	5,900	1,330
Difference	$2,700	1,470

3. Variable Cost per Room Sold $= \dfrac{\text{Mixed Cost Difference}}{\text{Rooms Sold Difference}}$

$$= \frac{\$2,700}{1,470}$$

$$= \$1.8367$$

This result means that for every additional room sold, the hotel will incur repair and maintenance variable costs of $1.8367.

4. Total Variable Cost of Repair and Maintenance Expense for December $=$ December Rooms Sold $\times$ Variable Cost

$$= 1,330 \times 1.8367$$

$$= \$2,442.81$$

5. Total Fixed Cost of   Total Repair and Maintenance
    Repair and Maintenance = Cost for December − Variable
    Expense for December   Repair and Maintenance Cost
                           for December

    = $5,900 − $2,442.81

    = $3,457.19

6. Check results by using the high month, August.

    Variable Cost = 2,800 × 1.8367
                  = $5,142.76

    Fixed Cost = 8,600.00 − 5,142.76
               = $3,457.24

    Compare the result in Step 5 with Step 6 as follows:

    Fixed Costs—Step 6 $3,457.24
    Fixed Costs—Step 5   − 3,457.19
                             .05 (minor difference due to rounding)

7. Calculate total fixed costs for the year.

    Total Fixed Costs = Fixed Costs per Month × 12 Months
                      = $3,457.19 × 12
                      = $41,486.28

8. Determine total variable costs of repair and maintenance expense for the year.

    Total Variable Costs = Total Mixed Costs − Total Fixed Costs
                         = $85,200 − $41,486.28
                         = $43,713.72

The high/low two-point method considers only two extreme periods and is a fairly simple way of estimating the variable and fixed elements of mixed costs. This approach assumes that the extreme periods are a fair reflection of the high and low points for the entire year; therefore, the results will be inaccurate to the degree that the two periods fail to represent fairly the high and low points of activity. The scatter diagram, though tedious, is a more accurate approach.

Scatter Diagram

The **scatter diagram** is a detailed approach to determining the fixed and variable elements of a mixed cost. The steps involved in this method are as follows:

1. Prepare a graph with the independent variable (sales volume) on the horizontal axis and the dependent variable (cost) on the vertical axis.

2. Plot data on the graph by periods.

3. Draw a straight line through the points, keeping an equal number of points above and below the line.

4. Extend the line to the vertical axis. The intersection indicates the fixed costs for the period.

5. Multiply the fixed costs for the period by the number of periods to determine the fixed costs for the time span.

6. Total variable costs are determined by subtracting total fixed costs (Step 5) from total mixed costs.

7. Variable costs per sales unit are determined by dividing total variable costs by total units sold.

Exhibit 9 is a scatter diagram of the maintenance and repair expense of the Mayflower Hotel. The scatter diagram was graphed with rooms sold as the independent variable (horizontal axis) and repair and maintenance expense as the dependent variable (vertical axis). Each monthly repair and maintenance expense was plotted and a straight line was drawn through the points. The line might vary depending on who draws it; however, it should approximate a "best fit." In this case, there are five points above the line, five points below the line, and two points on the line. The line intersects the vertical axis at $3,300. This is the fixed cost approximation per month. The estimated annual fixed costs are $39,600 ($3,300 × 12 months). Therefore, total variable repair and maintenance costs are $45,600, determined by subtracting total fixed costs of $39,600 from total costs of $85,200. Variable repair and maintenance costs per room sold is $1.75, determined by dividing the total variable costs of $45,600 by the number of rooms sold for the year (26,000).

The scatter diagram is an improvement over the high/low two-point approach because it includes data from all periods in the time span under consideration. In our example, the calculations use data from 12 months of a year. However, these calculations are time consuming, and the placement of the straight line between the data points is an approximation rather than a precise measurement. Regression analysis (discussed next) is a still more accurate approach. However, since an assumption when using regression analysis is a linear relationship between the two variables, a scatter diagram is still useful for determining linearity.

Regression Analysis

Regression analysis is a mathematical approach to fitting a straight line to data points perfectly—that is, the difference in the distances of the data points from the

Exhibit 9   Scatter Diagram

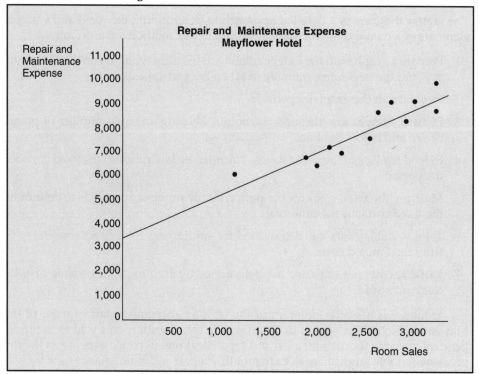

line is minimized. The formulas used in regression analysis allow us to make the calculations without plotting points or drawing lines.

As stated earlier, the formula for a straight line is $y = a + bx$. In our Mayflower Hotel example, y stands for repair and maintenance expense, x stands for rooms sold, a stands for the fixed cost element, and b stands for the variable cost per room sold. Therefore, the total repair and maintenance expense (y) for any period is the fixed cost element (a) plus the variable cost per room sold (b) multiplied by the number of rooms sold (x).

Once we know the monthly fixed cost element of the repair and maintenance expense, we multiply that figure by 12 months to calculate the annual total fixed cost element. The formula for determining the monthly fixed cost element is as follows:

$$\text{Fixed Costs} = \frac{(\Sigma y)(\Sigma x^2) - (\Sigma x)(\Sigma xy)}{n(\Sigma x^2) - (\Sigma x)^2}$$

The formula is explained as follows:

Σ the Greek letter sigma is read, and means, "the sum of." So, Σx and Σy mean the sum of all x values and the sum of all y values, respectively. Σxy means the sum of all x and y values that are multiplied together.

Exhibit 10   Calculating Values for Fixed Cost Elements

	(x) Rooms Sold	(y) Repair and Maintenance Expense	x^2	xy
Month				
January	1,860	$ 6,200	3,459,600	11,532,000
February	1,820	6,100	3,312,400	11,102,000
March	2,170	7,000	4,708,900	15,190,000
April	2,250	7,500	5,062,500	16,875,000
May	2,480	8,000	6,150,400	19,840,000
June	2,700	8,500	7,290,000	22,950,000
July	2,790	7,900	7,784,100	22,041,000
August	2,800	8,600	7,840,000	24,080,000
September	2,100	7,000	4,410,000	14,700,000
October	1,900	6,000	3,610,000	11,400,000
November	1,800	6,500	3,240,000	11,700,000
December	1,330	5,900	1,768,900	7,847,000
Totals	$\Sigma x = 26{,}000$	$\Sigma y = \$85{,}200$	$\Sigma x^2 = 58{,}636{,}800$	$\Sigma xy = 189{,}257{,}000$

Determination of Repair and Calculation of Values
for Maintenance Fixed Cost Element
Mayflower Hotel

y   stands for the dependent variable.

x   stands for the independent variable.

n   stands for the number of periods in the time span.

Exhibit 10 presents the calculated values for the Mayflower Hotel. Putting these values into the formula reveals that the monthly fixed cost element of repair and maintenance expense is $2,719.57.[2] Fixed cost per month multiplied by 12 equals the total fixed element of repair and maintenance expense for 19X1 ($32,634.84).

The total variable costs are determined by subtracting total fixed costs from total costs. Using the total cost figure for the Mayflower Hotel's repair and maintenance expense found in Exhibit 8, we can calculate the total variable cost element as follows:

Repair and Maintenance Expense	$85,200.00
Total Fixed Cost Element	− 32,634.84
Total Variable Cost Element	$52,565.16

The variable cost per room sold is determined by solving for the value of *b* using the formula for a straight line:

$$y = a + bx$$
$$85{,}200 = 32{,}634.84 + b(26{,}000)$$
$$b = \$2.02 \text{ per room sold}$$

These computations, performed manually, are too complex for practical application. Many computers and hand-held financial calculators have programs available to perform these calculations. The user simply enters the appropriate data. However, because this is so easy, there is a tendency for the user to feed raw data into the calculator or computer and accept the output as truth. The cliché "garbage-in, garbage-out" applies here. The user should select variables that have a logical relationship. For example, repair and maintenance expense and number of meals served may not be a meaningful relationship. If more guests dine in a hotel's restaurant, repair and maintenance expense in food service operations will increase, but dining in the restaurant does not affect repair and maintenance in other departments. Rooms sold, or even number of hotel guests, relates more logically to repair and maintenance expense.

As with the high/low two-point method, values representing abnormal operating conditions should not be included in regression analysis.

Evaluation of the Results

The three methods demonstrated to estimate the fixed and variable elements of the Mayflower Hotel's repair and maintenance expense produced the following results:

	Fixed	Variable	Total
High/low two-point method	$41,486.28	$43,713.72	$85,200
Scatter diagram	39,600.00	45.600.00	85,200
Regression analysis	32,634.84	52,565.16	85,200

The difference between the fixed cost amounts determined by the simplest (the high/low two-point method) and the most complex (regression analysis) methods is $8,851.44. This difference is more than 25% of the figure reached by regression analysis. Regression analysis is the most precise method and easily performed with a financial calculator or a computer. However, the major determination of which method to use is based on cost-benefit considerations.

Fixed Versus Variable Costs

Many goods and services may be purchased on either a fixed or variable cost arrangement. For example, a lease may be either fixed (offered at a fixed price) or variable (offered at a certain percentage of revenues). Management's decision to select a fixed or variable cost arrangement is based on the cost-benefit considerations involved. Under a truly fixed arrangement, the cost remains the same regardless of activity and, therefore, management is able to lock in a maximum amount. Under a variable arrangement, the amount paid depends on the level of activity. The level of activity at which the period cost is the same under either arrangement is called the **indifference point**. An example follows to illustrate this concept.

Assume that a food service operation has the option of signing either an annual fixed lease of $48,000 or a variable lease set at 5% of revenue. The indifference point is determined as follows:

Exhibit 11   Indifference Point

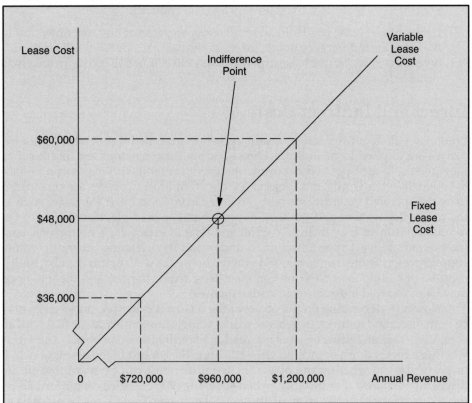

$$
\begin{array}{rcl}
\text{Variable Cost Percentage} \times \text{Revenue} & = & \text{Fixed Lease Cost} \\
.05\,(\text{Revenue}) & = & 48,000 \\
\text{Revenue} & = & \dfrac{48,000}{.05} \\
\text{Revenue} & = & \underline{\underline{\$960,000}}
\end{array}
$$

When annual revenue is $960,000, the lease expense will be $48,000, regardless of whether the lease arrangement is fixed or variable. Therefore, if annual revenue is expected to exceed $960,000, then management should select a fixed lease in order to minimize its lease expense. On the other hand, if annual revenue is expected to be less than $960,000, a variable lease will minimize lease expense. Exhibit 11 is the graphic depiction of this situation. A review of Exhibit 11 suggests the following:

1. Using a variable lease results in an excess lease expense at any revenue point to the *right* of the indifference point. For example, using the previous illustration,

if revenue is $1,200,000, the lease expense from a variable lease is $60,000, or $12,000 more than for a fixed lease of $48,000 annually.

2. Using a fixed lease results in an excess lease expense at any revenue point to the *left* of the indifference point. For example, using the previous illustration, if revenue is $720,000, the lease expense is still $48,000, or $12,000 more than for a variable lease.

Direct and Indirect Costs

When we talk about expenses, certain expenses are called direct while other expenses are implied to be indirect. Direct and indirect expenses are discussed as they pertain to the operated departments (profit centers) within a lodging establishment. In other words, the "objects" of direct/indirect expenses are considered to be the operated departments that generate income and incur expenses, such as the rooms department and the food department. For example, direct costs of the rooms department may include payroll and related expenses, commissions, contract cleaning, guest transportation, laundry and dry cleaning, linen, operating supplies, reservations, uniforms, and other expenses as well. In this context, undistributed operating expenses, management fees, fixed charges, and income taxes may be considered indirect (overhead) expenses.

However, depending on the object of the incurred expenses, many costs may be both direct and indirect. In general, a direct cost is one readily identified with an object, whereas an indirect cost is not readily identified with an object. Therefore, whether a cost is direct or indirect depends upon the context of the discussion and, in particular, on whether the object incurring the cost can be identified in the discussion's context. For instance, when speaking of the service center formed by the general manager's department, the general manager's salary can be ascribed as a direct cost of the service center and can be classified as a subset of administrative and general expense. However, in the context of discussing all operated departments (profit centers) and other service centers (for example, the marketing department), the general manager's salary would be ascribed as an indirect cost of these other departments, because the object of this cost in those departments cannot be directly identified.

This distinction is important because department heads are responsible for the direct costs of their departments since they exercise control over them; however, they are normally not responsible for indirect costs.

Overhead Costs

Overhead costs include all costs other than the direct costs incurred by profit centers. Thus, overhead costs are indirect costs when the cost objectives are the profit centers. Overhead costs include the undistributed operating expenses (administrative and general, information systems, human resources, transportation, security, marketing, franchise fees, property operation and maintenance, and utility costs), management fees, fixed charges (insurance, rent, depreciation, interest, property taxes, and so forth), and income taxes.

Exhibit 12   Sample Unallocated Income Statement

Unallocated Income Statement
Walters Motor Inn

	Rooms	Food & Beverage	Total
Revenue	$ 60,000	$ 40,000	$ 100,000
Cost of Sales	0	16,000	16,000
Payroll and Related Expenses	14,000	11,000	25,000
Other Direct Expenses	6,000	4,500	10,500
Total Expenses	20,000	31,500	51,500
Departmental Income	$ 40,000	$ 8,500	$ 48,500
Undistributed Operating Expenses:			
Administrative & General			12,000
Marketing			3,000
Property Operation and Maintenance			2,000
Utility Costs			4,000
Total Income After Undistributed Operating Expenses			27,500
Insurance			3,000
Depreciation			18,000
Total Insurance and Depreciation			21,000
Income Before Income Taxes			6,500
Income Taxes			2,000
Net Income			$ 4,500

Note: Information systems, security, human resources, and transportation expenses are insignificant and are not shown as separate cost centers.

Sometimes overhead costs are not distributed to profit centers. This is because these expenses are regarded as indirect costs, not readily ascribed to objects in the operated departments. However, management and the board of directors of a hospitality establishment may want to distribute overhead costs among the profit centers. This process is commonly called **cost allocation**.

Allocation of Overhead Costs

The Appendix to this chapter discusses and illustrates advanced cost allocation approaches. For our purposes here, however, we will consider a simplified approach that allocates overhead costs using a single allocation base (such as square footage). This method is referred to as the **single allocation base approach (SABA)**. We will illustrate this approach with the hypothetical Walters Motor Inn, whose unallocated income statement for a typical month is shown in Exhibit 12.

Exhibit 13   Overhead Costs

Overhead Costs
Walters Motor Inn

Overhead Cost Area (2)	Overhead Cost	Percentage		Amount (1)	
		Rooms	Food & Bev.	Rooms	Food & Bev.
A & G	$12,000	72.73%	27.27%	$ 8,728	$ 3,272
Marketing	3,000	72.73	27.27	2,182	818
POM	2,000	72.73	27.27	1,455	545
Utility Costs	4,000	72.73	27.27	2,909	1,091
Insurance	3,000	72.73	27.27	2,182	818
Depreciation	18,000	72.73	27.27	13,091	4,909
Total	$42,000			$30,547	$11,453

(1) All amounts are rounded to the nearest $1.
(2) A & G = administrative & general; POM = property operation and maintenance.

As the exhibit shows, the monthly net income for the entire operation is $4,500. The rooms and food and beverage departments have generated incomes of $40,000 and $8,500, respectively. The only overhead cost that will not be allocated among departments is income tax. All other costs will be allocated based on square footage. The square footage of the rooms department is 40,000, while the food and beverage department occupies 15,000 square feet. Therefore, 72.73% of the overhead costs will be allocated to the rooms department and 27.27% will be allocated to the food and beverage department.

Exhibit 13 illustrates this allocation. Exhibit 14 shows the allocated income statement of the Walters Motor Inn. The rooms department's bottom line after cost allocation is $9,453, while the food and beverage department's bottom line is $(2,953).

If an allocation base other than square footage had been used, there would have been different cost allocation amounts and, therefore, different departmental income reported after allocation. For example, the Walters Motor Inn employs 14 people in the rooms department and 20 people in the food and beverage department. If the SABA had used the number of employees in each department as the allocation base, the rooms department would absorb 41.18% of the overhead costs, while the food and beverage department would absorb 58.82%. The Walters Motor Inn allocated income statement, in very abbreviated form, would now appear as follows:

	Rooms	Food & Beverage	Total
Departmental Income	$40,000	$ 8,500	$48,500
Overhead Costs Allocated	17,296	24,704	42,000
Post Allocation			
Departmental Income	$22,704	$ (16,204)	$ 6,500

The above figures show that a different allocation base results in different allocated amounts and, therefore, in different departmental incomes following allocation. Ideally, costs should be allocated based on their actual usage by the profit

Exhibit 14   Sample Allocated Income Statement

	Rooms	Food & Beverage	Total
Allocated Income Statement			
Walters Motor Inn			
Revenue	$60,000	$40,000	$100,000
Cost of Sales	0	16,000	16,000
Payroll and Related Expenses	14,000	11,000	25,000
Other Direct Expenses	6,000	4,500	10,500
Total Expenses	20,000	31,500	51,500
Departmental Income	40,000	8,500	48,500
Allocated Overhead Costs:			
Administrative & General	8,728	3,272	12,000
Marketing	2,182	818	3,000
Property Operation and Maintenance	1,455	545	2,000
Utility Costs	2,909	1,091	4,000
Insurance	2,182	818	3,000
Depreciation	13,091	4,909	18,000
Total	30,547	11,453	42,000
Income Before Income Taxes	$ 9,453	$(2,953)	6,500
Income Taxes			2,000
Net Income			$ 4,500

centers and the nature of the expense involved. For example, if the hotel is leased on a square footage basis, then square footage is a suitable allocation base for the hotel's rent expense. On the other hand, since the general manager's supervisory role is often his or her primary role in managing the hotel, the general manager's salary may be allocated based on the number of employees supervised or even payroll expense by department.

Using different allocation bases to allocate different overhead costs among departments is referred to as the **multiple allocation base approach (MABA)**. MABA is generally preferable to SABA because MABA allocates overhead costs on the basis of an observed relationship between the cost and the profit center. The Appendix to this chapter contains a discussion of two multiple allocation base approaches.

After Cost Allocation

As Exhibit 14 shows, the food and beverage department of the Walters Motor Inn shows a $2,953 loss after cost allocation. Assuming the cost allocation was reasonable, what should be done, if anything? Management should consider at least four factors when deciding what to do about an underperforming department:

1. The underperforming department's income

2. The extent to which the overhead costs allocated to the underperforming department are fixed

3. The extent to which the presence and performance of the department affects other profit centers

4. Operating alternatives for the underperforming department

In our example, management of the Walters Motor Inn might propose closing the food and beverage department; however, this would result in the loss of the department's income of $8,500. Furthermore, assuming that the allocated overhead costs would be incurred anyway, the $11,453 allocated to the food and beverage department would be re-allocated to the rooms department. (To the extent that some of these costs could be avoided, closing down a "losing" department would be favorable to the overall profit picture. However, other factors must be considered.) The Walters Motor Inn would thus incur a $2,000 pretax loss by closing the food and beverage department, determined as follows:

Income before income taxes (per Exhibit 14)	$6,500
Loss of food and beverage department income	(8,500)
Net Result	$(2,000)

Management must also consider the food and beverage department's impact on other profit centers. For example, if the food and beverage department is closed, sales in the rooms department, and thus rooms income, might decrease. The final consideration is how the food and beverage operation is being managed. Perhaps a new menu, renovations, or other changes might correct the department's performance problems.

Controllable Costs

Managers should generally hold their subordinates responsible only for those costs they can control; to do otherwise may be counterproductive. Controlling costs means using judgment and authority to regulate costs—that is, keeping costs within certain limits rather than eliminating them. **Controllable costs** are costs over which a person is able to exert an influence. For example, the food department manager may be able to influence food usage, personnel preparing and serving food, and supplies used in food production and service. Therefore, cost of food sold, payroll expense, and food and service supplies expense are controllable costs for the food department manager. On the other hand, the food department manager generally has no control over rent paid for the space the restaurant occupies. However, the board of directors may be able to control the rent expense; therefore, from the board's perspective, rent is a controllable expense.

Several costs cannot be easily influenced or changed in the short run; these costs are often considered non-controllable. However, such costs can be regulated over the long run and from this perspective can be viewed as controllable. In general, all costs are controllable given sufficient time and input from a high enough level of management.

The income statement is organized on a responsibility accounting basis. The direct expenses of each profit center are those costs that the respective department heads control. For example, the food and beverage department manager has authority over (and can therefore control) cost of sales, payroll and related expenses,

Exhibit 15   The General Manager's Control over Selected Costs

Controlled Costs	Non-controllable Costs
Variable	
Cost of food sold	Rent expense (% of sales)
Cost of beverages sold	
Room supplies	
Food and beverage supplies	
Payroll costs—wages	
Fixed	
Payroll costs—salaries	Depreciation
Professional fees	Property taxes
	Property insurance
	Interest expense
	Rent expense (fixed portion)

and other direct expenses of the food and beverage department. Exhibit 15 is a table listing several costs as they relate to the general manager's ability to control them.

The general manager and department managers should be held accountable for costs they control. First, the controllable fixed costs incurred should be compared to the amounts budgeted for the period. Second, the controllable variable costs should be compared to the product of the variable unit costs times the unit sales. For example, assume that a food and beverage department's costs are budgeted at $2,000 of fixed costs per month and $3 per meal served. Further assume that 3,000 meals were served during the month and that the actual costs incurred were $2,200 for fixed costs and $9,300 for variable costs. A quick review reflects the following:

	Budget	Actual	Difference
Fixed costs	$ 2,000	$ 2,200	$ 200
Variable costs	9,000	9,300	300
	$ 11,000	$ 11,500	$ 500

The manager's performance reflects actual costs of $500 in excess of the budget. (In practice, costs and expenses are shown by account, rather than being categorized simply as fixed and variable.)

Differential Costs

In a decision-making situation, costs that differ between two alternatives are called **differential costs.** By focusing on differential costs, decision-makers can narrow the set of cost considerations to those that make a difference between two alternatives. For example, suppose management is considering the installation of a front office computer to replace two obsolete posting machines. In this situation, differential costs include the purchase price of the computer and any other costs associated with the new computer that differ from the costs involved in using the existing posting machines. Such costs might include labor, utilities, supplies, and insurance. Costs that remain the same with or without the new computer are non-differential and need not be considered in the decision-making process.

Relevant Costs

Relevant costs are those that must be considered in a decision-making situation. In order for a cost to be relevant, it must be differential, future, and quantifiable. The differential criterion demands that the cost between two or more alternatives be different. The future characteristic demands that the cost must not have already occurred, but must be incurred only after the decision is made. Finally, relevant costs must be quantifiable. The unquantifiable preference for Machine A over Machine B is not a cost consideration in the decision-making process. The following example illustrates the concept of relevant costs.

Happy Harry, owner of Harry's Place, has been approached by a salesperson selling ranges. The salesperson wants to sell Happy Harry a new range and provides the following information:

Cost of new range	=	$5,000
Estimated useful life of new range	=	Six years
Annual operating costs:		
Electricity	=	$800
Repairs	=	$200
Labor	=	$10,000
Estimated salvage value after six years	=	$500

Happy Harry believes his present range, with a major repair job, should last for six more years. In order to make a rational and informed decision, Happy Harry compiles the following data on his present range:

Original cost	=	$2,000
Estimated cost of required major repair	=	$1,200
Estimated salvage value now	=	$300
Estimated salvage value after 6 years	=	$100
Annual operating costs:		
Electricity	=	$700
Repairs	=	$500
Labor	=	$10,000

The relevant costs are listed in Exhibit 16. All of these costs are relevant because they are differential, future, and quantifiable. The original cost of the present range is irrelevant because it is not a future cost (but rather a *sunk cost*, discussed next), and the cost of labor is irrelevant because it is not differential. (The process of selecting an alternative is discussed later in this chapter.)

Sunk Costs

A **sunk cost** is a past cost relating to a past decision. A sunk cost may be differential yet irrelevant because it is not future. In the case of Happy Harry's decision, the original cost of the old range, $2,000, is a sunk cost.

Exhibit 16   Relevant Costs—Happy Harry's

	Alternatives	
Cost	Buy New	Keep Old
Cost of new range	$5,000	–
Electricity (annually)	800	$ 700
Repairs (annually)	200	500
Salvage value of present range now	300	–
Salvage value of range (end of 6th year)	500	100
Major repair job	–	1,200

In many decision-making situations, management will review financial records to determine the net book value (cost less accumulated depreciation) of a fixed asset that is to be replaced. This suggests that many managers consider the net book value of a fixed asset (rather than its original cost) the sunk cost. However, in this chapter, we will consider *both* the original cost and the net book value sunk costs. The relevant cost in replacing a fixed asset is the asset's current value. The current $300 value of Happy Harry's old range and its projected value of $100 at the end of six years are both relevant costs since they are differential, future, and quantifiable.

Opportunity Costs

The cost of the best foregone opportunity in a decision-making situation is the **opportunity cost**. Opportunity costs are among the relevant cost considerations in decision-making situations. If the decision-making process is rational, then the opportunity cost is less than the value associated with the outcome of the decision. For example, let's assume that $100,000 may be invested in one of three ways:

Investment	Annual Return
XYZ Corporation Bonds	10%
ABC Company Preferred Stock	12%
Uninsured Time Certificate of Deposit	9%

Assume that all three alternatives involve the same amount of risk—that is, the degree of certainty of receiving the specified return is the same for all three investment choices. Further assume that the ability of each investment to be converted into cash is the same for all three alternatives. Everything else being the same, the rational choice is to invest in ABC Company Preferred Stock. The best foregone opportunity is the investment in XYZ Corporation Bonds. Therefore, the opportunity costs associated with making the rational choice amount to $20,000 over two years ($100,000 × 10% × 2). The choice is a rational one because the return on the alternative selected ($24,000 from ABC stock) exceeds the opportunity costs of $20,000. The potential return of 9% on the Uninsured Time Certificate of Deposit is not an opportunity cost because it is not the best foregone opportunity. However, it is a relevant cost because it is future, differential, and quantifiable.

Average and Incremental Costs

The **average cost** to provide products and services is determined by dividing the total production and service costs by the quantity of production. For example, a food service operation may be able to produce the average meal served at breakfast for $3.00. The production costs include fixed, variable, and mixed costs. The calculation is as follows:

Cost of food (variable)	$200
Cost of labor (mixed)	200
Cost of supplies (variable)	10
Utilities (mixed)	10
Depreciation (fixed)	10
Other (mixed)	20
Total	$450
Number of meals produced	150

Average cost = $450 ÷ 150 = $3.00

The cost to produce and serve the next breakfast (number 151) is called the **incremental cost.** Incremental costs include the variable costs of food and supplies, as well as the variable portion of the mixed costs. Without providing detail, we will use $2.00 as the incremental cost. Thus, in this case, the incremental cost per meal is less than the average cost. In some cases, fixed costs or at least the fixed element of a mixed cost would have to be included in the incremental cost calculation. For example, if we wanted to know the cost of producing and serving 150 additional meals, we would include the cost of additional supervision and so on.

A common difference encountered between average and incremental costs concerns income taxes. To illustrate the difference, consider a simplified graduated tax rate as follows:

Taxable Income	Tax Rate
$20,000 and under	15%
Greater than $20,000	25%

The incremental taxes and average taxes paid on each dollar of taxable income up to $20,000 is 15 cents. Taxes on income in excess of $20,000 will be 25 cents for each dollar of taxable income. Thus, the incremental tax on the 25,000th dollar is 25 cents, while the average tax on $25,000 is 17%, calculated as follows:

Taxes on the first $20,000:	$20,000 × .15	=	$3,000
Taxes on the next $5,000:	$5,000 × .25	=	$1,250
Total taxes			$4,250

Average tax = $4,250 ÷ $25,000 = .17

Standard Costs

Standard costs are a forecast of what actual costs should be under projected conditions. These standards may serve as comparisons for control purposes and as evaluations of productivity. Generally, standard costs are established on a unit basis. For example, standard recipe costs consider the planned cost of a food serving such as a dinner or an à la carte item. Assume that the standard recipe cost for a dinner is $4.50. If 100 dinners are served, then the budgeted cost is $450. An actual food cost of $475 reveals a $25 variance. If the variance is significant, it is investigated to determine the probable cause(s) and appropriate corrective action.

Decision-Making Situations

Many situations call on management to make decisions using the cost concepts presented in this chapter. Several of these decision-making situations are listed below:

1. Which piece of equipment should be purchased?

2. What prices should be set for the hospitality operation's goods and services?

3. Can the hospitality operation ever afford to sell goods and services below cost?

4. During what time periods of a day should the hospitality establishment remain open?

5. When should a seasonal resort close?

6. Which business segment of the hospitality operation should receive the largest amount of funds?

7. Where should the hospitality enterprise expand?

In attempting to answer these and other cost-related questions, remember that there is no definitive method of evaluating costs. However, when applied correctly, the cost concepts presented in this chapter are useful in clarifying and helping to resolve these problems.

Illustration of Relevant Costs in Management Decisions

The selection process used to purchase a microcomputer will illustrate the application of relevant costs to a decision-making situation. Suppose a hotel wants to purchase a new microcomputer to be used by the controller for planning purposes. Even though the controller should become more productive by using the computer, his or her salary will not change because of the purchase. The costs associated with the purchase of either microcomputer #1 or microcomputer #2 are listed in Exhibit 17. Other information to consider includes:

1. Each computer is expected to have a useful life of five years, after which it would be considered completely worthless.

2. The different timing of costs that may be associated with each computer is ignored in this example, as well as any income tax implications.

3. The controller likes the appearance of computer #2 better; however, he or she is unable to place any value on this preference.

4. The value to the hotel of the controller's increased productivity is the same regardless of which microcomputer is purchased.

Exhibit 17   Illustration of Relevant Costs in Management Decisions

	Microcomputers	
	#1	#2
Costs—Hardware	$3,450	$4,250
Annual operating costs:		
Electricity	100	100
Supplies	200	200
Maintenance contract	200	100
Repairs (not covered by maintenance contract)	50	50
Software	2,000	1,800

Exhibit 18   Cost Analysis Solution

Cost Analysis		
	Microcomputers	
Relevant Cost	#1	#2
Hardware	$3,450	$4,250
Operating costs—maintenance contract for 5 years		
$200 × 5	1,000	–
$100 × 5	–	500
Software	2,000	1,800
Total cost	$6,450	$6,550

The irrelevant costs are the non-differential ones which include electricity supplies, and repairs. All other costs listed for the two computers are relevant because they are future, differential, and quantifiable. The controller's preference for microcomputer #2 is not directly considered since it has not been quantified. The value of the controller's increased productivity has not been quantified since it is non-differential between the two computers. In either case, the value to the hotel of this increase in productivity is expected to far exceed the cost of the computer.

Exhibit 18 presents a cost analysis useful in deciding which computer to purchase. Based on the lower cost, microcomputer #1 would be selected. If the $100 difference between microcomputers #1 and #2 were considered immaterial, then microcomputer #2 most likely would be purchased due to the controller's unquantified preference for it.

Computer Applications

Cost analysis is perhaps one of the best uses for the personal computer. With the help of a spreadsheet program, not only can cost analyses be performed, but "what if" situations can be examined. Any of the cost analysis methods described in this chapter can be used. Once the correct formulas are entered into the spreadsheet, it can be used over and over again. With the proper construction of a cost model,

Exhibit 19   Computer-Generated Rooms Department Rate Analysis

Rooms Department Rate Analysis						
AVAILABLE ROOMS FOR SALE	36,500	36,500	36,500	36,500	36,500	36,500
AVERAGE RATE	$ 40.00	$ 45.00	$ 47.50	$ 50.00	$ 52.50	$ 55.00
PROJECTED OCCUPANCY	77.5%	75.0%	72.5%	70.0%	65.0%	60.0%
Room Revenue	$ 1,131,500	$ 1,231,875	$ 1,256,969	$ 1,277,500	$ 1,245,563	$ 1,204,500
Room Variable Expenses	237,615	229,950	222,285	214,620	199,290	183,960
Room Profits	893,885	1,001,925	1,034,684	1,062,880	1,046,273	1,020,540

month-to-month variances can be determined instantly. Variances can be identified by specific cost (for example, food, room, or maintenance) for further analysis. A spreadsheet program can quickly perform tasks that, if done manually, might take several hours. Even complex calculations like regression analysis can be done in a matter of seconds.

The "what if" calculations allow the manager to analyze costs and revenues under different circumstances. Exhibit 19 shows how a manager might use a "what if" model to determine the best rate to charge hotel guests in order to maximize profits. In the example, the manager made the following assumptions:

$$\begin{array}{c}\text{Rooms}\\\text{Revenues}\end{array} = \begin{array}{c}\text{Available Rooms}\\\text{for Sale}\end{array} \times \begin{array}{c}\text{Average}\\\text{Rate}\end{array} \times \begin{array}{c}\text{Projected}\\\text{Occupancy}\end{array}$$

$$\begin{array}{c}\text{Rooms}\\\text{Variable}\\\text{Expenses}\end{array} = \begin{array}{c}\text{Available Rooms}\\\text{for Sale}\end{array} \times \begin{array}{c}\text{Projected}\\\text{Occupancy}\end{array} \times \begin{array}{c}\$8.40\\\text{per room}\end{array}$$

$$\begin{array}{c}\text{Rooms}\\\text{Profits}\end{array} = \begin{array}{c}\text{Rooms}\\\text{Revenues}\end{array} - \begin{array}{c}\text{Rooms Variable}\\\text{Expenses}\end{array}$$

The manager then copied these formulas to see the results in a number of different situations. In this case, the manager projected that, as the room rate increased, the occupancy decreased. However, the lower occupancy is offset by the increased total revenue. In this example, the rate of $50.00 and 70% occupancy maximizes revenues. In addition, in this example, room profits are highest at this level.

"What if" models can be designed to be very sophisticated. For example, in the illustration above, the model could have reflected the effect that the different levels of occupancy would have on food and beverage operations, telephone revenues, gift shop sales, and other profit centers.

Summary

This chapter highlighted the variety of definitions the term *cost* can have in the accounting world. In general, a cost as an expense is the reduction of an asset incurred with the intention of increasing revenues. Such costs include labor costs, cost of food sold, depreciation, and others.

There are many specific types of costs. A fixed cost is one that remains constant over a relevant range of operations for the short term. A variable cost is one that changes directly with the level of activity. Depreciation is usually considered a fixed expense, while cost of food sold is assumed to be variable. Many costs are mixed, a combination of fixed and variable elements. For example, telephone expense can be divided into a fixed portion (the cost of the system) and a variable portion (the cost of making calls). Step costs are constant within a range of activity but vary among ranges of activity.

Three methods of determining the fixed and variable elements of mixed costs were presented in this chapter. The simplest is the high/low two-point method, which examines the cost differences between the periods of lowest and highest activity. A scatter diagram can be used to visualize the relationship between all periods' activities and costs. Regression analysis, the most sophisticated method addressed, uses equations to determine the appropriate fixed-variable relationship.

Several types of costs are important in decision-making situations. Differential costs are useful when comparing two or more options; they are the costs that differ among the options. Relevant costs must be differential costs. In addition, relevant costs must be quantifiable and incurred in the future. Sunk costs are not considered in decision-making situations because they were incurred in the past.

Other costs include controllable costs. Controllable costs are costs that can be regulated. All costs before management fees and fixed charges are generally considered under the general manager's control.

Understanding the relationships among the different types of costs can be very beneficial to a hospitality manager. Different purchase or lease options can be more easily analyzed, operations can be monitored against standards, and costs can be broken into their fixed and variable portions in order to forecast future expenses.

Endnotes

1. This basic equation is most useful for forecasting purposes and for budgeting purposes.

2.
$$\text{Fixed Cost Element} = \frac{(85,200)(58,636,800) - (26,000)(189,257,000)}{12(58,636,800) - (26,000)(26,000)}$$

$$= \$2,719.57 \text{ per month}$$

Key Terms

average costs—Total production and service costs divided by the quantity of production.

avoidable costs—Costs that are not incurred when a hospitality operation shuts down (for example, when a resort hotel closes for part of the year).

capacity fixed costs—Fixed charges relating to the physical plant or the capacity to provide goods and services to guests.

controllable costs—Costs over which a manager is able to exercise judgment and hence should be able to keep within predefined boundaries or limits.

cost allocation—The process of distributing expenses among various departments.

differential costs—Costs that differ between two alternatives.

discretionary fixed costs—Costs that managers may in the short run choose to avoid. These costs do not affect an establishment's capacity.

fixed costs—Costs that remain constant in the short run even though sales volume varies; examples include salaries, rent expense, insurance expense.

high/low two-point method—The simplest approach to estimating the fixed and variable elements of a mixed cost. It bases the estimation on data from two extreme periods.

incremental cost—The cost to produce one more unit; includes the variable costs and the variable portion of the mixed costs.

indifference point—The level of activity at which the cost is the same under either a fixed or a variable cost arrangement.

mixed costs—Costs that are a mixture of both fixed and variable costs.

multiple allocation base approach (MABA)—The use of different allocation bases to allocate different overhead costs among departments.

opportunity cost—Cost of foregoing the best alternative opportunity in a decision-making situation involving several alternatives.

overhead costs—All expenses other than the direct costs of profit centers; examples include undistributed operating expenses, management fees, fixed charges, and income taxes.

regression analysis—A mathematical approach to fitting a straight line to data points such that the differences in the distances of the data points from the line are minimized; used in forecasting when a dependent variable (for example, restaurant covers) to be forecasted is thought to be causally related to one or more independent variables (for example, rooms sold).

relevant costs—Costs that must be considered in a decision-making situation; must be differential, future, and quantifiable.

scatter diagram—A graphic approach to determining the fixed and variable elements of a mixed cost.

single allocation base approach (SABA)—The allocation of overhead costs among departments using a single allocation base (such as departmental square footage).

standard costs—Forecasts of what actual costs should be under projected conditions; a standard of comparison for control purposes or for evaluations of productivity.

step costs—Costs that are constant within a range of activity, but different among ranges of activity.

sunk costs—Past costs relating to a past decision; for example, the net book value of a fixed asset.

variable costs—Costs that change proportionately with sales volume.

Review Questions

1. What are some of the different meanings of *cost?*

2. What is the difference between overhead costs and indirect costs?

3. What is an opportunity cost?

4. Which technique is the most accurate method of determining the fixed and variable elements of a mixed cost? Why?

5. What are the two definitions of sunk costs?

6. Which hotel costs are fixed in the short run? the long run?

7. Why would you consider allocating costs to the profit centers?

8. How are relevant costs defined? What is an irrelevant cost? Give an example.

9. Why are differential costs considered in a decision-making situation?

10. What is the difference between average costs and incremental costs?

Problems

Problem 1

Identify each expense in relation to sales volume as a fixed, variable, step, or mixed cost.

    a. Depreciation

    b. Cost of food sold

    c. Housekeeping salaries

    d. Telephone expense

    e. Guest supplies

    f. Property taxes

    g. Fire insurance

    h. Repair and maintenance

    i. Controller's salary

    j. Cost of beverages sold

Problem 2

Chico Hernandez, manager of the Texas Inn, desires to estimate the repair and maintenance expense for 19X4. Information from selected 19X3 monthly financial statements is as follows:

Month	Total Repair and Maintenance Expense	Paid Occupancy Percentage
January	$12,600	60%
April	13,800	70%
July	13,000	65%
October	14,000	68%

Required:

1. Using the high/low two-point method, estimate the monthly fixed repair and maintenance expense for 19X3.

2. What was the variable portion of repair and maintenance expense per 1% paid occupancy per month for 19X3?

3. Assuming an average monthly paid occupancy of 68% for 19X4 and a 5% increase is repair and maintenance costs, what is the estimated repair and maintenance expense for 19X4?

Problem 3

The following monthly income statement has been prepared by Dwayne Kris, CPA, for Troy Caballo, the owner of the Caballo Inn. As Mr. Caballo's private consultant, you are asked to explain several cost relationships.

Caballo Inn
Income Statement
For the month ended January 31, 19X1

	Net Revenues	Cost of Sales	Payroll and Related Expense	Other Expenses	Income (Loss)
Rooms	$ 105,430	$ -0-	$ 20,000	$ 1,450	$ 83,980
Food	52,400	18,864	15,000	1,000	17,536
Beverage	26,720	6,680	10,000	12,400	(2,360)
Other	4,000	-0-	-0-	-0-	4,000
	$ 188,550	$ 25,544	$ 45,000	$ 14,850	103,156

Undistributed Operating Expenses:	
Administrative and General	16,720
Information Systems	4,170
Marketing	3,400
Property Operation and Maintenance	5,080
Utility Costs	15,400
Income After Undistributed Operating Expenses	58,386
Rent	5,400
Property Taxes	1,220
Insurance	2,000
Interest	3,330
Depreciation	5,500

	Income (Loss)
Income Before Income Taxes	40,936
Income Taxes	15,136
Net Income	$ 25,800

Required:

1. What are the direct expenses of the rooms department?
2. What is the total of the overhead expenses for the period?
3. Which costs are controllable by the general manager or people under his/her supervision?
4. Which costs are considered fixed?
5. What is the relationship of the cost of sales to sales?

Problem 4

Jim Jones, the owner of Jim's Place, wants to analyze labor costs in his restaurant operations and has asked you for assistance. The operating statistics for the previous year are as follows:

	Number of Customers	Labor Costs
January	4,000	$15,500
February	2,400	10,450
March	3,700	18,500
April	4,450	19,000
May	4,400	19,000
June	4,800	20,250
July	5,000	20,500
August	3,900	18,500
September	3,800	18,000
October	3,100	15,500
November	2,900	15,250
December	3,000	16,650

Required:

1. Using the high/low two-point method, determine the variable labor cost per customer.
2. What is the monthly fixed labor cost at Jim's Place?
3. What is your estimate of total labor costs if 3,900 customers are served during the month? (Base this on your analysis in parts 1 and 2 above.)

Problem 5

Tanya Daniels has been successfully operating her restaurant, The Lion's Den, for the past five years. She has to renegotiate her lease and has two options: a $3,000 per month fixed charge or a variable rate of 5% of revenue. She has completed next year's budget to "Income Before Lease Expense" and expects annual sales of $1,000,000.

Required:

1. What is the indifference point (annual sales) for these lease options?
2. Which option should Ms. Daniels choose? Why?

Problem 6

The Gator Restaurant currently has a variable lease that is 6% of its total revenue. An alternative approach is $120,000 per year. Assume its average and marginal tax rates are 35% and 40%, respectively.

Required:

1. Determine its indifference point.
2. If its annual sales are expected to be $3,000,000, which type of lease do you recommend? Provide figures to support your recommendation.
3. Assume the Gator Restaurant's indifference point is $1,500,000. What is the net of tax cost of making an error in signing a variable lease when its annual sales are $1,700,000?

Problem 7

The D.K. Pizza House has provided you with the following information on its costs at various levels of monthly sales.

Monthly sales in units	3,000	6,000	9,000
Cost of food sold	$ 4,500	$ 9,000	$13,500
Payroll costs	3,500	5,000	6,500
Supplies	600	1,200	1,800
Utilities	360	420	480
Other operating costs	1,500	3,000	4,500
Building rent	1,000	1,000	1,000
Depreciation	200	200	200
Total	$11,660	$19,820	$27,980

Required:

1. Identify each cost as variable, fixed, or mixed.
2. Develop an equation to estimate total costs at various levels of activity.
3. Project total costs with monthly sales of 8,000.

Problem 8

Kent's Inn needs new laundry equipment. Paul Kent, the owner, is faced with the following two alternatives:

	Buy	Lease
Cost of equipment	$20,000	--
Semi-annual equipment rental	--	$ 3,000
Salvage value in five years	1,000	--
Annual costs:		
Labor	15,000	15,000

Supplies	1,000	1,000
Utilities	3,000	3,000
Interest expense	1,500	--
Repairs	200	--

Additional information:

Assume that the laundry equipment has a five-year life.

Required:

1. Which costs are irrelevant?

2. Prepare a five-year cost schedule for each alternative. (Ignore income taxes and the time value of money.)

3. Which alternative do you recommend?

Problem 9

Paul Smith is considering replacing Jones & Smith's present dishwasher with a new energy-efficient model. Although the old dishwasher has a present book value of $1,000, its current market value is $2,000 and, if held for five more years, this would drop to $300. If Paul decides not to buy the new machine, approximately $500 of repairs must be performed on the present dishwasher. The following is a schedule of expected annual expenses for each option over the next five years.

	Keep Present Dishwasher	Buy New Dishwasher
Maintenance	$ 400	$ 200
Labor	12,000	12,000
Energy	800	500
Water	400	400

The new machine would cost $7,000 and is expected to have a salvage value of $2,000 at the end of five years.

Required:

1. Which costs are irrelevant?

2. Which alternative should Paul choose? Support your decision with only relevant numbers.

Problem 10

Marita Lo desires to purchase a new front office computer system for her Lo Motel (LOMO). After considerable discussion with purveyors, she has narrowed her choices to systems sold by ABC Company and XYZ Computers. The system proposed by each company is expected to have a useful life of seven years. She believes the alternative systems are equivalent for providing services required by the LOMO; therefore, her focus is cost. The associated costs of each system are as follows:

	ABC Co.	XYZ Computers
Initial cost	$25,000	$30,000
Annual costs:		
Labor	25,000	25,000
Utilities	1,000	800
Supplies	2,000	2,000
Maintenance	3,000	2,500
Salvage value (in 7 years)	5,000	8,000

Required:

1. Which costs are irrelevant?
2. Which system should Marita purchase? (Ignore the time value of money). Support your decision with numbers.

Problem 11

Consider the following monthly income statement for the Double K Hotel:

Double K Hotel
Income Statement

	Rooms	Food	Gift Shop	Total
Revenue	$ 500,000	$ 500,000	$ 2,000	$1,002,000
Cost of Sales	-0-	180,000	1,000	181,000
Payroll & Related Expenses	120,000	130,000	400	250,400
Other Direct Expenses	40,000	45,000	100	85,100
Departmental Income	$ 340,000	$ 145,000	$ 500	$ 485,500

Undistributed Expenses:	Payroll & Related	Other	Total
Administrative and General	$ 60,000	$ 30,000	$ 90,000
Marketing	45,000	25,000	70,000
Property Operation & Maintenance and Utility Costs	30,000	40,000	70,000
Insurance	—	10,000	10,000
Depreciation	—	80,000	80,000
			320,000
Income Before Income Taxes			$ 165,000
Income Taxes			50,000
Net Income			$ 115,500

Indirect expenses will be allocated based on the number of employees, who are distributed as follows:

Department	Number of Employees
Rooms	55
Food	70
Gift Shop	$^{1}/_{2}$
Administrative and General	20
Marketing	15
Property Operation & Maintenance and Utility Costs	10

Required:

Prepare a fully-allocated income statement using the single allocation basis approach to cost allocation.

Problem 12

The owner of the Double K Hotel in Problem 11 would like to develop a fully-allocated income statement using the step method. (The unallocated income statement is presented in Problem 11.) Indirect expenses will be allocated on the following bases:

Indirect Expense	Basis
Insurance	Book value of fixed assets
Depreciation	Square footage
Property Operation & Maintenance and Utility Costs	Square footage
Marketing	Ratio of sales
Administrative and General	Number of employees

Additional information:

Department	Book Value of Fixed Assets	Square Footage	Number of Employees
Rooms	$8,000,000	120,000	55
Food	3,000,000	20,000	70
Gift Shop	20,000	500	$^{1}/_{2}$
Administrative and General	400,000	6,000	20
Marketing	200,000	4,000	15
Property Operation & Maintenance and Utility Costs	1,500,000	10,000	10

Service department expenses should be allocated in the following order:

1. Administrative and General

2. Property Operation and Maintenance and Utility Costs

3. Marketing

Required:

Prepare a fully-allocated income statement for the Double K Hotel using the step method. Note: The Appendix to this chapter discusses and illustrates the step method.

Problem 13

Sara Rose, owner of Rose Inn, is confused by the fully-allocated financial statements that suggest the Rose Inn's lounge is losing money. As she sees it, there are three alternatives:

1. Continue the lounge operation as is.
2. Close the lounge and convert the space to a small meeting room.
3. Lease the space to Bevco.

The following table summarizes the Rose Inn's fully-allocated monthly income statements:

	Rooms	Food	Lounge	Total
Departmental profit	$150,000	$30,000	$10,000	$190,000
Allocated overhead	100,000	25,000	15,000	140,000
Pretax income	$ 50,000	$ 5,000	$ (5,000)	50,000
Income taxes				20,000
Net income				$ 30,000

Additional information:

1. Closing the lounge would reduce overhead costs by $7,000. Leasing the lounge to Bevco would reduce overhead costs by $2,000.
2. The space can be leased to Bevco for 5% of sales. Bevco is a reputable operator, and Sara Rose believes that it will operate the lounge as effectively as Rose Inn has done in the past. Annual forecasted lounge sales are expected to be $150,000.
3. If the lounge is closed, room profits are expected to decrease by 2%, while food department profits are expected to increase by 20%.
4. The cost to convert the lounge for alternative use is assumed to be equal to the market value of the lounge equipment.
5. The lounge space, if used for small meetings, is expected to yield pretax profits of $3,000.

Required:

Based on the above information, recommend the best alternative to Sara Rose. Support your solution with numbers.

Problem 14

Peter John Star, owner of The Big Star Hotel, is confused by the fully-allocated financial statements that suggest The Big Star Hotel's lounge is losing money. As he sees it, there are three alternatives:

1. Continue the lounge operation as is.
2. Close the lounge and expand the restaurant.
3. Lease the space to Philip, Inc., a management company.

The following table summarizes the Big Star Hotel's fully-allocated monthly income statements.

	Rooms	Restaurant	Lounge	Total
Revenues	$250,000	$100,000	$40,000	$390,000
Department expenses*	100,000	70,000	20,000	190,000
Departmental profit	150,000	30,000	20,000	190,000
Allocated overhead	100,000	25,000	30,000	155,000
Pretax income	$ 50,000	$ 5,000	($10,000)	45,000
Income taxes				20,000
Net income				$ 25,000

*All departmental expenses are assumed to be variable.

Additional information:

1. Closing the lounge would reduce monthly overhead costs by $10,000. Leasing the lounge to Philip, Inc., would reduce monthly overhead costs by $5,000.

2. The space can be leased to Philip, Inc., for 10% of sales. Philip, Inc. is a reputable operator, and Peter John believes that it will operate the lounge as effectively as The Big Star Hotel has done in the past. Annual forecasted lounge sales are expected to be $550,000.

3. If the lounge is closed, room profits are expected to decrease by 2%, while food department sales are expected to increase by 20%.

4. The cost to convert the lounge for alternative use is expected to be $60,000. Assume the life of the equipment is five years and it will have no salvage value.

5. If the lounge is closed, the unneeded equipment can be sold on a contract over five years and $500 will be received each month.

Required:

Based on the above, advise Peter John Star. Use relevant numbers to support your recommendation.

Problem 15

Tammy's Motor Inn has been open for five months, and Tammy Weaver, the general manager, is conducting some cost analyses. She has not yet determined the amount of fixed and variable expenses the inn is incurring. The following is a summary of room sales and expenses incurred each month.

	Number of rooms	Costs
June	3,488	$122,319
July	3,842	128,940
August	3,584	124,320
September	3,333	119,431
October	3,261	117,642

Required:

1. Using regression analysis, determine the fixed cost per month for Tammy's Motor Inn.

2. What is the variable cost per room?

3. If Tammy's Motor Inn expects to sell 3,666 rooms in January of the next year, what are the fixed costs, total variable costs, and total expenses?

Appendix
Should overhead costs be allocated?*

By A. Neal Geller and Raymond S. Schmidgall

The allocation process is fairly complex, and is not well understood by the lodging industry. This article, therefore, has two purposes:

1) to discuss the advantages and drawbacks of allocation, and
2) to illustrate cost allocation.

Cost allocation is the assignment of overhead costs to operated departments according to benefits received, responsibilities, or other logical measures of use. Such overhead costs as the general manager's salary are spread across profit centers such as rooms and food and beverage.

Advantages of allocation

The major advantage of cost allocation is that it results in better decision-making by the general and departmental managers. These decisions are improved when based on fully allocated income statements:

PRICING. Pricing is best accomplished when the full costs of an operated department are known.

MARKETING. Management can best determine which services to emphasize after the full costs of each operated department are realized.

CHANGES IN CAPACITY. Expansion or reduction in the capacity of the hotel/motel operation should be based on the profit potential (net of indirect costs) of the operating departments.

STAFFING. More judicious staffing decisions are possible with the full cost of each operated department

known to management. In addition, cost allocation provides department heads with more realistic assessments of overhead costs their department must cover. Without the benefit of fully-allocated income statements, a rooms department manager, for example, may not understand why a 70% contribution from the rooms department is imperative for the firm to realize a profit.

Finally, fully-allocated income statements are useful in dealing with government regulations. They provide better information for wage-and-price guidelines, government per-diem rates and general lobbying efforts.

Drawbacks of allocation

The major drawbacks of cost allocation relate primarily to the managers of operated departments and to misunderstandings as to its use. For example:

- Department heads may not understand the process and may resist it.
- Department heads may defer discretionary costs such as repairs, or otherwise strive to achieve short-run profitability at the expense of the long-run profitability of the company.
- Fully-allocated department statements are not appropriate for performance evaluation.

The effects of these drawbacks will be minimized if top-level management will do the following:

This article first appeared in *Lodging*.

*Note: This article was written prior to the revision of the *Uniform System of Accounts for Hotels (USAH)*, which resulted in the 9th edition of the *Uniform System of Accounts for the Lodging Industry (USALI)*. However, in terms of allocating expenses, the approaches suggested here have not changed with the revision of the uniform system. Therefore, it is as relevant to cost allocation as when it was first written.

EXHIBIT 1
Suggested Allocation Bases

Allocated Costs	Allocation Bases
Rent	1. Percentage applicable to revenue sources 2. Square feet of area occupied (fixed rent)
Real Estate Taxes	Square feet of area occupied
Insurance—Building and Contents	1. Square feet of area occupied 2. Square feet plus investment in furniture and fixture
Interest	Same as above
Depreciation—Building	Square feet of area occupied
Depreciation—Furnishing and Equipment	1. Department asset records 2. Square feet of area occupied
Depreciation—Capital Leases	1. Department use of leased equipment 2. Square feet of area occupied
Telephone	Number of extensions
Payroll Taxes and Employee Benefits	1. Number of employees 2. Detailed payroll records 3. Salaries and wages
Administrative and General	1. Accumulated costs 2. Number of employees
Data Processing	1. Accumulated costs 2. Number of employees
Marketing	Ratio to sales
Guest Entertainment	Ratio to sales
Energy Costs	1. Sub-meters 2. Cubic feet of area occupied
Property Operation and Maintenance	1. Job orders 2. Number of employees 3. Square footage
Human Resources	Number of employees
Transportation	Number of employees

Source: *Uniform System of Accounts for Hotels,* 8th revised edition, p. 137.

1. Explain completely the process of cost allocation and emphasize the benefits to the hotel/motel (or company).
2. Emphasize the importance of management for the long-term rather than focusing all the attention on the current period.
3. Separate department costs in fully-allocated statements between direct and indirect. Further, separate the indirect costs between "controllable by department head"—if any—and "beyond the control of the department head."
4. Stress a team approach to managing the various profit and cost centers of the hotel/motel operation.

Bases of allocation

The *USAH* contains several suggested bases for cost allocation as you

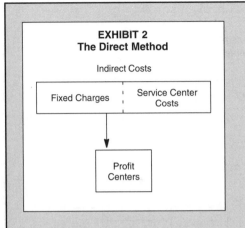

EXHIBIT 2
The Direct Method

Indirect Costs

Fixed Charges | Service Center Costs

Profit Centers

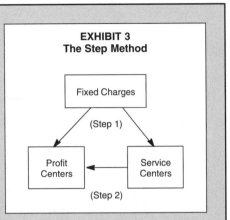

EXHIBIT 3
The Step Method

Fixed Charges

(Step 1)

Profit Centers ← Service Centers

(Step 2)

will see in Exhibit 1. A cost allocation base is a factor that determines how much is allocated to a cost objective (department). For example, the rent expense of a hotel may be allocated on the basis of square footage of each department. If the rent expense is $10,000 for the period and the square footage of the rooms and food departments are 18,000 and 6,000 square feet respectively, then 75% ($7,500) would be allocated to the rooms department and 25% ($2,500) to the food department.

It is important to note that the allocation bases should be chosen separately from the allocation method used. While the rent may be allocated to operated departments as shown in the above example, or indirectly through the service center, the allocation base can be the same. (Again, note Exhibit 1.)

Methods of allocation

The allocation method determines the degree of directness in allocating indirect costs from their cost centers to the profit centers. The three methods listed in the *USAH* are diagrammed and discussed briefly here.

The direct method (see Exhibit 2) results in all indirect costs flowing directly from the cost centers to the profit centers. With this approach, no

portion of fixed cost is allocated to service centers. The direct method is simple and easily understood.

The step method (see Exhibit 3) requires a two-step allocation process. First, fixed costs are allocated to the profit and service centers. Second, the costs of service centers, including the allocated fixed costs, are allocated to the profit centers. In the second step, the costs of the service centers providing the most services to the other service centers are allocated first.

Once a service center's costs are allocated, no additional costs are allocated to this service center. The step method does not consider the reciprocal provision of services among other service centers. The formula method incorporates this additional refinement. The step method is more realistic than the direct method because it recognizes services provided by some service centers to others.

The formula method also requires two steps in the allocation process (see Exhibit 4). The first step—the allocation of fixed costs—is the same as under the step method. The second step gives full consideration for services rendered by service centers to each other. The second step is gener-ally complex and requires mathematical computations best performed by a computer.

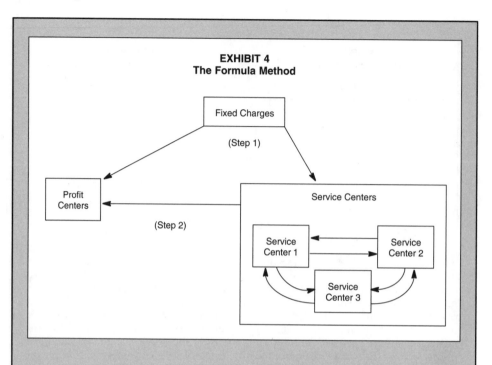

EXHIBIT 4
The Formula Method

Fixed Charges

(Step 1)

Profit Centers

(Step 2)

Service Centers

Service Center 1

Service Center 2

Service Center 3

Illustration of allocation

The direct and step methods of cost allocation are illustrated here by using Walters Motor Inn. The formula method is not illustrated because it is beyond the scope of this article.

The Walters Motor Inn is a 70-room property with food and beverage operations. It uses the *Uniform System of Accounts for Hotels.* To simplify the illustrations, we have included only three undistributed operating expense categories and two fixed charge categories. The Inn's income statement for March, developed in accordance with the *USAH,* is shown in Exhibit 5. Note that the indirect expenses have not been allocated to the profit centers so that the rooms and food and beverage departmental incomes, prior to cost allocation, are $34,000 and $14,500 respectively.

Regardless of the allocation method used, a cost allocation base must be selected for each indirect cost. The indirect expenses and the allocation bases selected for cost allocation of the Walters Motor Inn's indirect expenses are shown in Exhibit 5-A.

The bases selected were chosen on recommendations from the *USAH.* The notable exception is Property Operation & Maintenance and Utility Costs. To simplify the illustrations, these two costs (POM and UC) were combined and allocated using one of the recommended bases for property operation and maintenance. The information required to establish the allocation bases for the Walters Motor Inn is shown in Exhibit 5-B.

Illustration of direct method

The direct method of cost allocation is accomplished by allocating all indirect expenses to the profit centers and then preparing the fully-allocated income statement. For the Walters Motor Inn, four bases of allocation are used.

EXHIBIT 5
Unallocated Income Statement, Walters Motor Inn for the Month of March

	Rooms	Food & Beverage	Total
Revenue	$50,000	$50,000	$100,000
Cost of Sales	–0–	18,000	18,000
Payroll and Related Expenses	12,000	13,000	25,000
Other Direct Expenses	4,000	4,500	8,500
Total Expenses	16,000	35,500	51,500
Departmental Income (Loss)	$34,000	$14,500	48,500

	Payroll & Related	Other	
Undistributed Operating Expenses:			
Administrative & General (A & G)	$10,000	$2,000	12,000
Marketing	2,000	1,000	3,000
Property Operation, Maintenance and Utility Costs (POM & UC)	2,000	4,000	6,000
Total Income After Undistributed Operating Expenses			27,500
Insurance			3,000
Depreciation			18,000
Total Insurance and Depreciation			21,000
Income Before Income Taxes			6,500
Income Taxes			2,000
Net Income			$ 4,500

EXHIBIT 5-A

Indirect Expenses	Bases
Insurance	Book value of fixed assets (BV-FA)
Depreciation	Square footage (SF)
POM & UC	Square footage (SF)
Marketing	Ratio to sales (RS)
A & G	Number of employees (NE)

EXHIBIT 5-B

Department	Book Value of Fixed Assets	Square Footage	Number of Employees
Rooms	$900,000	40,000	14
Food & Beverage	300,000	15,000	20
A & G	50,000	2,500	4
Marketing	30,000	500	1
POM & UC	220,000	2,000	1

The base for allocating the Inn's insurance is the book value of fixed assets of the rooms and food and beverage departments. The total book value–fixed assets for the two profit centers is $1.2 million, of which $900,000 pertains to the rooms and $300,000 pertains to the food and beverage department. Since the book value–fixed assets of the rooms department is 75% of the combined book value–fixed assets for the two departments, the rooms department is allocated $2,250 of the insurance expenses

(.75 × $3,000).

The proportions of other indirect expenses and amounts allocated to the rooms and food and beverage departments were determined in similar fashion using the selected base of allocation as noted previously. Exhibit 6 contains the indirect costs, the amount to be allocated, the allocation base, the proportions to be allocated to rooms and food and beverage, and the amounts allocated to these two departments.

EXHIBIT 6
Allocation of Costs—Direct Method

Expense to be Allocated	Amount to be Allocated	Allocation Base	Proportion to		Amounts Allocated to	
			Rooms	Food & Beverage	Rooms	Food & Beverage
Insurance	$ 3,000	BV-FA	.7500	.2500	$ 2,250	$ 750
Depreciation	18,000	SF	.7273	.2727	13,091	4,909
POM & UC	6,000	SF	.7273	.2727	4,364	1,636
Marketing	3,000	RS	.5000	.5000	1,500	1,500
A & G	12,000	NE	.4118	.5882	4,942	7,058
TOTAL	$42,000				$26,147	$15,853

EXHIBIT 7
Fully Allocated Income Statement—Walters Motor Inn
Direct Method—For the Month of March

	Rooms	Food & Beverage	Total
Revenue	$50,000	$50,000	$ 100,000
Cost of Sales	–0–	18,000	18,000
Payroll and Related Expenses	12,000	13,000	25,000
Other Direct Expenses	4,000	4,500	8,500
Total Expenses	16,000	35,500	51,500
Departmental Income	34,000	14,500	48,500
Allocated Expenses (from Exhibit 6)	26,147	15,853	42,000
Departmental Income (Loss) after Allocation	$ 7,853	$ (1,353)	6,500
Income Taxes			2,000
Net Income			$ 4,500

Exhibit 7 contains the fully-allocated income statement. Under this method, the rooms department income after allocation is $7,853 while the food and beverage department loss after allocation is $1,353. Note that income taxes are not allocated to profit centers.

Illustration of step method

The step method of allocation requires two steps:

1. Allocate fixed charges to service centers and profit centers, and,
2. Allocate service center expenses to profit centers.

Following these steps, the fully-allocated income statement is prepared.

The bases for allocating indirect expenses of the Walters Motor Inn were the same as used to illustrate allocation by the direct method. The difference under the step method is that part of the indirect expenses was first allocated to service centers. Thus, in determining the proportionate share of a base for each cost objective, one must consider both the amounts pertaining to profit centers and to service centers.

The two fixed charges to be allocated are insurance and depreciation. The ratios used to allocate these expenses were calculated as shown in

EXHIBIT 8

		Insurance		Depreciation
Service and Profit Centers	BV-FA	Proportionate Share of BV-FA	Square Feet	Proportionate Share of Sq. Ft.
Rooms	$ 900,000	.6000	40,000	.6667
Food & Beverage	300,000	.2000	15,000	.2500
A & G	50,000	.0333	2,500	.0417
Marketing	30,000	.0200	500	.0083
POM & UC	220,000	.1467	2,000	.0333
TOTAL	$1,500,000	1.0000	60,000	1.0000

EXHIBIT 9
Step 1: Allocation of Fixed Charges to Profit Centers and Service Centers

				Allocated to		
Fixed Charge	Total Amount	Rooms	F & B	A & G	Marketing	POM & UC
Insurance	$ 3,000	$ 1,800	$ 600	$100	$ 60	$ 440
Depreciation	18,000	12,000	4,500	750	150	600
TOTAL	$21,000	$13,800	$ 5,100	$850	$ 210	$ 1,040

EXHIBIT 10

Department	Number of Employees	Proportioned Share of Total Employees	Amount Allocated
Rooms	14	.3889	$ 4,998
Food & Beverage	20	.5555	7,138
POM & UC	1	.0278	357
Marketing	1	.0278	357
TOTAL	36	1.0000	$12,850

Exhibit 8. Using the ratios thus calculated, the fixed charges were allocated as shown in Exhibit 9.

In Step 2, the service center expenses plus the fixed charges allocated to the service centers were allocated to the profit centers. A portion of these new totals was allocated directly to the profit centers with the remaining portion allocated in an established sequence to the service centers until all indirect expenses were allocated to the two profit centers.

Step 2 of the cost allocation of the Walters Motor Inn was accomplished by allocating Administrative and General expenses, Property Operation/ Maintenance expenses, Utility Costs, and Marketing expenses. The order is specified on the basis of service centers serving the largest number of service centers.

The Administrative and General expenses to be allocated in Step 2 total $12,850—$12,000 from the unallocated income statement plus $850 of fixed charges allocated in Step 1. Using the number of employees as the allocation base, the $12,850 was allocated to the two remaining service centers and two profit centers as shown in Exhibit 10.

EXHIBIT 11

Department	Square Feet	Proportioned Share of Square Footage	Amount Allocated
Rooms	40,000	.7207	$5,331
Food & Beverage	15,000	.2703	1,999
Marketing	500	.0090	67
TOTAL	55,000	1.0000	$7,397

EXHIBIT 12
Step 2: Allocation of Expenses from Service Centers to Profit Centers

	Service Centers			Profit Centers	
	A & G	POM & UC	Marketing	Rooms	Food & Beverage
Unallocated service center costs	$ 12,000	$ 6,000	$ 3,000	$ –0–	$ –0–
Allocated per Step 1	850	1,040	210	13,800	5,100
Costs to be allocated	12,850	7,040	3,210		
A & G	(12,850)	357	357	4,998	7,138
	$ –0–	7,397			
POM & UC		(7,397)	67	5,331	1,999
		$ –0–	3,634		
Marketing			(3,634)	1,817	1,817
TOTAL			$ –0–	$ 25,946	$ 16,054

Property Operation/Maintenance and Utility Costs are allocated next under Step 2. The total to be allocated is $7,397. This is the sum of $6,000 from the unallocated income statement, $1,040 from Step 1, and $357 from Administrative and General. The total was allocated to the marketing department and the two profit centers on the basis of square footage. The proportionate share and amounts of Property Operation/Maintenance and Utility Costs were calculated as shown in Exhibit 11.

Lastly, the Marketing expense was allocated to the two profit centers on the basis of ratio to sales. Therefore, the total Marketing expense of $3,634 ($3,000 from the unallocated income statement, $210 from Step 1, $357 from Administrative and General, and $67 from Property Operation/Maintenance and Utility Costs) was allocated $1,817 and $1,817 to the food and beverage depart-

ment. Exhibit 12 shows the step down process (Step 2) of the step method.

The fully-allocated income statement under the step method of cost allocation is shown in Exhibit 13. After cost allocation, the rooms department income is $8,054 while the food and beverage department shows a loss of $1,554.

Conclusion

The precision offered by the allocation procedures discussed and illustrated here increases from the direct to the step methods. So does the cost of preparation.

The decision to use a more sophisticated cost-allocation method must be made following a cost-benefit analysis. Hotel management must determine the value of the more precise information.

Cost allocation is an attention-getting tool. It should not lead to hasty

EXHIBIT 13
Fully Allocated Income Statement, Walters Motor Inn
Step Method—For the Month of March

	Rooms	Food & Beverage	Total
Revenue	$ 50,000	$ 50,000	$ 100,000
Cost of Sales	–0–	18,000	18,000
Payroll and Related Expenses	12,000	13,000	25,000
Other Direct Expenses	4,000	4,500	8,500
Total Expenses	16,000	35,500	51,500
Departmental Income	34,000	14,500	48,500
Allocated Expenses (from			
Exhibit 9)	25,946	16,054	42,000
Departmental Income (Loss)			
after Allocation	$ 8,054	$ (1,554)	6,500
Income Taxes			2,000
Net Income			$ 4,500

decisions. The results raise a number of questions for management; among them:

— What action should be taken if the departmental income after allocation is negative?
— Should a department's services be curtailed if a loss is shown after a full allocation?

— Should advertising for a department's services be increased if a loss is shown after full allocation?

Management decisions should be made only after careful cost-benefit analysis. Allocation of indirect costs allows management to make such decisions in a more informed and accurate manner.

Chapter 7 Outline

CVP Analysis Defined
    CVP Assumptions, Limitations, and
    Relationships
CVP Equation—Single Product
    CVP Illustration—Single Product
    Margin of Safety
    Sensitivity Analysis
CVP Equation—Multiple Products
    CVP Illustration—Multiple Products
    Additional Questions and Solutions
Income Taxes and CVP Analysis
Profit-Volume Graphs
Cash Flow CVP Analysis
Comprehensive Problem
Operating Leverage
Computer Applications

Cost-Volume-Profit Analysis

7

COST-VOLUME-PROFIT (CVP) ANALYSIS is a set of analytical tools used to determine the revenues required at any desired profit level. Many business people refer to CVP analysis as a **breakeven analysis**. However, the **breakeven point** of a firm is only one point among an infinite number of possible points that can be determined. When properly used, CVP analysis provides useful information about the structure of operations and answers many types of questions such as:

1. What is the breakeven point?

2. What is the profit at any given occupancy percentage above the breakeven point?

3. How will a $50,000 increase in property taxes next year affect the sales breakeven point?

4. How much must rooms sales increase next year to cover the increase in property taxes and/or other expenses and still achieve the desired profit?

5. How many rooms must be sold to achieve a $100,000 profit?

6. What is the effect on profit if prices, variable costs, or fixed costs increase?

This chapter begins with a definition of CVP analysis followed by a clarification of both the assumptions of the CVP model and the limitations of CVP as an analytical tool. Next, we will describe the relationships depicted in the CVP model, namely the relationships among revenues, variable costs, fixed costs, and levels of activity. We will then illustrate CVP analysis by discussing both the simple situation of a single product offering and the more complex multiple product situation. We will also discuss the effects of income taxes within the CVP model and modify the basic model to more adequately reflect cash flow considerations. Finally, we will consider the topic of the relative mix of fixed and variable costs through a discussion of operating leverage.

CVP Analysis Defined

CVP analysis is a management tool that expresses the relationships among various costs, sales volume, and profits in either graphic or equation form. The graphs or equations assist management in making decisions. A simple example may be used to illustrate this process.

Assume that the manager of the Red Cedar Inn, a 10-room motel, would like to know what price must be charged in order to make a profit of $2,000 in a 30-day period. The available information is as follows:

- Variable costs per room sold equal $5.

- If the average price is between $20 and $25, 250 rooms can be sold.

- Fixed costs for a 30-day period are $2,500.

Given these three pieces of information, using CVP analysis the manager is able to calculate that the selling price must average $23 in order to attain the goal of a $2,000 profit in a 30-day period. This selling price is determined on the basis of the CVP model by working through the calculations of the following formula:

$$\text{Selling Price} = \frac{\text{Variable Costs}}{\text{per Room}} + \frac{\text{Desired Profit} + \text{Fixed Costs}}{\text{Number of Rooms to be Sold}}$$

$$= \$5 + \frac{2,000 + 2,500}{250}$$

$$= \$23$$

Since the selling price of $23 suggested by the CVP analysis is within the range of $20 to $25 required to sell the specified number of rooms, the manager will be able to reach the desired goal of a $2,000 profit in 30 days by establishing the price at $23. The Red Cedar Inn's summarized operations budget for the 30-day period is as follows:

Room sales (250 × $23)		$5,750
Variable costs (250 × $5)	$1,250	
Fixed costs	2,500	3,750
Profit		$2,000

CVP Assumptions, Limitations, and Relationships

CVP analysis, like all mathematical models, is based on several assumptions. When these assumptions do not hold in the actual situations to which the model is applied, then the results of CVP analysis will be suspect. The commonest assumptions are as follows:

1. Fixed costs remain fixed during the period being considered. Over time, fixed costs do change. However, it is reasonable to assume that fixed costs remain constant over a short time span.

2. Variable costs fluctuate in a linear fashion with revenues during the period under consideration. That is, if revenues increase $x\%$, variable costs also increase $x\%$.

3. Revenues are directly proportional to volume—that is, they are linear. As unit sales increase by $x\%$, revenues increase by $x\%$. This relationship is shown in Exhibit 1.

Exhibit 1   Graphic Depiction of Revenue

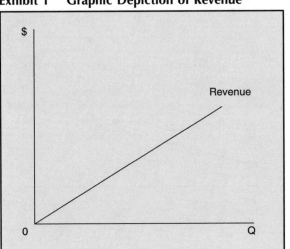

4. Mixed costs can be properly divided into their fixed and variable elements.

5. All costs can be assigned to individual operated departments. This assumption limits the ability of CVP analysis to consider joint costs. These are costs that simultaneously benefit two or more operated departments. Joint costs, or a portion thereof, are not eliminated by discontinuing the offering of services such as food, beverage, telephone, and so forth. Therefore, for the purposes of CVP analysis, joint costs cannot be assigned to individual operated departments. Because of the existence of joint costs, the breakeven point cannot be determined by operated department. However, it can still be determined for the entire operation.

6. The CVP model considers only quantitative factors. Qualitative factors such as employee morale, guest goodwill, and so forth, are not considered. Thus, management must carefully consider these qualitative factors before making any final decisions.

The cost-volume-profit relationships depicted in CVP equations and graphs consist of fixed costs, variable costs, and revenues. The relationships of fixed costs, variable costs, and revenues to volume and profits are graphically illustrated by Exhibit 2. The CVP graph shows dollars on the vertical axis and volume (rooms sales) on the horizontal axis. The fixed cost line is parallel to the horizontal axis from point A. Thus, the amount of the fixed costs theoretically would equal the loss the hospitality operation would suffer if no sales took place. The variable cost line is the broken straight line from point 0. This suggests that there are no variable costs when there are no sales and the straight line suggests that variable costs change proportionately with sales. The sum of variable costs and fixed costs equals total costs. The total cost line is drawn from Point A parallel to the variable cost line. This suggests that total

Exhibit 2   Cost-Volume-Profit Graph

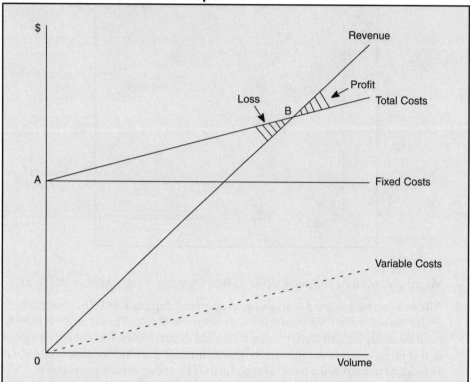

costs increase only as variable costs increase, and that variable costs increase only from increased sales.

The revenue line commences at point 0 and reflects a linear relationship between revenue and units sold. Point B is the intersection of the total cost line and the revenue line. At point B, revenues equal total costs; this is the breakeven point. The vertical distance between the revenue line and the total cost line to the right of point B represents profit, while the vertical distance between these two lines to the left of Point B represents operating loss.

In this way, the CVP model shows the relationship of profit to sales volume and relates both to costs. As the volume of sales increases and reaches the point where the amount of revenues generated by those sales equals the total costs of generating them, then the hospitality operation arrives at its breakeven point. As the volume of sales increases past the breakeven point, the amount of revenues generated by those sales increases at a faster rate than the costs associated with those sales. Thus, the growing difference between revenues and cost measures the increase of profit in relation to sales volume.

It is important to stress again that the CVP model of the relations of costs, sales volume, and profit is based entirely upon its assumptions about the relationship of costs and revenues to sales volume. Although both costs and revenues are assumed

Exhibit 3   Cost-Volume-Profit Analysis Equation—Single Product

A CVP analysis equation expresses the cost-volume-profit relationships as follows:

$$I_n = SX - VX - F$$

where:

I_n	=	Net income
S	=	Selling price
X	=	Units sold
V	=	Variable cost per unit
F	=	Total fixed cost

therefore:

SX	=	Total revenue
VX	=	Total variable costs

to increase in direct linear proportion to the increase of sales volume, revenues must increase at a faster rate than costs if the business is to succeed; in other words, revenues must exceed variable costs. When this is true, both revenues and costs increase in proportion to sales, but they do so at different rates. It is because of this difference in growth rates of revenues and costs in relation to sales that the total revenue and total cost lines are bound to intersect and reach a balance (breakeven point) as sales increase.

CVP Equation—Single Product

The CVP graph, although appealing in its simplicity, is not sufficiently precise, and it is often time-consuming to manually construct a graph for each question to be solved using CVP analysis. However, computers can produce these graphs quickly and easily. As an alternative, CVP analysis uses a series of equations that express the mathematical relationships depicted in the graphic model.

A CVP equation expresses the cost-volume-profit relationships and is illustrated in Exhibit 3. At the breakeven point, net income is zero and the equation is simply shown as follows:

$$0 = SX - VX - F$$

The equation may be rearranged to solve for any one of the four variables as follows:

	Equation	Determines
$X =$	$\dfrac{F}{S - V}$	Units sold at breakeven
$F =$	$SX - VX$	Fixed costs at breakeven
$S =$	$\dfrac{F}{X} + V$	Selling price at breakeven
$V =$	$S - \dfrac{F}{X}$	Variable cost per unit at breakeven

This CVP equation assumes the sale of a single product such as rooms or meals. Most hospitality firms sell a vast array of goods and services. However, before turning to this more complex situation, let's look at an illustration of this simple CVP analysis equation through the following example.

CVP Illustration—Single Product

The Michael Motel, a 30-room budget motel, has the following cost and price structure:

- Annual fixed costs equal $90,000.

- Average selling price per room is $20.

- Variable cost per room sold equals $8.

What is the number of room sales required for the Michael Motel to break even?

$$X \ = \ \frac{F}{S - V} \quad \text{(equation for units sold at breakeven)}$$

$$= \ \frac{\$90,000}{\$20 - \$8}$$

$$= \ \underline{\underline{7,500 \text{ rooms}}}$$

Exhibit 4 depicts the breakeven point of the Michael Motel at 7,500 rooms. The total revenue at the breakeven point is shown as $150,000 (the result of multiplying the selling price per room by the number of rooms sold).

What is the occupancy percentage at breakeven for the Michael Motel?

$$\text{Occupancy Percentage} \ = \ \frac{\text{Rooms Sold}}{\text{Rooms Available}}$$

$$= \ \frac{7,500}{365 \times 30}$$

$$= \ \underline{\underline{68.49\%}}$$

If the proprietor desires the Michael Motel to earn $12,000 for the year, how many rooms must be sold? This can be determined by modifying the equation for units sold at breakeven.

$$X \ = \ \frac{F + I_n}{S - V} \quad \text{(equation for units sold at \$12,000 profit level)}$$

$$= \ \frac{\$90,000 + \$12,000}{\$20 - \$8}$$

$$= \ \underline{\underline{8,500 \text{ rooms}}}$$

Exhibit 4   Breakeven Point—Michael Motel

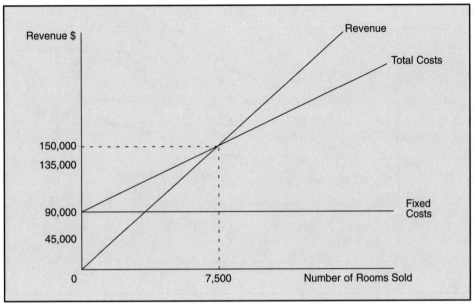

Therefore, for $12,000 to be earned in a year, the Michael Motel must sell 1,000 rooms beyond its breakeven point. The profit earned on these additional sales is the result of the selling price less variable cost per room multiplied by the excess rooms ($20 − $8 = $12; $12 × 1,000 = $12,000).

The difference between selling price and variable cost per unit is often called **contribution margin (CM).** In this example, the CM is $12—for each room sold, $12 is available to cover fixed costs or contribute toward profits. Beyond the breakeven point, 1,000 additional rooms sales result in a $12,000 profit (rooms sales beyond breakeven × CM = profit).

Exhibit 5 is a graphic depiction of the $12,000 of net income. When total revenue is $170,000 (8,500 × $20), expenses equal $158,000 (calculated by multiplying $8 by 8,500 and then adding $90,000), resulting in a $12,000 net income. The distance between the total revenue line and the total cost line at the 8,500 rooms point represents the net income of $12,000.

Likewise, if rooms sales are less than the 7,500 breakeven point, $12 (CM) is lost per room not sold. For example, we can calculate the loss for the year if the Michael Motel sells only 6,500 rooms. Based on the above information, the answer should be $12,000 (CM × rooms less than breakeven). Using the general formula, the proof is as follows:

$$
\begin{aligned}
I_n &= \text{SX} - \text{VX} - \text{F (general formula)} \\
&= \$20(6,500) - \$8(6,500) - \$90,000 \\
&= -\$12,000
\end{aligned}
$$

Exhibit 5   Net Income—Michael Motel

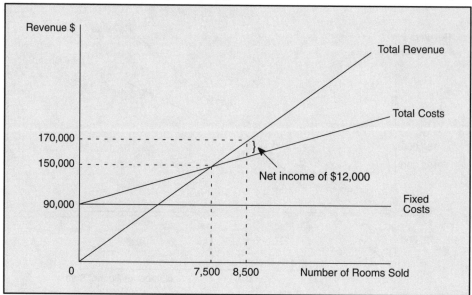

Thus, a loss of $12,000 would be incurred when rooms sales are only 6,500 for the year.

Margin of Safety

The **margin of safety** is the excess of budgeted or actual sales over sales at breakeven. For the Michael Motel above, the level of sales when net income of $12,000 is earned is $170,000. Since the breakeven sales were $150,000, the margin of safety for the Michael Motel when $12,000 of profit is generated is $20,000 and 1,000 rooms as follows:

	Breakeven	Profit of $12,000	Margin of Safety
Sales—$	$150,000	$170,000	$20,000
Sales—Rooms	7,500	8,500	1,000

Sensitivity Analysis

Sensitivity analysis is the study of the sensitivity of the CVP model's dependent variables (such as room sales) to changes in one or more of the model's independent variables (such as variable costs and selling prices). The CVP model shows how the dependent variable will respond to a proposed change.

Again we will use the Michael Motel to illustrate this concept. Assume that the Michael Motel's fixed costs increase by $12,000. How many more rooms must be sold in order to earn $12,000 of net income? (Assume that selling price and variable costs percentage remain constant.)

Exhibit 6   Cost-Volume-Profit Analysis Equation—Multiple Products

$$R = \frac{F + I_n}{CMR_w}$$

where F = Total fixed costs
I_n = Net income
R = Revenue at desired profit level
CMR_w = Weighted average contribution margin ratio

$$\text{Increased Rooms Sales} = \frac{\text{Increase in Fixed Costs}}{\text{Contribution Margin}}$$

$$= \frac{\$12,000}{\$12}$$

$$= \underline{\underline{1,000}}$$

Thus, a $12,000 increase in fixed costs (the independent variable) will require an increase in room sales of 1,000 units (the dependent variable) to cover the increased fixed costs and still make $12,000 in profits.

The proof is as follows:

Increased sales
1,000 rooms × $20   = $20,000

Increased variable costs
1,000 rooms × $8   =   8,000

Increased fixed costs   =   12,000

Bottom line impact $ –0–

CVP Equation—Multiple Products

Many hospitality operations, especially hotels, sell more than just a single product. In order to determine the operation's breakeven point (or any profit level) using CVP analysis, a different CVP equation is required. This equation is illustrated in Exhibit 6.

The **contribution margin ratio (CMR)** results from dividing CM by the selling price. (Remember that CM is determined by subtracting the variable cost per unit from the selling price.) Using the Michael Motel illustration, CMR is determined as follows:

$$CMR = \frac{CM}{S}$$

$$= \frac{\$20 - \$8}{\$20}$$

$$= \underline{\underline{.6}}$$

Exhibit 7   Weighted Average Contribution Margin Ratio

$$CMR_w = \frac{R_1}{TR} \times \frac{(R_1 - TV_1)}{R_1} + \frac{R_2}{TR} \times \frac{(R_2 - TV_2)}{R_2} + \frac{R_3}{TR} \times \frac{(R_3 - TV_3)}{R_3} +$$

$$\ldots + \frac{R_n}{TR} \times \frac{(R_n - TV_n)}{R_n}$$

where
R_1 = Revenue for operated department 1
R_2 = Revenue for operated department 2
R_3 = Revenue for operated department 3
R_n = Revenue for operated department n
TR = Total revenue
TV_1 = Total variable cost for operated department 1
TV_2 = Total variable cost for operated department 2
TV_3 = Total variable cost for operated department 3
TV_n = Total variable cost for operated department n

The CMR means that for every \$1 of sales for the Michael Motel, 60% is contributed toward fixed costs and/or profits. However, recall that in a multiple product situation, more than just rooms are being sold. Therefore, the CMR must be a **weighted average CMR (CMR$_w$).** That is, an average CMR for all operated departments must be weighted to reflect the relative contribution of each department to the establishment's ability to pay fixed costs and generate profits.

The weighted average CMR can be determined from more than one formula. In the more complex formula, a CMR is determined for each operated department and the weighted average of the various CMRs is determined as illustrated in Exhibit 7. To illustrate this calculation of CMR$_w$, assume that the Michael Motel adds a coffee shop. Exhibit 8 shows a partial income statement for the Michael Motel after the first year the coffee shop has been in operation. Using the equation in Exhibit 7, the CMR$_w$ of .5 for the Michael Motel is determined as follows:

$$CMR_w = \frac{R_1}{TR} \times \frac{R_1 - TV_1}{R_1} + \frac{R_2}{TR} \times \frac{R_2 - TV_2}{R_2}$$

$$= \frac{\$150,000}{\$200,000} \times \frac{(\$150,000 - \$60,000)}{\$150,000} + \frac{\$50,000}{\$200,000} \times \frac{(\$50,000 - \$40,000)}{\$50,000}$$

$$= .75(.6) + .25(.2)$$

$$= \underline{\underline{.5}}$$

Alternatively, the CMR$_w$ can sometimes be determined using a simpler formula using total revenues and total variable costs as follows:

Exhibit 8   Partial Income Statement—Michael Motel

Operated Department	Revenue		Variable Costs		Contribution Margin
Rooms	$150,000	(R$_1$)	$ 60,000	(TV$_1$)	$ 90,000
Coffee Shop	50,000	(R$_2$)	40,000	(TV$_2$)	10,000
	$200,000	(TR)	$100,000	(TV)	$100,000

$$CMR_w = \frac{TR - TV}{TR}$$

$$= \frac{\$200,000 - \$100,000}{\$200,000}$$

$$= \underline{\underline{.5}}$$

The simpler formula is easier to use when you know the breakdown of fixed and variable costs for the entire property. However, when calculating the effects of various changes within departments (for example, the sales mix), the formula in Exhibit 7 allows you to substitute figures more easily.

To further illustrate the use of the CMR_w formula, assume that forecasted activity at the Michael Motel shows the variable cost percentage of the rooms department dropping to 30%. Since the CMR equals one minus the variable cost percentage, the new rooms department CMR would be .7. Assuming the same sales mix (75% rooms, 25% coffee shop), the formula can be used to revise the CMR_w as follows:

$$\text{Revised } CMR_w = .75\,(.7) + .25\,(.2)$$

$$= \underline{\underline{.575}}$$

CVP Illustration—Multiple Products

The following series of questions and answers uses the Michael Motel to illustrate how the CVP calculations are used to analyze profit levels, sales mix, and break-even points in the more complex, and also more typical, situations where hospitality operations sell multiple goods and services. Consider the following information for the Michael Motel:

- Annual fixed costs are $150,000.

- Sales mix is 75% rooms, 25% coffee shop.

- The Rooms Department CMR is .6 and the Coffee Shop CMR is .2.

What is revenue when the Michael Motel breaks even?

$$R = \frac{F}{CMR_w} \quad \text{(equation for revenue at the breakeven point)}$$

$$= \frac{\$150,000}{.5}$$

$$= \underline{\underline{\$300,000}}$$

Therefore, the Michael Motel's breakeven point is reached when revenue is $300,000. Since, in this application of CVP analysis, multiple products are being sold, the breakeven point is expressed in dollars, not units sold, which is used when analyzing single product/service operations.

What is the Michael Motel's total revenue when a profit of $12,000 is earned?

$$R = \frac{F + I_n}{CMR_w}$$

$$= \frac{\$150,000 + \$12,000}{.5}$$

$$= \underline{\underline{\$324,000}}$$

In order for the Michael Motel to earn $12,000, its revenue must increase by $24,000 beyond its breakeven sales of $300,000. Alternatively, the additional revenues beyond breakeven could have been determined as follows:

$$\text{Revenue Beyond Breakeven} = \frac{I_n}{CMR_w}$$

$$= \frac{\$12,000}{.5}$$

$$= \underline{\underline{\$24,000}}$$

Failure to reach breakeven sales will result in a loss of $.50 for every $1 of sales that falls short of breakeven. For the Michael Motel, total sales of $280,000 will result in a $10,000 loss determined as follows:

$$I_n = R(CMR_w) - F$$

$$= \$280,000 \,(.5) - \$150,000$$

$$= \underline{\underline{-\$10,000}}$$

Additional Questions and Solutions

If net income is to be $20,000, how much must *rooms* revenue be, given a ratio of 75% of rooms revenue to total revenue?

$$R = \frac{F + I_n}{CMR_w}$$

$$= \frac{\$150,000 + \$20,000}{.5}$$

$$= \$340,000$$

$$\text{Rooms Revenue} = .75R$$

$$= .75(\$340,000)$$

$$= \underline{\underline{\$255,000}}$$

In this situation, rooms revenue must be $255,000. A total revenue of $340,000 is required to yield a net income of $20,000, and 75% of this total revenue represents the contribution of the rooms department.

If room prices increase by 20% and the number of rooms sold remains constant, what is the revised breakeven point?

In this situation, we can expect that the price change will affect the rooms department's relative contribution to the operation's ability to meet fixed costs or profit goals. Therefore, the CMR_w must first be recalculated. This is accomplished by recalculating the CMR for the rooms department and then determining the revised CMR_w. The 20% room price increase not only increases the CMR for the rooms department, it also changes the sales mix for the Michael Motel.

$$\text{Revised CMR for Rooms} = \frac{\$150,000(1.20) - \$60,000}{\$150,000(1.20)}$$

$$= \frac{\$180,000 - \$60,000}{\$180,000}$$

$$= \underline{\underline{^2/_3 \text{ or } .6667}}$$

$$CMR_w = \frac{\$180,000}{\$230,000}(.6667) + \frac{\$50,000}{\$230,000}(.2)$$

$$= \underline{\underline{.5652}}$$

$$\text{Revenue} = \frac{F}{CMR_w}$$

$$= \frac{\$150,000}{.5652}$$

$$= \underline{\underline{\$265,392.78}}$$

Thus, the effect on breakeven of a 20% rooms price increase is to reduce the amount of revenue needed to break even from $300,000 to $265,392.78.

If the sales mix changes to 60% rooms and 40% food from the prior mix of 75% rooms and 25% food, what happens to the breakeven point?

Again, the CMR_w must first be revised. The revised CMR_w is divided into total fixed costs to yield the new breakeven point.

$$\text{Revised } CMR_w = .6(.6) + .4(.2)$$

$$= .44$$

$$\text{Revenue} = \frac{F}{CMR_w}$$

$$= \frac{150,000}{.44}$$

$$= \$340,909.09$$

Thus, the changes in sales mix result in a reduction in the weighted average CMR from .50 to .44. This reduction, in turn, results in an increase of $40,909.09 in the amount of revenue needed for the operation to break even.

If fixed costs increase by $20,000 and all other factors remain constant, what is the revised breakeven point? (Assume a CMR_w of .5.)

In this situation, F is simply increased from $150,000 to $170,000. The new total for fixed costs is then divided by the CMR_w of .5 in order to calculate the new breakeven point.

$$\text{Revenue} = \frac{170,000}{.5}$$

$$= \$340,000$$

The breakeven point when revenues equal $340,000 could have been determined by dividing the increased fixed costs of $20,000 by .5 (the CMR_w) and adding the result ($40,000) to the original breakeven revenue of $300,000.

If fixed costs increase by $20,000, variable costs decrease by five percentage points, and all other factors remain constant, what is the revised breakeven point?

If variable costs decrease by five percentage points, then CMR_w increases by the same five percentage points. Thus, the revised CMR_w is .55.

$$\text{Revised } CMR_w = \text{Prior } CMR_w + \text{Variable Cost Decrease}$$

$$= .5 + .05$$

$$= .55$$

$$\text{Revenue} = \frac{\$170,000}{.55}$$

$$= \$309,090.90$$

Income Taxes and CVP Analysis

Up to this point, the CVP model has treated all costs as either fixed or variable in relation to revenues. However, income taxes vary, not with revenues, but with pretax income. Rather than simply treating income tax as a variable expense (which it is not), management can adjust the CVP equations to reflect this relationship between income taxes and pretax income. The CVP equations reflect this refinement by substituting I_b, the notation for pretax income, in place of I_n. When I_n and the tax rate (t) are known, I_b can be determined with the following formula:

$$I_b = \frac{I_n}{1 - t}$$

For example, assume that the Michael Motel desires to earn $12,000 of net income ($I_n$) and its tax rate is 20%. Pretax income (I_b) is determined as follows:

$$I_b = \frac{\$12,000}{1 - .2}$$

$$= \$15,000^*$$

*Proof:

Pretax income	$15,000
Taxes (20%)	− 3,000
Net Income	$12,000

The CVP equation is now altered for income taxes as follows:

$$R = \frac{I_b + F}{CMR_w}$$

This revised CVP analysis equation can be illustrated using the Michael Motel. Assume the following situation:

- Desired net income equals $30,000.
- Annual fixed costs equal $150,000.
- Tax rate equals 20%.
- CMR_w equals .5.

From this information, we can calculate the pretax income as follows:

$$I_b = \frac{\$30,000}{1 - .2}$$

$$= \$37,500$$

Once we calculate the pretax income as $37,500, we can then use the revised CVP equation to arrive at the breakeven point:

$$R = \frac{I_b + F}{CMR_w}$$

$$= \frac{\$37,500 + \$150,000}{.5}$$

$$= \$375,000^*$$

*Proof:

Revenue	$375,000
Variable costs (50%)	− 187,500
Fixed Costs	− 150,000
Pretax income	37,500
Income taxes	− 7,500
Net income	$ 30,000

When an enterprise breaks even, its net income and pretax income both equal zero. Therefore, the breakeven point for a given operation is the same regardless of the tax rate.

Profit-Volume Graphs

In CVP graphs such as Exhibit 2, profits and losses are represented by the vertical difference between the total revenue and total cost lines at any point. When management desires to focus on the impact on profits of changes in sales volume, a **profit-volume graph** is often used, because it more clearly depicts the relationship between volume and profits. In this graph, revenues and costs are not shown.

Exhibit 9 is the profit-volume graph (for the Michael Motel) which is used to illustrate the CVP analysis when a firm has multiple products. The breakeven point is reached when sales equal $300,000, as calculated earlier. If sales are $0, then losses are $150,000, which is the total amount of fixed costs. Likewise, if $150,000 of profit is to be earned, then total sales would have to be $600,000. Although the graph shows this result, one must question if this point is outside the Michael Motel's possible range of activity. If rooms revenue is 75% and the selling price per room is $20, then 22,500 rooms would have to be sold, determined as follows:

$$\text{Required Rooms Sales in Units} = \frac{\text{Rooms Revenue}}{\text{Room Selling Price}}$$

$$= \frac{.75(\$600,000)}{\$20}$$

$$= 22,500$$

Exhibit 9   Profit-Volume Graph

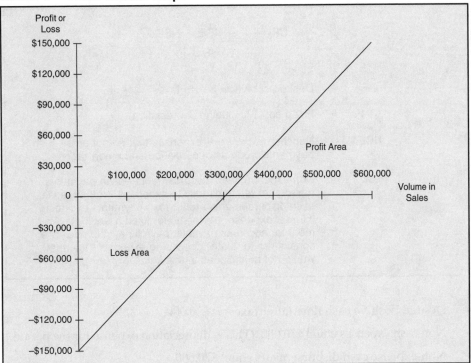

However, we established earlier in this chapter that the Michael Motel is a 30-room property. The total rooms it could sell in a year is 10,950; thus, 22,500 is beyond its reach. It would have to expand its size or increase its prices to achieve sales of $600,000 and net income of $150,000. The point to remember is: do not blindly use these analytical tools.

Cash Flow CVP Analysis

In addition to applying CVP analysis to evaluate profit levels, sales mixes, and pretax incomes, managers and owners are also interested in evaluating various levels of cash flow. They are interested in knowing the amount of revenues required to produce a sufficient flow of cash to reach such benchmarks as the breakeven point and other cash flow levels. The CVP analysis equations previously demonstrated may be modified to provide answers to these questions. The cash flow CVP equation is illustrated in Exhibit 10.

The application of CVP analysis to problems involving cash flow can be illustrated using the Michael Motel in light of the following information:

- Fixed costs equal $150,000.

- Tax rate equals 20%.

- CMR_w equals .5.

Exhibit 10   Cash Flow Cost-Volume-Profit Analysis Equation

$$R = \frac{CF_b + F - NCE + NECD}{CMR_w}$$

where

CF_b = Desired cash flow before taxes

F = Fixed costs (including depreciation)

NCE = Noncash expenses—expenses that do not entail cash payments, such as depreciation and amortization.

$NECD$ = Non-expense cash disbursements—cash payments that do not relate directly to expenses. Non-expense cash disbursements are for loan payments excluding interest expense, payments for fixed assets, etc. Payment for accounts payable, payroll payable, etc., are considered to relate "directly" to expense; thus, they would not be included in this figure.

- Desired positive cash flow (after taxes) is $30,000.

- Non-cash expenses equal $10,000. (This is depreciation expense for the period.)

- Non-expense cash disbursements equal $20,000.

In this situation, we can calculate the total revenue required to yield the desired positive cash flow (CF_d) of $30,000. But, first, we need to calculate the desired cash flow before taxes:

$$CF_b = \frac{CF_d + NECD - NCE}{1 - t} - NECD + NCE$$

$$= \frac{\$30,000 + \$20,000 - \$10,000}{1 - .2} - \$20,000 + \$10,000$$

$$= \underline{\underline{\$40,000}}$$

We can now calculate the total revenue required to yield the desired cash flow before taxes by using the following formula:

$$R = \frac{CF_b + F - NCE + NECD}{CMR_w}$$

$$= \frac{\$40,000 + \$150,000 - \$10,000 + \$20,000}{.5}$$

$$= \underline{\underline{\$400,000}}$$

Exhibit 11   Cash-Flow—Michael Motel

Cash receipts (revenue)	$ 400,000
Cash disbursements:	
Variable costs	200,000
Fixed costs	140,000*
Non-expenses (reduction in debt)	20,000
Income taxes	10,000**
Positive cash flow	$ 30,000

  * Total fixed costs less depreciation equals fixed costs cash disbursements
    ($150,000 − $10,000 = $140,000)

** Income Taxes = (Revenue − Variable Costs − Fixed Costs) (Tax Rate)
   Income Taxes = (400,000 − 200,000 − 150,000) (.2)
   Income Taxes = 50,000 (.2)
   Income Taxes = $10,000

Therefore, the Michael Motel must have total revenues of $400,000 in order to generate sufficient cash internally to make its payments and to attain the desired positive cash flow level. The proof of our calculations appears in Exhibit 11.

Alternatively, the total revenue at which the Michael Motel has breakeven cash flow (that is, CF_d equals 0) can be determined. First, we need to calculate the desired cash flow before taxes as follows:

$$CF_b = \frac{CF_d + NECD - NCE}{1 - t} - NECD + NCE$$

$$= \frac{0 + \$20,000 - \$10,000}{1 - .2} - \$20,000 + \$10,000$$

$$= \underline{\$2,500}$$

Now we calculate total revenue required to yield a breakeven cash flow as follows:

$$R = \frac{CF_b + F - NCE + NECD}{CMR_w}$$

$$= \frac{\$2,500 + \$150,000 - \$10,000 + \$20,000}{.5}$$

$$= \underline{\$325,000}$$

Therefore, the Michael Motel requires revenue of $325,000 to yield sufficient cash so that it does not have to borrow working capital funds. The revenue required for a breakeven cash flow of $325,000 is $25,000 greater than the breakeven revenue of

Exhibit 12   Income Statement—Smith Hotel

			Summary Income Statement Smith Hotel For the year ended December 31, 19X1			

	Revenue	Cost of Sales	Payroll and Related Expenses	Other Expenses	Income (Loss)
Operating Departments:					
Rooms	$4,000,000	$ 0	$ 500,000	$ 300,000	$3,200,000
Food	1,200,000	350,000	550,000	150,000	150,000
Beverage	600,000	150,000	150,000	50,000	250,000
Telephone	200,000	160,000	30,000	10,000	0
Total	$6,000,000	$ 660,000	1,230,000	510,000	3,600,000
Undistributed Operating Expenses:					
Administrative and General			100,000	50,000	150,000
Information Systems			50,000	50,000	100,000
Human Resources			30,000	260,000	290,000
Transportation			20,000	40,000	60,000
Marketing			100,000	300,000	400,000
Property Operation and Maintenance			100,000	100,000	200,000
Utility Costs			0	400,000	400,000
Income After Undistributed Operating Expenses			$ 1,630,000	$ 1,710,000	2,000,000
Rent, Property Taxes and Insurance				$ 200,000	
Interest				1,000,000	
Depreciation				500,000	1,700,000
Income Before Income Taxes					300,000
Income Taxes					60,000
Net Income					$ 240,000

$300,000 as computed previously. This difference is due to the excess of the required pretax cash flow and NECD over NCE, determined as follows:

$$\text{Difference in Revenue} = \frac{CF_b + NECD - NCE}{CMR_w}$$

$$= \frac{\$2,500 + \$20,000 - \$10,000}{.5}$$

$$= \underline{\underline{\$25,000}}$$

Comprehensive Problem

The Smith Hotel will be used to more fully illustrate CVP analysis. Exhibit 12 contains the income statement according to the *Uniform System of Accounts for the Lodging Industry (USALI)* format for the Smith Hotel for the year ended December 31, 19X1.

For CVP analysis, expenses need to be identified as either variable or fixed. For illustration purposes, the direct expenses of the operated departments for the Smith Hotel are assumed to be variable, while overhead costs (the undistributed operating

Exhibit 13   Relationship of Revenues, Variable Costs, and Contribution Margin—Smith Hotel

Relationship of Revenues, Variable Costs, and Contribution Margin
Smith Hotel
For the year ended December 31, 19X1

	Revenue	Variable Costs	Contribution Margin
Rooms	$4,000,000	$ 800,000	$3,200,000
Food	1,200,000	1,050,000	150,000
Beverage	600,000	350,000	250,000
Telephone	200,000	200,000	0
Total	$6,000,000	$2,400,000	3,600,000
Fixed Costs			3,300,000
Income Before Income Taxes			300,000
Income Taxes			60,000
Net Income			$ 240,000

expenses and fixed charges) are assumed to be fixed costs. Income tax is a function of income before income taxes. These assumptions are shown in Exhibit 13.

Given this information, we will now use CVP analysis to calculate each of the following situations for the Smith Hotel:

1. Weighted average contribution margin ratio

2. Breakeven point

3. Total revenue to yield a net income of $500,000

4. Rooms revenues when profit equals $500,000

5. Breakeven point if fixed costs increase by $300,000

6. Breakeven point if fixed costs increase by $300,000 and revenues increase 10% for each department through price increases

Situation #1: Determine the CMR_w.

From Exhibit 13, the CMR_w may be determined as follows:

$$CMR_w = \frac{\text{Contribution Margin*}}{\text{Total Revenue}}$$

$$= \frac{\$3,600,000}{\$6,000,000}$$

$$= .6$$

*Total operated departments income

Situation #2: Determine the breakeven point.

$$R = \frac{F}{CMR_w}$$

$$= \frac{\$3,300,000}{.6}$$

$$= \$5,500,000$$

Situation #3: Determine the total revenue required to yield $500,000 of net income. (Assume that the sales mix remains constant.)

First, the effect of income taxes on net income must be accounted for, assuming the Smith Hotel's income tax rate of 20%. The amount of income before income taxes that the hotel must generate in order to achieve the desired net income of $500,000 can be determined as follows:

$$I_b = \frac{I_n}{1 - t}$$

$$= \frac{\$500,000}{1 - .2}$$

$$= \$625,000$$

Second, the total revenue needed to yield this amount of income before income taxes is calculated as follows:

$$R = \frac{I_b + F}{CMR_w}$$

$$= \frac{\$625,000 + \$3,300,000}{.6}$$

$$= \$6,541,666.67$$

Situation #4: Determine the amount of room revenue when the Smith Hotel makes $500,000 of net income.

First, from the information provided on the Smith Hotel's summary income statement (Exhibit 12), we can determine the relative contribution of rooms revenue to total revenue.

$$\frac{\text{Rooms Revenue}}{\text{Total Revenue}} = \frac{\$4,000,000}{\$6,000,000}$$

$$= .6667$$

Second, we can then multiply .6667 by the total revenue and arrive at the required rooms revenue as part of the total revenue for the Smith Hotel to achieve $500,000 of net income.

$$\text{Rooms Revenue} = \$6,541,666.67 \times .6667$$
$$= \$4,361,329.17$$

Situation #5: Determine the breakeven point for the Smith Hotel if fixed costs increase by $300,000 and all other things remain constant.

The breakeven point is determined as follows:

$$R = \frac{F}{CMR_w}$$
$$= \frac{\$3,600,000}{.6}$$
$$= \$6,000,000$$

Note the Smith Hotel's breakeven point increases from $5,500,000 to $6,000,000 when its fixed costs increase by $300,000. Alternatively, the new breakeven point could have been determined by dividing the increased fixed costs ($300,000) by the CMR_w and adding the result to the previously calculated breakeven point of $5,500,000 as follows:

$$R = \$5,500,000 + \frac{\$300,000}{.6}$$
$$= \$6,000,000$$

Situation #6: Determine the breakeven point for the Smith Hotel if fixed costs increase by $300,000 and revenues increase 10% for each department through price increases. Assume that all factors remain constant.

First, a revised CMR_w must be determined as follows:

	Total Revenue	Total Contribution Margin
Prior	$6,000,000	$3,600,000
Increase	600,000	600,000
Revised	$6,600,000	$4,200,000

$$\text{Revised } CMR_w = \frac{\text{Revised Total Contribution Margin}}{\text{Revised Total Revenue}}$$
$$= \frac{\$4,200,000}{\$6,600,000}$$
$$= .6364$$

Exhibit 14   Cost Structures of Properties A and B

	Property A		Property B	
	$	%	$	%
Revenues	$500,000	100%	$500,000	100%
Variable costs	300,000	60	200,000	40
Fixed costs	200,000	40	300,000	60
Net income	$ 0	0%	$ 0	0%

Then the total fixed costs are increased by $300,000 to $3,600,000, and the breakeven point is determined as follows:

$$R = \frac{F}{CMR_w}$$

$$= \frac{\$3,600,000}{.6364}$$

$$= \$5,656,819.61$$

Operating Leverage

Operating leverage is the extent to which an operation's expenses are fixed rather than variable. If an operation has a high level of fixed costs relative to variable costs, it is said to be highly levered. Being highly levered means a relatively small increase in sales beyond the breakeven point results in a relatively large increase in net income. However, failure to reach the breakeven point results in a relatively large net loss.

If an operation has a high level of variable costs relative to fixed costs, it is said to have low operating leverage. A relatively small increase in sales beyond the breakeven point results in a small increase in net income. On the other hand, failure to reach the breakeven point results in a relatively small net loss.

For example, consider the cost structures of two hospitality operations illustrated in Exhibit 14. Note that both properties will break even when their revenues equal $500,000. However, Property A has a CMR of .4, while Property B has a CMR of .6. This reveals that, for each revenue dollar over the shared breakeven point, Property A will earn only $.40 while Property B will earn $.60. On the other hand, for each revenue dollar under the breakeven point, Property A loses only $.40 while Property B loses $.60. Both properties identify the same breakeven point as the difference between revenues and expenses, and, for both properties, the costs of failure equal the rewards of success. They both risk as much as they gain, but for Property B, the stakes are higher. Property B is more highly levered than Property A.

Exhibit 15 is a graphical representation of the cost structures of Properties A and B and reflects their identical breakeven points. However, it is the vertical distance between the total revenue and total cost lines that measures the degree of profitability for

Exhibit 15   Operating Leverages of Properties A and B

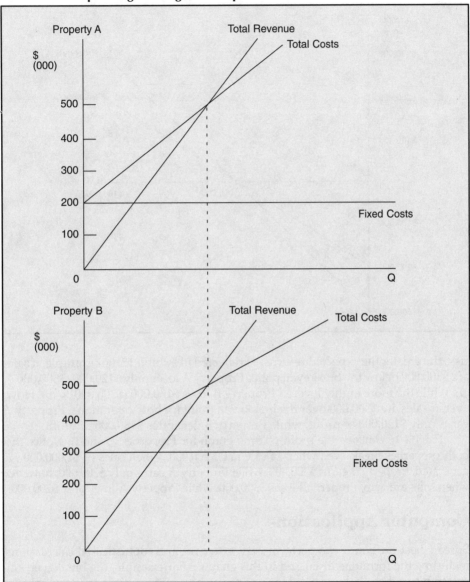

each property. Since Property B is more highly levered, the distance between the total cost and total revenue lines is greater at all operating levels compared to Property A, except at the breakeven point.

The degree of operating leverage desired by a hospitality property reflects the degree of risk that the operation desires to take. All other things being the same, the more highly levered the operation, the greater the risk. However, the greater the

Exhibit 16   Profit-Volume Graph for Properties A and B

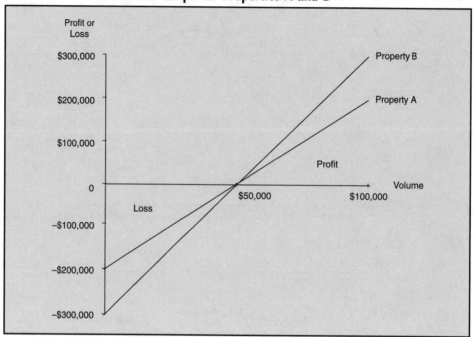

risk, the greater the expected returns, as reflected in Exhibit 15. For example, if sales are $300,000 below the breakeven point, Property A loses only $120,000 ($300,000 × .4), while the more highly levered Property B loses $180,000 ($300,000 × .6). However, if sales are $300,000 over the breakeven point for both operations, Property A earns only $120,000 of profit, while Property B generates $180,000 of profit.

Exhibit 16 contains the profit-volume graph for Properties A and B. Notice that both properties break even when sales equal $500,000. When sales of $1,000,000 are generated, Property B earns $300,000, while Property A earns only $200,000; however, when sales are zero, Property B loses $300,000, while Property A loses only $200,000.

Computer Applications

Spreadsheet programs can perform very extensive and sophisticated calculations, including the formulas discussed in this chapter. For example, the breakeven calculation could easily be entered into a spreadsheet and multiple levels of calculations could be performed quickly and accurately. These formulas can be repeated many times in the same model to determine the optimum solution to a question. In the case of CVP analysis, the breakeven point could be easily determined, and then the analysis could be conducted to find the revenues that would generate the desired net income.

Multiple-product CVP analysis is also ideally suited to spreadsheet programs. Contribution margins for each profit center can be quickly determined and combined

Exhibit 17 Computer-Generated Rooms Department Rate Analysis—Salem Hotel Company

Rooms Department Rate Analysis						
Salem Hotel Company						
Available Rooms for Sale	36,500	36,500	36,500	36,500	36,500	36,500
Average Rate	$ 40.00	$ 45.00	$ 47.50	$ 50.00	$ 52.50	$ 55.00
Projected Occupancy	77.5%	75.0%	72.5%	70.0%	65.0%	60.0%
Room Revenue	$1,131,500	$1,231,875	$1,256,969	$1,277,500	$1,245,563	$1,204,500
Room Variable Expense	237,615	229,950	222,285	214,620	199,290	183,960
Room Profits	893,885	1,001,925	1,034,684	1,062,880	1,046,273	1,020,540
F&B Revenue	424,313	410,625	396,938	383,250	355,875	328,500
F&B Variable Expense	318,234	307,969	297,703	287,438	266,906	246,375
F&B Profits	106,079	102,656	99,235	95,812	88,969	82,125
Total Departmental Profits	999,964	1,104,581	1,133,919	1,158,692	1,135,242	1,102,665
Contribution Margin Ratio	64.3%	67.2%	68.6%	69.8%	70.9%	71.9%
Fixed Expenses	$ 760,000	$ 760,000	$ 760,000	$ 760,000	$ 760,000	$ 760,000
Breakeven Point*	$1,182.461	$1,130,112	$1,108,518	$1,089,305	$1,072,100	$1,056,604

*Breakeven point was calculated by the computer using the formula that divides Fixed Expenses by the quantity (1 − Contribution Margin Ratio).

to create a total picture for the business. Exhibit 17 shows how this might be done with the Salem Hotel Company. In this example, the effects of the lower occupancy caused a reduction in food and beverage revenues. Food and beverage revenues equal the product of available rooms for sale × projected occupancy × $15 average check. This is based on past performance that suggests an average of $15 of food and beverage sales per room sold. The food and beverage variable expenses equal food and beverage revenue × .75.

With any reduction in business, variable costs would also be reduced. The effect is that profitability peaks at 70% occupancy and the combined contribution margin is 69.8%.

With this information, the breakeven point of the hotel is shown for each of the occupancy, revenue, and expense levels in the analysis. The breakeven point at the maximum profitability level is $1,089,305. Some managers might, however, prefer to operate under the scenario of $55 room rate and 60% occupancy because it has the lowest breakeven point and, all other things being equal, is therefore the least risky option. When the revenue and expense lines in the analysis are changed, the computer automatically calculates the contribution margin and the breakeven point.

In addition, computers can produce CVP graphs to reflect visually the results of CVP analysis. Many users find such graphs to be more understandable than a table of numbers.

Summary

Managers use cost-volume-profit (CVP) analysis as an analytical tool to examine the relationships among costs, revenues, and sales volume. By expressing these relationships in graphic form or by using mathematical equations, management can determine an operation's breakeven point, sales requirements for a specified net income level, and/or the mix of sales within the operation.

In order to use CVP analysis to determine the breakeven point, various relationships must be assumed. First, fixed costs are constant; they will not fluctuate within the range of operating activity being studied. Also, both variable costs and revenues fluctuate linearly with sales volume; that is, a percentage increase in sales volume (for example, rooms sold) will result in the same percentage increase in revenues and variable expenses. In a "shut-down" situation (when sales are zero), there are no variable costs or revenues, but the fixed costs will be at their constant level; therefore, the theoretical bottom line for such a shut-down period will be a net loss equal to the fixed costs of the period.

The breakeven point is defined as the level of sales that generates revenues equal to total (fixed and variable) costs. CVP analysis allows management selling a single product/service (for example, only rooms) to arrive at this breakeven level of revenues with the aid of the equation:

$$X = \frac{F}{S - V}$$

The $S - V$ element of the equation is the contribution margin, which is the amount of money generated by the sale that may be applied to cover fixed cost, or, beyond the breakeven point, to contribute to profit. Therefore, the equation reflects the fixed cost divided by the dollars provided to cover fixed costs per sales unit.

In the more complex situation where more than one good or service is sold, the CVP formula is as follows:

$$R = \frac{F + I_n}{CMR_w}$$

The CMR_w element of the equation reflects the weighted average of the CMRs for the profit centers. The CVP formulas for the multiple products operation may be used to determine breakeven points by substituting 0 for I_n. This formula may further be modified by substituting I_b for I_n to consider the effect of income taxes.

Once the CVP relationship is understood, it can become a vital tool offering aid in a number of situations. It can provide management with benchmark sales levels (such as the breakeven level, the amount needed to provide a specific net income, or the required level to provide for cash needs), prices, or sales mix. It can be used to examine the differences between levels of sales or costs. It can also be used to examine different cost structures, as the effect of differences in the CMR can be seen over different sales levels.

🔑 Key Terms

breakeven analysis—See cost-volume-profit analysis.

breakeven point—The level of sales volume at which total revenues equal total costs.

contribution margin—Sales less cost of sales for either an entire operating department or for a given product; represents the amount of sales revenue that is contributed toward fixed costs and/or profits.

contribution margin ratio (CMR)—The contribution margin divided by the selling price. Represents the percentage of sales revenue that is contributed toward fixed costs and/or profits.

cost-volume-profit (CVP) analysis—A set of analytical tools used by managers to examine the relationships among various costs, revenues, and sales volume in either graphic or equation form, allowing one to determine the revenue required at any desired profit level. Also called breakeven analysis.

margin of safety—The excess of budgeted or actual sales over sales at breakeven.

operating leverage—The extent to which an operation's expenses are fixed rather than variable; an operation that substitutes fixed costs for variable costs is said to be highly levered.

profit-volume graph—A graph that focuses on the impact on profits of changes in sales volume; revenues and costs are not shown.

sensitivity analysis—The study of the sensitivity of the CVP model's dependent variables (such as room sales) to changes in one or more of the model's independent variables (such as variable costs and selling prices).

weighted average contribution margin ratio (CMR_w)—In a multiple product situation, an average contribution margin for all operated departments that is weighted to reflect the relative contribution of each department to the establishment's ability to pay fixed costs and generate profits.

Review Questions

1. What are the assumptions underlying CVP analysis?

2. What does the term S − V represent in the CVP equation? How does its use differ from that of the CMR?

3. Draw a CVP graph of the following operation: F = $10; S = $1; V = $.50. What is the meaning of the regions (between the total revenue and total cost lines) to the left and right of 20 units sold?

4. What is income before taxes for a hospitality operation that generates no sales during a period?

5. What is the advantage of using CVP equations instead of CVP graphs to express relationships?

6. How does CMR for a single department, or for an enterprise selling only one product/service, differ from a weighted average CMR (CMR_w)? How is CMR_w determined?

7. What part of the CVP equation used to determine the breakeven point must be changed in order to produce the answer in terms of sales dollars versus sales units? Why is this so?

8. What is the sales mix? How does it affect CMR_w?

9. Why should noncash expenses be subtracted in the CVP formula used to determine the revenue level at the cash flow breakeven point?

10. If, by changing an operation's sales mix, the CMR_w decreases, how is the break-even level of sales affected?

Problems

Problem 1

The owner of Sullivan Foods is concerned about changing costs and the inability to increase prices. During 19X3, the average selling price per meal served was $10.25, the average variable costs were $5.25, and the average monthly fixed costs totaled $20,000.

During 19X4, the average variable costs are expected to increase $.25 per meal and the average monthly fixed costs are expected to increase by $2,000. No price increases are planned for 19X4.

Required:

1. Determine the breakeven point in meals sold for 19X3.

2. Determine the breakeven point in food revenue for 19X3.

3. Determine the breakeven point in meals sold for 19X4 given the expected cost increases.

4. Determine the breakeven point in food for 19X4 given the expected cost increases.

Problem 2

For promotional purposes, the Mackinac Fudge Company has enlarged its retail space at a cost of $20,000 to allow customers to view the fudge production process. In addition, it has started providing free samples of fudge estimated to cost $.25 per customer. The average customer buys a $10.00 box of fudge and the related cost of the fudge is $5.00 per customer.

Required:

Calculate how many boxes of fudge must be sold to cover the new promotional costs, including the cost of more space and the free samples.

Problem 3

The Karen Company owns the Center Road Motel, a 20-room rooms-only operation. In 19X2, the motel's average selling price was $25.00, its contribution margin ratio was 20%, and its annual fixed costs totaled $100,000.

Karen Schmidt (the owner) would like to know what amount of revenue must be generated in 19X3 to achieve a pretax profit of $50,000 for each independent situation listed below.

Required:

1. The motel desires to break even. The 19X3 selling price and expenses are the same as during 19X2.

2. The motel is able to increase its selling price by $2.00. Its expenses during 19X3 remain the same as during 19X2.

3. The motel's contribution margin ratio increases to 25% and other factors remain constant.

Problem 4

Keith Jones is considering investing $1,500,000 in a 60-room motel, The Olympia Inn. Based on his market research, he has determined that a reasonable room rate for the region is $39.95. He projects variable costs to be $12.00 per room, and his annual fixed costs are estimated at $400,000.

Required:

1. Determine the number of rooms sales required for The Olympia Inn to break even.

2. Assuming all 60 rooms will be available 365 days during the year, what is The Olympia Inn's projected breakeven occupancy percentage?

3. How many rooms must be sold if Mr. Jones is to make a 15% return on his investment? (Assume that there is no tax effect.)

Problem 5

John Rhoades, owner of Rhoades Inn, has requested your assistance in analyzing his 50-room rooms-only property. He provides you information as follows:

1. The average rooms sales price is $30.

2. Monthly fixed costs equal $20,000.

3. His variable costs per room sold equal $10.

Required:

1. Determine the Rhoades Inn's breakeven point in revenue.

2. If revenues equal $450,000, what is the Rhoades Inn's margin of safety in revenues and rooms sold?

3. If John desires his property to generate a pretax profit of $100,000, how many rooms must be sold?

4. What is the occupancy percentage for the Rhoades Inn when pretax profit earned is $100,000?

Problem 6

Sid Gull, the owner/operator of the Iowa Inn, is interested in determining the level of sales necessary to realize a net income of $500,000 next year. He has compiled records on each department's sales and costs, and assumes that the sales mix will be the same next year. The major department, the rooms department, had sales of $2,500,000, and its contribution margin was $1,750,000. The coffee shop had sales of $750,000 and variable costs of $300,000. The restaurant had sales of $1,200,000 and variable costs of $750,000. Mr. Gull assumes that the fixed costs will be $1,000,000.

Required:

1. What is the CMR_w?

2. What is the required level of total sales to generate $500,000 net income? (Assume that there are no income taxes.)

3. What is the required level of total sales to generate $500,000 net income if the income tax rate is 30%?

Problem 7

Dustin Gordon, the executive vice president of COB, is considering expanding the company's operations into the hospitality industry. The company's goals include diversification, but also require an 18% return on their investment after taxes. Mr. Gordon has studied a hotel property which yields the following results:

1. The rooms department generates 80% of the sales and operates with a CMR of .76.
2. The food and beverage department generates the other 20% of sales, and has a CMR of .55.
3. Fixed costs per year are estimated to be $240,000.
4. In order to purchase the hotel, COB would have to invest $1,500,000.
5. COB's tax rate is 30%.

Required:

What level of sales is required before Mr. Gordon would recommend investing in the hotel to COB's board of directors?

Problem 8

The M & L Inn's summary income statement is as follows:

	Rooms	Food	Total
Revenues	$1,500,000	$ 500,000	$2,000,000
Variable Costs	300,000	400,000	700,000
Contribution Margin	$1,200,000	$ 100,000	1,300,000
Fixed Costs*			1,000,000
Pretax Income			300,000
Income Taxes			75,000
Net Income			$ 225,000

*Includes Lease Expense of $480,000

Required:

1. What is the breakeven point for the M & L Inn?
2. If the fixed cost lease is traded for a variable lease of 20% of total sales, what is the revised breakeven point for the M & L Inn?

Problem 9

The Mackinaw and Minier Hotels' summarized operating results are as follows:

	Mackinaw Hotel	Minier Hotel
1. CMR_w	60%	50%
2. Annual fixed costs	$1,200,000	$1,000,000
3. Tax rate	20%	20%

Required:

1. Compute each hotel's breakeven point.
2. Draw a profit-volume chart, including a profit-volume line, for each hotel for sales volumes ranging from $0 to $3,000,000.
3. Which hotel is riskier? Why?

Problem 10

The KDJ Inn's summary income statement is as follows:

	Rooms	Food	Total
Revenues	$1,500,000	$ 500,000	$2,000,000
Variable Costs	300,000	400,000	700,000
Contribution Margin	$1,200,000	$ 100,000	1,300,000
Fixed Costs			1,000,000*
Pretax Income			300,000
Income Taxes			75,000
Net Income			$ 225,000

*Includes Lease Expense of $480,000

Required:

1. What is the breakeven point for the KDJ Inn?
2. If the fixed cost lease is traded for a variable lease of 20% of total sales, what is the revised breakeven point for the KDJ Inn?
3. If (independent of #2) the variable costs increase by 10%, by what percentage must sales increase in order for the KDJ Inn to earn its net income of $225,000?
4. If (independent of #2 and #3) the KDJ Inn is to earn net income of $300,000, what must its room sales equal? (Assume that the sales mix remains constant.)

Problem 11

Stephanie Miller, an experienced business person and consultant, realizes the importance of cash flow. Therefore, whenever she is requested to provide a client with a breakeven level of sales, she also provides them with a cash flow breakeven analysis. The present owner has provided Ms. Miller with the following information for BMS, Inc.

BMS Inc.
Monthly Condensed Income Statement

Rooms Revenues		$100,000
Food Revenues		40,000
Total Revenue		140,000
Departmental Expenses		
Rooms	$20,000	
Food	20,000	
Total Departmental Expenses		40,000
Contribution Margin		100,000
Fixed Costs		
Interest Expense	10,000	
Depreciation	20,000	
Other Fixed Costs	50,000	
Total Fixed Costs		80,000
Income Before Tax		20,000
Tax		5,000
Net Income		$ 15,000

Other information:

1. Assume the tax rate to be constant over any level of pretax income.
2. The monthly mortgage payment is $15,000, of which $10,000 is interest expense.
3. All inventories are purchased on a cash basis and are expensed when purchased since they are insignificant.
4. There is no major change in current assets, other than cash, or current liabilities from month to month.

Required:

You are to assist Ms. Miller in:

1. Determining the level of sales required to provide BMS, Inc. with $40,000 net income.
2. Determining the level of sales required to provide BMS, Inc. with $20,000 positive cash flow for a month.

Problem 12

Keith and Sue's Dude Ranch (KSDR) is a 40-room hotel near Denver with a 30-seat restaurant and stables (a profit center). Keith and Sue Cass, the owners, are interested in having you use CVP analysis to aid them in determining various sales levels for their resort. The following is a summary of the most recent annual income statement.

Keith and Sue's Dude Ranch
Condensed Income Statement
For the year ended December 31, 19X5

	Rooms	Food	Stables	Total
Revenues	$ 500,000	$200,000	$5,000	$705,000
Variable Expenses	150,000	150,000	4,000	304,000
Contribution Margin	$ 350,000	$ 50,000	$1,000	401,000
Fixed Expense				151,000
Income Tax				125,000
Net Income				$125,000

Required:

1. What is the food department's CMR?
2. What is the weighted average CMR for ECDR?
3. What is the breakeven point?
4. The Casses wish to increase net income by $30,000 and feel this can be done by increasing room sales *only*. Determine the necessary increase in room sales to meet this requirement.
5. Assume (independent of #4) that revenue from the stables can be increased, but only with a $500 increase in advertising (a fixed cost) for brochures to go in each room. What level of sales from the stables must be generated to cover this cost?
6. Assume that the brochures mentioned in #5 are used as a direct mailing. The cost would now be $1,500 to cover printing and mailing, but sales for each department would increase. Assuming that room sales, food sales, and stable revenue remain at a ratio of 5 to 2 to .05, how much must revenues increase for net income to remain constant?

Problem 13

The condensed income statement of the Sweetwater Hotel (SH) is as follows:

	Revenue	Variable Costs	Fixed Costs	Department Income
Rooms	$4,000,000	$ 800,000	$ 200,000	$3,000,000
Food	2,400,000	1,000,000	400,000	1,000,000
Telephone	300,000	200,000	100,000	–0–
Gift Shop	$ 300,000	$ 150,000	$ 100,000	50,000
Total Department Income				4,050,000
Other Variable Expenses*				700,000
Other Fixed Costs**				2,800,000
Pretax Income				550,000
Income Taxes				200,000
Net Income				$ 350,000

  * Management Fees (10% of total sales)
** Includes depreciation of $1,000,000

Required:

1.   Compute the SH's weighted average contribution margin ratio (CMR). Consider *all* variable costs.

2.   Compute the SH's breakeven point.

3.   Compute the total sales required to yield a *pretax* cash flow of $2,000,000. Assume a single payment during the accounting period to *reduce* the mortgage was for $200,000. Also assume other nonexpense cash disbursements of $100,000.

4.   The gift shop manager has proposed the development of a promotional piece to promote gift shop sales. The brochure would be mailed to area residents. The development cost is $4,000, and the expected mailing cost is $ .50 per person. The mailing is expected to go to 10,000 people. If $2,000 of profit (net of tax and management fees) is to be realized on this project solely from increased gift shop sales, what is the required increase in gift shop sales?

5.   Independent of #4, assume a sales mix as follows:

Rooms	50%
Food	35%
Telephone	5%
Gift Shop	10%
Total	100%

Assume the management fee remains at 10% of total revenue. What is the revised weighted average CMR?

Problem 14

The K&K Motel has 100 rooms and a swimming pool. Other activities such as vending machine sales and telephone sales are operated on a breakeven basis and may be ignored.

The cost structure of the K&K differs slightly by month based on season. The variable costs per occupied room are estimated as follows:

Housekeeping	$4.00
Operating supplies	2.00
Repair and maintenance	1.00
Utilities (summer)	.50
Utilities (winter)	2.00
Pool/maintenance (summer)	.50
Laundry	1.00

Fixed costs per month are estimated as follows:

Housekeeping-supervision	$2,000
Front office	3,000
Administration	6,000
Depreciation	5,000
Pool costs (summer)	2,000
Utilities	1,000
Insurance and other	2,500

Assume the average income tax rate is 30% of pretax income. The average daily rate of the K&K is estimated to be $35.00.

Required:

1. Compute the net income expected during June (a summer month) if 80% occupancy is achieved.

2. Compute the breakeven point in rooms sold during June. If 80% occupancy is achieved each night, on what day does the K&K break even?

3. Compute the net income expected during November (a winter month) if 70% occupancy is achieved.

4. Compute the breakeven point in rooms sold during November. If 70% occupancy is achieved each night, on what day does the K&K break even?

Problem 15

The condensed income statement of the Nazareth Inn (NI) is as follows:

	Revenue	Variable Costs	Fixed Costs	Department Income
Rooms	$5,000,000	$1,000,000	$ 500,000	$3,500,000
Food	3,000,000	1,000,000	1,000,000	1,000,000
Telephone	500,000	200,000	100,000	200,000
Total department income				4,700,000
Other variable expenses*				500,000
Other fixed costs**				2,000,000
Pretax income				2,200,000
Income taxes				600,000
Net income				$1,600,000

  * Rent (10% of room sales)
** Includes depreciation and amortization of $500,000

Required:

1. Compute the contribution margin ratio (CMR) for the rooms department.

2. Compute the NI's weighted average CMR.

3. Compute the NI's breakeven point.

4. If the NI wants to make $1,500,000, what must its *room sales* equal?

Chapter 8 Outline

The Importance of Pricing
Price Elasticity of Demand
Informal Pricing Approaches
Cost Approaches: Four Modifying Factors
Mark-Up Approaches to Pricing
Pricing Rooms
    $1 per $1,000 Approach
    Hubbart Formula
    Illustration of the Hubbart Formula
Yield Management
Bottom-Up Approach to Pricing Meals
Food Sales Mix and Gross Profit
Menu Engineering
Integrated Pricing
Computer Applications

Cost Approaches to Pricing

PRICING IS ONE OF THE MOST difficult decisions hospitality managers make. If prices are set too high, lower demand may result in reduced sales. When prices are set too low, demand may be high, but lowered sales revenue is likely to result in costs not being covered. Either way, the hospitality operation's profitability may be placed in jeopardy. How can a hospitality manager ensure that prices are neither too high nor too low?

Establishing prices that result in maximized revenues is extremely difficult. Some managers would suggest that the process of setting effective prices involves a bit of luck. Yet, while there may be no completely scientific method guaranteed to determine the best prices to maximize profits, good managers will seek to establish a rational basis for their pricing decisions. General approaches to the pricing problem provide ways of using relevant information and the manager's knowledge of the relationships among sales, costs, and profits to establish a reasonable basis for effective pricing.

Our discussion of cost approaches to pricing in this chapter will answer many of the important questions that come to mind regarding the pricing process, such as the following:

1. Which costs are relevant in the pricing decision?

2. What is the common weakness of informal pricing methods?

3. What are the common cost methods of pricing rooms?

4. What are common methods of pricing food and beverages?

5. How may popularity and profitability be considered in setting food prices?

6. Will departmental revenue maximization result in revenue maximization for the hospitality firm?

7. What is price elasticity of demand?

8. What is integrated pricing?

We will begin this chapter with a discussion of the importance of pricing and the need for profits by both profit-oriented and non-profit-oriented operations. Next, we will explain and illustrate the concept of the price elasticity of demand. We will then consider a variety of approaches to pricing both rooms and meals, discuss the effect of sales mix on profits, and address the topic of integrated pricing.

The Importance of Pricing

A major determinant of a hospitality establishment's profitability is its prices. Whether prices are set too low or too high, the result is the same—a failure to maximize profits. When prices are below what the market is willing to pay, the establishment will realize less revenues than it could generate through its operations. Alternatively, prices set too high will reduce sales and thereby fail to achieve the operation's potential for profit. Management's goal is to set prices that result in profit maximization.

Another factor to consider when setting prices is the "positioning" of the establishment's offerings within the marketplace. Prices set too low may tend to degrade the perceived quality of products, whereas inflated prices may tend to reduce the perceived value of products from the guest's perspective.

Profits should not result simply because revenues happen by chance or luck to exceed expenses. Profits should occur because revenues generated have been carefully calculated to exceed expenses incurred. The emphasis should not be defensive; that is, on keeping costs down to make a profit. Aggressive management should set out to generate sufficient revenues to cover costs. Cost containment is a respectable secondary objective *after* marketing efforts are undertaken to achieve a reasonably high level of sales.

In this chapter, prices will be approached from a cost perspective. However, this is not meant to suggest that non-cost factors such as market demand and competition are irrelevant. In some situations, they may be critical to the pricing decision.

For-profit operations desire to make profits for such reasons as expanding operations, providing owners with a return on capital invested, and increasing the share prices of stock. Many non-profit operations must also make a profit (often called "revenues in excess of expenses") for expanding operations, replacing fixed assets, and upgrading services. Since both types of operations need to generate profits, their approaches to pricing will not necessarily be different. The differences generally relate to costs and type of demand. For example, some non-profit food service operations, including some in the institutional setting, do not have to cover many capital costs such as interest expenses, property taxes, or depreciation. Further, the demand for the products and/or services may be different. The demand for food service in a hospital is quite different from the demand for food service in most hotels or restaurants. Many non-profit operations have less direct competition, so they may have greater leeway in pricing their products and/or services.

The emphasis in this chapter will be on commercial (for-profit) operations. However, since we will be discussing cost-oriented approaches to pricing, our discussion will apply to non-profit operations as well.

Price Elasticity of Demand

The concept of the **price elasticity of demand** provides a means for measuring how sensitive demand is to changes in price. In general, as the selling price of a product or service decreases, everything else being the same, more will be sold. When the price of a product is increased, only rarely is more of the product sold,

Exhibit 1   Price Elasticity of Demand Formula

$$\text{Price Elasticity of Demand} = \frac{\dfrac{\Delta Q}{Q_0}}{\dfrac{\Delta P}{P_0}}$$

where:

ΔQ	=	Change in quantity demanded
Q_0	=	Base quantity demanded
ΔP	=	Change in price
P_0	=	Base price

everything else being the same, and even then there may be other factors that account for the increased demand.

The demand for a product or service may be characterized as **elastic** or **inelastic.** Exhibit 1 illustrates the price elasticity of demand formula for mathematically determining whether the demand is elastic or inelastic. The base quantity demanded (Q_0) is the number of units sold during a given period before changing prices. The change in quantity demanded (ΔQ) is the change in the number of units sold during the period the prices were changed in comparison to the prior period. The base price (P_0) is the price of the product and/or service for the period prior to the price change. The change in price (ΔP) is the change in price from the base price. Strictly speaking, this equation will virtually always yield a negative number, since it is the result of dividing a negative change in quantity demanded by a positive price change or vice versa. (In other words, as price goes up, quantity demanded goes down and vice versa.) By convention, however, the negative sign is ignored.

If the elasticity of demand exceeds 1, the demand is said to be elastic. That is, demand is sensitive to price changes. With an elastic demand, the percentage change in quantity demanded exceeds the percentage change in price. In other words, any additional revenues generated by the higher price are more than offset by the decrease in demand. When demand is elastic, a price increase will decrease total revenues. Up to a point, price decreases will increase total revenues.

If elasticity of demand is less than 1, demand is said to be inelastic. That is, a percentage change in price results in a smaller percentage change in quantity demanded. Every operation desires an inelastic demand for its products and/or services. When prices are increased, the percentage reduction in quantity demanded is less than the percentage of the price increase. Therefore, revenues will often—but not always—increase despite some decrease in the quantity demanded.[1]

Let's look at an example illustrating the calculation of price elasticity of demand. A budget motel sold 1,000 rooms during a recent 30-day period at $30 per room. For the next 30-day period, the price was increased to $33, and 950 rooms were sold. The demand for the budget motel over this time period is considered to be inelastic, since the calculated price elasticity of demand is less than 1. The calculation of price elasticity of demand is as follows:

$$\text{Price Elasticity of Demand} \quad = \quad \frac{50}{1,000} \quad \div \quad \frac{3}{30}$$

$$= \quad .05 \quad \div \quad .1$$

$$= \quad \underline{\underline{.5}}$$

In general, the demand for products and services in the lodging and the commercial food service segments of the hospitality industry is considered to be elastic. Generally, demand will be elastic where competition is high due to the presence of many operations and where the products and/or services offered are fairly standardized. On the other hand, where competition is low or nonexistent or where an operation has greatly differentiated its products and/or services, then demand may be inelastic. At the extreme, some resorts, clubs, high-check-average restaurants, and luxury hotels are known to have an inelastic demand for their products and services. Generally, quick-service restaurants and medium and low priced hotels/motels are considered to have elastic demand for their products and services. However, these are generalizations, and there are exceptions.

This analysis of demand/price relationships assumes that other things are the same. However, hospitality operations seldom increase prices without effectively advertising their products in an effort to counter potential decreased demand. Therefore, the concept of the price elasticity of demand tends to be more theoretical than practical in nature.

Informal Pricing Approaches

There are several informal approaches to setting prices for selling food, beverages, and rooms. Since each of these approaches ignores the cost of providing the product, they are only briefly presented here as a point of departure for our discussion of more scientific approaches to setting prices.

Several managers price their products on the basis of what the competition charges. If the competition charges $80 for a room night, or an average of $20 for a dinner, then managers using competitive pricing set those prices as well. When the competition changes its prices, managers using this pricing approach follow suit. A variation of this approach is changing prices when the leading hospitality operation changes its prices.

Although these approaches may seem reasonable when there is much competition in a market, they ignore the many differences that exist among hospitality operations, such as location, product quality, atmosphere, customer goodwill, and so forth. In addition, they ignore the cost of producing the products and services sold. Hospitality operations must consider their own cost structures when making pricing decisions. A dominant operation with a low cost structure may "cause" competitors to go bankrupt if those competitors ignore their own costs and price their products following the competitive approach.

Another informal pricing approach used by some managers is intuition. Intuitive pricing is based on what the manager feels the guest is willing to pay. Generally, managers using this approach rely on their experience regarding guests' reactions to prices. However, as with competitive pricing, intuition ignores costs and may result in a failure not only to generate a reasonable profit, but even to recover costs.

A third approach is psychological pricing. Here, prices are established on the basis of what the guest "expects" to pay. This approach may be used by relatively exclusive locations (such as luxury resorts) and by operators who think that their guests believe "the more paid, the better the product." Although psychological pricing does possess a certain merit, it fails to consider costs and, therefore, may not result in profit maximization.

Finally, the trial-and-error pricing approach first sets a product price, monitors guests' reactions, and then adjusts the price based on these reactions. This approach appears to consider fully the operation's guests. However, problems with this method include:

- Monitoring guests' reactions may take longer than the manager would like to allow.

- Frequent changes in prices based on guests' reactions may result in price confusion among guests.

- There are many outside, uncontrollable factors that affect guests' purchase decisions. An example illustrates this problem: a 10% price increase in rooms may appear to be too high if occupancy is down by more than 10% over the next 30 days. However, other factors that may be part of the consumer decision include competition, new lodging establishments, weather conditions (especially if the lodging facility is a resort), and so on.

- The trial-and-error approach fails to consider costs.

Although all of the informal price approaches have some merit, they are most useful only when coupled with the cost approaches we are now going to consider.

Cost Approaches: Four Modifying Factors

Before looking at specific cost approaches to pricing, however, we need to set the stage. When pricing is based on a cost approach, four modifying factors to consider are historical prices, perceived price/value relationships, competition, and price rounding. These price modifiers relate to the pricing of nearly all products and services.

First, prices that have been charged in the past must be considered when pricing the hospitality operation's products. A dramatic change dictated by a cost approach may seem unrealistic to the consumer. For example, if a breakfast meal with a realistic price of $3.49 was mistakenly priced at $1.49 for five years, the food service operation may need to move slowly from $1.49 to $3.49 by implementing several price increases over a period of time.

Second, the guest must perceive that the product and/or service is reasonably priced in order to feel that he or she is getting a good value. Many guests in the 1990s appear to be more value-conscious than ever. Most are willing to pay prices much higher than a few years ago, but they also demand value for the price paid.

The perceived value of a meal includes not only the food and drink but also the atmosphere, location, quality of service, and many other often intangible factors.

Third, the competition cannot be ignored. If an operation's product is viewed as substantially the same as a competitor's, then everything else being equal, the prices would have to be similar. For example, assume that an operation's price calculations for a gourmet burger may suggest a $4.50 selling price; however, if a strong nearby competitor is charging $3.50 for a very similar product, everything else being the same, then competition would appear to force a price reduction. However, remember that it is extremely difficult for *everything* else to be the same: the location is at least slightly different, one burger may be fresher, one may be grilled and the other fried, and so on.

Finally, the price may be modified by price rounding. That is, the item's price will be rounded up to the nearest $.25 or possibly up to $X.95.

Mark-Up Approaches to Pricing

A major method of pricing food and beverages is marking up the cost of the goods sold. The mark-up is designed to cover all non-product costs, such as labor, utilities, supplies, interest expense, taxes, and also to provide the desired profit.

Under the mark-up approaches to pricing are **ingredient mark-up** and **prime ingredient mark-up.** The ingredient mark-up approach considers all product costs. The prime ingredient mark-up considers only the cost of the major ingredient.

The four steps of the ingredient cost approach are as follows:

1. Determine the ingredient costs.

2. Determine the multiple to use in marking up the ingredient costs.

3. Multiply the ingredient costs by the multiple to get the desired price.

4. Determine whether the price seems reasonable based on the market.

The multiple determined in Step 2 is generally based on the desired product cost percentage. For example, if a product cost percentage of 40% is desired, the multiple would be 2.5, determined as follows:

$$\text{Multiple} \ = \ \frac{1}{\text{Desired Product Cost Percentage}}$$

$$= \ \frac{1}{.4}$$

$$= \ \underline{\underline{2.5}}$$

The ingredient cost approach can be illustrated using the cost figures for a chicken dinner listed in Exhibit 2. Assuming a desired multiple of 3.5, the price of the chicken dinner is determined as follows:

$$\text{Price} \ = \ \text{Ingredients' Cost} \times \text{Multiple}$$

$$= \ \$1.32 \times 3.5$$

$$= \ \underline{\underline{\$4.62}}$$

Exhibit 2   Chicken Dinner Ingredients and Cost

Ingredient	Cost
Chicken—2 pieces	$ .59
Baked potato with sour cream	.19
Roll and butter	.09
Vegetable	.15
Salad with dressing	.18
Coffee—refills free	.12
Total cost	$1.32

If the result appears reasonable based on the market for chicken dinners, then the chicken dinner is sold for about $4.62. (In this instance, price rounding might set the price at $4.75 or $4.95.)

The prime ingredient approach differs only in that the cost of the prime ingredient is marked up rather than the total cost of all ingredients. In addition, the multiple used, all other things being equal, would be greater than the multiple used when considering the total cost of all ingredients. The multiple used would generally be based on experience; that is, what multiple has provided adequate cost coverage and desired profit. Using the same chicken dinner example, the prime ingredient cost is chicken with a cost of $.59. Using an arbitrary multiple of 7.8, the chicken dinner is priced at $4.60, calculated as follows:

$$\begin{aligned} \text{Price} \quad &= \quad \text{Prime Ingredient Cost} \times \text{Multiple} \\ &= \quad \$.59 \times 7.8 \\ &= \quad \underline{\$4.60} \end{aligned}$$

If the cost of chicken in the above example increases to $.69 for the dinner portion, then the new price would be $5.38 ($.69 × 7.8). The prime ingredient approach assumes that the costs of all other ingredients change in proportion to the prime ingredient; that is, when the prime ingredient's cost increases 10%, then other ingredients' costs have also increased 10%. When changes in the other ingredients' cost percentage differ from the prime ingredient's, then the product cost percentage will differ from the established goal.

Pricing Rooms

Two well-known cost approaches to pricing rooms are the $1 per $1,000 approach and the Hubbart Formula approach.

$1 per $1,000 Approach

The **$1 per $1,000 approach** sets the price of a room at $1 for each $1,000 of project cost per room. For example, assume that the average project cost of a hotel for each room was $80,000. Using the $1 per $1,000 approach results in a price of $80 per room. Doubles, suites, singles, and so on would be priced differently, but the average would be $80.

This approach fails to consider the current value of facilities when it emphasizes the project cost. A well-maintained hotel worth $100,000 per room today may have been constructed at $20,000 per room 40 years ago. The $1 per $1,000 approach would suggest a price of $20 per room; however, a much higher rate would appear to be appropriate. This approach also fails to consider all the services that guests pay for in a hotel complex, such as food, beverages, telephone, laundry, and so forth. If a hotel is able to earn a positive contribution from these services (and the successful ones do), then the need for higher prices for rooms is reduced.

Hubbart Formula

A more recently developed cost approach is the **Hubbart Formula,** which is a *bottom-up* approach to pricing rooms. In determining the average price per room, this approach considers costs, desired profits, and expected rooms sold. In other words, this approach starts with desired profit, adds income taxes, then adds fixed charges and management fees, followed by operating overhead expenses and direct operating expenses. It is called bottom-up because the first item, net income (profit), is at the bottom of the income statement. The second item, income taxes, is the next item from the bottom of the income statement, and so on. The approach involves the following eight steps:

1. Calculate the desired profit by multiplying the desired rate of return (ROI) by the owners' investment.

2. Calculate pretax profits by dividing desired profit (Step 1) by 1 minus tax rate.

3. Calculate fixed charges and management fees. This calculation includes estimating depreciation, interest expense, property taxes, insurance, amortization, rent, and management fees.

4. Calculate undistributed operating expenses. This calculation includes estimating administrative and general, data processing, human resources, transportation, marketing, property operation and maintenance, and energy costs.

5. Estimate non-room operated department income or losses; that is, food and beverage department income, telephone department income or loss, and so forth.

6. Calculate the required rooms department income. The sum of pretax profits (Step 2), fixed charges and management fees (Step 3), undistributed operating expense (Step 4), and other operated department losses less other operated department income (Step 5) equals the required rooms department income.

7. Determine the rooms department revenue. The required rooms department income (Step 6) plus rooms department direct expenses of payroll and related expenses plus other direct expenses equals rooms department revenue.

8. Calculate the average room rate by dividing rooms department revenue (Step 7) by rooms expected to be sold.

Illustration of the Hubbart Formula

The Harkins Hotel, a 200-room hotel, is projected to cost $9,900,000 inclusive of land, building, equipment, and furniture. An additional $100,000 is needed for working capital. The hotel is financed with a loan of $7,500,000 at 12% annual interest with the owners providing cash of $2,500,000. The owners desire a 15% annual return on their investment. A 75% occupancy is estimated; thus, 54,750 rooms will be sold during the year (200 × .75 × 365). The income tax rate is 40%. Additional expenses are estimated as follows:

Property taxes	$ 250,000
Insurance	50,000
Depreciation	300,000
Administrative & general	300,000
Information systems	120,000
Human resources	80,000
Transportation	40,000
Marketing expense	200,000
Property operation and maintenance	200,000
Utility costs	300,000

The other operated departments' income or losses are estimated as follows:

Food	$ 90,000
Beverage	60,000
Telephone	(50,000)
Rentals and other income	100,000

Rooms department direct expenses are $10 per room sold.

Exhibit 3 contains the calculations used in the Hubbart Formula and reveals an average room rate of $67.81.

The formula for calculating room rates for singles and doubles, where the doubles are sold at a differential of y from singles, is shown in Exhibit 4. For the Harkins Hotel, a double occupancy rate of 40% and a price differential of $10 would result in the calculation of single and double rates as follows:

$$\text{Doubles sold in one day} = \text{double occupancy rate} \times \text{number of rooms} \times \text{occupancy percentage}$$

$$= .4(200)(.75)$$

$$= \underline{\underline{60}}$$

$$\text{Singles sold in one day} = 150 - 60$$

$$= \underline{90}$$

$$90x + 60(x + 10) = (\$67.81)(150)$$

$$90x + 60x + 600 = \$10,171.50$$

$$150x = \$9,571.50$$

$$x = \frac{\$9,571.50}{150}$$

$$x = \$63.81$$

Exhibit 3   Calculation of Average Room Rate Using the Hubbart Formula

Item	Calculation	Amount
Desired net income	Owners' Investment × ROI 2,500,000 × .15 = 375,000	$ 375,000
Pretax income	Pretax income = $\frac{\text{net income}}{1 - t}$	$ 625,000
	Pretax income = $\frac{375,000}{1 - .4}$	
	Pretax income = $625,000	
Interest expense	Principal × int. rate × time = int. exp. 7,500,000 × .12 × 1 = 900,000	900,000
Income before interest and taxes		1,525,000
Estimated depreciation, property taxes, and insurance		600,000
Income after undistributed operating expenses		2,125,000
Undistributed operating expense		1,240,000
Required operated departments income		3,365,000
Departmental results excluding rooms		
Less: Food income		(90,000)
Beverage income		(60,000)
Rentals and other income		(100,000)
Plus: Telephone department loss		50,000
Rooms department income		3,165,000
Rooms department direct expense	54,750 × $10 = 547,500	547,500
Rooms revenue		3,712,500
		÷ 54,750
Required average room rate		$ 67.81

$$\text{Single Rate} = \underline{\underline{\$63.81}}$$
$$\text{Double Rate} = \$63.81 + \$10.00$$
$$= \underline{\underline{\$73.81}}$$

Alternatively, the double rate could be set as a percentage of the single rate. When this is the case, the formula is slightly altered as follows:

(Average rate) (Rooms sold)   =   (doubles sold)(x)(1 + percentage mark-up) + (single sold)(x)

The percentage mark-up is simply the percentage difference of the double rate over the single rate. To illustrate this approach, we will again use the Harkins Hotel example. Assume a 40% double occupancy and a mark-up of 15%.

Exhibit 4 Determining Single and Double Room Rates from an Average Room Rate

Singles Sold (x) + Doubles Sold (x + y) = Average Rate (Rooms Sold)

where:

x	=	Price of singles
y	=	Price differential between singles and doubles
x + y	=	Price of doubles

$$90x + 60(x)(1.15) = (\$67.81)(150)$$
$$90x + 69x = \$10{,}171.50$$
$$159x = \$10{,}171.50$$
$$x = \frac{\$10{,}171.50}{159}$$
$$x = \$63.97$$
$$\text{Single Rate} = \underline{\$63.97}$$
$$\text{Double Rate} = \$63.97(1.15)$$
$$= \underline{\$73.57}$$

The Hubbart Formula is most useful in setting target average prices as opposed to actual average prices. A lodging establishment does not generally earn profits in its first two or three years of operation. Thus, the average price determined using this formula is a target price at the point of profitability for the prospective property. As stated previously, even when this approach is used to set room prices, the four modifying factors must be considered. For example, assume that the average target price for a hotel is $75, when the average rate for competitive hotels is only $50. If the proposed hotel would be opening in two years, is the target price too high? By the end of the two years, the competitor's average price with annual 5% price increases would be $55.13 ($50.00 × 105% × 105%).

Since the proposed hotel would be new, a price premium could be expected; however, a difference of nearly $20, given a competitor's average price of just over $55, would appear to be too much. Therefore, a more reasonable price might be $65, which, after three years of successive price increases of 5% per year, would be increased to just over $75 as follows:

	Annual increase at 5%	Selling Price
Initial room rate		$65.00
At the end of year X3	$3.25	$68.25
At the end of year X4	$3.41	$71.66
At the end of year X5	$3.58	$75.24

Yield Management

For many years, lodging establishments have sold rooms strictly on the basis of room availability. In general, a transient hotel would sell its rooms Monday through Thursday (when it is busiest) at prices close to its targeted rate for each type of guest, while the weekend average room rates would be set at a much lower price. Such hotels sometimes offer weekend packages that include a hotel room and one or more meals to lure guests for the weekend. These approaches can be successful as long as the marginal revenue exceeds the marginal cost; that is, as long as the price exceeds the cost to provide food and services to the hotel guest.

However, in the past few years, hoteliers have become more aggressive in pricing rooms by using a concept popularly referred to as **yield management.** The focus of yield management is selling rooms in a way that maximizes total revenues, rather than trying simply to sell all available rooms. Yield management in substance considers room availability at the time of the advanced sale, compared to typical advanced sales at this time. That is, before selling a room in advance, the hotel considers the probability of being able to sell the room to other market segments that are willing to pay higher rates.

For example, assume for simplicity that the 100-room XYZ Hotel has business and group rates per room of $80 and $55, respectively. Further assume that the average group takes 20 rooms and is booked three weeks in advance, while the typical business person reserves his or her room seven days in advance. Further assume that, on the average, business people and groups stay two nights.

Given the above information, should a group desiring 20 rooms for April 21 and 22 be sold the rooms at $55 per room on April 1? Assume that 40 rooms have already been sold to business people at $80 per room, and the reservations agent believes 55 more rooms could be sold at $80 per person to business people. Based on the information, total room revenue is greater when the sale is *not* made to the group, and the rooms are held for business people. The analysis is as follows:

Alternative #1					
Group sales	20 rooms	@	$55	=	$1,100
Business sales	80 rooms	@	$80	=	6,400
Total					$7,500
Alternative #2					
Business sales	95 rooms	@	$80	=	$7,600

The difference of $100 per night favors Alternative #2. Of course, the illustration is fairly simplistic. Other considerations are the desired stay and income from other services provided by the XYZ Hotel to potential guests.

Bottom-Up Approach to Pricing Meals

A bottom-up approach similar to the Hubbart Formula may be used to determine the average meal price for restaurants. Seven steps for determining the average meal price are as follows:[2]

Exhibit 5   Essential Factors for Determining the Average Meal Price at Morgans

Item	Amount	Other
Owner's investment	$200,000	Desired ROI = 12%
Funds borrowed	500,000	Interest Rate = 10%
Tax rate	—	30%
Fixed charges (excluding interest)	100,000	Annual amount
Controllable expenses	500,000	Annual amount
Cost of food sold percentage	—	40%
Seat turnover	—	2 times per day
Days open (closed one day per week)	—	313 days
Desired food cost percentage	—	40%

1. Determine desired net income by multiplying investment by desired return on owners' investment (ROI).

2. Determine pretax profit by dividing the desired net income by 1 minus the tax rate.

3. Determine fixed charges.

4. Determine controllable expenses.

5. Determine food revenue by first adding figures from Steps 2–4 and then dividing this sum by 1 minus the desired food cost percentage.

6. Determine meals to be served by multiplying days open by number of seats by seat turnover for the day.

7. Determine price of the average meal by dividing the total food revenue by the estimated number of meals to be served.

To illustrate the average restaurant meal price calculation, Morgans, a 100-seat restaurant, will be used. Information regarding Morgans is found in Exhibit 5 Given this information, Exhibit 6 shows that the average meal price for Morgans, inclusive of beverage sales, desserts, and so forth, is $18.22. In those calculations, total food revenue is determined by dividing total expenses and net income (prior to cost of food sold) by 1 minus the cost of food sold percentage. If management could turn the seats over faster, everything else being the same, then the average meal price required to provide the owners with the desired 12% return would be reduced. For example, if the seat turnover could be increased to 3, then the average meal price is determined as follows:

$$\text{Average Meal Price} = \frac{\text{Food Revenue}}{\text{Meals Sold}}$$

$$= \frac{\$1,140,477}{93,900}$$

$$= \underline{\$12.15}$$

On the other hand, a less frequent turnover requires a higher average meal price, all other things being the same. For Morgans, a seat turnover of 1.5 requires an average meal price of $24.29.

The entire discussion of the bottom-up approach to pricing meals has centered on average meal prices. Few food service establishments price all meals at one price, or even all meals for a given meal period at one price. However, the average meal price per meal period can be determined as follows:

1. Calculate the revenue per meal period by multiplying the total food revenue by the estimated percentage of that total earned during that meal period.

2. Divide the revenue per meal period by the meals sold per meal period. (Meals sold per meal period is calculated by multiplying the days the food service business is open by the seat turnover by the number of seats.)

Once again, we will use Morgans to illustrate these calculations. Assume that management estimates the total food revenue to be divided between lunch and dinner revenue as 40% and 60%, respectively. Further assume that the luncheon seat turnover is 1.25 and the dinner seat turnover is .75. Using the total revenue for Morgans as calculated in Exhibit 6, the average meal prices by meal period are determined as follows:

Revenue per meal period:

Lunch 40%	$\times$	$1,140,477	=	$	456,191	
Dinner 60%	$\times$	$1,140,477	=		684,286	
	Total		=		$1,140,477	

Meals sold per meal period:

Lunch 313	$\times$	100	$\times$	1.25	=	39,125
Dinner 313	$\times$	100	$\times$	.75	=	23,475

$$\text{Average meal prices by meal period} = \frac{\text{Meal Period Revenue}}{\text{Meals Sold}}$$

$$\text{Lunch} = \frac{\$456,191}{39,125} = \underline{\$11.66}$$

$$\text{Dinner} = \frac{\$684,286}{23,425} = \underline{\$29.15}$$

Food Sales Mix and Gross Profit

Traditionally, restaurateurs have placed heavy emphasis on food cost percentage. The multiple in the mark-up approach used to price meals for many restaurants has been set at 2.5 times, so that a 40% cost of food sold could be achieved. This emphasis resulted in many managers evaluating the profitability of their food service operations by reviewing the food cost percentage. However, the food cost percentage is not the best guide to evaluating food sales, as will be shown below.

Exhibit 6 Calculation of Average Meal Price at Morgans

Item	Calculation	Amount
Desired net income	200,000 × .12	$ 24,000
Pretax profits	$\dfrac{24,000}{1-.3} = \dfrac{24,000}{.7}$	$ 34,286
Interest	500,000 × .10 × 1	50,000
Other fixed charges		100,000
Controllable expenses		500,000
Total expenses and net income prior to cost of food sold		$ 684,286
Total food revenue	$\dfrac{684,286}{.6}$	$1,140,477
Meals sold	313 × 100 × 2	62,600
Average meal price	$1,140,477 ÷ 62,600	$ 18.22

Exhibit 7 Sales Mix Alternatives and Number of Meals

	Sales Mix Alternatives		
	#1	#2	#3
Chicken	500	300	200
Fish	200	300	300
Steak	300	400	500
Total	1,000	1,000	1,000

Consider a restaurant that may sell one of three alternative sales mixes for the week as listed in Exhibit 7. Notice in each sales mix, the same number of meals is served. Exhibit 8 shows the total revenue, total cost of food sold, the gross profit, and food cost percentage for each alternative. The selling price and cost per meal remains constant for each menu item across the three alternative sales mixes.

Exhibit 9 compares the three alternatives. The sales mix with the lowest total food cost percentage is mix #1 at 39.56%, while mix #3 has the highest at 41.99%, or nearly 2.5% greater than mix #1. If the most desirable mix is based on food cost percentage, then mix #1 is selected. However, under mix #3, the gross profit is $4,670 compared to a low of $4,140 for mix #1. Gross profit generated by mix #3 is $530 more than the profit generated by mix #1. Therefore, all other things being the same, mix #3 is preferred, because a higher gross profit means a higher net income.

Exhibit 10 reveals the average gross profit for the three sales mix alternatives. The gross margin reflects the average gross profit per meal sold. The average gross margin under sales mix #3 ($4.67) is $.53 and $.22 higher than under mixes #1 and #2, respectively. Based on these results, fewer meals could be sold under mixes #2 and #3 than under mix #1, yet the gross profit under mix #1 still would be earned:

Exhibit 8   Profitability of Three Sales Mix Alternatives

	Selling Price	Cost Per Meal	Menu Item Food Cost Percentage	Meals Sold	Revenue	Total Cost of Food	Gross Profit
Alternative #1							
Chicken	$4.95	$1.65	33.33%	500	$2,475	$825	$1,650
Fish	6.95	2.75	39.57	200	1,390	550	840
Steak	9.95	4.45	44.72	300	2,985	1,335	1,650
Total				1,000	$6,850	$2,710	$4,140

$$\text{Food cost \%} = \frac{2,710}{6,850} = 39.56\%$$

	Selling Price	Cost Per Meal	Menu Item Food Cost Percentage	Meals Sold	Revenue	Total Cost of Food	Gross Profit
Alternative #2							
Chicken	$4.95	$1.65	33.33%	300	$1,485	$495	$990
Fish	6.95	2.75	39.57	300	2,085	825	1,260
Steak	9.95	4.45	44.72	400	3,980	1,780	2,200
Total				1,000	$7,550	$3,100	$4,450

$$\text{Food cost \%} = \frac{3,100}{7,550} = 41.06\%$$

	Selling Price	Cost Per Meal	Menu Item Food Cost Percentage	Meals Sold	Revenue	Total Cost of Food	Gross Profit
Alternative #3							
Chicken	$4.95	$1.65	33.33%	200	$990	$330	$660
Fish	6.95	2.75	39.57	300	2,085	825	1,260
Steak	9.95	4.45	44.72	500	4,975	2,225	2,750
Total				1,000	$8,050	$3,380	$4,670

$$\text{Food cost \%} = \frac{3,380}{8,050} = 41.99\%$$

Exhibit 9   Comparison of Sales Mix Alternatives

Sales Mix Alternative	Total Revenue	Total Cost of Food	Gross Profit	Food Cost %
1	$6,850	$2,710	$4,140	39.56%
2	7,550	3,100	4,450	41.06
3	8,050	3,380	4,670	41.99

$$\frac{\text{Gross Profit of Mix \#1}}{\text{Gross Margin of Other Sales Mix Alternatives}}$$

Mix #2 to Mix #1

$$\frac{\$4,140}{\$4.45} = \underline{930.34 \text{ meals}}$$

Thus, under sales mix #2, 930.34 meals sold at an average gross margin of $4.45 yields $4,140 of gross profit, which is the same as that generated under mix #1 when 1,000 meals are sold.

Exhibit 10   Average Gross Profit of Sales Mix Alternatives

Sales Mix	Gross Profit	Meals Sold	Gross Margin
1	$4,140	1,000	$4.14
2	4,450	1,000	4.45
3	4,670	1,000	4.67

Exhibit 11   Gross Profit Graph of Three Sales Mix Alternatives

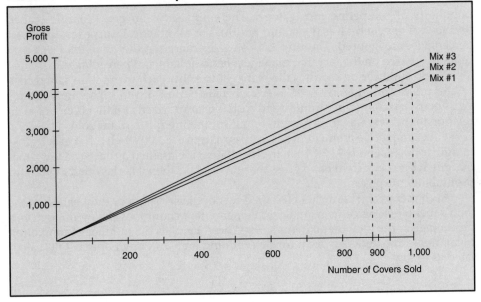

Mix #3 to Mix #1

$$\frac{\$4,140}{\$4.67} \quad = \quad \underline{\underline{886.51 \text{ meals}}}$$

Thus, under sales mix #3, 886.51 meals sold at an average gross margin of $4.67 yields $4,140, the same gross profit as that generated with mix #1 when 1,000 meals are sold.

These results are more clearly reflected in the graph found in Exhibit 11. The gross profit is related to meals sold in sales mixes #1 through #3. Gross profit increases progressively from sales mix #1 to sales mix #3. The same gross profit for sales mix #1 can be achieved by sales mixes #2 and #3 with fewer meals sold.

Menu Engineering

One method of menu analysis and food pricing is called **menu engineering**.[3] This sophisticated and fairly complex approach considers both the profitability and

Exhibit 12   Profitability/Popularity Classification of Menu Items

Profitability	Popularity	Classification
High	High	Stars
High	Low	Puzzles
Low	High	Plow Horses
Low	Low	Dogs

popularity of competing menu items. The emphasis is on gross margin (called *contribution margin* by Kasavana and Smith). For all practical purposes, food cost percentages are ignored. The emphasis on gross margin rather than food cost percentage is based on the fact that managers bank dollars, not percentages.

Menu engineering requires the manager to know each menu item's food cost, selling price, and quantity sold over a specific period of time. The menu item's gross margin (selling price minus food cost) is characterized as either high or low in relation to the average gross margin for all competing menu items sold.

For example, if a menu item has a gross margin of $3.00 when the average gross margin for the menu is $3.50, then the menu item is classified as having a low gross margin. If the menu item has a gross margin of $4.50, then it is classified as high for profitability purposes.

Each menu item is further classified by popularity (high or low) based on the item's menu mix percentage; that is, the menu item count for each menu item as a percentage of the total menu items sold. Where n equals the number of competing menu items, the dividing point for determining high and low popularity is calculated as follows:

$$70\% \quad \times \quad \frac{1}{n}$$

Therefore, if there are ten competing items on a menu, the dividing point is 7%, determined as follows:

$$70\% \quad \times \quad \frac{1}{10} \quad = \quad \underline{\underline{.07}} \text{ or } \underline{\underline{7\%}}$$

Given a ten-item menu, any menu items with unit sales of less than 7% of the total items sold would be classified as having a low popularity, while any equal to or greater than 7% would be classified as having high popularity.

The profitability and popularity classifications for each menu item result in four categories of menu items as shown in Exhibit 12. In general, stars should be retained, puzzles repositioned, plow horses repriced, and dogs removed from the menu. (For more discussion of management actions regarding the four classifications, see the sidebar on the following pages.)

Exhibit 13 is a graphic illustration of menu engineering results containing menu items in the four classifications. Eight menu items, identified by letters corresponding to the following table, are shown on the graph.

Exhibit 13   Graph of Menu Engineering Results

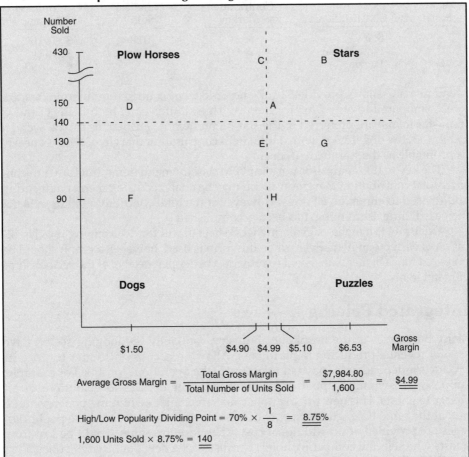

Average Gross Margin = $\dfrac{\text{Total Gross Margin}}{\text{Total Number of Units Sold}}$ = $\dfrac{\$7,984.80}{1,600}$ = $\underline{\underline{\$4.99}}$

High/Low Popularity Dividing Point = 70% × $\dfrac{1}{8}$ = $\underline{\underline{8.75\%}}$

1,600 Units Sold × 8.75% = $\underline{\underline{140}}$

Menu Item	Item Contribution Margin	Number Sold	Classification
A	$5.10	150	Star
B	$6.53	430	Star
C	$4.90	430	Plow Horse
D	$1.50	150	Plow Horse
E	$4.90	130	Dog
F	$1.50	90	Dog
G	$6.53	130	Puzzle
H	$5.10	90	Puzzle

In general, one prefers stars to dogs, puzzles, and plow horses. However, are stars *always* preferred to puzzles and plow horses? Specifically, is menu item A preferred to items C and G? Using the information for these menu items, we determine the following:

Menu Item	Classification	Item Contribution Margin	Number Sold	Total Item Contribution Margin
A	Star	$5.10	150	$ 765.00
C	Plow Horse	$4.90	430	$2,107.00
G	Puzzle	$6.53	130	$ 848.90

Menu items C and G provide $2,107 and $848.90 of contribution margin, respectively, compared to only $765 for item A. Thus, in this case, both items C and G (non-star items) are preferred to the star menu item A. Further, as can be seen on Exhibit 13, the dog item E, with a total item contribution margin of $637, is nearly as profitable as the star menu item A.

The key to this analysis is not simply to classify menu items, but rather to consider total contribution margin. A menu may be analyzed using menu engineering and revised to eliminate all dogs. However, if the total contribution margin is not increased, little, if anything, has been accomplished.

Exhibit 14 is a menu engineering worksheet useful for determining the classification of each menu item. Even when this form is used, however, a graph should be prepared for each menu analyzed to provide a better perspective of the relationships of menu items.

Integrated Pricing

Many businesses in the hospitality industry, especially the lodging sector, have several revenue-producing departments. Allowing each profit center to price its products independently may fail to optimize the operation's profits. For example, suppose the swimming pool department manager decides to institute a direct charge to guests. This new pricing policy may maximize swimming pool revenues, but, at the same time, guests may choose to stay at other hotels where pool privileges are provided at no additional cost. Therefore, revenues would be lost from guests who selected competing hotels because of the new pool charge policy.

Prices for all departments should be established such that they optimize the operation's net income. This will generally result in some profit centers *not* maximizing their revenues and thus their departmental incomes. This **integrated pricing** approach is essential and can only be accomplished by the general manager and profit center managers coordinating their pricing.

Computer Applications

Many of the pricing methods discussed in this chapter do not require sophisticated mathematical models to determine the desired price. However, even simple tasks can waste valuable time when they must be repeated many times. Because the standard formulas are frequently used, their computerization could benefit managers. This is especially true when management wants to view a number of scenarios in order to determine the best pricing options.

The Hubbart Formula can be translated into a computerized worksheet with relative ease. By entering each of the inputs into the formula separately, as shown in

Using Menu Engineering: A 14-Step Approach*

1. First, the operator lists all menu entrées in column A. Only entrée items are listed. Do not list appetizers, desserts, or other side items. Do not list alcoholic beverage sales on this list. The ratio of food to beverage sales is a key to successful merchandising in most restaurants. The analysis of beverage sales, however, should be done separately. While we separate sales for the purposes of our menu analysis, the successful operator is always concerned with the guests' total expenditure.

Daily specials must also be analyzed separately. By listing sales of daily specials separately, their impact on the menu is more easily identified. If the operator's suggestive selling program is effective, daily specials should become popular with relatively high contribution margins.

2. The total number of items sold for each item is listed in column B, menu mix, and the total is recorded in column N.

3. Each item's menu mix percentage is determined by dividing the number sold in column B by the total in column N.

4. Each item's menu mix percentage is categorized as either high or low. Any item that is equal to or exceeds the percentage in column Q is classified as high. All others are classified as low. The MM% category is recorded in column R.

5. Each item's standard food cost is listed in column D. An item's standard portion cost is composed of standard recipe costs, garnish cost, and supplemental food cost. Not all items, however, will have all three cost components.

6. Each item's published menu selling price is listed in column E.

7. The contribution margin for each item is listed in column F. Contribution margins are determined by subtracting the item's standard food cost (column D) from its selling price (column E).

8. In column G, the total menu food cost is determined by first multiplying each item's standard food cost (column D) by the number of items sold (column B). The sum of the amounts in column G is recorded in column I.

9. In column H, the total menu revenues are determined by multiplying the number of sales of each item (column B) by its selling price (column E). The sum of the amounts in column H is recorded in column J.

10. The total menu contribution margin is listed in column M. This is determined by first multiplying each item's contribution margin (column F) by the item's total number of items sold (column B). The contribution margin (by item) is recorded in column L. Then the sum of the item's contribution margins is recorded in column M.

11. The menu's average contribution margin is determined by dividing the total contribution margin (column M) by the total number of items sold (column N).

12. Each item's contribution margin is categorized as either high or low in column P, depending upon whether or not the item's contribution margin exceeds the menu's average contribution margin.

13. All the data that has been gathered is used to classify each item into categories in column S. Each menu item is classified as either a Star, Plow Horse, Puzzle, or Dog. These classifications are standard marketing theory terms (see the following page).

14. In column T, the decisions made on each item are listed. Should the item be retained, repositioned, replaced, or repriced?

How to Use the Categories

Once you have grouped your menu into the four key categories, you are ready to make decisions. Each category must be analyzed and evaluated separately.

*The process described here differs slightly from the process used to complete the menu engineering worksheet in Exhibit 14. The differences are not significant.

Stars. You must maintain rigid specifications for quality, quantity, and presentation of all Star items. Locate them in a highly visible position on the menu. Test them occasionally for price inelasticity. Are guests willing to pay more for these items, and still buy them in significant quantity? The Super Stars of your menu—highest priced Stars—may be less price-sensitive than any other items on the menu. If so, these items may be able to carry a larger portion of any increase in cost of goods and labor.

Plow Horses. These items are often an important reason for a restaurant's popularity. Increase their prices carefully. If Plow Horses are highly price-sensitive, attempt to pass only the cost of goods increase on to the menu price. Or, consider placing the increase on to a Super Star item. Test for a negative effect on demand (elasticity). Make any price increase in stages (from $4.55 to $4.75 then $4.95). Relocate non-signature and low contribution margin Plow Horses to a lower profile position on the menu. Attempt to shift demand to more profitable items by merchandising and menu positioning. If the item is an image maker or signature item, hold its current price as long as possible in periods of high price sensitivity.

Determine the direct labor cost of each Plow Horse to establish its labor and skill intensiveness. If the item requires high skills or is labor-intensive, consider a price increase or substitution. Also, consider reducing the item's standard portion without making the difference noticeable. Merchandise the Plow Horse by packaging it with side items to increase its contribution margin. Another option is to use the item to create a "better value alternative." For example, prime ribs can be sold by the inch, and steaks can be sold by the ounce. This offers guests an opportunity to spend more and get more value.

Puzzles. Take them off the menu. Particularly if a Puzzle is low in popularity, requires costly or additional inventory, has poor shelf life, requires skilled or labor-intensive preparation, and is of inconsistent quality. Another option is to reposition the Puzzle and feature it in a more popular location on the menu. You can try adding value to the item through Table d'Hôte packaging. Rename it. A Puzzle's popularity can be affected by what it is called, especially if the name can be made to sound familiar.

Decrease the Puzzle's price. The item may have a contribution margin that is too high and is facing price resistance. Care must be taken, however, not to lower the contribution margin to a point where the Puzzle draws menu share from a Star. Increase the item's price and test for inelasticity. A Puzzle that has relatively high popularity may be inelastic.

Limit the number of Puzzles you allow on your menu. Puzzles can create difficulties in quality consistency, slow production down, and cause inventory and cost problems. You must accurately evaluate the effect Puzzle items have on your image. Do they enhance your image?

Dogs. Eliminate all Dog items if possible. Food service operators are often intimidated by influential guests to carry a Dog on the menu. The way to solve this problem is to carry the item in inventory (assuming it has a shelf life) but not on the menu. The special guest is offered the opportunity to have the item made to order upon request. Charge extra for this service. Raise the Dog's price to Puzzle status. Some items in the Dog category may have market potential. These tend to be the more popular Dogs, and may be converted to Puzzles.

Whenever possible, replace Dogs with more popular items. You may have too many items. It is not unusual to discover a number of highly unpopular menu items with little, if any, relation to other more popular and profitable items held in inventory. Do not be afraid to terminate Dogs, especially when demand is not satisfactory.

Excerpted from an article by Donald Smith, Hospitality Publications, Okemos, Michigan.

Exhibit 14   Menu Engineering Worksheet

Menu Engineering Worksheet

Restaurant: _____

Date: _____

Meal Period: _____

(A) Menu Item Name	(B) Number Sold (MM)	(C) Menu Mix %	(D) Item Food Cost	(E) Item Selling Price	(F) Item CM (E–D)	(G) Menu Costs (D*B)	(H) Menu Revenues (E*B)	(L) Menu CM (F*B)	(P) CM Category	(R) MM% Category	(S) Menu Item Classification	(T) Decision
Column Totals:	N					I	J	M				

Additional Computations: $K = I/J$ $O = M/N$ $Q = (100\%/\text{items})(70\%)$

Exhibit 15   Computer-Generated Hubbart Formula Worksheet

	Alternatives				
INPUTS:	1	2	3	4	5
Investment	$2,000,000	$2,000,000	$2,000,000	$2,000,000	$2,000,000
ROI	16.0%	16.0%	16.0%	12.0%	16.0%
Tax rate	30%	30%	30%	30%	30%
Long-term debt	4,000,000	4,000,000	4,000,000	4,000,000	4,000,000
Interest rate	15.0%	15.0%	15.0%	15.0%	15.0%
Estimated fixed charges (excluding interest expense)	60,000	60,000	60,000	60,000	85,000
Undistributed operating expenses	600,000	600,000	600,000	600,000	650,000
Departmental profits					
Food	135,000	135,000	135,000	135,000	135,000
Telephone	10,000	10,000	10,000	10,000	10,000
Rooms department					
Variable costs per room sold	$15	$15	$15	$15	$18
Number of rooms	200	200	200	200	200
Occupancy rate	75%	80%	65%	75%	60%
	Hubbart Calculation				
Desired net income	$320,000	$320,000	$320,000	$240,000	$320,000
Pretax income	457,143	457,143	457,143	342,857	457,143
Interest expense	600,000	600,000	600,000	600,000	600,000
Income after undistributed operating expenses	1,117,143	1,117,143	1,117,143	1,002,857	1,142,143
Required rooms department income	1,572,143	1,572,143	1,572,143	1,457,857	1,647,143
Rooms revenue	2,393,393	2,448,143	2,283,893	2,279,107	2,435,543
Required average rate	$43.71	$41.92	$48.13	$41.63	$55.61

Exhibit 15, management can vary assumptions and see the results of "what if" questions. In the past, the number of scenarios considered was seriously limited by the time that a staff member could devote to number crunching. Now, suggestions can be calculated almost at will.

The personal computer also can be a tool for food and beverage outlets. There are menu engineering packages available that will calculate the contribution margins and menu mix percentages after the user inputs the menu items' sales prices, costs, and demands. Then, they determine the classification of each menu item and print the menu engineering graph for the manager. More sophisticated systems will interface a personal computer with the point-of-sale register and with the inventory information. Under this arrangement, it is possible to generate not only the outputs of menu engineering, but also to gather all of the inputs. When this type of a system is used, management can generate daily sales and cost reports so that pricing decisions can be made at any time. This is especially useful for restaurants that offer a large number of specials or vary their entrées based on market availability.

Summary

An optimal pricing structure can play a large role in the profitability of a hospitality operation. If rooms are underpriced, profits are lost. If meals are overpriced, demand may decrease, causing a decrease in profits. Management needs to be aware of these effects and set prices accordingly.

The relationship between the percentage change in price and the resulting percentage change in demand is called elasticity. In order to determine the price elasticity of demand for a product, the manager utilizes this formula:

$$\frac{\text{Change in Quantity Demanded}}{\text{Base Quantity}} \div \frac{\text{Change in Price}}{\text{Base Price}}$$

If the result (ignoring the negative sign) is greater than 1, the demand for the product is said to be elastic. In other words, a change in price results in a larger percentage change in the quantity demanded. Raising prices results in reduced revenues. Inelastic demand exists when the percentage change in price is greater than the percentage change in demand, and the formula results in an answer of less than 1. Every manager would prefer to have products with inelastic demand. When this is the case, raising prices results in increased revenues because the percentage decrease in demand is less than the percentage increase in prices.

There are a number of informal pricing methods. Some managers base prices on what the competition charges. Other managers assume that they intuitively know the price the public will accept. Still another method is psychological pricing by which managers determine what they think customers expect to pay.

These methods, although frequently used, fail to examine costs. More technical methods, such as the mark-up and the bottom-up approaches, start with costs to determine prices that result in adequate net income.

The mark-up approach multiplies cost by a mark-up based on the desired product cost percentage. There are two variations of this approach. One sets a mark-up factor for the total cost of the meal. The other multiplies only the prime ingredient cost by a factor. The result of either of these approaches should be a price that will cover not only the food cost, but also the labor and other costs.

The Hubbart Formula is a method used to price rooms. It begins with the required return on the investment and adds to it the costs of operation, including taxes, management fees, fixed charges, undistributed operating expenses, and other departmental income. Using this approach, departmental incomes (or losses) from other profit centers are added to (or subtracted from) the total indirect expenses of the hotel to determine the required rooms department income. The direct expenses of the rooms department plus the required rooms department income equal the required rooms department revenue. The average price per room is calculated by dividing the required rooms department revenue by the number of rooms expected to be sold during the period.

The cost approaches appear rigorous and objective; however, they generally are based on estimates. Further, when the proposed price is computed on the basis of one of the cost approaches presented, careful consideration must be given to prices being charged by the competition before the implementation of any price changes. Differences in price must be supported by a different offering, such as a better location, more amenities, and so on. Finally, in a multi-product situation, such as a hotel, prices of the various products, food, beverages, and rooms, must be set on an integrated basis.

Endnotes

1. A third situation occurs when the elasticity of demand is exactly 1. In this case, demand is said to be **unit elastic,** meaning that any percentage change in price is accompanied by the same percentage change in quantity demanded.
2. Based on terminology used in the *Uniform System of Accounts for Restaurants,* 6th rev. ed. (Washington, D.C.: National Restaurant Association, 1990).
3. Michael L. Kasavana and Donald I. Smith, *Menu Engineering—A Practical Guide to Menu Analysis,* rev. ed. (Okemos, Mich.: Hospitality Publications Inc., 1990).

Key Terms

elastic demand—A situation in which the percentage change in quantity demanded exceeds the percentage change in price.

Hubbart Formula—A bottom-up approach to pricing rooms. In determining the average price per room, this approach considers costs, desired profits, and expected rooms sold.

inelastic demand—A situation in which a percentage change in price results in a smaller percentage change in quantity demanded.

ingredient mark-up—See mark-up.

integrated pricing—An approach to pricing in a hospitality operation having several revenue-producing departments that sets prices for goods and/or services in each profit center so as to optimize the entire operation's net income.

mark-up—An approach to pricing of goods and services that determines retail prices by adding a certain percentage to the cost of goods sold. The mark-up is designed to cover all non-product costs (for example, labor, utilities, supplies, interest expense, taxes, and so forth) as well as desired profit. Ingredient mark-up is based on all ingredients. Prime ingredient mark-up bases the mark-up solely on the cost of the main ingredient.

menu engineering—A method of menu analysis and food pricing that considers both the profitability and popularity of competing menu items.

$1 per $1,000 approach—An approach to rooms pricing that sets the price of a room at $1 for each $1,000 of project cost per room.

price elasticity of demand—An expression of the relationship between a change in price and the resulting change in demand.

prime ingredient mark-up—See mark-up.

unit elastic—Elasticity of demand is exactly 1. Any percentage change in price is accompanied by the same percentage change in quantity demanded.

yield management—Selling rooms in a way that maximizes total revenues. Before selling a room in advance, the hotel considers the probability of being able to sell the room to other market segments that are willing to pay higher rates.

Review Questions

1. What are four methods of informal pricing?

2. What disadvantages are inherent with informal pricing?

3. How is the cost mark-up factor often calculated?

4. What is the difference between the mark-up and the prime ingredient mark-up pricing methods?

5. What is price elasticity of demand?

6. What is the philosophy behind bottom-up pricing?

7. What does menu engineering consider in its review of menu items?

8. What is the relation between contribution margins and cost percentages?

9. How is the $1 per $1,000 technique used to price rooms?

10. Which pricing method is the most applicable for restaurants? Why?

Problems

Problem 1

Kristy's has been charging an average of $45 for its hotel rooms and has operated at an 80% occupancy. A recent average room price increase to $50 has been proposed. The general manager expects the occupancy to decline to 77% as a result of the price increase.

Required:

1. Compute the price elasticity of demand.

2. How is demand characterized for Kristy's, based on your calculations in #1?

Problem 2

B.M. Andrews is switching to the markup approach for pricing entrées at her café. In the past, she has set prices based on intuition. The desired food cost percentage is 30%. Three entrées and their related past prices and costs are as follows:

	Ingredient Cost	Prior Price
Chicken Delight	$2.50	$6.95
Pork Squeal	$2.75	$8.95
Steak Supreme	$3.75	$12.95

Required:

1. Calculate the new prices based solely on the markup approach.
2. Discuss how the Chicken Delight should be repriced given the above calculation and the four modifying factors discussed in the chapter.

Problem 3

Hoatsie's Hotel has an average daily room rate (ADR) of $75.00. The breakdown of sales by type of room and the price differential is as follows:

	Mix of Sales	Price Differential
Singles	20%	------
Doubles	60%	$10 greater than the singles
Kings	20%	Twice the price of singles

Required:

1. Determine the ADR for each type of room.
2. Assume the sales mix is equal across each type of room. What would be the ADR for each type of room given the price differential above?

Problem 4

Bryan's, a proposed restaurant, is scheduled to open in two months. Bryan Murphy, the owner, seeks your advice on pricing. Although he knows he will have to modify your recommendations based on market prices, he would like a cost perspective. He gives you the following information:

Bryan's investment	$1,000,000
Bryan's desired return on investment (ROI)	20%
Bryan's tax rate	25%
Funds borrowed	$1,000,000
Interest rate	12%

Forecasted annual costs:	
Occupation costs other than interest and depreciation	$300,000
Depreciation costs	$120,000
Controllable expenses	$600,000
Cost of food sales*	30% of food sales

*in addition to other expenses

Bryan's will have 150 seats, and the average expected seat turnover per day is 2.5. The restaurant will be open 365 days per year.

Required:

Determine the average food service check.

Problem 5

The Squish, an upscale 150-seat restaurant, revises its menu every six months. The revisions are based, in part, on the price elasticity of demand for their menu items. During the 30-day periods before and after the last menu revision, the selling prices and quantity sold of three items were as follows:

Item	Prior to Revision		After Revision	
	Price	Quantity	Price	Quantity
Super Burger	$4.95	450	$5.45	400
Golden Chicken	$6.45	800	$5.95	1,000
Ocean Delight	$6.45	600	$6.95	400

The above sales quantities have remained fairly constant each month since the last menu revision.

Required:

1. Compute the price elasticity of demand for each menu item.
2. Advise Kay Rae, the manager, of the implications of your results for each menu item.

Problem 6

The Sugar Plum Inn had an average dinner cover charge of $8.75 during the month of June when 3,000 patrons were served. E.L. Plum, the owner/manager, increased the dinner menu prices by an average of $ .50 per item. During the first 30 days of July, 2,900 patrons were served dinner, and the average cover charge was $9.25.

Required:

1. Compute the price elasticity of demand.
2. How is demand characterized based on your calculations?

Problem 7

The proposed Harris Place (a 50-room, rooms-only lodging facility) is to be built in mid-Michigan. Jeremy Harris, the owner, is concerned about the average daily room rate (ADR), construction costs, borrowing costs, and their impact on profits. He provides you with the following information:

1. Proposed costs of the lodging facility:

    Land $400,000
    Building $2,000,000
    Equipment $1,000,000

2. Financing:

Equity (desired return on investment (ROI = 15%)	$1,000,000
Debt (8% annual interest rate)	$2,400,000

3. Income tax rate: 40%

4. Property taxes: $120,000 per year

5. Fire insurance: $30,000 (annual premium)

6. Depreciation:

   Building: 40-year life, straight-line method, $-0- salvage value
   Equipment: 10-year life, straight-line method, $-0- salvage value

7. Undistributed operating expenses: $300,000 annually and 5% of total room revenue

8. Management fee: 5% of rooms revenue

9. The telephone department is expected to just break even.

10. Rooms department expenses equal $30,000 annually plus 15% of room sales.

11. Expected paid occupancy is 70%.

Required:

Determine the required ADR to achieve Jeremy Harris' goal of earning an ROI of 15%.

Problem 8

Josie's Place Inn, a proposed 30-room motel with a fully-equipped restaurant, will cost $750,000 to construct. An estimated additional $50,000 will be invested in the business as working capital. Of the total $800,000 investment, $400,000 is to be secured from the Columbo Federal Bank at the rate of 10% interest. The projected occupancy rate is 80% for the year. The owners desire a 15% return on equity after the corporation pays income taxes of 25%. The estimated undistributable expenses, not including income taxes and interest expense, total $480,000. The estimated direct expenses of the rooms department are $7 for each room sold. Consider a year to have 365 days.

Required:

1. Determine the average price of a room using the Hubbart Formula, assuming the contribution from the restaurant department is $0.

2. If the double rooms are sold at a premium of $10 over singles, what is the price of singles and doubles? Assume a double occupancy rate of 40%.

3. If the restaurant generates a department profit of $20,000 per year, how much may average room rates be decreased and still meet the owners' financial goals?

Problem 9

A proposed dinner-only restaurant, Snickers, is scheduled to open in two months. The owner (Betsy Lab) seeks your advice on pricing. Although she knows she will have to modify your recommendations based on market prices, she desires a cost perspective. She gives you the following information:

Betsy's investment	$500,000
Betsy's desired ROI	15%
Betsy's tax rate	35%
Funds borrowed	$500,000
Interest rate	10% (annual)

Forecasted annual costs:

Occupation costs other than interest and depreciation	$100,000
Depreciation costs	$ 60,000
Controllable expenses	$750,000
Cost of food sales	35% of food sales

Snickers will have 150 seats and the average expected seat turnover per day is 1.0. The restaurant will be open 310 days per year.

Required:

1. Determine the average dinner check.
2. Assume non-food business provides $20,000 of pretax profits each year. Determine the average dinner check.

Problem 10

The Midday Cafe is located in the Midtown Mall which is open from 10 A.M. to 5 P.M. each day. The Midday Cafe sells ten different sandwiches as well as a variety of soft drinks. In a recent week, the following activity occurred:

Sandwich	Selling Price	Cost	Number Sold
Pork Barrel	$3.95	$1.30	50
Lamb Leg	3.75	1.00	40
Chicken Breast	3.95	1.40	150
Burger Delight	3.45	.85	300
Super Burger	4.95	1.25	190
Roast Beef	4.95	1.50	250
Ocean Catch	4.45	1.20	200
Tuna Salad	3.50	.60	175
Egg Salad	3.25	.35	150
Cheese Mix	2.95	.40	60

Required:

1. Determine the total sales for sandwiches for the week.
2. Determine the total cost of sandwich sales for the week.
3. Determine the food cost percentage for the week.
4. Determine the average contribution margin for all sandwiches sold.
5. Using menu engineering, determine the classification of each sandwich.

Problem 11

The Lynn Inn, a 100-room lodging facility, is proposed for construction in the north central part of the United States. The total cost of construction is $5,000,000. Another $200,000 is required for franchise costs and working capital purposes. Franchise costs of $100,000 are to be amortized over the first five years of operations. To simplify the problem, depreciation is calculated on a straight-line basis over 24 years (assume $200,000 of salvage value).

The owners will borrow $3,000,000 at an annual interest rate of 12%. The owners desire an 18% return on their equity investment. Other unallocable costs except for management fees total $1,500,000 annually. Management fees are based on 3% of room sales.

Assume that telephone department and food service department profits total $0 and $300,000, respectively. Further assume that all room department costs are variable and total 25% of room revenues, and that the Lynn Inn can achieve a 70% occupancy rate for the first year. Finally, assume an average tax rate of 25%.

Required:

1. Determine the average room rate for the Lynn Inn.

2. Assume that telephone department losses total $50,000. How much must the average room rate be modified to cover this loss?

3. Assume (independent of #2) that the Lynn Inn has singles, doubles, and suites. Further, the relationship between sales and prices are as follows:

	Price	Sales Mix
Singles	??	30%
Doubles	$10 premium over singles rate	50
Suites	125% of doubles rate	20
		100%

Determine the average room rate for suites and doubles.

Problem 12

Stan Rey, the manager of Masons, a casual dining facility, has just been exposed to the concept of analyzing a menu based on its gross profits rather than food cost percentage. The four major entrées at Masons and their selling prices (SP), food costs (FC), and contribution margins (CM) are as follows:

	SP	FC	CM
Chicken	$5.95	$1.78	$4.17
Fish	$6.95	$2.43	$4.52
Pork chops	$8.95	$3.58	$5.37
Steak	$11.95	$5.97	$5.98

Three alternative sales mixes are as follows:

	Sales Mixes		
	#1	#2	#3
Chicken	400	350	100
Fish	300	300	150
Pork chops	200	200	250
Steak	100	150	500
Total	1,000	1,000	1,000

Required:

1. Compute the total revenue, gross profit, and food cost percentage for each alternative.

2. How many meals would have to be sold for mixes #1 and #2 so that each would provide the gross profit earned with sales mix #3?
3. Which sales mix would you prefer? Why?

Problem 13

Barbara Rope, a wealthy investor, is considering investing $2,000,000 in a 300-room hotel. Debt financing would total $8,000,000. She desires to know the average rate her hotel will have to charge, given the following alternatives.

	Alternatives				
	#1	#2	#3	#4	#5
Desired ROI	14%	15%	16%	17%	18%
Interest rate	12%	12%	13%	14%	14%
Tax rate	30%	30%	30%	30%	30%
Estimated annual fixed charges (excluding interest)	$700,000	$700,000	$700,000	$700,000	$700,000
Management fees (% of room sales)	3%	3%	3%	4%	4%
Undistributed operating expense	$3,000,000	$3,000,000	$3,500,000	$3,500,000	$3,500,000
Departmental profits:					
Food	$300,000	$300,000	$400,000	$450,000	$450,000
Telephone	$10,000	$10,000	$10,000	$10,000	$10,000
Variable costs per room sold	$15	$15	$20	$20	$20
Occupancy rate	65%	70%	65%	75%	80%

Required:

Compute the average daily room rate for each alternative. To minimize the calculations, consider using a spreadsheet program.

Problem 14

Bobbie's Place has not changed its menu in three years. Recently, the owner, Bobbie Schmidt, read about menu engineering and desires your assistance in analyzing the dinner menu. The seven dinner entrées, their selling prices, costs, and the menu counts for a recent month are as follows:

	Selling Price	Food Cost	Number Sold
Sirloin steak	$ 9.95	$3.00	240
King crab	15.95	6.00	50
Lobster	18.45	8.00	60
Prime rib	14.50	4.25	300
Whitefish	8.75	2.50	80
New York strip	12.45	5.75	180
Chicken à la king	8.50	2.60	280

Required:

1. Complete a menu engineering worksheet using the format of Exhibit 14.
2. What recommendations would you offer the owner based on your analysis?

Problem 15

The K&S Restaurant desires to analyze its luncheon menu prior to making several changes. The manager, Louis Kass, has provided the following information:

	Selling Price	Food Cost	Number Sold
Hamburger Deluxe	$4.95	$1.50	180
Cheeseburger Deluxe	$5.25	$1.60	120
Turkey Sandwich	$4.25	$1.25	80
Ham & Cheese on Rye	$6.25	$1.70	220
Egg Salad Sandwich	$3.95	$1.10	50
Fishwich	$4.50	$1.30	80
Pizzaburger	$3.00	$ .85	100
Chicken Delight	$6.25	$2.10	140
Taco Salad	$3.25	$ .85	60
Chef Salad	$3.95	$1.25	100

Required:

1. Complete a menu engineering worksheet using the format of Exhibit 14. Alternatively, use a computerized menu engineering program.
2. Complete a second menu engineering worksheet after revising the menu as follows:
   A. Drop the poorest performing item (dog) and allocate the units sold of this item to the plow horses on a pro rata basis.
   B. Lower the prices of puzzle items by 5% and increase sales of each by 10%.
   C. Increase the prices of plow horses by 5% and decrease sales of each by 5%.
   D. Increase prices of each star to either the next $X.45 or $X.95 and assume that the number sold of each remains constant.
3. Compare the results of menu engineering of #1 and #2 above with regard to the following:
   A. Number of items sold
   B. Total sales
   C. Average contribution margin
   D. Total contribution margin
   E. Number of dogs and stars after each analysis

Chapter 9 Outline

Implicit Versus Explicit Forecasts
Forecasting in the Hospitality Industry
Personnel Responsible for Forecasting
The Nature of Forecasting
Underlying Pattern of the Data
Overview of Forecasting Methods
      Naive Methods
      Moving Averages
      Exponential Smoothing
      Causal Forecasting Approaches
      Limitations of Quantitative Forecasting Methods
      Qualitative Forecasting Techniques
Selection of a Forecasting Method
Short-Term Forecasts in the Lodging Industry
Forecasting Cases
      ARAMARK Corporation—Forecasting by Food Service
        Directors
      Pizza Hut—A Case in Forecasting
      Forecasting at Hilton Hotels
Computer Applications

9

Forecasting Methods

EVERY HOSPITALITY MANAGER'S JOB includes forecasting, which is the calculation and prediction of future events such as sales for the following day, week, or month. Forecasting is necessary in order to plan the most effective and efficient ways to meet expected sales volume. For example, if the food and beverage manager of a hotel forecasts 500 dinner guests, then food, beverages, and other supplies must be obtained, and the appropriate personnel must be scheduled to prepare and serve the food and beverages to the guests. Generally, the accuracy of sales forecasts is a major determinant of the cost effectiveness of the hospitality operation. For example, if 400 meals are forecast and 500 guests show up, the food and beverage provisions and the number of employees scheduled to work may not be adequate. This may result in poor service and overtime wages. On the other hand, if 600 meals had been forecast, service would probably have been outstanding; however, due to possibly excessive labor costs, efficiency would have been reduced. The general topic of forecasting raises several questions such as:

1. How important is forecasting?

2. Is forecasting limited to financial forecasts?

3. How is forecasting conducted by unit managers in the hospitality industry?

4. How does forecasting enable management to be successful?

5. What are the limitations to forecasting?

6. How does forecasting differ from planning?

7. What is the difference between seasonal and cyclical patterns?

8. How do quantitative and qualitative forecasting methods differ?

9. How is a moving average calculated?

10. When are causal forecasting approaches most useful in the hospitality industry?

This chapter begins by explaining the distinction between implicit and explicit forecasts. A general discussion of forecasting in the hospitality industry is followed by a discussion of the personnel who are responsible for preparing forecasts. Next, we turn to the nature of forecasting itself, focusing on the underlying patterns of data used in forecasts and providing an overview of various forecasting methods. The problem of selecting a forecasting method appropriate to individual hospitality operations is given special consideration. Finally, we will illustrate the chapter's discussion of forecasting by providing case studies of how forecasts are prepared by three different hospitality operations.

Implicit Versus Explicit Forecasts

Some hospitality managers may insist that they do not believe in forecasting. However, their actions almost always prove otherwise. For example, when the manager decides to replace an inoperative piece of equipment, such as a range, he or she is implicitly forecasting that profits will be higher if a new range is purchased.

This intuitive approach to managing may be useful, since unforeseen events often occur and must be resolved quickly. However, managing in this fashion on a daily basis is less than optimal. It is generally more useful to forecast consciously. Implicit forecasts are unsystematic, imprecise, and difficult to evaluate rationally. Explicit forecasts are systematic, may be reasonably reliable and accurate, and are easier to evaluate rationally.

Forecasting in the Hospitality Industry

A major function of management is planning, and a subset of the planning function is forecasting. Forecasting is generally used to predict what will happen in a given set of circumstances. The forecast gives an idea of expected results if management makes no changes in the way things are done. In planning, forecasts are used to help make decisions about which circumstances will be most desirable for the hospitality operation. Thus, if a forecast shows rooms demand will decrease next month, management should prepare an action plan to prevent rooms sales from declining. After the action plan is completed, a new forecast must be made to reflect the impact of the action plan.

Planning, and thus forecasting, is pervasive in hospitality operations. In a hotel operation, rooms sales and food and beverage sales account for approximately 85% of the total sales activity of a hotel. Many operations, especially food service and lodging chains, forecast sales for several years in long-range operating budgets. At the other extreme, sales are forecast for months, days, parts of a day, and sometimes even on an hourly basis, since management must plan to service the forecasted sales.

Hospitality establishments also provide estimates of future activity in management reports to stockholders, which include both qualitative and quantitative forecasts. For example, Host Marriott Services included the following in a recent annual report:[1]

> Host Marriott Services is committed to enhancing our customers' travel and entertainment experience with excellent food, beverage, and retail concepts and to becoming the first choice of our clients in our chosen markets. We intend to become a global company and will be internationally recognized by our clients and concept owners as the preferred provider of food, beverage, and retail concepts in travel and entertainment markets. Our reputation for quality, integrity, and for treating our associates, clients, and partners with dignity and respect will be unsurpassed.
>
> We will build on our excellent beginning in 1996 and look forward to the future. We expect our company to exceed $2 billion in annual revenues by the year 2001, and we anticipate that 25% of our revenues will come from new markets and venues by that time.

Exhibit 1   Personnel Involved in Making Short-Term Forecasts

	Rooms Forecast	Food & Beverage Forecast	Catering Forecast
Average number of personnel involved	3 people	3 people	2 people
Person responsible for final forecast	General manager (GM) and to a lesser extent the front office manager	Food and beverage director and to a lesser extent the GM	Director of catering and to a lesser extent the food and beverage director

Personnel Responsible for Forecasting

Forecasting of sales and related expenses is the responsibility not only of the accounting department, but also of management personnel in other departments. For example, the year-ahead forecast should include input from (1) the sales director's forecast of group rooms business, (2) the front office manager's forecast of rooms occupancy from all other sources, (3) a joint forecast of rooms business by the sales director and front office manager, (4) the controller, and (5) the general manager and management team review.

Exhibit 1 reveals the results of research regarding the number of people involved in making short-term (3- to 10-day) forecasts. Across all properties surveyed, the range of the number of personnel involved in the three areas shown was one to six people. The larger the property, the greater the number of personnel involved with the forecast. For example, the mega-hotels (1,000 or more rooms) that responded use six people in their rooms forecast, while hotels with fewer than 150 rooms involve an average of two people.

The Nature of Forecasting

It is important to understand the nature and limitations of forecasting. First, forecasting deals with the future. A forecast made today is for activity during a future period, be it tonight's dinner sales or next year's rooms sales. The time period involved is significant. A forecast today for tomorrow's sales is generally much easier than an estimate today of next year's sales. The more removed the forecast period is from the date the forecast is made, the greater the difficulty in making the forecast and the greater the risk that the actual results will differ from the forecast.

Second, forecasting involves uncertainty. If management were certain about what circumstances would exist during the forecasted period, the forecast preparation would be a trivial matter. Virtually all situations faced by managers involve uncertainty; therefore, judgments must be made and information gathered on which to base the forecast. For example, assume that rooms sales for a major hotel must be forecast for one year in advance. The manager (forecaster) may be uncertain about competition, guest demand, room rates, and so forth. Nevertheless, using the best information available and his or her best judgment, he or she forecasts that x rooms at an average room rate of $\$y$ will be sold.

Third, forecasting generally relies on information contained in historical data. Historical activity (for example, past sales) may not be a strong indicator of future activity, but it is considered a reasonable starting point. When historical data appear to be irrelevant to the future time period, the forecasts should be modified appropriately. For example, a successful World's Fair might have a major impact on hotel occupancies for several months. However, in projecting future hotel occupancies after the fair ends, the recent historical information may well be much less relevant.

Fourth, by their nature, forecasts are generally less accurate than desired. However, rather than discarding forecasts due to their inaccuracy, management should consider using more sophisticated forecasting models when their cost is justified, updating forecasts as necessary, and/or planning more carefully on the basis of the forecasted projections.

Naive forecasting models, such as using the most recent value plus $x\%$, may have been adequate in the past for small hospitality operations. However, more sophisticated models may be appropriate for larger properties. Forecasts should be revised as soon as there is a change in the circumstances on which the forecasts were based. For example, an enhanced food and beverage reputation due to favorable publicity may call for reforecasting next month's food and beverage sales.

Finally, management must plan to cover a deviation of an additional $x\%$ from the forecasted levels. Experience may be the best indication of the required planning. For example, if actual sales historically have exceeded projected sales by 10%, management should order sufficient provisions and schedule labor to cover such a deviation for the projected activity.

Underlying Pattern of the Data

Many forecasting methods assume that some pattern exists in past data that can be identified and used in making the forecast. The methods to be presented in this chapter make explicit assumptions about the type of underlying pattern. Thus, the forecaster must attempt to match the patterns with the most appropriate forecasting methods. Three types of pattern are trend, seasonal, and cyclical (discussed below and graphed for a hypothetical hotel in Exhibit 2).

The **trend pattern** is simply a projection of the long-run estimate of the activity being evaluated. The trend pattern of the data is often shown for several years. The trend of rooms sales in Exhibit 2 is an increasing one and could be determined by using methods presented later in this chapter.

A **seasonal pattern** exists when a series of data fluctuates over time according to some pattern. Business may vary regularly by season of the year, by month, by week, or even by the days of the week. Seasonal patterns exist in the hospitality industry primarily because of forces external to the industry. For example, many summer resort hotels experience high occupancy during the summer months, but are closed

Exhibit 2   Underlying Patterns of Data for a Hypothetical Hotel

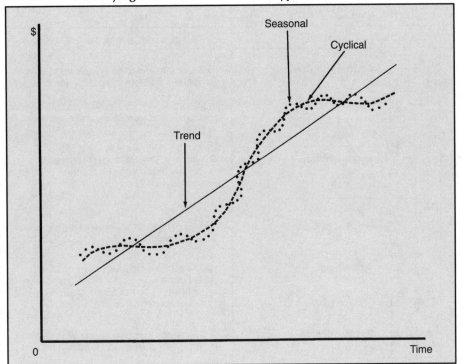

during the off-season. The manager of a hospitality operation affected by seasonal business swings must fully appreciate this impact in order to manage efficiently.

The final underlying pattern of data is called cyclical. **Cyclical patterns** are movements about a trend line that generally occur over a period of more than one year. Exhibit 2 shows that the cyclical pattern is similar to a seasonal pattern except for the length of the pattern. The cyclical pattern is the most difficult to predict because, unlike a seasonal pattern, it does not necessarily repeat itself at constant intervals.

Finally, random variations are also present in all historical data. By definition, there is no pattern in random variations. They occur for reasons that the hospitality manager cannot anticipate regardless of the forecasting method. Therefore, the actual observed result is a combination of trend and randomness. As long as randomness exists, uncertainty will be present. However, when the forecaster is able to identify the exact pattern of the underlying data, the random deviations are minimized.

Overview of Forecasting Methods

There are numerous ways to forecast, ranging from the simple, unsophisticated method of intuition to complex approaches such as econometric models, where sets of two or more multiple regression equations are used. Forecasting methods may be classified as shown in Exhibit 3.

Exhibit 3   Forecasting Methods

Approaches				Brief Description
Informal forecasting				Ad hoc, judgmental or intuitive methods
Formal Forecasting	Quantitative Methods	Causal Methods	**Regression Analysis**	Independent variables are related to the dependent variable using least squares: $y = A + Bx_1 + Cx_2$. Approaches include similar linear regression, multiple linear regression, and nonlinear regression.
			Econometrics	A system of interdependent regression equations describing one or more economic sectors.
		Time Series	**Naive**	Simple rules such as forecast equals last period's actual activity.
			Smoothing	Based on average past values of a time series (moving average) or weighting more recent past values of a time series (exponential smoothing).
			Decomposition	A time series that is broken down into trend, cyclical, seasonality, and randomness.
	Qualitative Methods		**Market Research**	Gathering information from potential customers regarding a "new" product or service.
			Juries of Executive Opinion	Top executives jointly prepare forecasts.
			Salesforce Estimates	A bottom-up approach to aggregating unit managers' forecasts.
			Delphi Method	A formal process conducted with a group of experts to achieve consensus on future events as they affect the company's markets.

The first breakdown is between informal and formal forecasting methods. Informal methods are based on intuition and lack systematic procedures transferable to other forecasters. Formal forecasting methods outline steps to be followed so they can be applied repeatedly. Formal forecasting methods are divided between **qualitative methods** and **quantitative methods.** The quantitative methods, which are the primary concern of this chapter, are further divided between causal and time series approaches.

The **time series approaches** always assume that a pattern recurs over time which, when identified, may be used to forecast values for any subsequent time period. For example, if a seasonal pattern of December hotel occupancies of 30% below the monthly average has been identified, then the estimated hotel occupancy for December of the following year would most likely be 30% below the monthly average for that year.

Time series approaches assume that the underlying pattern can be identified solely on the basis of historical data from that series. They do not consider the potential effects of certain decisions, such as pricing and advertising, that the manager makes for the future periods. Time series approaches presented in this chapter include naive methods and smoothing methods. The decomposition method is beyond the scope of this chapter.

The **causal approaches** assume that the value of a certain variable is a function of other variables. For example, the sale of food and beverages in a hotel is a function, among other things, of hotel occupancy. Thus, a food and beverage sales forecast is based in part on forecasted rooms sales. Causal methods include single and multiple linear regression, nonlinear regression, and econometric models. Only the single linear regression approach will be presented in this chapter.[2]

Naive Methods

The simplest time series approach to forecasting is to use the most recently observed value as a forecast. For example, a food service manager's sales projections of $50,000 for the current month may be based upon the $50,000 sales of the previous month. This naive approach to forecasting assumes that there is no seasonality affecting sales. To take seasonality into account, a forecaster might use sales from the same month of the previous year as a base and either add or subtract a certain percentage.

For example, assume that a hotel's January 19X1 rooms sales totaled $150,000. The projection for January 19X2, using an anticipated 10% increase due to expected increased rooms sales and prices, would be $165,000, computed as follows:

$$\text{Base}(1 + 10\%) = \text{Forecast for January 19X2}$$
$$\$150,000(1.1) = \underline{\$165,000}$$

Although naive methods are based on very simple rules, they may provide reasonably accurate forecasts, especially for estimates of up to one year. In some cases, more sophisticated methods do not sufficiently improve the accuracy of forecasts to justify their use—especially in light of their higher costs.

Moving Averages

In some cases, the major cause of variations among data used in making forecasts is randomness. Since managers do not make business decisions based on randomness that may never again happen, they attempt to remove the random effect by averaging or "smoothing" the data from specified time periods. One such approach to forecasting is the **moving average**, which is expressed mathematically as follows:

Exhibit 4   Weekly Meals Served—Bank of Hospitality

Week	Actual Meals Served
1	1,000
2	900
3	950
4	1,050
5	1,025
6	1,000
7	975
8	1,000
9	950
10	1,025
11	1,000
12	1,050

$$\text{Moving Average} = \frac{\text{Activity in Previous } n \text{ Periods}}{n}$$

where n is the number of periods in the moving average

This moving average method is illustrated using the contract food service operation at the Bank of Hospitality. Service Company, the contract feeding company, serves lunch five days a week at the Bank of Hospitality, and the manager needs to estimate sales for the thirteenth week. Exhibit 4 reveals weekly sales for weeks 1–12. Using a three-week moving average, the estimate for the number of meals to be served during the thirteenth week is 1,025, determined as follows:

$$\text{3-Week Moving Average} = \frac{1,025 + 1,000 + 1,050}{3}$$

$$= \underline{\underline{1,025}} \text{ meals}$$

As new weekly results become available, they are used in calculating the average by adding the most recent week and dropping the earliest week. In this way, the calculated average is a "moving" one because it is continually updated to include only the most recent observations for the specified number of time periods. For example, if 950 meals were served during week 13 at the Bank of Hospitality, then the forecast for week 14, using the three-week moving average, would be calculated as follows:

$$\text{Forecast for Week 14} = \frac{\text{Sum of Sales for Weeks 11–13}}{3}$$

$$= \frac{1,000 + 1,050 + 950}{3}$$

$$= \underline{\underline{1,000}} \text{ meals}$$

Alternatively, more weeks could be used to determine the weekly forecast. For example, a 12-week moving average to estimate meals to be sold during the thirteenth week results in a forecast of 994, determined as follows:

$$
\begin{aligned}
\text{12-Week Moving Average} \quad &= \quad \frac{\text{Actual Weekly Sales for Weeks 1--12}}{12} \\[2mm]
&= \quad \frac{11{,}925}{12} \\[2mm]
&= \quad 993.75, \text{ rounded to } \underline{\underline{994}}
\end{aligned}
$$

It should be noted that the more periods averaged, the less effect the random variations will have on the forecast. This can be seen in the above illustration. The three-week moving average forecast for week 13 was 1,025 meals, compared to the 12-week moving average forecast of 994. In this case, since the actual sales during the thirteenth week turned out to be 950 meals, the 12-week moving average forecast of 994 was more accurate than the forecast based on only three weeks. The increased accuracy is due to minimizing the effect of random variations by using data covering a greater number of time periods.

Although the moving average approach to forecasting is often considered to be more accurate and reliable than the naive methods, there are some disadvantages associated with this approach. One limitation is the need to store and continually update the historical data covering the most recent number of time periods used in calculating the moving average. This requirement would be quite costly for a large retail business, such as Sears or WalMart, which would have to keep track of sales data for a large number of different items. However, in the hospitality industry the cost of storing and maintaining historical data for moving average forecasts is not unreasonable, since hotels and restaurants sell a comparatively small number of different items.

A more serious limitation is that the moving average method gives equal weight to each of the observations gathered over the specified number of time periods. Many managers would agree that the data from the most recent time periods contain more information about what will happen in the future and, therefore, should be given more weight than the older observations that are calculated into the moving average. The exponential smoothing approach to forecasting not only satisfies this concern to count recent data more heavily than older data, but also eliminates the need for storing all of the historical data covering the specified time period.

Exponential Smoothing

Exponential smoothing is a forecasting method that uses a **smoothing constant** and recent actual and forecasted activity to estimate future activity. This approach has widespread appeal among business forecasters. It essentially says, "If the forecast for a particular period was too high, reduce it for the next period; if it was too low, raise it." A major benefit of this approach is that data for only two prior periods need to be retained, as the calculation of the smoothing constant is based on these limited data.

When the exponential smoothing method is used, the hospitality manager requires only two types of readily available data:

1. The forecasts from the two previous periods

2. The actual activity during the earlier of the two previous periods

These data are used to determine the smoothing constant as follows:

$$\frac{\text{Smoothing}}{\text{Constant}} = \frac{\text{Period 2 Forecast} - \text{Period 1 Forecast}}{\text{Period 1 Actual Demand} - \text{Period 1 Forecast}}$$

For example, consider an elementary school food service that uses exponential smoothing. Its period 1 forecast and actual demand were 200 and 220, respectively. The period 2 forecast was 210. The smoothing constant is .5, determined as follows:

$$x = \frac{210 - 200}{220 - 200}$$

$$= \underline{\underline{.5}}$$

The smoothing constant requires the manager to identify what is a good response rate. The smoothing constant should be small if sales have been relatively stable in the past, and large if the product/service is experiencing rapid growth.

Once the smoothing constant has been determined, it can be inserted into the general formula for exponential smoothing, which is as follows:

$$\frac{\text{New}}{\text{Forecast}} = \frac{\text{Past}}{\text{Forecast}} + \frac{\text{Smoothing}}{\text{Constant}} \times \left(\frac{\text{Actual}}{\text{Demand}} - \frac{\text{Past}}{\text{Forecast}} \right)$$

Using the previous illustration with the Bank of Hospitality, the weekly sales will be projected for week 13 using the exponential smoothing method of forecasting. Assume that the forecasted sales for week 12 were 1,020 and that .1 is the smoothing constant. The forecasted sales for week 13 of 1,023 meals is determined as follows:

$$\frac{\text{Week 13}}{\text{Forecast}} = \frac{\text{Week 12}}{\text{Forecast}} + .1(\text{Week 12 Actual Sales} - \text{Week 12 Forecast})$$

$$= 1,020 + .1(1,050 - 1,020)$$

$$= \underline{\underline{1,023}} \text{ meals}$$

The exponential smoothing method presented in this chapter is only one of several such approaches.[3] Exponential smoothing techniques are most useful when only short-term forecasts are required, and when reasonably accurate—rather than precise—forecasts are acceptable.

Causal Forecasting Approaches

Causal forecasting approaches include both single and multiple regression as well as econometric models. In this chapter, we will discuss only single regression analysis.

Regression analysis involves estimating an activity on the basis of other activities or factors that are assumed to be causes or highly reliable indicators of the activity. The activity to be forecasted (such as food sales) is the dependent, unknown variable, while the basis on which the forecast is made (such as room sales and/or advertising expenses) is the independent, known variable. Regression analysis is used to predict the dependent variable given the value of the independent variable.

The level of demand to be estimated is thought to depend upon, or be closely related to, the independent variable. In order to forecast the operation's demand, the closeness of the variables needs to be determined. For example, how closely related are a lodging property's rooms sales to food sales in its restaurant operation?

Two measures of closeness are the **coefficient of correlation** and the **coefficient of determination.** The coefficient of correlation is the measure of the relation between the dependent and independent variables, such as food sales and rooms sales. The formula for determining the coefficient of correlation is as follows:

$$r = \frac{n\Sigma xy - \Sigma x\Sigma y}{\sqrt{[n\Sigma x^2 - (\Sigma x)^2][n\Sigma y^2 - (\Sigma y)^2]}}$$

where x is the independent variable
y is the dependent variable
n is the number of observations
r is a positive relationship value[4] between 0 and 1

The closer the r value is to 1, the stronger the relationship between the dependent and independent variables being measured.

The square of the coefficient of correlation (r^2) is the coefficient of determination. This measure reflects the extent to which the change in the independent variable explains the change in the dependent variable.

Regression analysis is illustrated using data from the Forest Hotel. Exhibit 5 contains the number of room guests and meals served in the dining room for 19X1. Using these data, we can develop a regression equation that will allow us to forecast meals to be served based on our knowledge of the number of hotel guests. The regression formula is as follows:

$$y = a + bx$$

where y = Meals served
a = Meals served to non-hotel registrants
b = Average number of meals served to each hotel guest
x = Number of hotel room guests

Given the data in Exhibit 5 and using formulas[5] and a computer spreadsheet program to determine a and b, the regression equation becomes:

$$y = 370 + 1.254(x)$$

Exhibit 5   Room Guests and Meals Served

	x Room Guests	y Meals Served
January	4,060	5,200
February	4,100	5,360
March	4,200	5,720
April	4,250	5,430
May	4,200	5,680
June	4,150	5,520
July	4,300	5,800
August	4,350	5,910
September	4,400	6,020
October	4,200	5,840
November	4,080	5,510
December	3,600	5,020

This equation indicates that 370 people not registered as guests at the Forest Hotel dine there monthly and, further, that each registered room guest eats 1.254 meals at the hotel each day.

Assuming that the sales forecast for January, 19X2, is 3,000 rooms at an average occupancy per room of 1.5 people, the projected meals to be sold is determined as follows:

$$\text{Forecasted Meals Sold} = 370 + 1.254(3,000)(1.5)$$
$$= 370 + 5,643$$
$$= \underline{\underline{6,013}}$$

The forecasted 6,013 meals to be sold during the first week of January, 19X2, includes 370 meals for diners not registered as guests and 5,643 meals for hotel guests.

The coefficient of correlation (r) measures the relationship between hotel room guests and meals served. The r value for the above example is .8568, which suggests a strong relationship between the two variables. The coefficient of determination (r^2) for this example is .7341, which means that 73.41% of the change in meals served is explained by the change in hotel room guests.

Regression analysis forecasting used when two or more independent variables are related to the dependent variable is called **multiple regression analysis.** For example, the manager of the food and beverage department at a lodging operation may desire to forecast food sales on the basis of the number of room guests *and* advertising expenditures. Although multiple regression analysis is both interesting and challenging, it is beyond the scope of this chapter.[6]

The usefulness of these regression analysis techniques is a function of satisfactory dependent and independent variables. That is, the higher the correlation of the dependent and independent variables, the greater the probability regression analysis will yield meaningful forecasts.

Limitations of Quantitative Forecasting Methods

Although time series forecasting and causal forecasting can be quite useful, they have limitations. First, they are virtually useless when data are scarce, such as at the opening of a new hotel, restaurant, or club. In these instances, there is no sales history for the newly opened facility from which to collect the data needed to forecast demand. Second, they assume that historical trends will continue into the future and are unable to consider unforeseeable occurrences, such as the Gulf War in 1991 and its impact on lodging properties.

Qualitative Forecasting Techniques

When the limitations of quantitative approaches significantly affect a hospitality operation, qualitative forecasting methods are useful. These methods emphasize human judgment. Information is gathered in as logical, unbiased, and systematic a way as possible, and then judgment is brought to bear on the activity being forecasted. Qualitative forecasting methods include market research, jury of executive opinion, sales force estimates, and the Delphi method.

The market research method involves systematically gathering, recording, and analyzing data related to a hospitality operation's marketing of products and services. Large hotel chains generally conduct extensive market research before opening a new property to determine whether there is adequate demand. This market research provides data that can then be used in preparing formal sales forecasts.

The jury of executive opinion technique uses key financial, marketing, and operations executives to estimate sales for the forecast period. Generally, the person using this technique will provide the executives with expected economic conditions and changes in the establishment's services. The executives will then independently make their sales forecasts. The person using this technique will then reconcile differences among the executives' opinions.

The sales force estimates technique is similar to the jury of executive opinion in that opinions of corporate personnel are obtained. However, in this case, the input is from lower-echelon personnel who estimate their next year's sales. This approach is sometimes used by multi-unit food service operations. Unit managers are polled, and their immediate superiors review and discuss these estimates with each unit manager. Then, the separate sales estimates are combined to create a sales forecast for the food service operation.

The Delphi technique is used for making forecasts that are generally very futuristic in nature—for example, forecasting expected changes in international travel for the coming decade. This technique involves obtaining opinions from a group of experts to achieve consensus on future events that might affect an operation's markets. Rather than meeting together at one place, the group interacts anonymously. Questionnaires are often used. The responses are then analyzed and resubmitted to the experts for a second round of opinions. This process may continue for several rounds until the researcher is satisfied that consensus regarding the forecast has been achieved.

Selection of a Forecasting Method ——————————————

The specific forecasting method that a hospitality operation adopts will depend on several factors. The two most important are the method's effectiveness in providing usable projections from available data and the cost of using the method. Different methods will be used for different purposes as suggested throughout this chapter. Small establishments lacking personnel with forecasting skills will probably adopt the less sophisticated, but still highly useful, naive methods. On the other hand, large establishments may find the more sophisticated methods to be the most effective. Although these approaches may appear costlier, they may actually be less costly in the long run for large establishments.

In addition to the effectiveness and cost of different forecasting methods, other relevant factors include:

- Frequency with which forecasts will be updated
- Turnaround required for an updated forecast
- Size and complexity of the hospitality operation
- Forecasting skills of personnel involved in making forecasts
- Purposes for which the forecasts are made

Short-Term Forecasts in the Lodging Industry ——————————————

Exhibit 6 is a survey summary of lodging industry short-term sales forecasting approaches by three profit centers: rooms, food (restaurants), and catering (banquets). Short-term forecasts in this research refer to forecasts covering from 3 to 10 days.

The major purpose of each short-term forecast is to allow for staffing and, in food and catering, for ordering the food supplies to service the dining guests. A distant last purpose is the motivation of personnel (that is, using the short-term sales forecast as a target).

The methods used by the majority of respondents differ by profit center. Most hotels, especially those with reservation systems, forecast room sales using the rooms reservations at the time of the forecast plus an estimate for walk-ins. For example, a hotel may show 100 rooms reserved for the following Monday and add the average of walk-ins for the past four Mondays of 15 to equal a rooms sales forecast of 115 rooms. In this example, the short-term forecast is a combination of known sales plus a four-week moving average for the walk-ins.

A second approach is adjusting the prior period's sales based on intuitive expectations for the forecast period. Only 7% of the lodging establishments reported using this approach, and the majority of these users (60%) were establishments with fewer than 150 rooms.

The commonest approach used to forecast short-term food sales by hoteliers (46%) is using the prior period's sales figure and adjusting it for expected differences for the forecast period. For example, if 100 covers were served at the prior Monday evening dinner, the hotel's forecast for the coming Monday evening would be 100 plus or minus an adjustment for expected differences. These differences could be based on house guests, local events, weather forecasts, and other similar activities.

Exhibit 6 Summary of Lodging Industry Short-Term Sales Forecasting Approaches by Three Profit Centers

	Rooms	Food	Catering
Major purposes of forecast:	Staffing (98%) Motivating personnel (25%)	Staffing (100%) Order food (72%) Motivating personnel (19%)	Staffing (82%) Order food (72%) Motivating personnel (16%)
Methodology:	Room reservations plus estimated walk-ins (93%) Prior period sales adjusted based on intuition (7%)	Prior period sales adjusted based on intuition (46%) Meal reservations and estimate for walk-ins (28%) Capture ratios related to the rooms forecast (26%)	Booked catered events plus estimate of additional sales (90%) Prior period sales adjusted based on intuition (10%)
Expression of short-term forecast:	Daily number of rooms sold (80%) Daily sales dollars (55%) Daily number of rooms by type (35%) Daily sales dollars by type of room (20%)	Total covers (79%) Total sales dollars (61%) Food covers by meal period (60%) Sales dollars by meal period (44%)	Total sales dollars (70%) Total covers (67%) Sales dollars by catered event (47%) Covers by catered event (47%)

Twenty-eight percent of the hotels rely in part on meal reservations and estimated walk-ins, while 26% use **capture ratios**—that is, ratios based on hotel guests or some variation of hotel guests. For example, a hotel might estimate its dinner covers to be 40 plus one quarter of the estimated house guests for the night. If the estimated house guests total 200, then the dinner covers forecasted equal 90, determined as follows:

Forecasted dinner covers $= a + bx$

where a = estimated covers for walk-ins (non-hotel guests)
b = percentage of hotel guests expected to eat dinner
x = hotel guest count for evening

Forecasted dinner covers $= 40 + .25(200)$
$= \underline{\underline{90}}$

The sales forecasting methods reported for catered events include two alternatives:

- Ninety percent use the booked catered events plus an estimate for additional sales not booked when the forecast is made.

- Ten percent use prior period catered sales adjusted for expected differences.

Exhibit 7   Accuracy of Short-Term Sales Forecasts

Degree of Accuracy of Short-Term Forecast:*

	Rooms	Restaurant Food	Beverage	Catering
No difference	2%	1%	0%	5%
± 1.0% or less	20	12	8	15
± 1.1–2%	18	14	16	22
± 2.1–3%	17	18	18	13
± 3.1–5%	36	18	18	17
± >5%	7	37	40	28
Total	100%	100%	100%	100%

*Based on the percentage difference between the short-term forecast and the actual sales.

As Exhibit 6 shows, the short-term sales forecast is expressed in a variety of ways. For rooms, the commonest way is rooms sold (80%); for food sales, the commonest is total covers (79%); and for catering sales, the commonest is the total forecasted catering sales dollars (70%), followed closely by total covers (67%). Many hotels express the sales forecasts in more than one way.

Most hoteliers compare their actual results to their short-term sales forecasts in order to determine their forecasting accuracy, so that in the future they can refine their forecasting method and allow for forecasting error in staffing and ordering supplies.

Exhibit 7 contains a summary of the accuracy of the short-term sales forecasts for rooms, food, beverage, and catering activities. The rooms and catering sales forecasting appear to be the most accurate, as 40% and 42% respectively are accurate to within plus or minus 2% or less, compared with 27% for restaurant food forecasts and 24% for beverage sales forecasts. At the other extreme, only 7% of the hotels report their actual rooms sold differs by greater than 5% from their sales forecast, compared with 37%, 28%, and 40% for restaurant food, catering, and beverage forecasts, respectively. These results, especially in the restaurant food and beverage areas, clearly suggest there is room for improvement.

Forecasting Cases

To illustrate forecasting in hospitality industry firms, three companies from different segments have contributed overviews of one facet of forecasting at their companies. The case illustration from ARAMARK Corporation, which serves the business and industry segment of the hospitality industry, focuses on monthly forecasting at the unit level. A brief description of the calculation of the sales dollars is included as well as the two major expenses, cost of food sold and labor expense. Included with the case are two forms used for producing their forecasts.

The second case is from Pizza Hut. Its focus is the weekly sales forecast. This forecast is prepared by starting with the average of the past three weeks (effectively a three-week moving average). It is then adjusted based on several factors, such as local advertising. A major purpose of this forecast is scheduling labor. Included with the case are several forms, including a labor scheduling grid. This form is used to determine the number and types of personnel required on an hourly basis given the sales forecast.

The Hilton Hotels Corporation illustration focuses on the forecast for the annual budget. Several forms used in this process are shown.

The three cases cover three segments of the hospitality industry and three time periods—weekly, monthly, and annual. They are just a sampling of budgeting practices in hospitality corporations.

ARAMARK Corporation—Forecasting by Food Service Directors

ARAMARK Corporation is a leading competitor in the contract food service segment of the hospitality industry. ARAMARK is an international, privately-owned company with revenues over $6 billion. ARAMARK provides food services to all segments of the hospitality industry, including schools and colleges, hospitals, correctional institutions, sports and entertainment facilities, and business and industrial locations. ARAMARK's 140,000 employees provide a multitude of services to thousands of clients and millions of customers every day.

The Business Services Group of ARAMARK provides food service to business and industry clients. A monthly forecast for each month of the fiscal year is prepared for each operating account by the Food Service Director (FSD) using a personal computer. Historical data forms the basis of the forecast and is composed of:

- Sales:
    - Number of service days in the accounting period
    - Number of customers and participation rate
    - Sales by meal period
    - Menu offerings
- Food cost
- Labor cost
- Direct expenses

The historical data for each of the above categories are then adjusted for known changes that will affect the next fiscal year. Sales are adjusted for selling price increases and changes in customer count and participation, as well as menu programs that will increase average check size. Food cost is adjusted for anticipated cost increases, menu changes, and food cost ratios. Labor is adjusted by the change in hours needed for each fiscal period and changes in anticipated wages and tax rates.

The data in each category is prepared by the FSD and entered into the computer. This is an iterative process that allows the FSD to modify or adjust any account or category as necessary.

Prior to the completion of the process, the FSD reviews the forecast with regional management to obtain confirmation of the assumptions and financial data used to develop the forecast.

A summary forecast and a detailed forecast are compared to the actual results generated each month, and if an account has variances to forecast, appropriate action is taken by the FSD to correct the variances. These could include menu adjustments, selected price changes, and staffing adjustments.

Key performance indicators that are reviewed are total sales, total product cost, total labor cost, total direct expense, profit, and profit margin. A current sales analysis form is shown in Exhibit 8. Exhibit 9 is a six months manual operations forecast worksheet.[7]

Pizza Hut—A Case in Forecasting

Pizza Hut is the largest retail distributor of pizza in the world, with a distribution system of over 10,000 units, including approximately 8,800 in the United States, of which 5,500 are corporate-owned units and 3,300 are franchised units. This makes the Dallas, Texas–headquartered Pizza Hut one of the largest multi-unit food chains in the United States. The typical Pizza Hut operation consists of approximately 100 seats, 2,300 square footage, and has 25 employees. Pizza Hut's major items, familiar to most pizza lovers, include deep pan pizza and personal pan pizza.[8]

Forecasting pervades the entire organization. The emphasis here is on the store manager. The major forecasting by a unit manager is the preparation of the weekly sales forecast, which is reviewed and approved by his or her area supervisor. Area supervisors use unit sales forecasts in preparing their area sales forecasts, which then are used by district managers in preparing district forecasts, and so forth. The major uses of the weekly sales forecast by the unit manager are labor scheduling and preparing product ingredients for each day.

The weekly sales forecast is detailed by hour for each day. The manager starts with historical data—the average of the daily-hourly sales for the past three weeks. This historical hourly sales average is adjusted for several factors as follows:

- Advertising in local papers

- Local marketing, such as a Cub Scout troop of 20 boys expected between 6–7 P.M. on Tuesday

- Seasonality—including weather changes, time of year, and holidays

- Media advertising

- Trend for the past few weeks

Pizza Hut does not prescribe a formalized approach for adjusting the historical data for the above factors, but allows unit managers to use their judgment.

The forecasting form used by unit managers is titled the Hourly Reading Sheet (see Exhibit 10). After this is completed based on the discussion above, the Daily Labor Worksheet (see Exhibit 11) is completed, in part by using a labor scheduling grid similar to the illustration in Exhibit 12.

For example, assume that a Pizza Hut restaurant has forecast $250 of hourly sales between 6 and 7 P.M. The required staffing includes 10 people based on the labor scheduling grid column 9 as follows: 2—production, 3—service, 1—register/ telephone, 1—bus/dishwasher, 1—production leader, 1—host/hostess, and 1—floor manager.

Exhibit 8   Current Sales Analysis—Brand Profitability by Week

A	B					C	E=C/D	F	G=F/C	H=C−F	I=H/C	J	K=J/C	L	M=L/C	N=C−F−J−L		O=N/C
	Days Offered					(From 8steps Post Cost Sheets)						Direct Labor See Directions		Allocated Labor See Directions		Brand Profit or (Loss)		
						Sales		Food Costs		Gross Profit								
Brand	M	T	W	Th	F	$	%	$	%	$	%	$	%	$	%	$	%	$	%
Total						−	D		−				−			Input		

Courtesy of ARAMARK Corporation

Exhibit 9   Six Months Manual Operations Forecast Worksheet

Description	Acct. Code	October (4)	November (4)	December (5)	January (4)	February (4)	March (5)
Sales							
Cash	009.01						
Charge	009.02						
Cart	019.00						
*Grand Total**							
Product Cost							
Meat	209.01						
Produce	209.02						
Groceries	209.03						
Dairy	209.04						
Bakery	209.05						
Beverage	209.07						
Other	299.99						
*Grand Total**							
Labor							
Salary/Wages	301.00						
Payroll Adj.	302.00						
Accured Vac.	303.00						
Paid Vac. & Hol.	303.05						
Payroll Taxes	304.00						
Benefits	305.20						
*Grand Total**							
Directs							
Commissions	310.00						
Paper	312.00						
Cleaning	312.05						
Contracted Svcs.	313.14						
Repaires	314.99						
Tax & Licenses	315.99						
Vehicle Expense	316.01						
Gen. Insurance	317.00						
Travel	329.00						
Office	331.00						
Armored Car	344.95						
Uniform & Laundry	345.01						
Bank Charge	345.06						
Replacements	345.10						
Support Charge	345.86						
Other Expenses	345.99						
Buy Backs	381.03						
Assets Util.	381.50						
Depreciation	381.99						
*Grand Total**							
Other Income	199.99						
Total Net Costs*							
Subsidy/Refund**	101.01						
Contigent Refund***	101.02						
Level I Profit*							
Assets	510.10						

*Calculated

** Fee accounts enter minus if refund

***Limited P/L accounts enter minus if refund

Courtesy of ARAMARK Corporation

Exhibit 10   Hourly Reading Sheet

							HOURLY READING SHEET											

DAY		MARKETING WINDOW: LOCAL PROMOTION:																
Date	Open-12	12–1 PM	1–2 PM	2–3 PM	3–4 PM	4–5 PM	5–6 PM	6–7 PM	7–8 PM	8–9 PM	9–10 PM	10–11 PM	11–12 PM	12–1 AM	PROMO $	TOTAL SALES	COMMENTS

Courtesy of Pizza Hut, Inc.

Forecasting at Hilton Hotels

Hilton Hotels Corporation is the world's leading lodging and casino gaming company. Among its 247 properties are some of the most well-known hotels, including the Waldorf-Astoria and the Hilton Hawaiian Village. Hilton owns or has partial ownership of 31 hotels and manages 28 hotels for other owners. Hilton also has 172 franchised hotels, 12 hotel casinos, and four riverboats. Its total revenue in a recent year was nearly $4 billion, and its net income was $82 million. Its total assets exceed $7.5 billion.

The annual forecast at each property begins in mid-summer and is completed in September. Several steps are taken at the property level to arrive at the forecast, which is prepared in conjunction with Hilton's business plan for the year. Exhibit 13 is a form for comparing the 19X7 forecast of revenue, expenses, and other factors such as occupancy percentage and ADR to the 19X6 estimated results. In addition to this summary form, several additional detailed forms are provided for each property. A detailed form for the rooms department is shown in Exhibit 14. Similar detailed forms are required for each hotel's departments, including but not limited to food, beverage, telephone, and other operated departments.

Exhibit 15 includes an updated forecast for the month of November. An updated forecast is prepared on a monthly basis for each property. The updated forecast is compared to the current annual forecast (for November). The difference is shown in both dollars and as a percentage. In addition, the prior year's annual forecast and actual results ("last year" column) are also shown. For example, the rooms revenue for this property was originally forecasted to be $2,261,804. The updated forecast for November, most likely prepared in October, is $2,058,500. The difference is a reduction

Exhibit 11   Daily Labor Worksheet

DAILY LABOR WORKSHEET																													

Day:_____ Period _____

RESTAURANT NO.	PAN DOUGH	SPECIAL EVENTS/MARKETING	MARKETING WINDOW _____
	• # PPP's ____ x .0225 = ____	WK _____	
	• Morning Pan Batches (A.M.) ____	WK _____	
	• Afternoon Pan Batches (P.M.) ____	WK _____	
		WK _____	

HOUR	6	7	8	9	10	11	12	1	2	3	4	5	6	7	8	9	10	11	12	1	2		Promo $/Hrs	Total Sales/Hrs
PROJECTED SALES	PPP Hours	Basic Open	A.M. Pan	P.M. Pan																		Close All	Disc Hrs
GRID HOURS (DIRECT)		2.5																					
SCHEDULED DIRECT HOURS																							

JOB #	IN	OUT	6	7	8	9	10	11	12	1	2	3	4	5	6	7	8	9	10	11	12	1	2	3	IN	OUT	JOB #

Courtesy of Pizza Hut, Inc.

of $203,304 in rooms revenue, which is −8.99% when compared to the current annual forecast. In November of the prior year, the annual forecast was $2,282,233 in room sales, and the actual rooms revenue was $2,306,824.

Exhibit 12   Personal Pan Pizza Labor Scheduling Grid

PERSONAL PAN PIZZA
LABOR SCHEDULING GRID

COLUMN NUMBER	1	2	3	4	5	6	7	8	9	10	11	12	13	14	15	16
PROJECTED HOURLY NET SALES	0 TO 40	41 TO 59	60 TO 84	85 TO 115	116 TO 151	152 TO 174	175 TO 196	197 TO 237	238 TO 288	289 TO 331	332 TO 375	376 TO 436	437 TO 502	503 TO 594	595 TO 633	634 TO 673
PRODUCTION PERSON	0	1	1	1	1	1	1	1	2	2	2	2	2	2	3	3
SERVICE PERSON	1	1	2	2	2	2	3	3	3	4	4	4	4	4	4	5
REGISTER/TELEPHONE	0	0	0	0	1	1	1	1	1	1	2	2	2	3	3	3
BUS/DISHWASHER	0	0	0	0	0	0	0	1	1	1	1	1	2	2	2	2
BEVERAGE PERSON	0	0	0	0	0	0	0	0	0	0	0	1	1	1	1	1
PRODUCTION LEADER	1	1	1	1	1	1	1	1	1	1	1	1	1	1	1	1
HOST/HOSTESS	0	0	0	1	1	1	1	1	1	1	1	1	1	1	1	1
FLOOR MANAGER	0	0	0	0	0	1	1	1	1	1	1	1	1	1	1	1
TOTAL	2	3	4	5	6	7	8	9	10	11	12	13	14	15	16	17

OPENING ALLOWANCE
# of 6" PIZZAS PREPPED × .0225 HRS. = LUNCH PREP HOURS

Courtesy of Pizza Hut, Inc.

Finally, Exhibit 16 reflects the cumulative-to-date forecast of revenues and expenses for a Hilton property. At the bottom of this exhibit, note the occupancy, food cost, and beverage cost percentages. As expected, several of the numbers in Exhibit 16, such as the current monthly forecast for rooms, food, beverage, and total revenues, can be tracked to Exhibit 15.[9]

Computer Applications

Many of the forecasting methods discussed in this chapter would take a great deal of time to calculate manually. However, with the help of a computer and forecasting programs, they can be generated almost immediately. Even general software packages such as spreadsheets can calculate averages and perform trend extrapolation.

Exhibit 17 shows how management at the Jefferson Motel forecasts future room sales using moving averages. In order to do this, management first collects historical information—the number of rooms sold and the average rate for the last three weeks' business—and enters this information into the computer. At this point, the computer generates a forecast for the fourth week's sales by calculating the

Exhibit 13 Comparison of Annual Forecast to Estimated Results

HILTON HOTELS CORPORATION
For a Sample Property
Comparison of 19X7 Annual Forecast to 19X6 Estimated Results
(Amounts in thousands, except percentages)

	19X7 Annual Forecast	19X6 Estimated Results (1)	Increase (Decrease)
Revenue			
Rooms			
Food			
Beverage			
Telephone			
Other Operated Departments			
Interest Income			
Other Income			
Store/Office Building Rentals			
Total Revenue			
Departmental Profit			
Rooms			
Food			
Beverage			
Telephone			
Other Operated Departments			
Interest Income			
Other Income			
Store/Office Building Rentals			
Gross Operating Income			
Deductions From Income			
General and Administrative			
Accidents			
Marketing			
Property Operations			
Energy Costs			
Total Deductions			
Income Before Fixed Charges			
Capital and Other Expenses			
Site Rental			
Real Estate/Property Taxes			
Interest			
Depreciation			
Management Fee			
Sundry Capital Expenses			
Total Capital and Other Expenses			
Profit (Loss) Before Income Taxes			
Percentage of Occupancy			
Average Rate Per Room			
Guest Room Revenue			
Number of Rooms Available			

(continued)

Exhibit 13   *(continued)*

	19X7 Annual Forecast	19X6 Estimated Results (1)	Increase (Decrease)
Number of Rooms Occupied			
Convention			
Company Meetings			
Individual Business Traveler			
Leisure/Pleasure Traveler			
Permanents			
Total Occupied Rooms			
Average Room Rate			
Convention			
Company Meetings			
Individual Business Traveler			
Leisure/Pleasure Traveler			
Permanents			
Total Average Room Rate			
Room Revenue by Market Segment			
Convention			
Company Meetings			
Individual Business Traveler			
Lisure/Pleasure Traveler			
Permanents			
Total Segment Room Revenue			

Approved By: _____ _____
Regional Senior V.P.　　　　Date　　General Manager　　Date

(1) Based on eight months actual, September monthly forecast, and three months revised annual forecast.

Courtesy of Hilton Hotels Corporation

average of the same day of the week over the previous three weeks. In this case, it was estimated that 93 rooms would be sold on Monday, which is the average of 90, 95, and 93 (rounded to the nearest whole number). This information could be used for labor scheduling or for calculating the forecast of revenues. Average rate is calculated in the same fashion. The forecast of sales is the product of forecast room rate and rooms sold.

This worksheet can then be used to compare actual with forecast. For example, although 93 rooms were forecast to be sold on Monday, 95 rooms were actually sold, and management entered the actual results into the computer. When this number was input, the computer generated the variance figure between forecast and actual, and the forecast for the fifth week's rooms sold (the average of the second, third and fourth week's rooms sold). In this manner, management can enter each week's actual figures to calculate the next week's forecast. As a side effect, this also provides management with a record of performance that can be used in future periods as needed.

Exhibit 14   Annual Forecast for the Rooms Department

HILTON HOTELS CORPORATION
For a Sample Property
19X7 Annual Forecast
Rooms Department
(in thousands, except percentages)

	January	February	March	April	May	June	July	August	September	October	November	December	19X7 Annual Forecast	19X6 Estimated Results (1)
Revenue														
Guest Rooms Sales (2)														
Permanent Room Sales														
Public Room Sales														
Total Revenue														
Expenses														
Salaries & Wages														
P.T. & E.R. (Incl. meals)														
T.A. Commission														
Reservation Expense														
Laundry														
Guest & Other Supplies														
Operating Equipment														
Uniforms														
All Other Expenses														
Total Expenses														
Departmental Profit (Loss)														
Departmental Profit (Loss) as Percentage of Revenue														
Percentage of Occupancy (2)														
Average Room Rate (2)														

(1) Based on eight months actual, September monthly forecast, and three months revised annual forecast.

Approved By: _____   Date _____

Director of Front Office Operations

_____   Date _____

Director of Sales [as to (2) only]

Courtesy of Hilton Hotels Corporation

Exhibit 15   Comparison of Monthly Forecast with Annual Forecast

```
                              HILTON HOTELS CORPORATION
                                 FOR A SAMPLE PROPERTY
                     COMPARISON OF MONTHLY FORECAST WITH ANNUAL FORECAST
                                        NOVEMBER
```

	CURRENT MONTHLY FORECAST	CURRENT ANNUAL FORECAST	INCREASE (DECREASE) PROFIT**	VARIANCE %	PRIOR ANNUAL FORECAST	LAST YEAR
Revenue						
Rooms	2,058,500	2,261,804	(203,304)	-8.99%	2,282,233	2,306,824
Food	801,700	774,630	27,070	3.49%	782,120	876,732
Beverage	278,700	255,020	23,680	9.29%	322,000	229,791
Telephone	76,400	87,200	(10,800)	-12.39%	90,700	85,804
Other operated departments	21,600	23,200	(1,600)	-6.90%	24,800	29,778
Interest income	0	0	0	0.00%	0	0
Other income	26,600	35,300	(8,700)	-24.65%	41,950	47,883
Store/office building rentals	0	0	0	0.00%	0	0
Total revenue	3,263,500	3,437,154	(173,654)	-5.05%	3,543,803	3,576,812
Departmental profit (loss)						
Rooms	1,439,300	1,631,337	(192,037)	-11.77%	1,615,059	1,623,591
Food	60,100	34,540	25,560	74.00%	37,015	82,781
Beverage	167,800	155,916	11,884	7.62%	198,600	141,719
Telephone	10,000	21,300	(11,300)	-53.05%	23,000	17,527
Other operated departments	(1,800)	310	(2,110)	-680.65%	1,165	6,863
Interest income	0	0	0	0.00%	0	0
Other income	26,600	35,300	(8,700)	-24.65%	41,950	47,883
Store/office building rentals	0	0	0	0.00%	0	0
Gross operating income	1,702,000	1,878,703	(176,703)	-9.41%	1,916,789	1,920,364
Deductions from income						
General and administrative	223,100	236,600	13,500	5.71%	275,705	281,056
Accidents	85,000	85,000	0	0.00%	0	0
Marketing	230,800	204,485	(26,315)	-12.87%	207,980	205,837
Property operations	202,100	206,384	4,284	2.08%	220,800	155,936
Energy costs	144,000	143,991	(9)	-0.01%	138,800	154,209
Total deductions from income	885,000	876,460	(8,540)	-0.97%	843,285	797,038
Income Before Fixed Charges	817,000	1,002,243	(185,243)	-18.48%	1,073,504	1,123,326
Capital and other charges						
Site rental	0	0	0	0.00%	0	0
Real estate/property taxes	164,000	164,000	0	0.00%	164,000	148,877
Interest	0	0	0	0.00%	0	0
Depreciation	0	0	0	0.00%	0	0
Management fee	65,320	83,274	17,954	21.56%	90,500	97,071
Sundry capital/other expenses	15,000	15,000	0	0.00%	15,000	14,305
Total capital/other expenses	244,320	262,274	17,954	6.85%	269,500	260,253
Profit (loss) before income taxes	572,680	739,969	(167,289)	-22.61%	804,004	863,073
Percentage of occupancy	56.72	55.28	1.44	2.61%	55.65	59.30
Average rate per room	98.63	110.54	-11.91	-10.77%	110.65	105.69
Number of occupied rooms						
Convention	13,285	12,650	635	5.02%	12,980	15,259
Company Meetings	2,579	2,435	144	5.91%	2,825	1,488
Individual Business Traveler	2,250	2,925	(675)	-23.08%	2,925	2,543
Leisure/Pleasure Travlers	2,115	1,959	156	7.96%	1,375	1,965
Permanent	600	330	270	81.82%	330	519
Total Occupied Rooms	20,829	20,299	530	2.61%	20,435	21,774
Average Rate						
Convention	105.63	113.91	-8.28	-7.27%	109.41	109.11
Company Meetings	77.50	97.81	-20.31	-20.76%	100.78	100.35
Individual Business Traveler	116.75	126.04	-9.29	-7.37%	143.08	115.71
Leisure/Pleasure Travlers	80.14	93.51	-13.37	-14.30%	90.91	87.89
Permanent	32.00	39.00	-7.00	-17.95%	39.00	39.00
Total Average Rate	98.63	110.54	-11.91	-10.77%	110.65	105.69

Courtesy of Hilton Hotels Corporation

Exhibit 16   Cumulative-to-Date Forecast

HILTON HOTELS CORPORATION
FOR A SAMPLE PROPERTY
FORECAST OF BUSINESS FOR THE MONTH OF NOVEMBER
CUMULATIVE-TO-DATE

			REVENUES				COST OF SALES		PAYROLL		
									ROOMS	FOOD & BEVERAGE	ALL OTHERS
DAY	DATE	ROOMS	FOOD	BEVERAGE	OTHER	TOTAL	FOOD	BEVERAGE			
SUN	1	34,818	20,240	4,700	2,403	62,161	6,050	942	9,694	8,236	1,734
MON	2	42,647	27,710	7,300	4,604	102,261	8,283	1,464	19,144	18,333	13,140
TUE	3	109,959	40,300	11,300	7,356	168,915	12,046	2,266	28,697	28,512	24,714
WED	4	184,724	59,900	18,700	11,506	274,830	17,904	3,749	39,417	39,205	36,491
THU	5	263,154	107,990	25,000	16,085	412,229	32,278	5,013	51,357	51,751	48,687
FRI	6	334,172	139,870	33,100	20,757	527,899	41,807	6,637	63,530	63,923	60,367
SAT	7	384,535	178,720	41,550	24,452	629,257	53,419	8,331	74,644	73,427	62,222
SUN	8	417,213	196,300	45,850	30,054	689,417	58,674	9,193	84,091	82,023	63,956
MON	9	488,836	212,430	50,750	33,020	785,036	63,495	10,175	94,134	92,032	75,362
TUE	10	648,083	277,660	66,500	38,042	1,030,285	82,993	13,333	105,617	103,953	87,192
WED	11	813,453	349,160	82,350	43,476	1,288,439	104,364	16,511	119,320	116,154	99,174
THU	12	920,122	390,480	88,400	47,717	1,446,719	116,714	17,724	132,776	128,074	111,267
FRI	13	973,822	438,950	99,750	51,090	1,563,612	131,202	20,000	145,004	141,227	122,794
SAT	14	1,049,187	474,020	108,950	59,845	1,692,002	141,685	21,844	154,542	151,252	124,751
SUN	15	1,160,551	498,170	128,850	64,636	1,852,207	148,903	25,834	164,998	162,232	126,792
MON	16	1,265,155	519,470	151,250	68,883	2,004,758	155,270	30,326	178,277	174,669	138,403
TUE	17	1,389,782	541,560	174,050	73,467	2,178,859	161,872	34,897	191,048	186,693	150,233
WED	18	1,519,970	570,470	200,350	78,265	2,369,055	170,513	40,170	204,242	198,557	162,113
THU	19	1,644,714	597,690	225,050	83,279	2,550,733	178,650	45,123	216,769	210,590	174,309
FRI	20	1,718,273	649,500	233,800	89,135	2,690,708	194,136	46,877	230,279	223,233	185,989
SAT	21	1,769,690	686,140	244,000	93,043	2,792,873	205,087	48,922	240,699	232,734	187,844
SUN	22	1,779,642	696,580	246,700	94,897	2,817,819	208,208	49,463	249,985	240,560	189,526
MON	23	1,785,914	701,720	248,500	96,134	2,832,268	209,744	49,824	258,034	249,933	200,881
TUE	24	1,790,880	705,160	250,000	97,268	2,843,308	210,772	50,125	270,791	259,697	212,452
WED	25	1,798,862	711,300	251,900	98,618	2,860,680	212,608	50,506	278,729	269,080	223,948
THU	26	1,845,739	729,640	256,900	102,751	2,935,030	218,089	51,508	292,289	288,832	236,807
FRI	27	1,898,172	748,580	262,500	107,107	3,016,359	223,751	52,631	303,576	300,540	248,462
SAT	28	1,952,128	768,420	268,400	111,462	3,100,410	229,681	53,814	313,959	309,147	250,419
SUN	29	1,985,734	782,560	272,200	113,990	3,154,484	233,907	54,576	324,941	316,922	252,153
MON	30	2,058,500	797,300	277,500	130,200	3,263,500	238,313	55,639	335,400	327,300	263,500
LAST NOV		2,306,824	876,732	229,791	163,465	3,576,812	237,625	43,149	327,207	343,924	205,354
ANNUAL		2,261,804	774,630	255,020	145,700	3,437,154	228,400	50,140	323,151	327,400	260,379

	% OF OCCUPANCY	FOOD COST %	BEVERAGE COST %
MONTHLY FORECAST	56.72%	29.89%	20.05%
ACTUAL LAST NOV	59.30%	27.30%	18.90%
ANNUAL FORECAST	55.28%	29.73%	19.96%

Courtesy of Hilton Hotels Corporation

As an extension of this worksheet, management also has the computer generate a graph of the variance between actual and forecast room sales (see Exhibit 18).

OTHER EXPENSES	CAPITAL	PROFIT (LOSS)	LAST YEAR PROFIT (LOSS)	OCCUPIED ROOMS TODAY	TO DATE	AVERAGE RATE TODAY	TO DATE
33,230	5,657	(3,382)	35,756	320	320	108.49	108.49
62,068	8,834	(29,004)	86,393	313	633	88.59	98.65
95,324	14,011	(36,654)	124,952	500	1,133	94.62	96.87
135,198	21,978	(19,112)	168,797	868	2,001	85.99	92.15
182,762	31,145	9,236	224,191	976	2,977	80.14	88.22
225,387	39,152	27,096	266,507	946	3,923	74.89	85.00
266,418	47,029	43,767	313,232	661	4,584	76.04	83.71
298,641	52,656	40,183	315,182	315	4,899	103.58	84.99
336,349	60,143	53,345	357,334	552	5,451	129.03	89.45
400,679	77,870	158,648	400,512	1,135	6,586	139.95	98.15
467,492	96,177	269,247	436,839	1,181	7,767	140.03	104.52
516,992	107,374	315,797	484,788	834	8,601	127.72	106.77
561,091	114,711	327,583	530,932	580	9,181	92.50	105.87
605,117	125,188	367,623	577,519	887	10,068	84.77	104.01
652,788	138,395	432,265	667,006	1,016	11,084	109.61	104.52
698,796	149,652	479,366	755,789	855	11,939	122.23	105.79
748,042	162,779	543,295	860,562	993	12,932	125.34	107.29
800,264	176,916	616,279	926,728	1,044	13,976	124.55	108.58
851,253	190,423	683,617	924,335	1,104	15,080	112.63	108.88
899,170	199,540	711,485	911,323	891	15,971	82.11	107.38
940,103	207,607	729,877	946,981	712	16,683	71.86	105.87
966,877	210,594	702,606	977,584	136	16,819	73.18	105.60
991,603	211,921	660,328	1,031,951	78	16,897	77.85	105.47
1,015,690	212,498	611,283	1,042,103	61	16,958	78.13	105.38
1,041,028	214,015	570,766	996,320	124	17,082	63.65	105.07
1,076,361	218,072	553,071	958,724	807	17,889	58.09	102.95
1,112,794	223,839	550,766	915,035	891	18,780	58.85	100.86
1,149,695	231,166	562,529	848,693	887	19,667	60.83	99.06
1,181,274	236,263	554,448	826,147	412	20,079	81.57	98.70
1,226,348	244,320	572,680	863,073	750	20,829	97.02	98.64
1,296,227	260,253	863,073			21,774		105.69
1,245,441	262,274	739,969			20,299		110.54

This very quickly highlights the week's results; although the weekday sales were close to forecast, the weekend sales were significantly below forecast. This graph is

Exhibit 17 Moving Average Forecast Worksheet—Jefferson Motel

Moving Average Forecast Worksheet
Jefferson Motel

ROOMS SOLD Day	Historical Week 1	Week 2	Week 3	X	Forecast Week 4	Actual Week 4	Variance	X	Forecast Week 5	Actual Week 5	Variance
Monday	90	95	93	X	93	95	2	X	94		
Tuesday	92	90	92	X	91	92	1	X	91		
Wednesday	99	94	95	X	96	94	−1	X	95		
Thursday	89	85	99	X	91	94	3	X	92		
Friday	51	40	44	X	45	40	−5	X	43		
Saturday	33	30	32	X	32	30	−2	X	31		
Sunday	45	50	51	X	49	52	3	X	50		

AVERAGE RATE Day	Historical Week 1	Week 2	Week 3	X	Forecast Week 4	Actual Week 4	Variance	X	Forecast Week 5	Actual Week 5	Variance
Monday	$62.50	$61.50	$63.00	X	$62.33	$61.52	($0.81)	X	$62.28		
Tuesday	62.50	65.00	64.90	X	64.13	62.89	−1.24	X	64.68		
Wednesday	65.00	65.00	65.50	X	65.17	65.70	0.53	X	65.22		
Thursday	62.50	61.00	62.50	X	62.00	62.50	0.50	X	61.83		
Friday	50.00	47.00	43.00	X	46.67	44.44	−2.23	X	45.56		
Saturday	47.80	49.00	40.00	X	45.60	41.25	−4.35	X	44.87		
Sunday	$60.00	$59.80	$62.50	X	$60.77	$65.23	$4.46	X	$61.02		

SALES INFORMATION

Day	Forecast Week 4	Actual Week 4	Variance	X	Forecast Week 5	Actual Week 5	Variance
Monday	$5,776.22	$5,844.40	$68.18	X	$5,826.43		
Tuesday	5,857.51	5,785.88	−71.63	X	5,892.86		
Wednesday	6,256.00	6,175.80	−80.20	X	6,196.11		
Thursday	5,642.00	5,875.00	233.00	X	5,668.06		
Friday	2,100.00	1,777.60	−322.40	X	1,958.89		
Saturday	1,444.00	1,237.50	−206.50	X	1,400.84		
Sunday	$2,957.31	$3,391.96	$434.65	X	$3,044.33		

used because it quickly alerts managers to potential problems. They can then take timely actions.

Management could also use the computer to generate more sophisticated forecasts. There are programs available which perform linear regression, exponential smoothing, multiple regression, and many other methods mentioned in this chapter.[10]

Summary

Forecasting is simply the process of estimating the levels of some future activity such as sales. After an initial sales forecast has been made, the hospitality operation must plan to ensure the desired outcome is achieved.

Forecasts may be implicit or explicit. Implicit forecasts are implied by the expectations reflected by managers' actions when no explicit forecast has been made.

Exhibit 18   Forecast vs. Actual—Jefferson Motel

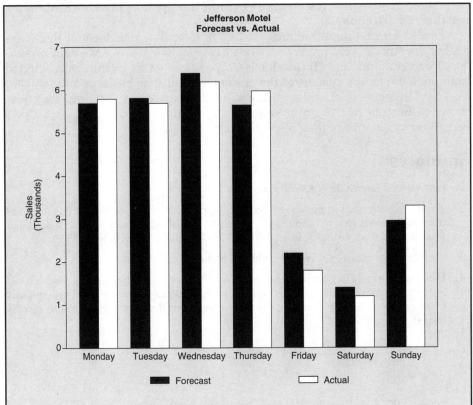

In this chapter, we focused on explicit forecasts; that is, on deliberate attempts to estimate levels of future activities. Explicit forecasting techniques provide managers with rational foundations for planning.

Since forecasting deals with the future, it inevitably involves uncertainty. In addition, since forecasts are made on the basis of historical data, they are predicated on the risky assumption that the past will be indicative of the future.

Patterns in existing data include trend, seasonal, and cyclical. A trend is simply the long-run projection of an activity being evaluated. Seasonal patterns exist when a series of data fluctuates according to a seasonal pattern, such as seasons of the year. Cyclical patterns represent movements along a trend line.

Forecasting methods covered in the chapter included both quantitative and qualitative approaches, with the emphasis on the former. Quantitative methods discussed included naive methods, moving averages, exponential smoothing, and single regression analysis. Limitations of quantitative methods, such as scarce data and the inability to consider unforeseeable occurrences, sometimes render quantitative methods less useful. When these limitations are significant, qualitative methods may be used. The qualitative methods covered briefly in this chapter included market research, jury of executive opinion, sales force estimates, and the Delphi technique.

Finally, forecasting techniques used by unit-level management at three hospitality operations were presented. The three operations—ARAMARK Corporation, Pizza Hut, Inc., and Hilton Hotels Corporation—were intentionally selected from three different segments of the hospitality industry: business and industry food service, commercial food service, and hotels, respectively. Although they were chosen to illustrate different applications of forecasting methods, they are not necessarily representative of their respective segments.

Endnotes

1. *Host Marriott Services 1996 Annual Report,* pp. 2–3.

2. The reader interested in pursuing forecasting approaches shown in Exhibit 3 that are not discussed in this chapter should see Steven C. Wheelwright and Spyros Makridakis, *Forecasting Methods for Management,* 5th ed. (New York: John Wiley & Sons, 1989).

3. For more information, see Wheelwright and Makridakis.

4. Using this formula, a number between 0 and -1 is also possible. Such a result would indicate a negative relationship. In practical terms, a negative result is extremely unlikely in hospitality forecasting because the forecasting variables generally used are directly related.

5. $a = \dfrac{\Sigma x^2 \Sigma y - \Sigma x \Sigma xy}{n\Sigma x^2 - (\Sigma x)^2}$ *or* $a = \dfrac{\Sigma y}{n} - \dfrac{b\Sigma x}{n}$

   $b = \dfrac{n\Sigma xy - \Sigma x \Sigma y}{n\Sigma x^2 - (\Sigma x)^2}$

6. The interested reader should see *Forecasting Methods for Management.*

7. This information was provided by Richard C. Sisca, Vice President—CFO, Correctional Services, ARAMARK Corporation.

8. This information was provided by Mike Landrum, Director of Training, Pizza Hut, Inc.

9. This information was provided by Fran Weigand, Vice President of Hotel Financial Operations, Hilton Hotels Corporation.

10. For more information on the use of spreadsheet programs for forecasting, see Hugh S. McLaughlin and J. Russell Boulding, *Financial Management with Lotus 1-2-3* (New York: Prentice-Hall, 1986).

Key Terms

capture ratios—Ratios based on hotel guests or some variation of hotel guests. For example, a hotel may estimate its dinner covers to be 40 plus one quarter of the estimated house guests for the night.

causal forecasting approaches—Forecasts made on the assumption that the future value of one variable is a function of other variables.

coefficient of correlation—A mathematical measure of the relation between the dependent variable and independent variables used in causal forecasting methods. May be any number between –1 and +1, inclusive.

coefficient of determination—A measure that reflects the extent to which the change in the independent variable explains the change in the dependent variable. The square of the coefficient of correlation; a number between 0 and +1.

cyclical pattern—A pattern of data (for example, sales activity) that fluctuates around a trend line according to some regular time period.

exponential smoothing—A forecasting method that uses a smoothing constant (a number between 0 and 1), along with recent actual and forecasted data, to reflect the relative stability or growth of the activity being forecasted.

moving averages—Averaging data from specified time periods in a continually updating manner such that as new results become available, they are used in the average by adding the most recent value and dropping the earliest value.

multiple regression analysis—Regression analysis forecasting used when two or more independent variables are related to the dependent variable.

qualitative forecasting methods—Forecasting methods that emphasize human judgment.

quantitative forecasting methods—Causal and time series approaches to forecasting.

regression analysis—A mathematical approach to fitting a straight line to data points such that the differences in the distances of the data points from the line are minimized; used in forecasting when a dependent variable (for example, restaurant covers) to be forecasted is thought to be causally related to one or more independent variables (for example, rooms sold).

seasonal pattern—A pattern of data (for example, sales activity) that shows regular fluctuations according to some time period (daily, weekly, monthly, yearly).

smoothing constant—A value used in the exponential smoothing forecasting method. Determined using forecasts from two consecutive previous periods and the actual demand from the earlier of these two periods.

time series forecasting approaches—Forecasts made on the assumption that an underlying pattern is recurring over time.

trend pattern—A pattern of data (for example, sales activity) characterized by a general direction whose long-run estimate is projected into the future.

Review Questions

1. What is the difference between implicit and explicit forecasts?
2. How do forecasting and planning differ?
3. What are the purposes and limitations of forecasting?
4. How do cyclical and seasonal patterns of data differ?

5. What are the differences between quantitative and qualitative forecasting methods?

6. How do causal forecasting methods differ from time series methods?

7. How is a moving average calculated?

8. When are exponential smoothing techniques most useful?

9. How can regression analysis be used to forecast food revenues based on occupancy percentage?

✎ Problems

Problem 1

The Oceanside Cafe bases its forecasts of monthly lunch sales on the lunch sales for the prior year. It projects customer counts will increase by 5% each month, and prices have been increased by $.50 per lunch served over the past year. Lunch sales for the first three months of 19X2 were as follows:

	Customers	Average Lunch Price
January	3,000	$7.95
February	2,750	$8.05
March	3,050	$8.00

Required:

Forecast the lunch sales in dollars for the first three months of 19X3.

Problem 2

The Aleidon Middle School forecasts its lunch meals using the exponential smoothing method discussed in this chapter. The recent results and forecasts have been as follows:

	Forecast	Actual Demand
Day 1	300	320
Day 2	310	330

Required:

1. Determine the smoothing constant.
2. Provide the forecast of lunch meals for Day 3.

Problem 3

The Rivera Golf Club's golf pro desires your assistance in forecasting rounds of golf for the months of June, July, and August of 19X4. She believes the activity for the past three years will be useful, but indicates they should be weighted by 1/6, 1/3, and 1/2 for the three years of 19X1–19X3, respectively. The rounds of golf played in the past were as follows:

	19X1	19X2	19X3
June	4,200	4,140	4,250
July	5,400	5,700	5,350
August	5,100	4,890	5,200

Required:

Forecast the rounds of golf for the months of June, July, and August of 19X4 based on the above information.

Problem 4

Mason High School's lunch covers are forecasted based on a moving average. The numbers of covers served by day for the past five weeks are as follows:

	Weeks					
	1	2	3	4	5	6
Monday	648	622	639	642	653	
Tuesday	610	618	623	609	630	
Wednesday	632	621	642	631	629	
Thursday	641	648	632	629	642	
Friday	751	730	756	740	745	

Required:

Forecast the number of meals for each day of week six using the five-week moving average method.

Problem 5

Mr. Jim Wheat, manager of the Plains Motel, has decided to forecast monthly room sales for the next three years. The monthly sales for 19X1 were as follows:

January	$194,321	July	$185,197
February	187,296	August	180,200
March	198,431	September	206,711
April	197,911	October	215,840
May	215,640	November	201,612
June	210,411	December	165,411

Jim believes that sales will increase 5% in 19X2, another 5% in 19X3, and another 6% in 19X4.

Required:

Using the above information, prepare the three-year sales forecast by month for the Plains Motel.

Problem 6

Servco operates the hot lunch program at Acres Elementary School. The weekly sales forecast necessary for ordering food provisions and scheduling labor is based on a three-week moving average, that is, Monday's forecast is based on the average sales of the prior three Mondays. The forecast is modified based on a number of factors, including weather. The weather modification is that sales are expected to increase moderately as the school year progresses into cooler weather and to decrease moderately with warmer weather in the spring. In addition, rainy days result in significant increases in sales.

The sales for weeks 4 through 6 were as follows:

	Week 4	Week 5	Week 6
Monday	$450	$460	$475
Tuesday	420	435	440
Wednesday	440	438	520
Thursday	430	445	450
Friday	410	420	435

Required:

Using the above results, answer the following questions:

1. What type of weather trend do the above figures suggest? Why?
2. Which day did it appear to rain?

Problem 7

This problem is a continuation of Problem 6. Karin Smith, manager of Servco, desires assistance in preparing the sales forecast for Week 7. To prepare the weekly sales forecast, the days' sales of the prior three weeks are averaged and modified by $20 for expected weather changes. In addition, if a rainy day is expected, an additional $70 of sales is expected.

Required:

Prepare the weekly sales forecast by day for Week 7. Assume that the winter season is approaching, that is, it is expected that Week 7 will be cooler than Week 6. Further, use $450 for sales for Wednesday of Week 6 in place of actual sales of $520. Finally, assume that Monday of Week 7 is expected to be a rainy day.

Problem 8

Part I

The Westsider has asked for your assistance in forecasting its room sales and food service sales. To forecast room sales for the week of May 18–24 (Week 4), it considers its group reservations and uses a moving average of the non-group hotel guests rooms sold for the prior three weeks. This moving average then is increased by 2%. Data for the past three weeks are as follows:

	Non-Group Hotel Guests Rooms			Week 4		
	Week 1	Week 2	Week 3	Group Reservations	Non-Group Guests	Total
Sunday	150	160	164	215	_____	_____
Monday	250	270	290	240	_____	_____
Tuesday	245	275	305	250	_____	_____
Wednesday	250	270	260	240	_____	_____
Thursday	240	240	249	200	_____	_____
Friday	120	110	130	50	_____	_____
Saturday	80	90	100	60	_____	_____

Required:

Complete the two right columns above. Round your forecast to the nearest whole number.

Part II

To forecast its food service breakfast sales, the Westsider uses the following formula:

$$y = a + bx_1 + cx_2$$

where	x_1	=	hotel guests
	x_2	=	hotel guests at the economy motel adjacent to the Westsider
	a	=	non-hotel (Westsider and the economy motel) guests eating breakfast
	b	=	percentage of hotel guests expected to eat breakfast
	c	=	percentage of economy motel guests that are expected to eat at the Westsider

Additional information is as follows:

1. $x_2 = 80$
2. $b = .8$
3. $c = .3$
4. $a = 20$

Required:

Forecast breakfast sales for Monday.

Problem 9

The Harris Hotel forecasts its breakfast covers based on (1) its prior night room guests count, (2) an estimated number of diners from the local community, and (3) an estimated number of guests who are staying at a nearby limited-service hotel and will have breakfast at the Harris Hotel. The formula used is as follows:

$$X = 30 + .8(B) + .2(C)$$

where	X	=	forecasted breakfast covers
	B	=	number of prior night room guests at the Harris Hotel
	C	=	number of prior night room guests at the nearby limited-service hotel

The estimated numbers of hotel guests are as follows:

	B	C
Sunday	200	100
Monday	300	140
Tuesday	310	120
Wednesday	320	130
Thursday	310	140
Friday	140	80
Saturday	100	90

Required:

1. Forecast the number of breakfast covers for Monday through Saturday.
2. Comment on the relevance of a three-period moving average and of the causal approach used by the Harris Hotel.

Problem 10

The Evergreen Hotel, a 200-room lodging facility, uses regression analysis to forecast dining room meals. Larry Spruce, the manager, has indicated the regression equations used are as follows:

$$y = 50 + .42x \text{ (breakfast)}$$
$$y = 200 + .21x \text{ (lunch)}$$
$$y = 450 + .35x \text{ (dinner)}$$

where y equals forecasted meals
  x equals the number of hotel guests

Further, the average check in the hotel's dining room is expected to be as follows:

Breakfast:	$ 3.25
Lunch:	$ 6.50
Dinner:	$12.95

Required:

Forecast daily sales by meal period when the occupancy percentage is expected to be 85% (all rooms are available for sale) and the average occupancy per room is expected to be 1.58.

Problem 11

The Marcus Motel uses the moving average approach to forecast its rooms sales for each week and linear regression for forecasting its food sales. The moving average approach utilizes the most recent five weeks of actual data. An adjustment is made for extremes as follows: If during the five weeks the actual rooms sold for a week differed by more than 30% from the budgeted room sales for that week, the actual is considered to an extreme. In such cases, the extreme is ignored and the budgeted number of rooms sold is used in its place.

The rooms sold for the five preceding weeks were as follows:

	Rooms Budgeted	Rooms Sold
May 24–31	660	460
June 1–7	710	700
June 8–14	720	710
June 15–21	710	930
June 22–28	715	710
June 29–July 5	??	??

The average occupancy per room sold is expected to be 1.8 for June 29–July 5. The regression equations used to forecast the number of meals to be sold are as follows:

Breakfast covers	=	50	+	.8(x)
Lunch covers	=	150	+	.2(x)
Dinner covers	=	60	+	.6(x)

where x = Number of motel room guests not committed to food functions for that day

Room guests committed to food functions (other than the restaurant) for June 29 are as follows:

Breakfast:	50
Lunch:	100
Dinner:	–0–

Required:

1. Calculate the expected number of rooms to be sold for the week of June 29–July 5.

2. Calculate the number of meals to be sold for breakfast, lunch, and dinner in the motel's restaurant for June 29. Assume 100 rooms are sold for June 29.

Problem 12

The Brunner forecasts its daily room sales based on the moving average of the prior three weeks' daily sales. Adjustments are made for holidays and seasonal trends as follows:

- If a holiday occurred during the prior three weeks, the day containing the holiday is adjusted by multiplying it by 1.67.

- If a holiday occurs during the forecast week, the forecasted daily sales based on the moving average are reduced by 40%.

- In estimating daily sales for the month of June, the moving average is adjusted upward by 3%.

Room sales for the prior three weeks were as follows:

	May 25–31	June 1–7	June 8–14	June 15–21
Sunday	160	165	168	_____
Monday	180 (holiday)	310	312	_____
Tuesday	300	315	318	_____
Wednesday	310	305	315	_____
Thursday	320	310	315	_____
Friday	180	185	190	_____
Saturday	170	174	177	_____

Required:

Calculate the expected room sales for the week of June 15–21. Round your answer to the nearest whole room. Show all of your work.

Problem 13

The Grand Hotel has 300 rooms and is expected to have a 90% occupancy for Monday through Thursday nights, June 16–19, and 50% occupancy the remaining nights of the week. The average occupancy per room of the Grand Hotel is 1.6 on weekends (Friday–Sunday) and 1.4 on weekdays. The expected luncheon average prices are $4.95 for weekdays and $5.95 for weekends. The regression equations to estimate luncheon covers are as follows:

Lunch covers for weekdays $= 50 + .6(x_1) + .1(x_2)$

Lunch covers for weekend days $= 150 + .4(x_1) + .2(x_2)$

x_1 = number of lodging guests at the Grand Hotel

x_2 = number of lodging guests at the Fairview Inn, a rooms-only lodging property

The projected room sales and average occupancy for the Fairview Inn for June 15–21 are as follows:

		Room Sales	Average Occupancy/Room
June 15	Sunday	60	1.2
June 16	Monday	80	1.1
June 17	Tuesday	80	1.05
June 18	Wednesday	80	1.05
June 19	Thursday	80	1.1
June 20	Friday	40	1.6
June 21	Saturday	30	2.0

Required:

Forecast the Grand Hotel's luncheon sales in dollars and covers for each day for June 15–21.

Problem 14

The Merry Motel uses the moving average approach to forecast its rooms sales for each week and linear regression for forecasting its food sales. The moving average approach utilizes the most recent five weeks of actual data. An adjustment is made for holidays as follows:

- If the holiday occurred during the prior five weeks, the week containing the holiday is adjusted by multiplying it by 110%.

- If the holiday occurs during the forecast week, the forecasted estimate based on the moving average is reduced by 10%.

The rooms sold for the five preceding weeks were as follows:

	Rooms Budgeted	Rooms Sold	Holidays
May 24–31	660	640	Memorial Day (May 30)
June 1–7	710	700	—
June 8–14	720	710	—
June 15–21	710	720	—
June 22–28	715	710	—
June 29–July 5	??	??	July 4

The average occupancy per room sold is expected to be 1.6 for June 29–July 5.

The regression equations used to forecast the number of meals to be sold are as follows:

Breakfast covers	=	50 +	.8(number of hotel room guests)
Lunch covers	=	150 +	.2(number of hotel room guests)
Dinner covers	=	60 +	.6(number of hotel room guests)

Required:

1. Calculate the expected number of rooms to be sold for the week of June 29–July 5.

2. Calculate the number of meals to be sold for breakfast, lunch, and dinner for the week of June 29–July 5.

Problem 15

The Sunset Inn's room guests and breakfast covers served in 19X1 were as follows:

	Room Guests	Breakfast Covers
January	1,010	1,200
February	960	1,010
March	1,100	1,260
April	1,050	1,230
May	1,210	1,350
June	1,190	1,280
July	1,150	1,320
August	1,200	1,340
September	1,180	1,260
October	1,120	1,250
November	1,010	1,160
December	910	1,005

Required:

1. Determine the coefficient of correlation for the Sunset Inn based on the above data.

2. Determine a regression equation for forecasting breakfast covers based on the number of room guests.

3. If 1,050 room guests are forecasted for January, how many breakfast covers are forecasted to be served?

Chapter 10 Outline

Types of Budgets
Budgeting Horizons
Reasons for Budgeting
Personnel Responsible for Budget Preparation
The Budget Preparation Process
    Forecasting Revenue
    Estimating Expenses
    Projecting Fixed Charges
    Budget Formulation Illustrated
    Flexible Budgets
    Budgeting for a New Lodging Property
Budgetary Control
Determination of Variances
Determination of Significant Variances
Variance Analysis
    Revenue Variance Analysis
    Cost of Goods Sold Analysis
    Variable Labor Variance Analysis
    Variance Analysis of Sands Motel's Significant Variances
Determination of Problems and Management Action
Reforecasting
    Reforecasting at The Sheraton Corporation
        The Three Month Outlook
        The Advanced Information for Outlook
        The Weekly Activity Report
Budgeting at Multi-Unit Hospitality Enterprises
Budgeting at The Sheraton Corporation

10

Operations Budgeting

Every rational manager plans for the future. Some plans are formal and others are informal. Budgets are formal plans reduced to dollars. Budgets provide answers to many questions, including the following:

1. What are the forecasted revenues for the month?

2. What is the budgeted labor for the year?

3. How many rooms are expected to be sold during any given month, and what is the expected average room rate?

4. What is the budgeted telephone department operating income for the month?

5. What is the estimated depreciation for the year?

6. How close were actual food and beverage revenues to the budgeted amounts for the month?

7. What is the projected net income for the year?

This chapter is divided into two major sections. The first section investigates reasons for budgeting, the process of preparing the operations budget, and the idea of budgeting horizons. The second section focuses on budgetary control and on how hospitality operations use budget reports in the budgetary control process. The Sands Motel, a hypothetical small lodging operation, is used to illustrate both budget preparation and control.

Types of Budgets

Hospitality operations prepare several types of budgets. The **operations budget,** the topic of this chapter, is also referred to as the revenue and expense budget, because it includes management's plans for generating revenues and incurring expenses for a given period. The operations budget includes not only operated department budgets (budgets for rooms, food, beverage, telephone, and other profit centers), but also budgets for service centers such as marketing, accounting, and human resources. In addition, the operations budget includes the planned expenses for depreciation, interest expense, and other fixed charges. Thus, the operations budget is a detailed operating plan by profit centers, cost centers within profit centers (such as the housekeeping department within the rooms department), and service centers.[1] It includes all revenues and all expenses that appear on the income statement and related subsidiary schedules. Annual operating budgets are normally subdivided into monthly periods. Certain information is reduced to a daily basis for management's use in controlling operations. The operations budget enables management to accomplish two of its major functions: planning and control.

Two other types of budgets are the cash budget and the capital budget. The cash budget is management's plan for cash receipts and disbursements. Capital budgeting pertains to planning for the acquisition of equipment, land, buildings, and other property and equipment.

Budgeting Horizons

The annual operations budget must be subdivided into monthly plans in order for management to use it effectively as an aid in monitoring operations. The monthly plans allow management to measure the operation's overall performance several times throughout the year. Certain elements of the monthly plan are then reduced to weekly and daily bases. For example, many lodging operations have daily revenue plans that differ by property, by day of the week, and by season. The daily revenue is compared to these daily revenue goals on the daily report of operations. Any significant differences (variances) require analysis, determination of causes, and, if necessary, corrective action. (Variance analysis will be discussed later in this chapter.) In addition, every month all revenue and expense amounts are compared to the budgeted amounts, and all significant variances are analyzed and explained.

Alternatives to the monthly breakdown of annual budgets are using thirteen 4-week segments or the 4-4-5 quarterly plan. The 4-4-5 plan consists of two 4-week plans followed by one 5-week, equaling the thirteen weeks in a quarter. Four of these quarterly plans serve as the annual operations budget.

Many hospitality organizations also prepare operations budgets on a long-range basis. A common long-range period is five years. A five-year plan consists of five annual plans. The annual plans for the second through fifth years are much less detailed than the current year's annual plan. When long-range budgets are used, the next year's budget serves as a starting point for preparing the operations budget. The long-range budget procedure is used to review and update the next four years and add the fifth year to the plan.

Long-range planning, also referred to as **strategic planning,** is recognized as essential to the controlled growth of major hospitality organizations. It not only considers revenues and expenses (as do annual operating plans), but also evaluates and selects from among major alternatives those that provide long-range direction to the hospitality operation. Major directional considerations may include the following:

- Evaluating whether a proposed acquisition will have a positive effect on existing operations or whether it will hinder or detract from existing operations

- Determining whether the hospitality operation should expand into foreign markets

- Determining whether a quick-service restaurant chain should add breakfast to its existing lunch and dinner offerings

- Considering whether a single-property operation should add rooms or possibly expand to include another property

Reasons for Budgeting

Many small organizations in the hospitality industry have not formalized their operations budgets. Often, the overall goals, sales objectives, expense projections, and the desired bottom line remain "in the head" of the owner/manager. However, there are many reasons every hospitality operation should use formalized budgeting. Several of these are briefly described below:

1. Budgeting requires management to examine alternatives before selecting a particular course of action. For example, there are pricing alternatives for each product and/or service sold. Also, there are many different marketing decisions that must be made, such as where to advertise, how much to advertise, how to promote, when to promote, and so on. There are also several approaches to staffing, each of which will affect the quality of service provided. In nearly every revenue and expense area, several courses of action are available to hospitality operations. Budgeting provides management with an effective means of evaluating these alternatives.

2. Budgeting provides a standard of comparison. At the end of the accounting period, management is able to compare actual operating results to a formal plan. Significant variances may be analyzed to suggest the probable cause(s) which require additional investigation and possibly corrective action. While the preparation of budgets is independent of budgetary control, it is inefficient not to use budgets for control purposes. The focus of the last part of this chapter is on the control process.

3. Budgeting enables management to look forward, especially when strategic planning is concerned. Too often, management is either solving current problems or reviewing the past. Budgeting requires management to anticipate the future. Future considerations may be both external and internal. External considerations include the economy, inflation, and major competition. Internal considerations are primarily the hospitality operation's reactions to external considerations. Hospitality operations should aggressively attempt to shape their environment rather than merely reacting to it.

4. When participative budgeting is practiced, the budget process involves all levels of management. This involvement motivates the lower level managers because they have real input in the process rather than being forced to adhere to budget numbers that are imposed upon them. Too often, autocratic budgeting approaches result in "unsuccessful" managers who blame the budget preparers (higher level managers) instead of accepting responsibility for poor operating results.

5. The budget process provides a channel of communication whereby the operation's objectives are communicated to the lowest managerial levels. In addition, lower level managers are able to react to these objectives and suggest operational goals such as rooms sold, rooms revenues, rooms labor expense, and so on. When the budget is used as a standard of comparison, the operating results are also communicated to lower level managers. This

allows for feedback to these managers. Further, lower level managers are required to explain significant variances—why they exist, what the causes are, and what action is to be taken.

6. Finally, to the degree that prices are a function of costs, the budget process (which provides estimates of future expenses) enables managers to set their prices in relation to their expenses. Price changes can be the result of planning, thereby allowing such changes to be properly implemented. Price changes made on the spur of the moment often result in unprofessional price execution, such as penciled changes on menus, poorly informed service staff who misquote prices, and other similar situations.

Personnel Responsible for Budget Preparation

The complete budget process includes both budget preparation and budgetary control. The major purpose of budgeting is to allow management to accomplish three of its functions: planning, execution, and control.

In most hospitality organizations, the board of directors approves the operating budget, the preparation of which has been delegated to the chief executive officer (CEO). The CEO generally enlists the controller to coordinate the budget preparation process. However, budgeting is not a financial function where bookkeepers, accountants, and the controller have the sole responsibility. The controller facilitates the budget preparation process by initially providing information to operating managers. The major input for the budget should come from operated department (profit center) managers working with their lower level managers and from service department managers.

The controller receives the department managers' operating plans and formulates them into a comprehensive operating budget. This is then reviewed by the CEO and a budget committee (if one exists). If the comprehensive operating budget is satisfactory in meeting financial goals, the CEO and the controller present it to the board of directors. If it is not satisfactory, then the elements requiring change are returned to the appropriate department heads for review and change. This process may repeat several times until a satisfactory budget is prepared.

The final budget should ideally be the result of an overall team effort rather than a decree dictated by the CEO. This participative management approach should result in maximizing departmental managers' motivation.

The Budget Preparation Process

The major elements in the budget preparation process are as follows:

- Financial objectives
- Revenue forecasts
- Expense forecasts
- Net income forecasts

The operations budget process begins with the board of directors establishing financial objectives. A major financial objective set by many organizations, both hospitality and business firms in general, is long-term profit maximization. Long-term profit maximization may mean that the operation does not maximize its profits for the next year. For example, in the next year, profits could be increased by reducing public relations efforts and major maintenance projects; however, in the long run, cuts in these programs may disturb the financial well-being of the hospitality establishment. An alternative objective set by institutional food service operations (for example, hospital food service) is cost containment. Since many of these operations generate limited food service revenues, cost containment is critical to enable these operators to break even.

Another objective may be to provide high quality service, even if it means incurring higher labor costs than allowable to maximize profits. Other objectives set by hospitality organizations have been to be the top establishment in one segment of the hospitality industry, to be the fastest growing establishment, and/or to be recognized as the hospitality operation with the best reputation. Many more objectives could be listed. The critical point is that the board must establish major objectives. These are then communicated to the CEO and are the basis for formulating the operations budget.

When a management company operates a hotel for independent owners, the owners' expectations for both the long and short term must be fully considered. Generally, the owners reserve the right to approve the operating budget. Therefore, failure to consider their views will most likely result in their rejection of the plan, as well as damaged relationships and the need to redo the budget. Several of the major hotel chains, such as Hilton, Hyatt, and Westin, manage many more hotels than they own. Thus, their management teams at the managed properties must work closely with the owners of each hotel.

Forecasting Revenue

Forecasting revenue is the next step in preparing the operations budget. In order for profit center managers (for example, rooms department managers) to be able to forecast revenue for their departments, they must be provided with information regarding the economic environment, marketing plans, capital budgeting, and detailed historical financial operating results of their departments.

Information regarding the economic environment includes such items as:

- Expected inflation for the next year

- Ability of the operation to pass on cost increases to guests

- Changes in competitive conditions—for example, the emergence of new competitors, the closing of former competitors, and so on

- Expected levels of guest spending for products/services offered by the hospitality operation

- Business travel trends

- Tourist travel trends

- For international operations, other factors such as expected wage/price controls and the political environment may need to be considered

Exhibit 1   Rooms Revenue Increases

	Amount	Increase over prior year	
		Amount	%
19X1	$1,000,000	—	—
19X2	1,100,000	100,000	10
19X3	1,210,000	110,000	10
19X4	1,331,000	121,000	10

In order for this information to be useful, it must be expressed in usable numbers. For example, regarding inflation and the ability of the operation to increase its prices, the information received by department heads may be phrased as follows: inflation is expected to be 4% for the next year and prices of all products and services may be increased by an average maximum of 5%, with a 2.5% increase effective January 1 and July 1.

Marketing plans include, but are not limited to, advertising and promotion plans. What advertising is planned for the upcoming year, and how does it compare with the past? What results are expected from the various advertising campaigns? What promotion will be used and when during the budget year? What results can be expected? Are reduced room prices and complimentary meals part of the weekend promotion? Answers to these questions and many others must be provided in order for managers to be able to prepare their budgets.

Capital budgeting information includes the time of the addition of property and equipment. For an existing property, the completion date of guestroom renovation must be projected in order to effectively estimate room sales. The renovation of a hotel's restaurant, the addition of rooms, and so forth are areas that must be covered before projecting sales and expenses for the upcoming year.

Historical financial information should be detailed by department. The breakdown should be on at least a monthly basis, and in some cases, on a daily basis. Quantities and prices should both be provided. That is, the number of each type of room sold and the average selling price by market segment—business, group, tourist, and contract—should be provided. Generally, financial information for at least the two prior years is provided. The controller should be prepared to provide additional prior information as requested.

Historical financial information often serves as the foundation on which managers build their revenue forecasts. This type of budgeting has been called **incremental budgeting.** For example, rooms revenue of a hotel for 19X1 through 19X4 is shown in Exhibit 1. From year 19X1 to 19X4, the amount of revenue increased 10% for each year. Therefore, if future conditions appear to be similar to what they were in prior years, the rooms revenue for 19X5 would be budgeted at $1,464,100, which is a 10% increase over 19X4.

An alternative approach to budgeting revenue based on increasing the current year's revenue by a percentage is to base the revenue projection on unit sales and

Exhibit 2   Rooms Revenue 19X1–19X4

Year	Rooms Sold	Occ. %	Average Room Rates	Rooms Revenues
19X1	25,550	70	$40	$1,022,000
19X2	26,280	72	42	1,103,760
19X3	26,645	73	45	1,199,025
19X4	27,375	75	49	1,341,375

prices. This approach considers the two variables of unit sales and prices separately. For example, an analysis of the past financial information in Exhibit 2 shows that occupancy percentage increased 2% from 19X1 to 19X2, 1% from 19X2 to 19X3, and 2% from 19X3 to 19X4. The average room rates have increased by $2, $3, and $4 over the past three years, respectively. Therefore, assuming the future prospects appear similar, the forecaster may use a 1% increase in occupancy percentage and a $5 increase in average room rate as the basis for forecasting 19X5 rooms revenue. The formula for forecasting rooms revenue is as follows:

$$\text{Rooms Available} \times \text{Occupancy Percentage} \times \text{Average Rate} = \text{Forecasted Rooms Revenue}$$

$$36{,}500 \times .76 \times \$54 = \$1{,}497{,}960$$

This simplistic approach to forecasting rooms revenue is meant only to illustrate the process. A more detailed (and proper) approach would include further considerations, such as: different types of rooms available and their rates, different room rates charged to different guests (for example, convention groups, business travelers, and tourists), different rates charged on weeknights versus weekends, and different rates charged based on seasonality (especially for hotels subject to seasonal changes), and so on. In addition, managers of other profit centers, such as food, beverage, telephone, and the gift shop, must forecast their revenue for the year.

Although sales forecasting is often used for short-term forecasts, many of its concepts are relevant to forecasting revenue for the annual budget. In addition to relying on historical information, many hotels, especially convention hotels which have major conventions booked a year or more in advance, are able to rely in part on room reservations in forecasting both room and food and beverage sales. Still, for activities not reserved so far in advance, forecasting must be done.

Estimating Expenses

The next step in the budget formulation process is estimating expenses. Since expenses are categorized both in relation to operated departments (direct/indirect) and how they react to changes in volume (fixed/variable), the forecasting of expenses is similar to the approach used in forecasting revenue. However, before department heads are able to estimate expenses, they must be provided with information regarding the following:

- Expected cost increases for supplies, food, beverages, and other expenses

- Labor cost increases, including the cost of benefits and payroll taxes

Department heads of profit centers estimate their variable expenses in relation to the projected revenues of their departments. For example, historically, the food department may have incurred food costs at 35% of food sales. For the next year, the food department manager decides to budget at 35%. Therefore, multiplying projected food sales by 35% results in the projected cost of food sales. Other variable expenses may be estimated similarly.

An alternate way to estimate expense is based on standard amounts. For example, a hotel may have a work standard that requires room attendants to clean two rooms per hour. Given this standard, if 800 rooms sales are budgeted during a month, 400 labor hours would be budgeted for room attendants' labor. If the average hourly wage is $7.50 per hour, $3,000 in wages is budgeted for room attendants for the period. Employee benefits related to room attendants are additional costs that also must be considered.

Another example is guestroom amenities. If the typical amenity package includes soap, mouthwash, shampoo, and so forth and costs $2 per room, then when 800 rooms sales are forecasted, the guest supplies—amenities budget would be $1,600.

Fixed expenses are projected on the basis of experience and expected changes. For example, assume that supervisors in the food department were paid salaries of $85,000 for the past year. Further assume that the new salary level of the supervisors is $90,000 plus another half-time equivalent to be added at a cost of $15,000 for the next year. Thus, the fixed cost of supervisor salaries for the next year is set at $105,000. Other fixed expenses are similarly projected.

The service center department heads also estimate expenses for their departments. The service departments in a hotel comprise the general expense categories of administrative and general, marketing, property operation and maintenance, utility costs, human resources, information systems, security, and transportation. Service center department heads will estimate their expenses based on experience and expected changes. Generally, the historical amounts are adjusted to reflect higher costs. For example, assume that the accounting department salaries of a hotel for 19X1 were $150,000. Further assume that salary increases for 19X2 are limited to an average of 5%. Therefore, the 19X2 accounting department salaries budget is set at $157,500.

A different budgeting approach, **zero-base budgeting (ZBB),** is applicable in budgeting for service departments. ZBB, unlike the incremental approach, requires all expenses to be justified. In other words, the assumption is that each department starts with zero dollars (zero base) and must justify all budgeted amounts. Let's look at an example that illustrates the differences between the incremental and ZBB approaches to budgeting.

Assume that the marketing department of a hotel had a total departmental budget of $500,000 in 19X1. In 19X2, cost increases are expected to average 5%, and

Exhibit 3   Interest Expense Budget for 19X2

Debt	Principal	Interest Rate	Time	Amount
Mortgage payment	$500,000	8%	Year	$ 40,000
Loan from partner A	500,000	12	Year	60,000
Working capital loans	200,000	7	6 mo.	7,000
			Total	$107,000

new advertising in the monthly city magazine is expected to cost $500 per month. Under the incremental approach, the marketing budget would be set at $531,000, determined as follows:

$$\$500,000 + \$500(12) + \$500,000(.05) = \$531,000$$

Under ZBB, the marketing department would have to justify every dollar budgeted. That is, documentation would be required showing that all budgeted amounts are cost-justified. This means all payroll costs, supplies, advertising, and so forth would have to be shown to yield greater benefits than their cost.

The ZBB approach to budgeting in hotels appears to be limited to the service departments. However, since the total cost of these departments is approximately 25% of the average hotel's total revenue, the total amount can be considerable.

More detailed discussion of ZBB is beyond the scope of this chapter.[2]

Projecting Fixed Charges

The next step in the budget formulation process is projecting fixed charges. Fixed charges include depreciation, insurance expense, property taxes, rent expense, and similar expenses. These expenses are fixed and are projected on the basis of experience and expected changes for the next year.

Exhibit 3 illustrates how the interest expense budget for 19X2 is determined by estimating interest expense based on current and projected borrowings. Based on calculations in Exhibit 3, the interest expense budgeted for 19X2 is $107,000.

Even though the above mentioned expenses are considered to be fixed, management and/or the board may be able to affect the fixed amounts for the year. For example, property taxes are generally based on assessed valuation and a property tax rate. A reduction in the assessed valuation will result in a reduction in the hotel's property taxes. Thus, if the property is over-assessed, management should pursue a reduction that, if successful, will lower the property tax expense. Some hotels have been successful in obtaining reductions in their assessments, thus reducing this "fixed" expense for the year.

The final step of the budget formulation process is for the controller to formulate the entire budget based on submissions from operated departments and service departments. The forecasted net income is a result of this process. If this bottom line is acceptable to the board of directors and/or the owners, then the budget formulation is complete. If the bottom line is not acceptable, then department heads are required to rework their budgets to provide a budget acceptable to the board and/or owners. Many changes may be proposed in this "rework" process, such as price changes, marketing changes, and cost reductions, just to mention a few. Often, the board or owner will provide a targeted bottom line number before the budget is prepared. More often than not, budgets must be reworked several times before an acceptable budget is produced.

Budget Formulation Illustrated

A very simplified lodging example will be used to illustrate the preparation of an operations budget. The Sands Motel is a 20-room, limited-service lodging facility—that is, it does not sell food and beverages. Each room is equipped with a telephone. Thus, the Sands Motel has two profit centers, the rooms department and telephone department. The Sands Motel also has two service centers, administration and a combined maintenance and utility cost department.

The board of directors has established the major financial goal of generating a minimum net income of 15% of sales. The income statements for the past three years are presented in Exhibit 4. An analysis of this financial information appears in Exhibit 5. Economic environment information relevant to the Sands Motel in 19X4 is summarized as follows:

- No new firms are expected to compete with the Sands Motel.

- Overall consumer demand for motel rooms is expected to remain relatively constant.

- Inflation is expected to be about 5% in the next year.

The major findings and projections for 19X4 are as follows:

Item	Analytical Findings	Projection for 19X4
1. Rooms Revenue		
Paid Occupancy	There is no new competition for next year, and the Sands has increased its paid occupancy one percentage point each year for the last three years. Assume a 1% increase in 19X4.	71%
Average Room Rate	This has increased by $2 each year, and the Sands Motel has still increased its occupancy percentage. An additional $2 increase appears to be reasonable for 19X4. Note: The $2 increase is 6% of the $33.50 average price for 19X3 and exceeds the expected inflation of 5%.	$35.50
2. Telephone Revenue	This has increased from 2% to 2.5%. A .2% increase appears reasonable for 19X4.	2.7%

Exhibit 4   Income Statements—Sands Motel

Income Statements
Sands Motel
For the years of 19X1–19X3

	19X1	19X2	19X3
Revenue:			
Rooms	$146,438	$158,634	$171,654
Telephone	2,962	3,466	4,246
Total	149,400	162,100	175,900
Departmental Expenses:			
Rooms:			
Payroll	21,966	23,000	27,465
Laundry	1,464	1,600	1,735
Linen	2,929	3,150	4,324
Commissions	1,470	1,578	1,650
All Other Expenses	1,500	2,380	2,575
Total	29,329	31,708	37,749
Telephone	2,850	3,350	4,285
Total	32,179	35,058	42,034
Departmental Income:			
Rooms	117,109	126,926	133,905
Telephone	112	116	(39)
Total	117,221	127,042	133,866
Undistributed Operating Expenses:			
Administration	27,470	30,105	32,795
Maintenance and Utility Costs	16,952	19,292	21,775
Total	44,422	49,397	54,570
Income After Undistributed Operating Expenses	72,799	77,645	79,296
Depreciation	15,000	15,000	15,500
Property Taxes	5,000	5,500	6,000
Insurance	5,000	5,000	5,000
Interest Expense	15,000	16,000	15,000
Income Before Income Taxes	32,799	36,145	37,796
Income Taxes	9,840	10,844	11,339
Net Income	$ 22,959	$ 25,301	$ 26,457

Item	Analytical Findings	Projection for 19X4
3. Rooms Expenses		
Payroll	This has fluctuated significantly due to labor unrest. Major pay increases this past year appear to be satisfying the two room attendants and part-time front office personnel. Keep the payroll percentage for 19X4 at 19X3 levels.	16%

Exhibit 5   Analysis of Income Statements—Sands Motel

Analysis of Income Statements
Sands Motel
For the years of 19X1–19X3

	19X1	19X2	19X3
Rooms Sold	4,964	5,036	5,124
Occ. %	68	69	70
Average Rate	$29.50	$31.50	$33.50
Rooms Revenue	$146,438	$158,634	$171,654
Telephone revenue as a % of room revenue	2%	2.2%	2.5%
Rooms expenses %			
Payroll	15%	14.5%	16%
Laundry	1	1	1
Linen	2	2	2.5
Commissions	1	1	1
All other expenses	1	1.5	1.5
Total	20%	20%	22%
Administration			
Payroll			
Fixed	$20,000	$22,000	$24,000
Variable	3%	3%	2.5%
Other	2%	2%	2.5%
Maintenance and Utility Costs			
Maintenance			
Fixed	$4,000	$4,500	$5,000
Variable	3%	3%	3%
Utility Costs			
Fixed	$1,000	$1,500	$2,000
Variable	5%	5.2%	5.4%
Fixed Charges			

Depreciation—based on cost of fixed assets, expected lives, and straight-line method of depreciation
Property taxes—historically has increased by $500 for 19X1 through 19X3
Insurance—a three-year policy for 19X1–19X3 was quoted at $5,000 per year
Interest expense—based on amount borrowed and prevailing interest rates
Income taxes—based on 30% of income before income taxes

	19X1	19X2	19X3
Profit margin %	15.36%	15.61%	15.04%

Item	Analytical Findings	Projection for 19X4
Laundry	This has remained constant at 1% of rooms revenue for three years.	1%
Linen	A .5% increase was experienced in 19X3 due to major purchases. The prior 2% appears adequate for 19X4.	2%

Item	Analytical Findings	Projection for 19X4
Commissions	The average for the past three years has been 1%. Continue to use 1% as an estimate for 19X4.	1%
All Other Expenses	These have stabilized for the past two years at 1.5%. This appears reasonable.	1.5%
4. Telephone Expense	This has nearly equaled telephone revenue each year. A breakdown situation is reasonable for 19X4.	100% of telephone revenue
5. Administration		
Payroll	The fixed portion has increased approximately $2,000 per year from 19X1–19X3. A $3,000 increase is scheduled for 19X4 to reward the general manager. Variable labor (as a percentage of total revenue) is expected to be 3% for 19X4.	$27,000 and 3%
Other	Although this increased to 2.5% in 19X3, it is expected to return to the previous level of 2% in 19X4.	2%
6. Maintenance and Utility Costs		
Maintenance	The fixed portion of part-time workers' pay has increased $500 each year over three years. An increase of $1,000 is scheduled for 19X4. Variable maintenance of 3% appears adequate for 19X4.	$6,000 and 3%
Utility Costs	The fixed portion has increased approximately $500 each year since 19X1. Therefore, the estimated fixed portion should be increased accordingly for 19X4. The variable portion has increased .2% from 19X1–19X3. Utility costs are expected to be moderate in 19X4 and 5.4% appears reasonable.	$2,500 and 5.4%
7. Fixed Charges		
Depreciation	The accountant's calculation of depreciation for 19X4 is $15,000 for existing fixed assets and an additional $700 for a new microcomputer to be purchased in 19X4.	$15,700
Property Taxes	This assessed valuation is expected to increase by 10% for 19X4. The tax rate is not expected to change; therefore, increase property taxes for 19X4 to $6,600.	$6,600

Item	Analytical Findings	Projection for 19X4
Insurance	The current three-year insurance policy expires on December 31. The new three-year policy requires a $6,000 premium each year.	$6,000
Interest Expense	The flexible interest rate presently at 15% is expected to average 14.5% for 19X4. The average debt outstanding for 19X4 will be $90,000. $90,000 × .145 = $13,050.	$13,050
Income Taxes	Income taxes for 19X1–19X3 were 30% of the income before income taxes. Due to reduced rates, the tax rate for 19X4 will be 25%.	25% of pretax income

The operations budget for 19X4 is shown in Exhibit 6. The projected 19X4 net income for the Sands Motel of $29,586 is 15.6% of sales, which exceeds the minimum requirement of 15%.

Flexible Budgets

The budgets we have discussed so far have been fixed (sometimes called static) in that only one level of activity was planned. However, no matter how sophisticated the budget process, it is improbable that the level of activity budgeted will be realized exactly. Therefore, when a fixed budget is used, variances from several budget line items, specifically for revenues and variable expenses, can almost always be expected. An alternative approach is to budget for several different levels of activity. For example, a hotel may budget at three paid occupancy levels, such as 69%, 71%, and 73%, even though it believes that the level of activity is likeliest to be at the 71% level. With flexible budgeting, revenues and variable expenses change with each level of activity, while fixed expenses remain constant.

Exhibit 7 contains three condensed operations budgets for the Sands Motel. The flexible budgeting reflects occupancy at 69%, 71%, and 73%. The static budget for the Sands Motel (Exhibit 6) was based on 71% occupancy. The kinds of observations that should be made in relation to flexible budgeting reflected in Exhibit 7 include the following:

- Revenues increase/decrease with occupancy.

- Departmental expenses increase/decrease with occupancy.

- Undistributed operating expenses increase/decrease only slightly, since a major portion of these expenses is fixed.

- Fixed expenses remain constant as expected.

- Net income changes with activity, but not as much as revenue.

- Net income as a percentage of total revenue for the three levels of activity is as follows:

Exhibit 6   Sample Operations Budget Worksheet

Operations Budget (Worksheet)
Sands Motel
For the year of 19X4

	Calculation	Amount
Revenue:		
Rooms	365 × 20 × .71 × 35.5	$183,996
Telephone	183,996 × .027	4,968
Total		188,964
Departmental Expenses:		
Rooms		
Payroll	183,996 × .16	29,439
Laundry	183,996 × .01	1,840
Linen	183,996 × .02	3,680
Commissions	183,996 × .01	1,840
All Other Expenses	183,996 × .015	2,760
Total		39,559
Telephone	(same as telephone revenue)	4,968
Departmental Income:		
Rooms		144,437
Telephone		–0–
Total		144,437
Undistributed Operating Expenses:		
Administration	27,000 + .05 (188,964)	36,448
Maintenance and Utility Costs	8,500 + .084 (188,964)	24,373
Total		60,821
Total Income After Undistributed Operating Expenses		83,616
Insurance		6,000
Property Taxes		6,600
Depreciation		15,700
Interest Expense		13,050
Income Before Income Taxes		42,266
Income Taxes	42,266 × .30	12,680
Net Income		$ 29,586

$$\text{At 69\% occupancy:} \quad \frac{\text{Net Income}}{\text{Total Revenue}} = \frac{27,237}{183,641} = \underline{\underline{14.8\%}}$$

$$\text{At 71\% occupancy:} \quad \frac{\text{Net Income}}{\text{Total Revenue}} = \frac{29,586}{188,964} = \underline{\underline{15.7\%}}$$

$$\text{At 73\% occupancy:} \quad \frac{\text{Net Income}}{\text{Total Revenue}} = \frac{31,935}{194,287} = \underline{\underline{16.4\%}}$$

Exhibit 7   Flexible Operations Budget—Sands Motel

Flexible Operations Budget
Sands Motel
For the year of 19X4

	Activity Levels—Occupancy %		
	69%	71%	73%
Revenue:			
Rooms	$178,813	$183,996	$189,179
Telephone	4,828	4,968	5,108
Total	183,641	188,964	194,287
Departmental Expenses:			
Rooms	28,445	39,559	40,673
Telephone	4,828	4,968	5,108
Total	43,273	44,527	45,781
Departmental Income:			
Rooms	140,368	144,437	148,506
Telephone	0	0	0
Total	140,368	144,437	148,506
Undistributed Operating Expenses:			
Administration	36,182	36,448	36,714
Maintenance and Utility Costs	23,926	24,373	24,820
Total	60,108	60,821	61,534
Income After Undistributed Operating Expenses:	80,260	83,616	86,972
Insurance	6,000	6,000	6,000
Property Taxes	6,600	6,600	6,600
Depreciation	15,700	15,700	15,700
Interest	13,050	13,050	13,050
Income Before Income Taxes	38,910	42,266	45,622
Income Taxes	11,673	12,680	13,687
Net Income	$ 27,237	$ 29,586	$ 31,935

Therefore, the minimum required profit margin percentage of 15% can only be realized at the budgeted occupancy levels of 71% and 73%. Since 69% yields less than the targeted 15% profit margin, management may be requested to review the budget at 69% in an attempt to achieve the desired net income.

The flexible budget is relatively easy to prepare using computers. The relationship between revenues and expenses is expressed in formulas, and the computer, with minor human assistance, is able to do the rest. The major benefit of the flexible budget is to provide management and owners with bottom line results for alternative levels of activity. Many activity levels can be projected.

As a note of caution, however, forecasters should realize that different levels of activity will most likely affect prices and possibly related expenses. For example, a room rate of $35.50 was used across the three occupancy levels used in the Sands Motel's flexible operations budget. However, in order to increase occupancy above 73%, an average price reduction may be necessary, and a still greater price reduction may be required beyond 80% or some other higher number.

Budgeting for a New Lodging Property

The preceding discussion covers budgeting for an existing lodging property. However, a hotel in its first year lacks a historical base. How can it prepare its budget?

Certainly one source for budgeting for a hotel's first year is the lodging feasibility study (LFS) that is generally prepared to secure the financing for the property. This study provides a summary of operations including sales, direct expenses of the profit centers, and operating overhead expenses. However, forecasters should not rely totally on these numbers for two major reasons. First, the study is prepared to secure financing, and the figures are not detailed by month, type of market, and so forth. Second, the LFS is prepared before the construction of the hotel, which is probably two years before the opening of the hotel; thus, the figures are somewhat dated. Nonetheless, it is a set of figures with which to start. These numbers should be updated on the basis of current room rates, labor costs, and other expenses.[3]

If a new hotel is part of a chain, cost information of similar properties can be obtained. When used cautiously, this information will be reasonably useful.

Finally, few if any new hotels or restaurants make a bottom line profit their first year. Unexpected expenses arise until the "bugs" are worked out and the market realizes the property exists. Therefore, the initial budget should allow for these higher than normal costs and possibly lower revenues than desired. A critical need is to have sufficient cash to carry the new property to the point of cash breakeven, which often is delayed until the second or third year of operation.

Budgetary Control

In order for budgets to be used effectively for control purposes, budget reports must be prepared periodically (generally on a monthly basis) for each level of financial responsibility. In a hotel, this would normally require budget reports for profit, cost, and service centers.

Budget reports may take many forms. Exhibit 8, a summary income statement used by The Sheraton Corporation, is prepared monthly and is the summary of the entire hotel operations. It is used by the hotel top management and is also made available to corporate executives and financial analysts. In addition to variances from budget, variances from last year's actual are also shown in order to put the budget in perspective and to provide management with trend information.

Exhibit 9 is a departmental budget report for the rooms department. It provides a further breakdown of the elements that make up revenues, wages, benefits, and other expenses. This report, which is available to corporate management, also goes to the next level of management below the general manager and controller.

In order for the reports to be useful, they must be timely and relevant. Budget reports issued weeks after the end of the accounting period are too late to allow managers to investigate variances, determine causes, and take timely action.

Exhibit 8   Monthly Summary Income Statement

	Month Actual	Month Budget	Month Prior Year	Budget Variance	Prior Year Variance
# of Hotel Rooms	0	0	0	0	0
Rooms Available	0	0	0	0	0
Rooms Occupied—Transient—Corporate	0	0	0	0	0
—Transient—Leisure	0	0	0	0	0
—Group—Corporate	0	0	0	0	0
—Group—Association	0	0	0	0	0
—Group—Leisure	0	0	0	0	0
—Airline	0	0	0	0	0
—Permanent	0	0	0	0	0
—Complimentary	0	0	0	0	0
Total Rooms Occupied	0	0	0	0	0
% Occupancy	--	--	--	--	--
Average Rate	--	--	--	--	--
Total Revenue	0	0	0	0	0
Rooms —Revenue	0	0	0	0	0
—Wages & Benefits	0	0	0	0	0
—Other Expenses	0	0	0	0	0
Total Rooms Profit	0	0	0	0	0
Food —Outlet Revenue	0	0	0	0	0
—Banquet Revenue	0	0	0	0	0
—Total Food Revenue	0	0	0	0	0
Beverage —Outlet Revenue	0	0	0	0	0
—Banquet Revenue	0	0	0	0	0
—Total Beverage Revenue	0	0	0	0	0
F & B —Other Income	0	0	0	0	0
F & B —Total Revenue	0	0	0	0	0
F & B —Cost of Sales	0	0	0	0	0
—Wages & Benefits	0	0	0	0	0
—Other Expenses	0	0	0	0	0
Total Food & Beverage Profit	0	0	0	0	0
Casino Profit	0	0	0	0	0
MOD Profit	0	0	0	0	0
Rents & Other Income	0	0	0	0	0
Total Operated Department Profit	0	0	0	0	0
Overhead Expenses					
Administrative & General	0	0	0	0	0
Marketing	0	0	0	0	0
Property Operations	0	0	0	0	0
Energy	0	0	0	0	0
Total Overhead Expenses	0	0	0	0	0
Gross Operating Profit	0	0	0	0	0
Capital Expenses					
Property & R/E Taxes	0	0	0	0	0
Insurance	0	0	0	0	0
Rent Non-Affiliate	0	0	0	0	0
Other (Adds) & Deducts	0	0	0	0	0
Total Capital & Other Expenses	0	0	0	0	0
Cash Earnings	0	0	0	0	0
Depreciation	0	0	0	0	0
Amortization of Pre-Opening	0	0	0	0	0
Hotel Operating Income	0	0	0	0	0
Interest Expense	0	0	0	0	0
Interest Income	0	0	0	0	0
State/Local Income Tax	0	0	0	0	0
Hotel Pretax Income	0	0	0	0	0
ITT Sheraton Pretax	0	0	0	0	0
Basic Management Fees	0	0	0	0	0
License Fees	0	0	0	0	0
Marketing Fees	0	0	0	0	0
Incentive Fees	0	0	0	0	0
Total Management Fees	0	0	0	0	0
Joint Venture Hotels Only:					
ITT Sheraton Pretax Equity (J.V. Hotels)	0	0	0	0	0
Interest Expense (3rd Party Debt)	0	0	0	0	0
State & Local Income Taxes	0	0	0	0	0
Operating Income	0	0	0	0	0
Total Fees & Operating Income	0	0	0	0	0

Courtesy of The Sheraton Corporation

Exhibit 9   Monthly Income Statement—Rooms Department

	Current Period						Year to Date					
	Actual	%	Budget	%	Last Year	%	Actual	%	Budget	%	Last Year	%
Revenue												
Transient	308,383	66.1	278,100	57.1	280,350	71.8	2,576,465	59.6	2,656,900	58.2	2,605,121	63.1
Group	126,466	27.1	172,800	35.5	85,962	22.0	1,454,681	33.6	1,581,400	34.6	1,241,069	30.0
Permanent	0	0.0	0	0.0	0	0.0	0	0.0	0	0.0	1,200	0.0
Airline	30,951	6.6	36,000	7.4	23,670	6.1	291,221	6.7	329,100	7.2	280,829	6.8
Extra Revenue	663	0.1	0	0.0	635	0.2	3,408	0.1	0	0.0	1,925	0.0
Total Revenue	466,463	100.0	486,900	100.0	390,617	100.0	4,325,774	100.0	4,567,400	100.0	4,130,145	100.0
Wages & Benefits												
Regular Wages	66,357	14.2	73,800	15.2	65,210	16.7	581,480	13.4	644,800	14.1	585,479	14.2
Premium Wages	2,934	0.6	0	0.0	2,078	0.5	31,794	0.7	0	0.0	30,978	0.8
Benefits	39,298	8.4	41,500	8.5	43,619	11.2	317,898	7.3	348,200	7.6	355,799	8.6
Total Wages & Benefits	108,588	23.3	115,300	23.7	110,907	28.4	931,172	21.5	993,000	21.7	972,256	23.5
Other Expenses												
Linen, China, Glass	0	0.0	4,200	0.9	3,581	0.9	22,729	0.5	38,500	0.8	24,795	0.6
Contract Cleaning	9,376	2.0	8,000	1.6	8,000	2.0	65,516	1.5	64,000	1.4	87,046	2.1
Laundry	10,007	2.1	8,600	1.8	8,449	2.2	83,710	1.9	73,900	1.6	77,973	1.9
Operating Supplies	15,606	3.3	10,700	2.2	9,680	2.5	125,659	2.9	99,000	2.2	87,787	2.1
Travel & Entertainment	0	0.0	0	0.0	0	0.0	1,499	0.0	0	0.0	0	0.0
Uniforms	1,500	0.3	2,200	0.5	1,319	0.3	13,443	0.3	20,200	0.4	14,311	0.3
Training	569	0.1	1,100	0.2	211	0.1	5,241	0.1	5,900	0.1	7,888	0.2
Rooms Commissions	12,666	2.7	11,100	2.3	13,177	3.4	95,025	2.2	106,300	2.3	99,572	2.4
Reservation	12,679	2.7	12,300	2.5	6,481	1.7	102,282	2.4	103,600	2.3	93,501	2.3
Comp Park & Trans	975	0.2	2,400	0.5	5,188	1.3	13,404	0.3	22,400	0.5	23,718	0.6
Cable TV & Video	814	0.2	2,000	0.4	1,900	0.5	15,499	0.4	16,000	0.4	20,248	0.5
Decorations	0	0.0	500	0.1	415	0.1	2,597	0.1	4,000	0.1	1,787	0.0
Rooms Cashier Over/s	20	0.0	100	0.0	0	0.0	493	0.0	800	0.0	0	0.0
Rooms After Departure	516	0.1	0	0.0	0	0.0	6,799	0.2	0	0.0	0	0.0
Miscellaneous	4,822	1.0	2,100	0.4	2,163	0.6	41,952	1.0	23,400	0.5	23,654	0.6
Total Other Expenses	69,550	14.9	65,300	13.4	60,565	15.5	595,848	13.8	578,000	12.7	562,281	13.6
Total Expenses	178,138	38.2	180,600	37.1	171,471	43.9	1,527,019	35.3	1,571,000	34.4	1,534,537	37.2
Department Profit	288,325	61.8	306,300	62.9	219,146	56.1	2,798,755	64.7	2,996,400	65.6	2,595,608	62.8

Courtesy of The Sheraton Corporation

Relevant financial information includes only the revenues and expenses for which the individual department head is held responsible. For example, including allocated overhead expenses such as administrative and general salaries on a rooms department budget report is rather meaningless from a control viewpoint, because the rooms department manager is unable to affect these costs. Further, they detract from the expenses that the rooms department manager can take action to control.

Relevant reporting also requires sufficient detail to allow reasonable judgments regarding budget variances. Of course, information overload (which generally results in management's failure to act properly) should be avoided.

There are five steps in the budgetary control process:

1. Determination of variances

2. Determination of significant variances

3. Analysis of significant variances

4. Determination of problems

5. Action to correct problems

Determination of Variances

Variances are determined by using the budget report to compare actual results to the budget. The budget report should disclose both monthly variances and year-to-date variances. Variance analysis generally focuses on monthly variances, because the year-to-date variances are essentially the sum of monthly variances.

Exhibit 10 is the January 19X4 summary budget report for the Sands Motel. This budget report contains only monthly financial information and not separate year-to-date numbers, as January is the first month of the fiscal year for the Sands Motel.

Variances shown on this report include both dollar variances and percentage variances. The dollar variances result from subtracting the actual results from the budget figures. For example, rooms revenue for the Sands Motel was $14,940, while the budgeted rooms revenue was $15,620, resulting in a difference of $680. The difference is set in parentheses to reflect an unfavorable variance. Dollar variances are considered either favorable or unfavorable based on situations presented in Exhibit 11.

Percentage variances are determined by dividing the dollar variance by the budgeted amount. For rooms revenue (Exhibit 10), the (4.35%) is the result of dividing $(680) by $15,620.

Variances should be determined for all line items on budget reports along with an indication of whether the variance is favorable or unfavorable. The kind of variance can be indicated by marking it " + " for favorable and " − " for unfavorable, "F" for favorable and "U" for unfavorable, or placing parentheses around unfavorable variances and showing favorable variances without parentheses as shown in Exhibit 10. Some enterprises simply asterisk unfavorable variances.

Determination of Significant Variances

Virtually all budgeted revenue and expense items on a budget report will differ from the actual amounts, with the possible exception of fixed expenses. This is only to be

Exhibit 10   Summary Budget Report—Sands Motel

Summary Budget Report
Sands Motel
For January 19X4

	Budget	Actual	Variances $	Variances %
Revenue:				
Rooms	$15,620	$14,940	$(680)	(4.35)%
Telephone	429	414	(15)	(3.50)
Total	16,049	15,354	(695)	(4.33)
Departmental Expenses:				
Rooms				
Payroll	2,500	2,243	257	10.28
Laundry	156	150	6	3.85
Linen	313	300	13	4.15
Commissions	156	150	6	3.85
All other expenses	234	200	34	14.53
Total	3,359	3,043	316	9.41
Telephone	422	380	42	9.95
Total	3,781	3,423	358	9.47
Departmental Income:				
Rooms	12,268	11,911	(357)	(2.91)
Telephone	0	20	20	NA
Total	12,268	11,931	(337)	(2.75)
Undistributed Operating Expenses:				
Administration	3,052	2,961	91	2.98
Maintenance and Utility Costs	2,169	2,220	(51)	(2.35)
Total Income After Undistributed Operating				
Expenses:	7,047	6,750	(297)	(4.21)
Insurance	500	500	0	—
Property Taxes	550	550	0	—
Depreciation	1,308	1,308	0	—
Interest Expense	1,087	1,087	0	—
Income Before Income Taxes	3,602	3,305	(297)	(8.25)
Income Taxes	1,081	992	89	8.23
Net Income	$ 2,521	$ 2,313	$(208)	(8.25)%

expected, because no budgeting process, however sophisticated, is perfect. However, simply because a variance exists does not mean that management should analyze the variance and follow through with appropriate corrective actions. Only significant variances require this kind of management analysis and action.

Criteria used to determine which variances are significant are called **significance criteria.** They are generally expressed in terms of both dollar and percentage

Exhibit 11   Evaluating Dollar Variance Situations

	Situation	Variance
Revenues	Actual exceeds budget	Favorable
	Budget exceeds actual	Unfavorable
Expenses	Budget exceeds actual	Favorable
	Actual exceeds budget	Unfavorable

differences. Dollar and percentage differences should be used jointly due to the weakness of each when used separately. Dollar differences fail to recognize the magnitude of the base. For example, a large hotel may have a $1,000 difference in rooms revenue from the budgeted amount. Yet the $1,000 difference based on a budget of $1,000,000 results in a percentage difference of only .1%. Most managers would agree this is insignificant. However, if the rooms revenue budget for the period was $10,000, a $1,000 difference would result in a percentage difference of 10%, which most managers would consider significant. This seems to suggest that variances should be considered significant based on the percentage difference. However, the percentage difference also fails at times. For example, assume that the budget for an expense is $10. A dollar difference of $2 results in a 20% percentage difference. The percentage difference appears significant, but generally, little (if any) managerial time should be spent analyzing and investigating a $2 difference.

Therefore, the dollar and percentage differences should be used jointly in determining which variances are significant. The size of the significance criteria will differ among hospitality properties in relation to the size of the operation and the controllability of certain revenue or expense items. In general, the larger the operation, the larger the dollar difference criteria. Also, the greater the control exercised over the item, the smaller the criteria.

For example, a large hospitality operation may set significance criteria as follows:

Revenue	$1,000 and 4%
Variable expense	$500 and 2%
Fixed expense	$50 and 1%

A smaller hospitality operation may set significance criteria as follows:

Revenue	$200 and 4%
Variable expense	$100 and 2%
Fixed expense	$50 and 1%

Notice that the change in criteria, based on size of operation, is generally the dollar difference. Both significance criteria decrease as the item becomes more controllable.

To illustrate the determination of significant variances, the significance criteria above for a small hospitality operation will be applied to the Sands Motel's January 19X4 budget report (see Exhibit 10). The following revenue and expense items have significant variances:

1. The unfavorable $680 difference between the budgeted rooms revenue and the actual rooms revenue exceeds the dollar difference criterion of $200, and the unfavorable 4.35% percentage difference exceeds the percentage difference criterion of 4%.

2. The favorable $257 difference between the budgeted rooms payroll expense and the actual rooms payroll expense exceeds the dollar difference criterion of $100, and the favorable 10.28% difference exceeds the percentage difference criterion of 2%.

3. Several rooms expense variances such as laundry, linen, and commissions exceed the percentage difference criterion, but do not exceed the dollar difference criterion, so they are not considered significant; therefore, they will not be subjected to variance analysis.

Variance Analysis

Variance analysis is the process of analyzing variances in order to give management more information about variances. With this additional information, management is better prepared to identify the causes of any variances.

We will look at variance analysis for three general areas—revenue, cost of goods sold, and variable labor. The basic models presented in these areas can be applied to other similar areas. For each area, formulas, a graph, and an example will be provided. In addition, the two significant variances of the Sands Motel, rooms revenue and rooms payroll expense, will be analyzed.

Revenue Variance Analysis

Revenue variances occur because of price and volume differences. Thus, the variances relating to revenue are called *price variance* (PV) and *volume variance* (VV). The formulas for these variances are as follows:

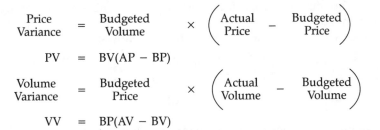

$$\text{Price Variance} = \text{Budgeted Volume} \times \left(\text{Actual Price} - \text{Budgeted Price} \right)$$

$$PV = BV(AP - BP)$$

$$\text{Volume Variance} = \text{Budgeted Price} \times \left(\text{Actual Volume} - \text{Budgeted Volume} \right)$$

$$VV = BP(AV - BV)$$

A minor variance due to the interrelationship of the price and volume variance is the *price-volume variance* (P-VV), calculated as follows:

$$\text{Price-Volume Variance} = \left(\text{Actual Price} - \text{Budgeted Price} \right) \times \left(\text{Actual Volume} - \text{Budgeted Volume} \right)$$

$$P\text{-}VV = (AP - BP)(AV - BV)$$

These formulas are illustrated by using the Sample Motel, whose budget and actual monthly results for rooms revenue appear in Exhibit 12.

Exhibit 12   Rooms Revenue: Budget and Actual—Sample Motel

	Room Nights	Average Price	Total
Budget	400	$20	$8,000
Actual	450	18	8,100
Difference	50	$ 2	$ 100(F)

The budget variance of $100 is favorable. Variance analysis will be conducted to determine the general cause(s) of this variance—that is, price, volume, or the interrelationship of the two. The price variance for the Sample Motel is determined as follows:

$$\begin{aligned} PV &= BV(AP - BP) \\ &= 400(\$18 - \$20) \\ &= -\$800 \text{ (U)} \end{aligned}$$

The price variance of $800 is unfavorable because the average price charged per room night of $18 was $2 less than the budgeted average price of $20.

The volume variance is computed as follows:

$$\begin{aligned} VV &= BP(AV - BV) \\ &= \$20(450 - 400) \\ &= \$1,000 \text{ (F)} \end{aligned}$$

The volume variance of $1,000 is favorable, because 50 more rooms per night were sold than planned.

The price-volume variance is determined as follows:

$$\begin{aligned} P\text{-}VV &= (AP - BP)(AV - BV) \\ &= (\$18 - \$20)(450 - 400) \\ &= -\$100 \text{ (U)} \end{aligned}$$

The price-volume variance is due to the interrelationship of the volume and price variances. Two dollars per room less than budgeted multiplied by the 50 excess rooms results in an unfavorable $100 price-volume variance.

The sum of the three variances equals the budget variance of $100 for room revenue as follows:

VV	$1,000 (F)
PV	−800 (U)
P-VV	−100 (U)
Total	$ 100 (F)

Exhibit 13   Revenue Variance Analysis—Sample Motel

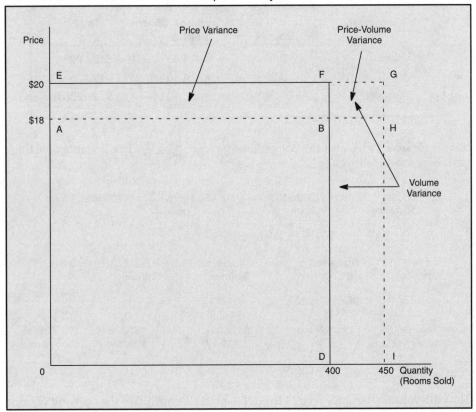

The price-volume variance in the analysis of revenue variances will be unfavorable when the price and volume variances are different—that is, when one is favorable and the other is unfavorable. When the price and volume variances are the same—that is, either both are favorable or both are unfavorable—then the price-volume variance will be favorable.

Exhibit 13 is a graphic depiction of the revenue variance analysis for the Sample Motel. The rectangle 0EFD represents the budgeted amount. The rectangle 0AHI represents the actual amount of rooms revenue. The price variance is the rectangle AEFB. The volume variance is the rectangle DFGI. The price-volume variance is the rectangle BFGH.

Cost of Goods Sold Analysis

The **cost of goods sold variance** occurs because of differences due to cost and volume. That is, the amount paid for the goods sold (food and/or beverage) differs from the budget, and the total amount sold differs from the budgeted sales. The detailed variances related to the cost of goods are called the *cost variance* (CV), the

Exhibit 14   Cost of Food Sold: Budget and Actual—Sample Restaurant

	Covers	Average Cost Per Cover	Total Cost
Budget	3,000	$ 4.00	$12,000
Actual	3,200	4.10	13,120
Difference	200	$ .10	$ 1,120(U)

volume variance (VV), and the *cost-volume variance* (C-VV). The formulas for these variances are as follows:

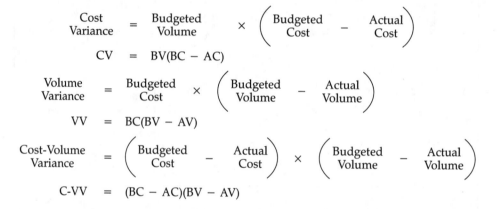

$$\begin{array}{rcl} \text{Cost Variance} & = & \text{Budgeted Volume} \times \left(\text{Budgeted Cost} - \text{Actual Cost} \right) \\ \text{CV} & = & \text{BV(BC} - \text{AC)} \\[10pt] \text{Volume Variance} & = & \text{Budgeted Cost} \times \left(\text{Budgeted Volume} - \text{Actual Volume} \right) \\ \text{VV} & = & \text{BC(BV} - \text{AV)} \\[10pt] \text{Cost-Volume Variance} & = & \left(\text{Budgeted Cost} - \text{Actual Cost} \right) \times \left(\text{Budgeted Volume} - \text{Actual Volume} \right) \\ \text{C-VV} & = & \text{(BC} - \text{AC)(BV} - \text{AV)} \end{array}$$

The cost-volume variance results from the interrelationship of the cost and volume variances.

The analysis of the cost of goods sold variance formulas is illustrated by using a food service example. The Sample Restaurant, open for dinner only, had cost of food sold results and budgeted amounts for January as shown in Exhibit 14. The budget variance of $1,120 is analyzed using variance analysis as follows:

The cost variance is determined as follows:

$$\begin{array}{rcl} \text{CV} & = & \text{BV(BC} - \text{AC)} \\ & = & 3,000(\$4.00 - \$4.10) \\ & = & -\$300 \text{ (U)} \end{array}$$

The cost variance of $300 is unfavorable because the cost per cover of 3,000 covers exceeded budget by $.10.

The volume variance is determined as follows:

$$\begin{array}{rcl} \text{VV} & = & \text{BC(BV} - \text{AV)} \\ & = & \$4(3,000 - 3,200) \\ & = & -\$800 \text{ (U)} \end{array}$$

The volume variance of $800 is also unfavorable because excessive volume results in greater costs than budgeted. Remember that this is from an expense perspective. Excessive volume from a revenue perspective is favorable.

The cost-volume variance is determined as follows:

$$
\begin{aligned}
\text{C-VV} &= (\text{BC} - \text{AC})(\text{BV} - \text{AV}) \\
&= (\$4.00 - \$4.10)(3,000 - 3,200) \\
&= \underline{\$20} \text{ (U)}
\end{aligned}
$$

The cost-volume variance of $20 is also unfavorable, even though the mathematical sign of the result is positive. The cost-volume variance will be unfavorable when the other two variances (cost and volume) are the same—that is, when both are favorable or unfavorable. When the cost and volume variances differ—that is, when one is favorable and the other unfavorable—then the cost-volume variance will be favorable.

The sum of the three variances is $1,120:

Cost Variance	$300 (U)
Volume Variance	800 (U)
Cost-Volume Variance	20 (U)
Total	$1,120 (U)

This sum equals the $1,120 budget variance shown in Exhibit 14. These results show that of the total $1,120, only $300 was due to cost overruns. Further investigation should be undertaken to determine why there were excessive food costs of $300. The volume variance of $800 should be more than offset by the favorable volume variance for the Sample Restaurant food revenue. The cost-volume variance of $20 is due to the interrelationship of cost and volume. It is insignificant and requires no additional management attention.

Exhibit 15 is a graphic depiction of the cost of food sold variance analysis. The original budget of $12,000 for cost of food sold is represented by the rectangle 0ABC, while the actual food cost for the period is the rectangle 0DFH. Therefore, the difference between these two rectangles is the budget variance. The budget variance is divided among the three variances of cost, volume, and cost-volume. The cost variance is represented by the rectangle ADEB. The volume variance is represented by the rectangle BGHC. The cost-volume variance is represented by the rectangle BEFG.

Variable Labor Variance Analysis

Variable labor expense is labor expense that varies directly with activity. Variable labor increases as sales increase and decreases as sales decrease. In a lodging operation, the use of room attendants to clean rooms is a clear example of variable labor. Everything else being the same, the more rooms to be cleaned, the more room attendants' hours are necessary to clean the rooms; therefore, the greater the room attendants' wages. In a food service situation, servers' wages are generally treated as variable labor expense. Again, the greater the number of guests to be

Exhibit 15   Cost of Food Sold Variance Analysis—Sample Restaurant

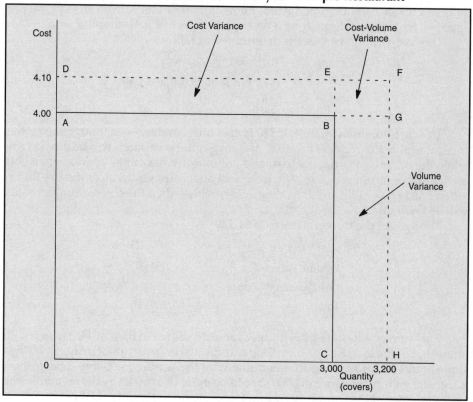

served food, the greater the number of servers; therefore, the greater the server expense. The remainder of the discussion of labor in this section will pertain to variable labor, which we will simply call labor expense.

Labor expense variances result from three general causes—volume, rate, and efficiency. All budget variances for labor expense may be divided among these three areas. *Volume variances* (VV) result when there is a different volume of work than forecasted. *Rate variances* (RV) result when the average wage rate is different than planned. *Efficiency variances* (EV) result when the amount of work performed by the labor force on an hourly basis differs from the forecast. Of course, as with revenue variance analysis and with cost of goods sold variance analysis, there is a variance (called the *rate-time variance*) due to the interrelationship of the major elements of the labor budget variance. The formulas for these variances are:

$$VV = BR(BT - ATAO)$$
$$RV = BT(BR - AR)$$
$$EV = BR(ATAO - AT)$$
$$R\text{-}TV = (BT - AT)(BR - AR)$$

Exhibit 16   Labor Expense: Budget and Actual—Sample Restaurant

	Covers	Time/ Cover	Total Time	Hourly Wage	Total
Budget	3,000	4 min.	200 hrs.	$2.50	$500
Actual	3,200	5 min.	266 2/3 hrs.	2.40	640
Difference	200	1 min.	66 2/3 hrs.	.10	$140(U)

where the elements within these formulas are defined as follows:

- BR (Budgeted Rate)—the average wage rates budgeted per hour for labor services.

- BT (Budgeted Time)—hours required to perform work according to the budget. For example, if the work standard for serving meals is 15 customers/hour per server, then servers would require 40 hours (600 ÷ 15) to serve 600 meals.

- ATAO (Allowable Time for Actual Output)—hours allowable to perform work based on the actual output. This is determined in the same way as budgeted time, except that the work is actual versus budget. For example, if 660 meals were actually served, the allowable time given a work standard of 15 meals/hour would be 44 hours (660 ÷ 15).

- AR (Actual Rate)—the actual average wage rate paid per hour for labor services.

- AT (Actual Time)—the number of hours actually worked.

The calculation of these formulas is illustrated in Exhibit 16. The work standard for servers of the Sample Restaurant is serving 15 meals per hour. Therefore, on the average, a meal should be served every four minutes (60 ÷ 15).

The volume variance is determined as follows:

$$VV \ = \ BR(BT - ATAO)$$
$$= \ \$2.50(200 - 213.33^*)$$
$$= \ -\$33.33 \ (U)$$

*The ATAO of 213.33 is determined by dividing the work standard of 15 covers per hour into the 3,200 covers served.

The volume variance of $33.33 is unfavorable, because more covers were served than budgeted. Normally, the volume variance is beyond the control of the supervisor of personnel to which the labor expense pertains. Therefore, this should be isolated and generally not further pursued from an expense perspective. In addition, an unfavorable volume variance should be more than offset by the favorable volume variance for the related food sales.

The rate variance for the Sample Restaurant is determined as follows:

$$RV = BT(BR - AR)$$
$$= 200(\$2.50 - \$2.40)$$
$$= \underline{\$20} \text{ (F)}$$

The rate variance of $20 is favorable because the average pay rate per hour is $.10 per hour less than the budgeted $2.50 per hour. The credit for this is normally given to the labor supervisor responsible for scheduling and managing labor.

The efficiency variance for the Sample Restaurant is determined as follows:

$$EV = BR(ATAO - AT)$$
$$= \$2.50(213.33 - 266.67)$$
$$= \underline{-\$133.35} \text{ (U)}$$

The efficiency variance of $133.35 is unfavorable, because an average of one minute more was spent serving a meal than was originally planned. The supervisor must determine why this occurred. It could have been due to new employees who were inefficient because of work overload, or perhaps there were other factors. Once the specific causes are determined, the manager can take corrective action to ensure a future recurrence is avoided.

The rate-time variance is determined as follows:

$$R\text{-}TV = (BT - AT)(BR - AR)$$
$$= (200 - 266.67)(\$2.50 - \$2.40)$$
$$= \underline{-\$6.67} \text{ (F)}$$

The rate-time variance of $6.67 is favorable, even though the negative sign seems to indicate otherwise. This compound variance is favorable when the individual variances within it differ. In this case, the rate variance was favorable; however, the time variance was unfavorable.

The sum of the four variances equals the budget variance of $140 (U) as follows:

Volume Variance	$ 33.33 (U)
Rate Variance	20.00 (F)
Efficiency Variance	133.35 (U)
Rate-Time Variance	6.67 (F)
Total	$140.01 (U)

The one cent difference is due to rounding.

Exhibit 17 is a graphic depiction of the labor variance analysis of the Sample Restaurant. The budget for labor expense is represented by the rectangle 0DEC, while the actual labor expense is represented by the rectangle 0AGH. The rate variance is represented by the rectangle ADEB. The volume variance is represented by the rectangle CEIJ. The rectangle JIFH represents the efficiency variance. The rate-time variance is represented by the rectangle BEFG.

Exhibit 17 Labor Variance Analysis—Sample Restaurant

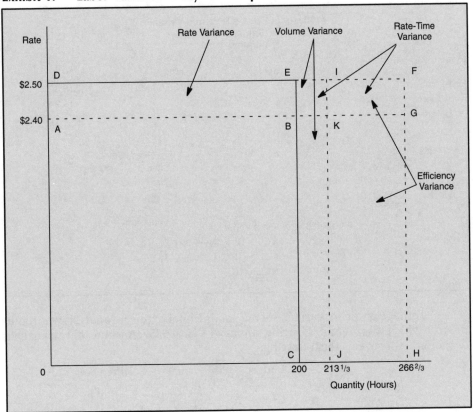

Variance Analysis of Sands Motel's Significant Variances

Exhibit 18 contains the analysis of the unfavorable rooms revenue variance of $680 identified earlier in the chapter for the Sands Motel. The breakdown is as follows:

Due to unfavorable volume differences	$887.50 (U)
Due to favorable price differences	220.00 (F)
Compound Variance	12.50 (U)
	$680.00 (U)

Management needs to investigate the causes of the failure to sell 25 additional rooms. This failure was partially offset by a favorable price variance.

If the volume variance was due to controllable causes such as price resistance or rooms being unavailable because they were out-of-order or simply not clean when potential guests desired them, then management action can be taken. If, on the other hand, the causes were beyond management's control, such as weather-related factors, then no specific management action appears to be required.

Exhibit 18   Rooms Revenue Variance Analysis—Sands Motel

Analysis of Rooms Revenue Variance
Sands Motel
January 19X4

	Room Nights	Price	Total
Budget	440	$35.50	$15,620
Actual	415	36.00	14,940
Difference	25	$ .50	$ 680 (U)

Volume Variance

$$VV = BP (AV - BV)$$
$$VV = 35.50 (415 - 440)$$
$$VV = \$887.50 \ (U)$$

Price Variance

$$PV = BV (AP - BP)$$
$$PV = 440 (36.00 - 35.50)$$
$$PV = \$220 \ (F)$$

Price — Volume Variance

$$P\text{-}VV = (AV - BV)(AP - BP)$$
$$P\text{-}VV = (415 - 440) (36.00 - 35.50)$$
$$P\text{-}VV = \$12.50 (U)$$

The other significant variance of the Sands Motel requiring analysis was rooms payroll, which was favorable during January 19X4, at $257. Assume that an analysis of rooms labor reveals the following:

	Budget	Actual	Difference
Room attendants	$ 737	$ 581	$ 156 (F)
Front office	1,763	1,662	101 (F)
	$2,500	$2,243	$ 257 (F)

Since the largest portion relates to room attendants' wages, only this portion is analyzed for illustrative purposes in Exhibit 19. The analysis of the $156 variance reveals favorable volume, rate, and efficiency variances.

When analyzing a variable labor variance, pay careful attention to each type of variance. Generally, a volume variance is beyond the scope of the labor supervisor's responsibility. For example, the $156 favorable room attendants' labor variance includes $41.88 of volume variance which is favorable. This results from fewer rooms being sold than budgeted—hardly a reason to praise the supervisor. Likewise, when more rooms are sold than budgeted, the room attendants' labor expense variance would contain an unfavorable volume variance. This portion of the total variance is not the fault of the supervisor and should be excluded when analyzing the budget variance.

Determination of Problems and Management Action

The next step in the budgetary control process is for management to investigate variance analysis results in an effort to determine the cause(s) of the variance. This

Exhibit 19   Rooms Payroll Variance Analysis—Sands Motel

Analysis of Room Payroll Variance
Sands Motel
January 19X4

	Room Nights	Time/ Room	Total Time	Hourly Wages	Total
Budget	440	30 min.	220 hrs.	$ 3.35	$737
Actual	415	28 min.	193 2/3	3.00	581
Difference	25	2 min.	26 1/3 hrs.	$ .35	$156(F)

Volume Variance

$$VV = BR (BT - ATAO)$$
$$VV = 3.35 (220 - 207.5)$$
$$VV = 3.35 (12.5)$$
$$VV = \$41.88 \ (F)$$

Rate Variance

$$RV = BT (BR - AR)$$
$$RV = 220 (3.35 - 3.00)$$
$$RV = 220 (.35)$$
$$RV = \$77 \ (F)$$

Efficiency Variance

$$EV = BR (ATAO - AT)$$
$$EV = 3.35 (207.5 - 193.67)$$
$$EV = 3.35 (13.83)$$
$$EV = \$46.33 \ (F)$$

Rate-Time Variance

$$R\text{-}TV = (BT - AT) (BR - AR)$$
$$R\text{-}TV = (220 - 193.67) (3.35 - 3.00)$$
$$R\text{-}TV = (26.33) (.35)$$
$$R\text{-}TV = \$9.22 \ (U)$$

Summation of Variances

Volume Variance	$41.88 (F)
Rate Variance	77.00 (F)
Efficiency Variance	46.33 (F)
Rate-Volume Variance	9.22 (U)
	155.99
Rounding Difference	.01
Total	$156.00 (F)

is needed because the analysis of a revenue variance will reveal differences due to price and/or volume, but not *why* the price and/or volume variances exist. Similarly, the analysis of variable labor expense will reveal differences due to rate, efficiency, and volume but, again, not the exact cause(s) of the variances. Additional investigation by management is required.

For example, assume that the analysis of the room attendants' labor variance reveals that a significant portion of an unfavorable variance is due to rate. Management must investigate the rate variance to determine why the average rate paid was higher than budgeted. An unfavorable labor rate variance may be due to staffing problems, excessive overtime pay, or a combination of these two factors. It may have been due to the scheduling of more higher paid room attendants than originally planned. There may be another reason. Each significant variance requires further management investigation to determine the cause(s).

The final step to complete the budgetary control process is taking action to correct a problem. For example, if a major cause of the rate variance for room attendants is that excessive overtime is paid, this may be controlled by requiring all overtime to be approved a specified number of hours in advance by the next highest management level.

Reforecasting

Regardless of the extensive efforts and the sophisticated methods used in formulating operations budgets, most large hospitality properties reforecast their expected operations as they progress through the budget year. This reforecasting is necessary only when the actual results begin to vary significantly from the budget. Some organizations will start reforecasting at the beginning of the budget year and continue to reforecast every month for the entire year.

Reforecasting at The Sheraton Corporation

For an example, we will look at how The Sheraton Corporation reforecasts. Reforecasting at Sheraton is a continuing process that begins immediately with the new year. It involves a three-step process as follows:

1. Three Month Outlook

2. Advanced Information for Outlook

3. Weekly Activity Report

The Three Month Outlook. Exhibit 20 is a short-term forecast used to update the annual budget on an ongoing basis. It is prepared monthly and covers the following 90-day period. The budget continues to be the standard against which goal achievement is measured. The outlook process enables management to evaluate the hotel's immediate future and to react accordingly by determining objectives, making plans, and assigning responsibilities. The general manager should be able to judge the performance of his or her team members relative to their outlook commitments.

The Three Month Outlook blends two types of forecast into its report format:

*   Sales forecast (revenues, occupancy, and average rate)

*   Profit and loss forecast (complete P & L)

While the general manager is the final approval authority, the hotel controller is responsible for overall coordination of the report preparation.

The Advanced Information for Outlook. Exhibit 21 is prepared each month in conjunction with the Three Month Outlook. Its purpose is to provide the home office with a weekly breakout of certain key outlook and budget figures on a month-to-date basis for the following month. The report is the basis for the home office's preparation of a consolidated report each week comparing month-to-date actual results with outlook and budget.

The Weekly Activity Report. Exhibit 22 is a calculated estimate of each hotel's key financial results. With the exception of fiscal year beginning and ending dates, the reporting periods cover 7-day time frames from Thursday through Wednesday. The reported information is on a cumulative (month-to-date) basis.

Exhibit 20   Three Month Outlook

THREE MONTH OUTLOOK

HOTEL_____   LOCATION_____

		Months:			19			19			19
Report 000.0		OUTLOOK	BUDGET	LAST YEAR	Outlook	Budget	Last Year	Outlook	Budget	Last Year		
Statistics												
% Occupancy	%											
Average Room Rate	$											
No. Rooms Occupied												
No. Rooms Available												
Total Revenue (Excl TVA)	$											
Total Revenue (Incl TVA)												

		$	%	$	%	$	%
Operated Departments							
Room	–Revenues		100		100		100
	–Wages & Benefits						
	–Other expenses						
	–Departmental Profit						
Food	–Revenues (Excl. O/L)		100		100		100
	–Cost of Sales						
	–Wages & Benefits						
	–Other Expenses						
	–Departmental Profit						
Beverage	–Revenues (Excl O/L)		100		100		100
	–Cost of Sales						
	–Wages & Benefits						
	–Other Expenses						
	–Departmental Profit						
Food & Beverage Other Income							
	–Food & Bev. Dept'l Prof						
Casino Departmental Profit							
Minor Operated Dept. Profit							
Convention Services Dept. Profit							
Rents & Other Income							
Total Operated Departments							
Overhead Departments							
Administrative & General							
Marketing							
Property Operation							
Total Overhead Departments							
Gross Operating Profit							
Taxes							
Insurance							
Rent Non-Affiliate							
Interest & Dept. Exp. Non-Affiliate							
(Interest Income) Non-Affiliate							
Other (Adds) & Deductions							
Cash Earnings (Loss)							
Depreciation/Replacement Reserve							
(Deferral) of First Year Loss							
Amortization of First Year Loss/Pre. Op.							
Profit Before Sheraton Charges							
Rent-Affiliate							
Inf. Exp. (Inc.) Affil.-Net							
Profit Before Sheraton Fees							
Fee	License						
	Management Basic						
	Management Incentive						
	Marketing						
Total Sheraton Fees							
Pretax Profit (Loss) Operations							

	Outlook	Budget	Last Year
Equivalent Full Time Employees			
Salaries & Wages			
Benefits			
Total Compensation			

Joint Ventures			
	Outlook	Budget	Last Year
Joint Venture Pretax Profit			
Partner(s) Equity			
Sheraton Gross Equity Before Deferral/Amort.			
Def./(Amort.) 1st Year Equity Loss			
(Def.)/Amort Fee Income			
Sheraton Net Equity			

International
Hotels Only
Rate of
Exchange

Outlook U.S.

$1.00_____

Budget U.S.

$1.00_____

Last Year U.S.

$1.00_____

Controller _____   Date _____   General Manager _____   Date _____

Courtesy of The Sheraton Corporation

Exhibit 21 Advanced Information for Outlook/Fiscal Budget

ADVANCED INFORMATION FOR OUTLOOK/FISCAL BUDGET
(Reported in U.S. Dollars and round to nearest thousand)

Refer to Financial Reports Calendar for Due Date.

INFORMATION FROM HOTEL: ____________

LOCATION: ____________

Signed: ____________ Hotel Controller

PERIOD FROM: ____________ TO: ____________

Date: ____________

MONTHLY OUTLOOK

Hotel Res. No.	Month	Excl. TVA	Title Rev. P/L	Rate	Avg. Occ.	% Fees	Equity	Hash Total
7 Days MO/	/W1							
14 Days MO/	/W2							
21 Days MO/	/W3							
28 Days MO/	/W4							
35 Days MO/	/W5							

MONTHLY BUDGET

Hotel Res. No.	Month	Excl. TVA	Title Rev. P/L	Rate	Avg. Occ.	% Fees	Equity	Hash Total
7 Days MB/	/W1							
14 Days MB/	/W2							
21 Days MB/	/W3							
28 Days MB/	/W4							
35 Days MB/	/W5							

Total Month Outlook

MPWR	COMP

Month: First three letters of the month being reported.
Total Rev: Total revenue excluding TVA's where applicable.
P/L: Owned & Leased report pre-tax income before Inter Co. Items. ie: before fees.
Managed & non-consolidated report gross operating profit.
Avg. Rate & %OCC: enter without decimals, ie: 28.70 Enter as 2870 76.2 enter as 762
Fees: Consolidated-Joint Ventures/Partnerships will report fees weekly.
Non-Consolidated will report fees weekly.
Equity: Consolidated & Non-consolidated Joint Ventures/Partnerships will report this field weekly.
MPWR: Average equivalent 40 hour employees, round to nearest whole number.
Comp: Total salaries/wages/benefits.

International Hotels Only – Rate of Exchange: Outlook U.S. $1.00 = Budget U.S. $1.00 =

	Month	Total Revenue Excl. TVA	Occupancy
Month 2			
Month 3			

Courtesy of The Sheraton Corporation

Each hotel uses its Weekly Activity Report as a primary source of financial performance, engaging in a review of its profit and loss (income) statement before the approved information is transmitted to headquarters.

At headquarters, the on-line information enters directly into a computer that generates a report showing actual results with variances to Budget and Outlook.

In addition to the Three Month Outlook, reforecasting is also done on a total year basis at least twice a year for strategic and operating plans.

Budgeting at Multi-Unit Hospitality Enterprises

This chapter has been oriented toward operations budgeting at a single hotel property. However, both lodging and food service chains continue to increase their dominance in their respective hospitality segments. The chains in the food service industry account for more than 50% of food service sales, and in the lodging industry, giants such as Holiday Inns and Marriott experience over $1 billion in lodging sales annually.

Research on budgeting at multi-unit food service and lodging chains has revealed the following significant results:[4]

Exhibit 22 Weekly Activity Report

The Sheraton Corporation

WEEKLY ACTIVITY REPORT
IN THOUSANDS OF DOLLARS)

FOR THE MONTH OF
WEEK ENDING DATE
WEEK
PAGE
OF

REVENUE						HOTELS	*PROFIT (LOSS)						AVG. ROOM RATE			%OCCUPANCY		
THIS WEEK			MONTH TO DATE				THIS WEEK			MONTH TO DATE			MONTH TO DATE			MONTH TO DATE		
	VARIANCE			VARIANCE				VARIANCE			VARIANCE			VARIANCE			VARIANCE	
ACTUAL	BUDGET	OUTLOOK	ACTUAL	BUDGET	OUTLOOK		ACTUAL	BUDGET	OUTLOOK	ACTUAL	BUDGET	OUTLOOK	ACTUAL	BUDGET	OUTLOOK	ACTUAL	BUDGET	OUTLOOK

Courtesy of The Sheraton Corporation

1. A majority of companies develop their overall corporate budgets using the bottom-up approach. That is, managers develop individual budgets that are accumulated through successive company layers until an overall corporate budget is proposed. The commonest reasons cited for using the bottom-up approach are (1) the need to increase the feeling of unit-level "ownership" in the budget, and (2) the ability of unit-level personnel to recognize specific problems affecting lower organizational levels.
2. A significant minority develop their budgets at the corporate level and then dictate the budgets to the lower levels in the corporate structure. The major reason cited for the top-down approach is that the sum of the individual restaurant budgets would not meet corporate expectations.
3. Several companies use a combination of the bottom-up and top-down approaches.
4. Whether the budgeting approach is bottom-up or top-down, most companies at the corporate level set financial goals before the budget process begins.
5. The major differences in budgeting by chains versus the single unit organization include:
    - Greater need for coordination

- Greater volume of information to be processed
- Use of more sophisticated and frequently computerized procedures
- Greater amount of time required
- Unique procedures to allocate costs between organization levels
- Greater extent of management attention to budget process

6. The percentage of lodging chains that reported allowable variance levels for selected costs is as follows:

	Food Costs	Beverage Costs	Labor Costs	Other Costs
< 1%	5%	5%	6%	6%
1–1.9%	26	28	23	6
2–2.9%	11	11	18	29
3–3.9%	5	6	12	18
4–4.9%	16	11	6	6
>4.9%	5	6	6	6
No set amount	32	33	29	29
Total	100%	100%	100%	100%

For those lodging chains that set tolerance criteria for variable costs, 1–1.9% was commonest for food costs, beverage costs, and labor costs, while 2–2.9% was commonest for other costs. Food service chains generally have even lower tolerances than lodging chains.

Budgeting at The Sheraton Corporation

Budgeting at The Sheraton Corporation involves a three-stage process as follows:

1. Long-range strategic plans
2. Shorter term operating plans
3. Detailed monthly budgets for the following year

The Strategic Plan is done each spring and is a projection of the financial objectives of the corporation over the next five years. It is generally a top-down approach with corporate strategies defined in the areas of marketing, development, and financial performance. The hotels participate individually by providing seven-year summary financial statements to their divisions' offices showing prior year actual, current year budget, forecast, variance, and projected earnings for the next five years (see Exhibit 23).

The One Year Operating Plan is done in the fall and is a refinement of Plan Year I of the Strategic Plan. Standardized workpapers are provided to each hotel for use in developing detailed backup for their Plan Year I revenue and expense projections. These workpapers are then subject to review by division operations and support

Exhibit 23   Strategic Plan: Comparative Income Statement

Sheraton

Weighted Avg. Exchange Rate–US $1

19___ STRATEGIC PLAN

COMPARATIVE INCOME STATEMENT
(Round to Nearest Thousand)

(HOTEL NAME:)

FRS NO

(DATE)   (REV NO)

Line Item	LINE NO	PRIOR YEAR ACTUAL 19__	% of Rev	CURRENT YEAR 19__ BUDGET	% Rev	FORECAST	% Rev	VARIANCE	PLAN YEAR I 19__	% Rev	PLAN YEAR II 19__	% Rev	PLAN YEAR III 19__	% Rev	PLAN YEAR IV 19__	% Rev	PLAN YEAR V 19__	% Rev
Total Revenue – Including TVA	1																	
Excluding TVA	2		100		100		100			100		100		100		100		100
Rooms – Revenues	3		100		100		100		100		100		100		100		100	
Wages & Benefits	4																	
Other Expenses	5																	
Departmental Profit	6																	
Food Revenues	7		100		100		100		100		100		100		100		100	
Cost of Sales	8																	
Wages - Benefits	9																	
Other Expenses	10																	
Departmental Profit	11																	
Beverage Revenues	12		100		100		100		100		100		100		100		100	
Costs of Sales	13																	
Wages & Benefits	14		100		100		100		100		100		100		100		100	
Other Expenses	15																	
Departmental Profit	16																	
Food & Beverage Other Income	17																	
Convention Services Deptl. Profit	18																	
Total Food & Bev. Profit	19																	
Minor Operated Deptl. Profit	20																	
Casino Departmental Profit	21																	
Rents and Other Income	22																	
Total Operated Deptl Profit	23																	
Overhead Departments	24																	
Administrative & General	25																	
Marketing	26																	
Property Operation	27																	
Total Overhead Departments	28																	
Gross Operating Profit (Loss)	29																	
Capital Expenses	30																	
Taxes	31																	
Insurance	32																	
Rent Non-Affiliate	33																	
Int. & Debt Exp. Non-Affiliate	34																	
(Int. Income) – Non-Affiliate	35																	
Other (Adds) & Deductions	36																	
Total Capital Exp. & Other	37																	
Cash Earnings (Loss)	38																	
Depreciation/Replacement Reserve	39																	
(Deferral) of First Year Loss	40																	
Amortization 1st Yr. Loss/Pre-Open Exp.	41																	
Profit Before Sheraton Charges	42																	
Rent – Affiliate	43																	
Int. Exp. (inc.) Affil. – Net	44																	
Marketing Fee	45																	
License Fee	46																	
Mgmt Fee – Basic	47																	
Management Fee – Incentive	48																	
Total Fees	49																	
Pretax Profit (Loss) Operations	50																	
Income Taxes	51																	
(Gain)/Loss Translation	52																	
Net Operations	53																	
Memo Sheraton Gross Equity	54																	
Def.(/Amort) 1st Yr. Equity Loss	55																	
(Def)/Amort Fee Income	56																	
Sheraton Net Equity	57																	
Total Salaries, Wages, Benefits	58																	
Avg. Equiv. Full-Time Employees	59																	
Headcount at 12/31	60																	
Overall Occupancy %	61																	
Average Rate	62																	
No. of Rooms Available	63																	
No. of Rooms Occupied	64																	
No. of Rooms at Year End	65																	

Courtesy of The Sheraton Corporation

staffs before final acceptance of the Operating Plan as local management's formal commitment to achieve these goals during the next year.

Upon final acceptance of the hotel's Operating Plan, the Annual Income Statement for Plan Year I automatically becomes the fixed budget against which actual performance will be measured for the next fiscal year. The budget is input into the computer at the corporate headquarters after the hotels break down the annual income statement by month and by departmental components on forms provided for that purpose.

Summary

The budgetary process is valuable to the operation of a hospitality establishment. In order to formulate a budget, the establishment's goals must be stated and each department must look ahead and estimate future performance. As the actual period progresses, management can compare operating results to the budget, and significant differences can be studied. This process forces management to set future goals and to strive to see that they become realized.

In order to formulate a budget, each department estimates its revenues and expenses. This is done by observing past trends and projecting them for another year. The manager must also take into account forces in the economy, new developments in the market, and other significant events that will affect the operation. These projections are then combined to form a budget for the next period's operations. At this point, the budgeted results are compared with the establishment's goals, and the budget is adjusted until these goals are met.

Once completed, the budget becomes a control tool. As the periods progress, management compares the budget with actual performance. The differences between each line item are calculated, and any significant differences are analyzed. Significance depends on both absolute dollar differences and percentage differences. The analysis includes dividing each line item into its components including price and volume for revenues and rate, volume, and efficiency for labor. Management can then address any deficiencies and take corrective action to keep the operations heading toward the defined goals.

Endnotes

1. A *service center* is a department outside the profit centers that provides services to the profit centers or the hotel as a whole—for example, the marketing department. A *cost center* is a department within a profit center for which costs are tracked—for example, housekeeping within the rooms department.

2. For more information on zero-base budgeting, see Peter A. Pyrrh, *Zero-Base Budgeting* (New York: John Wiley & Sons, 1973) and Lee M. Kruel, "Zero-Base Budgeting of Hotel Indirect Expense," *The Cornell Hotel & Restaurant Administration Quarterly*, November 1978, pp. 11–14.

3. For more information on lodging feasibility studies, see William P. Andrew and Raymond S. Schmidgall, *Financial Management for the Hospitality Industry* (East Lansing, Mich.: Educational Institute of the American Hotel & Motel Association, 1993), pp. 368–382.

4. Raymond S. Schmidgall and Jack D. Ninemeier, "Foodservice Budgeting: How the Chains Do It," *The Cornell Hotel & Restaurant Administration Quarterly*, February 1986, pp. 51–55. Raymond S. Schmidgall and Jack D. Ninemeier, "Budgeting in Hotel Chains: Coordination and Control," *The Cornell Hotel & Restaurant Administration Quarterly*, May 1987, pp. 79–84.

Key Terms

cost of goods sold variance—A group of variances used to examine differences between budgeted and actual amounts paid for goods sold and the total amount sold.

incremental budgeting—Forecasting budgets based on historical financial information.

operations budget—Management's detailed plans for generating revenue and incurring expenses for each department within the operation; also referred to as the revenue and expense budget.

revenue variances—A group of variances used to examine differences between budgeted and actual prices and volumes.

significance criteria—Criteria used to determine which variances are significant. Generally expressed in terms of both dollar and percentage differences.

strategic planning—Another name for long-range planning. It not only considers revenues and expenses, but also evaluates and selects from among major alternatives those that provide long-range direction to the hospitality operation.

variable labor variance—A group of variances used to examine differences between budgeted and actual variable labor expense.

variance analysis—Process of identifying and investigating causes of significant differences (variances) between budgeted plans and actual results.

zero-base budgeting—An approach to preparing budgets that requires the justification of all expenses; assumes that each department starts with zero dollars and must justify all budgeted amounts.

Review Questions

1. What are four future items that should be considered when formulating a budget?

2. How does a budget help an establishment to realize its operating goals?

3. How is the budget formulated?

4. Why should budgets be prepared at various levels of sales?

5. What constitutes a "significant" variance?

6. What do volume variances highlight for management?

7. Why is an increase in volume favorable in revenue analysis and unfavorable in cost analysis?

8. What does the formula $EV = BR(ATAO - AT)$ calculate?

9. What items should be considered when preparing the rooms revenue section of the budget?

10. What are three possible goals an establishment could set for its operations?

Problems

Problem 1

The manager of the 150-seat Broad Cafe requests your assistance in preparing the cafe's annual sales budget. The first day of the budget year is a Sunday, and the budget year has 365 days. In addition, the cafe is closed on Sundays.

The seat turnover (ST) and average check by meal period (AC) by day is as follows:

	Breakfast		Lunch		Dinner	
	ST	AC	ST	AC	ST	AC
M–F	1.2	$4.50	1.0	$7.20	.5	$9.80
S	.8	3.70	.5	6.70	1.5	11.45

In addition, miscellaneous sales (candy, etc.) are 3% of total sales.

Required:

Determine the Broad Cafe's sales budget for the year. Also show the sales budget by meal period.

Problem 2

The 100-room Delavan Inn's past three years of room sales for April are as follows:

Year	Rooms Sold	ADR	Room Revenues
19X1	$ 2,100	$ 45	$ 94,500
19X2	2,130	47	100,110
19X3	2,160	49	105,840

Required:

Analyze the past performance and project sales for April 19X4. Assume the trends of rooms sold and ADR continue for April of 19X4.

Problem 3

Turner's Eatery, a 50-seat restaurant, projects its seat turnover for June, 19X2, as follows:

Day of Week	Breakfast	Seat Turnovers Lunch	Dinner
Sunday	--------- Closed ---------		
Monday	1.3	1.5	.5

	Seat Turnovers		
Day of Week	Breakfast	Lunch	Dinner
Tuesday	1.2	1.3	.6
Wednesday	1.4	1.4	.6
Thursday	1.4	1.2	.5
Friday	1.3	1.3	1.0
Saturday	.5	.8	1.5
Average Food Service Check	$4.25	$6.85	$10.50

Required:

Determine the projected food sales by meal period for June, 19X2. Assume the first day of the month is a Sunday.

Problem 4

Horner's Corner projected 3,000 lunches to be sold for September at an average price of $5.50. The actual sales were 3,200 meals and food revenue of $18,400.

Required:

1. Determine the budget variance.
2. Determine the volume variance.
3. Determine the price variance.

Problem 5

The Summary Budget Report of the Hittle Cafe for the month of March is as follows:

			Variances	
	Budget	Actual	$	%
Food Sales	$50,000	$52,500	_____	_____
Miscellaneous Sales	3,000	3,200	_____	_____
Total	53,000	55,700	_____	_____
Cost of Food Sales	15,000	15,500	_____	_____
Other Cost of Sales	1,000	900	_____	_____
Total	16,000	16,400	_____	_____
Gross Profit	37,000	39,300	_____	_____
Controllable Expenses:				
Salaries and Wages	15,000	16,000	_____	_____
Employee Benefits	3,000	3,600	_____	_____
Marketing Expenses	2,000	2,500	_____	_____
Direct Operating Expenses	3,000	3,200	_____	_____
Repairs	2,000	2,100	_____	_____
Other	3,000	2,800	_____	_____

	Budget	Actual	Variances $	Variances %
Income before fixed expenses	9,000	9,100	_____	_____
Rent	2,000	2,000	_____	_____
Insurance	1,000	1,000	_____	_____
Property Taxes	1,000	1,000	_____	_____
Income before income taxes	5,000	5,100	_____	_____
Income taxes	1,500	1,530	_____	_____
Net Income	$ 3,500	$ 3,570	_____	_____

Required:

Complete the two variance columns of the Summary Budget Report and indicate unfavorable variances by using parentheses following Exhibit 10 as an example.

Problem 6

Jackie Jackson, the rooms department manager of Waverly Motor Hotel, is preparing a condensed 19X6 annual budget. She has the following information upon which to base her estimates.

- Estimated occupancy percentage: 75%

- Rooms: 100

- Average rate: $50.00

- Labor: Variable: $5.00/room
        Fixed: $100,000 (annual)

- Other operating expenses: $2.50/room

Required:

1. Prepare a condensed budget for the rooms department. (Assume that the hotel is open 365 days a year.)

2. The Waverly's management requires that the department have a departmental profit of at least $1,000,000 and 75% of revenue. Will Ms. Jackson's condensed budget projections be acceptable to the hotel's management?

Problem 7

Barbara Collins is the manager of Shives, a fine dining restaurant, and is preparing next year's budget. She wants to examine three different levels of sales as follows: $700,000, $1,000,000, and $1,300,000. The following information upon which to make the calculations is provided.

- Food cost percentage: 45%

- Labor: Variable: 23%
        Fixed: $80,000

- Other operating expenses: 8%

- Fixed charges: $100,000

- Income taxes: 30% of pretax income

Required:

1. Prepare the condensed operating budget for Shives at the three levels of sales indicated above.

2. Comment briefly regarding the impact of different levels of sales on the restaurant's profits.

Problem 8

Jim Smith is working on the operations budget for Smith's Place for 19X4. The estimated turn-over by meal period by day is as follows:

	Lunch	Dinner
Monday–Friday	1.5	.75
Saturday	.5	1.5
Sunday	1.5	.5

Smith's has 100 seats, and its average checks for lunch and dinner for 19X3 were $8.20 and $12.20, respectively. Jim Smith estimates his enterprise will be able to increase its average prices in 19X4 by 10% over 19X3.

Smith's Place has experienced a food cost of 35% in the past. However, by implementing new controls, Jim believes 32% can be achieved in 19X4. Labor is expected to average 32%, while other controllable expenses should total 15% of total sales. Fixed costs are expected to total $150,000, and Smith's tax rate is 30%.

Assume that 19X4 is a leap year and that the first day of the year falls on a Saturday.

Required:

Prepare the operations budget for 19X4 for Smith's Place.

Problem 9

The Mica Motel (MM), open 365 days a year, consists of an 80-room motel with a 60-seat coffee shop. J.D. Mica provides you with the following information:

1. Of the 80 rooms, 60 are doubles and 20 are singles.

2. The doubles are sold for $22 each and the singles are sold for $18 each.

3. Forecasted occupancy is 84% for doubles and 78% for singles.

4. The average occupancy per room is 1.8. (Only one person stays in a single but two or more may stay in a double for $22/night.)

5. Forty percent of those staying in the singles and 20% of those staying in the doubles eat breakfast in the coffee shop. (There is no walk-in business for breakfast.) The average check is $2.80.

6. The lunch and dinner business have seat turnovers and average checks as follows:

	Lunch		Dinner	
	Turnover	Aver. Ck.	Turnover	Aver. Ck.
Mon.-Fri.	1.25	$4.20	1.0	$10.75
Sat.	.5	4.50	1.0	12.50
Sun.	1.5	5.50	.5	11.25

7. The first day of the year for which you are to prepare the budget is Monday.
8. The food cost percentage is estimated to be 35%.
9. The labor cost percentages are as follows:

> Rooms: 20%
> Food: 32%

10. Other direct expenses of the operated departments are as follows:

> Rooms: 10%
> Food: 12%

11. Undistributed operating expenses include:

> $100,000 of fixed expenses and the remainder is 10% of total revenue

12. Other fixed costs include the following:

> | Property taxes | $30,000 |
> |---|---|
> | Depreciation | 60,000 |
> | Interest | 50,000 |

13. The MM's average income tax rate is 30% of income before income taxes.

Required:

Prepare, in reasonable form, the operations budget for the year.

Problem 10

For the week of June 6, Melvin Mince, the manager of Melvin's Hotel in northwestern Illinois, budgeted 600 hours for room attendants to clean rooms. This budget was based on a work standard of cleaning one room every 36 minutes. The rooms attendants actually worked 660 hours cleaning 1,050 rooms. The budgeted wage rate for room attendants is $3.40 per hour. The wages paid to room attendants totaled $2,178.00.

Required:

1. What is the amount of the budget variance?
2. What is the amount of the volume variance?
3. What is the amount of the efficiency variance?
4. What is the amount of the rate variance?

Problem 11

Harry Booky, the Happy Hotel's accountant, has just finished the hotel's monthly financial statements. He has shown an unfavorable budget variance for room attendants' wages, and the head housekeeper is in the "hot seat." However, since extra rooms were cleaned, the head housekeeper may not be totally responsible for the unfavorable variance. Ms. Edna Degree, the hotel's general manager, has requested that the unfavorable budget variance of $605 be analyzed.

The available information is as follows:

1. Budgeted rooms sales: 6,000

   Budgeted hourly pay rate for room attendants: $4.50

Work standard: clean 2 rooms per hour

2. Actual results—room sales: 6,400

Actual average hourly pay rate: $4.55

Actual hours attendants worked: 3,100

Required:

1. Is the unfavorable budget variance of $605 significant? Why or why not?

2. Compute the volume variance.

3. Compute the rate variance.

4. Compute the efficiency variance.

5. To what degree is the head housekeeper responsible for the unfavorable variance?

Problem 12

Amy Howe is the dining room manager of the Marathon Club. The wages budget for her department are divided between fixed and variable expenses. The work standard for waitpersons is to serve 12 members per hour. The average wage rate per hour is $6.00.

The variable wages budget for waitpersons for June is $14,400 based on $6.00 per hour, eight-hour shifts, 30 days in the month, and 10 waitpersons. Given the work standard, this is also based on servicing 28,800 people.

During the month of June, the waitperson wages totaled $15,600. During June, 2,500 hours were worked, and the average hourly pay was $6.24 per hour. In addition, 29,200 members were provided service by the waitpersons.

Required:

1. Determine the budget variance for waitperson variable wage expense.

2. Is the budget variance determined (in #1 above) significant? Explain.

3. Rate Amy Howe's performance in managing the waitpersons. Support your discussion with specific numbers.

4. What is the efficiency variance for waitperson wage expense for the month of June?

Problem 13

Part I

Holly's Hotel budgeted 800 room sales for the week ended March 10. The estimated average price per room was $18.50. The actual average price per room was 10% greater than anticipated, while room sales in units were 10% less than forecasted.

Required:

What is the budget variance for the week? Analyze the budget variance by calculating each revenue variance.

Part II

For the same week, Holly's Hotel's head housekeeper, based on the work standard, budgeted 400 hours for room attendants to clean the rooms sold. The actual hours worked totaled 380.

The estimated average wage rate for the attendants is $4.00 per hour. The wages paid totaled $1,444.

Required:

1. Were the room attendants efficient?
2. How much was the rate variance?
3. Based on the above, how would you rate the head housekeeper, considering the dollars spent? Use figures to support your answer.

Problem 14

The Armington Cafe appears to be having some difficulty controlling its food costs. The cafe's budgeted food cost percentage was 36% based on food sales of $100,000. However, the actual food sales were $110,000, and the actual food cost totaled $40,800. The proprietor, M.D. Schmidt, is concerned about the unfavorable food cost variance of $4,800. The number of covers budgeted and actually served totaled 15,000 and 16,000, respectively. The average food service check was budgeted for $6.6667. The average food service check for the month was $6.875.

Required:

1. Analyze the food revenue variance of $10,000, showing the amounts that relate to volume and price.
2. Analyze the cost of food sold variance and determine the amounts relating to the cost variance, volume variance, and cost-volume variance.

Problem 15

R. K. Dwight is interested in long-term operations planning for the rooms department of her hotel, the Dwight Inn. The budget detail for 19X5 is as follows:

	Rooms	Occ. %	ADR	Total
Singles	50	60%	$ 55	$ 602,250
Doubles	100	75%	$ 65	1,779,375
Suites	50	80%	$ 70	1,022,000
			Total	$3,403,625

Payroll costs:
  Fixed labor costs (annual)   120,000
  Variable labor costs   12% of room sales

Other expenses: (as a percent of room sales)
  Commissions   2.0%
  Laundry   2.0%
  Operating supplies   3.0%
  Linen   0.5%
  Uniforms   0.5%
  All other   1.5%

Assume that the rooms department for years 19X6–19X9 is able to realize occupancy increases of 0.5 percentage points per year for each type of room sales (for example, singles would be 60.5% for 19X6), and that ADR increases of $2 per year can be realized for each type of room. Further assume that variable labor costs increase by 4% each year and fixed labor costs increase by 6% each year. Finally, assume that the other expense percentages are maintained over the five years of 19X5–19X9. Round all figures to the nearest dollar.

Required:

Prepare the five-year budget for the rooms department of the Dwight Inn.

Chapter 11 Outline

Cash and Its Importance
Distinction Between Income and Cash Flows
Cash Budgeting
    Cash Receipts and Disbursements Approach
    Adjusted Net Income Approach
    Information for Cash Budgeting
    Illustration—Cash Receipts and Disbursements Approach
    Illustration—Adjusted Net Income Approach
Float
Cash Flow Information
    Enhancing Cash Flows
Management of Working Capital
Accounts Receivable
Inventory
Current Liabilities
Integrated Cash Management for Multi-Unit Operations
Computer Applications

11

Cash Management

CASH MANAGEMENT REFERS TO the management of a hospitality operation's cash balances (currency and demand deposits), cash flow (cash receipts and disbursements), and short-term investments in securities. Cash management is critical to both large and small hospitality operations. Insufficient cash can quickly lead to bankruptcy. This chapter will address many questions regarding cash management, including the following:

1. What is the difference between income and cash flows?

2. What is contained in a cash budget?

3. How are cash receipts forecasted?

4. How do short-term and long-term cash budgeting approaches differ?

5. What are the relevant factors to consider when investing working capital funds?

6. What are compensating balances?

7. How does a lockbox system speed up cash flow?

8. Why is depreciation expense irrelevant in cash flow considerations?

9. Why are investors interested in cash flow?

10. How are other (noncash) current assets related to cash flow?

Our discussion of cash management will identify the uses and importance of cash in a hospitality operation. We will consider the distinction between income and cash flows and explain what is meant by negative cash flow. We will discuss basic approaches to using cash budgets for planning purposes. We will also address the major areas of hospitality operations affecting the process of cash budgeting, such as management of working capital including accounts receivable, inventory, and current liabilities. Finally, we will address the special aspects of integrated cash management for multi-unit operations.

Cash and Its Importance

In hospitality establishments, cash consists of petty cash funds, cash on hand for operational purposes, and cash in the bank. Cash on hand includes both house banks and undeposited cash receipts. Cash in the bank includes demand deposits. Some operations also consider time deposits and certificates of deposit as cash. In our discussion, all of these elements will be considered cash.

Petty cash funds are established for making minor cash purchases. These funds are normally maintained on an **imprest basis**—that is, they are replenished by the amount of disbursements since the previous replenishment.

House banks are maintained in order to facilitate cash transactions with guests. Each cash drawer should hold only as much as is needed to transact business. Added together, the house banks in a hotel may total several thousand dollars. Since house banks do not generate earnings, these cash balances should be minimized.

Ideally, the hospitality operation's cash balance in a demand deposit bank account should be zero. That is, daily deposits should equal disbursements from the account. However, cash received and cash disbursed are generally not uniform because the cash receipts for a day seldom equal the cash disbursements for the same day. Therefore, most operations maintain minimum balances in their checking accounts to cover checks drawn. The reason for keeping these cash balances is commonly referred to as a **transaction motive**.

The size of the checking account balance is also influenced by banks. Some banks demand that depositors maintain substantial amounts in their accounts to cover bank services and to serve as compensating balances for bank loans. For example, an operation receiving a loan for $100,000 may be required to maintain a 10% compensating balance. This means $10,000 must be maintained in the checking account. Since no interest is earned on the compensating balance, the **effective cost** of the loan is higher than its stated interest rate. The effective cost is determined as follows:

$$\text{Effective Interest Rate} = \frac{\text{Annual Interest on Loan}}{\text{Loan} - \text{Compensating Balance Requirement}}$$

For example, assume that a hotel receives a one-year loan of $100,000 at 10% interest with a compensating balance requirement of $10,000. The effective interest rate is 11.1%, as illustrated below:

$$
\begin{aligned}
\text{Interest} &= \text{Principal} \times \text{Rate} \times \text{Time} \\
&= \$100,000 \times 10\% \times 1 \text{ year} \\
&= \$10,000 \\
\text{Effective Interest Rate} &= \frac{\$10,000}{\$100,000 - \$10,000} \\
&= \underline{\underline{11.1\%}}
\end{aligned}
$$

Aggressive financial managers attempt to keep cash balances as low as possible given in-house cash needs and banking requirements. The cost of maintaining excessive in-house cash or checking accounts is the opportunity cost. The opportunity cost equals the earnings available if the cash were invested. For example, if a hospitality operation has an average annual checking account balance of $40,000 when the bank requires only $25,000, the opportunity cost is the interest that could be earned on $15,000. At an interest rate of 10%, the opportunity cost is $1,500 annually ($15,000 × .1).

Exhibit 1   Sample Condensed Income Statement and Cash Flow Statement—Rambles Restaurant

Condensed Income Statement and Cash Flow Statement
Rambles Restaurant
For the year ended December 31, 19X3

Income Statement		Cash Flow Statement	
Sales	$ 600,000	Cash Receipts:	
Cost of Food Sold	200,000	Cash Sales	$ 300,000
Payroll Cost	200,000	Collection of Accounts	
Other Operating Expenses	100,000	Receivable	300,000
Depreciation	50,000	Total	600,000
Interest	25,000	Cash Disbursements:	
Income Taxes	10,000	Purchases of Food	200,000
Net Income	$ 15,000	Payment of Payroll	200,000
		Payment of Operating Costs	100,000
		Payment of Income Taxes	10,000
		Payment for Equipment	50,000
		Mortgage Payment	50,000
		Dividends Paid	10,000
		Total	620,000
		Excess Cash Disbursements	$ 20,000

Investors also have a keen interest in an operation's cash position. Investors make money in two ways: they receive cash dividends and their wealth increases as the stock prices increase. However, corporations are able to pay cash dividends only as cash is available. Therefore, those investing in corporations for dividends will review financial statements, especially the statement of cash flows, to determine whether the operation has sufficient cash to pay dividends and whether it will be operated in a manner that will allow dividend payments in the future.

Distinction Between Income and Cash Flows

Income flows result from operations generating revenues and incurring expenses. These flows are shown on the income statement and reflect the results of operations. **Cash flows** result from the receipt and disbursement of cash. It is possible for an operation to generate profits (income flow) yet have a negative cash flow (cash disbursements exceed cash receipts).

Exhibit 1 illustrates this situation. The statements are simplified for illustrative purposes. As the income statement shows, Rambles Restaurant generated net income flows of $15,000; however, cash disbursements exceeded cash receipts by $20,000. In this simplified illustration, the differences in income and cash flows are as follows:

Income Flows	Cash Flows
1. Depreciation $50,000	1. Depreciation has no effect on cash flows.

Income Flows	Cash Flows

2. Interest expense $25,000

2. Interest expense is part of the mortgage payment of $50,000. The $25,000 difference between the mortgage payment and the interest expense is the principal reduction portion of the mortgage payment.

3. The purchase of equipment has no direct effect on income flows. The write-off (depreciation) will affect income flows over several years.

3. Payment of $50,000 for equipment purchase (purchased in the last month of the year)

4. Dividends do not affect income flows.

4. Dividends paid of $10,000

Therefore, the $110,000 *cash* outflows listed above (mortgage payment of $50,000, payment of $50,000 for equipment, and dividends of $10,000 paid) exceed the sum of the two *income* outflows (depreciation and interest expense) of $75,000. The difference of $35,000 ($110,000 − $75,000) is the same as the difference between the income flows (net income of $15,000) and cash flows (net cash outflow of $20,000). Note that all other cash flows and income flows are the same in this simplified example. In more complex situations, there are usually additional differences between income and cash flows.

A hospitality operation may withstand negative cash flows for short periods of time if cash reserves are adequate to cover the deficits. However, over long periods, negative cash flows will most likely result in failure even if income flows are positive.

Most businesses, including hospitality establishments, have peaks and valleys in their operations. Generally, more cash is required during peak periods because cash is tied up in inventories and especially accounts receivable. Therefore, cash planning is important to ensure sufficient cash at all times. Cash planning is achieved by preparing cash budgets for several months in the future.

Cash Budgeting

Cash budgets are prepared to reflect the estimated cash receipts and cash disbursements for the period. In certain situations, cash may be in short supply and a cash deficit may be projected. If the estimated cash receipts and beginning cash (estimated available cash) are not sufficient to cover projected cash disbursements, management must take action. Even if estimated available cash is greater than projected cash disbursements, the projected cash balance must be reviewed to determine if it is a sufficient buffer for any cash receipt shortfalls and/or unplanned cash disbursements. If the estimated cash balance is insufficient, the operation must plan to increase cash receipts, decrease cash disbursements, or do both. Management actions to cover temporary deficits may include obtaining short-term bank loans, obtaining loans from owners, deferring equipment purchases, and deferring dividend payments or a combination of such actions.

If the estimated cash balance at the end of the period appears excessive, then the excess cash should be temporarily invested. The six factors management should consider when investing excess cash are risk, return, liquidity, cost, size, and time:

- *Risk* refers to the probability of losing the investment. Management should generally take a minimum risk when investing, especially when investing short-run funds. For example, investments in government securities such as Treasury bills are considered risk-free.

- *Return* refers to the rate of return that can be received on the funds. Generally, the greater the risk and the longer the investment period, the greater the return.

- *Liquidity* refers to the ability to convert the investment to cash. When cash is invested temporarily, it should generally be invested in fairly liquid investments so it can be quickly liquidated as required.

- *Cost* refers to the brokerage cost of investing.

- *Size* refers to the amount of funds available for investing. In general, the more money available for investing, the higher the return.

- *Time* refers to the amount of time the excess funds are invested. Generally, the longer the investment time, the higher the return.

Because managers need to know in advance whether cash shortages or excesses are likely, they project cash flows when they prepare cash budgets. There are two basic approaches to cash budgeting: the cash receipts and disbursements approach and the adjusted net income approach. The method used depends primarily on the length of time for which the cash budget is prepared.

Cash Receipts and Disbursements Approach

The **cash receipts and disbursements approach** is useful when forecasting cash receipts for periods of up to six months. It shows the direct sources of cash receipts, such as cash sales, collection of accounts receivable, bank loans, sale of capital stock, and so forth. It also reveals the direct uses of cash, such as payment of food purchases, payroll, mortgage payments, and dividend payments. Because the cash receipts and disbursements method reflects the direct sources and uses of cash, it is easy to understand. However, it should generally not be used for periods exceeding six months. Projected figures beyond this point become increasingly unreliable, especially when actual operations differ significantly from the operations budget.

Exhibit 2 illustrates the basic format of a cash budget based on the cash receipts and disbursements approach. This format consists of two major sections: estimated cash receipts and estimated cash disbursements. Estimated cash receipts are added to the estimated beginning cash to project the estimated cash available for the period. Estimated cash disbursements are subtracted from estimated cash available to determine estimated ending cash. This figure is then compared to the minimum cash required to identify any shortage or excess. (The process of estimating cash receipts and cash disbursements will be presented later in this chapter.)

Exhibit 2   Cash Budget—Cash Receipts and Disbursements Approach

Cash Budget
Cash Receipts and Disbursements Approach
For the months of Jan.–June, 19X1

	January	February	March	April	May	June
Estimated Cash—						
Beginning	$	$	$	$	$	$
Estimated Cash Receipts:						
Cash Sales						
Collection of Accounts Receivable						
Proceeds from Bank Loans						
Proceeds from Sale of Fixed Assets						
Other						
Total						
Estimated Cash Available						
Estimated Cash Disbursements:						
Inventory						
Payroll						
Operating Expenses						
Taxes						
Insurance						
Mortgage Payments						
Dividends						
Other						
Total						
Estimated Cash Ending						
Minimum Cash Required						
Cash Excess or Shortage	$	$	$	$	$	$

Adjusted Net Income Approach

The **adjusted net income approach** is generally preferable for budgeting cash for periods longer than six months. It also reflects the estimated cash balance for management's evaluation. In addition to its usefulness for longer periods of time, it emphasizes external, as opposed to internal, sources of funds. Exhibit 3 illustrates the format of a prepared cash budget using the adjusted net income approach.

The adjusted net income method is an indirect approach to cash budgeting because the sources and uses related to operations are indirect rather than direct; for example, direct sources from operations such as cash sales are not shown, nor are direct uses for operations such as disbursements for payroll. This approach has two major sections: sources and uses. The sources section consists of internal and external

Exhibit 3   Cash Budget—Adjusted Net Income Approach

Cash Budget
Adjusted Net Income Approach
For the year ended December 31, 19X1

Cash—Beginning of Year $

Sources of Cash:
   Net Income $
     Add: Depreciation
          Amortization
          Other   _____

Other Sources:
   Proceeds from Bank Loans
   Sale of Fixed Assets
   Sale of Capital Stock
   Other   _____

        Total   _____

Uses of Cash:
   Increase in Accounts Receivable*
   Increase in Inventories*
   Decrease in Current Liabilities*
   Purchase of Fixed Assets
   Reduction in Long-Term Debt
   Other   _____

        Total   _____

Estimated Cash—End of Year   _____

Minimum Cash Requirement   _____

Cash Excess or Shortage $ _____

*Decreases in accounts receivable and inventories and increases in current liabilities would be sources of cash.

Note: When a hospitality firm *pays* an amount of income taxes that differs from what is shown on the income statement, the difference must be included on the cash budget. This may be easily accomplished by showing the amount of income tax expense in the sources section, similar to depreciation, and the amount of taxes paid in the uses section of the cash budget.

sources. Internal sources are primarily cash from operations (chiefly reflected by net income plus income tax expense, depreciation, and other expenses that do not require cash). External sources of funds include proceeds from bank loans and the sale of capital stock. The sum of the beginning cash and the sources of cash is the estimated cash available.

The uses of cash are subtracted from cash at the beginning of the year plus sources of cash to find the estimated cash at the end of year. This figure is compared with the minimum cash requirement to determine any excess or shortage.

The adjusted net income approach, much like the statement of cash flows prepared on an indirect basis, focuses directly on changes in accounts receivable, inventories, and current liabilities. This requires management to consider the amount of cash tied up in accounts receivable and inventory and cash provided by current liabilities. Therefore, this approach encourages closer management review of these working capital accounts.

From a practical viewpoint, both cash budgeting approaches are useful. The cash receipts and disbursements approach should be used for short-term budgets prepared on a monthly or weekly basis. The adjusted net income approach is useful for long-term budgets. Many hospitality establishments prepare cash budgets for long-range periods corresponding to each annual operations budget prepared for several years into the future.

Information for Cash Budgeting

The operations budget is the major source of information for preparing a cash budget. For example, estimated cash sales for a period are based on total sales for the period and the estimated percentage of the sales that is paid for with cash.

In addition to the operations budget, the following information is necessary to prepare a cash budget:

- Estimated percentages of cash and credit sales.

- Estimated collection experience for credit sales—that is, when the credit sales will be collected. For example, the collection experience may be 30% during the month of sale, 60% in the following month, and 10% in the second month after the sale.

- Estimated other cash receipts including bank loans, sale of capital stock, and proceeds from sale of fixed assets and investments.

- Estimated payments for inventory items. For example, 10% of purchases may be paid during the month of purchase and 90% paid in the following month.

- Estimated payroll payments. A monthly payroll where all employees are paid on the last day of the month for that month means simply using the payroll expense estimates from the operations budget. Payroll distributed in any other way requires many more calculations.

- The payment schedules for other operating periods. Some operating expenses, such as utilities, are generally paid the month after they are expensed. Operating supplies are often paid for before the recognition of the expense when hospitality operations carry them as "supplies—inventory." Each type of expense must be reviewed to determine when the related cash expenditure is made.

- Capital expenses (such as property taxes and insurance) are paid only once or twice a year. In these cases, the payment date, not the expense from the operations budget, should be considered.

- A schedule of debt payments (not part of the operations budget). This is required to determine total debt payments.

- Additional information including, but not necessarily limited to, forecasted dividend payments and forecasted fixed asset and investment purchases.

Illustration—Cash Receipts and Disbursements Approach

The Greenery, a 100-seat restaurant, will be used to illustrate the cash receipts and disbursements approach to cash budgeting. In this illustration, cash budgets will

Exhibit 4   Operations Budget—The Greenery

Operations Budget The Greenery For the months of March–July, 19X1					
	March	April	May	June	July
Sales	$63,000	$60,000	$65,000	$70,000	$75,000
Cost of Sales	21,000	20,000	21,700	23,400	25,000
Gross Profit	42,000	40,000	43,300	46,600	50,000
Interest Income	2,000	2,000	2,000	2,000	2,100
Total Income	44,000	42,000	45,300	48,600	52,100
Controllable Expenses					
Salaries and Wages	17,000	16,000	18,000	19,000	20,000
Employee Benefits	3,000	2,500	3,000	3,000	3,500
Direct Operating Expenses	3,000	2,500	2,500	2,500	3,000
Marketing	4,000	4,200	4,000	4,500	5,000
Utility Costs	3,000	2,500	2,000	2,000	2,200
Administrative & General	2,000	1,800	1,700	1,800	2,000
Repairs & Maintenance	1,000	1,000	1,000	1,000	1,000
Income Before Occupation					
Costs, Interest, and Depreciation	11,000	11,500	13,100	14,800	15,400
Occupation Costs	4,000	4,000	4,000	4,000	4,000
Interest	1,000	1,000	1,000	1,000	1,000
Depreciation	1,700	1,700	1,700	1,700	1,700
Income Before Income Taxes	4,300	4,800	6,400	8,100	8,700
Income Taxes	1,400	1,600	2,100	2,700	2,900
Net Income	$2,900	$3,200	$4,300	$5,400	$5,800

be prepared for the three-month period of April–June, 19X1. Exhibit 4 contains the Greenery's operations budget for March–July, 19X1.

At the Greenery, cash receipts and sales relationships are as follows:

1. Cash sales represent 50% of each month's sales. Therefore, the Greenery's estimated cash receipts from cash sales in April are $30,000 ($60,000 × .5).

2. Charge sales represent the remaining 50%. Twenty percent of the charge sales are collected in the month of sale, while the remaining 80% are collected in the following month. The Greenery's estimated cash receipts from April charge sales total $6,000 ($60,000 × .5 × .2). In addition, March charge sales collected in April yield $25,200 of cash receipts ($63,000 × .5 × .8).

3. The Greenery receives cash each month for the projected interest income as shown in Exhibit 4. Therefore, the Greenery's cash receipts from interest income total $2,000 for April.

The Greenery's cash disbursements and expenses have the following relationships:

1. Food purchases (cost of sales) are paid during the current month as follows:

    30% of cost of sales of previous month
    70% of cost of sales of current month

Exhibit 5   Estimated Cash Disbursements—The Greenery

**Estimated Cash Disbursements in April
for Various Controllable Expenses
The Greenery**

	From March	For April	Total
Direct Operating Expenses	$1,500	$1,250	$2,750
Utility Costs	1,500	1,250	2,750
Administrative & General	1,000	900	1,900
Repairs & Maintenance	500	500	1,000
Total	$4,500	$3,900	$8,400

The Greenery's cash disbursements for food during April total $20,300 as follows:

$$\text{March cost of sales} \times .3 = \$21,000 \times .3 = \$\ 6,300$$
$$\text{April cost of sales}\ \ \times .7 = \$20,000 \times .7 = \underline{\$14,000}$$
$$\underline{\underline{\$20,300}}$$

2. Salaries, wages, and benefits are paid in the month they are expensed. The April cash disbursements for salaries, wages, and benefits total $18,500.

3. With the exception of marketing, 50% of all remaining controllable expenses are paid in the month expensed. The other 50% are paid in the following month. The Greenery's April cash disbursements of $8,400 for these expenses are shown in Exhibit 5.

4. Marketing expense is paid for as follows: In January, $24,000 was paid to an advertising agency for $2,000 of advertising for each month of 19X1. The remaining marketing expense (per the operations budget) is paid for during the month it is expensed. Therefore, The Greenery has an actual cash disbursement in April of $2,200 ($4,200 − $2,000) for marketing expense.

5. Occupation costs of $4,000 per month are paid during the month incurred.

6. Interest expense of $1,000 for April is included in the mortgage payment of $2,000 per month.

7. Depreciation is a write-off of fixed assets and requires no cash flow.

8. Income taxes are paid quarterly. The tax expense for April–June is paid in June.

Other information includes the following:

1. Assume that cash at the beginning of April is $5,000.

2. Equipment costing $5,000 is scheduled for purchase in May and is to be paid for in June.

The Greenery's three-month cash budget for April–June, 19X1, is shown in Exhibit 6. Exhibit 7 provides explanations for each cash budget line item.

Exhibit 6   Cash Budget—The Greenery

	April	May	June
Cash Budget			
The Greenery			
For the months of April–June, 19X1			
Cash—Beginning of Month	$ 5,000	$ 12,800	$ 20,110
Estimated Cash Receipts:			
Cash Sales	30,000	32,500	35,000
Collection of Accounts Receivable	31,200	30,500	33,000
Interest Received	2,000	2,000	2,000
Total	63,200	65,000	70,000
Estimated Available Cash	68,200	77,800	90,110
Estimated Cash Disbursements:			
Food Purchases	20,300	21,190	22,890
Salaries, Wages, and Fringe Benefits	18,500	21,000	22,000
Direct Operating Expenses	2,750	2,500	2,500
Marketing	2,200	2,000	2,500
Utility Costs	2,750	2,250	2,000
Administrative & General	1,900	1,750	1,750
Repairs & Maintenance	1,000	1,000	1,000
Occupation Costs	4,000	4,000	4,000
Mortgage Payment	2,000	2,000	2,000
Income Taxes	0	0	6,400
Payment of Equipment Purchase	0	0	5,000
Total	55,400	57,690	72,040
Estimated Cash—End of Month	$ 12,800	$ 20,110	$ 18,070

The Greenery has a relatively healthy cash flow, as cash at the beginning of the quarter (April 1) of $5,000 is projected to increase to $18,430 by the end of the quarter (June 30). If the Greenery's management considers cash at the end of any month to be in excess of its cash needs, then it should invest the excess. Many hospitality operations establish a minimum cash balance requirement. Any cash over this amount is available to invest on a temporary basis (if needed for future operations) or paid to the owners. Ideally, the minimum cash balance could be $0 as long as daily cash inflow were equal to daily cash outflow. However, this ideal situation is seldom achieved, so a cushion is maintained.

Assume that the Greenery maintains a cash cushion of $5,000 at the end of each month. Exhibit 8 presents the projected cash available to invest at the end of each month in the quarter. The Greenery is projected to have excess cash for investing of $7,800 and $7,310 in April and May, respectively. However, in June, temporary investments of $2,040 must be liquidated to provide the $5,000 minimum cash balance at the end of the month.

Illustration—Adjusted Net Income Approach

The adjusted net income approach can be used to prepare the Greenery's long-term cash budgets for 19X1–19X3. Exhibit 9 presents the Greenery's operations

Exhibit 7   Explanation of Cash Budget Line Items—The Greenery

Explanation of Cash Budget Line Items
The Greenery
April–June, 19X1

Monthly Budgets

Line Item	April	May	June
Cash—beginning of month (BOM)	*$5,000:* based on assumption provided	*$12,800:* cash-EOM, April 19X1	*$20,110:* cash-EOM, May 19X1
Cash sales	*$30,000:* April sales × .5 = 60,000 × .5 = $30,000	*$32,500:* May sales × .5 = 65,000 × .5 = $32,500	*$35,000:* June sales × .5 = 70,000 × .5 = $35,000
Collection of accounts receivable	*$31,200:* April sales × .5 × .2 = 60,000 × .5 × .2 = $6,000; March sales × .5 .8 = 63,000 × .5 × .8 = $25,200	*$30,500:* May sales × .5 × .2 = 65,000 × .5 × .2 = $6,500; April sales × .5 × .8 = 60,000 × .5 × .8 = $24,000	*$33,000:* June sales × .5 × .2 = 70,000 × .5 × .2 = $7,000; May sales × .5 × .8 = 65,000 × .5 × .8 = $26,000
Interest received	*$2,000*	*$2,000*	*$2,000*
Estimated cash available	*$68,200:* cash-BOM + total estimated cash receipts = 5,000 + 63,200 = $68,200	*$77,800:* cash-BOM + total estimated cash receipts = 12,800 + 65,000 = $77,800	*$90,110:* cash-BOM + total estimated cash receipts = 20,110 + 70,000 = $90,110
Food purchases	*$20,300:* March exp. × .3 = 21,000 × .3 = $6,300; April exp. × .7 = 20,000 × .7 = $14,000	*$21,190:* April exp. × .3 = 20,000 × .3 = $6,000; May exp. × .7 = 21,700 × .7 = $15,190	*$22,890:* May exp. × .3 = 21,700 × .3 = $6,510; June exp. × .7 = 23,400 × .7 = $16,380
Salaries, wages, and fringe benefits	*$18,500:* 16,000 + 2,500 = $18,500	*$21,000:* 18,000 + 3,000 = $21,000	*$22,000:* 19,000 + 3,000 = $22,000
Direct operating expenses	*$2,750:* March exp. × .5 = 3,000 × .5 = $1,500; April exp. × .5 = 2,500 × .5 = $1,250	*$2,500:* April exp. × .5 = 2,500 × .5 = $1,250; May exp. × .5 = 2,500 × .5 = $1,250	*$2,500:* May exp. × .5 = 2,500 × .5 = $1,250; June exp. × .5 = 2,500 × .5 = $1,250
Marketing expenses	*$2,200:* April exp. − 2,000 = 4,200 − 2,000 = $2,200	*$2,000:* May exp. − 2,000 = 4,000 − 2,000 = $2,000	*$2,500:* June exp. − 2,000 = 4,500 − 2,000 = $2,500
Utility costs	*$2,750:* March exp. × .5 + April exp. × .5 = (3,000 × .5) + (2,500 × .5) = 1,500 + 1,250 = $2,750	*$2,250:* April exp. × .5 + May exp. × .5 = (2,500 × .5) + (2,000 × .5) = 1,250 + 1,000 = $2,250	*$2,000:* May exp. × .5 + June exp. × .5 = (2,000 × .5) + (2,000 × .5) = 1,000 + 1,000 = $2,000
Administrative & general	*$1,900:* March exp. × .5 + April exp. × .5 = (2,000 × .5) + (1,800 × .5) = 1,000 + 900 = $1,900	*$1,750:* April exp. × .5 + May exp. × .5 = (1,800 × .5) + (1,700 × .5) = 900 + 850 = $1,750	*$1,750:* May exp. × .5 + June exp. × .5 = (1,700 × .5) + (1,800 × .5) = 850 + 900 = $1,750
Repairs & maintenance	*$1,000:* March exp. × .5 + April exp. × .5 = (1,000 × .5) + (1,000 × .5) = 500 + 500 = $1,000	*$1,000:* April exp. × .5 + May exp. × .5 = (1,000 × .5) + (1,000 × .5) = 500 + 500 = $1,000	*$1,000:* May exp. × .5 + June exp. × .5 = (1,000 × .5) + (1,000 × .5) = 500 + 500 = $1,000
Occupation costs	*$4,000*	*$4,000*	*$4,000*
Mortgage payment	*$2,000*	*$2,000*	*$2,000*
Income taxes	$ 0	$ 0	*$6,400:* April–June exp. = 1,600 + 2,100 + 2,700 = $6,400
Purchase of equipment	$ 0	$ 0	*$5,000*
Estimated cash—EOM	*$12,800:* Est. available cash − est. cash disb. = 68,200 − 55,400 = $12,800	*$20,110:* Est. available cash − est. cash disb. = 77,800 − 57,690 = $20,110	*$18,070:* Est. available cash − est. cash disb. = 90,110 − 72,040 = $18,070

Exhibit 8   Projected Cash Available to Invest—The Greenery

Projected Cash Available to Invest
The Greenery
For the months of April–June, 19X1

	April	May	June
Cash—BOM	$ 5,000	$ 5,000	$ 5,000
Plus: Total Estimated Cash Receipts	63,200	65,000	70,000
Less: Total Estimated Disbursements	55,400	57,690	72,040
Preliminary Cash EOM	12,800	12,310	2,960
Less: Cash Cushion	5,000	5,000	5,000
Excess Cash for Investing	$ 7,800	$ 7,310	($2,040)*

*If the excess cash is invested in April and May, The Greenery should prepare to liquidate $2,040 of these investments to maintain the desired cash cushion of $5,000 at the end of June.

Exhibit 9   Long-Range Operations Budget—The Greenery

Long-Range Operations Budget
The Greenery
For the years of 19X1–19X3

	19X1	19X2	19X3
Sales	$730,000	$850,000	$1,000,000
Cost of Sales	240,000	270,000	320,000
Gross Profit	490,000	580,000	680,000
Interest Income	25,000	30,000	35,000
Total Income	515,000	610,000	715,000
Controllable Expenses:			
Salaries and Wages	200,000	240,000	300,000
Employee Benefits	25,000	30,000	35,000
Direct Operating Expenses	28,000	30,000	32,000
Marketing	40,000	50,000	60,000
Utility Costs	30,000	35,000	40,000
Administrative & General	20,000	25,000	30,000
Repairs & Maintenance	12,000	14,000	16,000
Total	355,000	424,000	513,000
Income Before Occupation Costs, Interest, and Depreciation	160,000	186,000	202,000
Occupation Costs	50,000	50,000	50,000
Interest	15,000	15,000	15,000
Depreciation	20,000	22,000	24,000
Income Before Income Taxes	75,000	99,000	113,000
Income Taxes*	25,000	33,000	37,700
Net Income	$ 50,000	$ 66,000	$ 75,300

*The income tax paid each year is the same as the income tax expense in the long-range operations budget.

Exhibit 10   Long-Range Cash Budget—The Greenery

**Long-Range Cash Budget
The Greenery
For the years of 19X1–19X3**

		19X1	19X2	19X3
Cash—Beginning of Year		$ 5,000	$24,000	$ 52,500
Sources of Cash:				
Net Income		50,000	66,000	75,300
Add: Depreciation		20,000	22,000	24,000
Increase in Current Liabilities		2,000	3,000	3,500
	Total	72,000	91,000	102,800
Uses of Cash:				
Increase in Accounts Receivable		2,000	3,000	4,000
Increase in Inventory		1,000	1,500	1,500
Distributions to Owners		25,000	33,000	37,650
Purchase of Fixed Assets		10,000	10,000	10,000
Reduction in Long-Term Debt		15,000	15,000	15,000
	Total	53,000	62,500	68,150
Estimated Cash—End of Year		$24,000	$52,500	$ 87,150

budgets for 19X1–19X3. Additional information required to prepare cash budgets using the adjusted net income approach is as follows:

1. Equipment acquisitions, which will be purchased with cash, are projected at $10,000 per year for 19X1–19X3.

2. Distributions to owners are projected at 50% of net income.

3. Mortgage payments are estimated to be $30,000 per year for 19X1–19X3, of which 50% is interest expense.

4. The annual change in various current assets and current liabilities is estimated as follows:

	19X1	19X2	19X3
Accounts receivable	+2,000	+3,000	+4,000
Inventory	+1,000	+1,500	+1,500
Current liabilities	+2,000	+3,000	+3,500

The Greenery's long-range cash budget for 19X1–19X3 is shown in Exhibit 10. Overall, the cash budget shows a substantial increase in cash—from $5,000 at the beginning of 19X1 to $87,150 at the end of 19X3. This fully considers the distribution of 50% of net income to owners, the cash purchase of $10,000 of equipment each year, and the reduction of long-term debt by $15,000 each year. The Greenery's management must consider the best uses of the excess funds reflected by the cash budget. The factors relevant to short-term investing are also appropriate in a long-term situation, although liquidity is less important.

Float

The use of **float** is another element of cash management. Float is time between the subtraction or addition of cash to the company's books and the actual subtraction or addition to the company's bank account. For example, assume that the Greenery pays a supplier $1,000 on account. When the check is written, the cash is subtracted from the company's cash (general ledger) account. Assume that the check is mailed to the supplier, who receives it three days later. The supplier deposits the check the following day in its own bank, which is different from the Greenery's bank, and two days later the funds are deducted from the Greenery's bank account. The Greenery actually had use of the $1,000 for six days—from the day the check was written and deducted from the books until the day its bank paid the $1,000. This type of float is called **payment** or **disbursement float.** The Greenery benefits from this float, and any reasonable steps to increase payment float are to the Greenery's advantage.

On the other hand, when the Greenery deposits a guest's check into its bank account, it increases its cash account on the books but must wait to use the funds until its bank has received the funds from the guest's bank. This difference is called **collection float.** The difference between payment float and collection float is **net float.** Since management prefers a positive net float, it should take whatever legal actions it can (referred to as "playing the float") to increase payment float and decrease collection float.

Cash Flow Information

A recent study revealed that 39% of lodging firms want cash flow information for internal use by management more frequently than five years ago, and 52% want more detailed cash flow information. Further, the study revealed that 22% of external users (bankers, etc.) want more frequent cash flow information, and 33% of these users want more detailed cash flow information than five years ago.

Enhancing Cash Flows

The lodging firms in this study were asked which practices they use to enhance cash flows. Exhibit 11 lists the ways that lodging firms speed cash inflows and conserve cash outflows. The percentage of firms using each practice is shown.[1]

Management of Working Capital

The management of working capital is closely related to the management of cash. **Working capital** (current assets less current liabilities) is directly related to cash; Exhibit 12 depicts the effect of working capital on cash. These relationships assume that other activities (such as sales and expenses) remain constant. For example, if marketable securities decrease, cash increases, provided everything else remains the same. Therefore, it is imperative that hospitality managers understand the management of these elements of working capital.

Exhibit 11   Practices to Enhance or Conserve Cash Flows

Practices to Enhance Cash Inflows	Percentage of Lodging Firms Using the Practice
Use computerized credit card approvals.	91.2%
Send out bills within two or three days of completion of sale transaction.	77.8
Charge a cancellation fee when advanced notice for canceled rooms is too late.	72.5
Have accounting personnel of hotel meet with client to determine if the billing is correct while client (generally group business) is still in hotel.	72.5
Require more advanced deposits than in past.	66.1
After mailing bills, follow up with telephone calls when statements are over $10,000 to verify receipt.	63.7
Send invoice by overnight express service if amount charged is over some predetermined amount (such as $25,000) to ensure prompt receipt.	54.4
Use computerized deposit credit card vouchers.	53.7
Use Dunn & Bradstreet reports.	32.7
No longer offer cash discounts for early payment of accounts receivable.	29.2
Use lockboxes.	24.6
Practices to Conserve Cash Outflows	**Percentage of Lodging Firms Using the Practice**
Take 30-day terms to pay invoices when possible, except for cash discounts.	80.7%
Use computer programs to track payables.	67.3
Take all cash discounts offered by suppliers.	60.8
Pay personnel less frequently than in the past.	17.0

Accounts Receivable

Accounts receivable arise from sales on account. Hospitality operations would prefer to transact only cash sales. However, in order to increase sales, credit is often extended to guests. Credit commences when the guest checks into a room without paying for the room. Credit continues until the guest pays the bill—at check-out or after leaving the hotel. Credit should be monitored while the guest stays at the hotel.[2]

Exhibit 12 The Effect of Working Capital on Cash

Increases in cash result as:
- marketable securities decrease
- accounts receivable decrease
- inventories decrease
- current liabilities increase

Decreases in cash result as:
- marketable securities increase
- accounts receivable increase
- inventories increase
- current liabilities decrease

Accounts receivable statements should be mailed on a regular basis, usually monthly. A series of collection letters should be used to speed collection of accounts receivable. Delinquent accounts should be turned over to collection agencies only after the hospitality operation has made all reasonable collection efforts. Collection agency fees may range from 30% to 50% of the delinquent amount.

A **lockbox system** speeds the flow of cash from accounts receivable to the bank. This system consists of a post office box from which bank personnel collect all incoming mail and deposit any checks directly in the property's bank account. This process may speed the cash flow from collection of accounts receivable by up to three days by decreasing collection float. In addition, it enhances control over mail cash receipts because company personnel do not have access to this cash. However, the bank does charge for this service, usually by the number of checks handled. If the operation receives many small payments, the cost of a lockbox system may exceed the benefits.

A formula for considering the costs and benefits of a lockbox system provides a breakeven amount. This is the amount of a receivables account which, when invested for the number of days cash flow is speeded up, yields income equal to the added cost of the lockbox system. The formula is as follows:

$$B = \frac{C}{I \times T}$$

where B = Breakeven Amount

C = Bank Charge per Item

I = Daily Interest Rate

T = Change in Time

An example may best illustrate this formula. Assume that a hotel needs to know the breakeven amount for a lockbox system. The bank charges $.20 for each mail receipt processed, funds can be invested at 12% annually, and the lockbox system gets mail cash receipts to the bank two days faster. The breakeven amount per check is $304.14, determined as follows:

$$B = \frac{\$.20}{\dfrac{.12}{365} \times 2}$$

$$= \$304.14$$

That is, this hotel will benefit financially by using a lockbox system for processing mail receipts over $304.14. Therefore, this hotel should instruct its debtors with balances greater than $304.14 to mail their checks to its lockbox, while debtors owing less than $304.14 should send their payments to the hospitality operation for company personnel to process. This assumes that company personnel and related expenses are fixed and will not change by processing more or fewer mail cash receipts.

Accounts receivable, especially city ledger accounts, are monitored by the use of ratio analysis and the preparation of an aging schedule of accounts receivable. Three useful ratios are accounts receivable to sales, accounts receivable turnover, and number of days accounts receivable outstanding, which is a variation of the accounts receivable turnover. These ratios are useful in detecting changes in the overall accounts as they relate to sales.

An aging of accounts receivable is useful for monitoring delinquent accounts. Maximum efforts should be exerted to collect the oldest accounts. The aging schedule is also useful for estimating the uncollectible accounts at the end of the accounting period.

Inventory

Inventory is viewed by some as a necessary evil. Hospitality operations must maintain an inventory of food and beverages even though the cost of storing these items is relatively high. The benefit of having food and beverages for sale is obvious, however—they are generally sold at several times their cost.

The non-product costs of maintaining inventory need to be considered so that management will exercise tight control in this area. Several costs directly related to inventory include storage, insurance, and personnel. Inventory requires storage space, and many inventory items must be stored in temperature-controlled environments. Certain inventory items have a limited shelf life; thus, personnel need to monitor these items closely. Inventory must be counted periodically, which also requires personnel and therefore payroll dollars. Overall costs also increase when inventory items spoil and must be discarded. Insurance to cover inventory, although not expensive, is yet another cost. In addition to these costs, there is the opportunity cost of inventory. If funds were not tied up in inventory, they could be invested to provide a return to the hospitality operation. Therefore, management must closely monitor inventory to keep it at a minimum, while still having products available when customers wish to make purchases.

Assistance to food service operations in minimizing their inventories is available through computer programs that produce food purchase orders for required products. For example, when a 1,000-person banquet with ham as an entrée and various side dishes is entered into such a computer program, the program would produce an order for x pounds of ham and y cans of each side order. Since delivery is often available on short notice, these quantities can essentially be ordered on a "just-in-time" basis. The critical elements are forecasting meals to be served and using standard recipes.

Common means of monitoring inventory include the inventory ratios. The most commonly used ratio is inventory turnover, calculated by dividing cost of goods used by average inventory. This ratio should be computed not only for food but also for each category of beverages. The results are most meaningful when compared to the planned ratios and to ratios for past periods. These ratios can help management detect unfavorable trends. For example, food inventory turnovers of 2, 1.8, and 1.6 for three successive months suggest a major change in food inventory. Management should determine if the inventory is excessive and take the appropriate action to correct the situation.

Current Liabilities

A large portion of current assets is financed by current liabilities in hospitality operations. The current ratio (computed by dividing current assets by current liabilities) of approximately 1 to 1 for hospitality operations, especially in the lodging sector, reflects this situation. **Trade credit** is free—that is, suppliers do not charge interest to hospitality operations for amounts owed in the normal course of business. Everything else being the same, the longer a property has to pay its bills, the greater its reliance on trade credit to finance its operations.

Current liabilities consist primarily of trade payables, taxes payable, accrued wages, and the current portion of long-term debt. The remainder of this section focuses on trade payables, as the other payables must generally be paid on stipulated dates.

Trade payables resulting from purchases on account generally require payment in 30 days. Sometimes, suppliers offer cash discounts to hospitality operations to encourage their customers to pay their accounts early. For example, a supplier may provide a 2% cash discount if the invoice is paid within ten days of the invoice date. Thus, the terms of sale per the invoice are simply shown as $2/10, n/30$. The $n/30$ means that if the discounted invoice is not paid within 10 days of the invoice date, then the entire amount (net) is due within 30 days of the invoice date. The effective interest rate of the cash discount is determined as follows:[3]

$$\text{Effective Interest Rate} = \frac{\text{Cash Discount}}{\text{Invoice Amount} - \text{Cash Discount}} \times \frac{\text{Days in Year}}{\text{Difference between end of discount period and final due day}}$$

The following example illustrates the calculation of the effective interest rate. Assume that a hotel purchases a computer for $8,000 and is offered terms of $3/10$, $n/30$. The effective interest rate of 56.45% is the result of:

$$\text{Effective Interest Rate} = \frac{\$240^*}{\$8,000 - \$240} \times \frac{365}{20}$$

$$= 56.45\%$$

$$^*\text{Cash Discount} = \$8,000 \times .03 = \$240$$

Thus, the hotel would be wise to pay the invoice within the cash discount period, even if it had to borrow funds to do so, as long as the annual interest rate on the loan were less than 56.45%.

Alternatively, assume that the terms of sale are 1/10, *n*/30 and that this hotel must pay interest at an annual rate of 20%.

$$\text{Effective Interest Rate} = \frac{\$80}{\$8,000 - \$80} \times \frac{365}{20}$$

$$= 18.43\%$$

If the hotel has the cash available and management considers 18.43% to be an attractive return on a short-term investment, the hotel should pay the invoice within the cash discount period. However, if the cash is not available, the hotel should not borrow to pay the invoice, since the effective interest rate of 18.43% is lower than the rate at which the hotel can borrow funds. In this situation, the hotel should not take the cash discount, but rather should pay the full $8,000 30 days after the invoice date.

In general, management should pay bills only when they are due except when cash discounts are available for early payments and they result in lowering costs. The payment of invoices earlier than required results in a higher cost of doing business since the cash expended could have been invested. However, management must consider the intangible factor of supplier relations. Keeping on favorable terms with suppliers is especially advantageous when the hotel or restaurant occasionally needs special favors—such as receiving inventory two days sooner than normally available.

Integrated Cash Management for Multi-Unit Operations

So far, our discussion of cash management could most easily be applied to a single-unit operation. However, for multi-unit operations, an **integrated cash management system** should generally be installed.

An integrated cash management system consists of centralizing cash receipts and especially cash disbursements from the corporate office. Cash receipts, although initially received by the individual unit, are moved quickly to the corporate office. Cash disbursements, for the most part, are made from the corporate bank accounts. For example, payroll checks are prepared at the corporate office. Supplier invoices may also be paid from corporate accounts.

An integrated cash system's primary goal is to minimize the amount of cash the hospitality operation—both the corporate office and the individual facilities—holds. Cash balances at individual units may be reduced by having a centralized cash disbursement system. The checking accounts of individual units become, in essence, cash clearing accounts, maintained at balances just sufficient to facilitate required local disbursements. All excess cash is quickly transferred to the corporate accounts. More cash at the corporate level results in increased financial returns for two reasons. First, a large cash reserve increases the corporation's bargaining power with financial institutions. Second, the corporate office usually staffs more financial experts than individual operations can afford.

An integrated cash management system can pay real dividends. For example, assume that a chain's cash system is able to keep cash in its accounts (available for investment) for two days longer by increasing its net float. The interest earned for a chain with $1 billion of annual sales is $547,945, determined as follows:

$$\text{Interest} = \text{Principal} \times \text{Rate} \times \text{Time}$$
$$= \$100,000,000 \times .10 \times {}^{2}/_{365}$$
$$= \underline{\underline{\$547,945}}$$

An integrated cash management system results in better allocation of funds throughout the operation. When some properties need cash, they receive it from the corporate office rather than a local bank. Some experts suggest that an integrated cash system improves control over collection and disbursement procedures.[4] For example, individual properties may pay invoices before their due dates; however, a centralized system allows for proper monitoring of cash disbursements.

An integrated cash management system uses cash forecasting, including the preparation of cash budgets at both the unit and corporate levels. Both short- and long-term budgets should be prepared at both levels. The centralized system is designed to transfer as much cash as possible to corporate accounts. Some hospitality operations also have their own credit card systems, although most work directly with major credit card companies.

Computer Applications

Many large companies, including hotel firms, assign people to cash control. However, the typical hotel or restaurant is too small for such an arrangement; the labor cost would exceed the benefits derived.

A computer can help control cash easily and quickly. For example, the cash forecasts shown in Exhibits 6 and 7 can be computerized and used for weekly, or even daily, analysis. A general cash budget can be developed using the operations budget of the company as a starting point. In fact, because many of the line items in the operations budget affect the cash budget, an already-computerized budget process can be programmed to produce automatically a tentative cash budget for review and modification.

A computerized cash budget can be used for weekly and monthly forecasting of cash needs. The budget can reflect expected cash activity based upon cash incomes and outflows. Cash needed for major expenditures can also be projected in this plan, allowing for the anticipation of unusual items as well as daily transactions. While it

Exhibit 13   Computer-Generated Monthly Cash Budget

ABC Restaurant Company
Monthly Cash Budget
Month of July, 19X1

	Week 1	Week 2	Week 3	Week 4
Covers Served Restaurant	1,500	1,590	1,350	1,530
Covers Served Banquet	125	333	250	400
Average Price/Cover Restaurant	$ 12.40	$ 12.40	$ 12.40	$ 12.40
Average Price/Cover Banquet	$ 14.10	$ 14.10	$ 14.10	$ 14.10
Beverage Checks Restaurant	900	954	810	918
Beverage Checks Banquet	38	100	75	120
Average Beverage Sale Restaurant	$ 6.00	$ 6.00	$ 6.00	$ 6.00
Average Beverage Sale Banquet	$ 3.25	$ 3.25	$ 3.25	$ 3.25
Cash—Beginning of Week	$ 1,600	$ 6,784	$ 12,215	$ 13,961
Estimated Cash Receipts:				
Cash & Credit Card Sales	24,417	26,695	22,542	25,988
A/R Collections	2,199	3,397	2,966	1,854
Interest on Investments	6	6	6	6
Total Receipts	26,622	30,098	25,514	27,848
Estimated Cash Available	28,222	36,882	37,729	41,809
Estimated Cash Expenditures				
Food Purchases	6,951	8,074	6,740	8,050
Beverage Purchases	1,104	1,210	1,021	1,180
Salaries, Wages, & Benefits	8,507	10,056	8,369	10,089
Direct Operating Expenses	1,346	1,468	1,240	1,429
Marketing & Advertising	300	300	300	300
Administrative & General	1,597	1,806	1,531	1,671
Credit Card Commissions	551	601	507	585
Utility Costs	532	602	510	557
Repairs & Maintenance	300	300	300	300
Occupation Costs	250	250	250	250
Mortgage Payment	0	0	0	3,500
Capital Purchases	0	0	3,000	0
Income Tax Allowance	0	0	0	4,625
Total Cash Expenditures	21,438	24,667	23,768	32,536
Estimated Cash—End of Week	$ 6,784	$ 12,215	$ 13,961	$ 9,273

might take hours to develop such a plan manually every week, a computer can do it in just a few moments. Assuming basic ratios do not change (such as percentage of cash sales, average check sales, and cost of sales), a cash budget can be quickly developed whenever necessary. This will allow the manager to see what cash is required and decide how to invest any extra cash on hand. Exhibit 13 shows how this might be done for a food service operation.

Summary

Cash is a very important asset for hospitality operations. Although it may not earn interest, cash is used to pay debts, make other disbursements, and facilitate guest transactions. Management must try to minimize the operation's cash holdings by investing them in revenue-producing assets while, at the same time, not jeopardizing its operations. This chapter highlighted a number of cash management tools including cash budgets, the treatment of other current assets, and an integrated cash system.

Cash budgets are formulated to estimate the operation's future cash position. Two approaches, the cash receipts and disbursements approach and the adjusted net income approach, estimate the cash balance at the end of the period and give management the information necessary for planning.

The cash receipts and disbursements method is a direct approach that examines all cash inflows and outflows. Items found in this budget might include the amount of cash sales in the period, collection of accounts receivable, dividends and interest received, the operating expenses that were paid for during the period, and dividends paid. This type of budget is most useful for short-term periods because the estimates upon which it is based are less reliable the further the projections are made into the future.

The adjusted net income approach to cash budgeting is used for periods of over six months. The projected operations for each future year are adjusted to reflect cash flows. This approach also considers any expected changes in current accounts and any capital expenditures. Management should examine excess funds and determine the appropriate way to invest them.

Management must also monitor the activity in other current accounts in order to optimize the operation's liquidity position. Accounts receivable should be analyzed to ensure their timely collection. Inventory is expensive to store but is valuable to operations, so it should also be monitored. This is often done by analyzing the turnover ratio. Current liabilities should be studied with special consideration given to trade discounts. All of these procedures will aid management in cash control and overall operational efficiency.

An integrated cash system can minimize the total cash holdings of a multi-unit corporation. This is accomplished by maintaining a central account to which almost all receipts are deposited and from which almost all disbursements are made. Even when hospitality operations have this central account, it is important for them to make budgets, both for the long- and short-term horizons, and constantly update them as information becomes available.

Endnotes

1. For more information, see Agnes L. DeFranco and Raymond S. Schmidgall, "Cash Flow Practices and Procedures in the Lodging Industry," submitted to the *Hospitality Research Journal* for publication.

2. For a thorough discussion of this topic, see Ellis Knotts, "Handling the Credit Function at Small Hotels," *Lodging*, June 1979.

3. Alternatively, the effective interest rate can be calculated without using actual invoice amounts as follows:

$$\text{Effective Interest Rate} = \frac{\text{Percentage Discount}}{100\% - \text{Percentage Discount}} \times \frac{\text{Days in Year}}{\text{Difference between end of discount period and final due day}}$$

4. For a detailed discussion of integrated cash management systems for multi-unit firms, see Laurent P. Caraux and A. Neal Geller, "Cash Management: A Total System Approach for the Hotel Industry," *The Cornell Hotel & Restaurant Administration Quarterly,* November 1977.

🔑 Key Terms

adjusted net income approach—One of two basic approaches to cash budgeting. It is generally preferable for budgeting cash for periods longer than six months.

cash budget—Management's detailed plan for cash receipts and disbursements.

cash flow—A stream of receipts (inflows) and disbursements (outflows) resulting from operational activities or investments.

cash management—The management of a hospitality operation's cash balances (currency and demand deposits), cash flow (cash receipts and disbursements), and short-term investments in securities.

cash receipts and disbursements approach—One of two basic approaches to cash budgeting. It is useful when forecasting cash receipts for periods of up to six months. It shows the direct sources of cash receipts and the direct uses of cash.

collection float—The time between when a hospitality business deposits a guest's check (increasing its cash account on the books) and when the business can use the funds (that is, when the bank receives the funds from the guest's bank).

disbursement float—See payment float.

effective cost—The true cost when all elements are considered.

float—The time between the subtraction or addition of cash to the company's books and the actual subtraction or addition to the company's bank account.

imprest basis—Method of maintaining funds by replenishing the amount of disbursements since the previous replenishment.

income flow—Flow that results from operations generating revenues and incurring expenses. These flows are shown on the income statement and reflect the results of operations.

integrated cash management system—A cash management system for multi-unit operations. It consists of centralizing cash receipts and especially cash disbursements from the corporate office.

lockbox system—A system used to speed the flow of cash from accounts receivable to the hospitality operation's bank accounts consisting of a post office box from which bank personnel collect all incoming mail and deposit any checks directly in the operation's account with the bank.

net float—The difference between payment float and collection float.

payment float—The time between when a hospitality business writes a check (decreasing its cash account on the books) and when the funds are actually deducted from the business's bank account. Also called disbursement float.

trade credit—Term for credit offered by suppliers who do not charge interest to hospitality operations for amounts owed in the normal course of business.

transaction motive—The rationale for maintaining adequate balances in checking accounts to meet checks drawn on those accounts.

working capital—Current assets minus current liabilities.

Review Questions

1. What is meant by an *imprest basis?*
2. How is cash used by hospitality operations?
3. What are three items which exemplify the differences between income and cash flows?
4. What are the two different types of cash budget formats? In what circumstances would you use each one?
5. What are five informational items needed to prepare a cash budget using the cash receipts and disbursements approach?
6. What should management consider when investing excess cash?
7. Why must you analyze other current asset accounts when using the adjusted net income approach to cash budgeting?
8. How soon should you turn delinquent accounts receivable over to a collection agency? Why?
9. What is the value of a lockbox system to a hospitality operation?
10. What is an integrated cash management system?

Problems

Problem 1

Amy Jason is the accountant for the Jason Junction Inn and is unfamiliar with trade discounts. She has just been offered terms of 2/10, *n*/30 and turns to you for help.

Required:
1. Explain what 2/10, *n*/30 means.
2. What is the effective rate of interest under these terms of sale?

Problem 2

Warren Peace, owner of the War 'N' Peace Motel, is considering a lockbox system for some of his accounts receivable collections. He can program his computer to send statements with different return addresses depending on the amount of the balance. The bank charges $.25 per item for lockbox service. Warren can invest cash with the bank at an annual interest rate of 9%. He has estimated that using the lockbox would speed up collections by 3 days.

Required:

What is the breakeven amount—that is, the amount at which Warren Peace would be indifferent as to whether a customer sent the check directly to the motel or the post office lockbox?

Problem 3

Samuel Raymond, the manager of the Jayhawker, reports that there were changes during July in several current accounts as follows:

1. Accounts receivable increased by $4,000.
2. Inventory decreased by $2,500.
3. Accounts payable increased by $3,500.
4. Wages payable increased by $2,000.
5. Payroll taxes payable decreased by $1,200.
6. Dividends payable decreased by $10,000.
7. Marketable securities increased by $8,000.
8. Accrued expenses decreased by $3,500.

Required:

Indicate the impact on cash during the month of each change listed above.

Problem 4

The Green Meadows Motel borrowed funds of $30,000 from the Rolling Hills State Bank for one year. The annual interest rate is 10%. The bank requires the motel to have a compensating balance of $5,000 in its checking account.

Required:

1. Determine the effective interest rate.
2. Assume the motel normally maintains $2,000 in its checking account, so only an additional $3,000 must be left in its account related to this loan. What is the effective interest rate?

Problem 5

The Skyhorse Station has projected sales of $100,000, $120,000, and $110,000 for the months of October–December, respectively. Its sales on the average are 30% cash sales and 70% charge sales. Generally, 20% of the charge sales are collected in the month of sale, 70% in the month after the sale, and the final 10% in the following month.

Required:

Determine the estimated cash receipts from sales and collection of accounts for December.

Problem 6

The Murphy Motel's general manager, Bryan Murphy, has completed the operations budget for 19X6. He requests your assistance in developing equations for the cash budget.

He provides information as follows:

January	$250,000	April	$300,000
February	$225,000	May	$290,000
March	$280,000	June	$310,000

The division of sales is as follows:

Cash sales	40%
Regular credit	60%

Regular credit accounts are collected as follows:

Month of sale	10%
Month after month of sale	60%
Second month after month of sale	20%
Third month after month of sale	9%
Bad debts	1%
Total	100%

Required:

Determine the amount of cash expected to be received during May 19X6. (Show all of your calculations.)

Problem 7

The Drawbridge Corporation had net income of $100,000 for 19X2. Its income statement reflected depreciation of $50,000 and amortization expense of $10,000. Accounts receivable increased by $10,000 during 19X2 while accounts payable declined by $5,000. The mortgage payments for 19X2 totaled $75,000, of which $40,000 was interest expense. Dividends of $30,000 were paid during 19X2 while $35,000 of dividends were declared during 19X2.

Required:

Determine the net cash flow for 19X2. (Show all of your work.)

Problem 8

Use the following information to formulate a simplified cash budget for Heidi's Place.

	Dec.	Jan.	Feb.	Mar.
Sales	$40,000	$40,000	$50,000	$75,000
Inventory Purchases	15,000	17,000	18,000	30,000
Other Cash Expenses	15,000	15,000	22,000	37,000
Capital Purchases	–0–	–0–	10,000	–0–
(With cash)				

Sales:	60% of the sales are cash while the remaining 40% are credit sales. One half of the credit sales are collected in the month of sale and one half in the next month.
Purchases:	80% of the purchases are paid in the month of the purchase while 20% are paid in the next month.

Inventory: Assume that other cash expenses and capital purchases are paid for during the month indicated above
(for example, other cash expenses of $15,000 for De-
cember were paid in December).

Assume that the beginning cash balance of January 1 is $5,000.

Required:

Prepare a cash budget using the cash receipts and disbursements approach for the months of
January–March.

Problem 9

Topeka Corporation has just completed a long-range operations budget for 19X1–19X3. They
are interested in their ability to buy fixed assets in 19X2 and 19X3 from cash generated by the
business. They need tentative cash budgets for 19X1–19X3 to evaluate the situation. The following information is available:

Condensed Operations Budgets
Topeka Corporation
19X1–19X3

	19X1	19X2	19X3
Sales	$5,000,000	$6,000,000	$6,500,000
Operating expenses	4,000,000	5,000,000	6,000,000

	19X1	19X2	19X3
Depreciation	500,000	500,000	500,000
Income before taxes	500,000	500,000	-0-
Income tax expense*	200,000	200,000	-0-
Net income	$ 300,000	$ 300,000	$ -0-

*The income tax expense is recorded on the books only. The amount paid each year is as follows:

	19X1	19X2	19X3
Income tax liability for each year	$150,000	$ 150,000	$ 50,000
Increase in accounts receivable	10,000	20,000	10,000
Increase in accounts payable	5,000	15,000	20,000
Increase in inventories	5,000	2,000	1,000
Expected distributions to partners (owners)	100,000	110,000	120,000

Required:

Prepare cash budgets for the Topeka Corporation for 19X1–19X3 using the adjusted net income approach.

Problem 10

Eric Smith, the owner and manager of Eric's, has provided the following information about
his business for January–March 19X2. The cash balance on January 1, 19X2, is $10,000, and he
wants to maintain a minimum balance of $10,000 at the end of each month.

The estimated monthly sales are as follows:

January 19X2	$110,000
February 19X2	130,000
March 19X2	120,000

The sales are 30% cash and 70% credit card. The Smith Express Card is converted to cash each day after the sale; however, the brokerage charge is 4% on gross.

Other expected income is $2,000 from interest to be received in February. In addition, in February, a range with a net book value of $300 is expected to be sold for cash for a $700 gain on the sale.

Food and beverages are paid for the month following the sale, and they average 40% of sales. Sales in December 19X1 totaled $130,000. Employees are paid the last day of the month, and the total compensation is 35% of sales.

Other cash expenses approximate $10,000 per month. In the month of March, $40,000 is expected to be expended on new equipment. Funding for this expenditure comes in part from a long-term loan of $15,000 from the Kansas Bank and Trust.

Required:

Prepare the monthly cash budget for Eric's for January–March 19X2 using the cash receipts and disbursements approach.

Problem 11

Beth McNight is the manager of the Night Time Inn and has completed the operating budgets for the next three years as shown below. She is now ready to prepare the cash budget.

	Operating Budgets 19X1–19X3		
	19X1	19X2	19X3
Sales	$1,000,000	$1,200,000	$1,500,000
Direct Expenses	450,000	550,000	650,000

	Operating Budgets 19X1–19X3		
	19X1	19X2	19X3
Depreciation	200,000	200,000	200,000
Other Fixed Expenses	250,000	250,000	350,000
Income Before Taxes	100,000	200,000	300,000
Income Tax	40,000	100,000	150,000
Net Income	$ 60,000	$ 100,000	$ 150,000

Additional information:

A. Dividends paid in a given year are estimated to be 30% of net income for that year.

B. The following is a summary of the only current accounts that are expected to change:

	19X1	19X2	19X3
Accounts Receivable	+ 10,000	+ 5,000	+ 20,000
Accounts Payable	− 5,000	+ 5,000	+ 10,000

C. A major piece of equipment that costs $50,000 is scheduled for purchase during 19X3. Beth McNight would like to purchase the machine with company cash rather than borrow the necessary funds.

D. The cash balance at the beginning of 19X1 is $10,000.

E. Assume that the income tax for each year is paid in the year it is shown as expense.

Required:

Prepare cash budgets for 19X1–19X3 for the Night Time Inn using the adjusted net income approach.

Problem 12

The Redbird Restaurant's financial information for the months of July–September, 19X2, is as follows:

	Budgeted sales
July	$ 60,000
August	70,000
September	65,000

In the past, cash and charge sales have been 40% and 60%, respectively, of total sales. Actual sales for May and June totaled $62,000 and $58,000, respectively. Collections on charge sales average 75% in the month following the sale and 25% in the second month after the sale. Food costs average 35% of total revenue. Thirty percent is paid in the month of sale, while the remaining 70% is paid in the following month. Payroll costs are paid at the end of each month and average 30% of total sales.

Other budgeted expenses are as follows:

	July	August	September
Interest—loans	$1,500	$1,495	$1,490
Depreciation	1,000	1,000	1,000
Property taxes	500	500	500
Insurance	400	400	400
Other expenses	2,000	2,000	2,000

The interest is part of Redbird's $2,000 monthly mortgage payment. Property tax payments of $3,000 are made in July and December. The annual insurance premium of $4,800 was paid in January. Other expenses are paid each month as the expense is incurred.

During August, a new cash register is to be purchased for $8,000. The old register will be sold at an expected loss of $500; its net book value at that time will be $1,000. If necessary, the Redbird Restaurant can borrow money from the Illinois State Bank on a six-month note basis—that is, the note and interest would be paid in six months.

The cash balance on July 1, 19X2, is $5,000.

Required:

Prepare the Redbird Restaurant's cash budget for July–September 19X2 using the cash receipts and disbursements approach.

Problem 13

Claude Ziggy, owner of Ziggy's Diner, needs your assistance to prepare a cash budget for his restaurant. He estimates cash on July 1 will be $2,400. He wants to maintain a minimum of cash at the end of each month equal to one week's (7 days') disbursements for the next month, not including disbursements related to working capital loans. (Assume that disbursements are made evenly throughout a month.)

Total monthly sales are as follows:

March	$ 50,000
April	120,000
May	120,000
June	150,000
July (estimated)	159,000
August (estimated)	180,000
September (estimated)	142,000
October (estimated)	90,000

The sales are 40% cash and 60% regular credit. Regular credit sales are collected as follows:

Month of sale	10%
Month after sale	60%
Second month after sale	20%
Third month after sale	8%
Bad debts	2%
Total	100%

Interest income of $1,000 is expected in August. In September, the restaurant plans to sell some extra equipment. The chef estimates the equipment will bring $2,000; the book value of the equipment is $1,000. During September, 1,000 shares of capital stock with $1 par value are to be sold for $5 per share. Cash is to be received in September for the stock sales.

Payments for food are made one month after the sale. The food cost percentage is 35%. Beverages are purchased and paid for one month in advance and the beverage cost percentage is 25%. Beverages sales are 50% of food sales.

Labor is paid during the month wages are earned and represents 40% of total sales. Fixed expenses, except for insurance, depreciation, and property taxes, are $8,000 per month and are paid monthly.

Insurance premiums of $3,000 are paid quarterly in January, April, July, and October of each year. The property taxes of $20,000 for the year are paid in two installments of $10,000 each in July and December. Depreciation expense is $3,000 per month.

The Board of Directors is expected to declare a dividend per share of $.25 in July, payable in August (20,000 shares are outstanding).

In September, the firm plans to acquire fixed assets using cash totaling $20,000. If the firm is to borrow cash to maintain the desired cash balances, it must do so in increments of $1,000. The interest rate is 12% and principal and interest must be paid back in 30 days. (Assume that the funds borrowed, if any, are paid back in the following month.) Assume that a year has 365 days when calculating interest on short-term loans.

Required:

Prepare a monthly cash budget for Ziggy's Diner for July–September using the cash receipts and disbursements approach.

Problem 14

Stacey Williams, owner of the Williams Cafe, has requested your assistance in preparing a three-year cash budget. She provides the following financial data:

	19X1	19X2	19X3
Budgeted pretax income	$(20,000)	$ -0-	$150,000
Depreciation expense	30,000	30,000	30,000
Mortgage payments:			
Interest expense	20,000	19,500	19,000
Principal reduction	10,000	10,500	11,000
Expected changes in			
current accounts:			
Accounts receivable	5,000	5,000	(5,000)
Inventory	2,000	(3,000)	2,000
Accounts payable	5,000	(6,000)	7,000
Other planned activity:			
Sale of capital stock	100,000	-0-	-0-
Purchase of property	20,000	50,000	-0-

Additional Information:

1. Cash at the beginning of 19X1 was $30,000.
2. The average tax rate of the Williams Cafe is 25%.
3. Assume operating losses can be carried forward for up to five years and offset against operating profits prior to calculating income taxes.
4. Assume dividends are paid out during profitable years. The amount of dividends paid is equal to 50% of net income.

Required:

Prepare a cash budget for the years 19X1–19X3 for the Williams Cafe using the adjusted net income approach.

Problem 15

The Lakeland Diner has provided the information below for the preparation of its cash budget:

Beginning cash on July 1 is $5,000. The owner of the diner would like to maintain a minimum cash balance at the end of each month equal to one week's (7 days') disbursements for the current month, not including disbursements related to working capital loans. (Assume that disbursements are made evenly throughout a month.)

Monthly total sales are as follows:

March	$ 50,000	September (estimated)	$160,000
April	110,000	October (estimated)	150,000
May	130,000	November (estimated)	130,000
June	150,000	December (estimated)	120,000
July (estimated)	170,000	January (estimated)	100,000
August (estimated)	180,000	February (estimated)	90,000

The sales are 30% cash, 50% credit card, and 20% regular credit. The diner accepts only MasterCard. Cash is received from MasterCard for each day's sales, and the brokerage charge is 3%. Regular credit sales are collected as follows:

Month of sale	10%
Month after sale	70%

Second month after sale	10%
Third month after sale	9%
Bad debts	1%
Total	100%

Interest income of $3,000 is expected in July. In October, the firm plans to sell some extra equipment. The chef estimates the equipment will bring $5,000. The book value of the equipment is $2,000. During August, 2,000 shares of capital stock with $1 par value are to be sold for $4 per share. Cash is to be received in August for the stock sales. Investment dividends of $8,000 are expected to be received in November.

Payments for food are usually made one month after the sale, and the food cost percentage is 38%. Beverages are usually purchased and paid for one month in advance, and the beverage cost percent is 23%. Beverage sales are 75% of food sales.

Employee wages are paid during the month they are earned and represent 35% of total sales. Other expenses, except insurance, depreciation, and property taxes, are $20,000 per month and are paid on a monthly basis. Insurance premiums of $5,000 are paid quarterly in January, April, July, and October of each year. The property taxes of $30,000 for the year are paid in two installments of $15,000 in July and December. Depreciation expense is $5,000 per month.

The Board of Directors is expected to declare a dividend/share of $.25 in September, payable in October (24,000 shares are outstanding).

In August, the diner plans to acquire fixed assets totaling $20,000 with cash. If the diner is to borrow working capital, it must do so in increments of $1,000. The rate of interest is 12%, and principal and interest must be paid back in 30 days. (Assume that the funds borrowed, if any, are paid back the following month.) For the interest expense calculation, assume that a year has 365 days.

Required:

Prepare the cash budget for the Lakeland Diner for the months of July–December using the cash receipts and disbursements approach.

Chapter 12 Outline

Conditions for Fraud and Embezzlement
The Hospitality Industry's Vulnerability to Theft
Definition and Objectives of Internal Control
Characteristics of Internal Control
    Management Leadership
    Organizational Structure
    Sound Practices
    Fixed Responsibility
    Competent and Trustworthy Personnel
    Segregation of Duties
    Authorization Procedures
    Adequate Records
    Procedure Manuals
    Physical Controls
    Budgets and Internal Reports
    Independent Performance Checks
Internal Auditing
Basics of Internal Accounting Control
    Cash Control
        Cash Receipts
        Cash Disbursements
    Accounts Receivable
    Accounts Payable
    Purchasing and Receiving
    Payroll
    Inventories
    Fixed Assets
    Marketable Securities
Implementation and Review of Internal Controls
Internal Control in Small Operations
Additional Classification of Controls
Codes of Ethics
Computer Applications

Internal Control

$\mathbf{A}$LL BUSINESS OPERATIONS need strong internal controls to monitor and maintain the quality of goods and services they provide and thereby maximize profits, especially in the long run. Strong internal controls are critical for hospitality operations because (1) many sales transactions involve cash, (2) there are hundreds, and for some operations, thousands of transactions in a day, and (3) many employees handle cash at the front desk, in restaurants, and in beverage operations. However, as we will see in this chapter, internal control includes much more than control over cash and cash sales. This chapter will attempt to answer some of the following questions regarding internal control:

1. What is internal control?
2. What are the major objectives of internal control?
3. What are the differences between accounting and administrative controls?
4. What are the characteristics or principles of internal control?
5. How are internal controls documented?
6. How is flowcharting useful in documenting and monitoring internal control?
7. How does the segregation of duties enhance internal control?
8. What methods of internal control are necessary to safeguard cash?

In this chapter, we will first discuss conditions for fraud and embezzlement and the hospitality industry's vulnerability to theft. Then, we will provide a formal definition and some examples of internal control. Next, several internal control characteristics of hospitality operations are discussed, followed by the basic requirements of internal accounting control for various accounting functions, including cash receipts, cash disbursements, accounts receivable, accounts payable, payroll, inventories, fixed assets, and marketable securities. Next, the implementation and review of internal controls are presented. This is followed by discussions of internal controls applicable to small operations and of codes of ethics.

Conditions for Fraud and Embezzlement

A major focus of internal control systems in hospitality businesses is the prevention of fraud and embezzlement. According to the *Hotel Internal Control Guide*, three environmental conditions are necessary for fraud and embezzlement to take place. They are:

- Need

- Opportunity

- Failure of conscience

Need refers to the economic or psychological deficiencies that drive people to steal. It is an area that unfortunately has received much attention over the years. Hotel and restaurant operators are constantly admonished to "watch their employees' lifestyles" to assess whether employees, including top management, have economic and other needs. However, one could argue that economic needs drive good employees to produce. Focusing on employee needs puts managerial energy in the wrong areas—areas that managers can do little about.

It is the second condition, *opportunity*, upon which management can exert some influence. If management can preclude the opportunity for stealing, then it can truly prevent fraud and embezzlement. The purpose of this chapter is to discuss internal control characteristics and systems that will help eliminate the opportunity for theft. Clearly, the best way to prevent theft is to eliminate the opportunity.

The third condition, *failure of conscience,* involves conditions that allow a thief to rationalize the act of stealing. People need to rationalize theft. They need to convince themselves that they are somehow justified in taking what does not belong to them. Unlike economic and psychological needs, however, management can have some indirect influence on this need. Management can create an environment in which it is difficult to rationalize acts against the operation. This can be accomplished by applying internal control characteristics firmly but evenly throughout the organization—having the same rules for top management as for other employees. If a manager simply picks up a soft drink or pastry in a casual manner, this may cause other employees to think, "the boss takes what he or she wants. Why shouldn't I?" However, if all managers are required to sign a check for food and drink in the same manner as any hotel guest would, this creates an environment of control and recordkeeping. Similar situations exist for such issues as steward's sales (when merchandise is sold to staff at reduced rates), searching packages at the door, and punching in at the time clocks. The rules should be applied evenly across the board, thus precluding one form of rationalization.

Again, out of all three conditions necessary for fraud and embezzlement to take place, management has the most influence upon opportunity. Most of the characteristics of internal control discussed in this chapter are designed to prevent opportunities for theft.[1]

The Hospitality Industry's Vulnerability to Theft

Neal Geller has pointed out that hospitality businesses have general operating characteristics that render them relatively more vulnerable to theft than businesses in many other industries. These characteristics include the following:[2]

- There are many cash transactions.

- The industry provides many jobs requiring relatively low skills.

- Many hospitality positions are perceived as being of low social status.

- Items of relatively high value are commonly used in normal operations.

- Hospitality operations use many commodities that employees need and must buy for use in their own homes.

Many hotel and restaurant guests use cash to settle their accounts and to make other purchases during their stays. Even though credit cards are increasingly being used, a large number of transactions that involve cash occur each day. Many hotels have several profit centers that are open for much of the day (sometimes even 24 hours). These operations need cash banks. They also require several cashier shifts rather than the single shift many retail outlets can get by with.

Many hospitality positions are filled by relatively unskilled employees. These positions also tend to be low paying jobs with little social status. These factors further combine to contribute to high turnover. All of these factors do little to help the internal control environment.

In addition to Geller's list of hospitality business characteristics, many lodging properties are small. Even large hotels are often operated like a small business. Large hotels are aggregations of many relatively small revenue outlets. In a large, full-service hotel, the rooms department may be a major revenue center, but there will be many bars, food service outlets, and other revenue centers that individually are small operations. Thus, the critical mass or economics of scale that assist large operations with efficiency and control are often lacking.

These characteristics of the hospitality industry highlight the critical need for an effective internal control system.

Definition and Objectives of Internal Control

There are many definitions of internal control. One of the best known is provided by the American Institute of Certified Public Accountants (AICPA). This definition states, "Internal control comprises the plan of organization and all of the coordinate methods and measures adopted within a business to safeguard its assets, check the accuracy and reliability of its accounting data, promote operational efficiency, and encourage adherence to prescribed managerial policies."[3]

According to this definition, internal control consists of the plan of organization and the methods and measures within the operation to accomplish four major objectives. Several methods and measures used by hospitality operations will be discussed later in this chapter. At this point, it is important to realize that each hospitality operation must have a satisfactory plan of organization which should be in writing and which everyone in the operation should understand. Further, the organizational plan should provide for independence among operating, custodial, and accounting functions in order to prevent fraudulent conversion and assist in providing accurate and reliable accounting data. For example, in a restaurant operation, food should be stored and issued by custodians and requisitioned for use by preparation (operating) personnel. The accounting for the food should be accomplished by accounting personnel. Thus, the storing and issuing, preparation, and accounting functions are separate and independent of each other.

The four AICPA objectives of internal control can be defined as follows:

1. **Safeguard Assets.** A major objective of internal control is to protect company assets. This objective includes, but is not necessarily limited to, (1) the protection

of existing assets from loss such as theft, (2) the maintenance of resources, especially equipment, to ensure efficient utilization, and (3) the safeguarding of resources, especially inventories for resale, to prevent waste and spoilage. This objective is achieved by various control procedures and safeguards that might include the proper use of coolers and freezers for storing food, the use of locks to secure assets, the use of safes or vaults for cash, limiting personnel access to various assets, and segregating the operating, custodial, and accounting functions.

2. **Check Accuracy and Reliability of Accounting Data.** This objective consists of all the checks and balances within the accounting system to ensure the accuracy and reliability of accounting information. Accurate and reliable accounting information must be available not only for reports to owners, governmental agencies, and other outsiders; it is also necessary for management's own use in internal operations. For hospitality establishments, this objective may best be accomplished by adopting a uniform system of accounts. Because accounting information is most useful when received on a timely basis, regular reports for management's use must be prepared promptly.

3. **Promote Operational Efficiency.** Operational efficiency results from providing products and services at a minimum cost. In a hospitality establishment, training programs and proper supervision promote operational efficiency. For example, when room attendants are properly trained and supervised, the cost of cleaning rooms is lower. In addition, the use of mechanical and electronic equipment often improves operational efficiency. Point-of-sale (POS) devices in restaurant operations electronically communicate orders from server stations to preparation areas and often result in greater efficiency. POS devices in lodging operations also automatically post a restaurant sale to a guest's folio. This reduces labor and eliminates the possibility that the guest will check out before all charges have been properly posted to his or her account. Thus, the POS device also safeguards assets.

4. **Encourage Adherence to Prescribed Managerial Policies.** Another major objective of internal control is to ensure that employees follow managerial policies. For example, most operations have a policy that hourly employees must clock in and out themselves—one employee may not clock in another employee. Placing the time clock where managerial personnel can observe employees clocking in and out should encourage workers to adhere to the policy.

These four objectives may seem to conflict at times. For example, procedures to safeguard assets at a hotel may be so detailed that operational efficiency is reduced. Requiring four signatures to obtain a case of steaks from the storeroom may forestall theft, yet it may be so time-consuming that increased labor costs far exceed the potential losses without this elaborate control. Perfect controls, even if possible, generally would not be cost-justified. Management must weigh the cost of instituting a control against the benefit it would provide. When the proper balance of costs and benefits is achieved, management is performing efficiently.

The four objectives of internal control may be divided between the accounting and administrative functions. The first two objectives, safeguarding assets and ensuring the accuracy and reliability of accounting data, are considered **accounting**

controls. The last two objectives, promoting operational efficiency and encouraging adherence to managerial policies, are considered **administrative controls.** Historically, accountants (especially independent external auditors) have focused their attention on internal accounting controls. However, more recently, hospitality establishments are closely reviewing administrative controls, which are more applicable to operations than accounting controls. This focus is necessary if hospitality operations are to achieve their overall objectives of providing appropriate guest service and thereby maximizing their profits. The review of administrative controls is often assigned to internal auditors who, in addition to checking accounting controls, are looking at administrative controls more than in the past.

Internal accounting controls are not only highly desirable, they are also required by law. The Foreign Corrupt Practices Act (FCPA) of 1977, designed to stop illegal payments by publicly held corporations, contains the following provisions covering internal accounting control and recordkeeping:

1. Make and keep books, records, and accounts that, in reasonable detail, accurately and fairly reflect the transactions and dispositions of the assets of the company.

2. Devise and maintain a system of internal accounting control sufficient to provide reasonable assurances that:

   a. Transactions are executed in accordance with management's general and specific authorization;

   b. Transactions are recorded as necessary: (1) to permit preparation of financial statements in conformity with generally accepted accounting principles or any other criteria applicable to such statements, and (2) to maintain accountability of assets;

   c. Access to assets is permitted only in accordance with management's general and specific authorization; and

   d. The recorded accountability for assets is compared with the existing assets at reasonable intervals, and appropriate action is taken with respect to any differences.

The focus is on accounting controls, not administrative controls. The basic intent of the recordkeeping provision is to provide for reasonably accurate *external* financial reports, while the basic intent of the internal accounting control provision is to signal questionable or illegal payments. The FCPA pertains to those corporations subject to the Securities Acts, essentially corporations and their subsidiaries. Companies violating these provisions may be fined up to $10,000; company personnel may be fined up to $10,000 and imprisoned for up to five years.

Characteristics of Internal Control

The four major objectives of internal control can only be achieved by instituting the many methods and measures of control. For example, to help safeguard assets, an operation might maintain a safe for holding cash overnight. Another procedure to safeguard cash may require that cash receipts be deposited with the bank when they total (for example) $2,000. Before discussing other methods and measures of an internal control system, we will present several general characteristics of such a system. These characteristics include:

- Management leadership
- Organizational structure
- Sound practices
- Fixed responsibility
- Limited access
- Competent and trustworthy personnel
- Segregation of duties
- Authorization procedures
- Adequate records
- Procedure manuals
- Physical controls
- Budgets and internal reports
- Independent performance checks

These characteristics are sometimes referred to as elements or principles of internal control. They are essential to all effective internal control systems and apply to any business enterprise.

Management Leadership

Management's leadership is the key to any hospitality operation's system of internal control. The board of directors establishes the operation's highest level policies and management communicates and enforces these policies. These policies should be clearly stated and communicated to all management levels. In addition, the various management levels are responsible for ensuring that the internal control system is adequate. The tone they set in communicating and enforcing policies may determine the degree to which employees will accept them and carry them out. Although there may be exceptions to board and top-level management policies, these exceptions should be minimized so as not to render the policies useless.

Organizational Structure

Only in the smallest hospitality operations is one person able to supervise all employees personally. In most establishments, the organizational structure is divided into the functional areas of marketing/sales, production, accounting/finance, and personnel. The organization chart represents the organizational structure of an operation. Personnel must know the organization chart and follow the chain of command. Management policies usually prevent employees from circumventing the chain of command by requiring them to discuss any complaints or suggestions with their immediate supervisors or in some cases the human resources department. This approach not only reduces confusion but normally results in greater efficiency. Cases of management fraud constitute an exception to this general rule. In such extreme cases, employees must be able to communicate with the highest levels of management or with internal auditors.

Each position on the organization chart usually has a corresponding written job description. A job description consists of a detailed list of duties for the position. The procedure manual indicates how a job or duty should be performed.

In some hotel chains, the individual hotel controller answers directly to the area controller rather than to the hotel's general manager. Nevertheless, in this situation, the controller and general manager should work as a team, not as adversaries.

Sound Practices

Sound practices are policy measures generally set by the board of directors to create an environment conducive to excellent internal control. Several hospitality operations have adopted the following practices:

- Bonding employees—Employees in a position of trust are covered by fidelity insurance. Some operations carry a blanket bond for minimum coverage on all employees.

- Mandatory vacation policy—Employees are required to take annual vacations. This is rigidly enforced for employees in positions of trust. Other employees then perform the absent employees' duties. If the absent employees have engaged in dishonest practices, the replacements may discover them and management can take action.

- Code of ethics—Recently, some operations have required management personnel to follow a code of management ethics prohibiting illegal acts. Such codes are discussed later in this chapter.

Fixed Responsibility

Where practical, responsibility for a given activity should always be designated to a single individual. In that way, the person can be informed of his or her responsibilities, be given a set of standard operating procedures, and be expected to follow them. If the responsibility is given to one individual, then management knows where to start looking when there is a problem. This principle should also be viewed from the employees' perspective, however. The employees are held responsible for assets or actions, so they need the conditions to allow them to carry out their responsibilities. For example, a front office cashier should be solely and fully responsible for his or her bank. Consequently, no one but that individual should have access to that bank. There should be no sharing of banks and no sharing of custody. It is unfair to make a person responsible for a bank and then give others access to it.[4]

Competent and Trustworthy Personnel

A key characteristic of internal control—perhaps the most important—is personnel. In the hospitality industry, the major difference between competitors is generally the quality of service, which is often a result of staff competency. For example, "service with a smile" may often be more important than the quality of the food served. Personnel must exhibit a caring attitude toward their guests in order for the operation to be successful.

An operation's system of internal control may be rendered useless if personnel are not competent and trustworthy. Generally, systems of internal control are not designed to prevent collusion (two or more people working together to defraud the property). Therefore, the careful selection, training, and supervision of personnel is vital. The operation must hire people with potential and train them properly in the work to be accomplished. This includes not only communicating what the jobs are and how to do them, but following up to make sure that training has been effective. In addition, employees must understand the importance of their jobs in relation to the operation's overall objective.

Finally, employees must be properly rewarded for work performed. This includes not only compensation but also praise for a job well done and promotions when a person is ready and a position is available.

Segregation of Duties

The **segregation of duties** involves assigning different personnel to the functions of accounting, custody of assets, and production. Duties within the accounting function should also be segregated. The major objective of segregating duties is to prevent and detect errors and theft.

To illustrate the segregation of duties, consider the following description of a food service operation. A server takes a guest's order and records it on a guest check. A cook prepares the guest's food order from a copy of the guest check. The food itself was issued from storage by means of a requisition, submitted earlier in the day, based on estimated sales. The guest receives a copy of the guest check and pays the cashier. The cashier records the sale after checking the server's accuracy. In this example, the functions of order taker (sales), cook (production), storekeeper (custody of assets), and cashier (accounting) are separate. In addition to meeting the internal control objective of safeguarding assets by segregating duties, this separation promotes operational efficiency. Additional segregation of duties may further enhance operational efficiency. For example, the production area of a large restaurant may employ many people, including chefs, a garde-manger, a pastry chef, a butcher, a sous chef, and more.

Various tasks within the accounting department are divided among personnel to ensure proper checks and balances. For example, different personnel maintain the general ledger, the city ledger, and the guest ledger. Similarly, the cash reconciliation is prepared by personnel other than those accounting for cash receipts and/or disbursements.

Authorization Procedures

Management must properly authorize every business transaction. Management's authorization may be either general or specific. Management provides general authorization for employees to follow in the normal course of performing their jobs. For example, in a food service operation, servers are instructed to sell food and beverage items on the menu at the listed prices. No specific authorization is required to approve a sale in this case. In addition, a guest may pay for purchases with a credit card. If the guest's credit card is satisfactory, then the cashier may accept it and process the payment without specific authorization.

However, management may also require that certain transactions receive specific authorization. For example, suppose the purchase of fixed assets in excess of a certain amount requires the company president's approval. In this case, the transaction cannot be completed without the president's written authorization.

Adequate Records

Documents for recording transactions are essential to effective internal control. They include such forms as registration cards, folios, guest checks, payroll checks, receiving reports, purchase orders, time cards, and room out-of-order reports. Documents should be designed so that the preparer and ultimate user can understand them. Documents designed for multiple uses will minimize the number of different forms an operation needs. For example, a guest check for a food service operation could be a three-part form with the original copy serving as the customer's bill, the second copy used to communicate the order to production personnel, and the third copy for the server.

Documents are generally pre-numbered to facilitate control. Documents should be prepared when the transaction occurs in order to minimize errors. For example, when a hotel guest charges a meal to his or her room, a voucher is immediately prepared and transferred to the front office. This reduces the chance that the guest will check out without paying the food service charge.

Procedure Manuals

Each job within the hospitality operation can be reduced to writing. The procedure manual should list the details of each position, including how and when to perform each task. The procedure manual encourages consistent job performance, especially for relatively new employees who may be unsure about the details of their jobs. In addition, the procedure manual enables personnel to temporarily fill another position during a regular employee's absence.

Physical Controls

Physical controls are a critical element of safeguarding assets. Physical controls include security devices and measures for protecting assets, such as safes and locked storerooms. In addition, forms and accounting records need to be secured through proper storage and limited access. Mechanical and electronic equipment used to execute and record transactions also helps to safeguard assets. For example, cash registers that limit access to tapes help ensure the prompt and accurate recording of sales transactions in food service and beverage operations.

Budgets and Internal Reports

Budgets and other internal reports are essential elements of a system of internal control. These reports are an important part of an operation's communications system. When budgets are used for control purposes, they help to ensure that management's goals will be attained. If actual performance falls short of the goals, management is informed and able to take corrective action.

Other reports also alert management to operating performance and enable management to take corrective action as necessary. These reports include those prepared daily (daily report of operations), weekly (weekly forecasts), monthly (future bookings reports), and annually (long-range planning).

Independent Performance Checks

This characteristic of internal control is designed to ensure that the other elements of the internal control system are functioning properly. In order for a performance check to be successful, it must be independent—that is, the personnel performing the internal verification must be independent of the personnel responsible for the data being checked. In a number of hospitality operations, the independent performance check is conducted by the internal auditors. In order for the internal audit function to be successful, the auditors must be independent of both operations and accounting and must report directly to top management. (The internal audit function is discussed further in the next section of this chapter.)

Another independent performance check, especially in relation to the accounting function, is the work performed by the independent external auditors. The auditors not only verify financial statements, but also study the internal accounting control system and test it as a basis for how extensive the remaining audit will be. That is, the stronger the system of internal control is, the more reliance can be placed on it. Therefore, all other things being the same, a strong internal control system requires less extensive auditing.

Independent performance checks are the result of the segregation of duties. For example, the preparation of the bank reconciliation by personnel independent of those accounting for cash receipts and disbursements constitutes an independent check.

Internal Auditing

The internal audit function in many lodging and food service chains is a relatively recent development.[5] Some of the 100 largest lodging chains in the United States still do not have a chain-wide internal audit function, although several are in the process of establishing internal audit departments. The Institute of Internal Auditors defines internal auditing as "an independent appraisal activity within an organization for the review of operations as a service to management. It is a managerial control which functions by measuring and evaluating the effectiveness of other controls."[6]

In order for the internal audit function to be effective, it must be independent of the departments and functions that it audits. Since internal auditors review accounting functions, they should answer to the president of the organization or to the audit committee of the board of directors. However, in many firms, the audit function is part of the accounting department.

The above definition states that the internal audit is a "service to management." The ultimate purpose is to enhance profitability; thus, the internal auditor should be viewed as a partner seeking to assist management. The internal auditor's

Exhibit 1 Responsibilities of the Internal Audit Department

1. Develop a comprehensive long-term audit program.
2. Set policies for the audit activity.
3. Conduct financial audits.
4. Recommend improvements in control to strengthen protection of assets, promote corporate growth, and increase profitability.
5. Examine management's stewardship at all levels for compliance with company policies and procedures.
6. Review operations covering all controls.
7. Monitor the effectiveness of actions taken to correct deficiencies and see that "open" findings are appropriately resolved.
8. Conduct special examinations of sensitive areas.
9. Investigate fraud to discover the modus operandi, the extent of loss, and systems slippages or other deficiencies that warrant redress.
10. Assist the audit committee as needed.
11. Coordinate the work of the internal auditors with that of the independent public accountants.

Source: Paul J. Wendell, Editor, *Corporate Controllers' Manual* (Boston: Warren, Gorham, & Lamont, 1981).

reports should be constructive and contain explanations and recommendations for improvements. Internal auditors often follow up to ensure that their recommendations are implemented.

The internal audit focuses on both accounting and administrative controls. Like the independent external auditor, the internal auditor is concerned with safeguarding assets and ensuring the reliability of accounting records (and thus the financial statements). However, unlike the external auditor, the internal auditor is concerned with operational efficiency. The internal auditor's review of front office procedures may reveal a more efficient and profitable way to staff the front office. In addition, the internal auditor is concerned with adherence to managerial policies. For example, the internal auditor may investigate whether advance approval of overtime was sought and received as required. The internal auditor may also investigate compliance with a mandatory vacation policy for employees who handle cash.

Exhibit 1 lists typical responsibilities of the internal audit department of a large business. Of course, the responsibilities of the internal audit department should be tailored to each operation's needs.

Recent research of the 100 largest lodging chains in the United States reveals the internal audit procedures in lodging operations. Exhibit 2 lists four categories of activities and examples of both financial and non-financial data for each. Exhibit 3 reveals the percentage of respondents that reported conducting these internal audit activities, a range of activity of those responding, and the average percentage for each activity.

Exhibit 2   Chart of Internal Audit Activities

Categories of Internal Auditing Activities	Financial Data	Nonfinancial Data
Checking compliance with internal controls and procedures	1. Reviewing the bank reconciliation	5. Determining that there is adequate separation of duties in the handling of cash transactions
Checking compliance with applicable laws and procedures	2. Determining whether the hotel corporation's tax return is in compliance with Internal Revenue Service Code	6. Determining whether the food and beverage operations are in compliance with local health department regulations
Determining whether corporate resources are being used efficiently	3. Conducting analytical reviews on receivables, fixed assets, inventory, etc.	7. Determining the efficiency of the chain's marketing effort
Determining whether corporate resources are being used effectively	4. Determining whether the return on investment for a hotel is above the hotel's hurdle rate	8. Determining the effectiveness of community service projects

Source: Raymond S. Schmidgall and James W. Damitio, "Internal Auditing Activities of the Major Chains," *Hospitality Research Journal*, 1991, p. 262.

Basics of Internal Accounting Control

This section covers basic requirements of internal accounting control, including several methods of control for the various accounting functions. However, this list of methods is not exhaustive. Each hospitality operation must review these areas and determine control methods best suited to its needs.

Cash Control

Cash is the most vulnerable of all assets. It is therefore imperative to have an effective system of internal control over cash. The following list suggests commonly used cash control procedures.

1. All bank accounts and check signers must be authorized by the chief financial officer.

2. All bank accounts should be reconciled monthly, and the bank reconciliation should be reviewed by the controller.

3. The person reconciling bank accounts should receive bank statements (including canceled checks) directly from the bank. Employees who sign checks or have other accounting duties in connection with cash transactions should not reconcile the bank accounts. The reconciliation procedure should include examination of signatures and endorsements and verification of the clerical accuracy of cash receipt and disbursement records. Exhibit 4 presents a sample bank reconciliation.

4. The custody of cash should be the responsibility of the general cashier. Another employee should be assigned to account for cash received and to review

Exhibit 3　Internal Auditing Activity—Summary of Comparisons

Lodging Chains			
Using Financial Data	Percentage of Firms Reporting	Range of Activity	Average Percentage
Checking compliance with internal controls	100%	10–90%	42.47%
Checking compliance with laws	70%	0–30%	8.47
Checking on efficient use of resources	47%	0–10%	2.47
Checking on effective use of resources	50%	1–15%	2.97
Totals Using Financial Data			56.37%
Using Non-Financial Data	Percentage of Firms Reporting	Range of Activity	Average Percentage
Checking compliance with internal controls	87%	0–60%	27.83%
Checking compliance with laws	70%	0–25%	6.00
Checking on efficient use of resources	60%	0–27%	4.13
Checking on effective use of resources	60%	0–35%	5.67
Totals Using Non-Financial Data			43.63%
		Total	100.0%

Source: Raymond S. Schmidgall and James W. Damitio, "Internal Auditing Activities of the Major Chains," *Hospitality Research Journal*, 1991, p. 263.

cash transactions. This segregation of duties provides a check on the cashier's performance.

5. The general cashier must take annual vacations and his or her duties must be assumed by another employee.

6. House banks and petty cash funds should be counted at unannounced intervals by employees independent of the cash control function. Special attention should be given to the propriety of non-cash items such as IOUs and accommodation checks (that is, checks cashed for guests merely to provide them with cash).

7. Disbursements from petty cash funds should be supported by cash register tapes, invoices, or other documents. Such supporting data should be checked when funds are replenished and then canceled to prevent duplicate payment.

Cash Receipts. The following procedures are commonly used for the internal control of cash receipts.

1. Accounting and physical control over cash receipts should be established when the cash is first received, whether at the front desk, at a profit center, or through the mail. For example, incoming mail receipts should be initially listed by an employee independent of both the general cashier and the accounts

Exhibit 4   Bank Reconciliation—Hoosier Hotel

Bank Reconciliation
Hoosier Hotel
December 31, 19X2

Balance per bank statement—12/31/19X2		$14,622.18
Add: Deposit in Transit		3,641.18
Less: Outstanding checks		
Ck. 4315	$ 18.36	
Ck. 4422	156.14	
Ck. 4429	3,689.18	
Ck. 4440	172.47	
Ck. 4441	396.15	
Ck. 4442	100.00	
Ck. 4443	7.43	
Ck. 4444	799.18	−5,338.91
Other:		
Insufficient funds check received Dec. 31*		+ 324.32
Service charge—December, 19X2**		+ 15.24
Cash balance per books—12/31/19X2		$13,264.01
Prepared by _____		
Approved by _____		

*   Redeposited January 1, 19X3
** Amount recorded on books in January 19X3, since it was minor in amount.

receivable department. This procedure establishes an independent record that later can be checked against daily bank deposits and the general ledger posting to accounts receivable. Initial control of cash received in the hotel or restaurant is accomplished with cash registers and front office accounting machines.

2. Restrictive endorsements, such as "For deposit only to Hoosier Hotel's account," should be placed on checks when first received to guard against the obstruction or illegal diversion of such cash receipts.

3. Employees in the accounts receivable department should not handle checks or currency. Postings to accounts receivable ledger cards should be based on remittance advice or listings of cash receipts.

4. Cash received should be given to the general cashier as soon as is practical. Cash receipts should be deposited daily and intact. They should not be mixed with other cash funds used to pay invoices, incidental expenses, or cash accommodation checks.

5. The general cashier and his or her subordinates should not be responsible for any of the following activities:

a. Preparation or mailing of city ledger statements

b. Posting accounts receivable records or balancing detail ledgers with general ledger control accounts

c. Posting the general ledger

d. Authorizing rebates, allowances, discounts, or writing off uncollectible accounts

e. Preparing cash disbursements or reconciling bank accounts

These activities are prohibited in order to reduce the opportunity for the general cashier and his or her subordinates to steal from the operation.

6. General instructions for cashiers often include the following:

a. The cash drawer must be closed after each sale.

b. Cashiers must circle and initial any overrings on the tape at the time of occurrence.

c. Cash registers must be locked and keys removed when unattended.

d. Cash sales must be rung up when they are made. Sales made on an honor system are prohibited.

e. Cashiers may not have briefcases, handbags, purses, cosmetic bags, and so forth at cashier stations.

f. Cashiers should immediately inform the manager if they are experiencing problems with the cash register.

g. Cashiers should verify the amount of cash banks when they receive and sign for them and should not be allowed to count the banks after that time.

h. When feasible (or permitted by equipment), items should be rung up separately to allow the cash register to total the sale.

Cash Disbursements. There are several procedures that help to establish a strong system of internal control over cash disbursements.

1. Generally, all disbursements should be made by check. An exception is petty cash disbursements.

2. Checks should be pre-numbered and used in numerical sequence. In addition, it is a good idea to use a check protector (an imprinting device) to enter the amounts on the checks; this deters anyone from altering the amount.

3. Checks drawn in excess of a minimum amount (such as $50) should contain two signatures, while checks under this may require only one signature. Each check signer should carefully review supporting documents to ensure that the documentation has been properly audited and approved. Check signers should not be responsible for preparing checks and should not have custody of blank checks.

4. When a mechanical check signing device is used, only the employee authorized to use it should have the key. The operation should maintain an independent record of the number of checks processed through the device, and that number should be reconciled with the numerical sequence of the checks used.

5. Vouchers, invoices, and other documents supporting cash disbursements should be canceled by stamping them "PAID" when the check is signed. This procedure is designed to prevent duplicate payments should the document become detached from the check copy.

6. Signed checks and disbursement vouchers should not be returned to the check preparer but should be given to an employee independent of this function for immediate mailing.

7. Only authorized check preparers should have access to blank checks. Voided checks should be mutilated to prevent reuse by removing the signature line.

Accounts Receivable

Accounts receivable represent promises to pay the hospitality operation. A critical control in this area is the segregation of duties to prevent accounts receivable employees from pocketing cash received in payment of accounts. Control procedures for accounts receivable include the following:

1. Accounts receivable employees should not handle cash received in payment of accounts. Postings to accounts receivable for cash received should be made from remittance advice or check listings. Control totals for postings should be made independently of accounts receivable employees for posting by the general ledger clerk to the accounts receivable control account.

2. At the end of the month, the total of guest accounts should be reconciled with the independently determined balance in the general ledger control account. These procedures provide protection against manipulation by the accounts receivable employees. The failure to segregate cash handling and accounts receivable may facilitate **lapping,** a common fraudulent practice. Lapping occurs when an accounts receivable clerk steals cash received on an account, then posts cash received the next day on a second account to the first account. For example, assume that Guest A pays $100 on his or her account and the accounts receivable clerk takes the $100. The following day, Guest B pays $150. The accounts receivable clerk takes $50 for personal use and credits Guest A's account for $100. At this point, the accounts receivable clerk has stolen $150. This fraudulent activity may continue for quite some time when there is no segregation of duties or other compensating controls.

3. Noncash entries to receivable accounts, such as writing off an account as uncollectible, should originate with employees or managers who do not handle cash and are not responsible for maintaining accounts receivable.

4. The credit manager and a member of management should resolve disputed items. Clerical employees should not routinely adjust accounts receivable.

Exhibit 5   Voucher from Voucher System

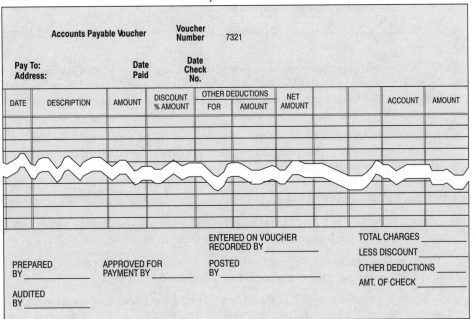

5. A key feature of control over receivables is an adequate system of internal reporting. Periodically, the accounts receivable should be aged, and special collection efforts should be applied to delinquent accounts. The trend of accounts receivable balances in relation to credit terms should be tracked over time.

6. All collection efforts should be carefully documented, and uncollectible accounts should be written off only with the approval of the controller.[7]

Accounts Payable

There are several internal control procedures for accounts payable. These procedures include the following:

1. Vendors' invoices should be routed directly to the accounts payable department. Purchasing personnel should not handle or approve invoices.

2. Control should be established over vendors' invoices when received. This may be accomplished by the use of a voucher system (see Exhibit 5). The voucher system uses pre-numbered vouchers that are prepared from vendors' invoices and recorded in a voucher journal. Invoices should be reviewed for possible cash discounts, and the due dates noted to take advantage of any available discounts.

3. The terms of sale, prices, and list of goods received on vendors' invoices should be checked against purchase orders and receiving reports. All amount

extensions and totals should be checked. The person auditing the vendors' invoices should initial these documents.

4. All vouchers, invoices, and supporting documents should be canceled when paid.

5. Only accounting personnel not responsible for the general ledger should maintain the accounts payable subsidiary ledger. The accounts payable subsidiary ledger should be reconciled monthly with the general ledger control account for accounts payable.

6. A monthly trial balance of accounts payable should be prepared for the controller's review. Suppliers should be paid on a timely basis in order to maintain good supplier relationships.

Purchasing and Receiving

This section covers only a few of the major controls of purchasing and receiving.[8] Common control procedures include the following:

1. To the extent practical, the purchasing agent should make all purchases acting upon approved purchase requisitions from department heads.

2. A written purchase order (PO) system should be used. Copies of each PO should be sent to receiving and accounting. In this way, receiving will be aware of materials ordered, while the accounts payable department can use the PO to audit the vendor's invoice.

3. A receiving department, separate from the purchasing agent, should receive all incoming goods. All materials received should be carefully checked.

4. The receiving department should prepare a receiving report for each vendor's delivery. A copy of the receiving report should be forwarded to the accounts payable department for verification against the vendor's invoice.

Payroll

Payroll is the largest expense for most hospitality operations. Therefore, controls in this area are critical if the operation is to meet its internal control objectives. Several common control procedures include:

1. Payroll functions should be segregated as follows:

   a. Authorizing employment and wage rates

   b. Reporting hours worked

   c. Preparing payroll

   d. Signing payroll checks

   e. Distributing paychecks to employees

   f. Reconciling payroll bank accounts

2. Only the human resources department or executives with hiring/terminating authority should authorize additions to, or terminations from, the staff. Generally, the human resources department carefully recruits new employees and provides the payroll department with all the relevant information on newly hired employees.

3. Procedures for reporting time worked should be clearly defined. Hourly personnel should use time clocks. Departmental supervisors should approve all hourly employees' time reports.

4. Employees should generally be paid with checks rather than cash. Separate payroll accounts should be maintained. An employee independent of the payroll department should reconcile the payroll bank account.

5. Payroll preparation procedures should include checking the clock card used for the department supervisor's approval and rechecking the hours worked.

6. Payroll sheets and net pay amounts should be checked independently.

7. Personnel independent of the payroll department should distribute paychecks. In addition, department heads should not distribute payroll checks.

8. Undelivered paychecks should be given to the controller or a person designated by the controller. This person should not be from the payroll department. The undelivered paychecks should be held until delivered or voided after a specified number of days.

Inventories

Purchasing and receiving control procedures apply to inventories also. Additional inventory control procedures include the following:

1. Accounting department employees should maintain inventory records. These employees should not have access to inventory, nor should employees with custody of inventory have access to inventory records.

2. Personnel independent of the storage function should periodically take a physical inventory. Accounting personnel should extend the physical inventory and compare it to the book inventory if a perpetual inventory record system is maintained. (*Extending* the physical inventory means listing the proper costs per unit and multiplying the counts of each item by the cost per unit.)

3. Taking physical inventory is best accomplished when:

    a. Like items are grouped together in the storeroom.

    b. Pre-printed inventory forms are used to list all inventory items.

    c. The inventory form is arranged in the same sequence as the inventory items are maintained in the storeroom.

    d. Two individuals conduct the physical inventory; one can count the items while the other records the count. (As noted earlier, the personnel should be independent of the storing function.)

4. The inventory records must be adjusted for any differences between the books and the physical inventory. The inventory adjustment must be approved by an executive such as the controller.

5. Any significant inventory overages or shortages should be investigated, the causes determined, and procedures designed to prevent recurrence of errors.

6. Other operating controls relating to inventory include the following:

   a. Control must be maintained over physical inventories. This is accomplished by storing inventory in the appropriate facilities; for example, food must be stored at proper temperatures.

   b. Daily inventories and usage rates of high priced items should be monitored.

   c. Access to inventory should be restricted to storage employees. Limiting access is accomplished, in part, by securing inventory in locked facilities.

   d. Personnel handling inventory (storage and production personnel) should leave the facilities by an exit easily observed by management.

   e. Records of spoilage, overcooked food, and so forth should be maintained for use in reconciling the physical inventory to the book inventory and for accounting for other discrepancies in food inventory.

Fixed Assets

Fixed assets generally constitute the largest percentage of most hospitality operations' assets. These assets are not liquid; however, controls must still be established to maintain these resources for their intended use—providing services to guests. Several common control procedures are listed below.

1. The board of directors usually issues formal policies establishing which executives and committees have the authority to purchase fixed assets.

2. A work order system should be established for the orderly accumulation of property costs when facilities are acquired. Each approved project is assigned a work order number, and all expenditures are charged to this number as the work progresses.

3. Accounting records maintained under a typical work order system include the following:

   a. An expenditure authorization that defines the project scope, purpose, cost justification, and budgeted amount.

   b. Cost sheets that summarize actual expenditures for comparison to budgeted amounts.

   c. Supporting evidence of costs charged to the project account. This evidence includes vendors' invoices, material requisitions, and labor time tickets.

4. General ledger control should be established for each principal classification of property cost and each related depreciation accumulation.

5. Physical inventories of fixed assets should be taken periodically by personnel independent of the person with custody of the assets and of the person maintaining the accounting records. The physical inventory should be compared to the equipment listed in the accounting records. Any discrepancies must be resolved and action taken to prevent recurrence of similar errors.

6. The sale, retirement, or scrapping of fixed assets requires formal executive approval. Approval must be from executives not having custody of the fixed asset. Accounting department personnel must determine that retired assets are removed from the books and that proceeds received are properly accounted for.

Marketable Securities

Marketable securities include investments in stocks and bonds of other corporations. Controls over marketable securities often include the following:

1. Accounting department records should identify each marketable security owned by name and certificate number.

2. All marketable security transactions should be approved by the board of directors or a designated committee.

3. Marketable securities should be kept in a safe deposit box to which only the custodian has access.

4. Periodically, independent physical counts of marketable securities should be taken and the count compared with the accounting records.

5. Income from marketable securities recorded in accounting records should be periodically compared to what the investment should be generating. For example, a $100,000 bond at 8% interest should provide $8,000 of interest annually.

Implementation and Review of Internal Controls

Top-level management is responsible for implementing and maintaining the system of internal controls. Since this system is critical to the well-being of the hospitality operation, management must regularly review it to ensure that it is adequate. The internal control system may break down periodically. New personnel may not understand procedures and thus not follow them. For example, a new employee may return disputed statements to the accounts receivable clerk for resolution, reasoning that the clerk can resolve such differences most efficiently.

The internal control system may also need restructuring due to changing business conditions and other circumstances. For example, ten years ago, a hospitality operation may have established a policy stating that cash receipts had to be deposited when they reached $1,000. Due to inflation, the amount might now be raised to $2,000.

An operation's internal controls may be documented and reviewed by flowcharting and by using internal control questionnaires. A **flowchart** diagrams the flow of documents through an organization, indicating the origin, processing, and final deposition of each document. In addition, the flowchart shows the segregation of duties. Exhibit 6 is a simplified flowchart of a club operation's payroll system.[9]

Exhibit 6   Flowchart of a Payroll System

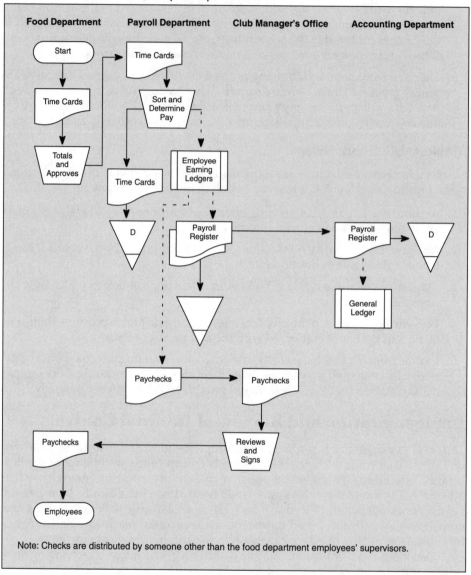

Note: Checks are distributed by someone other than the food department employees' supervisors.

Flowcharting is useful because it provides a concise overview of the internal control system. It facilitates review of the internal control system, enabling management to identify weaknesses for corrective action.

A second device for studying a hospitality operation's system of internal control is the **internal control questionnaire (ICQ).** The ICQ uses a series of questions about controls in each accounting area to identify weaknesses. ICQs generally provide complete coverage for each accounting area. However, they do not reveal document flows as do flowcharts. From a practical viewpoint, both flowcharts and ICQs should be used in documenting and reviewing an operation's system of internal control.

Once the review is completed, management must act to strengthen the internal control system. If a system is documented and reviewed without proper follow-up, then the real value of the review process is lost.

Internal Control in Small Operations

Although the hospitality industry has a number of giant firms with system-wide sales exceeding $1 billion, the vast majority of establishments are small. The elaborate control procedures presented thus far are not practical for operations with only a few employees because there are simply not enough people for the proper segregation of duties.

The key person in internal control of a small operation is the owner or manager. Several duties, if performed by the owner or manager, help to offset what might otherwise be weaknesses in the internal control system. These critical duties are outlined below.

1. Cash Receipts

    a. Open all mail and list cash receipts, retaining one copy of the list.

    b. Deposit all cash daily and compare the deposit with the cash receipts debit recorded by the bookkeeper.

    c. Reconcile cash receipts with cash register tapes.

2. Cash Disbursements

    a. Sign all checks, carefully review documentation, and cancel all supporting documentation.

    b. Use only pre-numbered checks and account for them as checks are signed.

    c. Total check disbursements periodically and compare the total to the bookkeeper's cash credit.

    d. Prepare the bank reconciliation.

3. Sales

    a. Keep all cash registers locked and remove cash register tapes when not in use.

    b. Compare cash register tape totals with the cash debit for the day and the cash receipts deposited.

4. Payroll

    a. Examine the payroll worksheet (or payroll journal), noting employees' names, authorized gross pay, hours worked, deductions, and net pay. Add the payroll and compare the net pay with the cash credit.

    b. Distribute payroll checks.

5. Accounts Receivable

   a. Review aging of accounts receivable.

   b. Compare statements with individual ledger accounts and mail statements.

   c. Resolve all disputed account balances.

6. Inventories

   a. Periodically supervise or take the physical inventory.

   b. Compare the physical inventory with the perpetual inventory on the books.

   c. Compare cost of goods sold with total sales each month, and investigate any major discrepancies in cost of goods sold percentages.

7. Purchases

   a. Randomly review price quotes for inventory items purchased.

   b. Use a purchase order system and account for all purchase orders.

   c. Randomly compare purchase orders with receiving reports, and vendors' invoices with vendors' statements.

8. General

   a. Review all general journal entries.

   b. Employ a competent, trustworthy bookkeeper.

   c. Engage an independent auditor to conduct an annual audit and to periodically conduct limited surprise audits of cash, inventory, and accounts receivable.

Additional Classification of Controls

At the beginning of this chapter, internal controls were classified as either accounting or administrative controls. Controls may also be classified based on whether they take effect before or after a problem occurs. **Preventive controls** are implemented before a problem occurs. They include such things as the use of locks to safeguard assets, the separation of duties to preclude operating personnel from controlling inventories, and general and specific authorization policies. Preventive controls are less expensive to establish than detective controls. **Detective controls** are designed to discover problems and to monitor preventive controls. Detective controls include external audits, surprise cash internal audits, and bank reconciliations. Detective controls may serve in part as preventive controls; for example, if employees know that audits will be conducted, they will be less likely to take advantage of their access to cash and other assets.

Codes of Ethics

Many hospitality companies have adopted a formal code of ethics for the personnel to follow, codifying unacceptable behavior. Recent research of 100 codes of ethics from

Exhibit 7   The Most Frequently Appearing Elements in Corporate Codes of Ethics

Elements	Frequency of Occurrence
Privacy of Communication	81
Conflict of Interest	70
Political Contributions in the U.S.	60
Company Records	58
Gifts, Favors, Entertainment, Trips and Outings	56
Use of Company Assets (i.e. Facilities, Airplane, etc.)	44
Anti-Trust Laws (Fair Competition)	43
Relations with Competitors	40
Relations with Suppliers	35
Relations with Customers	35
Insider Information	33
Security Regulations	26
Observing of Local Laws	26
Equal Employment Opportunities	25
Employees' Investments in Other Companies	24
Opportunities Resulting From Employment	24
Employees' Outside Business Interests	21
Penalties for Non-Compliance with the Codes of Ethics	21
Employees' Investments in the Company	19
Individuals' Political Involvement	18
Serving as Officers, or on Directorships	17
Quality of Products and Services	17
Voluntary Reporting of Violations of Companies' Codes of Ethics	14
Rendering of Service for Outside or Competing Concerns	14
Environment and Energy	14
Health and Safety	14
Rendering of Service for Outside or Competing Concerns	13
Foreign Corrupt Practices Act	13

Source: W. F. Edmonson, *A Code of Ethics: Do Corporate Executives and Employees Need It?* (Fulton, Miss.: Itawamba Community College Press, 1990).

America's largest corporations (not limited to hospitality) revealed the most common elements appearing in corporations' codes of ethics. Exhibit 7 lists these elements.

As an example from hospitality, consider Hilton Hotels Corporation's code of ethics. The code is strongly supported by corporate management. General managers and department heads in Hilton hotels are responsible for advising the employees under their supervision of the parts of the code that apply to them and their duties. An excerpt from Hilton's code dealing with the prohibition of substantial gifts reads as follows:

> Officers and employees shall not solicit, accept or agree to accept, at any time of the year, for themselves or on behalf of the Company, any gift which directly or indirectly

benefits them, from any person or firm having or seeking a business relationship with the Company, or from any employee or agent of such a person or firm; however, this prohibition does not apply to the acceptance over a twelve-month period (from each person or firm) of gifts of small value totaling not more than $200, except that in no event shall gifts of cash ever be accepted. In addition, the prohibition does not apply to free or reduced rate hotel accommodations, meals, entertainment and other services to the extent commonly furnished in the hotel industry on a reciprocal basis, and it does not apply to meals furnished in connection with a business purpose.

Computer Applications

Internal controls are an integral part of any accounting system. Computers can help to ensure adherence to the controls established by management.

Accounting software programs can edit data according to the controls. For example, accounts payable programs can verify whether an invoice has already been paid to help prevent duplicate payments. Accounts payable programs may also automatically calculate vendor discounts and verify that a master vendor record has been established before paying the vendor. Similar internal controls can be incorporated into programs for the general ledger, payroll, accounts receivable, fixed assets, and any other accounting functions. If someone attempts to bypass the controls, the computer can record the "error" and report it on an "exceptions report." For example, if the payroll program allows payroll checks to be written for no more than $5,000, an attempt to issue a check for $6,000 will be noted by the computer. Management can then access this information. A good computer control system will allow exceptions only with management override.

Computers can also assist management in internal controls by providing documentation. Word processing is an excellent way to create, revise, and distribute policies, procedures, and other documentation relating to internal controls. This is especially helpful in new operations, where controls are being tested and often revised. In addition, documentation stored on computer can be easily reproduced at a moment's notice. Since computers can store so much information, the operation can keep records of current and past control measures.

Computers can also help managers establish flowcharts and critical paths. For example, there are several flowcharting programs available that can design the exact flowchart for any given set of tasks. In addition, they can lay out a critical path, showing distribution of responsibilities, how long each task should take, and how the individual tasks relate to the entire process. One side benefit of this is a simple review of the separation of duties. A flowchart and critical path provide an overview of who is responsible for specific functions in an accounting office.

The security of the computer system itself can enhance internal controls. Most good data processing systems have a high level of security. They allow users to access specific functions only. For example, with a good security program, someone handling accounts payable would not be able to access payroll. Certain employees might be able to view an accounts payable vendor master record, but not post invoices. System security can also assist in the separation of duties. The system might prevent the person who enters invoices into the accounts payable system from printing the checks.

Summary

The hospitality industry has many characteristics that make it relatively vulnerable to theft. In part because of these traits, an effective internal control system is critical.

Internal control is the overall system of protecting the establishment's assets, ensuring the accuracy and reliability of its accounting records, promoting efficient operations, and encouraging adherence to management policies. An operation must have an adequate internal control system in order to operate profitably in the long run.

There are four main objectives of every internal control system. The first two, checking the accuracy of accounting data and safeguarding assets, are known as accounting controls. These controls ensure that assets are recorded properly and that they are safe from loss through negligence or theft. The other two controls are administrative controls. Promoting operational efficiency means that the operation's products and/or services are produced efficiently. Adherence to managerial policies is important because established rules are only effective if they are followed.

There are several characteristics of a strong internal control system. These characteristics include the physical control of assets, the development of budgets, management leadership, and organizational structure. Competent and trustworthy personnel are necessary for operational efficiency and adequate physical control of the assets.

Management needs to examine every function of the hospitality operation and establish controls for each one. For example, the cash account must have adequate controls because it is highly vulnerable to theft. Management should consider physical controls, segregation of duties, management policies, proper authorization procedures, and adequate performance checks. These characteristics of internal control can help protect the operation's cash.

Management must consider the costs and benefits of internal control policies. A "perfect" system—one that guarantees the safety of assets—would probably be cost-prohibitive. This is especially true for smaller operations that do not have enough personnel to completely segregate duties. In these instances, managers and managing owners must be aware of the available precautions and take an active role in the operation to ensure its success.

Many hospitality companies have adopted formal codes of ethics to spell out unacceptable behavior.

Endnotes

1. *AH&MA Hotel Internal Control Guide* (East Lansing, Mich.: Educational Institute of the American Hotel & Motel Association, 1997).

2. A. Neal Geller, *Internal Control: A Fraud-Prevention Handbook for Hotel and Restaurant Managers* (Ithaca, N.Y.: Cornell University Press, 1991).

3. Committee on Auditing Procedure, *Internal Control—Elements of a Coordinated System and Its Importance to Management and the Independent Public Accountant* (New York: AICPA, 1949), p. 6.

4. *AH&MA Hotel Internal Control Guide* (East Lansing, Mich.: Educational Institute of the American Hotel & Motel Association, 1997).

5. For further discussion of internal auditing, see the *AH&MA Hotel Internal Control Guide* (East Lansing, Mich.: Educational Institute of the American Hotel & Motel Association, 1997).

6. "Statement of Responsibilities of the Internal Auditor," *The Internal Auditor,* September/October 1971, p. 12.

7. The reader interested in the detailed procedures of the credit function at hotels should consider an article by Ellis Knotts in *Lodging,* June 1979, entitled "Handling the Credit Function at Small Hotels." This article covers credit extension, credit monitoring, and collection of hotel accounts receivable.

8. The reader interested in a detailed explanation of purchasing and receiving controls should read Chapter 6 of Jack D. Ninemeier's *Planning and Control for Food and Beverage Operations,* 3d ed. (East Lansing, Mich.: Educational Institute of the American Hotel & Motel Association, 1991).

9. Standardized flowcharting symbols help improve communication of details in an information system. Most flowcharting symbols were established by the United States of America Standards Institute. For information on the meaning of the different shapes used in a flowchart, see any standard flowcharting reference.

⚬═► Key Terms

accounting controls—Controls for safeguarding assets and ensuring the accuracy and reliability of accounting data.

administrative controls—Controls for promoting operational efficiency and encouraging adherence to managerial policies.

detective controls—Controls designed to discover problems and to monitor preventive controls. Detective controls include external audits, surprise cash internal audits, and bank reconciliations.

flowchart—A visual representation of the movement of information and documents within an operation.

internal control questionnaire (ICQ)—A second device for studying an operation's system of internal control. The ICQ uses a series of questions about controls in each accounting area to identify weaknesses.

lapping—A type of theft that occurs when an accounts receivable clerk steals cash received on an account, then posts cash received the next day on a second account to the first account.

preventive controls—Controls implemented before a problem occurs, including such things as the use of locks to safeguard assets, the separation of duties to preclude operating personnel from controlling inventories, and general and specific authorization policies.

segregation of duties—An element of internal control systems in which different personnel are assigned the different functions of accounting, custody of assets, and production; the purpose is to prevent and detect errors and theft.

Review Questions

1. What is internal control?

2. What are the four AICPA objectives of internal control?

3. What are four characteristics of internal control?

4. Which characteristic of internal control is most important? Why have you chosen this one?

5. Why is the control of cash important to a hospitality operation?

6. What is segregation of duties?

7. How can internal control systems be documented and reviewed?

8. How does flowcharting differ from an internal control questionnaire?

9. How can computers be used to strengthen an enterprise's internal control system?

10. What are three procedures to safeguard inventory?

Problems

Problem 1

Listed below are several control procedures used by the Shaftsburg Inn.

1. A safe is purchased for securing cash
2. Separation of accounting and cash activities
3. Division of duties in restaurant between waitstaff and buspersons
4. Two signatures required on checks written for $100 or more
5. Standard operating procedures manual for front desk positions
6. Internal auditors prepare the bank reconciliation

Required:

Indicate the objective of internal control that each procedure most likely is directed toward.

Problem 2

The Smooth Sailing Inn has instituted several new control procedures in regard to its cash activities as follows:

Procedure	Preventive Control	Detective Control
1. Cash receipts received through the mail are listed by the person opening the mail. The list is sent to the accounts receivable clerk and the checks are sent to the cashier.	_____	_____
2. Cash receipts are secured in the Inn's new safe until they are taken to the bank.	_____	_____
3. The internal auditor prepares the bank reconciliation.	_____	_____
4. All payroll checks require two signatures.	_____	_____
5. Cash register tapes are removed by the internal auditor, who also counts the cash received at the register.	_____	_____

Required:

Indicate whether each control procedure is most likely a preventive or detective control.

Problem 3

The Four Star Cafe's (FSC) procedures regarding service to its patrons are as follows:

1. Patrons seat themselves, as the FSC believes this saves money by not employing a host. During lunch several days of the week, the cafe operates at capacity for two hours.
2. A waitstaff of five takes the food orders and forwards them to the cooks. Generally, a server covers six tables with up to four people per table.
3. The servers also function as cashiers if the cashier is on break or simply away from the cash register when a patron decides to pay a bill.
4. Buspersons clear tables and set up tables for new patrons. Tips are split by the buspersons, servers, and the Four Star Cafe in a ratio of 1:3:1. That is, buspersons receive 20% of the tips, servers receive 60%, and the Cafe receives the remaining 20% of the tips.

Required:

1. Critique these procedures by indicating weaknesses (including violations of the law, if you notice any).
2. Recommend changes to counter any weaknesses.

Problem 4

Several controls currently used at the Lions Inn are listed below:

Control	Preventive/ Detective	Accounting/ Administrative
1. The Lions Inn uses a cash register.	_____	_____
2. The employee time clock is located just outside the manager's office.	_____	_____
3. An external auditor conducts a surprise cash audit quarterly.	_____	_____

Control	Preventive/ Detective	Accounting/ Administrative
4. Only the front office supervisor may approve room sales allowances.	_____	_____
5. Each room attendant's work in cleaning rooms is inspected by a housekeeping supervisor.	_____	_____
6. Cash receipts are deposited intact and on a daily basis.	_____	_____
7. The internal auditor prepares the monthly bank reconciliation.	_____	_____
8. Vegetables are stored in coolers at the proper temperatures.	_____	_____
9. Supplier invoices are reconciled to the suppliers' monthly statements.	_____	_____
10. Cash drawers must be closed after each sale in all revenue centers.	_____	_____

Required:

1. Indicate whether each control is preventive (P) or detective (D) and whether it is an accounting (AC) or administrative (AD) control.
2. If you believe a given control may be both P and D or AC and AD, provide your reasoning.

Problem 5

Several control procedures used at the Bulldog's Stop are listed below:

Procedure	Preventive/ Detective	Accounting/ Administrative
1. A cash bank is assigned to each waiter.	_____	_____
2. Guest checks are reviewed by the internal auditor.	_____	_____
3. Standard recipes are followed in preparing all entrées.	_____	_____
4. Payroll checks are distributed to employees by the owner.	_____	_____
5. Checks written to pay bills in excess of $100 require two signatures.	_____	_____
6. Written purchase orders are required for all equipment purchases.	_____	_____
7. Meat is stored in coolers at the proper temperature.	_____	_____
8. Cash is deposited nightly at the local bank using the bank's night depository service.	_____	_____

Required:

Indicate whether each control procedure is preventive (P) or detective (D), and whether it is an accounting (AC) or administrative (AD) control.

Problem 6

At the Divinity Hotel, a 150-room property, the procedure for handling checks returned by the bank marked "insufficient funds" was to carry them as part of the bank balance. That is, when the bank returned a check because payment was refused and charged it to the hotel's account, no entry was made in the books. The returned check was immediately redeposited, and the bank usually collected them. At the end of the month, those checks that had not been collected were treated as reconciling items (NSF checks) by the bookkeeper preparing the bank reconciliation. If the check was later collected, the bookkeeper made no formal entry; however, in preparing the next month's bank reconciliation, the bookkeeper reduced the amount of NSF checks. If the check was still uncollectible after three months, a journal entry was recorded charging "Bad Debt Expense" and crediting "Cash in Bank."

Required:

1. Explain any deficiencies in the Divinity Hotel's cash control system.
2. Provide the manager with suggestions for improving the system.

Problem 7

The January 31, 19X2, balance of the Hiatt Hotel's checking account was $10,420.00. The bank statement indicated a balance of $13,424.15 at the same date. Checks written before February 1, 19X2, that had not cleared the bank were as follows:

Check 1059	$ 246.81
Check 1072	$2,621.00
Check 1073	$ 349.06
Check 1074	$ 15.92
Check 1075	$1,123.46
Check 1076	$ 998.43

The bank statement reflected service charges of $32.46, which were not recorded on the books until February 19X2. A check marked "insufficient funds" for $168.24 was returned by the bank on January 31, 19X2, and was redeposited on February 2, 19X2. No entry was recorded on the books when the check was returned or redeposited. On February 1, 19X2, cash receipts of $2,149.83 from business on January 31, 19X2, were deposited in the bank. This cash was recorded as sales during January 19X2.

Required:

Prepare the Hiatt Hotel's bank reconciliation for January 19X2.

Problem 8

The Terica Cafe uses a standard cost approach to aid in controlling its food costs. Listed below are the sales price, standard food cost, and quantity sold for its five sandwiches for the week ended August 28.

Item	Selling Price	Standard Food Cost	Quantity Sold
Pork Barrel	$4.95	$1.60	50
Chicken Breast	4.45	1.40	100

Item	Selling Price	Standard Food Cost	Quantity Sold
Burger Delight	3.95	0.95	150
Ocean Catch	4.95	1.70	80
Egg Salad	2.95	0.45	40

The actual sales for the week equaled $1,799.00 while the total actual food costs equaled $547.00.

Required:

1. Calculate the standard food cost percentage based on the information above.

2. Calculate the standard food cost percentage assuming 100 of each item is sold during a week.

3. Calculate the actual food cost percentage for the week.

Problem 9

The Buckeye Motel's books indicated that the general checking account at the end of December 19X1 contained $6,523.34. The bank statement at December 31, 19X1, showed a closing balance of $7,432. Additional information includes:

1. Last month's bank reconciliation showed five outstanding checks:

Check 8923	$100.10
Check 8936	$248.15
Check 8944	$194.21
Check 8945	$648.49
Check 8946	$137.75

2. A comparison of the canceled checks from the bank with the check register revealed five checks written in December 19X1 that had not been paid by the bank:

Check 9164	$384.21
Check 9173	$439.42
Check 9190	$526.14
Check 9191	$422.15
Check 9192	$ 67.42

3. In addition, three checks were canceled in December that had been issued in the prior month:

Check 8944	$194.21
Check 8945	$648.49
Check 8946	$137.75

4. Cash receipts of $1,221.75 recorded on the books on December 31, 19X1, were deposited with the bank on January 2, 19X2.

5. A check for $57.18 received from a guest was returned by the bank on December 31, 19X1, marked "insufficient funds." The check was redeposited on January 2, 19X2. No entry was recorded to reflect the returned check on December 31, 19X1.

Required:

Prepare the Buckeye Motel's December 19X1 bank reconciliation.

Problem 10

Jeremy Harris, who has been working for 25 years as the bookkeeper for a family-owned restaurant, is planning to retire. Due to his loyalty, he has been given many additional responsibilities over the years. He is now responsible for the following:

a. Handling all cash receipts, including payments received on account

b. Preparing and distributing all checks, including all checks written on the payroll and general accounts

c. Signing checks when the owner/manager is absent, which amounts to about 15% of the checks

d. Preparing the bank reconciliations for both checking accounts

e. Performing all of the accounting related to accounts receivable

Required:

1. You have been asked to evaluate the above responsibilities and, from an internal perspective, advise the owner on how Harris' duties could be split between two people.

2. You are asked to tell the owner/manager what responsibilities currently handled by Harris should be handled by the owner/manager.

Problem 11

Many of the front office manager's headaches are caused by the skipper—the guest who departs without paying the bill. However, a dishonest employee can cause even more problems by using this situation as a cover-up. Consider the following situation. A guest checks in and is assigned to an $80 room. The clerk forgets to ask for a mailing address. The following day, the guest, hurrying to catch a flight, runs to the cashier's window, throws down $80 in cash, says "Check me out of 423," and rushes off.

The cashier looks at the bill in the file and notices that the guest left no address. The cashier reasons that the credit department will never track down the guest, so he pockets the $80 and leaves the bill in the file. The next day, room 423 is reported unoccupied. The bill by this time stands at $160 and is charged to "skippers."

Some hotels make no effort to locate skippers; at any rate, such attempts are usually without success. In this case, even finding the guest will not solve the problem; the guest has no receipt to prove his or her claim that the bill was paid.

Required:

What steps could be taken to adequately control cash in this situation?

Problem 12

At the Wolverine Inn, salaries and wages were paid semimonthly by individual checks to the order of each employee. These checks, drawn on a special payroll bank account, were signed jointly by the accountant and the payroll supervisor. Transfers for the total amount of the payroll for the period were made semimonthly to this special account by a check drawn on the regular bank account. In addition to the amounts periodically transferred, there remained a large balance from the period, representing the uncashed checks.

The Wolverine Inn's accountant had to be absent several days each month. It was her custom to leave a few signed blank checks to be used to pay employees who might quit during her absence.

With an assured minimum balance in the payroll account and the signed blank checks, the payroll supervisor saw an opportunity and seized it. He drew a check to his own order for an amount within the usual minimum balance. Since he always reconciled the monthly bank statements for this account, he was fairly safe from detection.

Required:

1. Which characteristics of internal control were violated in this situation?
2. How could this theft have been prevented?

Problem 13

Check-out time at the Wyman Hotel was 2 P.M. Guests checking out after that time were supposed to be charged for an extra day. However, the front office clerks did not post the extra charge on the guest folio until the money was paid. The usual procedure was to collect from those guests who failed to question the charge and then enter the amount on the folio. If the guest objected to the charge, the charge was dropped, as Wyman's management did not want unhappy guests.

One of the cashiers saw the opportunity for some personal gain in this procedure. The cashier would occasionally withhold the money paid by a hotel guest for the extra day, making no charge or credit for it on the guest's folio. The cashier did this only when the guest did not take the receipted statement. The cashier was able to add considerably to his monthly wages until by chance the assistant front office manager noticed his deceptive practices.

Required:

1. List weaknesses in Wyman's procedures for accounting for the extra charges.
2. What corrective action do you recommend?

Problem 14

The bookkeeper of Baylor's Fine Dining (BFD) has been unable to balance the firm's checkbook at December 31, 19X3, and has requested your assistance. Information is provided as follows:

1. Outstanding checks as of November 30, 19X3, were as follows:

Check 2186	$349.00
Check 2194	$115.21
Check 2210	$648.00
Check 2211	$ 18.76
Check 2212	$ 94.51

2. Outstanding checks as of December 31, 19X3, were as follows:

Check 2186	$349.00
Check 2212	$ 94.51
Check 2376	$153.40
Check 2377	$146.18
Check 2378	$349.00

3. Cash of $2,400.28 received on December 31, 19X3, was deposited on January 2, 19X4.

4. Bank service charges for December of $22.47 have not been recorded as of December 31, 19X3.

5. Checks returned by the bank on December 31, 19X3, were as follows:

   a. James Jones for $68.21, marked "insufficient funds"

   b. Wilma Hill for $157.83, marked "account closed"

   These items have not been recorded in the books since they have been received from the bank.

6. The cash balance per the bank statement as of December 31, 19X3, was $2,134.98, while the cash balance per the books is $3,691.68.

Required:

1. Prepare the bank reconciliation for December 31, 19X3.

2. Suggest the adjusting entries based on the above information.

Problem 15

Mr. Slippery, the chief accountant of a large hotel, in addition to his regular duties, had charge of the collection of city ledger and delinquent accounts and of returned checks. Thus, he was performing most of the duties of the credit manager.

In allowing Mr. Slippery to handle collection correspondence, prepare and send out the monthly statements, and receive the checks and cash in payment, the management was violating the most important of the fundamental principles of control in the hotel operation: *the bookkeeper must never be in charge of the cash.* The hotel was never audited by public accountants; if it had been, they would undoubtedly have recommended that the duties be shifted so as to take the collection of accounts out of the chief accountant's hands. That, however, would have meant giving the unpleasant duty to an assistant manager, and since the integrity of the chief accountant was considered to be above suspicion, such a recommendation would probably not have been heeded.

Mr. Slippery was fully aware of how easy it would be for him to appropriate money in various amounts and ways, with almost 100% protection against discovery. Accordingly, it did not take him long to make the most of the opportunities offered.

All mail concerning collections and remittances was placed on his desk. The envelopes addressed to him personally as credit manager were not opened, but those addressed to the hotel were opened by the manager's secretary and passed on to the chief accountant. Two rules were violated by this practice:

1. All business mail, regardless of the name or the position designated on the envelope, should be opened by someone in the manager's office.

2. Whoever opens the mail should make a record in triplicate of all remittances received, keeping a copy, sending the original to the head cashier, and the third copy to the credit department, so that the credit manager must account for all checks, money orders, etc.

In the course of the collection of the numerous city ledger accounts, a great many checks and money orders were received. Mr. Slippery had little trouble in appropriating some of them to his own use. He would destroy the remittance letter, and at the end of the month would dictate a letter asking the guest for payment. This, of course, never was mailed, but a copy was kept to support the eventual charge-off. He would get one of the front office cashiers to cash the withheld check, on the explanation that a friend upstairs in his office had asked him to cash a personal check. He would pocket the cash, the check going in with the other checks of the cashier through the hotel's account at the bank, and nobody being any the wiser.

When, once in a great while, somebody paid him personally in cash, it was still easier to get away with the money. And on one occasion, the head cashier, after having twice deposited a check only to have it come back marked "insufficient funds," turned it over to the chief accountant for collection. The latter, through correspondence, obtained a new check for the amount, drawn on another bank. This he personally cashed at the front office, and in time the old one was charged off.

By these operations, carried on with practically no risk, Mr. Slippery almost doubled his salary. All the book entries were regular, as he had not made any false entries or forced any footings—he did not have to!

When, occasionally, he forgot to destroy a statement which had been paid, there would of course be a protest from the guest or former guest. This would be referred by the manager to the accountant, and he would write an apologetic letter regretting that an "error" had been made.

Mr. Slippery never took a vacation and he was never sick; but one day he had the misfortune to have a serious automobile accident. While he was in the hospital, the city ledger bills were mailed, and a flood of complaints immediately poured in from persons who had already paid their bills. An audit and investigation by a firm of public accountants brought out the full details of the manipulations.

Required:

1. State the weaknesses in the hotel's system of internal control.

2. Indicate desired changes to overcome the weaknesses stated in #1.

Chapter 13 Outline

Relationship of Capital Budget to Operations Budget
Types of Capital Budgeting Decisions
Time Value of Money
Cash Flow in Capital Budgeting
Capital Budgeting Models
    Accounting Rate of Return
    Payback
    Net Present Value Model
    Internal Rate of Return
    Comparison of NPV and IRR Models
Mutually Exclusive Projects with Different Lives
Capital Rationing
Use of Capital Budgeting Models in the Lodging Industry
Computer Applications

13

Capital Budgeting

THE HOSPITALITY INDUSTRY, especially the lodging segment, is fixed-asset–intensive. This means that the majority of the assets of hospitality operations are fixed instead of current. This sets hospitality operations apart from many manufacturing firms, where most assets are current. Since establishments in the hospitality industry are so fixed-asset–intensive, capital budgeting becomes an important management concern.

Capital budgeting is the process of determining the amount to spend on fixed assets and which fixed assets to purchase. Capital budgeting addresses such questions as:

1. What piece of equipment among several alternatives should be purchased?
2. Should old equipment be replaced with new?
3. What is meant by the time value of money?
4. How is cash flow computed from an investment?
5. How is payback computed?
6. When is the net present value method preferred to the internal rate of return method?
7. How are alternative investments with different lives considered in the capital budgeting process?
8. Which fixed assets are purchased under capital rationing?

We will begin our consideration of the capital budget by comparing it with the operations budget and by identifying various types of decisions involving capital budgeting. We will then focus on the concept of the time value of money and the computation of cash flow and payback from fixed asset investments. Next, we will explain different models of capital budgets and see how they apply to choices among various kinds of projects. Finally, we will discuss capital rationing and identify special problems with capital budgeting.

Relationship of Capital Budget to Operations Budget

Preparing the operations budget is a prerequisite to capital budgeting for equipment. If the operations budget suggests that sales will increase beyond what present equipment is reasonably able to produce, then the present equipment has become functionally obsolete and must be replaced. For example, if a restaurant's budget is based on a realistic assumption that breakfast business will sizably increase, it may be necessary to invest in a large rotary toaster instead of continuing to use a four-piece drop-in toaster.

533

Capital budgets are prepared not only for the current year, but also are often projected for several years into the future. Construction projects undertaken by some hotel properties may take up to 24 months to complete. Even though capital budgets may be prepared for several years, they must be reviewed annually to consider the impact of changing economic conditions. The capital budget is adjusted as new information becomes available regarding changes in demand for the hospitality operation's goods and services, technological changes, and changes in the cost of providing goods and services. Evaluating past capital budgeting decisions in light of such current information is useful in determining whether those projects should be continued, expanded, reduced in scope, or possibly even terminated. Such current information may also affect the capital budgeting process itself.

Types of Capital Budgeting Decisions

Capital budgeting decisions are made for a variety of reasons. Some are the result of meeting government requirements. For example, the Occupational Safety & Health Administration (OSHA) requires certain safety equipment and guards on meat-cutting equipment. The hospitality operation may spend several hundreds or even thousands of dollars in order to upgrade equipment and meet OSHA's requirements. Regardless of the potential profit or cost savings (if any) from this upgrading of equipment, the government regulation forces the hospitality operation to make the expenditure.

A second capital budgeting decision is acquiring a fixed asset to reduce the operation's costs. For example, a lodging operation may have leased vehicles to provide airport transportation. However, to reduce this cost, a van could be purchased.

A third capital budgeting decision is acquiring fixed assets to increase sales. For example, a lodging operation may add a wing of 100 rooms or expand a dining facility from 75 to 150 seats. Another example is a lodging operation determining which franchise is most desirable. As a result of this expansion and/or franchise, both sales and expenses are increased, and, if the proper decision is made, total profits should increase to justify the capital expenditure.

A fourth capital budgeting decision is replacing an existing fixed asset. This replacement may be required because the present fixed asset is fully used up or functionally obsolete, or perhaps the replacement is simply more economical.

All four kinds of capital budgeting decisions require significant expenditures resulting in fixed assets. The return on the expenditures will accrue over an extended period of time. The expenditures should generally be cost justified in the sense that the expected benefits will exceed the cost. The more sophisticated capital budgeting models require a comparison of current cost expenditures for the fixed asset against a future stream of funds. In order to compare current year expenditures to future years' income, the future years' income must be placed on an equal basis. The process for accomplishing this recognizes the **time value of money**.

Time Value of Money

The saying, "$100 today is worth more than $100 a year from now" is true, in part because $100 today could be invested to provide $100 plus the interest for one year in the future. If the $100 can be invested at 12% annual interest, then the $100 will be worth $112 in one year. This is determined as follows:

Principal	+	(Principal	×	Time	×	Interest Rate)	=	Total
100	+	(100	×	1	×	.12)	=	$112

Principal is the sum of dollars at the beginning of the investment period ($100 in this case). Time is expressed in years, as long as an annual interest rate is used. The interest rate is expressed in decimal form. The interest of $12 plus the principal of $100 equals the amount available one year hence.

A shorter formula for calculating a future value is as follows:

$$F = A(1 + i)^n$$

where
$$F = \text{Future Value}$$
$$A = \text{Present Amount}$$
$$i = \text{Interest Rate}$$
$$n = \text{Number of Years (or Interest Periods)}$$

One hundred dollars invested at 12% for two years will yield $125.44, determined as follows:

$$F = 100(1 + .12)^2$$
$$= 100(1.2544)$$
$$= \$125.44$$

An alternative to using this formula to calculate the future value of a present amount is to use a table of future value factors, such as that found in Exhibit 1. The future value factors are based on present amounts at the end of each period. For example, the future amount of $100 two years from now at 15% interest is $132.25. This is determined by finding the number in the 15% column and the period 2 row (1.3225) and multiplying it by $100.

The present value of a future amount is the present amount that must be invested at $x\%$ interest to yield the future amount. For example, what is the present value of $100 one year hence when the interest rate is 12%? The formula to determine the present value of the future amount is as follows:

$$P = F \frac{1}{(1 + i)^n}$$

where
$$P = \text{Present Amount}$$
$$F = \text{Future Amount}$$
$$i = \text{Interest Rate}$$
$$n = \text{Number of Years}$$

Exhibit 1   Table of Future Value Factors for a Single Cash Flow

$$FV_{n,k} = (1 + k)^n$$

Number of Periods	1%	2%	3%	4%	5%	6%	7%	8%	9%	10%	12%	14%	15%	16%	18%	20%	22%	24%	26%	28%	30%	35%
1	1.0100	1.0200	1.0300	1.0400	1.0500	1.0600	1.0700	1.0800	1.0900	1.1000	1.1200	1.1400	1.1500	1.1600	1.1800	1.2000	1.2200	1.2400	1.2600	1.2800	1.3000	1.3500
2	1.0201	1.0404	1.0609	1.0816	1.1025	1.1236	1.1449	1.1664	1.1881	1.2100	1.2544	1.2996	1.3225	1.3456	1.3924	1.4400	1.4884	1.5376	1.5876	1.6384	1.6900	1.8225
3	1.0303	1.0612	1.0927	1.1249	1.1576	1.1910	1.2250	1.2597	1.2950	1.3310	1.4049	1.4815	1.5209	1.5609	1.6430	1.7280	1.8158	1.9066	2.0004	2.0972	2.1970	2.4604
4	1.0406	1.0824	1.1255	1.1699	1.2155	1.2625	1.3108	1.3605	1.4116	1.4641	1.5735	1.6890	1.7490	1.8106	1.9388	2.0736	2.2153	2.3642	2.5205	2.6844	2.8561	3.3215
5	1.0510	1.1041	1.1593	1.2167	1.2763	1.3382	1.4026	1.4693	1.5386	1.6105	1.7623	1.9254	2.0114	2.1003	2.2878	2.4883	2.7027	2.9316	3.1758	3.4360	3.7129	4.4840
6	1.0615	1.1262	1.1941	1.2653	1.3401	1.4185	1.5007	1.5869	1.6771	1.7716	1.9738	2.1950	2.3131	2.4364	2.6996	2.9860	3.2973	3.6352	4.0015	4.3980	4.8268	6.0534
7	1.0721	1.1487	1.2299	1.3159	1.4071	1.5036	1.6058	1.7138	1.8280	1.9487	2.2107	2.5023	2.6600	2.8262	3.1855	3.5832	4.0227	4.5077	5.0419	5.6295	6.2749	8.1722
8	1.0829	1.1717	1.2668	1.3686	1.4775	1.5938	1.7182	1.8509	1.9926	2.1436	2.4760	2.8526	3.0590	3.2784	3.7589	4.2998	4.9077	5.5895	6.3528	7.2058	8.1573	11.032
9	1.0937	1.1951	1.3048	1.4233	1.5513	1.6895	1.8385	1.9990	2.1719	2.3579	2.7731	3.2519	3.5179	3.8030	4.4355	5.1598	5.9874	6.9310	8.0045	9.2234	10.604	14.894
10	1.1046	1.2190	1.3439	1.4802	1.6289	1.7908	1.9672	2.1589	2.3674	2.5937	3.1058	3.7072	4.0456	4.4114	5.2338	6.1917	7.3046	8.5944	10.086	11.806	13.786	20.107
11	1.1157	1.2434	1.3842	1.5395	1.7103	1.8983	2.1049	2.3316	2.5804	2.8531	3.4785	4.2262	4.6524	5.1173	6.1759	7.4301	8.9117	10.657	12.708	15.112	17.922	27.144
12	1.1268	1.2682	1.4258	1.6010	1.7959	2.0122	2.2522	2.5182	2.8127	3.1384	3.8960	4.8179	5.3503	5.9360	7.2876	8.9161	10.872	13.215	16.012	19.343	23.298	36.644
13	1.1381	1.2936	1.4685	1.6651	1.8856	2.1329	2.4098	2.7196	3.0658	3.4523	4.3635	5.4924	6.1528	6.8858	8.5994	10.699	13.264	16.386	20.175	24.759	30.288	49.470
14	1.1495	1.3195	1.5126	1.7317	1.9799	2.2609	2.5785	2.9372	3.3417	3.7975	4.8871	6.2613	7.0757	7.9875	10.147	12.839	16.182	20.319	25.421	31.691	39.374	66.784
15	1.1610	1.3459	1.5580	1.8009	2.0789	2.3966	2.7590	3.1722	3.6425	4.1772	5.4736	7.1379	8.1371	9.2655	11.974	15.407	19.742	25.196	32.030	40.565	51.186	90.158
16	1.1726	1.3728	1.6047	1.8730	2.1829	2.5404	2.9522	3.4259	3.9703	4.5950	6.1304	8.1372	9.3576	10.748	14.129	18.488	24.086	31.243	40.358	51.923	66.542	121.71
17	1.1843	1.4002	1.6528	1.9479	2.2920	2.6928	3.1588	3.7000	4.3276	5.0545	6.8660	9.2765	10.761	12.468	16.672	22.186	29.384	38.741	50.851	66.461	86.504	164.31
18	1.1961	1.4282	1.7024	2.0258	2.4066	2.8543	3.3799	3.9960	4.7171	5.5599	7.6900	10.575	12.375	14.463	19.673	26.623	35.849	48.039	64.072	85.071	112.46	221.82
19	1.2081	1.4568	1.7535	2.1068	2.5270	3.0256	3.6165	4.3157	5.1417	6.1159	8.6128	12.056	14.232	16.777	23.214	31.948	43.736	59.568	80.731	108.89	146.19	299.46
20	1.2202	1.4859	1.8061	2.1911	2.6533	3.2071	3.8697	4.6610	5.6044	6.7275	9.6463	13.743	16.367	19.461	27.393	38.338	53.358	73.864	101.72	139.38	190.05	404.27
21	1.2324	1.5157	1.8603	2.2788	2.7860	3.3996	4.1406	5.0338	6.1088	7.4002	10.804	15.668	18.822	22.574	32.324	46.005	65.096	91.592	128.17	178.41	247.06	545.77
22	1.2447	1.5460	1.9161	2.3699	2.9253	3.6035	4.4304	5.4365	6.6586	8.1403	12.100	17.861	21.645	26.186	38.142	55.206	79.418	113.57	161.49	228.36	321.18	736.79
23	1.2572	1.5769	1.9736	2.4647	3.0715	3.8197	4.7405	5.8715	7.2579	8.9543	13.552	20.362	24.891	30.376	45.008	66.247	96.889	140.83	203.48	292.30	417.54	994.66
24	1.2697	1.6084	2.0328	2.5633	3.2251	4.0489	5.0724	6.3412	7.9111	9.8497	15.179	23.212	28.625	35.236	53.109	79.497	118.21	174.63	256.39	374.14	542.80	1342.80
25	1.2824	1.6406	2.0938	2.6658	3.3864	4.2919	5.4274	6.8485	8.6231	10.835	17.000	26.462	32.919	40.874	62.669	95.396	144.21	216.54	323.05	478.90	705.64	1812.78
26	1.2953	1.6734	2.1566	2.7725	3.5557	4.5494	5.8074	7.3964	9.3992	11.918	19.040	30.167	37.857	47.414	73.949	114.48	175.94	268.51	407.04	613.00	917.33	2447.25
27	1.3082	1.7069	2.2213	2.8834	3.7335	4.8223	6.2139	7.9881	10.245	13.110	21.325	34.390	43.535	55.000	87.260	137.37	214.64	332.95	512.87	784.64	1192.5	3303.78
28	1.3213	1.7410	2.2879	2.9987	3.9201	5.1117	6.6488	8.6271	11.167	14.421	23.884	39.204	50.066	63.800	102.97	164.84	261.86	412.86	646.21	1004.3	1550.3	4460.11
29	1.3345	1.7758	2.3566	3.1187	4.1161	5.4184	7.1143	9.3173	12.172	15.863	26.750	44.693	57.575	74.009	121.50	197.81	319.47	511.95	814.23	1285.6	2015.4	6021.15
30	1.3478	1.8114	2.4273	3.2434	4.3219	5.7435	7.6123	10.063	13.268	17.449	29.960	50.950	66.212	85.850	143.37	237.38	389.76	634.82	1025.9	1645.5	2620.0	8128.55
40	1.4889	2.2080	3.2620	4.8010	7.0400	10.286	14.974	21.725	31.409	45.259	93.051	188.88	267.86	378.72	750.38	1469.8	2847.0	5455.9	10347.	19427.	36118.9	*
50	1.6446	2.6916	4.3839	7.1067	11.467	18.420	29.457	46.902	74.358	117.39	289.00	700.23	1083.7	1670.7	3927.4	9100.4	20797.	46890.	*	*	*	*
60	1.8167	3.2810	5.8916	10.520	18.679	32.988	57.946	101.26	176.03	304.48	897.60	2595.9	4384.0	7370.2	20555.	56348.	*	*	*	*	*	*

*$FV_{n,k} > 99,999$

Therefore, the present value of $100 one year hence (assuming an interest rate of 12%) is $89.29, determined as follows:

$$P = 100 \frac{1}{(1 + .12)^1}$$
$$= 100(.8929)$$
$$= \underline{\underline{\$89.29}}$$

The present value of $100 two years hence (assuming an interest rate of 12%) is $79.72 determined as follows:

$$P = 100 \frac{1}{(1 + .12)^2}$$
$$= 100(.7972)$$
$$= \underline{\underline{\$79.72}}$$

An alternative to using this formula to calculate the present value of a future amount is to use a table of present value factors, such as that found in Exhibit 2. The present value factors in Exhibit 2 are based on future amounts at the end of the period. For example, the present value of $100 a year from now at 15% interest is $86.96. This is determined by finding the number in the 15% column and the period 1 row (0.8696) and multiplying it by $100. The present value of $100 today is simply $100.

Most capital investments provide a stream of receipts for several years. When the amounts are the same and at equal intervals, such as the end of each year, the stream is referred to as an **annuity.** Exhibit 3 shows the calculation of the present value of an annuity (at 15%) of $10,000 due at the end of each year for five years. The present value factors used in the calculation are from the present value table in Exhibit 2.

The present value of an annuity will vary significantly based on the interest rate (also called the **discount rate**) and the timing of the future receipts. Everything else being the same, the higher the discount rate, the lower the present value. Likewise, everything else being the same, the more distant the receipt, the smaller the present value.

An alternative to multiplying each future amount by the present value factor from the present value table in Exhibit 2 is to sum the present factors and make one multiplication. This is illustrated in Exhibit 4. Thus, the $33,522 calculated in Exhibit 4 equals the calculation performed in Exhibit 3. Rather than using the present values from Exhibit 2, present values for an annuity are provided in Exhibit 5. As a check on your understanding of the present value of an annuity table, locate the present value factor for five years and 15%. As you would expect, it is 3.3522. Thus, the present value for an annuity table is nothing more than a summation of present value factors from Exhibit 2. However, this table of present value factors for an annuity will save much time, especially when streams of receipts for several years must be calculated.

Exhibit 2 Table of Present Value Factors for a Single Cash Flow

$$PV_{n,k} = 1/(1 + k)^n$$

Number of Periods	1%	2%	3%	4%	5%	6%	7%	8%	9%	10%	12%	14%	15%	16%	18%	20%	22%	24%	26%	28%	30%	35%
1	.9901	.9804	.9709	.9615	.9524	.9434	.9346	.9259	.9174	.9091	.8929	.8772	.8696	.8621	.8475	.8333	.8197	.8065	.7937	.7813	.7692	.7407
2	.9803	.9612	.9426	.9246	.9070	.8900	.8734	.8573	.8417	.8264	.7972	.7695	.7561	.7432	.7182	.6944	.6719	.6504	.6299	.6104	.5917	.5487
3	.9706	.9423	.9151	.8890	.8638	.8396	.8163	.7938	.7722	.7513	.7118	.6750	.6575	.6407	.6086	.5787	.5507	.5245	.4999	.4768	.4552	.4064
4	.9610	.9238	.8885	.8548	.8227	.7921	.7629	.7350	.7084	.6830	.6355	.5921	.5718	.5523	.5158	.4823	.4514	.4230	.3968	.3725	.3501	.3011
5	.9515	.9057	.8626	.8219	.7835	.7473	.7130	.6806	.6499	.6209	.5674	.5194	.4972	.4761	.4371	.4019	.3700	.3411	.3149	.2910	.2693	.2230
6	.9420	.8880	.8375	.7903	.7462	.7050	.6663	.6302	.5963	.5645	.5066	.4556	.4323	.4104	.3704	.3349	.3033	.2751	.2499	.2274	.2072	.1652
7	.9327	.8706	.8131	.7599	.7107	.6651	.6227	.5835	.5470	.5132	.4523	.3996	.3759	.3538	.3139	.2791	.2486	.2218	.1983	.1776	.1594	.1224
8	.9235	.8535	.7894	.7307	.6768	.6274	.5820	.5403	.5019	.4665	.4039	.3506	.3269	.3050	.2660	.2326	.2038	.1789	.1574	.1388	.1226	.0906
9	.9143	.8368	.7664	.7026	.6446	.5919	.5439	.5002	.4604	.4241	.3606	.3075	.2843	.2630	.2255	.1938	.1670	.1443	.1249	.1084	.0943	.0671
10	.9053	.8203	.7441	.6756	.6139	.5584	.5083	.4632	.4224	.3855	.3220	.2697	.2472	.2267	.1911	.1615	.1369	.1164	.0992	.0847	.0725	.0497
11	.8963	.8043	.7224	.6496	.5847	.5268	.4751	.4289	.3875	.3505	.2875	.2366	.2149	.1954	.1619	.1346	.1122	.0938	.0787	.0662	.0558	.0368
12	.8874	.7885	.7014	.6246	.5568	.4970	.4440	.3971	.3555	.3186	.2567	.2076	.1869	.1685	.1372	.1122	.0920	.0757	.0625	.0517	.0429	.0273
13	.8787	.7730	.6810	.6006	.5303	.4688	.4150	.3677	.3262	.2897	.2292	.1821	.1625	.1452	.1163	.0935	.0754	.0610	.0496	.0404	.0330	.0202
14	.8700	.7579	.6611	.5775	.5051	.4423	.3878	.3405	.2992	.2633	.2046	.1597	.1413	.1252	.0985	.0779	.0618	.0492	.0393	.0316	.0254	.0150
15	.8613	.7430	.6419	.5553	.4810	.4173	.3624	.3152	.2745	.2394	.1827	.1401	.1229	.1079	.0835	.0649	.0507	.0397	.0312	.0247	.0195	.0111
16	.8528	.7284	.6232	.5339	.4581	.3936	.3387	.2919	.2519	.2176	.1631	.1229	.1069	.0930	.0708	.0541	.0415	.0320	.0248	.0193	.0150	.0082
17	.8444	.7142	.6050	.5134	.4363	.3714	.3166	.2703	.2311	.1978	.1456	.1078	.0929	.0802	.0600	.0451	.0340	.0258	.0197	.0150	.0116	.0061
18	.8360	.7002	.5874	.4936	.4155	.3503	.2959	.2502	.2120	.1799	.1300	.0946	.0808	.0691	.0508	.0376	.0279	.0208	.0156	.0118	.0089	.0045
19	.8277	.6864	.5703	.4746	.3957	.3305	.2765	.2317	.1945	.1635	.1161	.0829	.0703	.0596	.0431	.0313	.0229	.0168	.0124	.0092	.0068	.0033
20	.8195	.6730	.5537	.4564	.3769	.3118	.2584	.2145	.1784	.1486	.1037	.0728	.0611	.0514	.0365	.0261	.0187	.0135	.0098	.0072	.0053	.0025
21	.8114	.6598	.5375	.4388	.3589	.2942	.2415	.1987	.1637	.1351	.0926	.0638	.0531	.0443	.0309	.0217	.0154	.0109	.0078	.0056	.0040	.0018
22	.8034	.6468	.5219	.4220	.3418	.2775	.2257	.1839	.1502	.1228	.0826	.0560	.0462	.0382	.0262	.0181	.0126	.0088	.0062	.0044	.0031	.0014
23	.7954	.6342	.5067	.4057	.3256	.2618	.2109	.1703	.1378	.1117	.0738	.0491	.0402	.0329	.0222	.0151	.0103	.0071	.0049	.0034	.0024	.0010
24	.7876	.6217	.4919	.3901	.3101	.2470	.1971	.1577	.1264	.1015	.0659	.0431	.0349	.0284	.0188	.0126	.0085	.0057	.0039	.0027	.0018	.0007
25	.7798	.6095	.4776	.3751	.2953	.2330	.1842	.1460	.1160	.0923	.0588	.0378	.0304	.0245	.0160	.0105	.0069	.0046	.0031	.0021	.0014	.0006
26	.7720	.5976	.4637	.3607	.2812	.2198	.1722	.1352	.1064	.0839	.0525	.0331	.0264	.0211	.0135	.0087	.0057	.0037	.0025	.0016	.0011	.0004
27	.7644	.5859	.4502	.3468	.2678	.2074	.1609	.1252	.0976	.0763	.0469	.0291	.0230	.0182	.0115	.0073	.0047	.0030	.0019	.0013	.0008	.0003
28	.7568	.5744	.4371	.3335	.2551	.1956	.1504	.1159	.0895	.0693	.0419	.0255	.0200	.0157	.0097	.0061	.0038	.0024	.0015	.0010	.0006	.0002
29	.7493	.5631	.4243	.3207	.2429	.1846	.1406	.1073	.0822	.0630	.0374	.0224	.0174	.0135	.0082	.0051	.0031	.0020	.0012	.0008	.0005	.0002
30	.7419	.5521	.4120	.3083	.2314	.1741	.1314	.0994	.0754	.0573	.0334	.0196	.0151	.0116	.0070	.0042	.0026	.0016	.0010	.0006	.0004	.0001
35	.7059	.5000	.3554	.2534	.1813	.1301	.0937	.0676	.0490	.0356	.0189	.0102	.0075	.0055	.0030	.0017	.0009	.0005	.0003	.0002	.0001	*
40	.6717	.4529	.3066	.2083	.1420	.0972	.0668	.0460	.0318	.0221	.0107	.0053	.0037	.0026	.0013	.0007	.0004	.0002	.0001	.0001	*	*
45	.6391	.4102	.2644	.1712	.1113	.0727	.0476	.0313	.0207	.0137	.0061	.0027	.0019	.0013	.0006	.0003	.0001	.0001	*	*	*	*
50	.6080	.3715	.2281	.1407	.0872	.0543	.0339	.0213	.0134	.0085	.0035	.0014	.0009	.0006	.0003	.0001	*	*	*	*	*	*
55	.5785	.3365	.1968	.1157	.0683	.0406	.0242	.0145	.0087	.0053	.0020	.0007	.0005	.0003	.0001	*	*	*	*	*	*	*
60	.5504	.3048	.1697	.0951	.0535	.0303	.0173	.0099	.0057	.0033	.0011	.0004	.0002	.0001	*	*	*	*	*	*	*	*

*Rounds to zero

Exhibit 3   Present Value of a $10,000 Five-Year Annuity at 15%

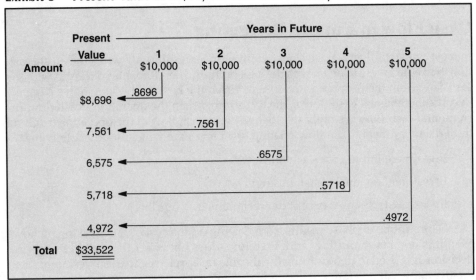

Exhibit 4   Shortcut Calculations of the Present Value of a $10,000 Five-Year Annuity at 15%

Years Hence	Present Value Factors at 15%
1	.8696
2	.7561
3	.6575
4	.5718
5	+ .4972
	3.3522
3.3522 × $10,000 =	$33,522

A problem that calls for the use of both present value factors (Exhibit 2) and present value factors for an annuity (Exhibit 5) is presented in Exhibit 6. This problem is solved by treating the stream of receipts as a $10,000 annuity and two separate payments of $5,000 and $10,000 due at the end of years two and four, respectively.

Similarly, to calculate future values of an annuity, it is simplest to refer to the table of future value factors for an annuity (Exhibit 7). For example, assume that a hotel company decides to invest $10,000 at the end of each year for five years at an annual interest rate of 10%, compounded annually. What will be the value of the investment at the end of year five? Using the factor for 10% and five periods from Exhibit 7, we can determine the answer as follows:

$$\$10,000 \quad \times \quad 6.1051 \quad = \quad \underline{\underline{\$61,051}}$$

Cash Flow in Capital Budgeting

In most capital budgeting decisions, an investment results only when the future cash flow from the investment justifies the expenditure. Therefore, the concern is with the cash flow from the proposed investment. From the hospitality operation's perspective, the incremental cash flow is the focus rather than the operation's cash flow. **Incremental cash flow** is simply the change in the cash flow of the operation resulting from the investment. Cash flow relating to an investment includes the following:

- Investment initial cost (cash outflow)
- Investment revenues (cash inflow)
- Investment expenses except depreciation (cash outflow)

Depreciation expense results from writing off the cost of the investment; however, it is not a cash outflow and, therefore, does not affect the capital budgeting decision. It is used in determining the income taxes relating to the investment since the IRS allows depreciation to be deducted in computing taxable income.

Exhibit 8 illustrates the relevant cash flows of a proposed investment of the Hampton Hotel. The Hampton Hotel is considering installing a game room. Since space is available with only minor modifications, the focus is on the cost of machines and related future revenues and expenses. Depreciation of $7,000 per year is used only in determining the pretax income from the investment. The cash flow generated by the investment in game machines is $36,840 for three years, resulting in an incremental net cash flow of $15,840 after the cost of the machines is subtracted. The means of financing the game machines is not considered. In capital budgeting models, the discount rate includes the interest cost, if any.

Capital Budgeting Models

Managers in hospitality operations use several different models in making capital budgeting decisions. The models vary from simple to sophisticated. The simple models are **accounting rate of return (ARR)** and **payback,** while more sophisticated models, which require the discounting of future cash flows, are **net present value (NPV)** and **internal rate of return (IRR).** The advantages and disadvantages of each model are addressed and illustrated using the investment data in Exhibit 9.

Accounting Rate of Return

The ARR model considers the average annual project income (project revenues less project expenses generated by the investment) and the average investment. The calculation of ARR is simply:

$$\text{ARR} \quad = \quad \frac{\text{Average Annual Project Income}}{\text{Average Investment}}$$

Exhibit 5 Table of Present Value Factors for an Annuity

$$PVA_{n,k} = \frac{1 - \dfrac{1}{(1+k)^n}}{k}$$

Number of Periods	1%	2%	3%	4%	5%	6%	7%	8%	9%	10%	12%	14%	15%	16%	18%	20%	22%	24%	26%	28%	30%	35%
1	0.9901	0.9804	0.9709	0.9615	0.9524	0.9434	0.9346	0.9259	0.9174	0.9091	0.8929	0.8772	0.8696	0.8621	0.8475	0.8333	0.8197	0.8065	0.7937	0.7813	0.7692	0.7407
2	1.9704	1.9416	1.9135	1.8861	1.8594	1.8334	1.8080	1.7833	1.7591	1.7355	1.6901	1.6467	1.6257	1.6052	1.5656	1.5278	1.4915	1.4568	1.4235	1.3916	1.3609	1.2894
3	2.9410	2.8839	2.8286	2.7751	2.7232	2.6730	2.6243	2.5771	2.5313	2.4869	2.4018	2.3216	2.2832	2.2459	2.1743	2.1065	2.0422	1.9813	1.9234	1.8684	1.8161	1.6959
4	3.9020	3.8077	3.7171	3.6299	3.5460	3.4651	3.3872	3.3121	3.2397	3.1699	3.0373	2.9137	2.8550	2.7982	2.6901	2.5887	2.4936	2.4043	2.3202	2.2410	2.1662	1.9969
5	4.8534	4.7135	4.5797	4.4518	4.3295	4.2124	4.1002	3.9927	3.8897	3.7908	3.6048	3.4331	3.3522	3.2743	3.1272	2.9906	2.8636	2.7454	2.6351	2.5320	2.4356	2.2200
6	5.7955	5.6014	5.4172	5.2421	5.0757	4.9173	4.7665	4.6229	4.4859	4.3553	4.1114	3.8887	3.7845	3.6847	3.4976	3.3255	3.1669	3.0205	2.8850	2.7594	2.6427	2.3852
7	6.7282	6.4720	6.2303	6.0021	5.7864	5.5824	5.3893	5.2064	5.0330	4.8684	4.5638	4.2883	4.1604	4.0386	3.8115	3.6046	3.4155	3.2423	3.0833	2.9370	2.8021	2.5075
8	7.6517	7.3255	7.0197	6.7327	6.4632	6.2098	5.9713	5.7466	5.5348	5.3349	4.9676	4.6389	4.4873	4.3436	4.0776	3.8372	3.6193	3.4212	3.2407	3.0758	2.9247	2.5982
9	8.5660	8.1622	7.7861	7.4353	7.1078	6.8017	6.5152	6.2469	5.9952	5.7590	5.3282	4.9464	4.7716	4.6065	4.3030	4.0310	3.7863	3.5655	3.3657	3.1842	3.0190	2.6653
10	9.4713	8.9826	8.5302	8.1109	7.7217	7.3601	7.0236	6.7101	6.4177	6.1446	5.6502	5.2161	5.0188	4.8332	4.4941	4.1925	3.9232	3.6819	3.4648	3.2689	3.0915	2.7150
11	10.3676	9.7868	9.2526	8.7605	8.3064	7.8869	7.4987	7.1390	6.8052	6.4951	5.9377	5.4527	5.2337	5.0286	4.6560	4.3271	4.0354	3.7757	3.5435	3.3351	3.1473	2.7519
12	11.2551	10.5753	9.9540	9.3851	8.8633	8.3838	7.9427	7.5361	7.1607	6.8137	6.1944	5.6603	5.4206	5.1971	4.7932	4.4392	4.1274	3.8514	3.6059	3.3868	3.1903	2.7792
13	12.1337	11.3484	10.6350	9.9856	9.3936	8.8527	8.3577	7.9038	7.4869	7.1034	6.4235	5.8424	5.5831	5.3423	4.9095	4.5327	4.2028	3.9124	3.6555	3.4272	3.2233	2.7994
14	13.0037	12.1062	11.2961	10.5631	9.8986	9.2950	8.7455	8.2442	7.7862	7.3667	6.6282	6.0021	5.7245	5.4675	5.0081	4.6106	4.2646	3.9616	3.6949	3.4587	3.2487	2.8144
15	13.8651	12.8493	11.9379	11.1184	10.3797	9.7122	9.1079	8.5595	8.0607	7.6061	6.8109	6.1422	5.8474	5.5755	5.0916	4.6755	4.3152	4.0013	3.7261	3.4834	3.2682	2.8255
16	14.7179	13.5777	12.5611	11.6523	10.8378	10.1059	9.4466	8.8514	8.3126	7.8237	6.9740	6.2651	5.9542	5.6685	5.1624	4.7296	4.3567	4.0333	3.7509	3.5026	3.2832	2.8337
17	15.5623	14.2919	13.1661	12.1657	11.2741	10.4773	9.7632	9.1216	8.5436	8.0216	7.1196	6.3729	6.0472	5.7487	5.2223	4.7746	4.3908	4.0591	3.7705	3.5177	3.2948	2.8398
18	16.3983	14.9920	13.7535	12.6593	11.6896	10.8276	10.0591	9.3719	8.7556	8.2014	7.2497	6.4674	6.1280	5.8178	5.2732	4.8122	4.4187	4.0799	3.7861	3.5294	3.3037	2.8443
19	17.2260	15.6785	14.3238	13.1339	12.0853	11.1581	10.3356	9.6036	8.9501	8.3649	7.3658	6.5504	6.1982	5.8775	5.3162	4.8435	4.4415	4.0967	3.7985	3.5386	3.3105	2.8476
20	18.0456	16.3514	14.8775	13.5903	12.4622	11.4699	10.5940	9.8181	9.1285	8.5136	7.4694	6.6231	6.2593	5.9288	5.3527	4.8696	4.4603	4.1103	3.8083	3.5458	3.3158	2.8501
21	18.8570	17.0112	15.4150	14.0292	12.8212	11.7641	10.8355	10.0168	9.2922	8.6487	7.5620	6.6870	6.3125	5.9731	5.3837	4.8913	4.4756	4.1212	3.8161	3.5514	3.3198	2.8519
22	19.6604	17.6580	15.9369	14.4511	13.1630	12.0416	11.0612	10.2007	9.4424	8.7715	7.6446	6.7429	6.3587	6.0113	5.4099	4.9094	4.4882	4.1300	3.8223	3.5558	3.3230	2.8533
23	20.4558	18.2922	16.4436	14.8568	13.4886	12.3034	11.2722	10.3711	9.5802	8.8832	7.7184	6.7921	6.3988	6.0442	5.4321	4.9245	4.4985	4.1371	3.8273	3.5592	3.3254	2.8543
24	21.2434	18.9139	16.9355	15.2470	13.7986	12.5504	11.4693	10.5288	9.7066	8.9847	7.7843	6.8351	6.4338	6.0726	5.4509	4.9371	4.5070	4.1428	3.8312	3.5619	3.3272	2.8550
25	22.0232	19.5235	17.4131	15.6221	14.0939	12.7834	11.6536	10.6748	9.8226	9.0770	7.8431	6.8729	6.4641	6.0971	5.4669	4.9476	4.5139	4.1474	3.8342	3.5640	3.3286	2.8556
26	22.7952	20.1210	17.8768	15.9828	14.3752	13.0032	11.8258	10.8100	9.9290	9.1609	7.8957	6.9061	6.4906	6.1182	5.4804	4.9563	4.5196	4.1511	3.8367	3.5656	3.3297	2.8560
27	23.5596	20.7069	18.3270	16.3296	14.6430	13.2105	11.9867	10.9352	10.0266	9.2372	7.9426	6.9352	6.5135	6.1364	5.4919	4.9636	4.5243	4.1542	3.8387	3.5669	3.3305	2.8563
28	24.3164	21.2813	18.7641	16.6631	14.8981	13.4062	12.1371	11.0511	10.1161	9.3066	7.9844	6.9607	6.5335	6.1520	5.5016	4.9697	4.5281	4.1566	3.8402	3.5679	3.3312	2.8565
29	25.0658	21.8444	19.1885	16.9837	15.1411	13.5907	12.2777	11.1584	10.1983	9.3696	8.0218	6.9830	6.5509	6.1656	5.5098	4.9747	4.5312	4.1585	3.8414	3.5687	3.3317	2.8567
30	25.8077	22.3965	19.6004	17.2920	15.3725	13.7648	12.4090	11.2578	10.2737	9.4269	8.0552	7.0027	6.5660	6.1772	5.5168	4.9789	4.5338	4.1601	3.8424	3.5693	3.3321	2.8568
35	29.4086	24.9986	21.4872	18.6646	16.3742	14.4982	12.9477	11.6546	10.5668	9.6442	8.1755	7.0700	6.6166	6.2153	5.5386	4.9915	4.5411	4.1644	3.8450	3.5708	3.3330	2.8571
40	32.8347	27.3555	23.1148	19.7928	17.1591	15.0463	13.3317	11.9246	10.7574	9.7791	8.2438	7.1050	6.6418	6.2335	5.5482	4.9966	4.5439	4.1659	3.8458	3.5712	3.3332	2.8571
45	36.0945	29.4902	24.5187	20.7200	17.7741	15.4558	13.6055	12.1084	10.8812	9.8628	8.2825	7.1232	6.6543	6.2421	5.5523	4.9986	4.5449	4.1664	3.8460	3.5714	3.3333	2.8571
50	39.1961	31.4236	25.7298	21.4822	18.2559	15.7619	13.8007	12.2335	10.9617	9.9148	8.3045	7.1327	6.6605	6.2463	5.5541	4.9995	4.5452	4.1666	3.8461	3.5714	3.3333	2.8571
55	42.1472	33.1748	26.7744	22.1086	18.6335	15.9905	13.9399	12.3186	11.0140	9.9471	8.3170	7.1376	6.6636	6.2482	5.5549	4.9998	4.5454	4.1666	3.8461	3.5714	3.3333	2.8571
60	44.9550	34.7609	27.6756	22.6235	18.9293	16.1614	14.0392	12.3766	11.0480	9.9672	8.3240	7.1401	6.6651	6.2492	5.5553	4.9999	4.5454	4.1667	3.8462	3.5714	3.3333	2.8571

Exhibit 6   Present Value of a Stream of Unequal Future Receipts

Problem:

Determine the present value of receipts from an investment using a 15% discount factor which provides the following stream of income.

Years Hence	Amount
0	$10,000
1	10,000
2	15,000
3	10,000
4	20,000
5	10,000

Solution:

Years Hence	Amount	Annuity	Excess of Annuity
0	$10,000	$10,000	$ 0
1	10,000	10,000	0
2	15,000	10,000	5,000
3	10,000	10,000	0
4	20,000	10,000	10,000
5	10,000	10,000	0

Calculation:

Present Value of amount due today	=	$ 10,000
Present Value of the $10,000 annuity for 5 years $10,000 × 3.3522	=	33,522
Present Value of $5,000 due 2 years hence $5,000 × .7561	=	3,781
Present Value of $10,000 due 4 years hence $10,000 × .5718	=	5,718
Total		$53,021

The average annual project income is the total project income over its life divided by the number of years. Average investment is project cost plus salvage value divided by two. The proposed investment is accepted if the ARR exceeds the minimum ARR required. For example, if the minimum acceptable ARR is 40%, a 52% ARR results in project acceptance.

The ARR model can be illustrated by using the Hampton Hotel's proposed investment in pizza equipment illustrated in Exhibit 9. The total project income over the five-year period is $89,000, which results in an average annual project income of $17,800. The average investment is $25,000, determined as follows:

Exhibit 7 Table of Future Value Factors for an Annuity

$$FVA_{n,k} = \frac{(1+k)^n - 1}{k}$$

Number of Periods	1%	2%	3%	4%	5%	6%	7%	8%	9%	10%	12%	14%	15%	16%	18%	20%	22%	24%	26%	28%	30%	35%
1	1.0000	1.0000	1.0000	1.0000	1.0000	1.0000	1.0000	1.0000	1.0000	1.0000	1.0000	1.0000	1.0000	1.0000	1.0000	1.0000	1.0000	1.0000	1.0000	1.0000	1.0000	1.0000
2	2.0100	2.0200	2.0300	2.0400	2.0500	2.0600	2.0700	2.0800	2.0900	2.1000	2.1200	2.1400	2.1500	2.1600	2.1800	2.2000	2.2200	2.2400	2.2600	2.2800	2.3000	2.3500
3	3.0301	3.0604	3.0909	3.1216	3.1525	3.1836	3.2149	3.2464	3.2781	3.3100	3.3744	3.4396	3.4725	3.5056	3.5724	3.6400	3.7084	3.7776	3.8476	3.9184	3.9900	4.1725
4	4.0604	4.1216	4.1836	4.2465	4.3101	4.3746	4.4399	4.5061	4.5731	4.6410	4.7793	4.9211	4.9934	5.0665	5.2154	5.3680	5.5242	5.6842	5.8480	6.0156	6.1870	6.6329
5	5.1010	5.2040	5.3091	5.4163	5.5256	5.6371	5.7507	5.8666	5.9847	6.1051	6.3528	6.6101	6.7424	6.8771	7.1542	7.4416	7.7396	8.0484	8.3684	8.6999	9.0431	9.9544
6	6.1520	6.3081	6.4684	6.6330	6.8019	6.9753	7.1533	7.3359	7.5233	7.7156	8.1152	8.5355	8.7537	8.9775	9.4420	9.9299	10.442	10.980	11.544	12.136	12.756	14.438
7	7.2135	7.4343	7.6625	7.8983	8.1420	8.3938	8.6540	8.9228	9.2004	9.4872	10.089	10.730	11.067	11.414	12.142	12.916	13.740	14.615	15.546	16.534	17.583	20.492
8	8.2857	8.5830	8.8923	9.2142	9.5491	9.8975	10.260	10.637	11.028	11.436	12.300	13.233	13.727	14.240	15.327	16.499	17.762	19.123	20.588	22.163	23.858	28.664
9	9.3685	9.7546	10.159	10.583	11.027	11.491	11.978	12.488	13.021	13.579	14.776	16.085	16.786	17.519	19.086	20.799	22.670	24.712	26.940	29.369	32.015	39.696
10	10.462	10.950	11.464	12.006	12.578	13.181	13.816	14.487	15.193	15.937	17.549	19.337	20.304	21.321	23.521	25.959	28.657	31.643	34.945	38.593	42.619	54.590
11	11.567	12.169	12.808	13.486	14.207	14.972	15.784	16.645	17.560	18.531	20.655	23.045	24.349	25.733	28.755	32.150	35.962	40.238	45.031	50.398	56.405	74.697
12	12.683	13.412	14.192	15.026	15.917	16.870	17.888	18.977	20.141	21.384	24.133	27.271	29.002	30.850	34.931	39.581	44.874	50.895	57.739	65.510	74.327	101.84
13	13.809	14.680	15.618	16.627	17.713	18.882	20.141	21.495	22.953	24.523	28.029	32.089	34.352	36.786	42.219	48.497	55.746	64.110	73.751	84.853	97.625	138.48
14	14.947	15.974	17.086	18.292	19.599	21.015	22.550	24.215	26.019	27.975	32.393	37.581	40.505	43.672	50.818	59.196	69.010	80.496	93.926	109.61	127.91	187.95
15	16.097	17.293	18.599	20.024	21.579	23.276	25.129	27.152	29.361	31.772	37.280	43.842	47.580	51.660	60.965	72.035	85.192	100.82	119.35	141.30	167.29	254.74
16	17.258	18.639	20.157	21.825	23.657	25.673	27.888	30.324	33.003	35.950	42.753	50.980	55.717	60.925	72.939	87.442	104.93	126.01	151.38	181.87	218.47	344.90
17	18.430	20.012	21.762	23.698	25.840	28.213	30.840	33.750	36.974	40.545	48.884	59.118	65.075	71.673	87.068	105.93	129.02	157.25	191.73	233.79	285.01	466.61
18	19.615	21.412	23.414	25.645	28.132	30.906	33.999	37.450	41.301	45.599	55.750	68.394	75.836	84.141	103.74	128.12	158.40	195.99	242.59	300.25	371.52	630.92
19	20.811	22.841	25.117	27.671	30.539	33.760	37.379	41.446	46.018	51.159	63.440	78.969	88.212	98.603	123.41	154.74	194.25	244.03	306.66	385.32	483.97	852.75
20	22.019	24.297	26.870	29.778	33.066	36.786	40.995	45.762	51.160	57.275	72.052	91.025	102.44	115.38	146.63	186.69	237.99	303.60	387.39	494.21	630.17	1152.2
21	23.239	25.783	28.676	31.969	35.719	39.993	44.865	50.423	56.765	64.002	81.699	104.77	118.81	134.84	174.02	225.03	291.35	377.46	489.11	633.59	820.22	1556.5
22	24.472	27.299	30.537	34.248	38.505	43.392	49.006	55.457	62.873	71.403	92.503	120.44	137.63	157.41	206.34	271.03	356.44	469.06	617.28	812.00	1067.3	2102.3
23	25.716	28.845	32.453	36.618	41.430	46.996	53.436	60.893	69.532	79.543	104.60	138.30	159.28	183.60	244.49	326.24	435.86	582.63	778.77	1040.4	1388.5	2839.0
24	26.973	30.422	34.426	39.083	44.502	50.816	58.177	66.765	76.790	88.497	118.16	158.66	184.17	213.98	289.49	392.48	532.75	723.46	982.25	1332.7	1806.0	3833.7
25	28.243	32.030	36.459	41.646	47.727	54.865	63.249	73.106	84.701	98.347	133.33	181.87	212.79	249.21	342.60	471.98	650.96	898.09	1238.6	1706.8	2348.8	5176.5
26	29.526	33.671	38.553	44.312	51.113	59.156	68.676	79.954	93.324	109.18	150.33	208.33	245.71	290.09	405.27	567.38	795.17	1114.6	1561.7	2185.7	3054.4	6989.3
27	30.821	35.344	40.710	47.084	54.669	63.706	74.484	87.351	102.72	121.10	169.37	238.50	283.57	337.50	479.22	681.85	971.10	1383.1	1968.7	2798.7	3971.8	9436.5
28	32.129	37.051	42.931	49.968	58.403	68.528	80.698	95.339	112.97	134.21	190.70	272.89	327.10	392.50	566.48	819.22	1185.7	1716.1	2481.6	3583.3	5164.3	12740.
29	33.450	38.792	45.219	52.966	62.323	73.640	87.347	103.97	124.14	148.63	214.58	312.09	377.17	456.30	669.45	984.07	1447.6	2129.0	3127.8	4587.7	6714.6	17200.
30	34.785	40.568	47.575	56.085	66.439	79.058	94.461	113.28	136.31	164.49	241.33	356.79	434.75	530.31	790.95	1181.9	1767.1	2640.9	3942.0	5873.2	8730.0	23222.
40	48.886	60.402	75.401	95.026	120.80	154.76	199.64	259.06	337.88	442.59	767.09	1342.0	1779.1	2360.8	4163.2	7343.9	12937.	22729.	39793.	69377.	*	*
50	64.463	84.579	112.80	152.67	209.35	290.34	406.53	573.77	815.08	1163.9	2400.0	4994.5	7217.7	10436.	21813.	45497.	94525.	*	*	*	*	*
60	81.670	114.05	163.05	237.99	353.58	533.13	813.52	1253.2	1944.8	3034.8	7471.6	18535.	29220.	46058.	*	*	*	*	*	*	*	*

*$FVA_{n,k} > 99{,}999$

Exhibit 8   Cash Flows from Game Room—Hampton Hotel

Cost of machines	$21,000
Life of machines	3 years
Tax rate	40%
Salvage value of machines	–0–
Annual revenues	$25,000
Related annual expenses including depreciation and income taxes	$10,000
Method of depreciation	Straight-line

Cash Flow Calculation

	Years		
	1	2	3
Revenues	$25,000	$25,000	$25,000
Expenses except for depreciation and income taxes	10,000	10,000	10,000
Income taxes	2,720(1)	2,720(1)	2,720(1)
Cash flow	$12,280	$12,280	$12,280

Net cash flow is determined as follows:

Cash flows from above $12,280 × 3 =	$36,840
Cost of machines	21,000
Net Cash Flow	$15,840

(1)   Income taxes:

Predepreciation income	$15,000
Less: depreciation	7,000(2)
Taxable income	8,000
Taxable rate	× .34
Income taxes	$2,720

(2)   Annual depreciation $= \dfrac{\text{Cost} + \text{Salvage Value}}{\text{Life}} = \dfrac{\$21,000 + 0}{3} = \$7,000$

$$\text{Average Investment} = \frac{\text{Project Cost} + \text{Salvage}}{2}$$

$$= \frac{\$50,000 + \$0}{2}$$

$$= \$25,000$$

Exhibit 9   Proposed Investment in Pizza Equipment—Hampton Hotel

Investment		Accept/Reject Criteria		
Cost of equipment	$48,000	APR	=	40%
Installation costs	2,000	Payback	=	3 years
		IRR	=	15%
Total	$50,000	NPV	=	0

Depreciation Consideration		Depreciation Percentages	
Salvage value	$–0–	Year	
Life for tax purposes	5 years	1	15%
		2	22%
		3	21%
		4	21%
		5	21%

Estimated Project Revenue and Expenses

	Years				
	1	2	3	4	5
Project revenues	$ 100,000	$ 120,000	$ 140,000	$ 160,000	$ 180,000
Project expenses:					
Labor	25,500	26,200	33,900	37,100	40,300
Cost of product	25,000	30,000	35,000	40,000	45,000
Supplies	5,000	6,000	7,000	8,000	9,000
Utilities	4,000	4,800	5,600	6,400	7,200
Depreciation	7,500	11,000	10,500	10,500	10,500
Other operating expenses	11,000	12,000	14,000	16,000	18,000
Income taxes	11,000	15,000	17,000	21,000	25,000
Project income	$ 11,000	$ 15,000	$ 17,000	$ 21,000	$ 25,000

Total project income for years 1–5 = $89,000

Cash flow:					
Project income	$11,000	$15,000	$17,000	$21,000	$25,000
Add: Depreciation	7,500	11,000	10,500	10,500	10,500
Total	$18,500	$26,000	$27,500	$31,500	$35,500

The ARR of 71.2% is determined as follows:

$$\text{ARR} = \frac{\text{Average Annual Project Income}}{\text{Average Investment}}$$

$$= \frac{\$17,800}{\$25,000}$$

$$= \underline{71.2\%}$$

If the Hampton Hotel were to use this capital budgeting model, management would invest in the pizza equipment since the project ARR of 71.2% exceeds the required minimum of 40%.

Some managers consider ARR to be useful because it relies on accounting income and, thus, it is easy to calculate and easy to understand. However, these advantages are more than offset by its disadvantages: ARR fails to consider cash flows or the time value of money.

Payback

The payback model compares annual cash flows to the project cost to determine a payback period. If the calculated payback period is equal to or less than the payback objective, then the project is accepted.

The payback model is reasonably popular in the hospitality industry because it is conceptually simple. Management simply sets the payback period at the determined length of time required for the operation to get its money back from the project.

The payback model is often used as a screening device in conjunction with more sophisticated models, especially in high-risk situations. Some operations will not consider evaluating proposed projects using the NPV or IRR approaches unless their initial review using the payback model suggests that the proposed project is viable.

When the annual cash flows are equal, the payback period is determined as follows:

$$\text{Payback Period} \quad = \quad \frac{\text{Project Cost}}{\text{Annual Cash Flow}}$$

When the annual cash flows are not equal, the payback period is determined differently. First, subtract as many full-year cash flows as possible from the project cost. If the numbers do not come out evenly, divide the amount remaining after all full-year cash flows have been subtracted by the cash flow for the year directly following those full-year cash flows. The payback period equals the number of years (including fractional years if applicable) it takes for cash flows to equal project cost.

Using figures from Exhibit 9, the payback period for the Hampton Hotel's proposed investment in pizza equipment can be calculated as follows:

Project Cost	=	$50,000
Less Year 1 Cash Flow	−	18,500
		31,500
Less Year 2 Cash Flow	−	26,000
		$ 5,500
Year 3 Cash Flow = $27,500 Portion of Year 3 needed to balance project cash flows with project cost:		$5,500 ÷ $27,500 = .2
Payback Period	=	2.2 years

Exhibit 10   Comparison of Two Mutually Exclusive Projects—Payback Model

		Project Cash Flows	
Years Hence		**Project A**	**Project B**
0	(cost of the projects)	$10,000	$10,000
1	(cash inflows)	5,000	3,000
2		4,000	4,000
3		3,000	5,000
4		2,000	6,000
5		1,000	7,000
Payback Period		2.33 years	2.60 years
Excess Cash Flow: Cash flow generated beyond payback period		$5,000	$15,000
Present value of all cash inflows discounted at 15%		$10,986	$15,833

Since the payback period of 2.2 years is less than the accept/reject criterion of 3 years as stated in Exhibit 9, based on the payback model, the Hampton Hotel would invest in the proposed pizza project.

Disadvantages to the payback model that require careful consideration are that it fails to consider either the time value of money or the project flows after the payback period. The latter disadvantage is readily apparent when comparing two mutually exclusive projects (A and B) as shown in Exhibit 10. Based on the payback method, project A would be accepted rather than project B, because the payback period of 2.33 years for project A is less than 2.6 years for project B. However, the excess cash flow is $10,000 larger for project B. The calculation of the present value of all cash flows of $10,986 and $15,833 for projects A and B, respectively, is convincing. If this is not readily clear, it will be as we now turn to consider the net present value model.

Net Present Value Model

Both the NPV and IRR models overcome the weaknesses of the previous models in that they consider the time value of money. The net present value approach discounts cash flows to their present value. The net present value is calculated by subtracting the project cost from the present value of the discounted cash flow stream. The project is accepted if the NPV is equal to or greater than zero. If the capital budgeting decision considers mutually exclusive alternatives, the alternative with the highest NPV is accepted and other alternatives are rejected.

The advantage of the NPV model over the ARR and payback models is the consideration of cash flows and the time value of money. Some managers have suggested that a disadvantage of the NPV model is its complexity. This argument may have been convincing to hospitality operations in the past, but as the hospitality industry continues to mature, the best methods of capital budgeting must be used if decision-making is to be optimized.

Exhibit 11   Illustration of NPV—Proposed Investment in Pizza Equipment by Hampton Hotel

Years Hence	Cash Flow	P.V. Factor (15%)	Present Value of Cash Flow
0	$(50,000)	1.0000	$(50,000)
1	18,500	.8696	16,088
2	26,000	.7561	19,659
3	27,500	.6575	18,081
4	31,500	.5718	18,012
5	35,500	.4972	17,651
		Net Present Value	$39,491

Using the Hampton Hotel's proposed investment in pizza equipment (Exhibit 9) and assuming a discount rate of 15%, Exhibit 11 shows the net present value to be $39,491. Therefore, based on the NPV model, the Hampton Hotel should make the proposed investment, because NPV is positive.

Internal Rate of Return

The IRR model is a capital budgeting approach that considers cash flows and the time value of money and determines the rate of return earned by a proposed project. In determining IRR, the net present value of cash flows is set at zero and the discount rate is determined. The formula is as follows:

$$0 = \frac{CF_1}{1 + r} + \frac{CF_2}{(1 + r)^2} + \cdots + \frac{CF_n}{(1 + r)^n} - PC$$

$$\text{where} \quad \begin{aligned} CF &= \text{Cash Flow} \\ r &= \text{Internal Rate of Return} \\ PC &= \text{Project Cost} \end{aligned}$$

Assume that a proposed project costs $6,850 and is expected to yield a cash flow stream of $3,000 for three years. The internal rate of return is 15%, which can be demonstrated as follows:

$$0 = \frac{\$3,000}{1.15} + \frac{\$3,000}{(1.15)^2} + \frac{\$3,000}{(1.15)^3} - \$6,850$$

$$0 = \underline{\underline{0}}$$

Using the IRR model, a project is accepted if the IRR is equal to, or greater than, the established minimum IRR, which is commonly called **hurdle rate** by hospitality financial managers.

Like the NPV model, the IRR model is superior to the ARR and payback approaches because it considers the time value of money. The IRR is also superior to

Exhibit 12   Illustration of IRR—Proposed Investment in Pizza Equipment by Hampton Hotel

Years Hence	Cash Flow	41% PV Factor (1)	41% PV Cash Flow	42% PV Factor (1)	42% PV Cash Flow
0	$ (50,000)	1.000	$ (50,000)	1.000	$ (50,000)
1	18,500	.7092	13,120	.7042	13,028
2	26,000	.5030	13,078	.4959	12,893
3	27,500	.3568	9,812	.3492	9,603
4	31,500	.2530	7,970	.2459	7,746
5	35,500	.1794	6,369	.1732	6,149
		Total	$ 349		$ (581)

(1) PV factors determined by the formula:

$$\frac{1}{(1+r)^1} \text{ , } \frac{1}{(1+r)^2} \text{ , } \frac{1}{(1+r)^3} \text{ , } \frac{1}{(1+r)^4} \text{ and } \frac{1}{(1+r)^5}$$

PV factor for 1 year at 41% is determined by dividing 1 by $(1.41)^1$ to equal .7092.

the ARR model because it considers cash flows. When there is a capital budgeting decision involving mutually exclusive projects, results from the IRR model may conflict with the NPV approach. This conflict may occur because of the IRR's assumption that all project cash flows are reinvested at the internal rate of return. Since operations normally invest in the most profitable projects first, one should not assume that other projects would result in the same return. This conflict will be discussed in greater detail later in this chapter.

The IRR model is illustrated using the Hampton Hotel's proposed investment in pizza equipment. Although the brief illustration of IRR above may have appeared simple, in practice, manual calculations are by trial and error. Various discount rates must be tried until the approximate net present value is found to be zero. The manual approach is illustrated in Exhibit 12. Alternatively, the IRR can be quickly and easily determined using a computer, which allows the user to insert and calculate potential IRR values virtually instantaneously.

The exact IRR lies between 41% and 42%. Interpolation would result in approximate determination of 41.5%. Since the IRR of 41.5% exceeds the target of 15%, using this capital budgeting model, the Hampton Hotel should invest in the proposed pizza equipment.

Comparison of NPV and IRR Models

As discussed previously, the NPV and IRR models are preferred to the simplistic ARR and payback models. However, which is preferred, NPV or IRR? The NPV and IRR models, when applied in most situations, provide the same solution whether the situation considers a single project or mutually exclusive projects. However, in some of the latter situations, the NPV could suggest one project while the IRR model suggests a different project. This outcome results from the assumed reinvestment rates of each model. The NPV model assumes reinvestment at the discount rate used (15% in the Hampton Hotel problem), while the IRR model assumes reinvestment at the computed IRR (41.5% in the Hampton Hotel problem). Even if the superior projects are first selected, it is doubtful that reinvestment would be at the calculated IRR. Reinvestment will likelier be at a lower rate. Therefore, when mutually exclusive projects are considered, the NPV approach is more useful.

The NPV is generally easier to compute than the IRR. However, computers and calculators have reduced the laborious calculations of the IRR model. On the other hand, many industry financial managers prefer the IRR model because the results are easier to interpret.

Mutually Exclusive Projects with Different Lives

To this point in our discussion, mutually exclusive projects have been assumed to have the same useful life. In reality, many mutually exclusive projects do not have equal lives. In such situations, three approaches to decision-making are as follows:

1. Assume that the shorter-lived project is followed with another project and that the combined lives of the two projects equal the life of the mutually exclusive longer-lived project.

2. Assume that the longer-lived project is disposed of at the end of the shorter-lived project's life.

3. Ignore the differences in lives of the two mutually exclusive projects.

The third approach is reasonable only if the lives are both long and the differences are inconsequential. For example, a difference of one year for proposed projects with fourteen- and fifteen-year lives may be immaterial.

The first approach is illustrated in Exhibit 13. In this example, a hotel is considering whether to replace its laundry washer with Machine A, which has a ten-year life and no salvage, or with Machine B, which has a five-year life and no salvage value. At the end of Machine B's life, Machine C, which will have a five-year life and no salvage, will be acquired. Thus, the life of Machine A (ten years) equals the combined lives of Machines B and C. The capital budgeting model and discount rate used are NPV and 15%, respectively. The results suggest that Machine B be purchased now followed by Machine C at the end of year five.

The second approach, that of assuming the longer-lived project is disposed of at the end of the short-lived project's life, is illustrated in Exhibit 14. The same situation is assumed as in Exhibit 13 except the comparison is only for five years as Machine B is totally used at the end of year five. In addition, at the end of year five, Machine A is assumed to have a salvage value of $7,000. The NPV of Machines A and B are −$1,463 and $4,057, respectively. Therefore, based on the available information, Machine B would be purchased.

Capital Rationing

Up to this point, no limit on projects has been discussed as long as the project returns exceeded the reject criteria. In reality, there are often limited funds available.

Exhibit 13   Comparison of Machine Acquisitions with Different Lives— Approach #1

	Cash Flows		
	Alternative A	**Alternative B**	
Years Hence	**Machine A (1)**	**Machine B (2)**	**Machine C (3)**
0	$(15,000)	$(6,000)	
1	3,000	3,000	
2	3,000	3,000	
3	3,000	3,000	
4	3,000	3,000	
5	3,000	3,000	$(11,000)
6	3,000		3,000
7	3,000		3,000
8	3,000		3,000
9	3,000		3,000
10	3,000		3,000

NPV—Alternative A	NPV—Alternative B
NPV = $3,000 (5.0188) − $15,000	NPV = $3,000 (5.0188) − $6,000 − $11,000 (.4972)
NPV = $56	NPV = $3,587

(1) Machine A costs $15,000 and provides a project cash flow of $3,000 per year for its ten-year life.

(2) Machine B costs $6,000 and provides a project cash flow of $3,000 per year for its five-year life of years 1 through 5.

(3) Machine C (purchased to replace Machine B) costs $11,000 at the end of year five and provides project cash flow of $3,000 per year for its five-year life of years 6 through 10.

For example, a parent corporation may limit funds provided to a subsidiary corporation, or a corporation may limit funds provided to a division. This concept of limiting funds for capital purposes, regardless of the expected profitability of the projects, is called **capital rationing.** Under capital rationing, the combination of projects with the highest net present value should be selected.

Exhibit 15 considers five proposed projects and calculates several possible combinations and their NPVs. In this illustration, projects B and C are considered to be mutually exclusive, and only $150,000 is available for capital projects.

The optimum combination is projects A, B, and E, because this yields the highest combined NPV. Other feasible combinations result in a lower NPV. In the several combinations where all funds would not be spent on projects, excess funds would be invested at the going interest rate; however, the present value of the return on the excess funds would be the amount invested, thus there would be no related NPV on these excess funds. (This assumes that the going interest rate is equal to the discount rate.)

Exhibit 14   Comparison of Machine Acquisitions with Different Lives— Approach #2

Machine A costs $15,000 and provides project cash flow of $3,000 per year for five years and then may be sold for $7,000. Machine B costs $6,000 and provides project cash flow of $3,000 per year for five years. At the end of five years, the machine is worthless.

	Cash Flows	
Years Hence	**Machine A**	**Machine B**
0	$(15,000)	$(6,000)
1	3,000	3,000
2	3,000	3,000
3	3,000	3,000
4	3,000	3,000
5	10,000	3,000

NPV—Machine A	**NPV—Machine B**
NPV $=$ $3,000 (3.3522) + $7,000 (.4972) − $15,000	NPV $=$ $3,000 (3.3522) − $6,000
NPV $=$ −$1,463	NPV $=$ $4,057

Exhibit 15   Capital Rationing—Five Proposed Projects

Project	Project Cost	NPV
A	$ 60,000	$ 30,000
B	70,000	20,000
C	50,000	15,000
D	100,000	40,000
E	20,000	10,000

Combination	Total Investment	Total NPV
A, B, & E	$ 150,000	$ 60,000
A, C, & E	130,000	55,000
A & B	130,000	50,000
A & C	110,000	45,000
C & D	150,000	55,000
D & E	120,000	50,000

Use of Capital Budgeting Models in the Lodging Industry

A recent survey of the 150 largest lodging chains revealed that 74% of the respondents use IRR, while 66%, 55%, and 32% use payback, NPV, and ARR, respectively.[1]

These results differ significantly from a similar survey in 1980 which showed that only 33% of hospitality businesses used IRR, while 71% and 36% used payback and NPV, respectively.[2] The more recent survey did not request reasons for the changes, but it seems likely that computer usage is a major reason. Calculations of NPV and IRR are virtually child's play for the computer.

Computer Applications

Spreadsheet programs on personal computers have automated many of the calculations discussed in this chapter. The internal rate of return and net present value calculations have been simplified into short computer instructions that execute the calculations automatically. For example, using *Lotus 1-2-3*, the "functions" typed to calculate the three formulas mentioned above are:

$$
\begin{aligned}
\text{Internal Rate of Return} &= @IRR(i, V1 .. Vn) \\
\text{Where:} \quad i &= \text{Guess at a rate of return} \\
V1 .. Vn &= \text{Range of cash flows, starting with the} \\
&\quad \text{first and ending with the last}
\end{aligned}
$$

$$
\begin{aligned}
\text{Net Present Value} &= @NPV(i, V1 .. Vn) \\
\text{Where:} \quad i &= \text{Interest rate to be used} \\
V1 .. Vn &= \text{Range of cash flows, starting with the} \\
&\quad \text{first and ending with the last}
\end{aligned}
$$

Exhibit 16 is an example of how some of these functions could be used. The first section examines two telephone systems by looking at their estimated cash savings due to decreased expenses over the system presently in use. The lower section demonstrates how a spreadsheet can compare various investments. It shows the two options' internal rates of return and states which option should be chosen.

There are two basic advantages to using a spreadsheet program to perform these calculations. First, once the format of the model is set, it can be used repeatedly. This ensures consistency in the evaluation of all projects. The model represents a standard methodology for determining which investments provide the best returns. Second, it is very quick and accurate. The actual calculation by a computer takes only a few seconds, and it is correct every time (assuming the formulas and data have been entered correctly). The computer allows more efficient use of management time, which should be spent evaluating projects, not calculating numbers.

Summary

Managers must carefully consider many necessary additions or changes in fixed assets in order to operate their businesses effectively. Projects are evaluated based on their costs and corresponding revenues. Projects that generate the most money for the firm should be accepted and the others should be rejected. This process is called capital budgeting.

Capital budgeting is appropriate in a number of decision-making processes. It can be used when purchasing equipment to meet government standards or to replace existing equipment. It is also valuable when considering the purchase of

Exhibit 16   Computer-Generated Telephone Investment Analysis

Washington Hotel Company
Telephone Investment Analysis

	Year				
	19X1	19X2	19X3	19X4	19X5
Proposed Telephone System 1					
Investment = $100,000					
Cash Savings:					
Long Distance Charges	$45,000	$46,350	$47,741	$49,173	$50,648
Yearly Maintenance	10,800	11,340	11,907	12,502	13,127
Depreciation	20,000	20,000	20,000	20,000	20,000
Total Pretax Savings	75,800	77,690	79,648	81,673	83,775
Plus Salvage Value					7,300
Net Pretax Cash Savings	75,800	77,690	79,648	81,673	91,075
Less Taxes @ 34%	(25,772)	(26,415)	(27,080)	(27,770)	(30,966)
Net Aftertax Savings	50,028	51,275	52,568	53,905	60,109
Less Depreciation Savings	20,000	20,000	20,000	20,000	20,000
Net Aftertax Cash Flow	$30,028	$21,275	$21,568	$33,905	$40,109
Net Present Value at 12%:	$49,231				
Proposed Telephone System 2					
Investment = $75,000					
Cost Savings:					
Long Distance Charges	$48,000	$49,440	$50,923	$52,451	$54,024
Yearly Maintenance	8,400	8,820	9,261	9,724	10,210
Depreciation	15,000	15,000	15,000	15,000	15,000
Total Pretax Savings	71,400	73,260	75,184	77,175	79,234
Plus Salvage Value					5,000
Net Pretax Cash Savings	71,400	73,260	75,184	77,175	84,234
Less Taxes @ 34%	(24,276)	(24,908)	(25,563)	(26,240)	(28,640)
Net Aftertax Savings	47,124	48,352	49,621	50,935	55,594
Less Depreciation Savings	15,000	15,000	15,000	15,000	15,000
New Aftertax Cash Flow	$32,124	$33,352	$34,621	$35,935	$40,594
Net Present Value at 12%:	$55,784				

Net Present Value Information

Cash Flows:						
Option 1:	($100,000)	$30,028	$31,275	$32,568	$33,905	$40,109
Option 2:	($75,000)	$32,124	$33,352	$34,621	$35,935	$40,594

Internal Rate of Return

Option 1:	19.15%	Choose Option:	2
Option 2:	39.58%		

equipment that could either increase the operation's revenues or decrease its costs. In each of these cases, budgeting is performed to determine if the revenues (or cost savings) generated by the equipment are greater than the corresponding expenditures, or to decide which option is best for the operation. By using capital budgeting models, management actively works to maximize the operation's profits.

Four capital budgeting approaches were examined in this chapter: accounting rate of return, payback, net present value, and internal rate of return. ARR is defined as the average annual project income divided by the average investment. Although it is a simple method, it does have a number of deficiencies and is, therefore, not used frequently. The payback method is also simple and is used more than the ARR in the hospitality industry. It examines the cash flows generated by the equipment and determines the number of years of cash flows required to recover the investment. The NPV approach looks at the cash flows relating to the project and discounts them to their present value. A project with NPV equal to or greater than zero is accepted. The final approach discussed, IRR, examines the cash flows to determine the rate of return the investment generates. In other words, it sets the project NPV equal to zero and calculates the discount rate.

The NPV and IRR methods are more complex than the ARR and payback approaches, but they also provide more valuable results. They both examine cash flows and recognize the time value of money. The major difference between the two is that IRR somewhat unrealistically assumes that the project cash flows will be reinvested in projects that generate the same return. Thus, when mutually exclusive projects are analyzed, the NPV method is preferred over the IRR.

Endnotes

1. Raymond S. Schmidgall and James W. Damitio, "Hotels and Long-Term Investment," *The Bottomline*, August–September 1990.

2. James J. Eyster, Jr., and A. Neal Geller, "The Capital-Investment Decision: Techniques Used in the Hospitality Industry," *The Cornell Hotel and Restaurant Administration Quarterly*, May 1981, pp. 69–73.

Key Terms

accounting rate of return (ARR)—An approach to evaluating capital budgeting decisions based on the average annual project income (project revenues less project expenses) divided by the average investment.

annuity—A stream of funds provided by a capital investment when the amounts provided are the same and at equal intervals (such as the end of each year).

capital rationing—An approach to capital budgeting used to evaluate combinations of projects according to their net present value (NPV).

discount rate—The term used for *k* when finding a present value.

hurdle rate—The established minimum internal rate of return that must be met or exceeded for a project to be accepted under the internal rate of return model of capital budgeting.

incremental cash flow—The change in cash flow of an operation that results from an investment.

internal rate of return (IRR)—An approach to evaluating capital budgeting decisions based on the rate of return generated by the investment.

net present value (NPV)—An approach to evaluating capital budgeting decisions based on discounting the cash flows relating to the project to their present value; calculated by subtracting the project cost from the present value of the discounted cash flow stream.

payback—An approach to evaluating capital budgeting decisions based on the number of years of annual cash flow generated by the fixed asset purchase required to recover the investment.

time value of money—The process of placing future years' income on an equal basis with current year expenditures in order to facilitate comparison.

Review Questions

1. What is capital budgeting?

2. What are four situations which might require capital budgeting?

3. Why is one dollar today worth more than one dollar a year from now?

4. How is the payback method of capital budgeting performed?

5. What is project cash flow?

6. What are the disadvantages of using the payback method of capital budgeting?

7. How can two mutually exclusive projects with different lengths of lives be analyzed?

8. What role does the accept/reject criterion play in the NPV and IRR methods of capital budgeting?

9. Which method of capital budgeting is the most effective? Explain your choice.

10. What is capital rationing?

Problems

Problem 1

Phil Rail, owner of the Rail Haven Motel, desires to know how much money must be invested in order to accumulate a total of $100,000 ten years hence. The options are as follows:

1. *X* amount is invested today at an annual interest rate of 12%.

2. *X* amount is invested today at a semi-annual interest rate of 6%.

3. *X* amount is invested today at a quarterly interest rate of 3%.

Required:

Determine the amount of *x* for each alternative.

Problem 2

Harry Hill wants to know the value of three possible investments 10 years hence.

1. Investment A: $100,000 is invested today at 12% annual interest. The interest is compounded quarterly.
2. Investment B: $15,000 is invested annually, starting today, and earns 10% interest compounded on an annual basis.
3. Investment C: $50,000 is invested today and $50,000 is invested five years hence. Assume quarterly compounding of 12% annual interest.

Required:

Determine the future value of each investment.

Problem 3

F. M. Knutson plans to finance an 18-month intensive culinary program for her eight-year-old son when he graduates from secondary school in ten years. She believes the total cost of this program will be $20,000 in ten years and wants to invest today whatever amount will provide the funds required.

Required:

1. Determine how much she should invest today if she receives annual interest of 10% compounded annually.
2. Determine how much she should invest today if she receives annual interest of 8% compounded quarterly.

Problem 4

James Wayne, proprietor of the Wayne Country Inn, desires to know the present value of various streams of dollars. Today is the beginning of year one. Assume an annual discount rate of 12% for all alternatives. The streams are as follows:

1. Ten thousand dollars received at the beginning of each year for ten years.
2. One hundred thousand dollars received at the end of the tenth year.
3. Ten thousand dollars received at the end of each year for ten years.
4. Twelve thousand dollars received at the end of each year for the first five years, and eight thousand dollars received at the beginning of each year for the last five years.

Required:

Determine the present value of each stream of dollars for the four scenarios.

Problem 5

T. M. Anderson is looking forward to his daughter, Sybil, attending a major western U.S. university to study hotel management. The dean of the school suggests annual costs beginning in ten years will most likely be $25,000 with expected annual increases of $2,000 per year thereafter for at least four years. T. M. would like to start investing funds in the form of an annuity at the end of the year to finance Sybil's education. Assume T. M.'s investments will earn an annual return of 8%.

Required:

1. Determine the amount T. M. must invest at the end of each year for ten years to finance Sybil's freshman year at college.

2. Determine the amount T. M. must invest at the end of each year (starting in one year) for ten years to finance Sybil's second year in college. Note: $27,000 will be needed for her second year; however, T. M.'s plan is to stop investing after ten years.

3. Determine the amount T. M. must invest each year for ten years for Sybil's college education. Assume she is on the *five*-year plan.

Problem 6

Martice Smith and Associates is considering investing $5,000,000 in a new motel and has predicted the following income stream over its ten-year life.

Year	Net Income
1	$ (245,000)
2	(115,600)
3	18,400
4	276,320
5	455,000
6	1,066,700
7	1,150,000
8	1,069,300
9	1,055,700
10	1,000,250

The motel is expected to have no salvage value at the end of its ten-year life.

Required:

1. Using the ARR method, what is the rate of return for this project?

2. If Martice Smith and Associates requires 35% return on its investment, should this motel be purchased?

Problem 7

Carol Rollins, owner of Carollins, is considering buying an energy-efficient oven for her restaurant. However, she is concerned that the cost savings adequately offset the purchase price; she would prefer the project to have no more than a 2.5-year payback period. She is basing her decision on the following information:

Project Cost: $23,500

Cost Savings:

			Years		
	1	2	3	4	5
Energy	$2,000	$2,500	$3,000	$3,000	$3,000
Maintenance	3,000	3,000	2,000	1,000	1,000
TOTAL	$5,000	$5,500	$5,000	$4,000	$4,000

Required:

1. Determine if Ms. Rollins should invest in this oven.

2. If there was an estimated cash savings of $4,500 for each year, would this oven be purchased, based on the payback criterion?

Problem 8

Susie Reed, owner of the Wild Life, an amusement park, is contemplating purchasing a new roller coaster/water combination ride for $1,500,000. She has determined that it would increase park revenues by $300,000 a year because of its originality, but it will cost approximately $70,000 a year to operate.

Assume a 15% discount rate and a ten-year life for the equipment.

Required:

Use the NPV model to determine if the equipment should be purchased.

Problem 9

The Jonathan Club is considering adding pizza to its menu. However, a conveyor oven that costs $20,000 will have to be purchased. It has an estimated seven-year life, and Jon Jones, the manager, has determined that the club could sell approximately $50,000 worth of pizzas each year with a food cost of 35%, labor cost of 30% and other negligible operating costs. At the end of seven years, the conveyor oven should be able to bring $2,000 at an auction.

Assume that the Club requires a 15% return on investment.

Required:

Use the IRR method to determine if the machine should be purchased.

Problem 10

The Apple Hill Club is considering the addition of a game room for the children of its members. The equipment is estimated to cost $100,000. Annual expenses related to the equipment are forecasted to be $20,000, and forecasted annual revenues equal $50,000. Assume the equipment is expected to have a five-year useful life and will be worthless at the end of five years. The equipment will be depreciated using the straight-line method. Assume the Apple Hill Club is a nonprofit club that does not pay income taxes.

Required:

1. Determine the payback period for this investment.

2. Determine the net present value. Assume a discount rate of 12%.

Problem 11

The Groesbeck Golf Club (GGC) has decided to construct forward tees on its 18-hole course. The estimated construction cost is $50,000. The GGC's owner, Gayle Groesbeck, believes many more rounds of golf will be played and other profit centers will also benefit. Her estimates on an annual basis for ten years are as follows:

a. Increased maintenance = $5,000

b. Increased green fees (2,000 rounds at $10 per round) = $20,000

c. Increased food sales (net of related costs) = $2,000

d. Increased miscellaneous sales (shirts, clubs, etc.) = $8,000

e. Increased cost of miscellaneous sales and related variable costs = $4,000

Required:

1. Determine the IRR for this investment.

2. Determine the NPV given a discount rate of 12%.

Problem 12

Jason and Jamie Hills, owners of the Hills Hotel, are considering upgrading their front office equipment by purchasing a new front office machine. The annual operating costs for front office machines are as follows:

Cost	Present Machine	Proposed Machine
Labor	$15,000	$12,000
Maintenance	500	200
Utilities	500	600
Insurance	60	100

The present machine has a present market value of $3,000 and will be useful for the next five years, but be worth $-0- at the end of five years. The proposed machine will cost $15,000.

To simplify the problem, assume that both machines would be depreciated by using the straight-line method of depreciation. Further assume a discount rate of 12% and a tax rate of 30%. Further assume that the proposed machine will be worth $5,000 at the end of year five.

Required:

Using the NPV model, should the new machine be purchased? Show all your work.

Problem 13

Leta O'Donnel, a wealthy Midwesterner, is considering the purchase of the Fairview Hotel for $20,000,000. The expected pre-depreciation earnings for years 1–10 are as follows:

Years	Pre-Depreciation Income
1	$ (500,000)
2	(100,000)
3	400,000
4	1,000,000
5	3,000,000
6	5,000,000
7	5,000,000
8	5,000,000
9	5,000,000
10	5,000,000

Assume that the hotel can be sold at the end of year 10 for $15,000,000.

For depreciation purposes, the depreciation methods and purchase cost of the Fairview Hotel are allocated as follows:

Land	10%	(no depreciation)
Equipment	20%	(double declining balance; 10 years)
Building	70%	(straight-line; $5,000,000 salvage value; 30 (years)
	100%	

Further assume an average income tax rate of 30% and that all net operating losses are carried forward for up to five years.

Required:

1. Assuming a discount rate of 12%, determine the net present value of this investment.

2. Determine the IRR of this investment.

3. Explain why the Fairview Hotel should or should not be purchased.

Problem 14

The Holt Company is considering selling one of its buildings and leasing it back for the remaining five years of the building's life. The building is to be demolished in five years to make way for a new highway. The restaurant's earnings before depreciation, interest, property taxes, insurance, and income tax for each of the next five years are estimated as follows:

Year 1	Year 2	Year 3	Year 4	Year 5
$121,000	$125,000	$131,000	$133,000	$135,000

If the building is not sold and leased back, the building depreciation, property taxes, insurance, and interest expense figures for the five years would be the following:

	Year 1	Year 2	Year 3	Year 4	Year 5
Depreciation	$10,000	$8,000	$6,000	$4,000	$2,000
Interest	??	??	??	??	??
Property taxes	3,000	3,200	3,400	3,600	3,800
Insurance	3,000	3,000	3,000	3,000	3,000

The depreciation expense over the next five years will result in a zero net book value at the end of year 5. Interest expense pertains to a mortgage of $10,000 with principal repayments of $2,000 at the end of each year. The interest rate is 10%. The Holt Company's average tax rate is 33%. The local government will pay only $20,000 for the land and building at the end of five years.

If the building is sold now, the price would be $50,000. Assume that a capital gains tax rate on gain on the sale is 25% and that any tax due will be paid at the time of the sale. The building could be leased back at $12,000 per year.

Required:

Use the net present value model to determine whether the building should be sold and leased back. Assume a discount rate of 12%.

Problem 15

Daniel David, president of the Grand Rabbits Corporation, is considering two investment projects. Only one of the two will be selected this year. Information regarding each project is as follows:

Investment Project #1: Renovate an existing motel for $1,000,000. After tax, cash flows are expected to be $200,000 per year for 20 years.

Investment Project #2: Build a new motel for $4,000,000. After tax, annual cash flows are expected as follows:

Year	
1	$ (200,000)
2	(50,000)
3	200,000
4	600,000
5–20	1,100,000

Assume a discount rate of 12%.

Required:

1. Based on the NPV model, which of the two projects should be selected?
2. Based on the IRR model, which of the two projects should be selected?

Chapter 14 Outline

Leases and Their Uses
    Advantages and Disadvantages of Leases
    Provisions of Lease Contracts
Lease Accounting
    Classification of Leases
    Accounting for Operating Leases
    Accounting for Capital Leases
    Illustration of Accounting for Capital Leases
Leasehold Improvements
Sale and Leasebacks
Leases and Their Effect on Financial Ratios

14

Lease Accounting

Leasing entitles someone to use equipment, land, or buildings without buying them. Leasing often provides a way to use resources when purchasing them is not possible or desirable. For example, a food service chain may lease space in a shopping mall because that space is not for sale. A hotel may lease equipment for a single day for a special function. This chapter will address several questions about lease accounting, including the following:

1. What are the advantages and disadvantages of leasing resources?

2. What are executory costs in relation to leases?

3. How are leases classified for accounting purposes?

4. What are the criteria for capitalizing leases?

5. How are leasehold improvements amortized?

6. What is a triple-net lease?

7. What is an incremental interest rate?

8. What is a sale and leaseback?

9. How are financial ratios affected by the accounting for leases?

10. What are several common provisions of lease agreements?

In this chapter, we will first consider the various uses of leases in the hospitality industry. We will discuss some of their advantages and disadvantages, as well as some provisions common to all leases. We will then focus on the differences between operating leases and capital leases and present guidelines for accounting for the different types of leasing arrangements. Finally, we will investigate the effects that leases may have on a hospitality operation's financial statements and ratios.

Leases and Their Uses

A **lease** is an agreement conveying the right to use resources (equipment, buildings, and/or land) for specified purposes and a limited time. From an operational perspective, the resource is available for use; operating personnel generally have little concern whether the company owns or leases it. Lease agreements govern the parties to the lease, usually the lessor and the lessee. The **lessor** owns the property and conveys the right of its use to the **lessee** in exchange for periodic cash payments called **rent**.

Leasing is popular in the United States with businesses in general and with the hospitality industry in particular. For example, restaurants may lease space in shopping malls, lodging companies may lease hotels, and gambling casinos may lease slot machines.

Historically, several hotel companies have leased many of their hotels from real estate and insurance companies. The **variable lease** was a common lease arrangement used by Holiday Corporation during the 1950s and 1960s. Holiday Corporation (the lessee) paid the lessors a percentage of rooms, food, and beverage revenues. For example, a 25–5–5 lease resulted in the lessee paying the lessor 25% of rooms revenue, 5% of food revenue, and 5% of beverage revenue. Since these rental payments were based on revenues and since the lessee corporation paid all operational expenses before generating any profits, the lessee shouldered much of the hotel property's financial risk.

The leasing of hotels is less popular today. Few hotel companies have signed new property leases in the 1980s and 1990s. Instead, they manage hotels under **management contract** arrangements. Under these contracts, the hotel owners make substantial payments from the hotel's gross revenues to the hotel management companies, much like the hotel companies used to pay lessors for leased properties.[1]

Many hotels continue to lease equipment ranging from telephone systems to computers to vehicles. Many food service corporations lease both their buildings and equipment. In part, the extent of leasing by hospitality companies is revealed in footnotes to their annual financial statements.

Advantages and Disadvantages of Leases

The following list presents some of the advantages of leasing.

- Leasing conserves working capital because it requires little or no cash deposit; cash equal to 20% to 40% of the purchase price is required when purchasing property and equipment. Therefore, for the cash-strapped operation, leasing may be the only way to obtain the desired property or equipment.

- Leasing often involves less red tape than buying with external financing. Although a lease agreement must be prepared, it usually is less complicated than the many documents required to make a purchase, especially when financing is involved.

- Leasing allows more frequent equipment changes, especially when equipment becomes functionally obsolete. However, the lessee cannot expect this flexibility to be cost-free. The greater the probability of technological obsolescence, the greater the lease payment (all other things being the same).

- Leasing allows the lessee to receive tax benefits that otherwise may not be available. For example, an unprofitable operation may not be able to take advantage of tax credits available to purchasers of certain equipment. However, a lessor, who can use the tax credits, may pass on part of the tax credit in the form of lower rental payments to the lessee.

- Leasing generally places less restrictive contracts on a lessee than financial institutions often place on long-term borrowers.

- Leasing has less negative impact on financial ratios, especially when the leases are not capitalized. Property acquired for use through an operational lease is not shown on the balance sheet. Future rent obligations also do not appear on the balance sheet, although some footnote disclosure may be required. For this reason, leases are often referred to as **off-balance-sheet financing.**

- Operating leases may allow an operation to obtain resources without following a capital budget.

Therefore, in many cases, leasing may be a lower overall cost alternative for many hospitality operations. However, there are also disadvantages of leasing, such as the following:

- Any residual value of the leased property benefits the lessor unless the lessee has the opportunity to acquire the leased property at the end of the lease.

- The cost of leasing in some situations is ultimately higher than purchasing. This is especially true when there are only a limited number of less-than-competitive lessors.

- Disposal of a financial lease before the end of the lease period often results in additional costs.

The above list of advantages and disadvantages is not exhaustive.[2]

Provisions of Lease Contracts

Each lease is a unique product of negotiations between the lessor and lessee that meets the specific needs of each party. However, all lease contracts normally contain certain provisions. The following list presents some of these common provisions.

1. Term of lease—The term of a lease may be as short as a few hours (usually for a piece of equipment) or as long as several decades (as is common with real estate). Leases should be long enough to ensure a proper return on the investment for leasehold improvements and other costs. A new food service operation may desire a relatively short initial lease (say, five years) with several five-year renewable options. This would allow the company to escape from an undesirable situation.

2. Purpose of lease—This provision generally limits the lessee to using the property for certain purposes. For example, a restaurant lease may state, "The lessee shall use the leased premises as a restaurant and for no other purpose without first having obtained the written consent of the lessor."

3. Rental payments—The lease specifies the amount of rental payment and when it is due. It also indicates any adjustments; for example, adjustments for inflation are often based on the consumer price index for a given city. **Contingent rent** is also specified. For example, a lease may stipulate that contingent rent equal to 3% of all annual food and beverage sales in excess of $700,000 is due the fifteenth day of the first month after the end of the fiscal year.

4. Renewal options—Many leases contain a clause giving the lessee the option to renew the lease. For example, a lease may provide "an option to renew this

lease for an additional five-year period on the expiration of the leasing term upon giving lessor written notice 90 days before the expiration of the lease."

5. Obligations for property taxes, insurance, and maintenance—Leases, especially long-term leases, specify who shall pay the **executory costs**—that is, the property taxes, insurance, and maintenance costs—on the leased property. A lease in which the lessee is obligated to pay these costs in addition to the direct lease payments is commonly called a **triple-net lease.**

6. Other common lease provisions include:

   • The lessor's right to inspect the lessee's books, especially when part of the lease payment is tied to sales or some other operational figure.

   • The lessor's obligations to restore facilities damaged by fire, tornadoes, and similar natural phenomena.

   • The lessee's opportunity to sublease the property.

   • The lessee's opportunity to make payments for which the lessor is responsible, such as loan payments to preclude default on the lessor's financing of the leased property.

   • Security deposits, if any, required of the lessee.

   • Indemnity clauses protecting the lessor.

Lease Accounting

Historically, leases were accounted for simply as executory contracts—that is, the rental expense was generally recognized with the passage of time. Leases were not capitalized as assets, nor were liabilities recognized for the lessee's obligations under lease contracts. However, as leases have become more sophisticated and economically similar to sale/purchase transactions, many accountants have argued for a change in lease accounting.

The Accounting Principles Board, the past accounting rule-making body, issued four opinions regarding lease accounting. The Financial Accounting Standards Board (FASB), the present rule-making body, has issued more than ten statements relating to lease accounting. A major result of these rules is that many long-term leases are now capitalized—that is, they are recorded as fixed assets with recognition of a liability.

Most of the remainder of this chapter presents lease accounting guidelines for lessees. Lease accounting for lessors is beyond the scope of this chapter. Our discussion is meant to cover the major elements of lease accounting and is certainly not exhaustive. The student interested in further study of lease accounting should consult an intermediate accounting text and/or FASB statements.

Classification of Leases

In general, lessees classify leases for accounting purposes as either operating leases or capital leases. At the extremes of what is essentially a continuum, operating leases differ substantially from capital leases. Depending on their specific provisions, however, they can also be hard to distinguish. **Operating leases** (also called service leases) are normally (but not always) of relatively short duration, and the lessor retains the responsibility for executory costs. They can usually be canceled easily. **Capital leases** (also called financing leases) are of relatively long duration, and the lessee often assumes responsibility for executory costs. In addition, they are generally non-cancelable or at least costly to cancel. Capital leases are capitalized, while operating leases are not.

The FASB has established four capitalization criteria for determining the status of non-cancelable leases. If a non-cancelable lease meets any one of the four criteria, the lessee must classify and account for the lease as a capital lease. Non-cancelable leases not meeting any of the four criteria may be accounted for as operating leases. The FASB criteria are reproduced below:[3]

1. The property is transferred to the lessee by the end of the lease term, referred to as the **title transfer provision.**

2. The lease contains a bargain purchase option, referred to as the **bargain purchase provision.**

3. The lease term is equal to 75% or more of the estimated economic life of the leased property, referred to as the **economic life provision.**

4. The present value of minimum lease payments (excluding executory costs) equals or exceeds 90% of the excess of fair market value of the leased property over any investment tax credit retained by the lessor, referred to as the **value recovery provision.**

The bargain purchase option (criterion #2) means that the purchase price at the end of the lease period is substantially less than the leased property's expected market value at the date the option is to be exercised. The bargain price is generally considered substantially less than the market value only if the difference, for all practical purposes, ensures that the bargain purchase option will be exercised. The "economic life" (criterion #3) refers to the useful life of the leased property. The following list explains several terms in the value recovery provision (criterion #4):

- *Present value* refers to determining present value.

- *Minimum lease payments* consist of minimum rental payments during the lease term and any bargain purchase option. If no bargain purchase option exists, the minimum lease payments include any guaranteed residual value by the lessee or any amount payable by the lessee for failure to renew the lease. Minimum lease payments do not include contingent rent (such as a percentage of sales). Executory costs are also excluded in determining minimum rental payments when the lease specifies that lease payments include these costs.

- *Fair market value* represents the amount the leased item would cost if it were purchased rather than leased.

- *Investment tax credit* is a credit that the federal government used to allow against the federal income tax liability of the hospitality operation. When it was allowed, up to 10% of the cost of qualifying equipment could typically be taken as a credit. The credit generally applied to personal property (such as equipment), but not to real property (such as land and buildings). Investment tax credits are no longer allowed by current tax laws; however, if they are reinstated, they would be treated as indicated by criterion #4. Note that, when there is no investment tax credit, criterion #4 in effect states that if the present value of minimum lease payments (excluding executory costs) equals or exceeds 90% *of the fair market value* of the leased property, the lease must be capitalized.

- *Residual value* refers to the estimated market value of the leased item at the end of the lease term. When the residual value is guaranteed by the lessee, then the lessee is ultimately liable to the lessor for the residual value.

Accounting for Operating Leases

Operating leases are accounted for as simple rental agreements—that is, the expense is generally recognized when the rent is paid. For example, if a restaurant company leases space in a shopping mall for $5,000 per month and pays rent on the first day of each month, the monthly rental payment would be recorded as follows:

Rent Expense	$5,000	
Cash		$5,000

When rent is paid in advance, it should be recorded in a prepaid rent account. For example, if the restaurant company had paid three months' rent in advance, the proper entry would be:

Rent Expense	$ 5,000	
Prepaid Rent	10,000	
Cash		$15,000

This accounting entry recognizes rent expense for the current month and delays recognition of rent for the following two months (based on the matching principle).

In the event rent is paid for a period beyond twelve months from the balance sheet date, the rental payment should be recorded as "deferred rent" and shown as a deferred charge on the balance sheet. Any rent paid for future periods is recognized during the period to which it relates by an adjusting entry. In the example above, the adjusting entry to recognize the second month's rent would be:

Rent Expense	$5,000	
Prepaid Rent		$5,000

Accounting for Capital Leases

A capital lease is similar to the purchase of a fixed asset. Therefore, the accounting for capital leases recognizes an asset and applicable liabilities. The amount to be recorded as an asset and a liability is the present value of minimum lease payments, as defined earlier in relation to the fourth capitalization criterion. The lease payments are discounted using the lessee's incremental borrowing rate, or, if known, the lessor's implicit rate of interest in the lease *if* it is lower than the lessee's incremental borrowing rate. The former is used more often because the lessee does not usually know the lessor's implicit interest rate in the lease. The lessee's **incremental borrowing rate** is the rate of interest the lessee would have to pay if financing the purchase of the leased item.

Executory costs included with the lease payments must be excluded in determining the present value of minimum lease payments. However, a bargain purchase option or a lessee's guaranteed residual value must be included. For example, a lease agreement may require a monthly payment of $1,000, of which $200 is for maintenance. This $200 for maintenance is excluded in determining the present value of minimum lease payments. On the other hand, if the lessee guarantees a residual value of $2,000 for the leased item, the present value of $2,000 should be included in determining the present value of minimum lease payments.

When the lessee makes subsequent lease payments, the lease obligation is reduced by the difference between the lease payment (excluding executory costs) and the interest on the lease obligation. The interest is calculated by using the effective interest method, which results in a constant rate of interest throughout the lease term. This is accomplished by multiplying the interest rate used in discounting the minimum lease payments by the lease obligation for the lease period. For example, assume that a lease payment is $5,000 for the month, including $500 for property taxes, and the lease obligation for the period is $480,000. Further assume that the lessee's incremental borrowing rate is 10%. The entry to record the lease payment is as follows:

Property Tax Expense	$ 500	
Interest Expense	4,000	
Lease Obligations	500	
Cash		$5,000

The interest expense of $4,000 is determined as follows:

$$\text{Interest} = \frac{\text{Lease}}{\text{Obligation}} \times \frac{\text{Incremental}}{\text{Borrowing Rate}} \times \frac{\text{Time}}{\text{(in Years)}}$$

$$= \$480,000 \times .10 \times \frac{1}{12}$$

$$= \underline{\underline{\$4,000}}$$

Therefore, the lease obligation is debited by $500, determined as follows:

$$\frac{\text{Reduction in}}{\text{Lease Obligation}} = \frac{\text{Lease}}{\text{Payment}} - \frac{\text{Executory}}{\text{Costs}} - \frac{\text{Interest}}{\text{Expense}}$$

$$= \$5,000 - \$500 - \$4,000$$

$$= \underline{\underline{\$500}}$$

Illustration of Accounting for Capital Leases

Assume the Chambers Hotel signs a lease agreement with a major computer manufacturer for the use of a front office computer. Provisions of the lease agreement and other relevant facts for classifying the lease are as follows:

1. The term of the lease is five years, commencing on January 1, 19X1. The lease is non-cancelable.

2. Annual payments of $55,000 are due at the beginning of each year.

3. The leased computer has a fair market value of $200,000 at January 1, 19X1.

4. The estimated economic life of the computer is seven years, and there is no expected residual value.

5. The Chambers Hotel is to pay all executory costs directly except for annual maintenance costs of $10,000 which are included in the annual lease payments.

6. The lease contains no renewal or bargain purchase options, and the equipment reverts to the lessor at the end of the lease period.

7. The Chambers Hotel's incremental borrowing rate is 12%.

8. The Chambers Hotel depreciates its own computer equipment on a straight-line basis.

9. The lessor's implicit rate of return on leasing the computer to the Chambers Hotel is unknown.

10. There are no tax credits applicable to this situation.

The Chambers Hotel must determine whether the lease should be capitalized by comparing the lease provisions to the FASB lease capitalization criteria. Exhibit 1 illustrates this comparison. As the exhibit indicates, the lease should be capitalized, based on criterion #4, because the present value of lease payments, excluding executory costs, exceeds 90% of the fair market value of the leased equipment. The calculations are as follows:

Fair market value of leased equipment	$200,000
90% factor	× .9
	$180,000
Present value of lease payments	$181,678
(see Exhibit 2)	
Excess of lease payments	$ 1,678

The journal entry to record the capitalization of the leased equipment accompanied by the first payment of $55,000 is as follows:

Leased Equipment Under Capital Leases	$181,678	
Prepaid Maintenance	10,000	
Cash		$ 55,000
Obligations Under Capital Leases		136,678

Exhibit 1   FASB Lease Capitalization Criteria

**FASB Lease Capitalization Criteria
and the lease of computer equipment
by the Chambers Hotel**

Lease Capitalization Criteria	Computer Lease Provisions	Capitalize Yes/No
1. Title transfer provision	Item 6 states the "equipment reverts to the lessor at the end of the lease."	No
2. Bargain purchase provision	Item 6 states the lease contains no bargain purchase options	No
3. Economic life provision	$\dfrac{\text{Life of lease}}{\text{Useful life of equipment}} = {}^5/_7 = 71.4\%$ 71.4% < 75%	No
4. Value recovery provision	$45,000 (4.0373)* = $200,000 (.9) = excess of PV of lease payments over 90% of FMV is	\$181,678** (180,000) \$ 1,678 — Yes

* For the derivation of this factor, see Exhibit 2.
** This amount is actually \$181,678.50; however, the detail of cents is dropped here and throughout the rest of this illustration.

Exhibit 2   Present Value of Five Lease Payments—Chambers Hotel

Annual lease payments	\$ 55,000
Less: Amount for executory costs	10,000
Net lease payment	45,000
Present value of an annuity for 4 payments at 12% (3.0373)	
Plus present value factor for the initial (undiscounted) payment (1.0000) = 4.0373	× 4.0373
	\$181,678

This single entry consists of the capitalization of the lease at \$181,678 (the present value of the five lease payments), the recognition of the related liability at \$136,678, and the initial payment of \$55,000, of which \$10,000 relates to maintenance and the remaining \$45,000 to the lease.

The single entry could have also been recognized in two parts:

(1) Capitalization of lease

Leased Equipment Under Capital Leases	\$181,678	
Obligations Under Capital Leases		\$181,678

This entry simply records the present value of the five lease payments.

(2) Lease payment

Obligations Under Capital Leases	$45,000	
Prepaid Maintenance	10,000	
Cash		$55,000

This entry records the initial cash payment, the $10,000 executory payment, and the reduction in the "obligation" account.

The prepaid maintenance would be written off throughout the year by a monthly entry of $833 ($1/12$ of the annual payment):

Maintenance Expense	$833	
Prepaid Maintenance		$833

Future payments will result in the recognition of interest expense, the reduction of the obligation under capital leases, and prepayment of maintenance for the next year. In practice, at year-end (December 31, 19X1), interest expense would be accrued by debiting interest expense by $16,401 and crediting accrued interest by $16,401 because of the matching principle.

The Chambers Hotel would record its second lease payment on January 1, 19X2, as follows:

Interest Expense	$16,401	
Obligations Under Capital Leases	28,599	
Prepaid Maintenance	10,000	
Cash		$55,000

The interest expense of $16,401 results from multiplying the $136,678, recorded as "obligations under capital leases" throughout the year, by the Chambers Hotel's incremental borrowing rate of 12%. The reduction in the liability "obligations under capital leases" of $28,599 is the difference between the *net* lease payment of $45,000 and the interest expense of $16,401. Exhibit 3 shows the amortization of the $136,678 lease obligation over the term of the lease.

The leased equipment should be depreciated over its lease term of five years. The annual entry for depreciation expense (based on straight-line) would be as follows:

Depreciation Expense	$36,336	
Accumulated Depreciation—Capital Leases		$36,336

Exhibit 3   Lessee's Amortization of Obligation under Capital Leases—Chambers Hotel

Date of Payment	(1) Annual Lease Payment	(2) Interest Expense[1]	(3) Reduction in Liability[2]	(4) Balance of Liability Account[3]
1/1/X1				$136,678
1/1/X2	$ 45,000	$16,401	$ 28,599	108,079
1/1/X3	45,000	12,969	32,031	76,048
1/1/X4	45,000	9,126	35,874	40,174
1/1/X5	45,000	4,826*	40,174	$ –0–
	$180,000	$43,322	$136,678	

*Rounding error of less than $5.

Note: The total annual lease payments ($180,000) less the balance of the obligation at January 1, 19X1 ($136,678) equals the interest expense of $43,322.

[1]Interest expense is calculated by multiplying the annual interest rate (12%) by the prior balance of the liability account.

[2]The reduction in the liability is computed by subtracting the interest expense (column 2) from the annual lease payment (column 1).

[3]The balance of liability account (column 4) is reduced each year by the amount in column 3.

This entry assumes a zero salvage value because the equipment reverts to the lessor at the end of the lease term. At the end of the five-year term, the leased equipment is returned to the lessor and the two accounts, "leased equipment under capital leases" and "accumulated depreciation—capital leases," each at $181,678, are reduced to zero:

Accumulated Depreciation—Capital Leases	$181,678	
Leased Equipment Under Capital Leases		$181,678

Throughout the five-year period, the following expenses related to the leased item were incurred:

Maintenance—$10,000/year	$ 50,000
Depreciation—the capitalized cost of the lease	181,678
Interest Expense—the sum of the five net lease payments less the capitalized cost of the lease ($225,000 − $181,678):	43,322
Total Expense	$275,000

Notice that the total expense equals the five annual payments of $55,000.

Leasehold Improvements

Buildings that are leased for several years, such as restaurants in shopping malls, often require extensive improvements before the commencement of operations. Often, the space leased is not capitalized since none of the capitalization criteria is met. However, any improvements to the space must be capitalized as **leasehold improvements.** For example, the cost of walls, ceilings, carpeting, and lighting installed in leased space is capitalized. The leasehold improvement is recognized as an intangible asset, and the cost must be amortized against revenue over the life of the lease or the life of the leasehold improvement, whichever is shorter. For example, assume that the Chambers Hotel leased three acres of adjoining land for parking facilities and the land was improved by adding storm sewers, sidewalks, lighting, and pavement at the cost of $200,000. Further assume that the life of the improvement is ten years, while the land was leased for 30 years. The annual amortization of the leasehold improvement would be $1/10$ of the cost—$20,000 per year for ten years. This expense is generally recognized monthly ($1/12$ of annual amortization) as follows:

Amortization of Leasehold Improvement	$1,667	
Leasehold Improvement		$1,667

Sale and Leasebacks

Sale and leasebacks are transactions whereby an owner of real estate agrees to sell the real estate to an investor and then lease it back. The original owner's use of the property continues without interruption. The property is sold to the investor (lessor) at market value and then leased back to the seller (lessee) for an amount equal to the investor's cost plus a reasonable return.

The major reason for sale and leaseback transactions is to raise capital that was previously tied up in the property. The investors in these transactions are usually looking for a financial return, as they have no interest in managing hospitality operations.

The lessee should account for the lease based on the FASB's four criteria for classifying leases. If the seller (lessee) makes a profit from the sale of the now leased assets, such profit should generally be deferred and amortized over the lease term. Losses should be recognized in their entirety when the sale and leaseback agreement is signed. The student interested in a more detailed discussion of this topic is encouraged to consult an intermediate accounting text.

Leases and Their Effect on Financial Ratios

Whether a leased item is accounted for as a capital lease or an operating lease can have a major impact on the financial statements, especially the balance sheet. Therefore, several financial ratios are also affected. Property leased under an operating lease is not shown on the balance sheet, while property leased under a capital

Exhibit 4   Financial Ratios Most Affected by Lease Accounting

Ratio	Ratio Formula	How capital lease affects ratio
1. Asset turnover	revenue ÷ average total assets	Capitalizing leases results in increasing the average total assets, therefore reducing the asset turnover ratio.
2. Return on assets	net income ÷ average total assets	Increased average total assets will also reduce the return on assets.
3. Debt-equity ratio	total debt ÷ total equity	Capitalizing leases results in increasing the total debt, therefore increasing the debt-equity ratio.
4. Number of times interest earned ratio	earnings before interest and taxes ÷ interest expense	Capitalizing leases results in increased interest expenses, therefore reducing this ratio.

lease is shown. The balance sheet disclosure of capital leases includes both assets and liabilities. Therefore, most financial ratios involving noncurrent assets and long-term liabilities are affected by how leases are accounted for. Four financial ratios affected by capitalizing leases are shown in Exhibit 4.

In general, capitalizing leases negatively affects these ratios—that is, the ratios suggest a less desirable financial situation than they would if the leases had been accounted for as operating leases. For example, if a lease is capitalized, the assets and liabilities increase. This means the net income must also increase in order to maintain a constant return on assets. Thus, many hospitality operations prefer not to capitalize leases. They often negotiate lease provisions so that the lease does not qualify as a capital lease under any of the FASB's four capitalization criteria.

Summary

Leasing is a special type of financing used by many hospitality businesses. By entering into a lease agreement, the lessee acquires the right to use specific resources for a limited time and a specific purpose. The advantages for the lessee include the conservation of working capital, the benefits of tax deductions that might not otherwise be available, and, in some cases (when the lease is accounted for as an operating lease), a favorable effect on the balance sheet ratios. In exchange for these advantages, the lessee must make some sacrifices. In many instances, the residual value of the property remains with the lessor, there may be substantial penalties for termination of the lease contract, and the cost of leasing may be higher than purchasing the leased item. The operator contemplating a lease arrangement must weigh the advantages and disadvantages before entering into the contract. In many cases in the hospitality industry, the lease contract proves advantageous.

There are many aspects common to most leases. Provisions contained in most lease contracts include the length and purpose of the contract, the specific rent payments, any lessee obligations, and renewal options.

When deciding between leasing and purchasing an asset, many businesses consider how the agreement will affect the financial statements. Depending upon its terms, a lease will either be capitalized (recorded on the balance sheet as an asset and liability) or treated as an operational lease (expensed as the payments are made). If capitalized, certain financial ratios can be negatively affected. Some managers avoid capital leases because of this effect.

In addition to accounting for the initial lease, leasehold improvements must be recorded and subsequently amortized over either the life of the lease or the life of the improvement, whichever is shorter.

Management should study all the variations of the lease agreement before signing any contract. Establishments judged solely on their financial ratios will probably be more interested in whether a lease is capitalized. Other establishments may value the difference between the total lease payments and the benefits of having a present cash flow.

Historically, leases have been a popular way to finance assets. The trend indicates that leases will continue as viable means of hospitality financing, especially for equipment.

Endnotes

1. The reader interested in studying management contracts is referred to James J. Eyster's *The Negotiation and Administration of Hotel and Restaurant Management Contracts,* 3d ed. (Ithaca, N.Y.: School of Hotel Administration, Cornell University, 1988).

2. For more detail on this topic, see Pietrat Elgers and John J. Clark, *The Lease-Buy Decision* (New York: The Free Press, 1980) and T. M. Clarke, *Leasing* (London: McGraw-Hill, 1978).

3. FASB Financial Accounting Standard #13, *Accounting for Leases,* 1976.

Key Terms

bargain purchase provision—One of four Financial Accounting Standards Board capitalization criteria for determining the status of non-cancelable leases. Under this provision, if a lease has a bargain purchase option, the lessee must classify and account for the lease as a capital lease. A bargain purchase option gives the lessee the option to purchase the leased property at the end of the lease at a price substantially lower than the leased property's expected market value at the date the option is to be exercised.

capital lease—A classification of lease agreements that are of relatively long duration, generally non-cancelable, and in which the lessee assumes responsibility for executory costs. For accounting purposes, capital leases are capitalized in a way similar to the purchase of a fixed asset (that is, recorded as an asset with recognition of a liability).

contingent rent—Rent based on specified variables, such as a percentage of revenues above a given amount.

economic life provision—One of four Financial Accounting Standards Board capitalization criteria for determining the status of non-cancelable leases. If the lease term is equal to 75% or more of the estimated economic life of the leased property, the lessee must classify and account for the lease as a capital lease.

executory costs—Obligations for property taxes, insurance, and maintenance of leased property.

incremental borrowing rate—The rate of interest a lessee would have to pay if financing the purchase of the item to be leased.

lease—An agreement conveying the right to use resources (equipment, buildings, and/or land) for specified purposes for limited periods of time. The lessor owns the property and conveys the right of its use to the lessee in exchange for periodic cash payments called rent.

leasehold improvements—Renovations or remodeling performed on leased buildings or space prior to the commencement of operations. For accounting purposes, all leasehold improvements are capitalized (that is, recorded as an asset with recognition of a liability).

lessee—Party that makes periodic cash payments called rent to a lessor in exchange for the right to use property.

lessor—Party that owns property and conveys the right of its use to the lessee in exchange for periodic cash payments called rent.

management contract—Contract under which hotel owners make substantial payments from the hotel's gross revenues to hotel management companies.

off-balance-sheet financing—Term sometimes applied to leasing, because property acquired for use through an operational lease is not shown on the balance sheet. Future rent obligations also do not appear on the balance sheet, although some footnote disclosure may be required.

operating lease—A classification of lease agreements that are usually of relatively short duration, easily cancelled, and in which the lessor retains responsibility for executory costs. For accounting purposes, operating leases are not capitalized, but simply recognized as an expense when rent is paid.

rent—Cash payments made by a lessee to a lessor.

residual value—With regard to leasing, the estimated market value of a leased item at the end of the lease term.

sale and leaseback—A transaction whereby an owner of real estate agrees with an investor to sell the real estate to the investor and simultaneously rent it back for a future period of time, allowing uninterrupted use of the property while providing the operation with capital that was previously tied up in the property.

title transfer provision—One of four Financial Accounting Standards Board capitalization criteria for determining the status of non-cancelable leases. If the property is transferred to the lessee by the end of the lease term, the lessee must classify and account for the lease as a capital lease.

triple-net lease—A form of lease agreement in which the lessee is obligated to pay property taxes, insurance, and maintenance on the leased property.

value recovery provision—One of four Financial Accounting Standards Board capitalization criteria for determining the status of non-cancelable leases. If the present value of minimum lease payments (excluding executory costs) equals or exceeds 90% of the excess of fair market value of the leased property over any applicable investment tax credit retained by the lessor, the lessee must classify and account for the lease as a capital lease.

variable lease—A form of leasing agreement in which rental payments are based upon revenues.

? Review Questions

1. What are three major advantages to the lessee of lease financing?

2. What are some provisions common to most leases?

3. What are the FASB's four criteria for determining if a lease is a capital or an operating lease?

4. If a hotel operation enters into a capital lease agreement, what effect will it have on the debt-equity ratio?

5. What major effects do capital leases (compared to operating leases) have on an operation's balance sheet?

6. What are leasehold improvements?

7. What is a sale and leaseback agreement?

8. What are lease executory costs and how do they influence the determination of whether a lessee should capitalize a lease?

9. What is meant by guaranteed residual value? How does it affect the present value of lease payments?

10. At what value is a capitalized lease recorded?

Problems

Problem 1

Kathy Waltz, owner of the new Trio Cafe, signed a building lease for three years for $1,000 per month on April 1, 19X4. She has paid $3,000 for the first three months' rent covering April–June, 19X4.

Required:

1. Prepare the journal entry to recognize the payment and the rent expense for April.

2. Prepare the adjusting entry to recognize lease expense for May.

Problem 2

The Green River Eatery (GRE) has signed a five-year contract with Mall, Inc., for 2,000 square feet of space in the River Mall. The contract requires payments of $3,000 per month payable on the first of each month. The contract also requires a $5,000 security deposit which is to be refunded at the end of the lease. The GRE spent $100,000 on leasehold improvements that should have a useful life of eight years.

Required:

1. Prepare the journal entry to record the rental payment for the first month.

2. Prepare the journal entry to record the payment of the security deposit.

3. Prepare the journal entry to recognize one month's amortization of the leasehold improvement.

Problem 3

Jimmy Ko, proprietor of Jimmy's Place, has recently leased a computer that does not meet any of the FASB's accounting requirements for capitalizing the lease. The three-year lease contract requires Jimmy to make an original payment of $4,000 on July 1, 19X1, for the first and last month's rent expense of $2,000 each.

On August 1, 19X1, Jimmy is required to make the next month's payment of $2,000. Jimmy's Place maintains its books on a strict accrual accounting basis.

Required:

1. Prepare the journal entry to record the original payment for July 1, 19X1.

2. Prepare the adjusting journal entry for July 31, 19X1.

3. Prepare the journal entry for the August 1, 19X1 payment.

Problem 4

Soonmi Lee is considering signing a ten-year lease for her Oriental Garden Inn. Her two best alternatives are as follows:

	Alternative #1	Alternative #2
Monthly rent	$2,000	7% of sales
Energy costs	Paid by lessee	Paid by lessor
Repairs to building	Paid by lessee	Paid by lessor
Building insurance	Paid by lessee	Paid by lessor

The average monthly revenues over the ten-year period are expected to start at $40,000 and increase by $1,000 per month each year. The estimated monthly costs for energy, repairs, and building insurance total $1,000 and are expected to increase by $50 per month each year.

Required:

1. Determine the annual costs of each alternative over the ten-year period.

2. Based on cost minimization, which lease do you recommend? Why?

Problem 5

Fidencio Lopez, owner of Fido's Pizzeria, has just signed a lease contract for several major machines (ovens and so forth). The lease required an initial payment of $10,000 when the lease was signed and five future payments of $10,000 each at one-year intervals. The restaurant's incremental interest rate is 12%. Mr. Lopez's accountant has determined that the lease must be capitalized.

Required:

1. Determine the amount of the capitalized lease.

2. Prepare an amortization table for the liability related to the capitalized lease. (Use the format provided in Exhibit 3.)

Problem 6

Sun Pak, owner of Pak Inns, has just leased two vans for guest transportation. The term of the lease is three years. The lease requires quarterly payments of $2,000 at the beginning of each quarter. Assume an incremental borrowing rate of 12%.

Required:

1. Determine the present value of the lease payments.

2. If the lease is capitalized, how much rent expense is recorded over the life of the lease?

3. If the lease is capitalized, how much interest expense is recorded over the life of the lease?

Problem 7

The Jerusalem Inn has just leased a new computer as of January 1, 19X1. The terms of the contract allow the lessee to buy the computer for $500 at the end of the lease five years hence. ABC Computer's salesperson believes the computer would have a fair market value of $1,500 at the end of the lease period.

Other lease terms are as follows:

Estimated useful life of computer:	7 years
Incremental cost of debt:	12%
Average cost of debt:	11%

Semi-annual lease payments are due at the beginning of each six-month period starting on July 1, 19X1.

Semi-annual payments *inclusive* of insurance:	$2,500
Semi-annual insurance cost:	$200
Fair market value:	$15,000

The lessor's implicit interest rate is 10% for this venture.

Required:

1. Should the lease be capitalized? Why?

2. Assuming the lease is capitalized, provide the journal entry to record the lease at the beginning of the lease period. (Include calculations to support your entries.)

Problem 8

On January 1, 19X1, Brian's Bungalow leased a 100-room motel property for 25 years. The estimated life of the property is 35 years. The lease is not capitalized since it does not meet any of the FASB's requirements. The business also leased a posting machine on July 1, 19X2, for a five-year period. The machine's life is seven years, and the equipment reverts to the lessor at the end of five years. The cost of the posting machine, if purchased, would be $6,000; annual lease payments are $1,525, payable at the beginning of each year. Brian's has an incremental borrowing rate of 12%, and the present value of $1 for four periods is 3.0373.

The rooms are to be renovated effective July 1, 19X2, at a cost of $2,000 per room. The life of the renovation is estimated at 30 years.

Required:

1. Should the lease of the posting machine be capitalized? If so, at what amount?
2. Should the renovation be capitalized? If so, at what amount?
3. If the renovation is capitalized, what is the annual amortization?

Problem 9

The Irish Inn is contemplating the purchase or lease of a new dryer. Tip O'Reilly, owner of the Irish Inn, believes that the lease would not be capitalized and thus his financial ratios would not be adversely affected by the lease. He has asked you to examine the proposed arrangement, which is as follows:

Term of lease:	6 years
Estimated life of dryer:	9 years
Average cost of debt:	11%
Incremental cost of debt:	12%
Lease payments due:	
—first payment due at signing (January 1, 19X1)	
—next five payments annually beginning January 1, 19X2	
Annual lease payment:	$1,000
First lease payment:	$1,000
Fair market value:	$4,500

There is also no option to buy at the end of lease; the dryer reverts to lessor at the end of the lease period.

Required:

1. Is the owner correct in his belief that the lease would not be capitalized? Show all your work in arriving at your decision.
2. What is the present value of the lease payment stream?
3. Prepare the journal entry to record the lease assuming it will be capitalized.
4. What is the amount of interest for 19X1?
5. What is the amount of interest over the life of the lease (19X1–19X5)?

Problem 10

The Betonya Hotel has decided to lease its computer system from IMC Corporation. The lease is for a five-year period commencing on January 1, 19X1. Details of the lease and other information are as follows:

1. Quarterly lease payments are $5,500.
2. The lease payments include $200 for maintenance.
3. The first lease payment is to be made on March 31, 19X1.
4. The 19 additional future quarterly payments start on June 30, 19X1.

5. The estimated life of the computer system is eight years and the computer system's estimated market value at the end of the five years is $5,000.

6. The fair market value of the computer system is $75,000 on January 1, 19X1.

7. The lessee has agreed to guarantee a residual value of $4,000.

8. The lessor's implicit interest rate is 10%.

9. The lessee's average and marginal interest rates are 9% and 11%, respectively.

Required:

1. Should the lease be capitalized? Why or why not? Be specific.

2. Assuming the lease is capitalized, provide the journal entry to record the capitalization of the lease on January 1, 19X1.

3. Again assuming the lease is capitalized, provide the journal entry to record the second payment.

Problem 11

Alfredo Salvador is contemplating the purchase or lease of a new computer for his hotel. The proposed lease arrangement is as follows:

Term of lease:	5 years
Estimated life of computer:	10 years
Average cost of debt:	10%
Incremental cost of debt:	9%
Lease payments due:	
—first payment due at signing (January 1, 19X1)	
—next four payments annually beginning January 1, 19X2	
Annual lease payment:	$10,000
Fair market value:	$50,000
Lessee's guarantee of residual value:	$5,000

Required:

1. Determine the present value of the payment stream.

2. Prepare the journal entry to record the initial lease payment and capitalization (if necessary) of the lease.

3. Prepare the journal entry to record the second lease payment.

Problem 12

On January 1, 19X5, the Clairemount Hotel plans to sign a five-year lease for its telephone system. Provisions of the lease are as follows:

1. The lease is non-cancelable.

2. Annual payments beginning on January 1, 19X5, are $35,000 each for five years.

3. The telephone system has a fair market value of $140,000 at January 1, 19X5.

4. The estimated useful life of the system is seven years.

5. Included in the $35,000 annual payment is $5,000 for maintenance costs.
6. The Clairemount Hotel's average and incremental interest rates are 12% and 11%, respectively. The lessor's implicit interest rate is 10%.
7. The Clairemount Hotel agrees to guarantee a residual value of $10,000.

Required:

1. Determine the present value of the lessee's payments related to the lease.
2. Should the lease be capitalized? Explain your position.

Problem 13

The Koelling Hotel has just signed a lease with IRC, Inc., for a new front office computer. Lease provisions and other relevant information are as follows:

1. The lease term is five years starting on January 1, 19X2.
2. Annual payments are $60,000 starting on January 1, 19X2.
3. The fair market value of the computer at January 1, 19X2, is $225,000.
4. The estimated economic life of the computer is seven years.
5. The lease payments include $10,000 for maintenance and $3,000 for insurance.
6. The Koelling Hotel's incremental borrowing rate is 10%, while IRC's implicit rate of return on leasing the computer is 12%.

Assume that the lease is capitalized.

Required:

1. Provide the journal entry to record the first lease payment and the lease.
2. Provide the journal entry to record the second payment.
3. Calculate the total interest expense over the five years.

Problem 14

Robert Traub, owner/manager of Traub's Place, has just signed a seven-year lease for kitchen equipment. Details are as follows:

1. The estimated life of the equipment is ten years.
2. Semi-annual lease payments commencing with the signing of the lease on January 1, 19X3, are $10,000.
3. Each lease payment includes executory costs of $500.
4. Traub's incremental interest rate is 10%, while its average interest rate is 9%.
5. Traub's guarantees a residual value of $10,000.
6. The fair market value of the leased equipment is $90,000.

Assume that the lease is capitalized.

Required:

1. Record the initial lease payment and the lease.
2. Prepare an amortization schedule for the lease liability.

Problem 15

The King's Inn's financial situation at the end of 19X3 and 19X4 is summarized as follows:

	19X3	19X4
Total property and equipment (fixed assets)	$5,800,000	$6,000,000
Total assets	$6,500,000	$6,750,000
Interest expense (for the year)	$ 600,000	$ 625,000
Income taxes (for the year)	$ 400,000	$ 420,000
Net income (for the year)	$ 500,000	$ 550,000

On January 1, 19X4, the King's Inn leased adjoining sporting facilities for its guests' use. The lease was negotiated so that it was not capitalized. However, *if* any of the capitalization criteria had been met, the above accounts would have been affected at the end of 19X4 as follows:

Total property and equipment—increase by $850,000

Total assets—increase by $850,000

Interest expense for 19X4—increase by $100,000

Note: Income taxes and net income would not be affected as rent expense (for operating leases) would equal the depreciation and interest expense (for the capitalized lease).

Required:

1. Calculate the following ratios given that the King's Inn did *not* capitalize the lease of the sporting facilities:

   a. Return on fixed assets

   b. Return on total assets

   c. Number of times interest earned

2. Calculate the same ratios listed in #1 for the King's Inn assuming that the lease was capitalized.

3. Based on your calculations, was the King's Inn wise in negotiating an operating lease? Why?

Chapter 15 Outline

Tax Considerations in Economic Decisions
History and Objectives of Federal Income Taxes
Tax Basics
      Income, Income Exclusions, and Adjustments
      Deductions, Exemptions, and Taxable Income
      Taxes and Credits
      A Tax Illustration
Tax Avoidance
Forms of Business Organization
      Sole Proprietorship
      Partnerships
      Limited Partnerships
      Limited Liability Companies
      Corporations
      S Corporation
Minimizing Taxes
Accounting Methods
      Cash Method Versus Accrual Method
      Installment Sales Method
Accounting Income Versus Taxable Income
      Accelerated Depreciation
      Pre-Opening Expenses
      First-Year Losses
      Loss Carrybacks and Carryforwards
State and Municipal Taxes
Property Taxes

Income Taxes

In 1789, Benjamin Franklin wrote, "But in this world nothing can be said to be certain, except death and taxes."[1] Most businesses and individuals view taxes similarly—as a necessary evil. Most also try to pay as little tax as legally possible. Hospitality managers must attempt to minimize the operation's income taxes in order to increase the owners' financial returns. Questions about taxes addressed in this chapter include the following:

1. Are taxes a major consideration when purchasing capital assets?

2. What is the difference between income exclusion and deductions?

3. How do tax deductions differ from tax credits?

4. How do tax avoidance and tax evasion differ?

5. What are the advantages of a sole proprietorship form of organization?

6. What is double taxation?

7. How can double taxation be avoided by a corporate form of organization?

8. What is a limited partnership and what are its advantages over a general partnership?

9. Which federal tax forms does each type of organization file?

This chapter begins with a discussion of the effect of taxes on business decisions. It presents a brief history and explanation of the objectives of federal income taxes. Next, tax basics for the individual taxpayer are covered. Tax avoidance and tax evasion are discussed, followed by an overview, including the tax advantages and disadvantages, of the various forms of business organization. We then discuss cash versus accrual accounting and accounting income versus taxable income. Finally, state, municipal, and property taxes are discussed briefly.

The purpose of this chapter is not to explain all of the ramifications of the various tax laws, most of which are very complex. Rather, this chapter attempts to illustrate the importance of taxes in a hospitality operation's economic decisions.

Tax Considerations in Economic Decisions

Taxes are an important consideration in most major financial decisions. For example, the purchase of furniture and equipment may be delayed because a new tax incentive will take effect the following year. This is not to suggest that an investment in fixed assets should be delayed simply because of a tax advantage. Other business goals may indicate that the purchase should be made immediately. However, when current business objectives allow a choice of timing, management should plan acquisitions to gain tax advantages that will lower the net cost of acquiring the asset and result in greater net income. Similarly, the disposition of marketable securities, investments, fixed assets, or even an entire business should be considered with the tax effects of the proposed transaction in mind.

Because federal, state, and city taxes may consume over 50% of a business's earnings, management must be ever vigilant to the effect that tax rules may have on business decisions. One major purpose of hospitality associations such as the American Hotel & Motel Association and the National Restaurant Association is to lobby for tax legislation beneficial to the hospitality industry.

History and Objectives of Federal Income Taxes

Although the United States government first used an income tax to raise revenue during the Civil War, it was not until 1913 that the Sixteenth Amendment established the constitutionality of such a tax and cleared the way for federal income tax as we know it today. Since 1913, Congress has made amendments to the original law and charged the Treasury Department with its enforcement through the Internal Revenue Service (IRS), a branch of the Treasury Department.

Until the late 1960s, major tax law changes were infrequent—often seven to ten years apart. In recent years, however, significant changes have been made to the Internal Revenue Code nearly every year. The most recent major tax law was the Tax Reform Act of 1986. The law and its accompanying explanations are over 1,500 pages long.

To illustrate the increase in tax regulations, consider the following example. According to Sheldon S. Cohen, a Washington lawyer and former IRS Commissioner, the tax code in 1952 was only about three-fourths of an inch thick, and regulations fit into one volume about half an inch thick. Today, the code is $4^{1}/2$ inches thick, and regulations take up six volumes with a total thickness of about $9^{3}/4$ inches.[2]

The primary objective of income taxes is to raise revenue necessary for the operation of the federal government. This goal has been expanded at various times to include stimulating certain aspects of the economy and accomplishing various social goals.

Tax Basics

Taxes are levied on individuals and corporations. The income of a sole proprietorship must be reported on the proprietor's individual tax return. Similarly, partnerships are not generally taxed, but their partners are. That is, partnerships must report their incomes to their partners, who must include their share of partnership income on their individual returns. The members of limited liability companies similarly must include their company incomes on their individual returns. Although corporations are separate legal entities in themselves, they are ultimately owned by individual investors. Therefore, corporate tax decisions are often based on the impact they may have on the individual investors. For example, the use of an accelerated method of depreciation reduces taxable income, which in turn reduces taxes and the cash paid in taxes. This allows more cash to be invested or more cash dividends to be paid to investors.

In other words, all of these forms of business organization ultimately affect individual tax returns. Thus, a brief discussion of individual income taxes is warranted.

The individual income tax return is Form 1040 (shown later in Exhibit 3). In 1996, individuals with gross income above a certain amount had to file Form 1040 or one of its variations, Form 1040A or Form 1040EZ. An individual's tax is determined as follows:

	Income
	Income
Less:	Adjustments to Income
Equals:	Adjusted Gross Income (AGI)
Less:	Deductions
Less:	Amount for Exemptions
Equals:	Taxable Income
Times:	Tax rate
Equals:	Federal Income Tax
Less:	Tax Credits
Plus:	Other Federal Taxes
Equals:	Total Tax

In addition to Form 1040, several schedules must be filed, when appropriate. For example, Schedule C summarizes a sole proprietor's business for the year. Discussing all of the numerous schedules is beyond the scope of this chapter. All IRS offices provide all federal tax schedules and materials explaining these schedules.

The following brief discussion covers the major elements of Form 1040.

Income, Income Exclusions, and Adjustments

Income on Form 1040 includes, but is not limited to, wages, salaries, and tips (as reported on Form W-2), as well as interest and dividend income, business income or loss from a sole proprietorship, capital gains or losses, rents, royalties, partnership income or loss, and S corporation income or loss (S corporations are discussed later in this chapter).

Certain non-taxable income (such as interest from state and local government bonds), often referred to as **income exclusions,** is reported on the individual's tax return but excluded from income for tax purposes.

Gross income less adjustments to gross income equals adjusted gross income (AGI). Adjustments to gross income include, but are not limited to, individual retirement account deductions and some other retirement investments.

Deductions, Exemptions, and Taxable Income

Individual taxpayers should itemize **tax deductions** if their total deductions exceed the standardized deduction. For example, in 1996, it was beneficial for married taxpayers (if neither was 65 or older or was blind) filing jointly to itemize if their deductions exceeded $6,700. Itemized deductions include medical and dental expenses in excess of 7.5% of AGI, other taxes (such as state and local income taxes) paid during the tax year, real estate taxes, home mortgage interest expense, contributions to charitable organizations, limited amounts for casualty and theft losses, and the portion of certain summed miscellaneous deductions (such as union and professional dues and tax preparation fees) that exceed 2% of AGI.

In 1996, $2,550 was allowed for each exemption. In general, a taxpayer is allowed one exemption for himself or herself and one for each dependent.

Taxes and Credits

Income taxes are calculated on the basis of taxable income. The current tax rate system for individuals is graduated, with rates ranging from 15% to 39.6%. In addition, the tax code provides for minimum taxes (the *alternative minimum tax*) for certain individuals who would otherwise not have to pay income taxes. Income taxes less credits plus other applicable taxes equal the total taxes due.

In contrast to tax deductions, which are deducted from AGI to determine taxable income, **tax credits** are deducted directly from taxes due. Credits deductible from income taxes include credit for child and dependent care expenses and foreign tax credit.

Other taxes that must be added to the income taxes due include self-employment tax, commonly known as social security for the sole proprietor, and social security taxes on tip income not reported to the employer.

The tax code is quite complex, as are the many forms and schedules required to complete some individual tax returns. Individuals with complicated returns should consider obtaining assistance from a tax expert.

A Tax Illustration

Warren and Beth Schmidt have four children and own Snicker's Restaurant, an unincorporated business. Exhibit 1 presents a summary income statement of their restaurant operation, managed by Warren. Beth earns $40,000 as a part-time education specialist at the local community college. Her W-2 shows $10,000 withheld for federal income taxes. Exhibit 2 shows the Schmidts' other income, adjustments to income, deductions, and other taxes. Exhibits 3 through 5 illustrate the Schmidts' Form 1040, Schedule A, and Schedule C, respectively. Schedule SE—Computation of Social Security Self-Employment Tax and Form 4562—Depreciation must also be filed with the Schmidts' return. These schedules are not included as exhibits here, but their results appear as appropriate on the exhibits; for example, the total depreciation of $50,000 from Form 4562 is shown on line 13 of Schedule C (Exhibit 5), and the self-employment tax of $9,998 from Schedule SE is shown on line 45 of Form 1040. The self-employment tax is computed as follows:

Net profit (from Schedule C)	$83,000
Reduced by .9235 factor	× .9235
Net earnings from self-employment	$76,551

Exhibit 1   Summary Income Statement—Snicker's Restaurant

Summary Income Statement
Snicker's Restaurant
For the year ended December 31, 1996

Sales		$1,000,000
Cost of Sales		350,000
Gross Profit		650,000
Controllable Expenses:		
Payroll	$ 300,000	
Employee Benefits	30,000	
Laundry	5,000	
Supplies	10,000	
Utilities	35,000	
Advertising	18,000	
Car Expenses	8,000	
Legal and Professional	8,000	
Office Expense	3,000	
Telephone	3,000	
Travel	5,000	
Dues and Publications	1,000	
Profit Sharing Plans	8,000	
Repairs and Maintenance	10,000	444,000
Income Before Occupation Costs		206,000
Rent		10,000
Property Taxes		18,000
Insurance		15,000
Interest		30,000
Depreciation		50,000
Income Before Taxes		$ 83,000

		Tax Rate*		
Earnings subject to social security portion	$62,700	×	.124	= $7,775
Earnings subject to medicare portion	$76,551	×	.029	= 2,223
		Total self-employment taxes		$9,998

* The first $62,700 of net earnings is subject to the social security tax portion of the self-employment taxes. All net earnings are subject to the medicare portion of the self-employment taxes.

Notice that income from the restaurant, shown on Schedule C, is entered on Form 1040, line 12. Further, note that a refund of $9,330 is due the Schmidts.

Exhibit 2   Information about the Schmidt Family Income

Other Income:	
Interest income of $600	
Adjustments:	
A Keogh retirement plan of $10,000 (for Warren)	
Deductions:	
Medical—	
Prescribed drugs	$ 500
Doctor bills, etc.	1,500
Insurance	8,000
Taxes—	
Property taxes—house	6,500
State income taxes	6,000
Personal property taxes	500
Interest—	
Mortgage on house	12,000
Contributions—$6,000 to Evangel Center	12,000
Professional dues—Beth Schmidt	500
Tax return preparation fee for 1995 tax return	500
Other Taxes:	
Self-employment tax	9,998*
Federal taxes paid during year by Warren	$ 19,000

* Per Schedule SE (not included)

Tax Avoidance

Tax avoidance—that is, planning a transaction to mitigate the tax impact or to avoid the application of taxes completely—is entirely legal and should be aggressively pursued. Judge Learned Hand stated it well:

> Over and over again courts have said there is nothing sinister in so arranging one's affairs as to keep taxes as low as possible. Everybody does so, rich or poor; and all do right, for nobody owes any public duty to pay more than the law demands: taxes are enforced extractions, not voluntary contributions. To demand more in the name of morals is mere cant.[3]

Management can and should conduct the hospitality operation's business so as to achieve the lowest possible tax cost within the constraints of other business considerations and the prevailing tax laws and regulations. Good tax planning is simply good business management.

Exhibit 3 Schmidt Family Income Tax Return (Form 1040)

Form **1040**	Department of the Treasury -- Internal Revenue Service **U.S. Individual Income Tax Return** 1996	IRS Use Only -- Do not write or staple in this space.

For the year Jan. 1–Dec. 31, 1996, or other tax year beginning , 1996, ending ,19 | OMB No. 1545-0074

Use the IRS label. Otherwise, please print or type.

Warren B. Schmidt
Beth J. Schmidt
1415 Redbird Av.
Topeka   KS xxxxx

Your social security number XXXXXXXXX
Spouse's social security no. XXXXXXXXX

Note: Checking "Yes" will not change your tax or reduce your refund.

Presidential Election Campaign ▶
Do you want $3 to go to this fund? .... Yes [X] No
If a joint return, does your spouse want $3 to go to this fund?..................... Yes [X] No

Filing Status

Check only one box.

1 Single
2 [X] Married filing joint return (even if only one had income)
3 Married filing separate return. Enter spouse's SSN above & full name here. ▶
4 Head of household (with qualifying person). (See instructions.) If qualifying person is a child but not your dependent, enter child's name here. ▶
5 Qualifying widow(er) with dependent child (yr. spouse died ▶19). (See instructions.)

For help finding line instructions, see pages 2 and 3 in the booklet.

Exemptions

If more than six dependents, see the instructions for line 6c.

6a [X] Yourself. If your parent (or someone else) can claim you as a dependent on his or her tax return, **do not** check box 6a. ....
b [X] Spouse ....

c Dependents: (1)First name Last name	(2) Dependent's social security number. If born in Dec. 1996, see inst.	(3)Dependent's relationship to you	(4)No. of mos. lived in home in 1996.
Ami A. Schmidt	XXXXXXXXX	Daughter	12
Heidi M. Schmidt	XXXXXXXXX	Daughter	12
Eric W. Schmidt	XXXXXXXXX	Son	12
Samuel R. Schmidt	XXXXXXXXX	Son	12

No. of boxes checked on lines 6a and 6b: **2**
No. of your children on line 6c who:
● lived with you **4**
● did not live with you due to divorce or separation (see instructions)
Dependents on 6c not entered above
Add numbers entered on lines above ▶ **6**

d Total number of exemptions claimed ....

Income

Attach Copy B of your Forms W-2, W-2G, and 1099-R here.

If you did not get a W-2, see the instructions for line 7.

Enclose, but do not attach, any payment. Also, please enclose Form 1040-V (see the instructions for line 62).

7	Wages, salaries, tips, etc. Attach Form(s) W-2	7	40,000.
8a	Taxable interest. Attach Schedule B if over $400.	8a	600.
b	Tax-exempt interest. DO NOT include on line 8a 8b		
9	Dividend income. Attach Schedule B if over $400	9	
10	Taxable refunds, credits, or offsets of state and local income taxes (see instructions)	10	
11	Alimony received	11	
12	Business income or (loss). Attach Schedule C or C-EZ...........................	12	83,000.
13	Capital gain or (loss). If required, attach Schedule D	13	
14	Other gains or (losses). Attach Form 4797	14	
15a	Total IRA distributions .. 15a	b Taxable amount (see inst.)..	15b	
16a	Total pensions and annuities . 16a	b Taxable amount (see inst.)..	16b	
17	Rental real estate, royalties, partnerships, S corporations, trusts, etc. Attach Schedule E ...	17	
18	Farm income or (loss). Attach Schedule F.....................................	18	
19	Unemployment compensation	19	
20a	Social security benefits . 20a	b Taxable amount (see inst.)..	20b	
21	Other income.	21	
22	Add the amounts in the far right column for lines 7 through 21. This is your **total income**. ▶	22	123,600.

Adjusted Gross Income

If line 31 is under $28,495 (under $9,500 if a child did not live with you), see the instructions for line 54.

23a	Your IRA deduction (see instructions) 23a		
b	Spouse's IRA deduction (see instructions)........... 23b		
24	Moving expenses. Attach Form 3903 or 3903-F......... 24		
25	One-half of self-employment tax. Attach Schedule SE 25	4,999.	
26	Self-employed health insurance deduction (see inst.)..... 26	2,400.	
27	Keogh & self-employed SEP plans. If SEP, check... ▶ ☐ 27	10,000.	
28	Penalty on early withdrawal of savings.................. 28		
29	Alimony paid. Recipient's SSN ▶ 29		
30	Add lines 23a through 29...	30	17,399.
31	Subtract line 30 from line 22. This is your **adjusted gross income** .... ▶	31	106,201.

For Privacy Act and Paperwork Reduction Act Notice, see page 7.   Preparers Edition   Form **1040** (1996)

CAA   104012   NTF 5326
Copyright Forms Software Only, 1996 Nelco, Inc. N9610401

(continued)

Exhibit 3   *(continued)*

Warren B.   Schmidt   SSN: xxxxxxxxx

Form 1040 (1996)   Page **2**

	32	Amount from line 31 (adjusted gross income)	32	106,201.
Tax Computation	33a	Check if: ☐ You were 65/older, ☐ Blind; ☐ Spouse was 65/older, ☐ Blind.		
		Add the number of boxes checked above and enter the total here .... ▶ 33a ☐		
	b	If you are married filing separately and your spouse itemizes deductions or you were a dual-status alien, see instructions and check here .... ▶ 33b ☐		
	34	Enter the larger of your: **Itemized deductions** from Schedule A, line 28, OR **Standard deduction** shown below for your filing status. But see the instructions if you checked any box on line 33a or b or someone can claim you as a dependent. ● Single -- $4,000 ● Married filing jointly or Qualifying widow(er) -- $6,700 ● Head of household -- $5,900 ● Married filing separately -- $3,350	34	39,035.
	35	Subtract line 34 from line 32	35	67,166.
If you want the IRS to figure your tax, see the instructions for line 37.	36	If line 32 is $88,475 or less, multiply $2,550 by the total number of exemptions claimed on line 6d. If line 32 is over $88,475, see the worksheet in the inst. for the amount to enter	36	15,300.
	37	**Taxable income.** Subtract line 36 from line 35. If line 36 is more than line 35, enter -0-	37	51,866.
	38	**Tax.** See instructions. Check if total includes any tax from **a** ☐ Forms(s) 8814		
	b	☐ Form 4972 .... ▶	38	9,312.
Credits	39	Credit for child & dependent care exp. Attach Form 2441	39			
	40	Credit for the elderly or the disabled. Attach Schedule R	40			
	41	Foreign tax credit. Attach Form 1116	41			
	42	Other. Check if from **a** ☐ Form 3800 **b** ☐ Form 8396 **c** ☐ Form 8801 **d** ☐ Form _____	42			
	43	Add lines 39 through 42		43	
	44	Subtract line 43 from line 38. If line 43 is more than line 38, enter -0- .... ▶	44	9,312.
Other Taxes	45	Self-employment tax. Attach Schedule SE	45	9,998.
	46	Alternative minimum tax. Attach Form 6251	46	360.
	47	Social security and Medicare tax on tip income not reported to employer. Attach Form 4137 ...	47	
	48	Tax on qualified retirement plans, including IRAs. If required, attach Form 5329	48	
	49	Advance earned income credit payments from Form(s) W-2	49	
	50	Household employment taxes. Attach Schedule H	50	
	51	Add lines 44 through 50. This is your **total tax** .... ▶	51	19,670.
Payments	52	Federal income tax withheld from Form(s) W-2 and 1099	52	10,000.		
	53	1996 estimated tax payments & amt. applied from 1995 return .	53	19,000.		
	54	**Earned income credit.** Attach Schedule EIC if you have a qualifying child. Nontaxable earned income: amt. ▶ [ ] and type ▶	54	NO		
Attach Forms W-2, W-2G, and 1099-R on page 1.	55	Amount paid with Form 4868 (request for extension)	55			
	56	Excess social security and RRTA tax withheld (see inst.)	56			
	57	Other payments. Check if from **a** ☐ Form 2439 **b** ☐ Form 4136 .	57			
	58	Add lines 52 through 57. These are your **total payments** .... ▶	58	29,000.
Refund	59	If line 58 is more than line 51, subtract line 51 from line 58. This is the amount you **OVERPAID** .	59	9,330.
Have it sent directly to your bank account! See inst. and fill in 60b, c, and d.	60a	Amount of line 59 you want **REFUNDED TO YOU** .... ▶	60a	9,330.
	b	Routing no. [ ] **c** Type: ☐ Checking ☐ Savings		
	d	Account no. [ ]		
	61	Amount of line 59 you want **APPLIED TO 1997 EST. TAX.** .. ▶	61	0.
Amount You Owe	62	If line 51 is more than line 58, subtract line 58 from line 51. This is the **AMOUNT YOU OWE.** For details on how to pay and use Form 1040-V, see instructions .... ▶	62	0.
	63	Estimated tax penalty. Also include on line 62	63	0.

Sign Here	Under penalties of perjury, I declare that I have examined this return and accompanying schedules and statements, and to the best of my knowledge and belief, they are true, correct, and complete. Declaration of preparer (other than taxpayer) is based on all information of which preparer has any knowledge.		
Keep a copy of this return for your records.	Your signature ▶	Date	Your occupation **Businessman**
	Spouse's signature. If a joint return, BOTH must sign. ▶	Date	Spouse's occupation **Educator**
Paid Preparer's Use Only	Preparer's signature ▶	Date	Check if self-employed ☐	Preparer's social security no.
	Firm's name (or yours if self-employed) and address ▶		EIN	
			ZIP code	

CAA   **104012**   NTF 5329
Copyright Forms Software Only, 1996 Nelco, Inc. N9610402

Preparers Edition

Exhibit 4   Schedule A: The Schmidts' Itemized Deductions

SCHEDULE A (Form 1040)	Schedule A — Itemized Deductions	OMB No. 1545-0074 **1996**
Department of the Treasury Internal Revenue Service	▶ Attach to Form 1040. ▶ See Instructions for Schedule A (Form 1040).	Attachment Sequence No. **07**

Name(s) shown on Form 1040   Warren B.   Schmidt   Beth J.   Schmidt   Your social security no.   XXXXXXXXX

Medical and Dental Expenses

Caution: Do not include expenses reimbursed or paid by others.
1 Medical and dental expenses _____

1	10,000.	
2 Enter amount from Form 1040, line 32 .. **2** 106,201.		
3 Multiply line 2 above by 7.5% (.075) **3**	7,965.	
4 Subtract line 3 from line 1. If line 3 is more than line 1, enter -0- **4**		2,035.

Taxes You Paid

(See page A-1.)

5 State and local income taxes.............................. **5**	6,000.	
6 Real estate taxes (see page A-2) **6**	6,500.	
7 Personal property taxes................................. **7**	500.	
8 Other taxes ▶ _____ **8**		
9 Add lines 5 through 8 .... **9**		13,000.

Interest You Paid

(See page A-2.)

Note: Personal interest is not deductible.

10 Home mortgage interest and points reported to you on Form 1098 .. **10**	12,000.	
11 Home mortgage interest not reported to you on Form 1098. If paid to seller, show that person's name, ID no., & address ▶ _____ **11**		
12 Points not reported to you on Fm 1098. See pg. A-3 for special rules **12**		
13 Investment interest. If required, attach Form 4952. (See page A-3.) .. **13**		
14 Add lines 10 through 13 .... **14**		12,000.

Gifts to Charity

If you made a gift and got a benefit for it, see page A-3.

15 Gifts by cash or check _____ **15**	12,000.	
16 Other than by cash or check. If any gift of $250 or more, see page A-3. If over $500, you **MUST** attach Form 8283 .... **16**		
17 Carryover from prior year **17**		
18 Add lines 15 through 17 .... **18**		12,000.

Casualty, Theft   19 Casualty or theft loss(es). Attach Form 4684. (See page A-4.) **19**

Job Expenses and Most Other Miscellaneous Deductions

(See page A-4 for expenses to deduct here.)

20 Unreimbursed empl. exp. If required, you **MUST** attach Form 2106 or 2106–EZ ▶ _____ **20**		
21 Tax preparation fees.................................... **21**	500.	
22 Other expenses ▶ _____ Dues 500. **22**	500.	
23 Add lines 20 through 22 .... **23**	1,000.	
24 Enter amount from Form 1040, line 32 .. **24** 106,201.		
25 Multiply line 24 above by 2% (.02) .. **25**	2,124.	
26 Subtract line 25 from line 23. If line 25 is more than line 23, enter -0- **26**		0.

Other Miscellaneous Deductions

27 Other — from list on page A-4. List type and amount ▶ _____ **27**	

Total Itemized Deductions

28 Is Form 1040, line 32, over $117,950 (over $58,975 if married filing separately)?
   NO.   Your deduction is not limited. Add the amounts in the far right column for lines 4 through 27. Also, enter on Form 1040, line 34, the **larger** of this amount or your standard deduction.
   YES.   Your deduction may be limited. See page A-5 for the amount to enter.   ▶   **28**   39,035.

For Paperwork Reduction Act Notice, see Form 1040 Instructions.   CAA   **AB12**   NTF 5338   Prepares Edition   **Schedule A (Form 1040) 1996**
Copyright Forms Software Only, 1996 Nelco, Inc.   N96SCHA1

Exhibit 5   Schedule C: The Schmidts' Profit or Loss from Business

SCHEDULE C (Form 1040)	**Profit or Loss From Business** (Sole Proprietorship)	OMB No. 1545-0074 **1996**
Department of Treasury Internal Rev. Service (99)	▶ Partnerships, joint ventures, etc., must file Form 1065. ▶ Attach to Form 1040 or Form 1041. ▶ See Instructions for Schedule C (Form 1040).	Attachment Sequence No. **09**

Name of proprietor   Warren B.   Schmidt   Social security number (SSN) XXXXXXXXX

A Principal business or profession, including product or service (see page C-1)
foodservice   food
B Enter principal busn. code ▶ **3079**

C Business name. If no separate business name, leave blank.   Snickers Restaurant
D Employer ID no. (EIN), if any   XXXXXXXXX

E Business address, ▶ 1950 Main Street
City, State, ZIP   Topeka   KS xxxxx

F Accounting method: (1) ☒ Cash (2) ☐ Accrual (3) ☐ Other (specify) ▶

G Did you "materially participate" in the operation of this business during 1996? If "No," see page C-2 for limit on losses .... ☒ Yes ☐ No

H If you started or acquired this business during 1996, check here .... ▶ ☐

Part I   Income

1 Gross receipts or sales. Caution: If this income was reported to you on Form W-2 and the "Statutory employee" box on that form was checked, see page C-2 and check here .... ▶ ☐	1	1,000,000.
2 Returns and allowances..	2	
3 Subtract line 2 from line 1...	3	1,000,000.
4 Cost of goods sold (from line 42 on page 2)	4	350,000.
5 Gross profit. Subtract line 4 from line 3	5	650,000.
6 Other income, including Federal and state gasoline or fuel tax credit or refund (see page C-2)	6	
7 Gross income. Add lines 5 and 6 .... ▶	7	650,000.

Part II   Expenses. Enter expenses for business use of your home **only** on line 30.

8 Advertising...............	8	18,000.	19 Pension & profit-sharing plans .	19	8,000.
9 Bad debts from sales or services (see page C-3)	9		20 Rent or lease (see page C-4): a Vehicles, machinery, & equip...	20a	10,000.
10 Car and truck expenses (see page C-3)	10	8,000.	b Other business property ...... 21 Repairs and maintenance	20b 21	10,000.
11 Commissions and fees.......	11		22 Supplies (not included in Part III)	22	10,000.
12 Depletion................	12		23 Taxes and licenses	23	18,000.
13 Depreciation and section 179 expense deduction (not included in Part III) (see page C-3)..	13	50,000.	24 Travel, meals, & entertainment: a Travel	24a	5,000.
14 Employee benefit programs (other than on line 19)	14	30,000.	b Meals and entertainment c Enter 50% of line 24b subject to limitations (see pg. C-4)		
15 Insurance (other than health)..	15	15,000.			
16 Interest: a Mortgage (paid to banks, etc.).	16a	30,000.	d Subtract line 24c from line 24b	24d	
b Other	16b		25 Utilities....................	25	35,000.
17 Legal and professional services..................	17	8,000.	26 Wages (less employment credits) 27 Other expenses (from line 48 on	26	300,000.
18 Office expense.............	18	3,000.	page 2)	27	9,000.

28 Total expenses before expenses for business use of home. Add lines 8 through 27 in columns .... ▶	28	567,000.
29 Tentative profit (loss). Subtract line 28 from line 7	29	83,000.
30 Expenses for business use of your home. Attach Form 8829	30	
31 Net profit or (loss). Subtract line 30 from line 29. • If a profit, enter on Form 1040, line 12, and ALSO on Schedule SE, line 2 (statutory employees, see page C-5). Estates and trusts, enter on Form 1041, line 3. • If a loss, you MUST go on to line 32.	31	83,000.

32 If you have a loss, check the box that describes your investment in this activity (see page C-5).
 • If you checked 32a, enter the loss on Form 1040, line 12, and ALSO on Schedule SE, line 2 (statutory employees, see page C-5). Estates and trusts, enter on Form 1041, line 3.
 • If you checked 32b, you MUST attach Form 6198.

32a ☒ All investment is at risk.
32b ☐ Some investment is not at risk.

For Paperwork Reduction Act Notice, see Form 1040 instructions.   Schedule C (Form 1040) 1996

CAA   **C12**   NTF 5474
Copyright Forms Software Only, 1996 Nelco, Inc. N96SCHC1

For example, consider the purchase or sale of a hospitality establishment. An incorporated seller must decide whether to sell the stock of the company or its assets. Assuming a gain on the transaction, the after-tax differences between these two alternatives can be dramatic. Even in a situation generating an overall loss, tax recognition of gain may be required on certain elements of the transaction if the decision was to sell assets rather than stock.

Conversely, a buyer will be reluctant to acquire the stock of a corporation if the tax basis of the corporation's assets is substantially below the selling price of the stock. In this situation, the buyer's goal is generally to acquire the assets of the corporation at their fair market value in order to preserve this higher base for future depreciation purposes. Even if the stock must be acquired, it is usually possible to effect a tax reorganization to realize a step-up in tax basis.

The point of all this is that, with proper tax planning, tax laws frequently allow both buyer and seller to realize most of their opposing goals. This fairly complex example also illustrates the need for most investors to consult tax experts in order to minimize their taxes. Recognizing these opportunities for tax planning and avoiding excessive or burdensome taxes is perfectly legal and represents a key management responsibility.

In contrast to tax avoidance, **tax evasion** is the fraudulent denial or concealment of a current or future tax liability, such as under-reporting income or claiming unsubstantiated or excessive deductions. For example, a business that intentionally fails to report or under-reports revenues, dividends, interest, fees, or profits from business transactions is guilty of tax evasion. Similarly, tax evasion occurs when non-deductible expenses (such as personal expenses or costs related to personal use of business property) are intentionally deducted on tax returns as business expenses. Activities of this nature are illegal and untenable for the management of any business.

Forms of Business Organization

The importance of addressing tax questions early is perhaps best illustrated by looking at a new business. One of the basic decisions a business person must make is determining the legal form of operation: sole proprietorship, partnership, limited liability company, corporation, or one of their hybrid forms such as limited partnership and S corporation.

Each of these entities offers tax advantages and disadvantages. Tax considerations, however, are only one factor in such a decision. There are practical business and legal considerations, as well as governmental regulatory requirements. The following sections briefly discuss the forms of business organization and the major advantages and limitations of each. Exhibit 6 presents an outline of this information.

Sole Proprietorship

The **sole proprietorship** is the most common form of organization in the hospitality industry. As the name implies, the business is owned by a single individual. This form of organization is popular because it is easy to form. Establishing a sole proprietorship may only require filing an assumed business name statement with the proper authorities (such as the county government) and filing a Schedule C on the owner's federal, state, and local tax returns.

Exhibit 6   Operating Forms for the Hospitality Business

	Sole Proprietorship	Partnership		Limited Liability Company	Corporation	
		General	Limited		Regular	S Corporation
Instrument of Creation	None (assumed name statement may be required)	Agreement—oral or written	Certificate of limited partnership	Articles of organization	Articles of incorporation	Articles of incorporation, file election with IRS
Organizational Documents	None	Partnership agreement	Certificate of limited partnership agreement	Operating agreement	Articles of incorporation, bylaws, minutes	Articles of incorporation, bylaws, minutes
Type of Tax Return	Schedule C for Form 1040	Form 1065	Form 1065	Form 1065	Form 1120	Form 1120S
Tax Rates	Individual	Individual	Individual	Individual	Corporate	Individual
Limited Liability	No	No	Yes—Limited Partners; No—General Partners	Yes	Yes	Yes
Recognition of Losses	Owner	Partners	Partners	Members	Corporation	Shareholders

The following list indicates some advantages of the sole proprietorship form of organization.

1. Proprietorship eliminates double taxation (defined later under corporate disadvantages). Income is reported only on the owner's individual tax return.

2. Expected losses during start-up and the early years can offset the owner's other income. Losses that exceed the owner's other income may result in net operating losses that can be used to recover some or all of the owner's taxes for the previous year(s).

3. Business tax credits retain their character—that is, if they are tax credits to the business, they are tax credits to be used directly by the owner.

4. The owner maintains complete control over the business by being the sole owner.

Several disadvantages may discourage a hospitality business owner from operating as a sole proprietor. These disadvantages include:

1. Hospitality operations may be risky. The sole proprietor does not enjoy the limited liability available with some other organizational forms; that is, he or she is personally liable for the obligations of the business. However, adequate insurance can at least partially alleviate this problem.

2. Most benefits are severely limited or completely disallowed as deducted tax expenses if they are for the benefit of the sole proprietor. For example, only 30% of the cost of medical insurance for the sole proprietor can be included as a deductible tax expense.

3. The transfer of a portion of the ownership interest in a sole proprietorship requires a change to either partnership or corporate form. In addition, the continuity of the business is not assured at the death of the owner. By contrast, a corporation is legally separate from its owners.

4. The sole proprietor is generally unable to raise large amounts of capital, while a corporation may be able to issue stock or sell bonds.

The sole proprietorship may be an ideal form of organization if the anticipated risk is minimal and is covered by insurance, if the owner is either unable or unwilling to maintain the necessary organizational documents and tax returns of more complicated business entities, and if the business does not require extensive borrowing.

Partnerships

The **partnership** consists of two or more owners joined together, but not incorporated, for the purpose of operating a business. A partnership offers most of the tax and other advantages and disadvantages of a sole proprietorship. The advantages include the following:

1. More than one owner results in greater financial strength. The added capital can provide greater resources for expansion of the business.

2. Partnership arrangements allow flexibility in the allocation of profits, losses, and certain tax benefits among the owners. Such allocations must be reasonable and justified as having economic substance in order to satisfy the IRS.

3. Profits, losses, and tax credits pass through the partnership entity to the owners' individual returns, thus preventing double taxation.

4. Control of the business resides with the partners.

Major disadvantages of the partnership include the following:

1. Partners are taxed on their share of the profits, regardless of whether the partnership actually provides a cash distribution to the partners.

2. Partners may become frustrated in sharing the decision-making process. They may hold different opinions, and, theoretically, each has an equal right to manage the business.

3. Partners generally have unlimited legal liability for the obligations of the business. This can be a significant factor when uninsurable business risks exist. This disadvantage may be partially overcome by the use of a limited partnership form of organization.

Limited Partnerships

A **limited partnership** is a partnership of two or more individuals having at least one **general partner** (a partner with unlimited liability) and at least one **limited partner.** Unlike a general partnership agreement (which can be oral), the limited partnership agreement must be in writing, and the **certificate of limited partnership** must be filed with the proper governmental authorities. Most states regulate the public sale of limited partnership interests. The process of filing documents with the

Securities and Exchange Commission to sell limited partnership interests may result in sizable legal fees and other costs. Smaller private issues (issues not generally available to the general public) generally seek an exemption from registration.

The major distinguishing feature of limited partnerships is the limited liability afforded to limited partners: their liabilities are limited to their investments. However, limited partners cannot actively participate in controlling or managing the business. If they do, they will generally lose their limited liability status in any legal matters.

In recent years, the limited partnership has become an attractive financing vehicle for the expansion of hospitality operations. Limited partnerships have been formed for specific projects, with the hospitality establishment acting as the general partner and investors as the limited partners. The limited partnership enables the hospitality establishment to obtain needed capital and still maintain control over operations.

The basic tax advantages available to general partners are also available to limited partners. In addition to limited liability, another advantage available to limited partners (but not to general partners) is that, within certain limits, the limited partners' interests may be assigned without prior approval of the general partners.

Limited Liability Companies

A **limited liability company (LLC)** is a form of business that is relatively new in the United States. The LLC files articles of organization and is controlled by its operating agreement. It is an unincorporated organization that limits the liability of its owners (called *members*) to their investment, much as corporations do for stockholders and limited partnerships do for limited partners. In addition, the LLC is treated like a partnership for tax purposes, so income and losses pass through to the members. This eliminates the double taxation faced by regular corporations.

An LLC should be considered as the organizational format of choice for anyone who would have formed an S corporation, a general partnership, or a limited partnership. It offers more protection than a general partnership and is more flexible than an S corporation or a limited partnership. Unlike an S corporation, an LLC is not restricted to 75 or fewer owners; also, it can be layered with partnerships and corporations. An LLC can have different types of memberships and is not limited to one type of stock as the S corporation is. All members of an LLC have limited liability, unlike the partners of a general partnership or the general partner(s) of a limited partnership. Furthermore, the members can have an active role in management, unlike limited partners of a limited partnership.

Yet an LLC is not for everyone. To begin with, LLCs must have at least two members, so this format is not an option for a sole proprietor. Also, because some states do not recognize the tax exemption status of LLCs, LLCs are liable to corporate income taxes in those states. In addition, an LLC does not have a perpetual life like a corporation.

Corporations

A **corporation** is a legal entity created by a state or another political authority. The corporation receives a charter or articles of incorporation and has the following general characteristics:

1. An exclusive name

2. Continued existence independent of its stockholders

3. Paid-in capital represented by transferred shares of capital stock

4. Limited liability for its owners

5. Overall control vested in its directors

While hospitality businesses organized as sole proprietorships account for the largest number of businesses, hospitality corporations account for the greatest volume in terms of sales, assets, profits, and employees. Revenues from corporate lodging businesses constitute nearly two-thirds of the total lodging revenues across the United States.[4] Several hospitality corporations, such as Holiday Inns, Marriott International, and McDonald's Corporation have annual sales in excess of $2 billion. The major advantages of the corporate form over other forms of business organization include the following:

1. Its shareholders' liability is normally limited to their investments.

2. Owners are taxed only on distributed profits.

3. Employees can be motivated by equity participation (such as stock bonus plans and stock options) and by certain tax-favored benefits.

4. Equity capital can be raised by selling capital stock to the public.

5. A corporation can use its stock to acquire other companies and thereby offer the sellers a tax-free exchange.

6. Tax rates are often lower for small corporations than for individuals.

7. There is free transferability of capital stock by owners.

8. The corporation exists independently of the owners.

As with the other forms of business organization, there are disadvantages of the corporate form. Some of these include the following:

1. **Double taxation**—corporate profits are taxed twice. First, they are taxed on the corporation's own income tax. Then, any profits paid out as dividends are considered taxable income to the individual stockholders. Exhibit 7 illustrates that the effective tax rate on the second $100,000 of corporate pretax income could be as high as 63% (based on 1996 tax rates). The calculations assume that the individual stockholder/taxpayer's marginal tax rate is 39.6% and that all after-tax profits are distributed. Thus, the corporate tax of 39% plus the individual tax of 24% (39.6% of 61%) equals 63%, the effective tax rate. If this business had been unincorporated, the maximum effective tax rate would have been only 39.6%.

2. The corporation cannot pass on tax advantages (such as operating losses and tax credits) that might be more advantageous to the owners than to the corporation.

Exhibit 7   Illustration of Double Taxation

	Dollars	Percentage
Corporate Pretax Income over $100,000	$100,000	100.00%
Less: Corporate Tax (39%)	39,000	39.00
Dividend Distribution	61,000	61.00
Less: Individual Income Taxes (39.6%)	24,156	24.16
After-Tax Benefit to Stockholder	$ 36,844	36.84%

S Corporation

Some of the tax drawbacks of the corporate form of organization can be overcome by filing as an **S corporation** (the *S* merely refers to subchapter S of the code). In essence, this filing allows the corporation to be taxed like a partnership.

The philosophy behind the S corporation provisions of the Internal Revenue Code is that a firm should be able to select its form of organization free of tax considerations. The S corporation is a hybrid form allowing limited liability for owners but avoiding the corporate "curse" of double taxation.

To qualify as an S corporation, the corporation must meet several tests, including, but not limited to, (1) having 75 or fewer stockholders, (2) being a domestic corporation, and (3) having only one class of stock.

This form of organization can be very useful when corporate losses are anticipated and owners have taxable income that can absorb the losses. It can also be very useful when corporations are profitable without having uses for extra capital; since profits are passed through to stockholders, they are not taxed as accumulated earnings.

Minimizing Taxes

As pointed out earlier, all taxpayers wish to pay as little tax as possible. An example will illustrate how a business can accomplish this end. The owners/managers of a corporation may receive compensation in the form of benefits, salary, and dividends; this package should be structured to minimize taxes. Consider the taxability of these three compensation elements to both the corporation and the sole stockholder:

	C Corporation	Owner/Manager
Fringe benefits	Deductible	Non-taxable
Salary	Deductible	Taxable
Dividends	Non-deductible	Taxable

Certain benefits, such as health insurance, are a tax-deductible expense for a **C corporation** (the term often used in tax literature to refer to all non–S corporations) and are not taxable to the recipient, in this case the owner/manager. On the other hand, the corporation may deduct salaries in determining its federal income taxes, but the owner/manager must pay taxes on his or her own salary. Dividends are not a deductible expense to the corporation, and they are taxable to the owner/manager.

To further illustrate these concepts, consider George Brown, the sole stockholder of Brown's Eatery, an incorporated restaurant business. George has invested $200,000 in the business. In 19X1, he received a salary of $100,000 and the business had net income of $100,000. George received no benefits or dividends.

For the purpose of simplicity, assume a corporate tax rate of 20% on the first $200,000 of taxable income and an individual tax rate of 25% on the first $100,000 of earnings. George Brown and Brown's Eatery paid taxes in 19X1 totaling $45,000, determined as follows:

Taxpayer	Taxable Income	Tax Rate	Taxes
Brown's Eatery	$100,000	20%	$ 20,000
George Brown	100,000	25%	25,000
		Total	$ 45,000

In this case, the IRS may rule that part of George Brown's salary is dividends, especially if his salary is considered unreasonably high. Assume that the IRS rules $20,000 of his salary to be dividends. The total taxes increase by $4,000 to $49,000—the salary deduction of $20,000 denied to the corporation times the corporation's tax rate of 20%.

The IRS considers the following factors in determining whether salaries are reasonable:

- The amounts being paid by corporations of similar size in the same industry

- The economic conditions and salary levels in the geographic region in which the corporation operates

- The nature of the shareholder/employee responsibilities and the amount of time the shareholder/employee devotes to the business

- The shareholder/employee's qualifications in terms of education and experience

The owner/manager must formally document the basis of a relatively large salary; that is, he or she must explain the duties and functions performed to justify the salary. The corporation's board of directors should approve the owner/manager's salary.

In this example, we initially assumed that George did not receive any benefits. Suppose that George's effective salary of $80,000 is reduced to $70,000 and he receives $10,000 in benefits (such as health and life insurance). Assume that these benefits are 100% deductible by the corporation and non-taxable to George. The taxes paid by George and his corporation now total $44,500, determined as follows:

Taxpayer	Taxable Income	Tax Rate	Taxes
Brown's Eatery	$110,000*	20%	$ 22,000
George Brown	90,000**	25%	22,500
		Total	$ 44,500

* original net income	$ 100,000
salary declared by IRS as dividends	20,000
cost of fringe benefits	(10,000)
Total	$ 110,000
** salary	$ 70,000
dividends	20,000
Total	$ 90,000

The total tax bill is $4,500 less than it would be if Brown's Eatery provided George with no benefits. The $4,500 reduction is, in effect, the combined tax rates multiplied by the cost of the benefits:

$$(.20 + .25)\$10,000 = \$4,500$$

Thus, to minimize taxes, the preferred order is benefits, salary, and dividends. However, just as the IRS is vigilant to determine that salaries are reasonable and do not include dividends, the IRS also has rules regarding benefits. Certain benefits are taxable, such as the premiums paid on life insurance policies when the insurance coverage exceeds $50,000 and the insured is the owner of the policy. The IRS treats the premium on the excess coverage as taxable income to the benefiting employee.

It might appear at this point that a small C corporation is better off not declaring dividends above a required minimum that satisfies the IRS. However, if corporations accumulate earnings in order to avoid double taxation, they may be subject to an **accumulated earnings tax.** The current rate is 39.6% on accumulated earnings in excess of $250,000. Specifics of this tax are beyond the scope of this chapter; however, the tax can be avoided by showing a reasonable need for accumulating earnings (such as business expansion).

How would George Brown's taxes change if he had filed as an S corporation? This example assumes that the benefits under an S corporation would be nontaxable, as they were for the C corporation. The restaurant's taxable income of $110,000 would be passed directly to George for tax purposes. Therefore, his 19X1 taxes would have been $50,000, determined as follows:

George's salary	$ 90,000
Brown's Eatery income taxable to George	110,000
Total taxable income	200,000
George's tax rate	× .25
Total taxes	$ 50,000

Thus, the S corporation form of organization costs George an extra $5,500. This result is due entirely to the 5% difference in the Eatery's tax rate of 20% as a C corporation and George's tax rate of 25%.

The tax rates vary for C corporations and individuals. At lower taxable income levels, individual rates exceed corporate rates. Thus, based on the assumed rates used in our illustration, the C corporation is better than the S corporation for Brown's Eatery.

The 1996 federal tax rate schedules for individuals and corporations were as follows:

Individual (Married filing joint)

Taxable Income	Tax Rate
$0–$40,100	15%
$40,100–$96,900	$6,015 + 28% of the amount over $40,100
$96,900–$147,700	$21,919 + 31% of the amount over $96,900
$147,700–$263,750	$37,667 + 36% of the amount over $147,700
over $263,750	$79,445 + 39.6% of the amount over $263,750

Corporation

Taxable Income	Tax Rate
$0–$50,000	15%
$50,000–$75,000	$7,500 + 25% of the amount over $50,000
$75,000–$100,000	$13,750 + 34% of the amount over $75,000
$100,000–$335,000	$22,250 + 39% of the amount over $100,000
$335,000–$10,000,000	$113,900 + 34% of the amount over $335,000
$10,000,000–$15,000,000	$3,400,000 + 35% of the amount over $10,000,000
$15,000,000–$18,333,333	$5,150,000 + 38% of the amount over $15,000,000
over $18,333,333	$6,416,666.55 + 35% of the amount over $18,333,333

For example, $100,000 of taxable income to a married individual filing a joint return results in federal income taxes of $22,880.00.

First	$ 40,100	×	.15	=	$ 6,015.00
Next	56,800	×	.28	=	15,904.00
Next	3,100	×	.31	=	961.00
Total	$100,000				$22,880.00

Thus, the effective average rate is 22.88%.

For a C corporation, the first $100,000 is taxed as follows:

First	$ 50,000	×	.15	=	$ 7,500
Next	25,000	×	.25	=	6,250
Next	25,000	×	.34	=	8,500
Total	$100,000				$22,250

Thus, the effective average rate is 22.25%.

Accounting Methods

There are different accounting methods available. After the legal form of operation has been chosen, management must determine which accounting method best reflects the type of business and provides optimum ability to minimize or postpone taxes. Minimizing or postponing taxes is achieved by effectively timing the recognition of income and deduction of expenses.

Cash Method Versus Accrual Method

Tax laws require the taxpayer to use the method of accounting that most clearly reflects income. The accrual method of accounting is appropriate for taxpayers with significant inventories. Further, the use of the accrual method of accounting is required if the taxpayer is a corporation or a partnership with a C corporation as a partner. However, if the business is small (average annual sales of $5,000,000 or less), the cash method of accounting may be used for tax purposes. Under this method, items of income and expense are generally reported for tax purposes when cash is actually received or paid out.

Even under the cash method, there are exceptions. For example, fixed assets must generally be depreciated over the life of the asset rather than being deducted as an expense in the year paid. Exhibit 3 shows that Snicker's Restaurant was accounted for on a cash basis. For tax purposes, food inventories were $-0-; however, there was depreciation of $50,000 for 1996.

A cash-basis taxpayer has some flexibility in reporting income and expenses. The timing of income collection, or the payment of expenses, can be controlled to some extent, particularly near year-end.

The accrual method of accounting reports income when it is earned, rather than when the cash is collected. It reflects expenses when they are incurred, rather than when they are paid. As is the case with many areas of tax law, there are exceptions to the general rule. Under the accrual method, some items of income (such as advance rentals) are taxed when collected rather than when earned. Similarly, an expense item must be fixed and determinable before it can be deducted for tax purposes. Estimated expenses, while generally acceptable for financial accounting, may not be deducted for tax reporting until all factors that affect the expense item have become fixed and determinable.

Installment Sales Method

For financial accounting purposes, when goods or property is sold on the installment method (that is, the sales price is received in periodic payments over time), the entire sales price is recognized at the time of sale, and the entire cost of goods sold deducted as an expense of sale. Tax reporting, however, allows recognizing the profit on sales made on the installment method on a prorated basis as cash is received. This method is frequently chosen upon the sale of a business such as a hotel or restaurant.

Accounting Income Versus Taxable Income

Thus far, the importance of tax planning for a transaction at an early stage of its development has been emphasized. In addition, several options for selecting the legal entity within which to conduct a business have been presented. After the form of organization is selected, the method of accounting (cash versus accrual) most suitable for mitigating the tax costs of operation is chosen. All of these choices are made with the overall business objectives of the operation in mind.

These choices can result in differences between the amount and timing of income or expenses reported in financial statements and the amounts reported on the tax return. Other tax requirements or choices can cause further differences in the amount or timing of the reporting of income and expenses.

Accelerated Depreciation

Tax legislation in 1981 and 1982 liberalized tax depreciation rules with enactment of an Accelerated Cost Recovery System (ACRS) which provided for faster recovery (depreciation) of capital expenditures. The 1986 tax law significantly tightened the tax rules for depreciating real estate, but retained the liberal rules for depreciating personal property such as equipment and furniture. Since 1986, the depreciation rules have been based on the **Modified Accelerated Cost Recovery System (MACRS).**

In financial accounting, a building may be depreciated over 30 years or more. MACRS currently requires, for tax purposes, recovery over 39 years. (For property placed in service before May 13, 1993, recovery may be over 31.5 years.) Similarly, furniture and equipment may be depreciated over seven to ten years (or more) for financial accounting purposes, while the same items are depreciated for tax purposes over five years under MACRS. (Within certain limits, the first $17,500 of equipment purchases may be expensed immediately for tax purposes, while for accounting purposes, the equipment would be depreciated as normal.) Thus, the timing of reporting net income for financial purposes can be significantly different from that for taxable income.

In the later years of an asset's life, the deduction for depreciation, especially with furniture and equipment, will be greater for financial accounting than for tax accounting. At the end of the asset's life, the deduction for depreciation will be the same in total for both financial reporting and tax accounting. The difference is in the timing of the deduction.

Exhibit 8   Depreciation of Equipment for Tax and Financial Reporting Purposes

Year	MACRS Recovery[1]	Straight-Line Recovery[2]	Difference
19X1	$ 200,000	$ 100,000	$ 100,000
19X2	320,000	100,000	220,000
19X3	192,000	100,000	92,000
19X4	115,200	100,000	15,200
19X5	115,200	100,000	15,200
19X6	57,600	100,000	(42,400)
19X7	0	100,000	(100,000)
19X8	0	100,000	(100,000)
19X9	0	100,000	(100,000)
19X0	0	100,000	(100,000)
Total	$1,000,000	$1,000,000	$ 0

[1] The MACRS for 5-year tax life is calculated using the double declining method and the half-year convention; that is, one half of a year's depreciation is taken in the year of the purchase (19X1) and one half in 19X6.

1st year	–	20.00%
2nd year	–	32.00
3rd year	–	19.20
4th year	–	11.52
5th year	–	11.52
6th year	–	5.76
Total		100.00%

[2] Assuming a zero salvage value. Annual depreciation is determined by dividing the cost ($1,000,000) by the life (10 years) to equal the annual depreciation ($100,000).

Exhibit 8 uses a purchase of $1,000,000 worth of equipment to illustrate the difference between MACRS recovery expense and depreciation using the straight-line method. For tax purposes, the MACRS allows the cost of the equipment to be recovered over five years, while for financial reporting purposes, the hospitality operation chooses to depreciate the equipment over ten years using the straight-line method. In the first five years, MACRS results in $442,400 more expense (cost recovery) than the straight-line method, while the reverse results in the last five years.

Pre-Opening Expenses

For many years, hospitality firms were able to deduct, for tax purposes, many expenses as they were incurred before formally opening a new hotel, even if such expenses were deferred for financial reporting purposes. This was especially true if the operation was not the first hotel in the business. The current tax law disallows immediate write-off and requires pre-opening expenses to be amortized over a five-year period beginning with the month the hotel or restaurant opens for business.

First-Year Losses

First-year losses of a hospitality operation are usually capitalized as a deferred charge and amortized over several years for financial accounting purposes.

However, for tax purposes, such costs are generally deductible as incurred, so taxable income is lower than financial accounting income, improving the first-year cash flow by deferring taxes. This situation reverses after the first year. As the first-year losses are amortized for financial accounting with no offsetting amortization for tax accounting, the result is a higher taxable income than book income and a corresponding higher tax payment.

Loss Carrybacks and Carryforwards

A final example of the differences between financial and tax accounting is the treatment of operating losses sustained by a business. Current tax laws allow a net operating loss to be carried back and applied as a deduction against prior taxable income, resulting in a refund of taxes previously paid. Losses may be carried back three years and carried forward fifteen years.

For financial accounting purposes, an operating loss will generally flow through to reported earnings. In certain situations, the tax benefit may then reduce this pretax book loss by up to the amount of previously paid taxes. Financial accounting rules permit the recording of a tax benefit on an operating loss if it can be carried back and used against taxable income for the previous year. For example, assume that an enterprise incurs a $100,000 pretax loss that can be carried back against prior years' taxable income. Further assume that $30,000 of previously paid taxes can be recovered. The pretax loss is then reduced by the $30,000 recovery.

State and Municipal Taxes

Until recently, managers paid little attention to state and local taxes because rates were low and the amounts involved did not warrant serious study. This has changed in recent years as state and local governments have been increasing tax rates and seeking new ways to generate tax revenues. Today's manager should realize that state and local taxes also require planning to reduce the overall tax burden.

The financial manager of a multi-state operation should be aware that the manner in which business is conducted in a state determines whether and how the business is subject to that state's tax laws. Early tax planning is as important here as it is in all areas of tax planning.

Planning is also important in a multi-corporate form of business when one corporate unit is profitable and a second is unprofitable. The manager should investigate whether state tax laws allow consolidation of operations to offset the income of one corporation with the loss of another, minimizing the total tax burden. If state laws do not permit consolidation and the mix of profit and loss is expected to continue for some time, the manager should consider whether a corporate reorganization is desirable. A reorganization that merged the losing operation into the profitable one would achieve the same tax results as filing a consolidated return. Of course, in this situation, other business objectives should also be weighed.

Property Taxes

Taxes levied on real estate and personal property such as furniture, fixtures, and equipment are commonly called **property taxes.** In recent years, property taxes for hotels have approximated 3% of gross revenues, which may seem insignificant. However, a .5% reduction for a hotel with $20,000,000 in sales would save the business $100,000.

Property taxes are generally levied at the local level. The tax is a result of the assessed value of the property and the tax rate. Property taxes differ by state and locality; for example, the general property tax formula in Michigan is:

$$\text{Property Taxes} = \frac{\text{Assessed Valuation}}{1,000} \times \text{Tax Rate}$$

In this formula, the **assessed valuation** is the value the tax assessor places on the property to be taxed. The tax rate is stated in *mills,* which is tax dollars per $1,000 of assessed valuation. Assume that Rocky's Hotel had an assessed valuation of $10,000,000 and a tax rate of 60 mills. The annual property tax would be calculated as follows:

$$\text{Property Taxes} = \frac{\$10,000,000}{1,000} \times 60$$

$$= \$600,000$$

Although property taxes are normally viewed as a fixed cost (that is, not controllable by management), management should challenge any assessed valuation considered to be excessive. For example, in Michigan the assessed valuation is by law 50% of market value. Assume that Rocky's Hotel had recently been purchased for $18,000,000. Based on Michigan law, the assessed valuation for Rocky's Hotel should be reduced to $9,000,000, which is 50% of the market price. The $1,000,000 assessed valuation reduction, given the tax rate of 60 mills, reduces property taxes by $60,000 annually.

Summary

Governments levy income taxes to raise the revenue they need to provide their constituents with services and to achieve a variety of social goals. Both individuals and businesses pay taxes. Most financial business decisions have tax implications. Therefore, hospitality managers must understand taxes in order to make sound decisions.

Federal income taxes are based on a self-reporting system, whereby the taxpayer prepares the appropriate tax forms. For the individual, tax considerations include income, adjustments to income, deductions, exemptions, credits, other taxes, and taxes paid. Form 1040, Form 1040A, or Form 1040EZ must be filed by all qualifying taxpayers.

Tax avoidance refers to legally paying the least amount of tax. Tax evasion is the illegal attempt to pay less or no tax. Hospitality managers should strive for tax avoidance.

One major tax consideration is the form of organization a business selects. The major forms are the sole proprietorship, the partnership, the limited liability company, and the corporation, while hybrid forms include the limited partnership and the S corporation. Each form offers advantages and disadvantages. The disadvantage of individual unlimited liability can be overcome by incorporating; however, incorporation results in double taxation. Avoiding double taxation and unlimited liability can be achieved by filing as an S corporation and a limited liability company; however, S corporations are limited to one type of stock and 75 or fewer stockholders. An operation should consider the size, goals, and riskiness of its business, then select a form that minimizes the disadvantages and maximizes the advantages.

Just as there are different business forms, there are different accounting methods. Businesses must decide whether cash accounting or accrual accounting better meets their needs. There are also differences between accounting for financial purposes and accounting for tax purposes. These differences may involve the treatments of depreciation, pre-opening expenses, first-year losses, and loss carrybacks and carryforwards.

State, municipal, and property taxes all deserve the manager's attention. These taxes, which used to be negligible, have been growing. Although property taxes are thought of as fixed expenses, attentive managers may be able to successfully challenge assessed valuations and reduce the property tax burden.

Endnotes

1. Letter to Jean Baptiste Le Roy, 13 Nov. 1789.

2. "Is This Progress?" *The Wall Street Journal*, 28 May 1997, Central edition.

3. Commissioner v. Newman (CA-2), 47-1 USTC 99175, 159 Fed.(2d)848.

4. Albert J. Gomes, *Hospitality in Transition* (New York: American Hotel & Motel Association, 1985).

Key Terms

accumulated earnings tax—A tax designed to prevent corporations from accumulating earnings in order to avoid double taxation. The tax can be avoided by showing a reasonable need for accumulating earnings (such as business expansion).

assessed valuation—With regard to property taxes, the value the tax assessor places on the property to be taxed.

C corporation—The term often used in tax literature to refer to all non–S corporations.

certificate of limited partnership—A document that must be filed with the proper governmental authorities. Unlike a general partnership agreement (which can be oral), the limited partnership agreement must be in writing.

corporation—A form of business organization that provides a separate legal entity apart from its owners.

double taxation—Occurs when both corporate profits and dividends paid to stockholders are taxed.

general partner—A member of a partnership with unlimited liability for the debts of the partnership.

income exclusions—Income that is reported on federal tax returns but not subject to taxation; exclusions from income shown on tax forms include amounts for dividends and a portion of long-term capital gains.

limited liability company—A form of business organization that combines the corporate feature of limited liability with the favorable tax treatment of partnerships and sole proprietorships. May have an unlimited number of owners (who are referred to as members) and is not restricted to one class of stock.

limited partner—A member of a limited partnership having limited liability. Limited partners may not actively participate in managing the business.

limited partnership—A form of business organization consisting of a partnership between two or more individuals having at least one general partner and one limited partner in which the latter's liabilities are limited to investments.

loss carryback—The application of a net operating loss as a deduction against prior years' taxable income, resulting in a refund of taxes previously paid.

loss carryforward—The application of a prior year's net operating loss as a deduction against subsequent taxable income.

modified accelerated cost recovery system (MACRS)—The legal basis for depreciation rules since 1986; allows for faster "recovery" (depreciation) of capital expenditures for tax purposes.

partnership—A form of business organization involving two or more owners that is not incorporated.

property taxes—Taxes levied on real estate and personal property such as furniture, fixtures, and equipment.

S corporation—A hybrid form of organization that allows a corporation to be taxed in the same manner as a partnership.

sole proprietorship—An unincorporated business organized by one person.

tax avoidance—Planning transactions to mitigate the impact of taxes or avoid the application of taxes in such a manner as to achieve the lowest possible tax cost within the constraints of other business considerations and the prevailing tax laws and regulations.

tax credits—Amounts that are subtracted directly from income taxes calculated on taxable income in accordance with prevailing tax laws.

tax deductions—Amounts that are deducted from taxable income in accordance with prevailing tax laws.

tax evasion—The fraudulent denial or concealment of a current or future tax liability such as the underreporting of income and claiming unsubstantiated or excessive income deductions.

Review Questions

1. What are five types of income that must be reported on an individual's tax return?

2. How do tax deductions differ from tax credits?

3. What are the major advantages of a sole proprietorship?

4. What are the major advantages of a corporation?

5. How may the disadvantage of unlimited liability be overcome in selecting a form of organization?

6. Why are limited partnerships so useful in raising capital funds for hospitality operations?

7. How does accelerated depreciation (as opposed to straight-line depreciation) save profitable hospitality businesses tax dollars?

8. What are two limitations to S corporations?

9. What is double taxation?

10. Under what circumstances is the sole proprietorship form best?

Problems

Problem 1

Terri Bensen, a married taxpayer who files jointly with her husband, has taxable income for 19X6 of $120,000.

Required:
1. Determine Terri's federal income taxes based on the 1996 rates.
2. What are Terri's average and marginal tax rates?

Problem 2

The Blueball Inn has an assessed valuation of $5,000,000. The property tax rate is 60 mills.

Required:
Determine the Blueball Inn's annual property taxes.

Problem 3

Leslie Boyer is considering opening a franchised quick-service restaurant (QSR). He believes that in a typical year he will gross nearly $1,200,000 and net $100,000 before income taxes. Angela, his wife, is expected to have taxable income of $100,000 from her apartment rentals. Her business is not incorporated. Leslie wants to avoid double taxation but also wants to limit his liability.

Required:
1. What form of organization do you suggest? Assume that the LLC has not been approved by the state where Leslie lives.
2. How might Leslie overcome the liability problem without incorporating?

Problem 4

Based on the information in the previous problem, calculate income taxes for the Boyers (ignore exemptions and deductions) and their businesses in the following situations:

1. Assume that the Boyers' average tax rate is 25% and that both the QSR and the real estate business are unincorporated.
2. Assume that the Boyers' average tax rate is 25%, the average corporate rate is 20%, and the QSR is incorporated.
3. Assume the same situation as in #2 above and that the QSR pays Leslie $50,000 in dividends that are taxed at the Boyers' average tax rate.
4. Assume that the Boyers' average tax rate is 25%, the average corporate rate is 20%, and the QSR is incorporated but is treated as an S corporation for tax purposes.

Problem 5

Jacob Mark's tax information for 19X6 is as follows:

Salary	$60,000
Interest income	$ 3,000
Individual retirement account	$ 2,000
Exemptions	four
Deductions	$12,000
Tax credits	$ 500
Federal income taxes withheld	$ 5,000

Required:

Based on the above and using the 1996 tax rates for a married individual filing jointly, determine how much Jacob must pay or will receive as a refund for 19X6.

Problem 6

Jerome Woods, owner of Woods Place, wants to know the potential tax liability of his restaurant given various levels of taxable income and different forms of organization. Assume that Woods Place potentially generates pretax income at three levels:

Low level	$ 50,000
Medium level	$ 80,000
High level	$150,000

Required:

1. Using the 1996 tax rates, calculate the income tax liability if Woods Place is incorporated and files its tax returns as a C corporation.
2. Using the 1996 tax rates for a married individual filing jointly, calculate the income tax liability for Jerome Woods, assuming Woods Place is unincorporated. (Ignore Jerome's deductions and exemptions.)

Problem 7

Nicole Bustle is earning a mint selling real estate. During the past five years, she has had average annual taxable income of $200,000. Her husband, Richie, would like to open a 100-unit motor hotel. The feasibility study conducted for the lodging facility suggests losses of $150,000, $100,000, and $50,000 for the first three years, respectively. The following three years, the motor hotel is expected to generate pretax profits of $100,000 per year. Assume that the Bustles' average tax rate is 28%. Further assume that the average corporate tax rate is 20% and that corporate tax losses can be carried forward for up to five years.

Required:

Based on the above information, how should Richie Bustle organize his motor hotel business? Note: consider providing "tax savings" to support your answer.

Problem 8

J. Deere Restaurants, Inc., must decide whether to use the cash or accrual method of accounting for tax purposes. The chairperson, John Deere, has provided you with the following information:

	Basis	
	Cash	Accrual
Sales	$1,000,000	$1,100,000
Cost of Sales	350,000	325,000
Labor	300,000	310,000
Other Expenses (excluding taxes)	200,000	190,000

John believes that the approach that minimizes taxes for the first year is the preferred method. Assume that the taxes for J. Deere Restaurants, Inc., will be based on the following tax structure:

Taxable Income	Tax Rate
$0–$50,000	15%
$50,000.01–$75,000	$7,500 + 25% of the amount over $50,000
$75,000.01–$100,000	$13,750 + 34% of the amount over $75,000
$100,000.01–$335,000	$22,250 + 39% of the amount over $100,000
over $335,000	$113,900 + 34% of the amount over $335,000

Required:

Determine which method J. Deere Restaurants, Inc., should use.

Problem 9

The Waterloo Inn is an unincorporated lodging facility owned by James Waters. During 19X1, the inn provided its owner with $55,000 in net income. In addition, James received $1,000 in interest and dividend income for 19X1. James's deductions and exemptions for 19X1 are as follows:

Exemptions: his wife, Sally, and their two children, Lisa and Dianne. Assume that $2,600 is allowed for each exemption.

Deductions:	Home mortgage interest	$7,000
	Real estate taxes	3,000
	Contributions	5,000

Since the above deductions exceed the standard deduction, James will itemize deductions.

James also must pay self-employment taxes of 15.3% on his first $65,400 of earned income and 2.9% on anything above that amount. He has paid estimated federal income taxes and self-employment taxes of $20,000 during 19X1.

Required:

1. Compute Waters' self-employment taxes for 19X1.
2. Compute his federal income taxes for 19X1. Assume that Sally and James are filing a joint return and that their average tax rate is 28%. (Hint: use Exhibits 3 through 5 as a guide for determining parts 2 and 3 of this problem.)
3. Determine how much Mr. Waters owes or has coming from the federal government for 19X1.

Problem 10

The Celtic Corporation has purchased $2,000,000 worth of equipment for its hotels in the current year. The President, Fred Boston, has heard that using the MACRS recovery offers cash savings over the straight-line method. The equipment could be depreciated over five years for tax purposes using the recovery rates shown in Exhibit 8. It could also be depreciated over ten years using the straight-line method and have zero salvage value. The marginal tax rate for the Celtic Corporation is 30%. Taxes saved due to the difference between MACRS and straight-line depreciation are invested at the end of each year at 10% interest compounded annually.

Required:

1. Determine the amount of the "tax savings fund" from taxes saved and interest earned over the first five years. Use the half-year convention for depreciation as shown in Exhibit 8.
2. Calculate the interest earned over the ten-year period. Assume that for the sixth through tenth years the taxes paid due to excess straight-line depreciation over MACRS come at the end of each year from the "tax savings fund."

Problem 11

Jill Wiggins, who is self-employed, provides you with her tax information for 19X1:

Professional earnings from self-employment:	$50,000
Dividend income:	$20,000
Three exemptions:	$2,300 allowed per exemption

Assume tax rates are as follows:

Taxable Income	Tax Rate
<$20,000	15%
$20,001–$40,000	25%
>$40,000	35%

Itemized deductions total $15,000.

The self-employment tax rate is 15.3% on the first $66,000 of earned income.

Jill has paid estimated taxes of $15,000.

Required:

Determine the following:

1. Self-employment taxes for 19X1
2. Income taxes for 19X1
3. Amount due or refund due to Jill Wiggins for 19X1

Problem 12

Zera Adams owns a very successful food service chain. The chain is incorporated and generates net income of $300,000 each year. Her salary is $40,000 a year and she receives no benefits. The food service chain pays her dividends equal to 40% of its net income each year. Zera's average tax rate is 28%. Assume the corporate income tax rates are as follows:

Taxable Income	Tax Rate
$0–$50,000	15%
$50,000.01–$75,000	$7,500 + 25% of the amount over $50,000
over $75,000	$13,750 + 34% of the amount over $75,000

Zera is an excellent owner/manager, but does not know much about taxes. At a recent conference for entrepreneurs, she heard about S corporations, double taxation, excessive salary being considered dividends, and other related matters. She is the sole owner of her business and insists the business retain its corporate form; however, she wants to minimize taxes.

Required:

1. Based on the above information, calculate the income taxes paid by the corporation and Zera (ignore deductions and exemptions in calculating her personal income taxes).
2. How would you advise Zera to minimize her taxes? Consider that the minimum dividends would have to be 12% of net income and the maximum salary could be $100,000. The maximum benefits would cost $20,000. Assume that these benefits are deductible to the corporation and non-taxable to Zera. She still wants to receive salary, dividends, and benefits totaling $160,000.
3. Based on your advice, what would be the tax reduction?

Problem 13

Gayle Koelling owns and manages the unincorporated Christmas Inn. She and her husband Melvin file a joint return. Their tax situation for 19X2 is as follows:

A. Income

Income from the Christmas Inn	$ 60,000
Interest income	600
Dividend income	2,000
Capital gain from sale of investment	10,000
Melvin's salary	75,000

B.   Adjustments to Income

Keogh retirement plan investment $ 10,000

C.   Exemptions

Four (two children) at $2,600 each

D.   Itemized Deductions (Schedule A)

Medical	$ 3,000
Property taxes	4,000
State income taxes	4,000
Intangibles tax	300
Home mortgage interest	6,000
Personal interest	1,500
Charitable contributions	8,000

E.   Tax Rate

Average federal income tax rate—25%

Self-employment tax rate—15.3% on the first $65,400 of earned income and 2.9% on anything above that amount

Note: Social security taxes were properly withheld from Melvin's paychecks. Self-employment taxes need to be calculated for Gayle.

F.   Tax Payments

- Melvin's employer withheld $10,000 of federal income tax during 19X2.
- Gayle paid estimated federal taxes of $20,000 during 19X2.

Required:

Calculate the amount of federal taxes due or to be refunded to the Koellings for 19X2. Note: Follow Schedule A (Exhibit 4) to determine the deductibility of the Koellings' itemized deductions in determining their taxable income.

Problem 14

Mark Reed is the sole owner of a successful lodging chain. The chain is unincorporated and generates pretax income of $300,000 each year. At the present time, he receives no tax-free benefits. Assume Reed's average tax rate is 30%. Mark draws $90,000 from the chain each year for his personal use and leaves the remainder in the chain to finance growth. The $90,000 has *not* been subtracted in determining the pretax income of $300,000.

Mark is an excellent owner/manager, but weak in taxation. At a conference for entrepreneurs, he recently heard about S corporations, double taxation, excessive salary being labeled as dividends by the IRS, and so forth. Assume corporation income tax rates as follows:

Taxable Income	Rate
0–$100,000	15%
$100,001–$200,000	25%

Over $200,000   35%

Required:

1. Based on the above, calculate the income taxes paid by him. (Ignore deductions, exemptions, and so forth in calculating his personal income taxes.)
2. How would you advise him to minimize the taxes he pays? If he incorporates, dividends would have to be at least equal to $10,000 (unless the company files as an S corporation) and the allowable benefits maximum should be assumed to be no more than $15,000. Any benefits in excess of $15,000 should be considered salary. Further, consider the maximum salary allowable by the IRS (if his corporation files as a C corporation) is $75,000. He desires to continue receiving a total of $90,000 annually in cash and/or benefits.

Problem 15

Mike Miller owns a successful food service chain. The chain is incorporated and generates net income of $300,000 each year. His salary is $80,000 a year. At the present time, he receives benefits worth $5,000. The corporation chain pays him dividends equal to 60% of its net income. Assume corporation income tax rates are as follows:

Taxable Income

Over	Not Over	Rate
$ 0	$200,000	18%
$200,000	$350,000	24%
$350,000		33%

Assume Miller's average tax rate is 36%.

Miller is an excellent owner/manager, but weak in taxation. At a conference for entrepreneurs, he recently heard about S corporations, double taxation, excessive salary being labeled as dividends by the IRS, and so forth. He is the sole owner of his business and insists the business retain its corporate form; however, he desires to minimize taxes.

Required:

1. Based on the above, calculate the income taxes paid by his corporation and by him. (Ignore deductions, exemptions, and so forth in calculating his personal income taxes.)
2. How would you advise him to minimize the taxes he and his corporation pay? Assume dividends would have to be at least equal to 10% of net income (unless the company files as an S corporation) and the allowable benefits maximum should be assumed to cost no more than $15,000. Anything in excess of $15,000 should be considered salary. Further, assume the maximum salary allowable by the IRS (if his corporation files as a C corporation) is $100,000 in total. He desires to continue receiving $265,000 annually in benefits, salary, and dividends.

Index